W9-AKX-097

HAIDA ART

289 ~
50

HAIDA ART

GEORGE F. MacDONALD

University of Washington Press
Seattle

PLATE 1A, 1B (opening pages)
A complex transformation mask.
Closed, the mask depicts a
Whale with a Seagull on its head
(left, PLATE 1A). When the
Whale's face is opened, the dorsal fin and the gull's head both
fold back to reveal the humanlike inner face (right, PLATE 1B).
Copper eyebrows, lips and cheek
decorations complete this mask.
Collected on Haida Gwaii in 1879
by Israel W. Powell. CMC VII-B-23
(s92-4172 closed, s92-4174 open)

PLATE 2 (frontispiece)
A pair of interior house posts
from Grizzly Bear House, which
belonged to Chief Xa'na of
Masset. Richard Maynard notes
in his log for 1884 that he assembled these items, including the
war daggers and model totem
poles, when the residents of
Masset refused to pose for him.
The large posts, collected by the
Berlin Museum, were removed
to East Germany at the end of
World War II, but are now in
the Dahlem Museum, Berlin.
Photograph by Richard Maynard,
1884. CMC 100462

Copyright © 1996 by Canadian Museum of Civilization

All rights reserved. No part of this publication may be reproduced or transmitted in any
form or by any means, electronic or mechanical, including photocopying, recording, or any
information storage or retrieval system, without permission in writing from the publisher.

Published in the United States by the
University of Washington Press
P.O. Box 50096
Seattle, WA 98145-5096

Published simultaneously in Canada by
Douglas & McIntyre Ltd.
1615 Venables Street
Vancouver, British Columbia V5L 2H1

LIBRARY OF CONGRESS CATALOGING-IN-PUBLICATION DATA
Haida art / George F. MacDonald.
    p.   cm.
    Includes bibliographical references and index.
    ISBN 0-295-97561-X (alk. paper)
    1. Haida art. 2. Haida Indians—Material culture. 3. Haida Indians—Social life and customs. I. Title.
E99.H2M3   1996   96-7727
704'.03972—dc20   CIP

The paper used in this publication meets the minimum requirements
of American National Standard for Information Sciences—Permanence
of Paper for Printed Library Materials, ANSIZ39.48—1984. ∞

Editing by Saeko Usukawa
Design by Barbara Hodgson

Front cover photograph of mask of a young woman wearing a small
    labret of abalone shell, collected on Haida Gwaii in 1879 by Israel W. Powell,
    CMC VII-B-928A (s85-3284), by Harry Foster
Back cover photograph of frontlet depicting a young woman, carved by Simeon Stiltla,
    collected at Masset before 1884 by Dr. William F. Tolmie, CMC VII-B-25 (s86-3275),
    by Harry Foster
Publication co-ordination at Canadian Museum of Civilization by Cathrine Wanczycki
Printed and bound in Canada by Hemlock Printers Ltd.

CONTENTS

I am flying high above the Queen Charlotte Islands as I write this, bound from Vancouver to Taipei. What better time to ask myself what it is about these islands—which the Haida people call Haida Gwaii—that captures the imagination. They exist somewhere in time immemorial when nature and culture were in balance among the Haida, the original inhabitants of these islands. This state of equilibrium was not destined to last forever, and indeed it was dashed with the arrival of Europeans and Americans who also brought with them a host of viruses that killed over 95 per cent of the population and most of the cultural meaning of being Haida as well.

Even in my own time, I have seen these islands change greatly. The forests of fir, spruce and cedar, recording in their growth rings many centuries of botanical and climatic histories, have been cut down, leaving terrible tangles of indistinguishable roots and stumps. As if to confirm that the cosmic world of the Haida is in upheaval, the root masses of trees torn from their underworld realm reach raggedly for the sky.

My first visit to the Kaigani Haida village of Kasaan in southeast Alaska was, I recall, an experience in the archaeology of the senses. I had gone there on a research vessel of the Department of Archaeology at Simon Fraser University as a guest of Professor Roy Carlson, who was the skipper and field director. When we landed on the beach, I desperately tried to establish co-ordinates and recall the many photos I had seen, taken the century before, depicting the village and the impressive front it presented to the ocean.

As I waded into a sea of shore grasses that came first to my knees, then to my hips, then my shoulders, until my head slipped beneath the spindly stalks that supported a canopy of salmonberry bushes, I entered an alternate world where I gradually found my bearings. It was a world of the past, a dreamtime landscape, known to me only from pale reflections in photographic images. But I recognized the Eagle with its tightly flexed talons grasping the ridge pole of Eagle House, and I recognized the Beaver with its huge incisor teeth. I thrust out my arms to part the light green stalks, using a breast stroke. It was like swimming through a kelp bed, a place that often appears in north coast myths. Kelp beds are part of the nether world where birds, animals and fish disport together yet none dominate. I was reminded of the myth in which the Raven chose his landing spot on earth after stealing the sun, moon and stars from the house of the Sky Chief. Raven had seen the disastrous consequences of the choice made by his brother Lagabula who had decided to land in a kelp bed, never to be seen again and relegated to an eternal limbo in a liminal zone between memory and reality. This place, where the flotsam and jetsam of myth and memory coincided, impressed me deeply.

By concentrating, I called to mind the old photographs I had seen in the archives of the Smithsonian Institution. I remembered that Ensign Alfred P. Niblack had approached Kasaan in the spring of 1883, not long after the death of its powerful Chief Skowl and sixteen years after the United States had purchased southeast Alaska from the Czar of Russia, who had grown weary of his rarely lucrative trading empire. I tried, as I swam through the green branches, to remember the impressions Niblack had described on entering Skowl's house and viewing the chief's coffin placed between his objects of wealth laid out for visitors to admire.

Suddenly, another memory pulled me to the mid-1960s when I first visited Haida Gwaii. It was at the very spot where Europeans had made their first landfall among the Haida in 1774, in Cloak Bay between Langara and Graham Islands. Langara was named for a Spanish admiral by Jacinto Caamano, who in 1792 sailed his ship to this far corner of Haida Gwaii, where he encountered Chief Cunnyha, whose name survives among the chiefly names of Skidegate as Gunia.

Marius Barbeau of the Canadian Museum of Civilization summed up the significance of the achievement of the early carvers on the Northwest Coast when he wrote (1950:vol. 1, dedication): "Their genius has produced monumental works of art on a par with the most original the world has ever known. They belong one and all to our continent and our time, and have shown how creative power may thrive in remote places."

The aim of this book is to take the beached remnants of Haida culture, objects which are now part of one of the world's best collections at the Canadian Museum of Civilization, and to reflect on the shape and depth and texture of that culture in the past and its continuing strength today.

Writing this book was a most agreeable undertaking made easier by a large number of friends and colleagues. I would like to acknowledge the people who originally stimulated my interest in things Haida: Wilson Duff of the University of British Columbia; Marius Barbeau of the Canadian Museum of Civilization; Tom McIlwraith, my first professor of Northwest Coast studies at the University of Toronto; Charles Borden of the University of British Columbia; Robert Bruce Inverarity provided one of my earliest contacts with Haida art through his 1950 book.

I would also like to thank those who shared and encouraged my enthusiasm over Haida art. My wife Joanne, daughter Christine and son Grant have always shared my interests and been lifelong critics whose encouragement on projects like this is to a large part responsible for their completion. Bill Reid has been a constant friend who poses challenging questions to every statement and is always suggesting new avenues to explore. Robert Davidson has been another Haida friend and inspiration, as has Jim Hart of Masset. Many Haida elders have contributed through their conversations with me over the years, including Peter Hill, Florence Edenshaw Davidson and Frank Collison of Masset, as well as Rufus Moody of Skidegate. Dan Savard, photo archivist at the Royal British Columbia Museum, has helped with photos, as has Margery Toner of the Canadian Museum of Civilization.

I am especially grateful for the artistry of Harry Foster and Richard Garner, many of whose photographs enhance these pages. They took the colour plates over a period of more than a decade, as I discovered each piece in our museum collections and researched it between other duties. Michelle Labelle and Sylvie Jourdain are responsible for preparing the manuscript. Saeko Usukawa deserves my profound thanks for her patient editorial hand that left a strong imprint on the final product.

Finally, I would like to express my admiration for the Haida people, who have created a cultural style worthy of endless study and perpetual preservation. The living culture is growing stronger each day as the Haida regain their numbers, their pride and control of their own destinies.

George F. MacDonald
President
Canadian Museum of Civilization

HAIDA ART

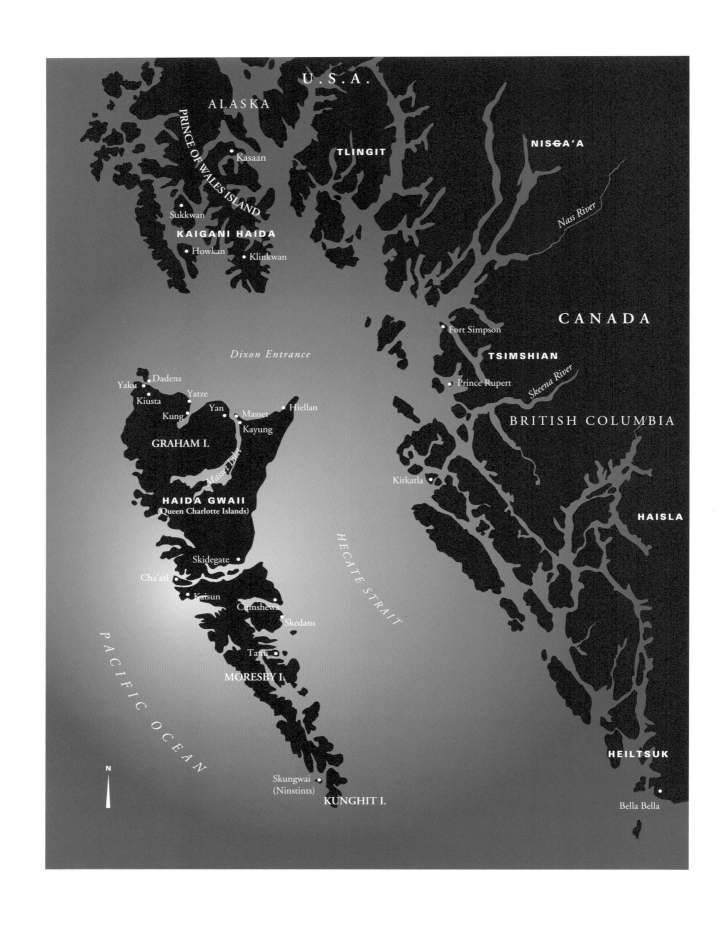

U · S · A ·

ALASKA

PRINCE OF WALES ISLAND

• Kasaan

TLINGIT

NISGA'A

Nass River

• Sukkwan

KAIGANI HAIDA

• Howkan   • Klinkwan

CANADA

Dixon Entrance

• Fort Simpson

Yaku • • Dadens
        Yatze •
Kiusta •   Yan •   Masset •   • Hiellan
  Kung •   Kayung •

GRAHAM I.

TSIMSHIAN

• Prince Rupert   Skeena River

BRITISH COLUMBIA

Masset Inlet

HAIDA GWAII
(Queen Charlotte Islands)

• Kitkatla

HAISLA

Skidegate •

Cha'atl •

Kaisun •
        Cumshewa •
          Skedans •

HECATE STRAIT

Tanu •

MORESBY I.

PACIFIC OCEAN

N

Skungwai •
(Ninstints)

KUNGHIT I.

HEILTSUK

•

• Bella Bella

FROM TIME IMMEMORIAL | Chapter One

PREHISTORY OF HAIDA GWAII

Haida Gwaii is an archipelago of islands (the Queen Charlotte Islands) off the northern coast of British Columbia near the province's border with Alaska (PLATE 3). The southern islands are mountainous, with Moresby Island predominating. The large northern island, Graham Island, where the Haida people now live, is mountainous on its western side but to the east is flat with isolated outcrops of rock. North of Dixon Entrance are the Kaigani Haida, as the Haida in Alaska are named. Their territory encompasses the southern half of Prince of Wales Island in Alaska.

During the end of the last ice age between 13,000 and 11,000 years ago, events resulted in very low water levels around Haida Gwaii. What is now Hecate Strait, the body of water that separates Haida Gwaii from the mainland, was for the most part dry land. Throughout this area of dry land, there were lakes and small rivers draining north and south to the Pacific Ocean. Soil samples from Hecate Strait indicate that many areas were habitable in the last ice age. After 10,000 years ago, the melting glaciers contributed to a rise in the sea level that resulted in a flooding of the Northwest Coast, temporarily creating beach lines high above today's high tide marks.

The memory of this drastic fluctuation of sea levels is preserved in the widespread flood myths of people along the Northwest Coast. Scores of these stories have been recorded. In 1892, James Deans, a Hudson's Bay Company employee, was told a legend that was very specific about glacial events at the Honna River on Haida Gwaii (1899:67):

> This is the story of the long long ago told amongst our people, the Hidery, that at Quilh-cah about three miles west from the village of Illth-cah-geetla, or Skidegate's town, lived a boy whose name was Scannah-gan-nuncus . . .
>
> . . . One day, making a further venture than usual, he sailed up the Hunnah, a mountain stream emptying its waters into Skidegate channel, four or five miles [6.5 to 8 km.] west from the place where he lived.
>
> Tradition says that this river in those days was three times larger than it is nowadays. At present there is seldom water enough to float a canoe, unless at high water. It is also related that the waters of the sea stood higher on the land than is now the case. Of the rise of the land, evidence is everywhere to be seen; old landmarks show thirty feet [9 m].

PLATE 3

Map of Haida Gwaii (the Queen Charlotte Islands) and Kaigani Haida territory on Prince of Wales Island.

After pulling up stream, he became tired; so, in order to rest, he pulled ashore and lay down. In those days at the place where he went ashore were large boulders in the bed of the stream, while on both sides of the river were many trees. While resting by the river, he heard a dreadful noise up stream, coming toward him. Looking to see what it was, he was surprised to behold all the stones in the river coming toward him. The movement of the stones frightened him so much that he jumped to his feet and ran into the timber. Here he found he had made a mistake, because all the trees were cracking and groaning; all seemed to say to him, "Go back, go back at once to the river, and run as fast as you can." This he lost no time doing. When again at the river, led by his curiosity, he went to see what was crushing the stones and breaking the trees. On reaching them, he found that a large body of ice was coming down, pushing everything before it. Seeing this, he got into his canoe and fled toward home.

Deans speculates, with some insight, on a problem that still puzzles us today (1899:70-71):

Who was the author of this story, or when was it adopted by the Scannahs [Killer Whale phratry], I cannot say. Doubtless a tradition of ice coming down the Hunnah was current at the time when the Scannahs chose that fish as their crest. This event must have happened very early in the settlement of these islands, for tradition says at the time only two or three families lived on the southeast side of these islands, and that, excepting our hero and his grandmother, who lived at Quilh-cah, all the others dwelt in a small village on Maud Island, a mile and a half west from the others at Quilh-cah.

According to Haida tradition, there was a remnant of an earlier population on the west coast of Haida Gwaii. Marius Barbeau of the Canadian Museum of Civilization collected a flood legend from Henry Young of Skidegate (Barbeau, no date:MS). Intensive review of the body of flood and related myths of the Haida is likely to prove that they have inhabited Haida Gwaii since the end of the last ice age and thus constitute one of the oldest traceable populations of any in the New World.

The first indications of the Haida presence consist of roughly flaked stone tools found in intertidal areas that were once dry land. Ocean-going canoes enabled these earliest inhabitants to communicate with neighbours to the north, from whom they adopted new forms of tools such as sharp stone flakes called microblades. These were preferably made of obsidian, a volcanic glass that can be precisely fingerprinted to identify its place of origin. The presence on the islands of obsidian from mainland sources long distances away provides a clue to the maritime skills of the ancient people of Haida Gwaii.

Archaeological surveys have located sites in all parts of Haida Gwaii that indicate the population was sizable by 5,000 years ago. At about that time, their economy was expanding from a primary reliance on hunting and fishing to include harvesting shellfish from the huge intertidal areas that surround many of the more protected waterways of the islands. The abundance of shellfish provided a virtually inexhaustible supply of food; it also made possible a stability of residence that allowed the establishment of more permanent villages where food, tools and other material objects could be safely stored, as well as the development of craftsmen who could devote more time to art. These changes led to the refinement of woodworking tools and skills, which, in turn, allowed for the construction of bigger and more elaborate canoes as well as larger plank houses.

Improved watercraft also meant that people were able to travel to food resources in far-flung areas and that warfare, particularly against mainland tribes, was a profitable venture. In fact, at the time of first contact with Europeans, the Haida could strike out from their island fortress and cross the treacherous waters of Hecate Strait, which they alone had mastered, with little fear of retribution from their mainland enemies.

The first archaeological excavation on Haida Gwaii was that of a shell midden near Masset, conducted in 1919 by Harlan I. Smith of the Canadian Museum of Civilization (PLATE 4). He was following up on his earlier work with the Jesup North Pacific Expedition headed by anthropologist Franz Boas. Smith had served as a photographer on that expedition, taking thousands of photographs of coastal villages from Washington State to Alaska. Unfortunately, his wonderful plates do not include Haida Gwaii villages. Another member of the Jesup Expedition, John R. Swanton, the principal ethnographer of the Haida, did do work at Masset and Skidegate, and Smith may have been influenced by the expedition connection with him to undertake archaeological work near Masset. Since precise techniques like radiocarbon dating were not then available, Smith (1919:MS) greatly underestimated the maximum age of the shell middens on Haida Gwaii and in the Prince Rupert area on the mainland where he also dug.

My own archaeological work on Haida Gwaii was an offshoot of excavations in Prince Rupert harbour that began in 1966. Then in 1968, Wilson Duff of the Royal British Columbia Museum encouraged me to investigate observations he had made on Graham Island of shell middens on raised terraces that marked ancient strandlines from times of higher sea levels. The brief excavations I conducted there at Honna River yielded dates in the 3,000 to 4,000 year range and much evidence of burials and utensils roughly equivalent to those of similar date from the Prince Rupert harbour sequence.

That same year, we discovered another midden at Blue Jackets Creek on Masset Inlet on

PLATE 4

The first scientifically documented archaeological excavations on Haida Gwaii were conducted in 1919 at shell middens near Masset. Harlan I. Smith of the Canadian Museum of Civilization attempted to date the most recent occupations by reference to the age of trees growing on the surfaces of the middens and concluded that the majority were from prehistoric times. *Photograph by Harlan I. Smith, July 1919.* CMC 46,683

5

the north coast of Graham Island, which Patricia Severs (1974) later excavated. The artifacts from 3,000 to 5,000 years ago were strikingly different from those found in the Prince Rupert area, but those from about 2,000 years ago showed strong influences from the adjacent mainland. This indicates the beginning of a trading pattern among the Haida and the neighbouring Tsimshian and Tlingit that led to increased sharing of symbols of wealth and materials of exchange, and eventually to closely parallel art styles that were different from those of groups to the south.

Although many water-logged archaeological sites on Haida Gwaii contain wood objects that would document fully the development of Haida art styles, none has been excavated. The excavation of such sites would be very productive, as was demonstrated in water-logged sites several thousand years old in Prince Rupert harbour, from which decorated wooden bowls, boxes, canoe paddles, etc. were successfully recovered and their artistic qualities preserved, using specialized techniques. And few shell midden sites on Haida Gwaii have been excavated, compared to the mainland, partly due to more expensive and difficult logistics of mounting archaeological expeditions there, but also because the Haida themselves have not encouraged such work. All of the old village sites and shell middens contain numerous skeletons, a reminder of "the great dying" that carried off most of their population in the last century. This has made the Haida particularly aware of the near-impossibility of conducting archaeological research without disturbing many such burials.

SOCIAL ORGANIZATION

The Haida were divided into two social groups, or moieties, called Raven and Eagle. The Raven moiety was subdivided into twenty-two lineages, or families, and the Eagle moiety into twenty-three; the lineages were not grouped into clans. According to John R. Swanton (1905:66), "in olden times each town was inhabited by one family only," but by historic times, all villages contained representatives of several lineages and most contained members of both moieties. Marriages had to take place between Eagles and Ravens, rather than those who belonged to the same moiety, and children became members of the same moiety as their mother.

Each lineage provided its members with entitlement to a range of economic resources such as fishing spots, hunting or collecting areas, and house sites. Other prerogatives included rights to a wealth of myths and legends, dances, songs and musical compositions. Names were a highly coveted lineage property and were bestowed to mark different stages of people's lives. Names were also given to important material belongings such as fish traps, houses, canoes, feast dishes and even feast spoons. Face painting and tattoo designs were also lineage property, as were all crests, of which Swanton (1905:113–15) lists over seventy.

Each household, whose average size was around thirty to forty people (consisting of about ten closely related nuclear families of a lineage), was headed by a chief. The houses of powerful chiefs were large and could contain up to a hundred individuals, including slaves.

Each lineage also recognized the authority of a chief who could act as a war chief in times of conflict. The town chief was the head of the most wealthy or populous lineage in a village, but changed from time to time in accordance with the general fortunes of the lineage or because of the respect commanded by a certain chief. During the last century, for instance, there was intense rivalry between Chief Ninsingwas and Chief Skidegate. According to Newton H. Chittenden (1884:81), a surveyor for the British Columbia provincial government, "They quarrelled bitterly over their rank for a long time, Ning-Ging-Wash, by means of his more liberal potlatches finally prevailing, but not until two of their adherents had been killed."

Chiefly rank was passed down by inheritance through the matrilineal line, usually to a chief's oldest sister's son. Inherited positions determined the order in which chiefs or people of high rank were seated at potlatches and feasts. Those who had not had potlatches given for them, or who did not own houses or major property, were considered commoners. The Haida also owned slaves, who were war captives or the children of captives, often taken from neighbouring tribes on Vancouver Island or the mainland.

The potlatch was the most important Haida ceremony and accompanied the progress of high-ranking people through the social order to mark the giving of names, marriages and deaths. Years of preparation were required to amass the food to feed invited guests and the wealth to distribute gifts to pay for the witnessing of events. The building of a house and the raising of a frontal pole usually called for the major potlatch any chief would give in his lifetime.

MYTHOLOGY AND CRESTS

The mythology of the Haida, like that of other tribes on the central and northern coast, is based on the epic cycle of stories about the Raven and his various exploits. The Raven is truly a trickster who liberates humankind from a clamshell, then in one story sets the universe in order, only to threaten it with chaos in the next. The Raven is the most greedy, mischievous and lecherous creature imaginable, but almost without meaning to, teaches humans the arts of living a good life. Haida artist Charles Edenshaw alone could recount several hundred different Raven stories from memory.

One of the best-known of these stories tells how the Raven disguised himself in order to enter the house of the Sky Chief, from whom he stole the sun, moon and stars to give to humankind. In another popular tale, the Raven was hungry, so decided to swim underwater to eat the bait off the hooks of some halibut fishermen. However, the hook lodged solidly in his beak. The fishermen banded together to haul up what they thought was a huge halibut, but got the Raven's beak instead.

Many stories describe the Raven's encounters with supernatural beings and how he acquired other useful things for humans from them, such as fresh water, salmon, the fish weir and the house—the latter from the Beaver.

Most Haida objects are decorated with crests—figures of animals, birds, sea creatures and mythic beings—that immediately identify the moiety (Raven or Eagle) and often the lineage of the owner. On a more subtle level, the placement of a crest figure, and especially the smaller figures attached to its ears, chest or mouth, refers to a specific myth involving that crest. An example is the Edenshaw family's frequent use of the Butterfly on the chest of the Raven, which refers to a series of myths in which the Butterfly is the Raven's travelling companion in the Masset series of stories (Swan 1883:MS, Aug. 10). In the Skidegate series of myths (Swanton 1905A), however, it is the Eagle who accompanies the Raven on his travels. Details such as these make it difficult to read the full range of meaning on a totem pole without a thorough knowledge of the mythology, but there is no one alive today who is familiar with the thousands of myths that have been recorded in various museum archives. Hence, the "text" that can be associated with a particular pole is similar to a Mayan text, in that only glimpses of meaning are possible.

Around 1900, John R. Swanton worked out a list of crests with information from such knowledgeable Haida artists as Charles Edenshaw of Masset, John Cross and John Robson of Skidegate, and Tom Price of Ninstints. These men all had an intimate working knowledge of the mythology and how crest designs should be used on everything from tattoos to totem poles. Tattoos were put on the thighs, chest, shoulders, forearms, backs of the hands and even all of the joints of the fingers.

Although the Haida have almost seventy crest figures, less than a score are in general use. A few crest figures were used by many lineages, and a larger number were exclusive to a few lineages. The Killer Whale, which is a particularly strong feature of Haida art and myth, is a popular crest. All Raven lineages use forms of the Killer Whale as a crest; one of them, the Raven-Finned Killer Whale, refers to the myth in which the Raven pecked himself out of the body of a Whale through the end of its dorsal fin. Eagle lineages of Ninstints use only the Five-Finned Killer Whale, which links them to specific Killer Whale chiefs whose undersea village was near their own and with whom their mythic ancestors had a profitable experience. The tall dorsal fin of Killer Whale crests that belong to Ravens are always black, while those of Eagles have a diagonal white stripe.

All of the land mammals used as crests, except for the Beaver, belong to the Raven moiety. Some of these crests such as the Mountain Goat, the Wolf and the Grizzly are of animals that do not occur on Haida Gwaii; their use was transferred from Tsimshian chiefs on the mainland. All crests of amphibious creatures such as the Beaver and the Frog are the exclusive prerogative of the Eagle moiety and also originated with the Tsimshian. Sea mammals mostly belong to the Ravens, although many Eagle lineages use the Blackfish as a crest. Fish crests are heavily weighted in favour of the Eagle moiety, who use the Sculpin, Skate, Dogfish, Starfish and Halibut. The Ravens share with them the Dogfish and the Skate.

The Raven moiety does not use the Raven as a crest, but the Eagle moiety does use its namesake frequently, as well as many other bird crests including the Raven, Cormorant, Heron, Hawk and Hummingbird. The only bird crests the Raven moiety uses are the Flicker, Hawk and Horned Owl.

The Haida fashioned for themselves a world of costumes and adornments, tools and structures, with spiritual dimensions appropriate to each. The decorations on the objects they created were statements of social identity, or reminders of rights and prerogatives bestowed on their ancestors by supernatural beings, or of lessons taught to them through mythic encounters with the animals, birds, fish or other beings whose likenesses were embodied in the crests passed down through generations.

The abstract concept of art for art's sake had little meaning for the Haida, but they had exceptionally high standards of craftsmanship and the desire to constantly improve their skills. As inhabitants of an archipelago that lacked many of the prized natural resources available on the mainland—such as mountain sheep or goats, major runs of eulachon fish, mineral pigments, and specialized stones and metals for tools—the Haida began about 2,000 years ago to trade in order to maintain status among their neighbours. What they offered in exchange were products of skilled workmanship, especially their exceptional canoes, but ranging over a great variety of objects such as carved and painted chests, as well as other furnishings appropriate to the potlatch feasts of all the other north coast tribes.

They imported the raw materials that they lacked and processed them into highly refined products that they then exported to other tribes on Vancouver Island and the mainland. Such items included copper shields, silver and copper jewellery (after the late eighteenth century), as well as horn bowls, ladles, spoons, and possibly goat's wool blankets. The Haida excelled in making and engraving copper shields, and examples of their work have been collected from the Tsimshian, Tlingit, Kwakwaka'wakw (or Kwakiutl) and most other peoples of the coast.

From the first days of contact, the Haida tailored their production of art to European and American requirements. Just as the traders catered to the Haida by setting up the shipboard manufacture of iron and copper implements and even items of clothing, the Haida developed art and crafts that appealed to the traders. Most popular were small carvings made of argillite (a soft black stone), items of ivory and silver, as well as a wide variety of wooden and basketry "souvenirs." Literally thousands of such items, collected before the end of the sea otter trade in the 1830s, have turned up in the New England states and the British isles. Numbers of them have found their way into museum collections.

The North Coast Art Style

Many features of what is recognized as the north coast art style are shared by the Haida and their mainland neighbours, the Tsimshian to the east and the Tlingit to the north. This is particularly true of flat designs, which use formlines and ovoids. Primary formlines, which are generally black, outline the parts of each figure. Secondary formlines occur within the primary spaces and are usually red. In rare instances, the two colours are reversed for dra-

matic effect. There is a formal grammar of formlines, in which rules control the thickness of the line and the changes of direction.

A rounded, bulging oval-to-rectangular shape called an ovoid is a feature unique to Northwest Coast art. Ovoids are used to portray a creature's eyes and joints, and sometimes teeth or orifices like nostrils and ears. Small faces are often placed within such ovoids; these refer to the loss of the soul as a prelude to death, for the Haida believe that the soul leaks out of the joints or orifices of the body.

The most common Haida artistic motif is the symmetrical flat design, made up of a complex pattern of components, that represents the Chief of the Undersea World (PLATE 5). This supernatural being is prevalent throughout the Northwest Coast, from the prehistoric levels of the Ozette archaeological site in the State of Washington to the ancient burial chests found in caves in Alaska. One of the favourite designs of the Haida, it is a two-dimensional flat depiction of a being with a small body and an inordinately large, broad head that has a cleft in the forehead. The eyes often contain small creatures ranging from profile heads of salmon to double-profile heads similar in form to the larger head itself. The hands are also oversize, with emphasis on the palms, which in rare cases have separate faces portrayed within them. The arms, which are narrow and tightly folded, often have fins hanging from them. All the joints of the being's body are marked with eyes, heads of salmon or human faces. The overall impression is of undulating black bands that sketch out a broad face teeming with other life forms, which some interpret as souls of humans or other beings temporarily contained within this creature and awaiting rebirth into the world above the sea. George T. Emmons (1907:330), who was the major recorder of Tlingit culture and a collector of Tlingit objects for a number of museums, made the following observation:

> The belief in the mythical being Gonaqadet occurs along the whole coast. He lives in the sea, and brings power and fortune to all who see him. Sometimes he rises out of the water as a beautifully painted house-front inlaid with the much-prized blue and green haliotis-shell [abalone], again as the head of an immense fish or as an elaborately painted war-canoe. In decorative art he is generally represented as a large head with arms, paws, and fins.

Despite the great frequency with which the Haida depicted the Chief of the Undersea World on all types of containers such as food vessels, storage chests, chief's seats and even housefronts, they rarely identified it by name. We know, however, from Swanton's observations (1905:18) on Haida cosmology, that this ubiquitous being is called Konankada (or Gonankadet among the mainland tribes of the north coast). In the most general terms, it is the Master of Souls. Its nature is hinted at in the Haida myth of Master Gambler, whose house is mid-way on the journey to the land of souls, or the realm of Konankada. If those who pause to gamble lose to Master Gambler, more people will soon die in their village. If they win, however, the salmon runs in their village streams will increase. This alternation of souls between human and salmon forms one of the central equations of north coast art. The

PLATE 5

A red cedar bentwood Haida storage chest carved and painted with the protective image of Konankada, Chief of the Undersea World. *Collected at the Nass River in 1905 by W. A. Newcombe.* CMC VII-C-109 (s94-6802)

paradigm into which this and many other equations fit is the recycling of souls between human and animal (most frequently salmon) from one generation to another.

Flat Design

Elaborate two-dimensional designs called "flat designs" are characteristic of Northwest Coast art and are tightly controlled by formal canons of both line and form. The Haida made far fewer large-scale paintings, such as housefronts and screens, than their Tsimshian neighbours. The Haida were, however, the masters of subtly sculpted flat design—a kind of bas-relief—in which the secondary and tertiary spaces were enhanced with gently swelling or concave planes between the primary formlines. In the past, the Haida used less complex textured zones of cross-hatching or parallel lines around eye forms than did Tsimshian and Heiltsuk artists. Although early Haida artists are not known by name, art historian Bill Holm (1981:199), after a close study of disparate works such as totem poles, housefront paintings, chief's seats and argillite carvings, identified one early master painter and sculptor as "the Master of the Chicago Settee," after the first piece of his work to attract the appreciation of experts like Holm, Wilson Duff and Haida artist Bill Reid.

From the 1870s on, numerous Haida artists who are known by name became remarkably free and innovative in their paintings, depicting animal, fish and bird forms with a greater degree of realism than before, and often in quite a narrative dimension. This creative development is undoubtedly related to the fact that these artists, of which there were several dozen, were working in both argillite and paint, using formline designs on a variety of objects intended to appeal to foreign visitors.

The best known of these artists were Charles Edenshaw, Tom Price, John Robson and John Cross, but there were many others. A small number of Skidegate artists also applied radical painting styles to box or drum designs with intriguing results. It is virtually impossible to differentiate the nineteenth-century boxes decorated in the various villages of the north coast groups, as these served as containers of trade items among those communities. However, tribal styles are distinctive in boxes and chests owned by chiefs for storing wealth items and for burial chests (or coffins).

John Cross, John Robson, Tom Price and Charles Edenshaw also produced many flat designs that fit into the category of "ledger drawings," a form common to Indian art of the late nineteenth century. These were often elaborate drawings based on tattoo designs, done from memory in ledgers or copybooks provided by the administrators and missionaries who entered Indian communities to educate and Christianize them. Drawing skills were considered important and were encouraged by supplying coloured pencils, crayons and paper. The Haida needed little encouragement in adopting these new materials to provide samplers of totemic and other designs that were much in demand by collectors.

Haida flat design has survived and is in fact thriving in the limited edition print market that sprang up in the late 1960s. Many artists like Don Yeomans, Gerry Marks and Reg

Davidson have produced hundreds of images that are sold in fine art galleries throughout the world. The current master of this form of painting and printmaking is Robert Davidson (a descendant of Charles Edenshaw), whose work is featured in more detail in the final chapter.

Sculpture

Haida sculptures range from 20-metre (65-foot) tall totem poles to the equally complex carved handles of horn spoons. This ability to express artistic concepts over a range of sizes and forms has attracted the admiration of art aficionados worldwide over the past two centuries.

The earliest known Haida sculptures are from cave sites or remote graves of shaman that date from the mid-eighteenth century. The oldest carved poles are undoubtedly shaman grave posts, some of which are late eighteenth and early nineteenth century. They portray primarily human figures, whereas the monumental poles standing in the villages display crests and supernatural beings from mythology. The earliest surviving poles include triple mortuary posts circa 1830 from Kiusta (MacDonald 1983:259) and a large house frontal pole circa 1840 from Hiellan village (PLATE 140) (MacDonald 1983:236). On these four poles, the figures are very large and few in number, with many small faces appearing at the joints, eyes and ears.

The oldest burial chest is from the Gust Island burial cave (MacDonald and Cybulski 1973:26), while a slightly later example from an eighteenth-century mortuary at Kiusta is now in the Royal British Columbia Museum (1321). In both examples, the eye forms are very elongated, with slits in the pupils. Another early piece is a sea lion-shaped bowl (PLATE 25) that is characteristic of the eighteenth-century pieces collected by early explorers.

The majority of Haida carvings created during the last half of the nineteenth century belong to the classic style. Facial features such as eyes, ears, nostrils and lips are very large, and occupy about the same space as the forehead, cheeks and jaw. This gives the animal or bird forms a youthful or even naive look that viewers find appealing. The formal symmetry of the crest art also provides a serenity and charm akin to Egyptian art. Smaller sculptures such as masks and frontlets range from the mystic to the frightening, and occasionally the comical.

Following the tragic depopulation of the late 1860s due to epidemics and the deculturation of the survivors by Indian agents and missionaries in the 1870s and 1880s, the monumental sculptural tradition was abandoned. Carvers miniaturized their production into models of houses and poles, tailoring their art to the tourist market. Few new artists were trained, and eventually the canons and tenets of the distinctive Haida style were lost. The story of the rediscovery of those traditions by the current generation of artists who learned by studying models on dusty museum shelves is told in the final chapter of this book.

14

CHIEFLY POSSESSIONS

Over time, trade among the people of the north coast groups—the Haida, Tsimshian, Tlingit and Nisga'a—led to the mutual adoption of a limited range of objects and materials that symbolized wealth and prestige. These included the regalia used by chiefs, such as headdresses decorated with ermine skins. Other prestigious objects included artistically decorated chests, boxes and bowls used to store and display the food and wealth that characterized the potlatches.

Chiefs of all the tribes of the north coast possessed an array of regalia, which was documented in drawings by the Russian artist Mikhail Tikanov as early as 1818 and which was compared by travellers and missionaries to robes of the Masonic order with regard to their importance in denoting status. For chiefs, this regalia provided a shared frame of reference for the exchange of wealth between nations with different languages and belief systems.

The full set of chiefly regalia consisted of a Chilkat blanket, leggings, an apron, a frontlet and a pair of Raven rattles (or a drum). A chief was also likely to own a shield-shaped plate of native copper; this was a symbol of wealth that was displayed at feasts and could be exchanged or substituted for other commodities (PLATE 6). After a chief's death, his coppers were often fastened on his memorial pole.

The Haida adopted most of these symbols of chiefly rank, particularly the items of clothing, from the Tsimshian and Nisga'a, and either manufactured their own or acquired them through trade with mainland groups. Very few Chilkat blankets appear to have been woven on Haida Gwaii, however; there was no local supply of goat wool, and the pattern boards from which the blankets were woven are missing from collections from Haida Gwaii, although they are common among the Tlingit. The Haida made their own frontlets and Raven rattles, although on occasion they obtained these items in trade from the mainland.

People of classes other than chiefs, such as shaman or members of secret societies, also had their own particular regalia.

PLATE 6

The chief whose name means Highest Peak in a Mountain Range stands in front of House Where People Always Want To Go at Haina village. This photograph shows a Haida chief of the previous century in traditional dress, displaying his wealth of coppers before his lineage house. *Photograph by Richard Maynard, 1888.*

Clothing

In precontact times, most items of Haida clothing were woven from red or yellow cedar bark. After the bark was peeled in long strips from the trees, the outer layer was split away, and the flexible inner layer was shredded and processed. The resulting felted strips of bark were soft and could be plaited, sewn or woven into a variety of fabrics that were either dense and watertight, or soft and comfortable. Women wore skirts and capes of cedar bark, while men wore long capes of cedar bark into which some mountain goat wool was woven for decorative effect.

PLATE 7

A Chilkat-style blanket of mountain goat wool and cedar bark. The centre figure, an Eagle, is flanked by two profile Ravens. *Collected from a Kaigani Haida village in Alaska circa 1900 by George T. Emmons.* CMC VII-X-1491 (S91-946)

Early examples of chief's capes have repetitive patterns of trophy heads, but after warfare was suppressed by the traders, the trophy heads were replaced with crest figures, and the amount of wool used was increased to the point where the cedar bark warps could not even be seen. The fur of sea otter or other animals was added to the neckline of capes for those of chiefly rank.

After contact, the everyday wear of men and women was an unadorned trade blanket, worn as a wraparound garment during the day and used as a covering at night. Slaves were clothed in handed-down blankets.

Chilkat Blankets

Chilkat blankets were the specialty of the Chilkat tribe of the Tlingit, whose territory was at the mouth of the Chilkat River in southeast Alaska. This group refined the style to its highest level in the late nineteenth century, but it had initially been developed among the Tsimshian-speaking people who lived along the Skeena and Nass Rivers on the mainland and had easy access to mountain goats in their hunting territories. Early explorers like Captain James Cook collected cedar bark capes decorated with small amounts of goat's wool; not until the early nineteenth century did full Chilkat-style blankets appear in collections.

Although Chilkat blankets have many design variations (PLATE 7), the most favoured one on those owned by the Haida is a double-profile view of Konankada in the guise of a Killer Whale, flanked by two profile Ravens. This design, according to George T. Emmons (1907:330), is a reference to the first potlatch in the world, which was given by Konankada in honour of the Raven. A vivid description of the first potlatch according to the Tsimshian is provided by Franz Boas (1916:285).

Painted Leather Capes

The Haida were also fond of large elkskin capes with painted panels and fringes on the sides (PLATE 8). The design on these is most frequently that of the Killer Whale, with the Raven, usually in human form, within it. It can thus be equated with the same designs on a Chilkat blanket. The homogeneity of the designs on these capes and their collection provenance sug-

gest they originated among the Kaigani Haida of the Prince of Wales archipelago in Alaska. Many early traders made special efforts to acquire elkskins from the tribes at the mouth of the Columbia River, where elk were abundant, in order to resell them to the Haida.

Tunics, Dance Aprons and Leggings

Another popular item of clothing in the late nineteenth century was a cloth tunic with a single crest on the front and sometimes another crest on the back (PLATE 9). The most prestigious kind was the woven Chilkat tunic, which probably preceded the cloth one. The Chilkat tunic, like the blanket, was a specialty of the Tlingit, and the rare Haida examples were probably obtained in trade. Considerably more common among the Haida were Chilkat woven aprons and leggings, probably also imported from the Tlingit. The design fields on Chilkat tunics, aprons and leggings followed those of the blanket, with slight adaptations because of differences in size and shape.

Clothing worn by chiefs under the Chilkat blanket typically included a dance apron (or wraparound skirt), leggings of leather or cloth, and simple undecorated moccasins. Early aprons were made of tanned deerskin, painted in red and black with elaborate formline designs similar to those on boxes and even housefronts. There is usually a single large Konankada figure, often embellished with human heads in its mouth, but Whale and Raven designs are also common. A few examples, possibly traded from the mainland, are decorated with porcupine quill embroidery. The aprons are fringed at the bottom, a holdover from the ancient skin apron of the shaman. To the fringes are attached deer hooves or brass thimbles to produce a distinctive sound as the wearer moves.

Late in the last century, dance aprons of heavy wool cloth appeared among the Haida but never replaced leather aprons to the same degree as they did among mainland peoples. The decoration consists of a single family crest, cut from red cloth and appliquéd onto the dark blue apron.

Leggings are decorated in much the same way as dance aprons. Early leggings were made of leather, with complex figures painted on them and quill embroidery. After contact, cloth leggings with appliquéd crest figures became popular. The Haida often added puffin beaks or deer hooves as janglers.

Button Blankets

The button blanket, which came into use after contact, has now become the most popular piece of contemporary feast attire. At first, crest designs decorated with dentalium shells were sewn onto wool blankets acquired from maritime fur traders and later the Hudson's Bay Company (PLATE 10). By the middle of the last century, the favoured blanket was made of blue duffle, with the designs appliquéd in red stroud (PLATE 11). Squares of abalone shell were sewn to the eyes and joints of the crest figures to reflect bits of light as the wearer

PLATE 8

An elkskin cape painted with a Killer Whale design on the borders. Such capes were especially popular among the Kaigani Haida and commonly bore this identical design, perhaps symbolizing an honorary rank like captain of a war canoe. *Probably acquired circa 1900 by George T. Emmons for the Lord Bossom collection.* CMC VII-X-783 (s94-6729)

PLATE 9

The bold design of a Mountain Goat crest on a clan tunic of red and dark blue wool trade cloth, adorned with pieces of abalone shell. *Probably acquired at Kasaan village in Alaska circa 1900 by George T. Emmons for the Lord Bossom collection.* CMC VII-X-1078 (s94-6740)

PLATE 10

A trade wool blanket decorated with a human figure outlined by dentalium shells, pieces of abalone shell and trade buttons. *Probably acquired at Kasaan village in Alaska circa 1900 by George T. Emmons for the Lord Bossom collection.* CMC VII-B-1525 (S92-4307)

PLATE 11

A dark blue trade wool blanket with the design of a double-headed Eagle appliquéd on it in red. Trimmed with dentalium shells, ovoid pieces of abalone shell and a border of mother-of-pearl buttons. *Lord Bossom collection, circa 1900.* CMC VII-B-1521 (S92-4306)

danced around a fire. When pearl buttons obtained from fur traders came into use, they proliferated onto the formlines. Today, buttons are sometimes used to fill entire zones of the design elements and even the whole field of the background.

A modern potlatch can bring forward a hundred or more button blankets from the participants. At a traditional naming ceremony, it is now considered essential to present the recipient with a special blanket decorated with a family crest. A century after the button blanket was first developed, it has become a symbol of social and artistic rebirth among the Haida. One Kaigani Haida artist, Dorothy Grant, has initiated a fashion house specializing in appliquéd clothing that she labels "Feastwear" (PLATE 12).

Headdresses

Headdresses worn by chiefs included carved frontlets and painted hats. The item of chiefly regalia that had the most prestige and recognition among the northern tribes was the frontlet, a carved wooden plaque worn on the forehead. The frontlet plaque was carved of yellow cedar, birch or maple, in bas-relief, affixed to a cap that was edged with stiff sea lion whiskers and that had a train of ermineskin. This headdress appears to have originated with the Nisga'a and been adopted into the chiefly regalia of other tribes. The train of densely packed ermineskins may be conceptually linked to Konankada, who is sometimes depicted as a painted housefront surrounded by white clouds or flocks of seagulls that signal the beginning of eulachon runs on the Nass River. The Whale tail of Konankada is always attached to the back of this type of headdress.

Frontlets

All the north coast groups adopted the frontlet, but they each developed distinctive styles. The typical Tsimshian frontlet is a human figure with a head larger than its body and limbs, squeezed into a rectangular or dome-topped plaque that is surrounded by small human or crest animal figures. The frontlet of the Nisga'a of the Nass River has shallow rounded carving of the central human figure with squares of abalone shell surrounding it. The Tlingit frontlet has a more irregular pattern of small figures around the central figure, which is usually a crest animal rather than a human; the colours are more variable than the standard black and red used by the Haida, with a preference for green and grey.

The Haida frontlet is mid-way between those of the Tsimshian and Tlingit, in that animal figures are common in the centre but human figures are not rare. The Haida carve the central figure in higher relief and outline its eyes with a black line (PLATE 13) that among the Tsimshian is rendered by a change in sculptural plane between the eyelid and the eye. Haida frontlet plaques are round or oval as often as they are rectangular. One classic Haida frontlet uses a rectangular frame with a high relief figure of Dogfish Woman (PLATE 14).

The north coast frontlet embodies a complex cosmological message in which the domi-

PLATE 12

A button blanket by Dorothy Grant, Kaigani Haida, depicting the Raven bringing light to the world. This piece was commissioned by Dr. Margaret Hess for the Canadian Museum of Civilization on the occasion of the unveiling of a bronze sculpture on the same theme by Robert Davidson at the Museum of Anthropology in Vancouver, 1986. CMC VII-B-1832 (S95-26,944)

PLATE 13 (page 24)

This chief's frontlet representing the Moon is similar to the one worn by John Robson in PLATE 103. The abalone shell inlays on the face and rim of the Moon reflected the firelight, while the flicker feathers served as an invocation to that bird to carry the chief's prayers skyward. *Probably acquired at Skidegate before 1899 by James Deans for the A. Aaronson collection.* CMC VII-B-690 (S85-3282)

nant reference, conveyed both by the visual forms and by the materials used, relates to beings of the sea and the under world. However, images of humans representing the middle world, and birds the upper world, are not excluded. The sea world and under world references include the painted leather Whale tail that projects from the back and the sea lion whiskers on top that form the cage into which eagle down is placed. The flicker feathers that adorn the sides of the headpiece represent the role of messenger played by these birds, which are said to travel up and down the world tree, or *axis mundi,* and serve as messengers between worlds. Similarly, the ermineskin train refers to the role that creature plays in marking the seasons through its change of colour. The abalone shell, which comes from the sea, is thought to reflect the sky world.

Painted Woven Hats

Early engravings by Russian artists depict north coast chiefs wearing woven hats painted with formline crest designs at the period of first contact. Haida women made these very finely woven spruce root hats that were then painted by male artists with the crests of the commissioning family. Often, the hats had woven basketry rings added to the crown to designate high chiefs. It is claimed that each ring commemorates a potlatch feast the wearer has given, or at least the number of times the owner has been asked to dance at other feasts. Some hats from the north coast have more than twenty such rings.

Haida women excelled in basketry, particularly of spruce root, making not only woven hats but baskets and mats. Their work is different from that of Tsimshian women, who worked mostly with cedar bark strips. This distinction appears to go back at least 2,000 years, to judge from the basketry recovered from Prince Rupert harbour (Inglis 1976).

Both hats and baskets were woven on a stand with a wooden form appropriate to each size and shape (PLATE 15). Designs were either painted on or woven in. The colours of paint were restricted to red and black, with occasional touches of blue or green (PLATE 18). For woven designs, naturally dark-coloured bark was used as a contrast, but plant fibres were also dyed brown, black, red or yellow.

In early historic times, Haida women also sold their baskets and hats to Europeans and Americans who were trading or travelling in Haida territory. Painted woven hats became a popular tourist item late in the last century, and a number of leading Haida artists of the era, such as Tom Price, John Robson and Charles Edenshaw, painted many wonderful examples. Isabella, the wife of Charles Edenshaw, was a very skilled hat weaver and, according to their daughter, Florence Edenshaw Davidson (in Blackman 1982:40), her parents spent many winters producing painted spruce root hats, trays and baskets for sale (PLATE 16). The hats made by the Edenshaws are distinguished by a compasslike design at the top of the crown (PLATE 17).

PLATE 14 (page 25)
Although frontlets were acquired from the Nisga'a people, the Haida elaborated the three-dimensional sculptural qualities of the form. This portrayal of the mythic Dogfish Woman is one of the finest examples from Skidegate village. It has a train of ermineskin, flicker feathers at the sides, and sea lion whiskers at the top; the eyes and joints are inset with pieces of abalone shell. *Collected circa 1898 by Charles F. Newcombe.* CMC VII-B-1102 (S92-4298)

PLATE 15
A woman from Masset weaving a basket of spruce root on a stand. Such baskets provided women with an important source of income in the early tourist economy. *Photograph by Edward Dossetter, 1881.* CMC 74-15907

PLATE 16

Shallow trays of tightly woven
spruce root, such as this one
with a Beaver crest, were
suitable for display in a
Victorian home. This one was
created by Isabella and Charles
Edenshaw for sale to travellers,
although it is totally traditional
in style and manufacture.
*Collected at Masset in 1898 by
Charles F. Newcombe.* CMC VII-
B-1135 (s94-6777)

PLATE 17

A woven cedar bark hat, hand
painted with a Frog by Charles
Edenshaw. The four-pointed
star with bicoloured points is
the signature of this artist.
*Collected at Masset in 1911 by
C. C. Perry.* CMC VII-B-899
(s92-4284)

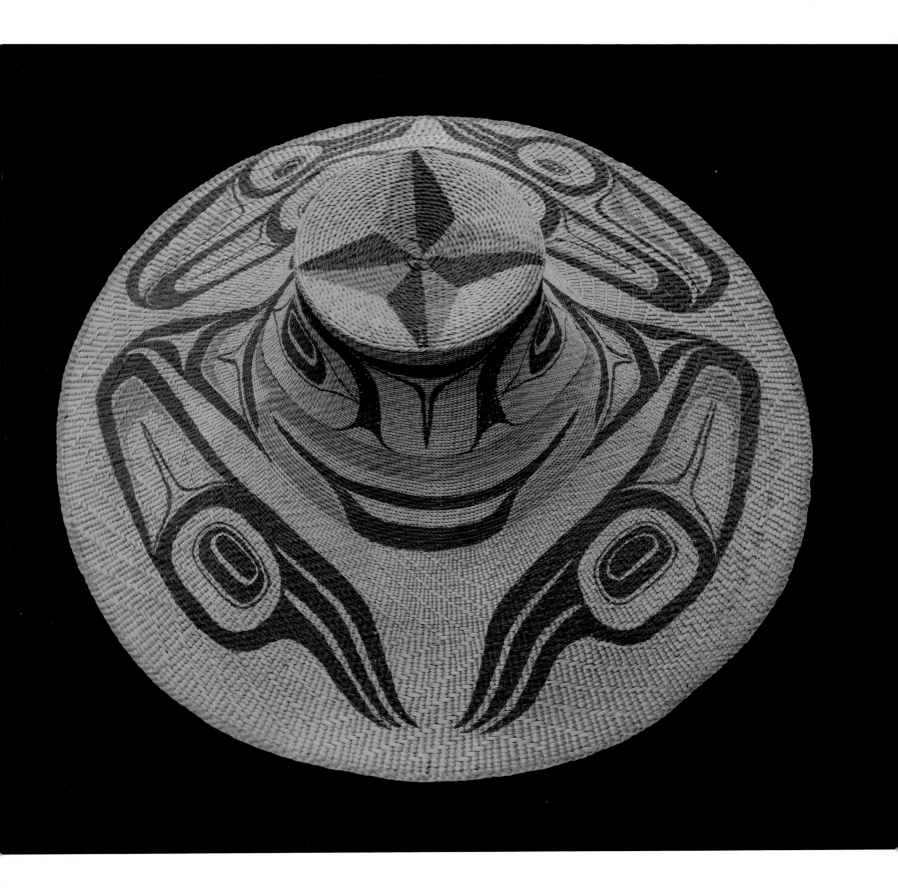

Raven Rattles

Another standard accoutrement of a north coast chief was a pair of Raven rattles (PLATE 19). The basic form is that of the Raven holding a small object in its beak, in reference to the Raven's bringing sunlight to mankind. On the Raven's breast is a flat design image of Konankada. Up to this point of comparison, the symbols are parallel to those of the Chilkat blanket: that is, the image of Raven centred by that of Konankada. The symbolism of the Raven rattle, however, elaborates upon this basic reference to the first potlatch. On the Raven's back is a small human, whose extended tongue is joined to that of a woodpecker type of bird.

Many rattles have a Frog in the place of the woodpecker, and on some, the Raven even holds a Frog in its beak in place of the sun. This may be a mythic reference to the blind Frog People who lived at the mouth of the Nass River and whose plight prompted Raven to steal the sun (Boas 1916:62).

These rattles are complex in their meaning and as yet have not been fully decoded. A possible clue is provided by the Tsimshian myth about the Raven who returns to earth after stealing the sun from the Sky Chief and lands on his back in Prince Rupert harbour (where a large petroglyph marks the spot). The Raven is freed from the rock by a flicker, which uses its sharp tongue to free it. Another Tsimshian myth tells of how the first Raven rattle was brought up on the hook of a fisherman from the Skeena River; from there, its use spread to other people on the north coast. The Haida themselves have no such origin myths and probably received the Raven rattle through prehistoric trade with the mainland.

Raven rattles were usually used in pairs, which associates them with ceremonies elsewhere on the coast to mark the start of salmon runs into the rivers. The swishing noise of the rattles is said to sound like the fins of salmon breaking the surface of the water, which encourages the fish to come past the villages.

Copper Shields

Copper was the ultimate symbol of wealth among the Haida and is associated with Copper Woman of Haida myth. Throughout the coast, shields made of copper were exchanged at ever higher values between chiefs at potlatch feasts. Among the Kwakwaka'wakw (or Kwakiutl) to the south of Haida Gwaii, coppers were particularly associated with the distribution of wealth at wedding feasts. The Haida used coppers as a marker and symbol of wealth, and some wealthy chiefs owned a dozen or more (PLATES 20, 21, 106, 156).

In the Prince Rupert harbour shell middens, the use of copper in the form of bracelets, pendants and tubes can be traced back more than 2,000 years (MacDonald and Inglis 1981:50) and thus appears to be an early feature of north coast trading and warfare. According to tradition, copper came from the territory of the Eyak people in the Copper River area of Alaska, where it occurs with some frequency as pure nuggets in the river gravels.

PLATE 18
Decorated paintbrushes with porcupine hair bristles and traces of pigment, collected from three different villages in 1905 by Charles F. Newcombe. *Left:* The brush from Skidegate is one of the gems of Haida miniature art. It depicts a hunter climbing a tree with his bow and arrow to shoot a bird at the top. CMC VII-B-1022 (S92-4388) *Centre:* The brush from Masset portrays a human figure with an enormous tongue that reaches to its feet. Greatly extended tongues are associated with bears, and the position of the hands pointing downward is also bearlike. The lower figure is the head of a Thunderbird. CMC VII-B-1024 (S92-4388) *Right* The third brush from Kasaan, Alaska, is decorated with the standing figure of a Bear. CMC VII-B-1021 (S92-4388)

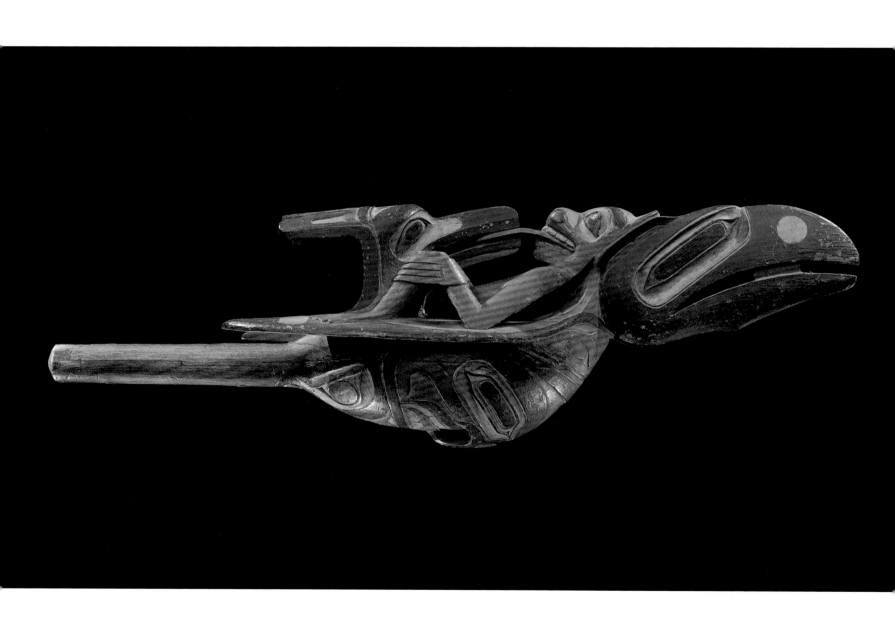

Alexander McKenzie, the Hudson's Bay Company agent at Masset, recorded the following information, which he elicited from local chiefs (1891:12):

> The original coppers were brought from the northern portion of Alaska, and the tradition is . . . that they were first made out of lumps of native copper which were found in the bed of a river there, but latterly the Indians bought sheet copper from the Russians at Sitka, and also in Victoria, and several natives along the coast commenced manufacturing spurious coppers from this material, which ultimately produced a fall in the value of coppers, and by glutting the market destroyed the romance of the idea that the copper was one of the earthliest rarest and choicest treasures fit only to be purchased by great chiefs.

McKenzie also notes that, among the Haida, each copper had its own name. He records the history of a copper called Taow-kee-ass, which belonged to Albert Edward Edenshaw; it was sold to a Tsimshian chief for eight slaves, one large cedar canoe, one hundred elkskins and eighty boxes of eulachon grease.

A number of studies have tried to unwrap the cosmological meaning of the copper shield with varying success. On one level, it represents the ancestors of the owner, and the raised T-shaped bar that divides it is the backbone or skeleton of the ancestors. McKenzie (1891:11) also comments on this feature of the copper:

> A conspicuous mark was always on these, the (T) cross, and on the skill with which this was executed depended in a great measure the value of the copper: This T or indentation is called in Haida *taow-tsoe-h*, namely, "back bone of the *taow*." It was fashioned by hammering on a wooden pattern by a particular process known only to skilful workers, with the result that when the *taow* was finished, the indentation of the T was the same thickness as the rest of the copper plate. If the T proved thinner, the value was considerably diminished; in fact, the copper was considered not genuine.

The portion above the T-bar is often bulbous and represents the head of the ancestor/crest, although among the Haida the rest of the body of the crest is often incorporated above the T-bar. The Haida engraved the design deeply into this upper portion and frequently chiselled out the background to provide a higher relief.

Very small coppers were sewn in numbers onto dance aprons and skirts, and the shape of the copper shield was often used for other objects of wealth such as abalone earrings. Neck-rings made of copper were popular, and copper figurines of humans were also fairly common, but there are no indications as to their use. They invariably have large heads, sometimes with pierced facial features, and even wear small copper armbands. It is possible they were used in curing rites or by shaman at first salmon ceremonies. Much rarer were copper masks (PLATE 22), though similar ones are frequent among the Tlingit.

PLATE 19
Raven rattles such as this one were used by a chief in ceremonies. The different sounds and rhythms produced by a pair of such rattles enhanced the drama of his oratory. On this rattle, the Raven supports a shaman initiate who is drawing inspiration and knowledge from the animal world through the link between his tongue and that of a mythical bird. *Collected on Haida Gwaii (probably Skidegate) in 1876 by Lord and Lady Dufferin.* CMC VII-C-2149 (s85-3308)

33

PLATE 20

This beautifully engraved copper depicting a Sculpin is a classic Haida object. The bulbous top panel displays the crest of the owner, and the well-fashioned T-bar in the lower half represents the backbone of an ancestor. *Acquired from the Kaigani Haida circa 1900 by George T. Emmons for the Lord Bossom collection.* CMC VII-X-1080 (S94-6768)

PLATE 21

A large copper decorated with a double-headed Eagle. The double-headed Eagle is not a traditional Haida crest but was adopted from the Imperial Russian form of this bird introduced by Russian fur traders in Alaska. *Collected from Skedans before 1900 by Charles F. Newcombe.* CMC VII-665 (S92-4244)

Dishes, bowls, trays, ladles and spoons in a variety of shapes and sizes were part of the expected settings for a feast, and those that were particularly well designed drew much comment from guests. Dishes and bowls were carved out of blocks of wood, moulded out of horn, or constructed by bending boards into a box shape. Bill Holm (1974:31) eloquently captured the essence of these dishes:

> The containers of the northern coast illustrate the remarkable technology of wood and horn working practiced by the native craftsmen. Many different techniques were utilized in making these containers, including carving from solid blocks of wood, shaping carved horn by means of steam, bending planks at steamed kerfs, and fastening joints by pegging or sewing them. The resulting vessels were utilitarian and functional. Their utilitarian roles, however, are over-shadowed by the subtleties of structural form, the richness of surface carving, or the strength of sculptural detail. Function, form, and decoration come together in pieces of aesthetic merit that express the strength and life of a rich culture.

Ladles and Horn Spoons

Ladles and spoons were used to transfer food from serving containers to dishes and to eat with. Ladles were elegantly plain or might have handles embellished with an ancestral figure or a crest design.

Antler spoons with crest figures on the handle appeared on the mainland at the Musqueam northeast site near the mouth of the Fraser River 3,000 years ago (Borden 1982:135), and mountain goat horn cores for spoon handles from 4,000 years ago were found in the Prince Rupert middens. Unfortunately, there are no prehistoric examples of horn spoons from Haida sites, but it is likely that they acquired such spoons very early from mainland groups as part of the intertribal potlatch system.

Individual horn spoons were the most elaborately decorated items at a feast. The bowl of the spoon was made from cream-coloured mountain sheep horn, steamed and bent in a mould. The curved handles were made from black mountain goat horn that provided a field for artistic display second only to that of totem poles. In fact, many spoon handles were faithful replicas of the poles in front of their owners' houses. Some of the most elaborate spoon handles have a dozen or more diminutive figures writhing around and seeming to devour each other on a handle that rarely exceeded 15 cm (6 inches) in length (PLATES 23, 24). Thousands of these exquisite works survive in museums.

Some foods, like soapberries (or Indian ice cream), required special eating utensils. Spoons for eating whipped soapberries were shaped like miniature paddles, which people used to literally shovel the delicacy into their mouths.

PLATE 22

A copper mask, evidently used in rituals since there is a fringe of eagle down glued with pine pitch around the outer edge. This mask was said to have been dug up at an ancient village site at the south end of Masset Inlet and reused in a ceremony at Masset village. *Collected at Masset in 1884 by Israel W. Powell.* CMC VII-B-108 (S92-4185)

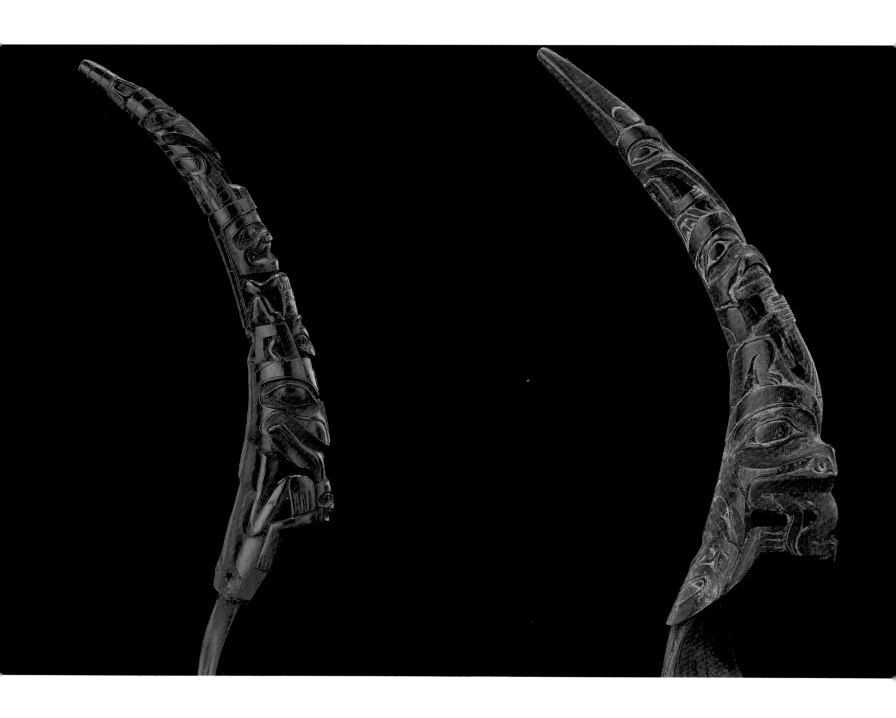

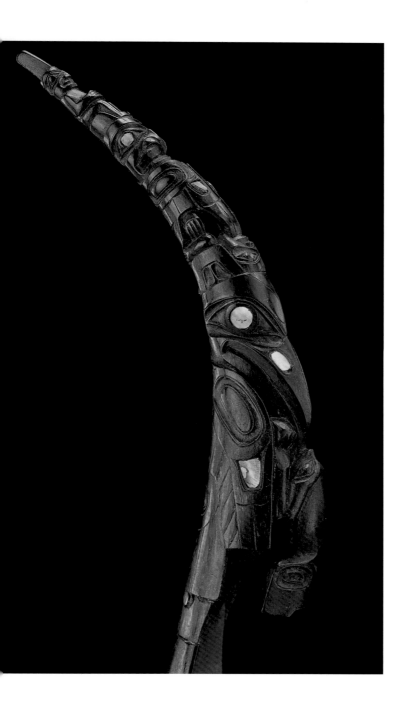

PLATE 23A, B, C

Feast spoons made of mountain goat horn. Each is a miniature version of the same family crests displayed on the totem pole in front of the owner's house.

Left: This spoon handle refers to two well-known Haida myths. The lowest figure represents the story of the hero Nansimget, who is shown grasping the dorsal fin of the Whale that is taking the soul of his dead wife to the undersea world. She is held upside-down in the Whale's large mouth. On top is the Raven holding his beak, in reference to the myth of the halibut fisherman. *Acquired on Haida Gwaii before 1908 for the A. Aaronson collection.* CMC VII-B-719 (S92-4260)

Centre: This spoon handle illustrates the Bear Mother myth. At the base of the handle, the Bear Father attacks the Bear Hunter while his wife and one of their cubs watch from above. The Raven with a raven fin on its head completes the composition. *Collected at Masset before 1894 by Charles F. Newcombe.* CMC VII-B-492 (S92-4221)

Right: On this spoon handle, the Raven holding an otter is the dominant figure on the lower part. Above are two human figures, the first a chief in ceremonial robes, then a shaman with a dorsal fin on his head. Pieces of abalone shell have been set into the handle to make it flash in the firelight. *Collected at Masset before 1901 by Charles F. Newcombe.* CMC VII-B-483 (S92-4212)

PLATE 24A, 24B, 24C
Feast spoons made of
mountain goat horn.
Left: The culture hero Raven
perches on a personified rock
at the base of the spoon
handle. The Killer Whale at
the top grasps a drowned
human whose soul is being
taken to the undersea world.
*Collected at Masset before 1901
by Charles F. Newcombe.* CMC
VII-B-475 (s92-4209)
Centre: This spoon handle
illustrates the Nansimget story.
The large Whale at the base is
grasping the hero's wife in its
mouth while the hero rides its
dorsal fin. The Bear completes
the composition. Abalone shell
inlays enhance the prestige of
the owner of this piece.
*Collected from the Kaigani
Haida before 1901 by Charles F.
Newcombe.* CMC VII-B-470
(s92-4204)
Right: At the base of the spoon
handle, a large Whale holds a
halibut in its mouth. On the
Whale's head is the hunter
from the Bear Mother story,
holding the Bear. *Collected at
Masset before 1894 by Charles F.
Newcombe.* CMC VII-B-472
(s92-4205)

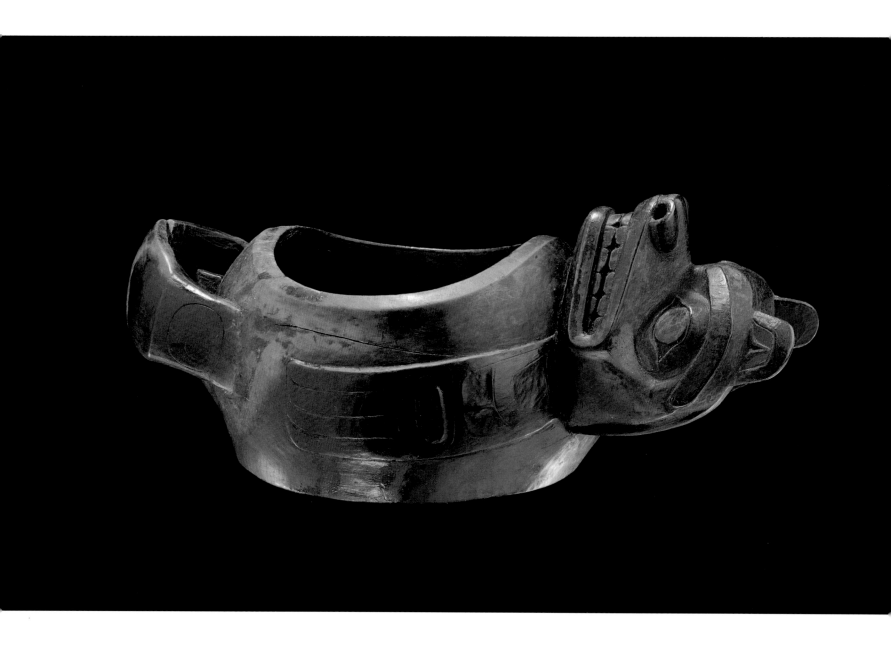

Food Dishes and Bowls

An individual who possessed a personal or family food dish (PLATE 25) was expected to bring it along to a feast and to use it afterwards to take food home to relatives (Newcombe 1902:MS). The personal food dish, called a *kihle,* is about 30 cm (12 inches) in length, although smaller ones were made for children. A personal "grease" dish was often carved from a solid block of wood, usually alder, which grows on Haida Gwaii, or maple, which was traded in finished form from the Tsimshian. Bill Holm (1974:28) argues convincingly that the prototype for this sort of dish was originally birchbark, with folded and sewn seams at each corner.

Most dishes have decorated ends only, emblazoned with the owner's crest incised in shallow formlines enhanced by red and black paint, though green is sometimes used. The rims often have inlays of shell—operculum, abalone or dentalium—or in historic times, white beads or brass tacks. A significant number also have decorations on the sides, including a broad range of creatures such as Thunderbird, Eagle, Bear, Whale, Beaver and various unidentified mythological beings. The major collector of Haida artifacts, Charles F. Newcombe of Victoria, describes the design of a Thunderbird on a grease dish as follows (1902:MS):

> In these dishes the head occupies nearly all of the surface of the ends. The eyes are the most conspicuous parts and are indicated by the rounded oblong figures on each side with a black center. Above these are the ear symbols, and below the long narrow space with, usually, a curved line above and a straight one below, is the mouth. At the center of the mouth is generally a wedge shaped mark. If complete, this should have its base joined to the upper lip and the point overhanging the lower one. It is more usual to find this V-shaped mark wanting some of its proper characters than to find a perfect one. It indicates the beak of the bird as seen from full front. A few horizontal markings under the mouth are intended to show the foot.

Another kind of dish favoured by the Haida was made of mountain sheep horn that was steamed and bent over a wooden form. The exterior was usually engraved with a complete creature, often a Hawk or Thunderbird. Since sheep horn had to be imported to Haida Gwaii, these are relatively rare in comparison with wooden bowls, and often glow with the patina of long and careful use.

Serving bowls provided by the hosts are the most sculptural of Haida food containers. They are often decorated with human and animal faces and give full expression to the animal forms they emulate (PLATE 26). The most common form of zoomorphic bowl is in the shape of a Seal, often shown holding a small human figure in its mouth or under its chin, a gesture that undoubtedly had some mythical significance. Incised formlines delineate the Seal's joints and front flippers. The seal-shaped dish was used to serve seal oil. Other figures such as the Beaver, Sea Otter or even Dragonfly also decorate serving bowls. The rims of

PLATE 25

This ancient style of carved wooden food bowl, which depicts a Sea Lion in a floating position, is heavily impregnated with grease. The creature's head resembles that of a bear, with prominent ears that are not possessed by sea lions. *Acquired on Haida Gwaii in the early nineteenth century by Philip Henry Hind, later in the James Hooper collection, London.* CMC VII-X-1458 (S94-6747)

these vessels are often embellished with opercula shell or sea otter teeth.

Dishes for serving seal or eulachon oil, to judge from their glossy patina, were also frequently made in the shape of canoes. Most are plain, perhaps to emphasize the abstract sculptural form of the canoe, but some have incised designs similar to those painted on actual canoes.

Bentwood Trays and Serving Dishes

PLATE 26

This small alder food bowl portraying a Frog was used to serve special condiments such as fermented fish eggs. This piece in the Canadian Museum of Civilization collection is the personal favourite of Haida artist Bill Reid. *Collected at Skidegate circa 1900 by Charles F. Newcombe.* CMC VII-B-464 (s94-6782)

A variety of containers for the feast, including trays and serving dishes, were made by the bentwood technique, in which a single plank was kerfed, steamed and bent at three corners, then pegged together at the fourth. Bases were morticed and pegged to the sides.

Shallow rectangular bentwood trays were standard items at a feast. Some large trays for serving smoked or roasted fish were up to 1.5 m (5 feet) in length. The sides were often of alder, and the bottom was generally red cedar. The shape of the top of the rim alternates between concave and convex on each of the four sides. Most trays have a raised flat pedestal at each end, on which to rest spoons.

A deeper version of the bentwood tray is actually a serving dish, ranging from large shallow-sided soup dishes to deep-sided boxes for berries or crabapples in eulachon grease (PLATES 27 to 34). These bentwood dishes were often made in the shape of animals or humans, with faces and hands at one end, and hips, legs and feet at the other. The sides of some dishes bulge out, considerably enhancing their zoomorphic nature, and are usually embellished with two-dimensional bas-relief carving or painting. Some examples position the decorative figures upside-down, but the majority are right-way up. The most elaborate example has a sculptured face and tail on the ends, and bas-relief arms, legs and hip joints on the bulging sides. This type of bentwood dish is often so animated in design and execution that it appears to be alive. Covers made of tightly woven cedar bark were used to keep dirt and insects out of the food (PLATE 27).

PLATE 27

A bentwood food dish with its cover of woven cedar bark. The main figure is that of a Hawk; at the opposite end is an inverted human figure. This dish belonged to Chief Klue of Tanu, who took it with him when he moved to Skidegate. *Collected at Skidigate circa 1900 by Charles F. Newcombe.* CMC VII-B-740 (s92-4270)

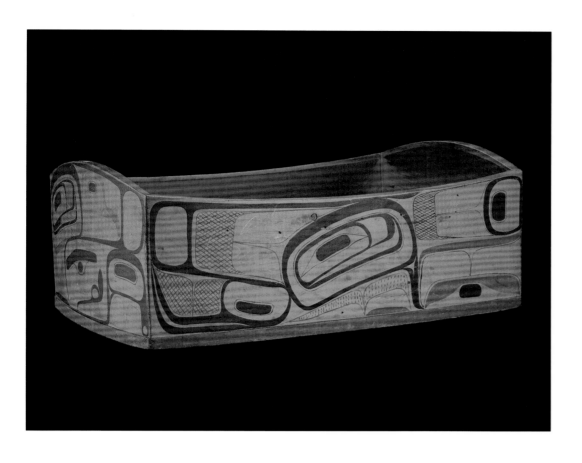

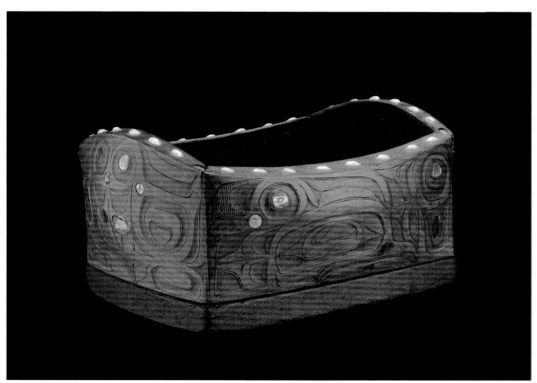

PLATE 28

The isolated decorative
elements on this bentwood
food dish do not form a
coherent design. Such
fractured designs seem to have
appeared more frequently in
the late nineteenth century,
perhaps as a result of the
disappearance of the traditions
that guided the art forms. As
well, pieces with such designs
were sold mostly to artistically
naive travellers. *Collected in
1914 by Thomas Deasey, the
Indian agent at Masset.* CMC
VII-B-1158 (s94-6748)

PLATE 29

An exquisite example of a deep
bentwood food dish of yellow
cedar. The complex Whale
designs are inlaid with two
kinds of shell, opercula and
abalone. *Acquired about 1900
for the Lord Bossom collection.*
CMC VII-X-1093 (s94-6746)

PLATE 30

A deep bentwood food dish. The design on it, originally painted in black and red, is that of a Whale with Nansimget hanging onto its head. Large feast dishes like this one could hold an entire 22.7-kg (50-pound) roasted salmon. *Collected at Skidegate in 1897 by Charles F. Newcombe.* CMC VII-B-739 (s92-4266)

PLATE 31

A bentwood food dish made about 1850, decorated with brass corner plates. The design depicts a bird, possibly the Thunderbird, with a profile human figure on its back between the wing and tail feathers. The theme of carrying ancestors or mythic heros to the sky or undersea world is a recurrent one. *Collected on Haida Gwaii in 1898 by Charles F. Newcombe.* CMC VII-B-142 (s94-6799)

PLATE 32 (facing page)

A deep bentwood food dish depicting the wings and tail of a bird. An unusual quartered device appears beside the wing joint on the long side. The rim is decorated with opercula shells. *Collected at Masset before 1901 by Charles F. Newcombe.* CMC VII-B-334 (s94-6753)

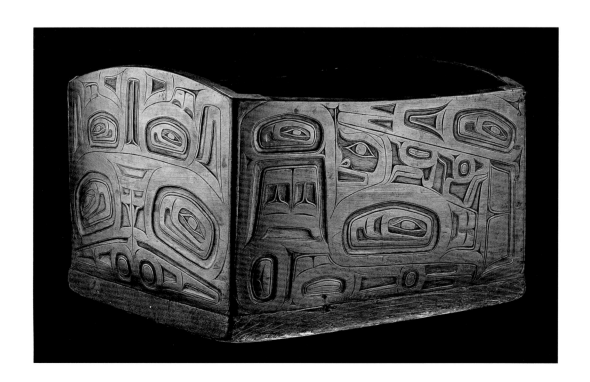

PLATE 33

A deep bentwood food dish with a bird design. The slightly bulbous sides are incised and painted, with a particularly fine inverted human head over the forehead of the bird. *Collected at Skidegate in 1899 by Charles F. Newcombe.* CMC VII-B-341 (S92-4201)

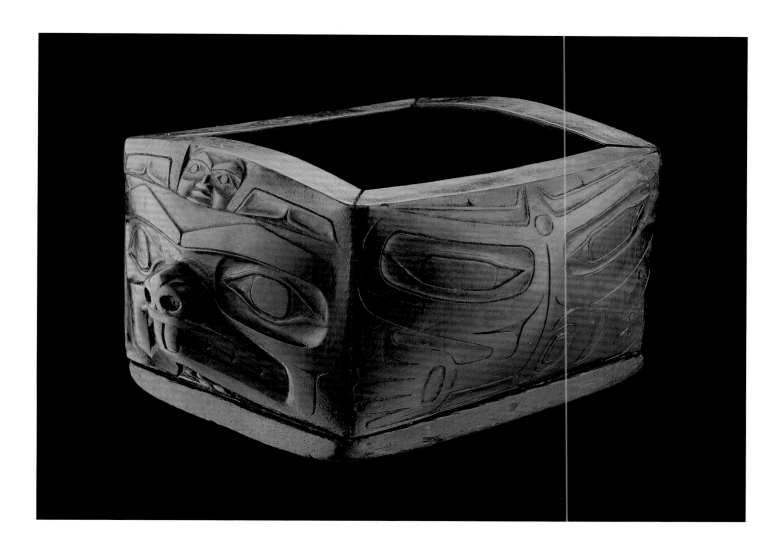

PLATE 34

This fine example of a bentwood food dish portrays a Beaver crest in which a human figure is manifested by hands on the sides and a face between the ears of the Beaver. *Collected at Skidegate in 1886 by Reverend Thomas Crosby.* CMC VII-B-97 (S94-6739)

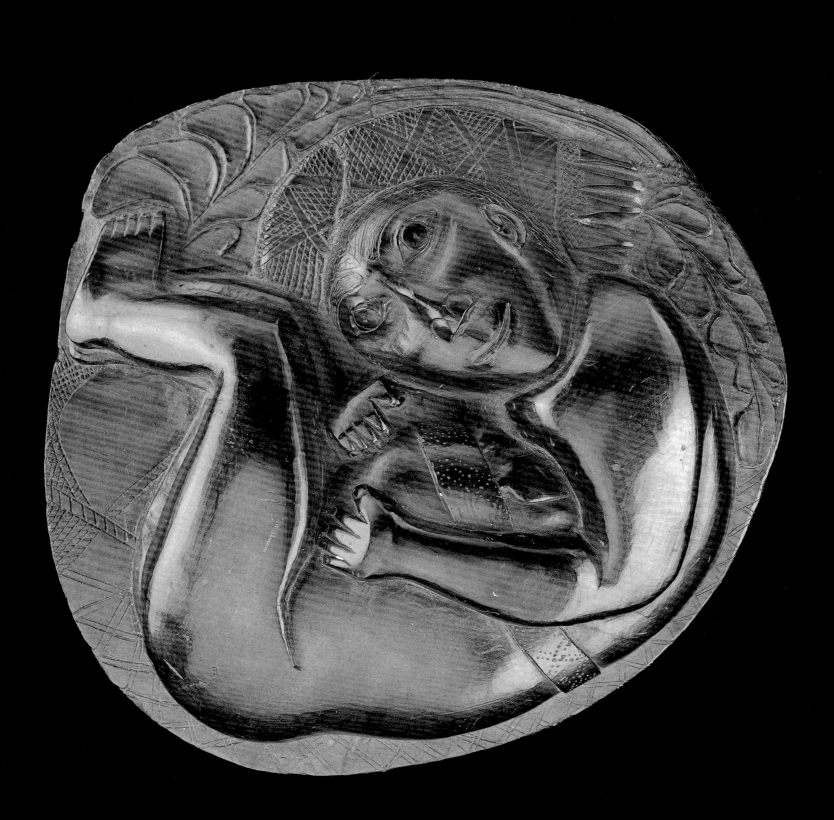

SHAMANISM

The Haida and their neighbours held in common a set of beliefs about the way the human world interacted with the natural and supernatural worlds, though the Haida also had some profound differences in outlook. The shared concepts centred around curing the sick, ensuring the supply of fish and game, and controlling or at least influencing the weather. Among the ranks of shaman were specialists whose powers were particularly effective within a selected range of tasks such as securing the outcome of major enterprises like trading expeditions or warfare.

Both genders could be shaman, but more often it was men who chose the calling. Women shaman focussed more on curing illnesses and the difficulties of childbirth (PLATE 35) and, in rare cases, on power over animals and fish. Although shaman could come from any rank except slaves, they were usually members of high-ranking families, often even the brother of a chief; thus, together they combined both secular and supernatural control at the head of a lineage. John R. Swanton was able to secure detailed information as to how a person became a shaman (1905:38):

> A shaman was one who had power from some supernatural being (*sga'na*) who "possessed" him, or who chose him as the medium through which to make his existence felt in the world of men. When the spirit was present, the shaman's own identity was practically abolished. For the time he was the supernatural being himself. So the shaman must dress as the spirit directed him, and, when the spirit was present, spoke in the latter's own language . . .
>
> The calling of a shaman was generally hereditary in his family, the order being usually from maternal uncle to nephew. Before he died he revealed his spirits to his successor, who might start with a comparatively feeble spirit and acquire stronger and stronger ones. The principal classes of supernatural beings who spoke through shamans were the Canoe-People, the Forest-People, and the Above-People.

Alexander McKenzie (1891:57) also made some observations about shaman in Masset:

> There were no prescribed stages or degrees in the initiation of a medicine-man. (Haida *Sahgah*). The aspirant to that office was instructed by another medicine-man, generally his uncle,

PLATE 35

An argillite birth charm depicting a woman in labour. She is sitting on a cedar bark mat and resting her head on a cedar bark pillow. Around her waist is a ceinture used to constrict the upper abdomen and aid in the delivery. Marks on the piece suggest it is a talisman rather than a tourist piece. *Collected on Haida Gwaii in 1879 by Israel W. Powell.* CMC VII-B-779 (S94-6827)

to whom he succeeded, and on his aptitude to learn the system did the length of his proba-
tion depend . . .

. . . Haida doctors never used the drum by way of divination, nor did they employ
passes or signs among themselves. Their great aim was to avoid meeting, as they professed to
be afraid of each other, and the custom was for each doctor to magnify himself and reduce
his rival. They professed to fight in visions.

Much of what we know about shaman is provided by commentary on particular individuals, sometimes by traders, travellers and ethnographers, but mostly by missionaries,
although the latter and shaman were mutually suspicious of each other as competitors. The
most famous shaman was, without doubt, Dr. Kudé of Masset; numerous photographs taken
of him in the 1880s and 1890s show that he fitted the image of a shaman perfectly. Dr. Kudé
left his shamanic paraphernalia, including fish effigies he must have used for first salmon ceremonies, to the Pitt Rivers Museum at Oxford University. He appears in a famous photograph of three shaman from Masset dressed in a mixture of sacred and secular clothing
(PLATE 138).

The dress of a male shaman is described by Swanton (1905:40):

The dress of a shaman differed somewhat in accordance with the kind of spirit speaking
through him. Usually he wore a dancing blanket (Chilkat Blanket), carried an oval rattle, and
had a number of bone "head-scratchers" hung around his neck. His hair was allowed to grow
long, and was never combed or cleaned. Sometimes he wore a bone stuck through it; at others he wore a cap slanting upon either side to a ridge at the top; sometimes he wore a circular
fillet. He always wore a long bone through the septum of his nose.

The traditional clothing of a shaman is particularly well documented in the art of the
Haida, who portrayed the shaman on the pair of posts that flanked his or her mortuary to
warn off trespassers. The costume depicted is invariably a fringed apron ornamented with
deer hooves or puffin beaks. A male shaman always wore his hair long, collected in a bun on
top of his head, topped with a wedge-shaped or pointed hat, or a crown of grizzly bear claws.
The crown of claws (or occasionally goat horns) is more usual among the Tsimshian but was
frequently depicted in Haida argillite portraits of shaman, perhaps because it appealed to
tourists (PLATES 36, 37).

Wooden carvings of shaman are often very naturalistic, and a dozen or two were made by
Simeon Stiltla, Charles Edenshaw and possibly by others (PLATE 38). New documentation
indicates that the works once attributed to Gwaitilth are actually by Simeon Stiltla
(1833–1883). The most elaborate of these pieces, such as the one collected by John R. Swanton for the American Museum of Natural History, show the dead shaman laid out, knees
bent, in his mortuary house; often he is clutching in one hand a globular rattle with a human
or animal face on it, and in the other a soul catcher (PLATE 39).

PLATE 36

An argillite figure of a *skaga*, or shaman, with all of the accoutrements of his trade, including a nose pin as well as a bone tube in his hair knot. In his right hand, he holds a bone soul catcher, and in his left a carved rattle. He wears only a decorated apron of fringed deerskin, and his box of charms is placed conveniently before him. *Possibly acquired by James Deans in 1899 for the A. Aaronson collection.* CMC VII-B-812 (S92-4272)

It is said that shaman on the north coast could see the soul departing from a patient's body, as if it were a firefly or small light darting around, and the Haida also seemed to identify the Dragonfly and Butterfly with human souls. The shaman's task was to capture the lost soul in a double-ended soul catcher, then trap it inside with a plug of shredded red cedar bark until it could be blown back into the patient. According to Reverend Charles Harrison (1925:98), "Another familiar of Haida shaman was the killerwhale that was considered to be a bearer for the souls of those who drowned to the realm of the sea chief who was the master of drowned souls."

The shaman wore a neckring of hide over a frame of wood, from which were suspended a dozen or more charms (PLATE 40). Thousands of these charms survive in museum collections, unfortunately without specific documentation. Bird and otter figures are the most common, followed by fish and whales, though many necklaces have only pointed bone pins or bear or beaver teeth attached to them. Rarer shaman charms depict human parts like legs or a hand, or monstrous figures with no natural counterparts. Halibut figures seemed to be a favourite of the shaman, perhaps as art historian Aldona Joanitis (1981) suggests because of the liminal state that halibut fishing, which is done at great depths, represents. Hauling up a 136-kg (300-pound) halibut on a kelp line from a depth of hundreds of metres must have called on supernatural strength more then anything else a Haida fisherman did. McKenzie (1891:59) notes that "To catch eight halibut was a subject for congratulations."

The Haida preferred to obtain their charms from Tsimshian or Nisga'a shaman, who were thought to be especially powerful. The large number of shaman charms that has survived may be due to the fact that they were made of enduring materials like teeth, bone, antler and stone; the Haida often inlaid theirs with small pieces of abalone shell. Also, they were placed in shaman's tombs well away from villages and could be touched only by other shaman.

Haida shaman employed three types of rattles. One is globular in shape and filled with pebbles, or later trade beads, to produce a distinctive sound when shaken in a variety of rhythmic ways appropriate to the purpose of the ceremony. One side of the rattle usually has a human or animal face in full sculptural form, and the other side an engraved and painted flat design of stylized formlines (PLATES 41, 42, 43, 110). Some rattles, however, are sculpted on both sides.

The second type of rattle consists of hoops of wood with crossbars, to which are attached deer hooves or puffin beaks. Deer hooves have been used by shaman in the northern hemisphere since palaeolithic times, and it is claimed that fetal caribou hooves made a sound that was particularly attractive to herds of caribou, which would be lured to approach the shaman and of course his hunter companions.

A third type of rattle, unique to Haida shaman, was the double-headed dance wand hung with puffin beaks (PLATES 44, 45). Puffins were significant because they were diving birds that suddenly disappeared into another cosmic zone beneath the sea. Puffin beaks were also suspended on a circle of wood that represented a cosmic doorway.

PLATE 37A, 37B
Front and rear views of an argillite carving of a shaman with a chief and his slave, which relates to a story about a shaman from Tanu. It was probably carved at Skidegate. *Collected at Carcross, Yukon Territory, in 1972 by Dr. Catherine McClellan.* CMC VII-X-484 (S94-6805 front, S94-6806 back)

PLATE 38

This wooden figure of a shaman has a large Killer Whale fin protruding from his head. The face of the same creature is portrayed on his apron. The symmetrical position of the hands is unusual for a shaman and may indicate that he is diving or swimming in the undersea world of the Killer Whale chief. *Purchased in London, England, in 1976.* CMC VII-B-1654 (S94-6774)

PLATE 39

A model of a shaman's mortuary showing the placement of his body with his head resting on his box of charms. The image of the shaman is repeated on the corner posts, and the large Raven stands guard on the top. Many actual mortuaries like this were placed on small islands near the old villages, but all of them have been looted by curiosity seekers. This fine model was made by Simeon Stiltla in 1900 for John R. Swanton and is now in the American Museum of Natural History.

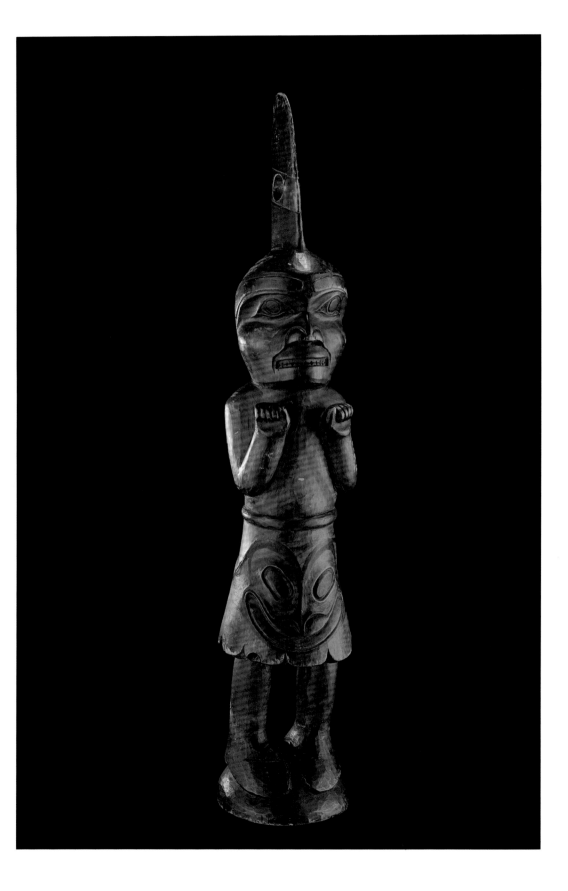

PLATE 40

A shaman's charm necklace for effecting cures. The fishlike figure at the centre is a "mountain demon" according to James Deans. John R. Swanton (1905:275) identifies this as a *sangu*, or "halibut gills," a crest of the Stastas Eagles lineage. *Acquired on Haida Gwaii in 1899 for the A. Aaronson collection.* CMC VII-B-871 (s92-4280)

PLATE 41

Robins were thought to be familiar spirits of shaman, perhaps because of their migratory behaviour. The wormholes and decay in this shaman's rattle indicate that it was taken from a grave on Haida Gwaii. *Collected at Masset at the turn of the century by Edward Harris, a Hudson's Bay Company fur trader.* CMC VII-X-276 (s94-6776)

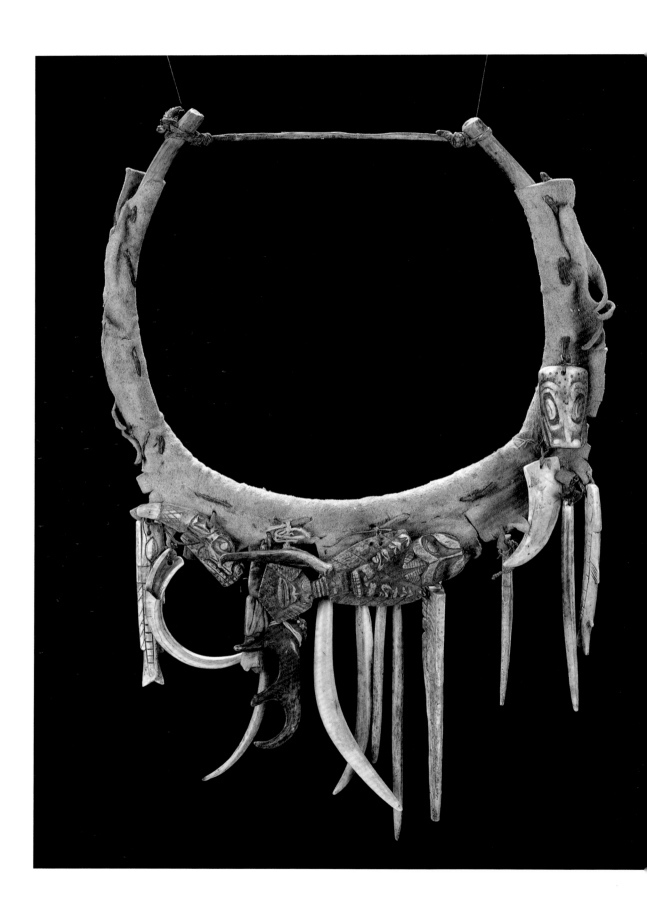

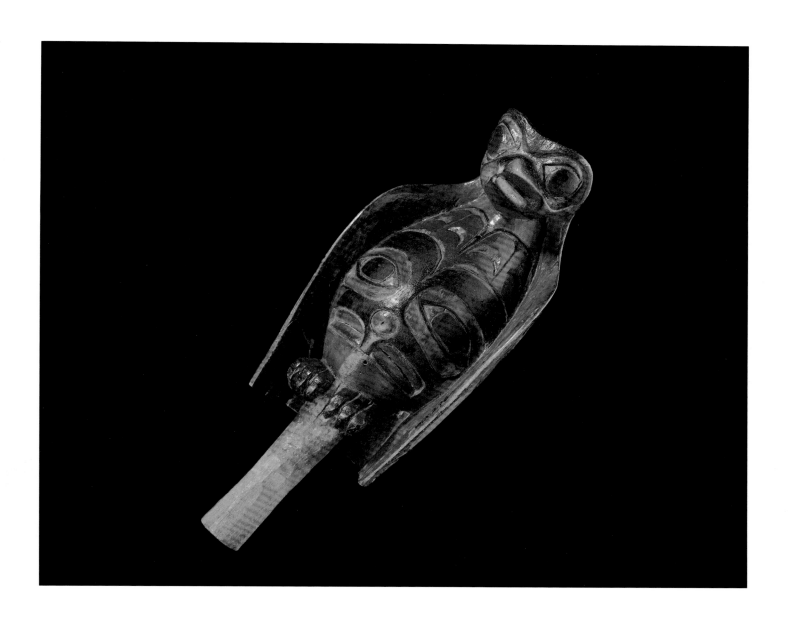

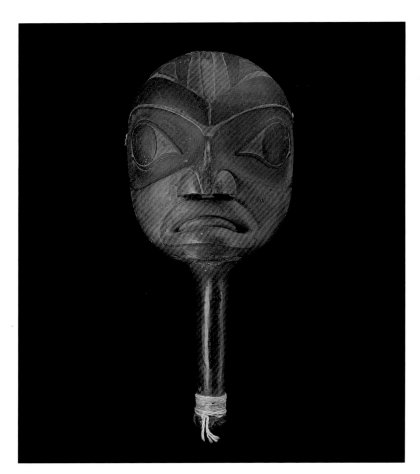 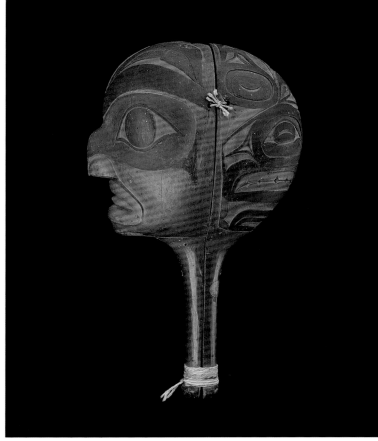

PLATE 42A, 42B

Front (*left*) and side views of a
shaman's curing rattle, with a
human face sculpted on one
side and a two-dimensional
design of a Sculpin on the
other. *Acquired on Haida Gwaii
in 1899 for the A. Aaronson
collection.* CMC VII-B-672 (SS92-
4249 front, S92-4250 side)

PLATE 43A, 43B

On the front of this shaman's curing rattle (*left*) is a Bear with the head of a Frog in its mouth. The back portrays a Sculpin head. *Collected on Haida Gwaii in 1884 by Alexander McKenzie for Dr. W. F. Tolmie of the Hudson's Bay Company.* CMC VII-B-669 (s92-4247 front, s92-4248 back)

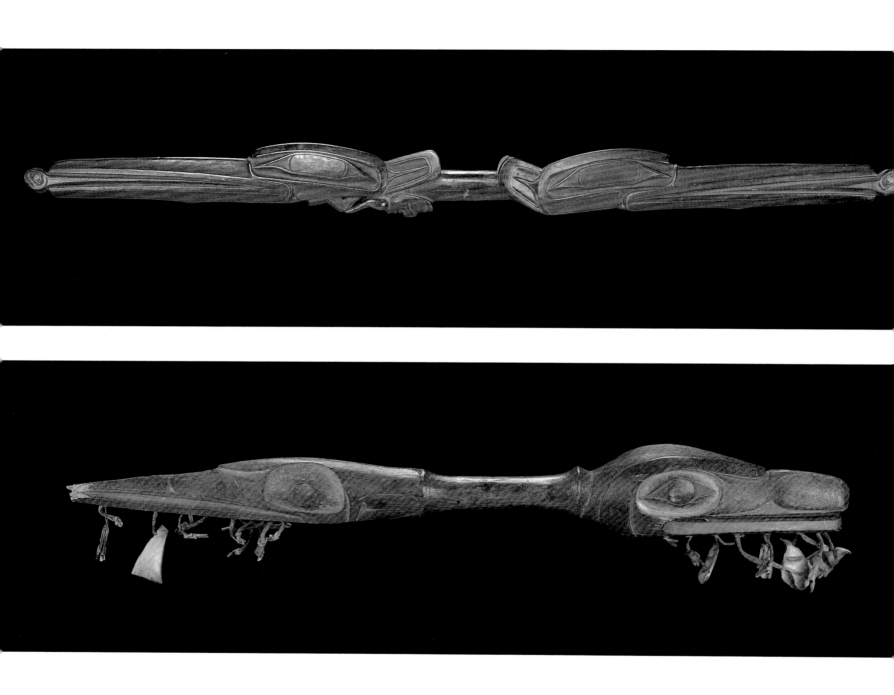

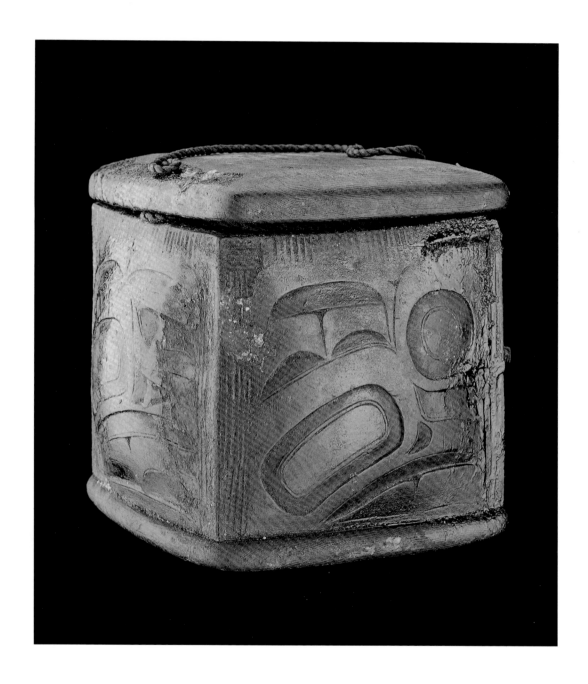

PLATE 44

A shaman's dance wand with the symmetrical heads of two Cranes eating some kind of fish, a variation on the double-headed pattern of the soul catcher itself. This very early piece was probably removed from a shaman's gravehouse. *Collected on Haida Gwaii in 1879 by Israel W. Powell.* CMC VII-B-117 (S92-4189)

PLATE 45

This shaman's dance wand has puffin beak rattles attached to it. One end depicts a Crane's head and the other end a Sea Lion's head. *Possibly acquired by James Deans before 1899 for the A. Aaronson collection.* CMC VII-B-686 (S92-4252)

PLATE 46

A red cedar bentwood box used to hold a shaman's charms. The highly stylized design includes a bird's head on one side. The wear and grease on the box indicate long service. *Probably removed from a shaman's grave on Haida Gwaii before 1899 by James Deans for the A. Aaronson collection.* CMC VII-B-726 (S94-6800)

The shaman kept his paraphernalia in a special box that was distinctive in form and decoration. It was stoutly made to serve the shaman for his lifetime and bore protective animal images (PLATE 46). In it, he kept his soul catcher, charms, rattles and, in some larger boxes, a set of masks. According to Franz Boas (in Swanton 1905:43), Haida shaman do not wear masks, though Tlingit shaman do. However, there is some evidence that Haida shaman did wear masks on rare occasions (PLATE 47).

Objects and motifs associated with shamanism were not appropriate for trade; they were custom made for individual shaman and buried with them. Consequently, the range of motifs and styles associated with shamanism are archaic in many respects. There is a heavy emphasis in shamanic artifacts on Killer Whale motifs or creatures from the liminal space of the intertidal zone, like octopus, or the depths of the ocean, like halibut.

SECRET SOCIETIES

Secular power in Haida society was wielded by the chiefs, who, unlike their Kwakwa̲ka'wakw (or Kwakiutl) neighbours to the south, never yielded their power each winter to the heads of the secret societies. Nevertheless, by the mid-eighteenth century, the Haida began to practise much weaker forms of secret society winter dances, which they learned from captives taken in wars against the Heiltsuk in particular. However, as many of the captives were of low rank and had not been fully initiated into secret societies, the Haida were copying poorly understood models. Like the Tsimshian, the Haida were late recipients of these winter dance societies and never elaborated them further. Photographer Edward Curtis (1916:130) noted that the Haida knew little of the underlying myths or esoteric features of the winter dances, though they did preserve the names of a dozen different kinds and performed them at all winter festivities, including those to mark the raising of a totem pole or the building of a house.

The Tsimshian have a well-known story about how secret societies were acquired by two brothers out fishing (Boas 1916:285). The Haida version is different: according to it, secret societies were stolen by one of their own supernatural beings, Qingi, who travelled from Haida Gwaii in a small black canoe called Tobacco Canoe to the house of the Chief of the Undersea World. One part of the long story illuminates some features of Haida dance hats (Swanton 1905:157):

> Qi'ngi sat by himself on one side of the house, and at intervals opened his bag, took out a piece of dried salmon, and ate it. For this all of the supernatural beings laughed at him. Then he put on a tall dance-hat and began to dance. At once they heard the "spirits" (secret-society whistles), —the first time that human beings had heard them. These whistling sounds were caused by flickers. Qi'ngi's hat now began to grow; and as it grew, sea-gulls and cormorants flew from the joints, and scattered their excrement over everybody, so that the supernatural beings covered up their faces. By and by his hat shrank again, and he took it off.

PLATE 47
A shaman's mask of red cedar trimmed with eagle down. The crown of grizzly claws was copied from Tsimshian shaman. Masks were only very rarely used by Haida shaman, so this one was probably made for sale to visitors. *Collected on Haida Gwaii by Israel W. Powell in 1879*. CMC VII-B-11 (s92-4165)

PLATE 48

A wooden Killer Whale dorsal
fin ornament with streamers of
human hair. As many as five
similar fins were tied to dance
cloaks, or a single one was tied
to the head of a dancer. From
a donated collection, no
specific acquisition
information. CMC VII-X-31
(s94-6783)

PLATE 49 (facing page)
A dancing spear that belonged
to the Warrior Society. The
alternating thick and thin
spiral lines imitate patterns
observed on the legs of tables
and chairs aboard European
ships. *Collected on Haida
Gwaii in 1879* by *Israel W.
Powell.* CMC VII-B-129.2
(s4192.2)

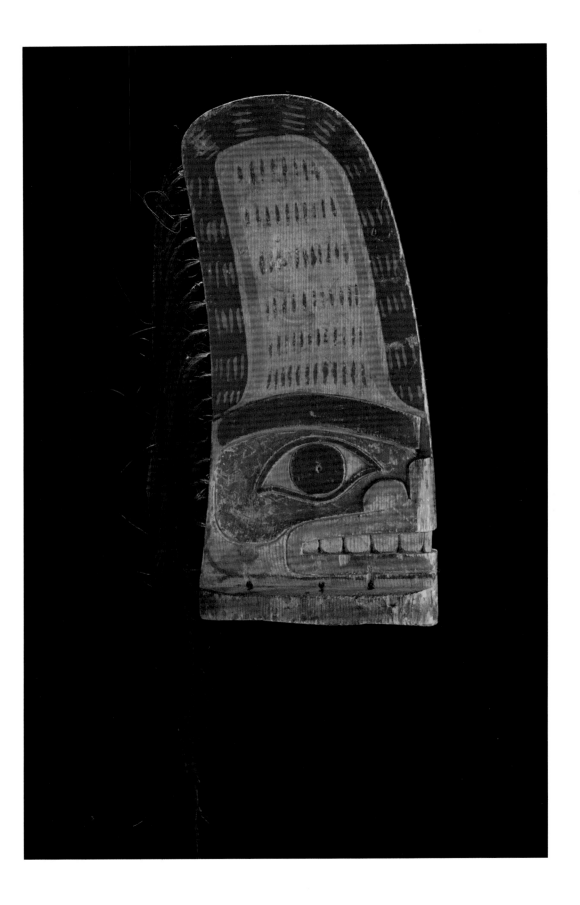

The living beings flying out from the joints of the stack of rings on the dance hat are a revealing reference to the Haida belief that the rings represent the spinal column of supernatural beings and are a source of new emerging life. The story ends with Qingi escaping with the new dances he had seen to introduce them to the Haida.

Among the Haida, the winter dances began to die out in the mid-1870s, although they were held sporadically for another decade. There are, consequently, few eyewitness accounts of the performances. Nevertheless, Curtis (1916:142–43) was able to find Haida who still vividly recalled such events from their childhood:

> Little children could be initiated into the society . . . They spent the eleven days behind the curtain, supposedly dead for eight days and absent with the spirits for the remaining three, and when the dancing began they came out and stood in front of the curtain . . .
>
> After retiring behind the curtain the elder initiates also remained in concealment for eleven days, except that in the evenings of the first eight days they came out in full paraphernalia and went with characteristic actions through the village. During the day they too were supposedly lying dead behind the curtain.
>
> At the end of eight days many whistles sounded in the woods, and gradually receded, and it was said that the spirits of the initiates were being carried away by supernatural beings. For the next three days the initiates remained in constant hiding. Then on the twelfth morning those initiates who were to represent dancers appeared on the beach as if they were wild creatures just come out of the woods after their absence with the supernatural beings. The members of the fraternity proceeded in a body to catch them with ropes, and dragged them into a house (not the *skasnai*) and behind a curtain. In the evening all the people, regardless of membership in the society, assembled in the *skasnai* to exorcise the spirit that possessed the initiates.
>
> The female members danced in their various characters, and then the initiates, led in through the front door by their attendants, danced round the fire and retired behind the curtain. They reappeared and performed several times in different costumes until they were "tamed." The night was passed in dancing and performing sleight-of-hand tricks such as seemingly decapitating an initiate and restoring his life.

Each dancing society had its own distinctive features (PLATES 48, 49). Some societies were the exclusive right of particular village chiefs and not widely distributed on Haida Gwaii. Swanton and Curtis interviewed many informants sufficiently long after the passing of the societies that they revealed some facts which otherwise would have been kept secret.

Swanton (1905:16) claims that the secret societies were merged with the shamanic beliefs of the Haida:

> Just as a shaman was supposed to be inspired by some supernatural being who "spoke," or, as they generally preferred to translate it to me, "came through" him, so the U'lala spirit, the Dog-eating spirit, the Grisly-Bear spirit, and so on, "came through" the secret-society novice.

One of the main societies was the Ulala (or Wilala), similar to the Hamatsa (or Cannibal) among the Kwakwa̲ka'wakw (or Kwakiutl), which was danced only by men. A long pole with a crossbar projected through the roof from behind the dance curtain and had cedar bark streamers suspended from it. This pole was rotated to signal to those outside that the Ulala was about to emerge. According to Curtis (1916:145), "Various masks were worn by Ulala, depending on the supposed source of his supernatural power."

Much of what shocked and repelled the early missionaries about the winter dances was the stagecraft, which they took very literally. Curtis (1916:144) describes some such enactments by the Ulala:

He made the gestures and facial expressions of the Hamatsa, and pretended to bite either forearm of several persons. Actually he did not bite at all. Those who were to be "bitten" had previously raised a blister on the forearm by burning cedar-bark over a round spot, so that after the "biting" they could exhibit a raw wound. Many of the oldest men have numerous such scars extending along the arm.

On appearing at the edge of the woods, Ulala mounted a mortuary hut and took out an image closely resembling a corpse. It was covered with the dark skins of scoters, and looked much like a dried, mouldy corpse. Inside the belly was a mass of cooked spruce-bast, or a long string of flour paste colored bluish so as to resemble intestines. Sometimes the initiate would tear the belly skin open and there on the beach devour the contents, but usually the "corpse" was taken from him and carried into the house, where he ate and passed portions among the other Ulala.

MASKS

Secret societies and their performances began to disappear with the arrival of the missionaries in the mid-1870s. A photograph documents the participants in the last secret society dances at Skidegate in the 1880s (PLATE 124), showing some of the young women wearing masks while others wear frontlets or have painted their faces (PLATES 50, 51).

Among the Haida, masks were used mostly by members of the secret societies (PLATES 1, 52 to 56, 58 to 71). Secret society dances frequently used both masks and puppets to represent wild spirits of the woods, which the Haida called *gagiid*. They are distinguished by an emaciated or wrinkled face and grimacing mouth, and are often blue-green in colour, to indicate that they portray a person who has narrowly escaped drowning and whose flesh has gone cold from long exposure in cold water (PLATES 56, 57).

Like their Tsimshian neighbours, the Haida also employed masks in potlatch performances to illustrate the spirit beings (*geni loci*) encountered by their ancestors. Unfortunately, much less is known about such supernatural being masks among the Haida than about the *nox nox* (or supernatural spirit) masks of the Tsimshian, who to this day have maintained their traditions in some interior villages.

PLATE 50

This deerskin bag, which held powdered red ochre for paint used in a variety of ceremonies, has seen much wear. The double-headed Thunderbird on the front is a rarity among the Haida, who usually portray it with a single head. It is very similar in form to a tattoo design and may have been used as such by the owner. *Collected from Skidegate between 1890 and 1904 by Charles F. Newcombe.* CMC VII-B-538 (S92-4235)

PLATE 51

The style of the painting on this deerskin bag (used to store red ochre for paint) is truly outstanding and was done by an unknown master artist of the middle of the last century. On the bag are two classic opposites: the Thunderbird, which is the supreme sky being, and the Killer Whale, which is one manifestation of the Chief of the Seas. *Collected at Skidegate between 1890 and 1904 by Charles F. Newcombe.* CMC VII-B-537 (S92-4233)

71

PLATE 52

A secret society mask with face painting and copper inlay. Both types of decoration were actually used by dancers, who in addition to painting their faces sometimes attached cutouts of copper and abalone shell to them with halibut glue. This mask was probably made for ceremonial use in the 1850s and was extensively trimmed with fur to form a goatee, fringe beard and hairline, but only the leather that once held the fur remains. *Collected at Masset before 1884 by Alexander McKenzie of the Hudson's Bay Company.* CMC VII-B-1554 (s85-3286)

PLATE 53

A mask of a young woman wearing a small labret of abalone shell and with face painting. The red scalelike carving around the rim is an unusual feature. *Collected on Haida Gwaii in 1879 by Israel W. Powell.* CMC VII-B-928A (s85-3284)

The influence of the tourist market on Haida mask-making is difficult to evaluate. After the 1840s, masks and argillite carvings were the items most sought after by seamen, traders and tourists, and probably several thousand Haida masks are held in private and museum collections around the world. Deciding which masks were made for traditional use rather than for sale is largely a matter of judgement. Indicators of actual use include signs of wear on the leather ties and interior surface, the functionality of the eyeholes, the allowance for facial fit for wearing, evidence of attachment of headcloths or animal fur that was stripped off before sale, and traces of glue and down or cedar bark. The opposite factors such as no means for attaching the mask to the wearer's head, no preparation of the interior to avoid rubbing the wearer's nose and no functional eyeholes indicate that a mask was made for tourists.

Famous artists like Simeon Stiltla and Charles Edenshaw are known to have made masks for ceremonial use. One such example is the elaborate transformation mask by Charles Edenshaw now in the Pitt Rivers Museum at Oxford University.

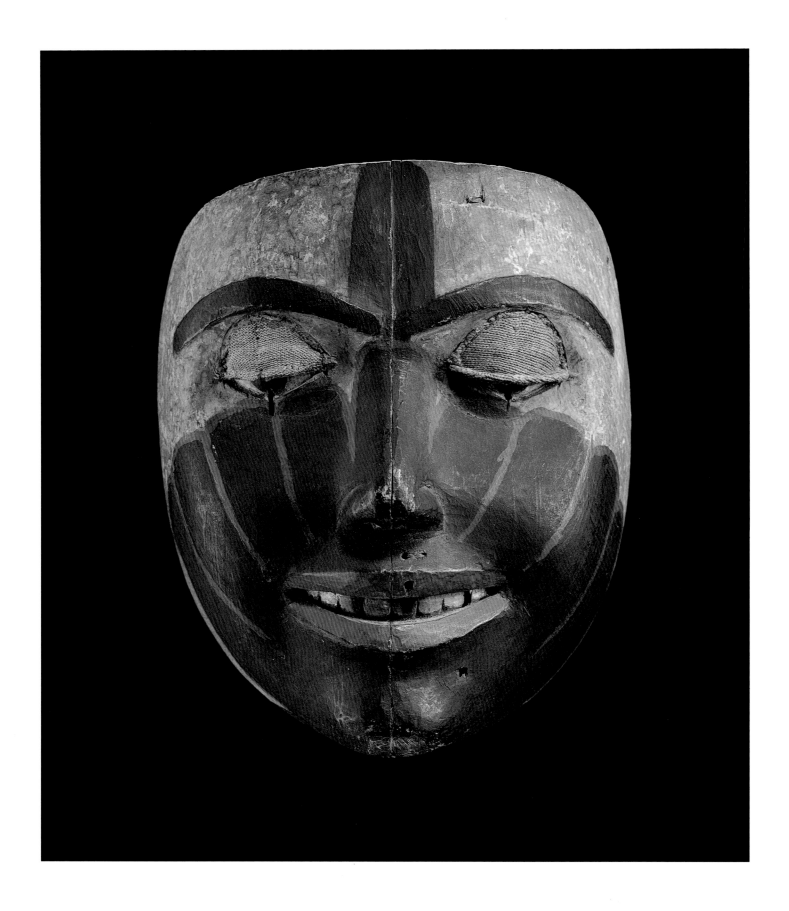

PLATE 54

A secret society mask made by
Simeon Stiltla (1833–1883).
Raven feather patterns are
painted around the mouth.
The face is fuller than on most
of this artist's works, but the
narrow eyebrows, pointed chin
and movable eyes are all
characteristic of his style.
Collected at Masset before 1884
by Alexander McKenzie of the
Hudson's Bay Company. CMC
VII-B-1 (S92-4160)

PLATE 55

A portrait mask by Simeon
Stiltla of an old woman
wearing a large labret.
Streamers of red wool
originally decorated the ears.
Stiltla usually incised the hair
in plaited grooves to look like
the folk carvings made by
sailors on New England ships,
but on this rare example he
painted the hair pattern,
perhaps to differentiate it from
the wrinkles on the old
woman's face. *Collected at*
Masset before 1884 by Alexander
McKenzie of the Hudson's Bay
Company. CMC VII-B-7 (S92-
4163)

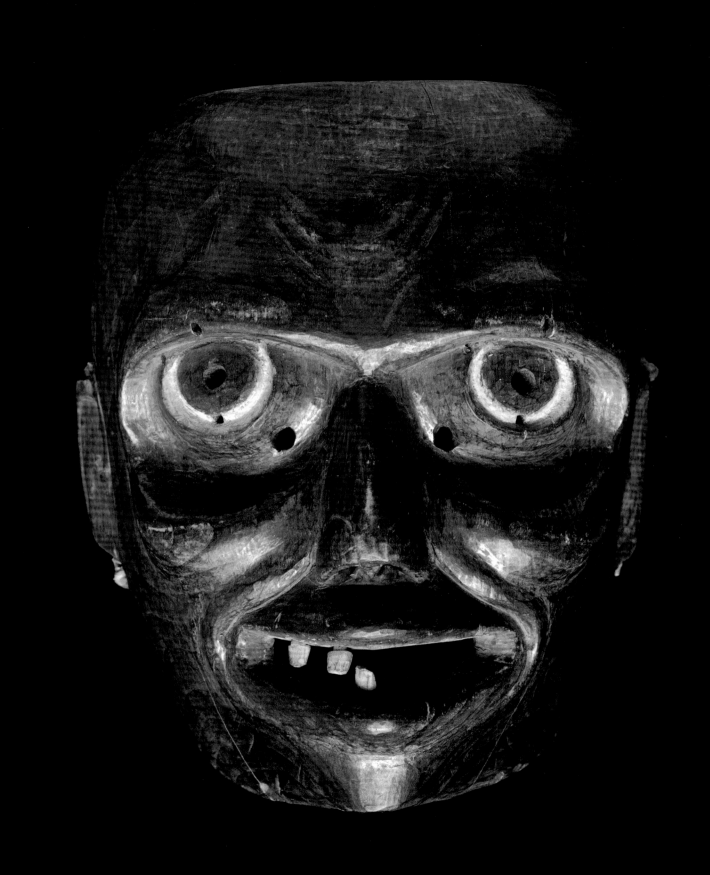

PLATE 56

This mask used in secret society dances represents a *gagiid*, or wild spirit of the woods, someone who narrowly escaped drowning but whose flesh has changed colour from long exposure in cold water. *Collected on Haida Gwaii in 1879 by Israel W. Powell.* CMC VII-B-109 (S92-4186)

PLATE 57

The head of a *gagiid* doll used in secret society dances. The cloth body as well as the wooden hands and feet have been lost. *Collected at Masset before 1900 by Charles F. Newcombe.* CMC VII-B-526 (S94-6728)

PLATE 58

This very fine mask made in the middle of the nineteenth century once had a moustache and goatee made of bear fur. *Collected on Haida Gwaii (probably Skidegate) in 1879 by Israel W. Powell.* CMC VII-B-3 (s85-3270)

PLATE 59

The relatively small upper incisors of this Marmot mask and the lack of a stick in its mouth distinguish it from a Beaver. *Collected by Alexander McKenzie of the Hudson's Bay Company, who commented it was used in a social dance at a house-warming potlatch in Masset before 1884.* CMC VII-B-136a (s85-3277)

This forehead mask represents a Beaver characteristically gnawing a stick, which it holds with humanlike hands. There is abalone shell inlay on the teeth and eyes, and streamers of human hair. Some Tsimshian influence is evident in the form and decoration of the eyebrows. *Collected on Haida Gwaii in 1879 by Israel W. Powell.* CMC VII-B-17 (S92-4168)

PLATE 61

This dance mask dating from about 1860 has unusual red eyes, with peepholes beside each pupil rather than in the centre of them, lending a blank or neutral expression to the face. Red cedar bark and eagle down are still attached. *Collected on Haida Gwaii in 1879 by Israel W. Powell.* CMC VII-B-4 (S92-4161)

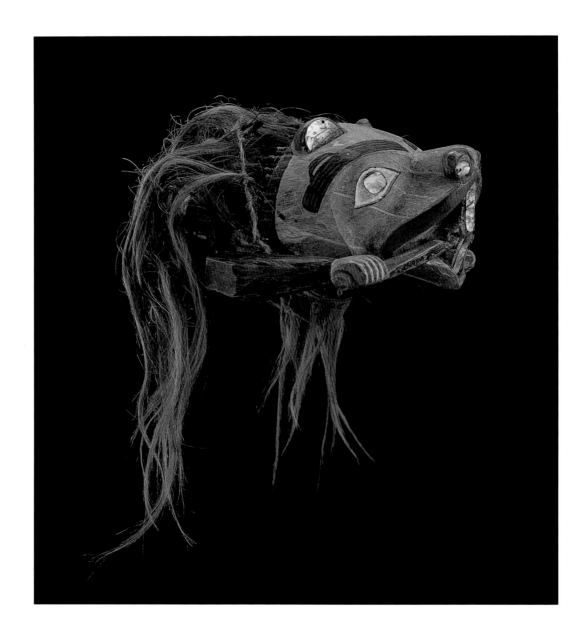

PLATE 62 (facing page) A dance mask with a movable attachment of a White Squirrel on top. The style is markedly Tsimshian, including the dashed and crosshatched zones on the face, as well as the White Squirrel crest. Masks like this one were probably acquired by the Haida in trade at Fort Simpson. *Collected on Haida Gwaii in 1879 by Israel W. Powell.* CMC VII-B-21 (S92-4171)

PLATE 63 A mask with unusually large eyeholes, peaked eyebrows and thick lips. It appears to have been made by the same artist as the masks in PLATES 64, 65, 66, 67. The extensive face painting on it is crudely done and gives no indication of what it represents. *Collected on Haida Gwaii (probably at Skidegate) in 1879 by Israel W. Powell.* CMC VII-B-135 (S92-4195)

PLATE 64 A Moon mask with painted eyebrows and delicate feminine features. *Collected on Haida Gwaii (probably at Skidegate) in 1879 by Israel W. Powell.* CMC VII-B-9 (S85-3273)

PLATE 65

On the top of this mask of a supernatural Killer Whale is a dorsal fin, which can be pulled upright with hidden strings. The lower jaw is also movable. Other stylistic features such as the peaked eyebrows, large eye openings and thick lips indicate it is also by the same artist who made the masks in PLATES 63, 64, 66, 67. CMC VII-B-13 (S94-6724)

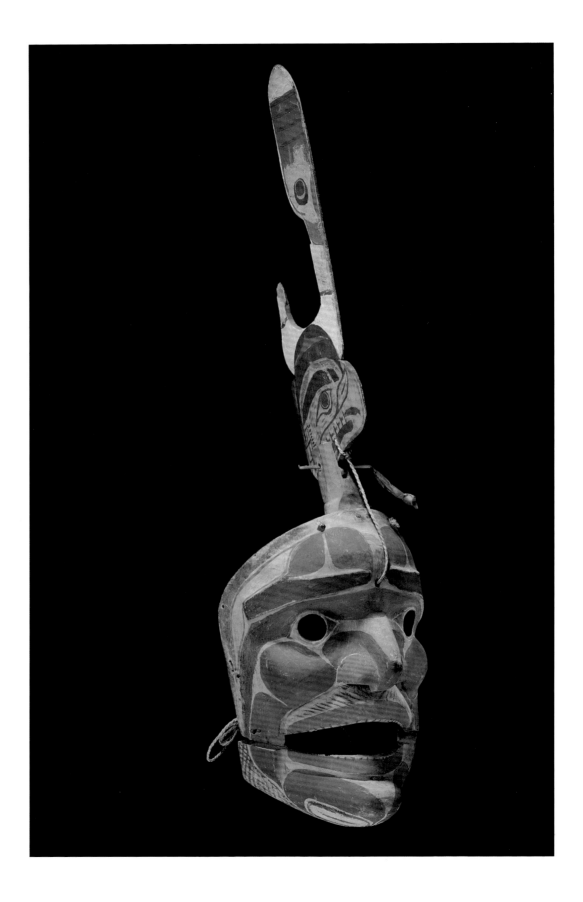

84

PLATE 66

A Moon mask with robust male features. There are traces of a cloth hood that was once attached to it. The style of a broad face and thick lips looks is similar to Heiltsuk masks but may have been used by Haida to suggest the full face of the Moon. *Collected on Haida Gwaii (probably Skidegate) in 1879 by Israel W. Powell.* CMC VII-B-19 (S92-4170)

PLATE 67A, 67B

This spectacular transformation mask, when closed, represents an Eagle or Thunderbird; open (*right*), it portrays the Moon. Human hair attachments add to the drama of the powerfully serene face of a supernatural being. The transformation of the mask is accomplished by pulling cords attached to the hinged panels that extend to form the corona. *Collected on Haida Gwaii (probably at Skidegate) in 1879 by Israel W. Powell.* CMC VII-B-20 (s86-386 closed, s86-387 open)

LUCK OF THE GAMBLER

The Haida had several popular games that involved gambling, and a lull in any social activity was a good reason to play. One was a simple game similar to pickup sticks. The thin playing sticks were quickly made and never decorated, so they were not sought by collectors and no examples are preserved in museums.

Another game consisted of three sets of sticks, named after different animals or birds, which, according to Charles F. Newcombe (1902:MS), were known only to the owner and his family. The sticks have rings and spiral markings to distinguish them, but the most elaborate sets are a veritable gallery of Haida art and may contain fifty or more unique drawings (PLATE 72). The sticks were made of hard maple and were decorated by carving, painting and pyro-engraving with a hot poker; many were inlaid with abalone shell or copper. The burning-in of designs with a hot poker demanded different skills from Haida artists, who responded admirably to the challenge. The drawings are difficult to appreciate at first glance, since they are wrapped completely around the sticks, which must be rotated slowly to unlock their form. Some have jumping shaman figures that resemble an animated cartoon; as the stick is rotated, one shaman after another jumps into view. Flying birds are also common, along with jumping killer whales.

There are also scores of examples of very complex scenes such as war parties in canoes, sea otter hunters in action, or fishermen and their catch—each entire composition no more than 2 cm (¾ inch) in length. These gaming pieces seem to offer the only decorative field in which the Haida artist felt free to become truly documentary. Drawings of half a dozen sets of these decorated sticks have been published by Franz Boas (1927:figs. 200, 201), Swanton (1905:149–54) and others, but many await study. George T. Emmons (no date) recorded in meticulous detail the identifications by a Tlingit owner of a full set of sticks now in the National Museum of the American Indian.

These gambling sticks were used on a special leather mat that was often decorated with painted or pyro-engraved images that appear to be regular crests. This is appropriate, since crests are generally considered to bring good fortune to those who have the inherited the right to use them.

PLATE 72

A set of Haida gambling sticks decorated with pyro-engraved crest images. They were kept in the painted deerskin bag. *Collected at the Nass River village of Gitlaxdimiks in 1905 by Charles F. Newcombe.* CMC VII-C-142 (S92-4313)

Like other north coast peoples, the Haida believed that the souls of the deceased travelled first to the sky world in their cycle of reincarnation (Swanton 1905:35). Both prayers and souls could be helped on their journey by means of smoke rising from the central hearth of the house or by smoke rising from pipes. Prior to contact, the Haida used local tobacco. Pipe smoking became strongly associated with the extraordinary powers initially attributed to Europeans, particularly firearms, which not only smoked but brought instant injury or death. Many early pipes were made from the walnut of gunstocks and parts of gun barrels in order to capture and transfer the power of guns to pipes (PLATE 73).

At some point, argillite replaced recycled gun parts for the making of pipes, but fixing upon a date for the beginning of argillite carving has been something of a challenge to scholars. One clue was found by archaeologist Knut Fladmark (1973:90) of Simon Fraser University, who discovered a chiefly burial inside a house floor at Lawn Hill, on the east coast south of Rose Spit. A well-sculpted argillite pipe of a clam with a human face on it is related to this burial, which associated trade goods date to before 1820.

Next to totem poles, argillite carvings are probably the best known art form of the Haida (Barbeau 1944, 1954, 1957; Macnair and Hoover 1984; Sheehan 1981; Wright 1985). They alone produced works in argillite, since they controlled the supply of the soft black stone, which came from Slatechuck Creek on a mountainside near the village of Skidegate. Argillaceous slate does occur elsewhere on the Northwest Coast, but the lustrous black variety found near Skidegate is unique. Although Skidegate controlled the supply of argillite, it was Masset artists who produced some of the most famous pieces. A much inferior form of the stone, red in colour with mottled yellowish inclusions, occurs as surface boulders around Masset. Works made of this stone can be considered as invariably coming from there, for it was used only by Masset artists who sometimes did not find it convenient to travel to Skidegate to obtain prime black argillite.

The ability of Haida artists to work in stone is well documented in prehistoric carvings, particularly tobacco mortars and pestles (PLATES 74, 75). One interesting stone bowl, probably dating from the eighteenth century, depicts a Dragonfly carrying a human, possibly in reference to myths about Dragonflies transporting human souls. A later piece in argillite on the same theme portrays a human figure riding on the back of a Dragonfly.

The transition of argillite pipes from a ceremonial function to an item of exchange or sale is quite clear. By the 1830s, the sea otter trade that had brought the Haida so much wealth so quickly was over. However, as ships engaged in the trade for other furs continued to ply the coast, the Haida attempted to find substitutes for sea otter pelts by offering potatoes as well as fresh and dried fish. The sale of artworks also became increasingly important to the Haida economy. When the Hudson's Bay Company established a trading post at Fort Simpson on the mainland, British gunboats replaced maritime traders as customers to a large extent. Hundreds of pieces of carved argillite were purchased and taken home as

PLATE 73

On this wooden pipe with a brass bowl, the design of the Raven (with another bird's head on its tail) is very similar to one on a Raven rattle (PLATE 19), with the notable absence of the human figure on its back. *Purchased from Douglas Ewing of New York City in 1976.* CMC VII-B-1659 (S92-4313)

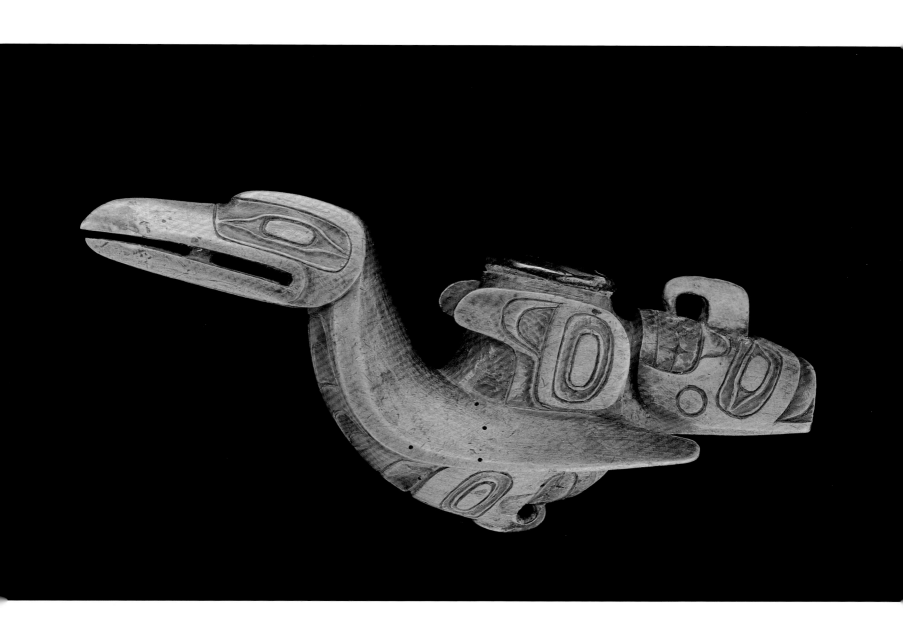

souvenirs by sailors from New England, Britain and elsewhere.

When Reverend Jonathan Green (1915:86) stayed near Skidegate in 1829, he noted that "pipes which the Haida make of a kind of slate stone are curiously wrought." Art historian Robin Wright (1985) has documented in detail the florescence of the panel pipe form, which lost its original funeral function and became a medium for the expression of myths and even for the recording of historical events.

Although panel pipes were the first form of argillite carving sold to tourists, the Haida soon began making and ornamenting other objects that appealed to Europeans. Dishes were particularly successful, since Victorians delighted in displaying plates, bowls and platters in cabinets, on sideboards and on special rails around their parlours (PLATES 76, 154, 157, 158). Pipes appealed enormously to seamen, while plates and platters were equally attractive to their sweethearts back home.

Throughout the 1850s, the design of panel pipes became more baroque. Other forms of pipes, more in the European style but with Haida images, were also produced, along with ever more elaborate plates and platters. It is worth noting that in Britain during the Victorian era, jet carving was popular. Jet is a type of metamorphosed coal that occurs in association with many coal deposits in Britain, and crippled or retired miners often took up jet carving after they could no longer work. The jet jewellery and figurines they produced as a livelihood were well suited to the funeral rituals and long mourning periods of the time. This may explain why the lustrous black carvings of the Haida, especially of familiar forms like pipes, mugs, dishes and platters, were readily accepted by the people of Victorian Britain. Haida argillite carvings, along with African carvings in ebony, found ready markets throughout the Victorian age.

Miniature totem poles in argillite were introduced in the 1860s and became increasingly popular in the 1870s and 1880s. Reverend William H. Collison, a missionary, provides a rare note about the argillite carving that had by the 1870s become a major source of income to the people of Skidegate (in Lillard 1981:173):

The Haida of Skidegate possess a deposit of black stone [argillite] in the vicinity of their village, from which they obtain material to keep them engaged, during their spare moments, in designing and carving a variety of articles for sale. Miniature totem poles for mantelpiece ornaments, of various sizes, large and small dishes, sometimes inlaid with abalone and ornamented with rows of the teeth of marine animals and fishes and many other designs, are carved, and then smoothed by rubbing them with the dried skin of the shark. During the winter this tribe continues to prepare a stock of ornamental articles from this black stone, which takes a fine polish, and brings them a good sum of money when sold at various centres. The possession of this stone is quite a treasure to them, as it tends to preserve and improve the art of carving and designing amongst them, besides bringing in a revenue.

By the turn of the century, the wide dispersal of tens of thousands of argillite carvings

PLATE 74

A sandstone mortar for grinding burned clamshells to make lime, which was then mixed with flakes of dried native tobacco leaves; the lime chemically released the psychogenic compounds in the tobacco, much like the use of lime and betel nut in southeast Asia and other parts of the Pacific. The hands holding the stick that identify this as a Beaver emerge from the creature's own mouth, presumably to keep the sculpture very compact since more anatomically correct arms would easily break off.

Collected on Haida Gwaii in 1879 by Israel W. Powell. CMC XII-B-318 (S91-946)

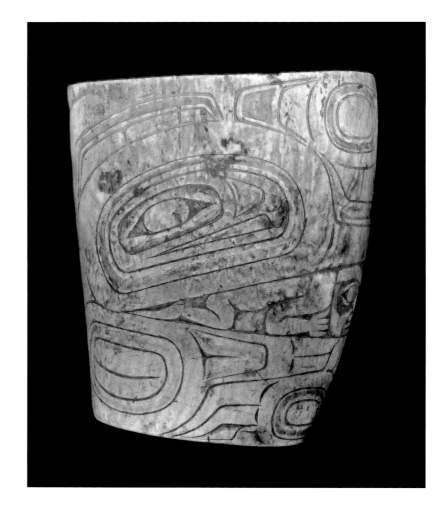

PLATE 75

A mortar of walrus ivory
engraved with an image of the
Raven holding a human being
in its beak. Pieces of burned
clamshell were crushed in this
mortar to make lime for use
with tobacco. *Collected at
Masset before 1884 by James
Deans for Dr. W. F. Tolmie of
the Hudson's Bay Company.*
CMC VII-B-1001 (S92-4292)

PLATE 76

An argillite dish made circa
1835 depicts European women
apparently dancing, and it is
also adorned with the leaves
and berries of the native Haida
tobacco plant. Rosettes and
chrysanthemumlike motifs are
also common in the work of
this unnamed artist. Another
plate by the same carver is in
the Bristol Museum in
England (Drew and Wilson
1980:205, top). CMC VII-C-1036
(S92-4293)

had led to the recognition by discerning collectors of the works of particular artists like Charles Edenshaw and John Cross. John Cross was trained first in tattooing in the 1870s (Barbeau 1957:124–25) and later turned his talents to argillite carving. No argillite carvings were signed, although a few have artists' names written on them by collectors themselves.

Thomas Deasey, the federal government Indian agent at Masset, assembled hundreds of examples of the works of many Masset artists early this century. His collection was donated to the Florida State Museum in Gainesville (PLATE 153).

Argillite carving went into decline after the First World War until the 1950s and was relegated to a minor place in the tourist market. The style of the poles was limited to the repetition of a narrow range of crests and figures compared to the innovative period in the last century. Now, most of the poles for sale in shops in Vancouver and Victoria are cast in simulated argillite and are not even made by Haida artisans.

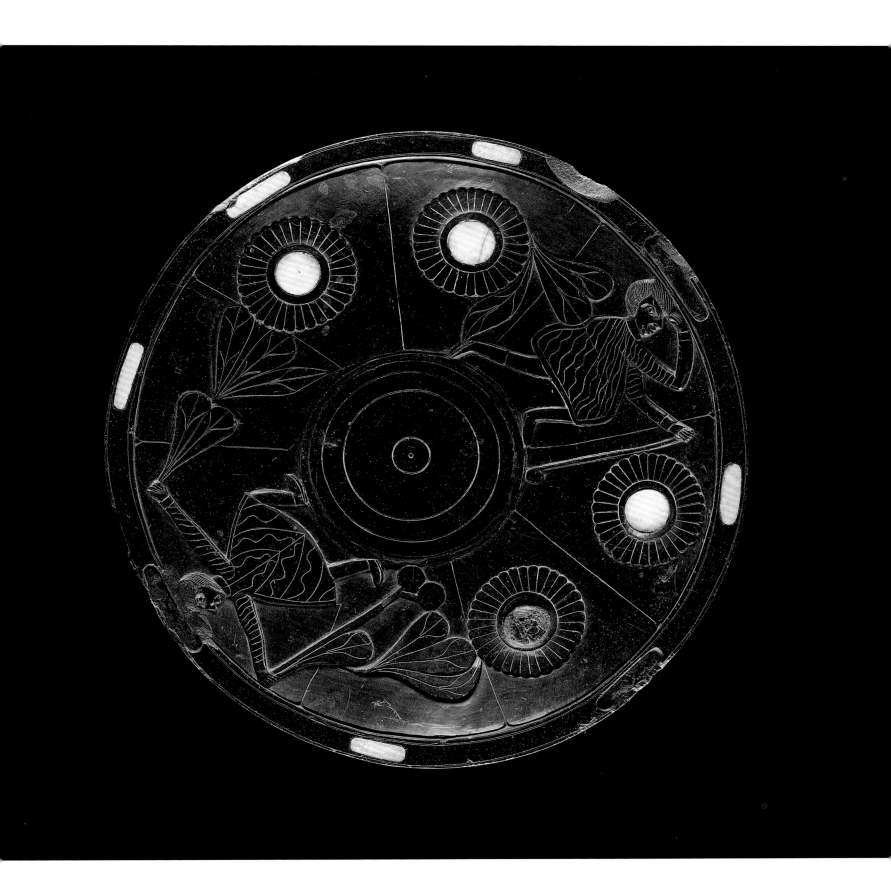

HOUSES

Permanent Haida villages consisted of one or more rows of houses strung along a beach. Double-row villages were quite common, but villages with up to five rows of houses existed only in myth time. Generally the house owned by the town chief was larger than the rest and stood near the middle of the village.

The most extensive early reconnaissance of north coast native villages was carried out by Ensign Albert Niblack, who first visited them during tours of duty with the U.S. Navy. Later, in the 1880s, he returned for a number of years to photograph and record them in detail for the Smithsonian Institution. He was most impressed by the houses built by the Haida (Niblack 1890:384):

> Their houses are exceptionally well constructed, and the custom of erecting the carved column in contact with the front of the house and cutting a circular doorway through both, seems to be nowhere so universally practiced.

According to ancient myth, the house was one of the main contributions that the Raven made to Haida life after he stole the idea from the Beaver (Robert Davidson in Thom 1994:19). The house was the centre of Haida social, political and economic life. Certain aspects and themes related to the house call for some elaboration in order to better understand the setting within which all Haida art was created and used. The subject of houses and their decoration is dealt with extensively in the book *Haida Monumental Art* (MacDonald 1983).

Haida houses were constructed of western red cedar with a framework of stout corner posts that supported massive beams. The frame was clad with wide planks. The tools required for building houses included sledgehammers, adzes, hand mauls and wedges for splitting wood. Most housebuilding tools were not decorated, but a few examples in the collection of the Canadian Museum of Civilization are quite remarkable (PLATES 77,78).

Small houses averaged 6 by 9 m (20 by 30 feet) and were occupied by thirty to forty closely related family members, while large houses were up to 15 by 18 m (50 by 60 feet) with twice as many residents, including immediate family and slaves. The ideal house had a large pit in the central area, often lined with a vertical box structure of massive planks. The hearth occupied the centre, directly under a smokehole, which had a plank flap that could be moved

PLATE 77

An elaborately carved basalt hand maul that was used for driving wooden wedges into red cedar logs to split off planks. James Deans identifies the lower face as that of a Bear, with the naturalistic head of a hunter above. The hunter's conical hat forms the traditional top of a nipple-top maul, suggesting this may have been an old maul that was later enhanced with a carved design. The accession record claims it was once in the collection of Sir Matthew Begbie, chief justice of British Columbia. *Acquired with the A. Aaronson collection in 1899, but probably originally collected by James Deans in the early 1890s on Haida Gwaii.* CMC VII-B-908 (s82-269)

with ropes to control the draft for the fire. Usually the house of the town chief had the largest or deepest housepit. The roofs of houses belonging to people of rank were covered with overlapping planks, anchored in placed with large rocks. The houses of poorer people and canoe sheds had roofs of cedar bark that had to be replaced frequently.

The people of the northern and southern regions of Haida Gwaii have different approaches to house construction. In the north, including the villages of the Prince of Wales archipelago, Haida houses resemble the large gable-roofed plank structures found throughout other north coast villages. This house has an *internal* frame consisting of four or more massive vertical posts spanned by equally massive round beams up to 15 m (50 feet) or more in length, covered with a cladding of wide planks.

In the south, houses have an *external* frame, with plank cladding that fits precisely between the parallel timbers of the house frame. This more elaborate style of house, with mortice and tenon joints and low-tolerance carpentry, probably did not develop until steel tools became available in the late eighteenth century. The greatest incidence of the exterior frame house occurs at the village of Ninstints at the southern tip of Haida Gwaii.

A third type of house occurs predominantly among the Kaigani Haida of the Prince of Wales archi-

PLATE 78

A sledgehammer used to drive wedges into cedar trees to split off planks. This fine specimen has the head of the Thunderbird holding a small Whale. *Collected on Haida Gwaii in 1879 by Israel W. Powell.* CMC VII-B-924 (K85-2630)

pelago in Alaska. It is a blend of the two basic styles, in having both an interior frame based on four massive posts as well as a system for the walls and gables supported by four smaller exterior corner posts. Large houses, like that of Chief Skowl at Kasaan village, have a heavy horizontal timber between the front corner posts (repeated at the back wall) that effectively divides the cladding on the front and back gables above and below this beam into shorter boards.

The terms applied to a house's structural members are the same as for the bones of a human skeleton, or more specifically the bones of the collective ancestor. The two front vertical support posts are the arm bones, the two rear posts are the leg bones, the longitudinal beams are the backbone, the rafters are the ribs, and the exterior cladding is the skin. The inhabitants are the spirit force of the ancestor/house.

In addition to being a place of shelter, the house had a cosmological meaning for the

PLATE 79

This model of a double-post mortuary made by Charles Edenshaw contains two burial chests with model corpses inside. The crest of the Bear in a nest belongs to a chief of Skedans village. On the actual mortuary, the Bear is holding the chief's copper (MacDonald 1983:plate 98); this original front panel is now in the Museum of Northern British Columbia in Prince Rupert. *Collected at Masset between 1895 and 1901 by Charles F. Newcombe.* CMC VII-B-661 (S92-4243)

Haida, who thought of the house as a very large box and often decorated its walls to coincide with the images used on boxes. The concept of boxes within boxes is central to Haida beliefs about containers and the spiritual beings who safeguard their precious contents.

The wealth contained by the house-sized box was in the form of human souls. The Haida believed that the fish stored in food boxes retained their souls until they were consumed, when their souls were released to become new fish and continue the cycle. Similarly, a house protected the souls of its inhabitants until they died, whereby their souls were released to newborn members of the family. The Haida were always concerned to know which child had inherited the soul of a recently deceased relative and would search the faces and actions of the newborn to determine that affiliation. The deceased were placed in burial boxes in mortuary houses or on posts, as close as tolerable to the house of their surviving kin (PLATES 79, 80). Reverend William H. Collison (in Lillard 1981:86) comments on this after his first night in a house at Masset village:

> When opening my door the following morning, I was startled at receiving a smart lash as though from a whip on the side of my face. Looking up to see the cause, I perceived that the wind had blown the side out of a mortuary chest, which was supported by two great posts. In this receptacle lay the skeleton of a woman, her long black hair was being blown to and fro by the wind as it hung down fully three feet from the scalp.

The Haida viewed the universe as a large house (the World Box or World House), with the sides being the four cardinal directions. After the Raven brought the sun to this World Box from another box in the house of the Sky Chief, the sun entered the World House each day and passed over its roof at night. The stars were sunlight shining through holes in roof of the World House. The seasons were tracked by marking the position of the sun at daybreak on the wall opposite the hole where the sunlight entered.

Through the middle of each house ran an axis that centred the resident family at the centre of the world, where the contact between the various levels of the universe was the greatest. The smoke from the household fire signified this axis of conjunction of various worlds and the hearth was the site of daily prayers to the supernatural forces that determined people's destiny. The houses of important chiefs had a succession of box-shaped pits extending symbolically down into the underworld. The living compartment of the chief was like a smaller box at the back of the house.

Not a single complete original Haida dwelling survives, but there are historical photographs of about four hundred Haida houses in twenty-five villages, taken in the last half of the nineteenth century. In addition, nearly one hundred house models survive in museum collections. The Field Museum in Chicago has the entire village of Skidegate, some thirty houses in model form, commissioned by James Deans for the Columbian World Exposition in Chicago in 1893 (PLATE 81).

Deans spent considerable time in Skidegate in the 1880s and was able to recruit craftsmen from each lineage group to make models of the houses connected to their families. It must have been a terrific undertaking on his part to negotiate the rights, fees, and schedules of so many artists to deliver the complete model within a year. The model even has carvings of figures engaged in various rituals from funeral ceremonies to potlatches, and the house belonging to Chief Skidegate includes a detailed reconstruction of the interior house pit.

Another excellent piece that is part of the model of Skidegate village is the mortuary that stood behind Chief Skidegate's house. It is a shedlike building with a painted housefront depicting a Wasgo (or Sea Wolf) that once lived in a lake behind Skidegate. When its roof is removed, stacks of burial chests are revealed, including the highly decorated ones of former Chiefs Skidegate resting on a huge carving of a Wasgo. Such supports (called *manda'a* by the Haida) were often placed at the foot of the mortuary post to which the chief's burial box was moved two years after his death (PLATE 166). Many of these carved supports can be seen in historical photos of Haida villages.

Housefront Paintings

Despite the fact that all of the mainland tribes between Vancouver Island and central Alaska had painted housefronts, they were rare among the Haida. This is surprising, since the Haida were the most accomplished artists on the coast in flat design as applied to canoes, chiefs' seats and storage chests. One example from the Skidegate area of Haida Gwaii is on the

PLATE 80

This central panel from a double-post mortuary in Skidegate village portrays the Grizzly Bear with a protruding tongue and prominent ears. *Collected circa 1900 by Charles F. Newcombe.* CMC VII-B-668 (s92-4246)

house of Chief Gold, who together with his wife was the first to report the discovery of gold on the islands to Albert Edward Edenshaw in 1849. At the time, Chief Gold was head chief of Kaisun village, but later he moved his people to Haina village (now New Gold Harbour) near Skidegate. He rebuilt his own house at First Beach between Skidegate and Haina to maintain ancient rights of his family to that site.

When Chief Gold rebuilt his house, he added a housefront that follows the precise template of many such paintings among the Tsimshian, especially popular at Fort Simpson (PLATE 82). That pattern consists of a Master of Souls flat design with multiple faces in the eyes and human figures in the mouth. The remarkable feature of the housefront is the profile of Thunderbird flanking each side of the main design. Since the Haida from the Skidegate area travelled regularly to Fort Simpson to trade, Chief Gold may have either received the right to use the pattern as a gift or purchased it from a Tsimshian chief. Chief Gold subsequently commissioned a local Haida artist to execute this housefront painting. Bill Holm (1981:199) convincingly argues that this artist is also "the Master of the Chicago Settee." The closest Tsimshian example is the house of Chief Skagwait, the second-highest in rank to Chief Legaic at Fort Simpson. In Haida society, Chief Gold had a comparable position as second in rank to Chief Skidegate. Chief Gold added a distinctive Haida touch by putting his Moon-Hawk crest on the gable of his house.

Another Haida housefront painting exists only as a photograph of a collection of boards from an exquisite housefront, assembled somewhat randomly on a chief's grave in the cemetery of the Kaigani Haida village of Howkan in Alaska. In the photo, about a quarter of the painted boards are missing, most are out of order, and some are upside-down (PLATE 148). A number of detailed features of this painting suggest that it was commissioned from an artist at Fort Simpson, as it closely resembles about ten other housefronts from that town. Collectively, these are the finest corpus of two-dimensional design from the Northwest Coast.

There is evidence of two other painted housefronts in Skidegate village proper. The first belonged to the town chief, Skidegate, whom collector James G. Swan (1893:MS 49) referred to as "Skidegate the Great," the highest-ranking chief on the central and southern islands and equal in rank to Chief Wiah of Masset. We know of this housefront painting only from a model, which probably exaggerates reality. The model depicts a Konankada flat design, almost identical to that on many carved storage chests. There are no flanking bird or animal figures as in the Tsimshian examples, but Killer Whale designs are painted on the side walls of the model. In concept, this design is comparable to the Tsimshian housefront painting from Fort Simpson now in the Smithsonian Museum. This assemblage has been interpreted as the Tsimshian figure Hakulack, a variant of Gonankadet (or Konankada), flanked by two Killer Whales (MacDonald 1981:230, fig. 5).

Although nothing has survived of the housefront painting owned by Chief Skidegate, historical photos of his house reveal that it had no frontal pole (although that of his predecessor stood nearby). The housefront was an unusually plain one for such a high-ranking chief, and the implication is that it was decorated for potlatches by the erection of a painted plank

PLATE 81
This model of Skidegate village was commissioned for the Columbian World Exposition in Chicago in 1893. James Deans hired most of the artists active in Skidegate at the time to make models of their own lineage houses.

PLATE 82

A rare example of a painted housefront from Moon House, which Chief Gold built at First Beach near Skidegate. According to Bill Holm (1981:197), the painting was done by the unknown artist referred to as "the Master of the Chicago Settee." The Moon-Hawk plaque at the top, which was moved by Chief Gold from his previous house at Kaisun village, is now in the Field Museum. *Photograph by Richard Maynard, 1881.*

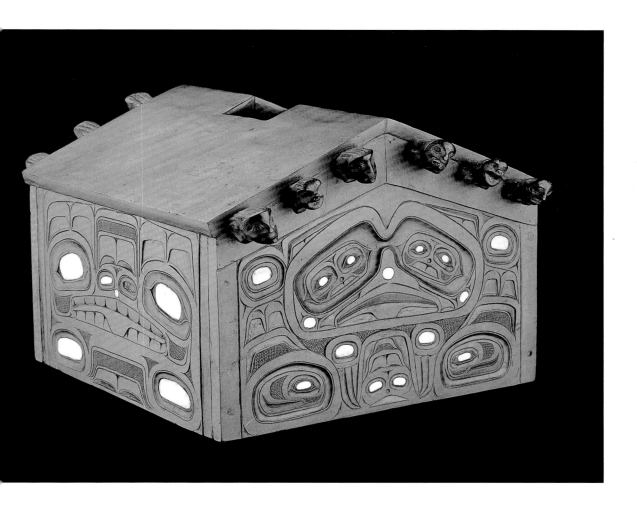

PLATE 86

An interior house pole of
Chief Wiah (*right*), displaying
his crest of a standing Beaver
with a Dragonfly on its belly.
The Beaver is gnawing a stick
inlaid with nearly one hundred
pieces of abalone shell. This
pole was probably carved
when the house was
constructed circa 1850. It now
stands before the Haida house
in the Grand Hall of the
Canadian Museum of
Civilization. *Acquired from
Chief Henry Wiah of Masset in
1901 by Charles F. Newcombe.*
CMC VII-B-1130 (S92-4407)

PLATE 87

An argillite model of a house
in which the figures at the
ends of the rafters portray
singers who perform when
anyone approaches. The
housefront is decorated with
the image of a Grizzly Bear.
*Acquired on Haida Gwaii
(probably Skidegate) circa 1892
by James Deans for the A.
Aaronson collection.* CMC VII-B-
816 (S92-4274)

the screen (Swanton 1905:fig. 6). The most spectacular surviving Haida screen is from How-kan village in Alaska (PLATE 149). George T. Emmons, who collected this piece, identifies its images in his unpublished notes (no date) but does not identify the house from which it came.

Other features of the Haida house that were sometimes elaborated with carving or paint-ing were the rafters (PLATE 87), the retaining planks that framed the housepit surrounding the central fireplace, and the timbers around the smokehole above the fireplace. No carved housepit planks survive for the Haida (though there are Tlingit and Tsimshian examples), but the most elaborate of all known examples from anywhere on the coast belonged to Charles Edenshaw's son Henry in the village of Klinkwan, Alaska (PLATE 142). The design is composed of elaborately carved and painted chests (with opercula shell inlay) that alternate with engraved coppers. Although Henry Edenshaw inherited this house, it was probably built by Albert Edward Edenshaw, who may have commissioned his nephew Charles Eden-shaw to create this design.

The smokehole had mythical significance among the Haida, as it was the opening through which souls entered and left the house at birth and death, following the pathway of smoke uniting this world to the upper world and the Milky Way, which was the pathway of souls in the sky. It was also the opening through which the trickster-hero Raven escaped to carry his gifts of the sun, the moon and the stars to humans. It was while flying through this opening that the White Raven, the primal form, turned black in the smoke.

One notable smokehole carving depicts a double-headed Killer Whale with prominent dorsal fins (PLATE 88). In form, it resembles the double-headed soul catchers traditionally used by Tsimshian shaman but on occasion by Haida shaman as well. The placement of a soul catcher as a device to protect souls in the smokehole of a house presents some intriguing equations in the cycles of birth and death.

FURNISHINGS

Haida houses had little in the way of furnishings in the European sense. Sleeping compart-ments and privacy were provided by plank partitions that were often elaborately decorated. During ceremonies, additional screens were added to the back of the house to create a back-stage area for dancers and initiates to put on their costumes. These screens were often made of canvas obtained in trade and were painted with crest designs. Storage boxes were stacked around the sides of the house. Formal seats were reserved for the chief and his wives, while others sat on boxes or on mats on the floor.

The chief's seat of honour in each house was located along the back platform on the cen-tral axis of the house, facing the door. The seat was thought of as a box that protected the spirit of the chief. Hence, the decoration is typically either the Konankada design or a crest belonging to the chief (PLATE 114). The decoration on a chief's seat is on the inside, so the seated chief was shown to public view surrounded by his carved and painted crests.

PLATE 88

A small human figure crouches between two Killer Whales on this protective device made in the form of a shaman's soul catcher. It may have been placed in the smokehole of a house to prevent the souls of its inhabitants from wandering away during illness. The painted details are Tsimshian in style, but the piece is recorded as Haida in the catalogue of the Lord Bossom collection. *Acquired by George T. Emmons before 1900 for the Lord Bossom collection.* CMC VII-B-1821 (S92-4385)

Boxes and Chests

Boxes were used to store food stuffs, clothing, regalia and ritual paraphernalia such as rattles and whistles. Some boxes were simply made of bent sheets of cedar bark sewn at the corners and base to provide disposable containers for trade items, while others were more substantial and durable bentwood boxes. Bentwood boxes for food (PLATE 89) ranged in capacity from a couple of litres (quarts) up to 225 L (50 gallons). George M. Dawson (in Cole and Lockner 1989:475) observed that boxes of eulachon grease brought to the islands for trade by the Tsimshian required two men each to pack them up the beach from the canoes.

Bentwood storage boxes destined to store important wealth objects were provided with a guardian spirit decoration in the form of supernatural marine beings and more familiar animals (PLATES 90, 91). They also had heavy plank lids, whose edges were decorated with vertical rows of opercula shells. For transport, the lids were tied in place with elaborate knotwork of cedar bark cordage (PLATE 91).

The design field of a bentwood box has provided a constant challenge for art historians and native scholars alike to interpret. Although the design is standard, the variations are endless and intriguing. The "front" of the box normally depicts Konankada (the Chief of the Undersea World), with fins as well as human hands. The face has double-eye forms (two salmon heads joined at the nose). The "back" of the box is a variation of this creature with single-pupil eyes. This supernatural being may be modified by the addition of such markers as large incisors (Beaver), gill slits (Dogfish), large canines (Wolf), tall ears and protruding tongue (Bear), and so on. The side panels of the box have much simpler designs, which are only painted and not carved.

A variation of the standard box design is to spread the traditional front and back image of the supernatural being over the two sides, so that its protective power is continuous around the box.

Some box designs defy a simple analysis. They do not relate to a supernatural guardian figure but use multiple elements, including human faces manipulated freely. Franz Boas (1955:fig. 287) challenged Charles Edenshaw to provide an interpretation for such a box, which is now in the collection of the American Museum of Natural History in New York City. Edenshaw provided an explanation of each panel as part of a Raven myth, but few others have been able to comprehend the shorthand interpretation of the visual symbolism he provided. Bill Reid refers to this box as "the final exam" in understanding Northwest Coast art. Few manage to pass that exam.

Large bentwood chests, approximately the size of two storage boxes, were favoured by chiefs to store and protect their regalia, particularly their costumes of Chilkat or button blankets, aprons, leggings and frontlets. Important chiefs owned up to half a dozen such chests (PLATES 5, 92, 94). The major centres of production for these chests throughout the nineteenth century were at Bella Bella and Fort Simpson. Since Fort Simpson was viewed by all the tribes of the north coast as the hub of trade for expensive goods, including high-quality items of native manufacture, and also had the largest cadre of professional artists throughout the last two-thirds of the nineteenth century, it was probably the source of chests acquired by the Haida, who visited the post annually.

PLATE 89

Food storage boxes were usually not decorated, but occasionally one such as this example was painted with the image of the supreme Chief of the Seas, the being ultimately responsible for all of the other sea creatures that the Haida used for food. Their flesh was under its guardianship while in such a box, which in turn honoured that supernatural being. *Collected at Masset circa 1895 by Charles F. Newcombe.* CMC VII-B-324 (S92-4198)

PLATE 90A, 90B, 90C, 90D

The unusual decoration on all four sides of this bentwood storage box displays the idiosyncratic style practised by some Skidegate Inlet artists towards the end of the nineteenth century. *From the Lord Bossom collection.* CMC VII-X-621 (S94-6786/6787/6788/6789)

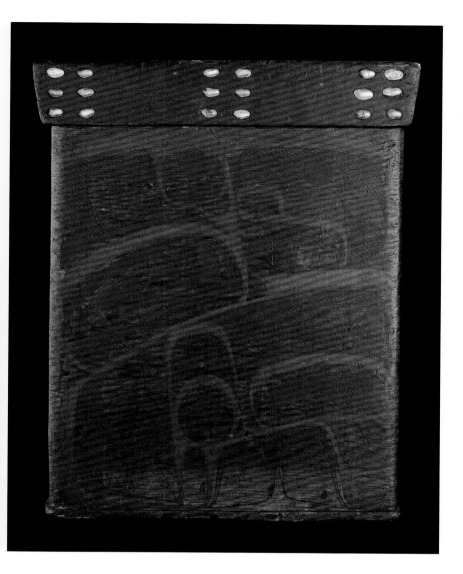

PLATE 91

This painted bentwood storage box shows the typical lashing and knotwork of twisted cedar bark cordage used to secure the contents during transport in freight canoes. *Collected on Haida Gwaii before 1901 by Charles F. Newcombe.* CMC VII-B-929 (S94-6759)

PLATE 92

A large bentwood storage chest. The front of the chest portrays the face of Konankada, Chief of the Undersea World. The bas-relief sculpture and incised formlines of the ovoids and eyes represent the highest level of surface decoration achieved by Haida artists. *Collected on Haida Gwaii in 1898 by W. A. Newcombe.* CMC VII-B-129.3 (S92-4193)

PLATE 93A, 93B, 93C

This exquisite bentwood burial chest is one of the finest in the collection of the Canadian Museum of Civilization. On the front panel (*facing page*), the hands are inlaid with separately carved faces. At each corner, the salmon trout head ovoids indicate the work of an exquisite craftsman. The circles around the eyes of the human face in the lower centre of the panel are the signature feature of an unknown artist whose work was widely traded on the north coast in the mid-nineteenth century. The front, back and one side are shown here. *Collected at Skedans in 1932 by Robert Bruce Inverarity.* CMC VII-B-1881 (S92-4379 front, S92-4381 back, S92-4382 left)

The design of the standard chest uses the face of the double-eyed supernatural being on the front panel, while the back portrays the single-eyed being. The sides are often decorated with simple formlines and ovoids, but on a series of chests that were probably imported to Haida Gwaii, the side panels have full designs that resemble the fronts of storage boxes.

After protecting the wealth of a chief during his lifetime, such a chest often became his burial box and the protector of his soul after death (PLATES 93, 95, 96, 105, 111, 120).

Basketry

Haida women made a range of baskets from large coarsely woven ones that would allow clams to drain, to drinking cups so tightly woven they would hold water. Every woman had her work baskets, which were usually hung from the walls or rafters of the house. Other baskets were made for the storage of clothes, as well as roots and vegetables. Cooking baskets of red cedar bark with an open weave were used to boil berries, prior to mashing and drying them for winter use. Woven strainers were used to skim off the grease when boiling black cod. Potato baskets became a common item when, as part of the nineteenth-century economy, the Haida grew potatoes to sell to mainland natives and maritime traders.

Containers were also woven for a great many other specific functions such as burden baskets, bait baskets, basket quivers for arrows and even stout baskets for anchor stones. Cradles were also fashioned of basketry, although wooden ones were more popular. Fancy baskets for storing soapberry spoons became something of a specialty, as did drinking cups, and very fine examples were woven for domestic use as well as for trade.

Women also wove many types of basketry mats for household use. Meals were eaten on them, babies were born on them, people slept on them and the dead were wrapped in them for burial. Old mats were recycled as covers for boxes or for covering canoes to keep them from checking in the sunlight. Designs on mats were geometric but could be quite complex. Some patterns had individual names and meanings, and specific designs belonged as a privilege to certain families of high rank. These design motifs have not been thoroughly analysed, but in his unpublished notes, Charles F. Newcombe (1902:MS) documented the names of many of them, such as "slug trail," "comb pattern," "shadow," "small waves in calm waters," "the crossing of the sticks of a drying frame for fish," "little breeze on the water" and so on. Museum collections contain numerous painted mats, some of which may be attributed to the Haida, but many appear to be intended for the early tourist trade and there is no evidence they were ever produced in Haida country.

Although the art of weaving hats, mats and baskets almost disappeared from the 1930s until the late 1950s, the recent renaissance of feasting has encouraged young women to learn basketry from their grandmothers. Dorothy Grant from Hydaburg, Alaska, typifies the younger generation who have mastered this skill, and she has produced a wide range of hats and baskets. The Haida artist Robert Davidson has painted crest designs on many pieces of her work, including hats. These new pieces are as fine as any old examples and are sought after by museums in North America and Japan.

PLATE 94

One of the painted end panels of a large bentwood chest. This particular style of chest with carved front and back panels, as well as elaborately painted end panels, was produced by specialized craftsmen at Bella Bella and Fort Simpson. *Collected at Masset in 1898 by Charles F. Newcombe.* CMC VII-B-457.2 (S92-4203)

PLATE 95

The back of a bentwood burial chest that has both painted and incised formline designs wrapping around two sides. The ovoids are extremely thick at the top, and the inner ovoids have simple slits indicating closed eyes. Such chests were often found in burial caves, although this example was never used. *Acquired by Charles F. Newcombe in 1898.* CMC VII-B-1559 (S92-4311)

128

PLATE 96

On this bentwood burial chest, the face of the Beaver crest projects from the front in high relief. It was created, according to Wilson Duff (personal communication) by Charles Edenshaw during his residence at Port Essington at the mouth of the Skeena. Its form bears a striking resemblance to the sculpted facade of Grizzly Bear's Mouth House at Skidegate, where Edenshaw grew up. Here, however, the design is totally rearranged to be displayed entirely on the front panel rather than being wrapped around all four sides in the usual fashion, a further indication that it was a burial chest meant to be seen only from one perspective. The artist may have intended to use it for his own funeral, but he sold it to another chief instead. *Collected by Harlan I. Smith in 1926 from a chief at the Gitksan village of Kitwanga on the Skeena River.* CMC VII-C-1183 (K84-274)

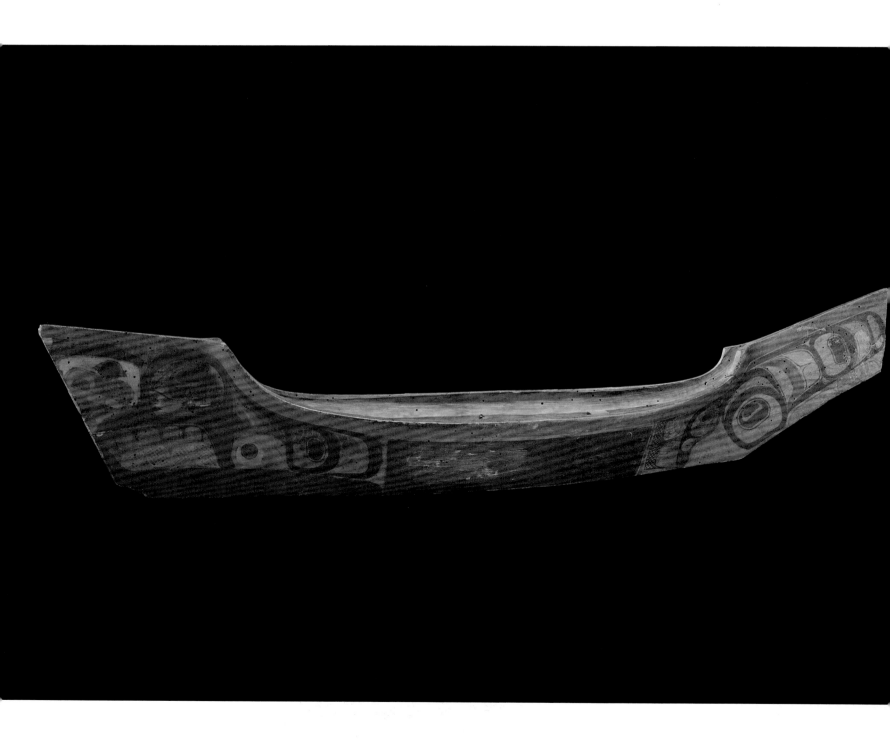

CANOES AND TRADE

Haida canoes were exquisite craft hewn from the gigantic red cedar that grows on Haida Gwaii and were highly prized by chiefs of other nations throughout the coast. The combination of beautiful lines that pleased the most demanding navigator with the fine craftsmanship and the superior quality of the cedar available on Haida Gwaii literally made Haida canoes the Cadillacs of the coast.

Canoemakers in each village worked on their new craft throughout the autumn at sites where the very best red cedars stood. After an appropriate snowfall that facilitated sledding, the roughed-out canoes were moved from the woods to the nearest beach and towed to the home village, where they were finished over the winter. In the spring, lightly manned flotillas of new canoes left Skidegate Inlet, Masset and Rose Spit on the north coast, braving the seasonal storms to head for the mainland. If these vessels could withstand a crossing of the treacherous Hecate Strait, they could withstand any weather the coast could provide. At the Nass River, the canoes were traded to coastal tribes assembled to take advantage of the spring eulachon fishery. Old canoes were taken in trade by the Haida for their return journey home.

When the first Europeans arrived, they made drawings depicting the Haida in their large war canoes with high prows emblazoned with the crests of the owners. Although there are many models of these canoes, called "head canoes," no full-sized ones have been preserved.

By the end of the eighteenth century, the Haida had learned from visiting sailors and sea captains how to rig sails, and thereafter most large canoes were fitted with two or three masts and sails of canvas or cedar bark mats. These faster, more manoeuvrable craft were capable of carrying 20 000 kg (10 tons) of freight.

The development of this new craft was probably responsible for the disappearance of the "head" type of canoe. The head canoe had a massive prow extending far in front, which was ideal for bearing the crests of the war chief but was a detriment to manoeuvrability under sail. Models of head canoes continued to be made until they began to fade in the memories of carvers (PLATE 97).

War canoes had the same sharp projecting prow as the freight canoes but, in addition to the two-dimensional painted designs on the hull, they often had separate carved crests at the prow or stern (PLATE 98). A stunning example of this style of war canoe was made by Alfred Davidson and other master canoemakers (including Robert Davidson Sr., Robert Davidson's

PLATE 97

A model of an ancient style of war canoe, often called a "head canoe," whose broad prow was designed to display the crests of the chief who owned it. This type of canoe had disappeared from use by the middle of the nineteenth century, although models were still made after that date. *Collected on Haida Gwaii (probably at Masset) before 1892 by Edward Harris, a Hudson's Bay Company fur trader.* CMC VII-X-280 (S94-6773)

grandfather) for a world's fair in the United States (PLATES 99, 100). The paintings on it were designed and executed by Charles Edenshaw. When the final price proved too high for the fair's budget, the craft was purchased for the Canadian Museum of Civilization. At 17 m (56 feet) in length, this is the largest Haida war canoe that has survived (although the Heiltsuk war canoe at the American Museum of Natural History in New York is considerably longer).

In 1985, Bill Reid was commissioned to make a 15-m (50-foot) dugout canoe for Expo 86, the world's fair in Vancouver. This beautiful craft he called *Lootas* (or *Wave Eater*). After the fair, several replicas were made in fiberglass, the first two of which were for the Canadian Museum of Civilization. The original canoe was taken to France and paddled up the Seine to Paris, in honour of the bicentennial of the French Revolution. Later, it undertook a much-publicized voyage from Vancouver to Haida Gwaii and has since been kept at Skidegate for ceremonial occasions.

WARFARE

The Haida were feared along the coast because of their practice of making lightning raids against which their enemies had little defence. Their great skills of seamanship, their superior craft and their relative protection from retaliation in their island fortress added to the aggressive posture of the Haida towards neighbouring tribes. Diamond Jenness, an early anthropologist at the Canadian Museum of Civilization, caught their essence in his description of the Haida as the "Indian Vikings of the North West Coast" (1934:243):

> Those were stirring times, about a century ago, when the big Haida war canoes, each hollowed out of a single cedar tree and manned by fifty or sixty warriors, traded and raided up and down the coast from Sitka in the north to the delta of the Fraser River in the south. Each usually carried a shaman or medicine man to catch and destroy the souls of enemies before an impending battle; and the women who sometimes accompanied the warriors fought as savagely as their husbands.

The Haida went to war to acquire objects of wealth, such as coppers and Chilkat blankets, that were in short supply on the islands, but primarily for slaves, who enhanced their productivity or were traded to other tribes. High-ranking captives were also the source of other property received in ransom such as crest designs, dances and songs.

Even prehistorically, the Haida engaged in sea battles. They tied cedar bark ropes to heavy stone rings that were hurled to smash enemy canoes and that could quickly be retrieved for subsequent throws. A stone weighing 18 to 23 kg (40 to 50 pounds) could shatter the side of a dugout canoe and cause it to founder. Most tribes avoided sea battles with the Haida and tried to lure them ashore for a more equitable fight. The Tsimshian developed a signal-fire system to alert their villages on the Skeena River as soon as Haida invaders reached the mainland (MacDonald, no date).

PLATE 98

A Bear crest from the prow of a Haida war canoe. Such figures were added for ceremonial occasions and removed when the canoe had to be stripped for battle. *Collected on Haida Gwaii in 1879 by Israel W. Powell.* CMC VII-B-1054 (S92-4297)

PLATE 99

The only surviving Haida war canoe, 17 m (56 feet) in length with a beam of nearly 2 m (6 feet). It was commissioned for the 1904 American world's fair from Alfred Davidson and other Masset carvers, including Robert Davidson Sr. The original paddles were lost en route to Ottawa, but Charles Edenshaw made a replacement set. *Collected at Masset in 1908 by Reverend William Hogan and R. W. Brock.* CMC VII-B-1128 (S92-4299)

PLATE 100

Alfred Davidson of Masset, shown carving the canoe that was commissioned for the 1904 American world's fair. It was painted with Sea Wolf designs by Charles Edenshaw and is now on display at the Canadian Museum of Civilization (PLATE 99). *Photograph by Edward Sapir, 1914.* CMC 26665

PLATE 101

This heavy wooden war
helmet in the form of a Seal's
head, with copper eyes and
teeth, was probably made
around 1820 and preserved as
an heirloom. *Collected on
Haida Gwaii in 1897 by
Charles F. Newcombe.* CMC VII-
B-1543 (S92-4308)

The florescence of warfare was undoubtedly accelerated in the half century from 1780 to
1830, when the Haida had no effective enemies except the many European and American
traders on their shores who would rather trade than fight. During this period, the Haida successfully captured more than half a dozen ships. One was the ship *Eleanora,* taken by chiefs
of the village of Skungwai (or Ninstints) in retaliation for the maltreatment Chief Koyah had
received from its captain (MacDonald 1983:46). An even more spectacular event was the capture of the ship *Susan Sturgis* by Chief Wiah of Masset and the rescue of its crew by Albert
Edward Edenshaw. In such conflicts, the Haida quickly learned the newcomers' fighting tac-
tics, which they used to good effect in subsequent battles (Brink 1974:38):

As early as 1795, a British trading ship fired its cannons at a village in the central part of the
archipelago because some of the crew had been killed by the inhabitants, and the survivors had
to put hastily to sea when the Indians fired back at them. They found out later that the Indians
had used a cannon and ammunition pilfered from an American Schooner a few years earlier.

Swivel guns were added to many Haida war canoes, although initially the recoil on discharge caused the hulls of many craft to split.

Fortified sites were part of the defensive strategy of all Northwest Coast groups for at least 2,000 years. Captain George Dixon (Dixon 1789) was so impressed with one Haida fort off the west coast of Graham Island that he called it Hippah Island after the Maori forts he had seen in New Zealand. Military defences at Haida forts included stout palisades, rolling top-log defences, heavy trapdoors and fighting platforms supplied with stores of large boulders to hurl at invaders.

Warriors wore various kinds of armour including war helmets (PLATE 101), wooden visors to protect their necks, and breastplates that were often concealed under a leather tunic emblazoned with their crests. Few Haida wooden slat breastplates have survived, although numerous Tlingit examples exist in museums. There are, however, many Haida painted leather tunics.

Haida body armour favoured the war coat, which was made of the thick hides of sea lions (PLATE 102) or of several layers of elkskin. The former was available through trade on the Nass River while the latter was acquired from European and American traders who obtained them from tribes at the mouth of the Columbia River.

The Haida replaced the bow and arrow and short spear with firearms as soon as they became available early in the nineteenth century, and some proud owners carved their crests onto the stocks of their muskets. War daggers, however, continued to be used in close combat, and many hundreds of them have been collected from northern tribes. These daggers became something of an art form in themselves and were treasured for many generations within the families of chiefs. The descendants of the famous Tsimshian Chief Legaic kept his war dagger until the 1980s, when its value had climbed to over a hundred thousand dollars.

By the 1830s, endemic warfare had given way to the Pax Britannica on the Northwest Coast, as warfare became too costly for the land-based fur traders to tolerate. John R. Swanton was struck by the similarity between war and potlatching among the Haida (1905:155): "Feasts . . . and the potlatches were the Haida roads to greatness more than war. The latter, when not waged to avenge injuries, was simply a means of increasing their power to give the former."

PLATE 102

The full outfit of a north coast warrior: a round wooden helmet, a bentwood visor, and a painted leather tunic over a breastplate made of interlocking wooden slats. This type of armour had its origins in the bronze age of China and Japan. Its use in the New World was limited to the west coast, but elements of the outfit, particularly wooden slat breastplates, spread as far south as California. CMC VII-X-1073 (S94-13,386)

THE HAIDA HOMELAND | Chapter Six

HAIDA GWAII

Today, most of the Haida population in Canada lives on Haida Gwaii, particularly Graham Island, but in prehistoric times they were much more evenly distributed throughout the archipelago. According to the early fur traders, there were concentrations of population in the south at Skungwai (or Ninstints) village and in the north at Cloak Bay, where there was a cluster of villages, including Kiusta, Dadens and Yaku. On the north coast, on Masset Inlet, there were the major villages of Masset, Yan and Kayung; and on Skidegate Inlet, there was the village of Skidegate. The locations chosen for these settlements protected them from the winter storms that lash the Pacific coast and Hecate Strait.

Although the Haida spent most of the year in their sizable towns, during the fishing season they dispersed to every stream or river that had a fish run. Salmon were the primary food species, although they run only on alternate years on Haida Gwaii. All Haida had access to the rich halibut fishing grounds, and villages on the west coast relied heavily on black cod. Shellfish was readily available, except on the west coast. Eulachon, a variety of herring rich in oil, was not indigenous to on Haida Gwaii, so the Haida travelled to the huge runs on the Nass River on the mainland, where they traded for other foods and rare materials that were not available in their homeland.

A late visitor to Haida Gwaii, Newton H. Chittenden (1884:75), who went to the villages of Cumshewa, Skedans, Tanu and Skungwai as part of a survey for the British Columbia government, reported:

> All the villages named are beautifully situated, facing the south from cosy sheltered nooks, with splendid beaches, and abundant supplies of food conveniently near. Besides the halibut bank marked on the chart, there is one near all of the villages mentioned, and inexhaustible quantities of clams and mussels along the neighbouring shores. This is certainly one of the most favoured regions in the world for the abode of the Indian.

Skungwai (Ninstints)

Ninstints, the name under which this village was declared a World Heritage Site by UNESCO in 1983, is also the name of the town chief in the middle of the last century (PLATE 103). An

PLATE 103

A portrait of Chief Ninstints (Tom Price, *left*) and Chief Giatlins (John Robson, *right*). Tom Price (circa 1860–1927) was the last traditional chief of Ninstints (Skungwai) to live in the village and was also a talented carver of argillite. John Robson, a famous carver, was the successor to Chief Giatlins and stepfather of Charles Edenshaw. *Studio portrait by an unknown Victoria photographer circa 1884.*

earlier town chief in the late eighteenth century whose name was Koyah (Work in Dawson 1880:173B) had his attack on a trading ship immortalized in a folk song popular among New England whalers (Howay 1929:15):

Come all ye bold Northwestmen who plough the raging main,
Come listen to my story, while I relate the same;
'Twas of the *Lady Washington* decoyed as she lay,
At Queen Charlotte's Island, in North America.

On the sixteenth day of June, boys, in the year Ninety-One,
The natives in great numbers on board our ship did come,
Then for to buy our fur of them our captain did begin,
But mark what they attempted before long time had been.

PLATE 104

Four mortuary posts and two house frontal poles at Skungwai (Ninstints) convey some idea of the artistry that led to this village being declared a UNESCO World Heritage Site. *Photograph by Charles F. Newcombe, 1897.*

The Haida name of Skungwai (or Red Snapper Island Town) refers to the small island behind which the village shelters. The island on which the village sits is called Kunghit (or Anthony) Island. Skungwai has taken on a symbolic status today, primarily because its remote location helped to preserve more *in situ* totem poles there than in any other Haida village. Two tragedies, however, claimed some of the beautiful poles from Skungwai. The first was a fire in the last century, which burned one end of the village and half a dozen poles; it was supposedly set by the Heiltsuk people in retaliation for a raid. The second was another fire, which destroyed the workshop of the Queen Charlotte Islands Museum at Skidegate, where seven poles from Skungwai had been sent for restoration. These lost poles were part of a collection of more than a dozen of the finest poles from Skungwai that had been taken to the Royal British Columbia Museum in Victoria by a salvage expedition in 1957 under the leadership of Professor Harry Hawthorn, Professor Wilson Duff, Michael Kew and Bill Reid. The museum lent some of the poles to the University of British Columbia Museum of Anthropology, where they are still located, and returned the remaining seven to Skidegate, only to meet the tragic end already described.

About a dozen poles still stand at Skungwai, all mortuary posts, now missing their frontal boards (PLATES 104, 105). The bones and objects they once held, such as coppers and labrets (PLATE 106), were scattered or stolen by enthusiastic collectors over the course of more than a century.

Tanu

Tanu, which is located on Laskeek Bay, is an important Haida village whose name refers to a type of sea grass found nearby. It was often called Kloo's village (also spelled Clue or Klue), meaning "southeast (wind)," after the name of its town chief. The town was founded sometime after 1725 and abandoned in the 1880s. The last chief, Gitkun, died in Skidegate early this century.

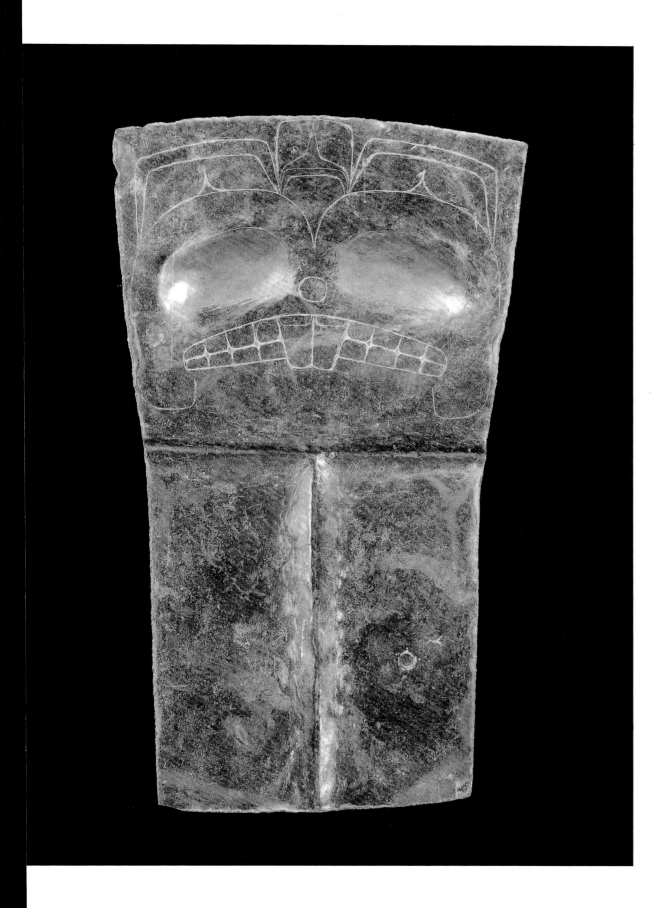

PLATE 105

The front of a chief's burial
chest from Skungwai
(Ninstints), made in the style
of the early nineteenth
century. The central figure of a
Bear is in high relief and once
had abalone shell inlay in the
eyes, ears, hands and knees.
The bas-relief carvings on the
flanking panels were also once
inlaid with abalone shell.
*Collected at Skungwai
(Ninstints) in 1897 by Charles
F. Newcombe.*

PLATE 106

From Skungwai (Ninstints)
village, a small copper shield
depicting a Beaver. The
protruding eyes on this figure
appear to have been reworked
from the original heavily
oxidized metal but were not
engraved with the expected
salmon-head eye designs.
*Collected at Skungwai
(Ninstints) in 1897 by Charles
F. Newcombe.* CMC VII-B-377
(s94-6769)

144

In 1967, I recorded (but did not excavate) a mass grave at Tanu that represented the last mortuary ceremony performed about 1885, just before the remaining occupants left their village to the encroaching forest. Prompted by the missionaries to inter their dead, the people of Tanu collected all of the remains from the mortuaries and laid them in a common grave of more than fifty individuals (MacDonald and Cybulski 1973:60–113).

George M. Dawson (1880:169B), who visited this village in 1878 during his work for the Canadian Geographical Survey, wrote a vivid description of a Haida house:

> The village consists of perhaps twelve or fourteen of the large houses usual on the coast, & bristles with totem poles carved into Grotesque figures. Some of the houses entered through holes in the bases of the poles, but Clue's by an ordinary door. Descending some steps one is in a rectangular area depressed somewhat below the level of the ground outside, with several broad steps running round it, on which the family goods, bedding &c. placed. In the Centre a square area not boarded in which a bright fire of small logs burns, the smoke passing off through apertures in the roof above. Clue with some of his friends occupied positions on the further side of the fire from the door. Squatting on Clean mats, several women, who however kept in the background.

Dawson went on to add (1880:169B): "There are about 32 upright totem poles in the village of all ages, heights, & styles . . . about sixteen, including one unfinished, though evidently some time under way." He was also fortunate enough to witness the raising of a totem pole, which he describes (1880:169B):

> There were a considerable number of strangers here at the time of our visit in July, 1878, engaged in the erection of a carved post and house for the chief. The nights are given to dancing, while sleep and gambling divided the portions of the day which were not employed in the business at hand. Cedar planks of great size, hewn out long ago in anticipation, had been towed to the spot, and were now being dragged up the beach by the united efforts of the throng, dressed for the most part in gaily coloured blankets. They harnessed themselves in clusters to the ropes, as the Egyptians are represented to have done in their pictures, shouting and ye-hooing in strange tones to encourage themselves in the work.

Dawson also took a photograph of Tanu (PLATE 107): "Present Chief Klue with a pound of tobacco, & finding no objection take a photo of the village. Would have taken several but the rain threatening all the morning now began." The photograph is the only one that portrays Haida village life of the time as it might have been observed on a casual visit. At least a dozen people appear in the photo, including a totem pole carver at work, not to mention several dogs. Domestic enterprises are evident in clothing hung to air next to a rain barrel, and halibut fillets and other foodstuffs drying on a rack. The greatest activity occurs at the door to Chief Gitkun's house, beside a double row of food boxes covered with cedar bark

PLATE 107

The village of Tanu in July 1878. George M. Dawson (1880:169B) notes that the community was undergoing a succession of town chiefs; a trading party of Tsimshian, gathered before the entrance of the town chief's house, were gambling as they waited for the raising of the new chief's pole, to which the carver is shown applying the finishing touches. *Photograph by George M. Dawson. National Archives of Canada* 242

PLATE 108

This interior house pole from
Easy to Enter House at Tanu
was carved by the artist known
as "the Master of the Chicago
Settee," according to Bill
Holm (1981:197). The pole
belonged to the chief's wife
and displays the Sea Grizzly
Bear crests of her father, the
chief of Skedans. *Photograph
by Charles F. Newcombe, 1901.*

mats and tied neatly with cords for a sea journey.

James G. Swan visited Tanu in 1883, just five years after Dawson.
He was accompanied by Chief Gitkun's son Kitkune, who volunteered to show him his father's great house (Lucile McDonald 1972:
190–91):

> He entered it by knocking off one of the massive planks, crawled
> inside and unfastened the door so that Swan's party could bring
> their cargo kit inside . . . The place was of huge proportions, fifty
> feet [15 m] long and with walls eight inches [20 cm]thick. Young
> Kitkune opened a hidden door and revealed a chamber where
> sacred emblems of the old chief were kept. The owner was reluc-
> tant to part with many and then only for a large price.

Swan (1883:Sept. 18) notes in his diary: "I would have been will-
ing to pass several days at Laskeek [Tanu] as there is more of interest
there than at any village I have seen." He wanted to experience as
much as possible and persuaded Kitkune to show him more
(McDonald 1972:191): "Young Kitkune took Swan to an uncle's
tomb, a small structure behind the big house. The sepulchre con-
tained an elaborately carved box, two guns, ammunition boxes, and the carved stick the dead
man had held when distributing presents at potlatches."

For the Columbian World Exposition in Chicago in 1893, Swan collected an exceptional
interior central pole about 5 m (16 feet) high, which stood in Easy to Enter House (PLATE
108, 109). The crests on it belong to the chief's wife, who claimed rights to the crests of the
chief of Skedans village. After the fair, the pole was deposited in the Field Museum, which
sold the pole but kept a unique talking stick (shaped like a narwhal tusk and inlaid with
abalone shell) that was attached to it. The pole went through several private owners before it
was purchased by the Canadian Museum of Civilization. The Field Museum kindly restored
the talking stick to the pole, where it now protrudes prominently from the forehead of the
lowest of two Wasgo (or Sea Wolf) figures. The myth associated with this pole is that of the
Wasgo, who lived in the lake behind Skidegate village and had the ability to transform
between the form of a Wolf and a Killer Whale. The pole shows the Wasgo in two states,
with and without his Whale attributes. According to Bill Holm, the pole was carved by the
unnamed artist whom he has dubbed "the Master of the Chicago Settee." Several of the
house frontal poles collected by Swan for the exposition passed through various owners until
they were eventually acquired by the Canadian Museum of Civilization.

At the time of Swan's visit, only fifteen people were living at Tanu. The mortuary
columns outnumbered the totem poles and houses of the inhabitants.

PLATE 109

The same interior house pole from Easy to Enter House in Tanu as in PLATE 108, restored and on display in the Grand Hall of the Canadian Museum of Civilization. The narwhal tusk talking stick, which was separated from the pole for a number of years, has been replaced in its original position. CMC VII-B-1797A (pole), CMC VII-B-1797B (talking stick)

Skedans

PLATE 110

One side of this shaman's
rattle portrays a Bear with an
extended tongue. The other
side (not shown) has the face
of Hawk. *Collected from
Skedans in 1897 by Charles F.
Newcombe.* CMC VII-B-544
(s92-4238)

Skedans village is located on the neck of a peninsula of land at the head of Cumshewa Inlet (PLATE 112). A high rocky prominence at the end of the peninsula offered a perfect site for a fort to protect the village. Skedans is a European rendering of the name of the town chief, Gida'nsta. The Haida name for this town is Koona, or in the old days Huadji-lanas, which means Grizzly Bear Town. Chief Gida'nsta maintained a special relationship with Chief Tsebassa, town chief of the Tsimshian village of Kitkatla opposite Skedans on the mainland. According to a charter myth, both town chiefs had a common ancestor who had migrated from the Nass River (Swanton 1905:79). This alliance provided the main channel through which trade and potlatching took place.

The Haida exchanged their dried halibut, dried seaweed, herring roe and canoes with the Tsimshian for eulachon grease, dried berries, goat wool and horns. Friendly competition in the potlatch system encouraged the exchange of crests, songs and stories, and it appears that the secret society structure of the Nuxalk and other central coast tribes moved from Kitkatla to Skedans via this connection (PLATE 111).

George M. Dawson's recently published field notes provide a much richer insight into Haida life than his official monograph issued a year after the expedition, such as this record of his impression of Skedans during a visit in July 1878 (in Cole and Lockner 1989:473):

> Skedan's village shows signs of having passed its best days some time since, though not quite so deserted as Cumshewa's. It has always been a larger village & many of the houses are still inhabited. Most, however, look old & moss grown & the totem poles have the same aspect. Of houses there are about sixteen, of totem poles about 44. These last seem to be put up not merely as hereditary family Crests, but in memory of the dead . . . The flat topped, boarded totems are more frequent in this village than elsewhere seen. One of these shows a curious figure leaning forward & holding in its paws a genuine *Copper* like those described to me by Mr. Moffat as in great request & much worth among the Ft Rupert Indians. At least one other *Copper* in view on the posts here, but the second observed not in Evident relation to any of the Carved figures.

Dawson (in Cole and Lockner 1989:474) was a keen observer of the routine activities that occupied the community:

> About sundown two large Canoes with two masts Each, & the forward one with a large flag hoisted, hove in sight round the point. Turn out to be Kit-Katla Chimseyan Indians with loads of oolachen grease for Sale. They have slept only two nights on the way from Kit-Katla. They come here on a regular trading expedition, & expect to carry back chiefly blankets in place of their oil . . . Quite a picturesque scene when the Canoes grounded & the Kit-Katlans assisted by the Haidas carry up blankets used as bedding, miscellains little things & the Cedar bark boxes which hold the precious oil.

The surprising feature of this event is that the traders from Kitkatla were seeking woven Chilkat blankets from the Haida. Since the Tsimshian were the providers of goat wool to the Haida, this suggests that the Haida either wove the blankets or traded blankets they had obtained from the Tlingit to the north.

The inhabitants of Haida villages like Skedans probably traded several thousand objects to travellers (PLATE 110); of these, perhaps one thousand are now in museums, but only a few score have been specifically documented as to their village of origin. Dawson (in Cole and Lockner 1989:472) made interesting observations about how the trade in curios took place:

> Besieged by Indians with various things to sell this morning, curiosities, new potatoes about the size of wallnuts . . . Soon after dark Capt Klue & three of his people arrived, disgusted that they had not been knowing enough to offer *items* for Sale when we were [in] their country, & having heard that Skedan was making a big thing out of us. Brought with them one remarkable mask with a nose about 6 feet [1.8 m] long, a dancing pole highly prized & gaily painted & a head ornament composed of a cedar bark ring into which a great number of imitation arrows, in wood & feathered, were stuck. All these they valued much & had evidently brought their best things to cut out Skedan & his friends.

The village of Skedans has a special aura it presents even to contemporary visitors. Robert Bruce Inverarity (1932:MS 60), an art historian, collector and museum director, visited the site in 1932 and describes his impressions:

> Last night I thought I heard voices in the wind and at first thought the sealers had landed on the beach. But then when I heard women's voices thought perhaps a party had come from Skidegate, but when the voices came no closer and drifted no farther away, I knew I was wrong. They all seemed to be singing. The men's voices were low and the women's voices were very high and sustained. I got up and gazed at the beach,— there was no sign of anyone. In the morning I looked at the beach but could find no sign of any boat having landed. Later I learned that other people had also heard ghosts here and when I described the singing to some old Indians, they told me that it was a funeral dirge I had heard.

PLATE 111

This burial chest intended for the chief of Skedans bears his Mountain Goat crest, which he obtained from the chief of the Tsimshian village of Kitkatla. The chest is now in the American Museum of Natural History. *Collected by Charles F. Newcombe in 1897.*

PLATE 112

Panorama of Skedans village from the eastern end. *Photograph by George M. Dawson, July 1878. National Archives of Canada 249*

Cumshewa

The village of Cumshewa is on the northern shore of Cumshewa Inlet, an hour's paddle from Skedans (PLATE 113). In 1840, the village had about twenty houses and slightly fewer than three hundred inhabitants (Work in Dawson 1880:173B), who belonged to three closely related Eagle lineages.

Cumshewa was an anglicized version of the name of the town chief, Gomshewah, a Heilt-suk word meaning "rich at the mouth of the river." This alludes to the teeming life at a river mouth where seagulls, seals and killer whales congregate to feed upon the salmon that pool there prior to making their spawning run up the river. When the first European ships with their white sails arrived on the coast, the Haida compared them to the flocks of seagulls at spawning time and gave the name Cumshewa to the white people associated with this appari-tion. The Haida name for the village was Thlinul, anglicized as Tlkinool by John Work (in Dawson 1880:168B), who carried out the first census of the Haida for the Hudson's Bay Com-pany in 1839; the Tsimshian called the village Kit-ta-was.

Joseph Ingraham's journals of 1791 and 1792 (in Kaplanoff 1971:MS 134) record numerous trading activities with Chief Cumshewa and his people, although Ingraham did not leave his ship: "The people of these Isles in generall possess a truly merchantile spirit but none more so than the tribe of Cummashawaa for they will not part with a single skin till they had exerted their utmost to obtain the best price for it."

Reverend Jonathan Green (1915:64), who visited Cumshewa in 1829 when there was a war in progress between that village and the Tsimshian town of Kitkatla, did not leave his ship either:

> We came down opposite Kumshewa village, and several of the Indians came off to see us. This is the tribe, several of whom were killed by the Shebasha men. Some of the sufferers of that quarrel were on board. One lost a child, another a sister, another his wife, besides receiving a wound himself. Their badge of mourning is a face painted horribly black, with their hair cut very short.

George M. Dawson (1880:169) was the first outside visitor to actually enter the village:

> The village generally known as Cumshewas is situated in a small bay facing toward the open sea, but about two miles [3.2 km] within the inlet to which the same name has been applied. The outer point of the bay is formed by a little rock islet, which is connected to the main shore by a beach at low tide . . . There are now standing here twelve or fourteen houses, several of them quite ruinous, with over twenty-five carved posts. The population is quite small, this place having suffered much from the causes to which the decrease in numbers of the natives have already been referred.

Cumshewa was occupied until 1905, when Methodist missionaries encouraged the remaining few inhabitants to move to Skidegate.

PLATE 113A, 113B

(pages 152/153)

A panorama of the village of Cumshewa in July 1878. Most of the houses have been abandoned, and the new mortuary posts attest to the deaths of many chiefs in quick succession. *Photographs by George M. Dawson.* CMC 244 (left) and 245 (right)

PLATE 114

The ceremonial seat of honour of Chief Skotsgai of Kaisun village. This piece led Bill Holm (1981:197) to name the artist who made it "the Master of the Chicago Settee" and to identify many other works by this unknown carver in various museums. The seat was collected at Skidegate in 1901 by Charles F. Newcombe and is now in the Field Museum of Natural History, Chicago (79595). *Photograph by Charles F. Newcombe, 1901.*

Kaisun

Kaisun is a village on the west coast of Moresby Island (PLATE 115). It is located at the east end of Inskip Channel, due south of Cha'atl village, with which it has close ties. The town chief of Cha'atl owned a large house in Kaisun, called Dogfish House, which he used when he resided there. Around 1840 there were over three hundred people living in twenty houses in Kaisun (Work in Dawson 1880:173B). All of the inhabitants belonged to an Eagle lineage known as the People of Sea Lion Town.

Skotsgai, the town chief of Kaisun, owned three houses; the principal one was House Upon Which Are Clouds, a Haida equivalent of "skyscraper house." In 1849, the discovery of gold in the area started a short-lived gold rush on the islands. Chief Skotsgai changed his name to Chief Gold, and his town became known as Gold Harbour. A decade later, he moved his villagers to Haina (or New Gold Harbour) near Skidegate on the east side of Haida Gwaii. Charles F. Newcombe purchased several items from Skotsgai, including his beautifully decorated chief's seat (PLATE 114).

PLATE 115

The village of Kaisun as it appeared in 1901. The discovery of gold in nearby Mitchell Harbour in 1849 started a gold rush that lasted for a few years and attracted miners from the California rush. *Photograph by Charles F. Newcombe.*

PLATE 116

The frontal pole of House Waiting for Property (*right*) in Haina was exhibited at the Columbian World Exposition in Chicago in 1893. It has now been fully restored and stands in the Grand Hall of the Canadian Museum of Civilization. *Photograph by Richard Maynard, 1884.* CMC VII-B-1127 (20,529)

Haina (New Gold Harbour)

Haina in Haida means Sunshine Town, and the village is situated at the end of a small island looking east into the rising sun over Skidegate Bay (PLATE 117). Haina was occupied in the late 1850s, on a much older site, by the people of Kaisun (Gold Harbour) and Cha'atl villages. Dawson (1880:173B) explains that the reason for the move to Haina was the drastic decline of population in all the west coast towns due to the introduction of diseases like smallpox and tuberculosis by the miners in the short-lived gold rush that Chief Gold and his wife started.

The town chief was Ganai of the Eagle clan, who owned two houses in the village. His main residence was called House Always Looking for Visitors, and the other was Lightning House. On the frontal poles of both houses, the main figure wears an immense hat with alternating light and dark rings, on which sits a Raven. This main figure represents a mythical being who taught the chief the dances of the Dog-Eater Society.

Chief Ganai's main house was distinguished by having two oval entrances on either side of the frontal pole, as well as by smaller versions of the dog-eater figure or watchmen on the corner posts. The Raven on the top of the pole ensured that no one overlooked Ganai's wealth, as it held a large copper in its beak. Although the pole of the main house eventually

PLATE 117

A panorama of the village of Haina (or New Gold Harbour), showing the ten original houses of the chiefs in a row; three more modest dwellings have been added nearer to the beach at left. *Photograph by Richard Maynard, 1884.*

PLATE 118

On this model totem pole, the second figure from the top is that of a shaman holding puffin beak rattles over two patients. *Collected at Haina in 1884 by Alexander McKenzie of the Hudson's Bay Company.* CMC VII-B-842 (s92-4275)

158

fell down and decayed, the pole from Lightning House is now at the Canadian Museum of Civilization.

The pole that stood in front of House Waiting for Property belonged to a Raven lineage, and it is also now at the Canadian Museum of Civilization (PLATE 116). The top figure is a Killer Whale person flanked by two watchmen. The large beak on the figure below belongs to an Eagle crest, and below that is a *tcamaos* (a supernatural snag that devoured canoes) grasping a six-section potlatch cylinder emerging from the head of a Whale.

When I made a very brief test excavation at the edge of one of the house pits at Haina, I found piles of chips of argillite as well as pieces of broken and unfinished argillite carvings. This confirmed various reports that many argillite carvers had lived and worked at Haina, although they may have sold most of their output in Skidegate or Victoria (PLATE 118).

Haina struggled on through the 1880s, and the inhabitants even built a church, but they finally abandoned the town in about 1890.

Cha'atl

Cha'atl is located on Skidegate Inlet and is partly exposed to swells from the open Pacific Ocean (PLATE 119). The shoreline is steep and mostly rocky, with only a few places to draw up large canoes, but the site does enjoy a southern exposure and is far enough up the channel for protection from storms. During the early nineteenth century, the town was a large community: John Work's census (in Dawson 1880:173B) counts 561 people, making it the third-largest community on Haida Gwaii after Masset and Skidegate. The population consisted of both Raven and Eagle families, who lived in about three dozen houses scattered in several rows.

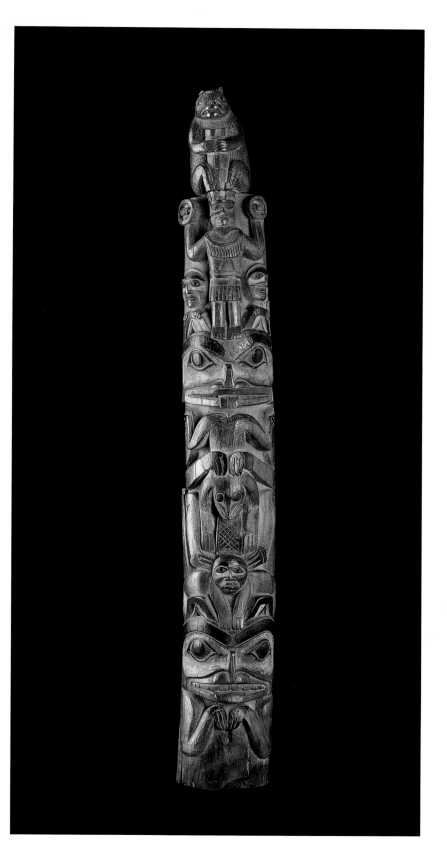

PLATE 119

A view of Cha'atl village,
looking west to the Pacific
coast of Graham Island with
Skidegate Channel to the left.
The old houses have
disappeared, leaving only the
house frontal poles and
mortuary posts among the
bushes. The heyday of the
village was over by the 1860s.
*Photograph by Charles F.
Newcombe, 1903.* CMC J20558-13

PLATE 120

On this mortuary box from
Cha'atl village, a particularly
impish-looking Raven peers
from between its wings. The
box may date from the
smallpox epidemic that swept
the village in the 1860s.
*Collected in 1897 by Charles F.
Newcombe.* CMC VII-B-547
(s85-3278)

While the location of Cha'atl gave it ideal access to passing trading vessels, the switch in trade after 1834 to the Hudson's Bay Company at Fort Simpson put the town into decline. The town chief of Cha'atl was Wadatstaia, brother of Chief Skotsgai of Kaisun. The discovery of gold on the islands in 1849 led to a gold rush that sustained Cha'atl until the 1860s, when devastating epidemics greatly depopulated the community. The inhabitants began to move to the eastern end of Skidegate Inlet in the 1850s, but Cha'atl was still used by Haida seal hunters until after the turn of the century.

At the end of the nineteenth century, Charles F. Newcombe made a complete photographic and oral history record of Cha'atl and collected many artifacts that are now scattered among museums around the world (PLATE 120). The site was by then heavily overgrown with only four small fish camp houses still habitable. The tangled growth was an extra inducement to the British Columbia artist Emily Carr, who painted one of her most famous Haida scenes from the beach at Cha'atl village.

Although a large fire destroyed part of the town after George M. Dawson's visit in 1878, it is still remarkable today for its well-carved house frontal poles. Unfortunately, none of the magnificent free-standing poles were removed to museums, and today only one, which belonged to the late Solomon Wilson of Skidegate, still survives at the site.

The modern-day village of Skidegate displays little evidence of its creative and tumultuous past. The single exception is the Band Council office building, designed by Rudy Kovaks and enhanced by a pole carved by Bill Reid.

The first contact between Europeans and the people of Skidegate appears to have been made by Captain George Dixon (1789), who in July 1787 anchored off the entrance to Skidegate Inlet. He did not visit the village but does provide the first description of Chief Skidegate:

> Of all the Indians we had seen, this chief had the most savage aspect, and his whole appearance sufficiently marked him as a proper person to lead a tribe of cannibals. His stature was above the common size; his body spare and thin, and though at first sight he appeared lank and emaciated, yet his step was bold and firm, and his limbs apparently strong and muscular.

Dixon's use of the term "cannibals" is an exaggerated reference to the ritual eating of human flesh by the initiates of secret societies. Although in some ceremonies the Tsimshian, Haida and the Kwakwaka'wakw (or Kwakiutl) did bite high-ranking people, it is likely that the Haida only pretended to eat human flesh from cadavers. The care with which they prepared artificial human and dog carcasses in order to fool spectators at the winter dances and initiations is described earlier in this book.

Within a few years of Dixon's visit, many ships included Skidegate in their itinerary while pursuing the trade in sea otter pelts. The name of the town chief was, as usual, applied by the traders to the community itself. Skidegate in Haida means "son of the chiton" (Swanton 1905A:434). One of the best observers is Joseph Ingraham, who recorded his first meeting in 1791 with the town chief of Skidegate in his journal (in Kaplanoff 1971:MS 135–36):

> At 10 oclock in the evening a small canoe was seen coming to us in which was 4 men as she was so small I let them come alongside they said they were of the tribe of Skeetkiss and had furr for sale they sold us but one skin when they could better examine our articles of trade as the least flaw in our chizzles or daggers was sufficient to condemn them as unfit for their purpose . . . Towards night a large war canoe came into the bay and after holding a conversation with some other canoes (perhaps relative to the trade) they came alongside in this canoe was Skeetkiss a chief of the first consequence among these people as at every place we visited they spoke of him as a man of great power and of whom they were afraid.

James Deans, a Hudson's Bay Company employee, describes that chief's successor, who was called Skidegate the Great (1899:77):

> He was named the Great because he was large in body and wealth, if not in good deeds . . . He was a man about six feet in height, had a very small head on an exceedingly large body, so

large that a belt he wore round his waist could go around three ordinary sized men. He was the richest chief of his day. It is said he had thirty slaves, male and female . . . He also had all the neighbouring tribes under his tribute.

Maritime fur traders were cautious about venturing ashore and usually chose to conduct their trade from the relative safety of a well-armed ship. Ingraham (in Kaplanoff 1971:MS 148–49) provides graphic details of the traders' fear of the Haida during his stay in Skidegate Inlet:

The Evening of the 25 we observed severall war canoes cross the port from Skeetkiss to Cummashawaas village I determin'd to watch them closely for fear of any design upon us therefore doubled our watch severall canoes took up their quarters in the cove about 2 oclock next morning the watch inform'd me the Indians were mustering in the woods as something uncommon was about to take place I order'd all hands immediately and we were soon in readiness to receive them after being on deck about 5 minutes I observed the fires on shore increase and a canoe put off from the beach and paddle towards us a man in her called out to me to look they were going away at the same time they advanced fast towards us I therefore answered him with a swivell and severall musketts on which every fire was immediately extinguished and all silent.

By the 1820s the supply of sea otter furs was beginning to dwindle over much of the north coast, except for Skidegate. In the meantime, the written accounts of maritime traders had begun to interest the mission churches of New England, which had achieved rapid success in Hawaii and were aware of the expanding Russian missions in Alaska. In 1829, Reverend Jonathan Green, who had served the Hawaiian missions, was sent to the Northwest Coast, and provides this description in his journal (1915:84):

Just before we cast anchor, we passed the village of Skidegas. To me the prospect was almost enchanting, and, more than any thing I had seen, reminded me of a civilized country. The houses, of which there are thirty or forty, appeared tolerably good, and before the door of many of them stood a large mast carved in the form of the human countenance, of the dog, wolf, etc., neatly painted. The land about the village appeared to be in a good state of cultivation. The Indians do not raise much, excepting potatoes, as they have not a variety of seeds; yet, from the appearance of the land, I presume they may greatly vary their vegetable productions.

Reverend Green (1915:85) attempted to preach to the chiefs of Skidegate on board the ship but observed: "When I had finished, they insisted upon my giving them a small drink of rum! . . . On board the ship of a north-west trader is a place very unsuitable to preach temperance to an Indian, and indeed to attempt anything in the form of Christian instructions." He abandoned all plans for a mission at Skidegate.

During the 1830s, whalers began to arrive. In 1832, one whaling captain, a Mr. C. Jefferson, married a daughter of Chief Skidegate the Great and built a residence called Mosquito Hawk House. As he did not own any crests, Jefferson was permitted to use one of his wife's crests, the Raven with a broken beak (a reference to the Raven and the halibut fisherman myth), at the base of his house frontal pole. He filled in the space above the Raven with seven coppers stacked three across as a sign of his wealth.

The fur trade after 1834 swung heavily to the Hudson's Bay Company's new Fort Simpson on the mainland in Tsimshian territory. The Haida from Skidegate visited the fort regularly to trade their potatoes and tobacco to the Tsimshian, who acted as intermediaries.

The discovery of gold in the Queen Charlotte Islands in 1849 brought the first mass influx of whites to the area, but by 1854 the gold rush had subsided. A couple of ships that visited the area in search of gold were wrecked, and James Deans (1899:285) reports that the Skidegate chiefs profited considerably both from the brief gold rush and the ransom of shipwrecked sailors. This windfall led to a flurry of raising new poles and building new houses, but it also gave such a bad reputation to Skidegate that ships stopped calling for a while.

The Haida were bothered by the lack of trading contacts, and in 1853 five hundred of them canoed south to the colonial outposts of Victoria and Nanaimo. Their arrival in Victoria frightened the small settlement, and Governor James Douglas sent them home. However, a few weeks later, a smaller flotilla of five canoes quietly returned to Victoria. This was the beginning of an annual migration that lasted for two decades, leaving Skidegate almost empty for much of each year.

Two things came back to the village with the returning families: wealth, which allowed them to build larger houses and raise more poles, and a variety of diseases that ravaged the populace. Only the influx of survivors from the southern Haida villages that had been hit even harder by disease kept Skidegate alive. The new villagers brought with them many family treasures, which they mostly sold to travellers and collectors.

The worst epidemics hit Skidegate in the late 1860s, and many of the houses abandoned in the back row were never rebuilt, though the frontal poles of these dwellings and their massive frames can be seen in photographs taken by George M. Dawson in 1878.

Two visitors to Skidegate within a short time of each other provide an insight into Haida ceremonial life as the final curtain fell. Reverend William H. Collison of Masset, who visited Skidegate in 1876 with Albert Edward Edenshaw and his son Cowhoe (later baptized George), describes his reception thus (in Lillard 1981:123):

Cedar bark mats were spread for us to the rear of the lodge in the centre . . . Water, soap, and towels were first brought, and each of us invited to wash our hands. The first food offered us was dried salmon and eulachon grease . . . The next dish was boiling dulse, which, when gathered, is made up into square cakes about twelve inches by twelve [30.5 × 30.5 cm] and about one and a half inches [3.8 cm] in thickness, and dried in the sun. Before boiling, this is chopped fine, and it is also mixed with eulachon grease before being served out. Large horn spoons were then handed round, those given to the chiefs being inlaid with abalone or mother-of-pearl. As a special mark of honor, I was given a large silver-plated tablespoon, which became so heated with the boiling seaweed that I could not permit it to touch my lips. Accordingly I called upon them to change it for one of their horn spoons. This caused much hilarity among them to find that the *Yetz haada* preferred a spoon of their manufacture to that made by his own countrymen.

After this dish we were served with dried halibut and grease, and then with boiled herring spawn. During this repast I had remarked two young men, stripped to the waist, beating up in tubs dried berries with water until it became a frothy substance, not unlike ice cream in appearance. This was served up last as dessert.

Dawson attended a potlatch at Skidegate on 24 July 1878 and furnishes a rich description of the proceedings (in Cole and Lockner 1989:478–81):

The smoke from the fire,—which the only light—escaped by wide openings in the roof . . . The performers in this instance about twenty in number, dressed according to no uniform plan but got up in their best clothes, or at least their most gaudy ones, with the addition of certain ornaments &c. appropriate to the occasion. All or nearly all wore head-dresses, variously constructed of cedar bark rope ornamented with feathers &c. or as in one case with a bristling circle of the whiskers of the Sea-lion. Shoulder girdles made of Cedar-bark rope, variously ornamented & coloured, with tassels &c. very common. One man wore gaiters covered with fringes of strung puffin bills which rattled as he moved. Nearly if not all held sprigs of fresh spruce, & were covered about the head with downy feathers which also filled the warm atmosphere of the house. Rattles were also in order. Different from the rest however, five women who stood in front, dressed with some uniformity, Several having the peculiarly beautiful mountain goat shawls which are purchased from the Mainland Indians. The head-dresses of these women were also pretty nearly the same consisting of Small mask faces Carved in wood & inlaid with haliotis [abalone] shell, these Attached to Cedar bark & built round with gay feathers &c. stood above the forehead. The faces of the women—as if All engaged in the dance—gaily painted, vermillion being the favourite colour. Another important feature the master of the ceremonies, who stood in the middle of the back row, slightly higher than the rest, not particularly gaily dressed, but holding a long thin stick with which he kept time & led off the singing . . .

The performer on the drum—a flat tambourine-looking article formed of hide stretched on a hoop—Sat opposite the dancers & near the fire, So that they Could mutually see each others movements. The drum beaten very regularly in "double knocks," thus—tum tum—tum tum—tum tum—&c!

With this the dancers kept time in a sort of Chant or Song to which words appeared Set, & which rose to a loud pitch or fell lower according to the motions of the Master of the Ceremonies, who besides keeping up the time now & then slips in a few words of direction or exhortation. To the drumming the dancing also keeps time, following it closely . . . When the chorus swells to *forte,* the rattles are plied with tenfold vigour & the noise becomes very great. After a performance of ten Minutes or so the Master of Ceremonies gives a sign & all stop, ending with a loud *Hugh!* After a few minutes repose the movement begins again, with the drum.

The people of Skidegate asked Reverend William Duncan of Metlakatla to send a missionary to them, and he sent Edward Mathers, a Tsimshian teacher. This was not what the Haida wanted, so they sent a party led by Chief Nanjingwas to Metlakatla to plead their case again with Reverend Duncan (Lillard 1981:123): "You have gone to Masset . . . and made your residence there, while you have only sent a Tsimshian to teach us. This is not as it should be, as Skidegate was formerly just as powerful as the north, and we should have a white teacher also." This statement illustrates the long-standing rivalry between Skidegate and Masset, and between the Haida and the Tsimshian peoples. That rivalry was one of the driving forces in the production of impressive artworks that are now considered of world significance.

The Methodist mission at Fort Simpson sent the Haida a white teacher, George Robinson, in 1883. The effects of a permanent mission at Skidegate were rapid and profound. Within a year, the traditional plank houses were replaced with single-family dwellings of frame construction, and the rows of houses along the shore were replaced with streets on a grid pattern. The church became the major focus of community life, though there is no evidence that totem poles were destroyed at the instigation of missionaries, as had happened at Masset (Henderson 1974:104).

Edward Dossetter, a Victoria photographer aboard the ship *Rocket,* had stopped at Skidegate in 1881 and took some excellent photographs (PLATE 121). At the time of his visit, several new houses were under construction and a few new memorial poles had been raised, but this activity marked the end of the erection of traditional monuments in the village; the few remaining master carvers received no new commissions after the mid-1880s (PLATE 122).

In 1884, when Richard Maynard, another Victoria photographer who accompanied Newton H. Chittenden on a provincial survey of the Queen Charlotte Islands, visited Skidegate, most of the old houses had been pulled down or were in ruins and many poles had fallen (PLATE 123). The people of Skidegate had decided to adopt the ways of the white man (PLATE 124).

PLATE 121

Chief Nanjingwas wearing a
naval uniform (*left*) and
another man, probably Chief
Skidegate VII, stand before the
former's Raven crest at Chief's
House in Skidegate.
*Photograph by Edward
Dossetter, 1881.*

167

PLATE 122

This panorama of Skidegate
village from the east shows
Grizzly Bear's Mouth House
(*second from right*). The figures
of Judge Pemberton and the
court clerk from Victoria who
once imprisoned Chief
Giatlins, the owner of this
house, can be seen on the
corner posts. John Robson,
who inherited this house,
married Qwa'Kuna, the
widowed mother of Charles
Edenshaw. The pole with the
Eagle on top (*centre*) was a
memorial to her. *Photograph
by O. C. Hastings, 1879.*

PLATE 123

The frame of the abandoned
Grizzly Bear House at
Skidegate. The waning
fortunes of this family are
revealed by the shack they
have built inside the frame of
their former dwelling.
*Photograph by Richard
Maynard, 1884.* CMC 67236

Kiusta

The name Kiusta means "where the trail comes out," in reference to a trail from Lepas Bay to the village. The first European to see the village was Captain George Dixon in July 1787. Kiusta was first portrayed in 1799, in a drawing in the journal of the ship *Eliza,* a fairly accurate panorama of the town from the water. The largest house belonged to the town chief Itl-tini, of a branch of the Stastas Eagles whose head chief was Cunnyha (now Gunia). Cunnyha's house was on Lucy Island near Kiusta, but in about 1800 he moved his people to the Prince of Wales Island area of Alaska to join the group known as the Kaigani Haida.

Kiusta, along with the adjacent village of Yaku, was identified by John Work (in Dawson 1880:173B) as Lu-lan-na. The remains of twelve houses at Kiusta indicate the population was then just over three hundred people.

The name Edenshaw is first mentioned by fur traders of the 1790s. As with all Haida chiefly names, it was passed down the matrilineal line to a chief's eldest sister's son. At least one Chief Edenshaw preceded the one who dominated most of the nineteenth century, Albert Edward Edenshaw. He was born in 1812 and grew up in his uncle's village of Hiellan, but moved to Kiusta after 1834 when he was involved in an unsuccessful attempt to loot the *Vancouver,* a stranded Hudson's Bay Company ship. The captain and crew burned the vessel, nearly killing Edenshaw, but he later salvaged many rifles from the sandbar and replaced their badly burned stocks with ones he carved himself. These he traded to other Haida and converted his new wealth into slaves, of which he eventually owned a dozen.

Albert Edward Edenshaw built his house in Kiusta around 1840 after the details of the carvings on the corner posts, rafter ends and frontal pole were revealed to him in a dream. He named it Story House, and it stood on the site of his predecessor's dwelling, called Property House. When Story House was finished, Albert Edward gave a great potlatch and invited guests from Masset, Skidegate, Kaisun and Cha'atl, as well as from Kaigani Haida villages.

The noted artist Charles Edenshaw, who was Albert Edward's nephew and heir, made a model of Story House for John R. Swanton, and it is now at the American Museum of Natural History in New York (MacDonald 1983:plate 257). Swanton (1905:125–26) notes that Albert Edward intended to leave Story House to his son rather than his nephew, but abandoned the idea and, in fact, the village itself, moving to Kung village in 1850, just before the capture of the ship *Susan Sturgis* by Chief Wiah of Masset.

Just west of Kiusta are three mortuary posts that once supported a communal mortuary box, now completely overgrown with mosses and ferns (PLATE 125). In 1932, Robert Bruce Inverarity (1932:MS 19) saw these mortuary poles and recorded his observations of them:

> The centre pole of the three carved poles was half round, and hollow, while the other two were solid. The two outer poles and the plain pole behind are notched in the top to receive a burial box at a height of about fifteen feet. The box was gone. On both sides of this mortuary

PLATE 124

A number of young Skidegate women wearing secret society regalia are surrounded by men, including Chief Tom Price (*right*) in a white shirt. Reverend Charles Harrison arranged this photograph in 1890 in an attempt to discourage face painting, masks and secret societies. *Photograph by Reverend Charles Harrison.* CMC 71-6778

PLATE 125

The centre pole of this
unusual mortuary monument
at Kiusta was probably the
interior pole from the house of
an early Chief Edenshaw who
died in the 1830s. The two
flanking poles were carved by
the same artist as the original
one and display the Bear and
Beaver crests of the family.
CMC uncatalogued

PLATE 126

Yaku village near Kiusta was
founded by refugees from the
southwest coast of Haida
Gwaii who fled their enemies
from Skungwai. An epidemic
wiped out most of the
community in 1852, and the
survivors eventually settled at
Masset. *Photograph by Charles
F. Newcombe, 1913.*

group were the remains of burial platforms. Both were broken and well pilfered like the cave
we had visited, by fisher folk. From the box sides I found there must have been from twenty
to thirty boxes on each side of the two platforms.

Remains of the timbers that formed the burial platforms were still evident in the 1990s.
The central pole of this mortuary appears to once have been an interior pole of a chief's
house, for the back of it is hollowed out, as Inverarity notes above, and it also has a small oval
doorway only 30 cm (1 foot) high in the base. The opening is clearly symbolic rather than
functional, but it is similar to other known examples of interior central poles from the backs
of houses; they appear to be thought of as small frontal poles for the chief's compartment.

When Marius Barbeau went to Kiusta for the Canadian Museum of Civilization in 1939,
he photographed several monuments there and at Yaku (PLATE 126). On my first visit to
Kiusta in 1967 to map the village, there was but one other pole left standing, with the face of
a Bear on it. This carving was removed to the CMC, where a replica was made; the original
was then returned to the community museum in Masset (MacDonald 1983:plate 255).

Kung

Kung (or Dream Town) was a thriving community of fifteen houses and 280 inhabitants in 1840, according to John Work (in Dawson 1880:173b). On the east side of the village, the remains of a row of houses that appear to be at least several hundred years old suggest an even larger population long ago. The village chief in 1840 was Gulas of the Up-Inlet Town People of the Eagle moiety. A closely related Eagle family shared the eastern half of the town with them, while the Stastas Eagles and a single household of Rose Spit Ravens lived in the western half.

In 1850, Albert Edward Edenshaw, realizing that Kiusta had lost its economic and strategic importance, abandoned his Story House there (Dalzell 1973:443). He resettled at Kung and built an elaborate dwelling named House That Can Hold a Great Crowd of People (PLATES 128, 129). Its architecture has many features of the Kaigani Haida style, such as tall square corner posts, which reveal Chief Edenshaw's strong ties with Haida towns in Alaska. He also erected a pole in the early 1860s in Kung in honour of Governor James Douglas's fairness to native people; the pole portrays Douglas dressed in his frock coat and tall hat. At about the same time, villages in Alaska were raising poles in Abraham Lincoln's honour for freeing the slaves.

About 1875, Albert Edward Edenshaw moved again, this time to Yatze (or Knife Village) at the head of Naden Harbour, in the hope of encouraging more Alaskan trade (PLATES 127, 130). George M. Dawson (1880:163B) notes on his 1878 visit to Kung:

> The village just within the narrow entrance to Virago Sound, from which these people are removing, is called Kung; it has been a substantial and well constructed one, but is now rather decayed, though some of the houses are still inhabited. The houses arranged along the edge of a low bank, facing a fine sandy beach, are eight to ten in number, some of them quite large. The carved posts are not numerous, though in a few instances elaborate.

By the time Newton Chittenden, a provincial government surveyor, stopped at Kung in 1884, it had been abandoned as a permanent village. Yatze had been abandoned the year before, when Albert Edward Edenshaw moved to Masset, but the site continued to be used as a halibut fishing camp until at least the First World War, and smaller temporary houses were built near the beach.

Very few objects were collected at Kung, since it was off the usual visitors' track. Most of the valuable items were taken along by their owners when they moved to Masset. George A. Dorsey, an anthropologist, helped himself to the contents of many Haida graves at Kung, and these objects are now in the Field Museum in Chicago. Dorsey (1897:169) describes one unusual grave (MacDonald 1983:plate 249):

> The grave of the old chief at Kung was the best I had seen. Four short, stout posts had been

PLATE 127

This pole was erected by Albert Edward Edenshaw at the village of Yatze in 1878. The bottom figure may have been carved by Charles Edenshaw or John Robson. The Raven at the top sits on a mythic being called Kaga, who was his uncle and with whom he had a quarrel. The Raven landed on Kaga with such force that he split him open. The next figure is a Sea Wolf, followed by a Beaver with prominent incisors. The small figure below that at the front of the pole is a Mountain Hawk, and at the base is a Mountain Goat that is similar to the one on Chief Skedans's mortuary post at Skidegate. *Photograph by Marius Barbeau, 1947.*

PLATE 128

House That Can Hold a Great Crowd of People (*left*) was built in the village of Kung by Albert Edward Edenshaw in the 1850s when he moved there from Kiusta. The house next to it (*right*) is Steel House, so called because it was fortified with the addition of extra horizontal planks to the walls so that no one could shoot the inhabitants through the cracks. *Photograph by George M. Dawson, 1878. National Archives of Canada 264*

PLATE 129

The interior pole of Albert
Edward Edenshaw's house at
Kung. The figure at the top is
Skungo, a man who dwelt in
cave near Kiusta and who was
transformed into a monster
because he was living on raw
fish and birds. The Bear and
Frog at the centre are crests
often used by Edenshaw, while
the large figure at the base
looks like a bear but is similar
to a being on an interior house
pole from Skidegate carved by
his nephew Charles Edenshaw
(MacDonald 1983:plate 52),
which retains its beak and is
clearly a Thunderbird.
Photograph by Charles F.
Newcombe, 1913.

firmly planted in the ground, and on the inner corners of each grooves had been cut out to receive the beams that supported the little house, in which lay the chief in state. The structure was nearly buried in a thick growth of vegetation, and much work with the axe was needed before the beautifully carved posts could be rendered visible to the camera.

Dorsey (1897:169) explored numerous other graves at Kung, including those of shaman:

What proved of special interest were several very old graves which faced the beach on the east side of the village. These were the burial places of medicine men or Shamans, and quite different from the ordinary grave, instead of a single pole in which the body is placed through a hole in the top or at the side, or from the double pole platform grave which we saw at Kung. We found a little house built of short cedar logs. Inside was placed the Shaman in a long coffin-box reclining at full length with his rattles and other ceremonial paraphernalia about him. With one had been placed several very fine masks, but they were almost entirely crumbled into dust.

PLATE 130

Albert Edward Edenshaw and Wiah, the town chief of Masset, on the beach at Yatze village. *Photograph by George M. Dawson, 1878. National Archives of Canada* 38147

PLATE 131

A panorama of the village of Yan from the south a few years after people began leaving it for Masset. By 1885, Yan was deserted. *Photograph by Edward Dossetter, 1881.*

PLATE 132

Women and children of Yan pose for the camera in front of Flicker House and a memorial pole to an Eagle chief, Ildjiwas. *Photograph by Edward Dossetter, 1881.*

Yan

Yan means Beeline Town (literally, "to proceed in a straight line"). It was a large village of seventeen houses established in the late eighteenth century when a split occurred between two Masset families, one of which, the Masset Inlet Rear-Town People, moved across the inlet to Yan. Other Raven and Eagle families joined them there, but were segregated into Eagles in the north end of town and Ravens in the south.

The town chief of Yan, named Stiltla, was an accomplice of Chief Wiah of Masset in the capture of the ship *Susan Sturgis* in 1852. After its seizure, the ship was brought to Yan, then looted and burned a short distance offshore from Stiltla's House Looking at Its Beak. Stiltla built another large house at Masset, on which he displayed a carved eagle from the stern-board of the ship.

Shortly after photographer Edward Dossetter visited Yan in 1881 when the town was booming, Henry Wiah, the new town chief of Masset, invited the population to move there, and Yan was abandoned (PLATES 131, 132).

Kayung

Kayung was an important village from at least the late eighteenth century, and it appears prominently on maps of that period. By the early 1880s, it had been abandoned in the consolidation of north coast villages to Masset that was encouraged by town chief Henry Wiah.

One fine pole stood in front of Chief Na'qadjut's House That Wears a Tall Dance Hat, so named in reference to the figure at the top of the pole, a chief wearing a hat with eight rings. The chief's tongue is joined to the tongue of a bearlike animal that he is holding. The depiction of joined tongues is rare on a totem pole, though it was a common feature on argillite carvings in the middle of the last century when this pole was probably created. The middle figure is a Whale with human arms holding its fins. The lowest figure is a Bear with a small Raven in its mouth. This pole was removed from Kayung at the turn of the century by Charles F. Newcombe for E. E. Ayers, a Chicago philanthropist who gave it to the Field Museum. After passing through the hands of several owners, the pole was purchased by the Canadian Museum of Civilization, which painstakingly restored it and erected it in front of the Haida house in the Grand Hall.

A second exquisite pole tells the story of the lazy son-in-law (PLATE 133). The son-in-law is depicted at the level of the gable board on the pole, on the back of a Sea Wolf that is eating a Killer Whale. His mother-in-law, who thinks she has a shaman's power to bring in whales (which in actuality her son-in-law has caught), is lodged above him between two Whales. The house chief holding his club sits at the top.

When Richard Maynard arrived in 1884 to take the first photographs of Kayung, fourteen houses of the old style were still standing. The first five houses at the south end of the village belonged to the Eagles while the remainder all belonged to the Ravens.

Masset

The Haida called this town Uttewas (or White Slope Town), after the shells from countless mollusc dinners of the past scattered on a nearby hill (PLATE 134). The hill itself was called Idjao, and the houses south of it formed a separate village when the first Europeans and New Englanders arrived. The two settlements amalgamated in the middle of the last century to form Masset.

In 1792, while on board the ship *Columbia* commanded by Captain Robert Gray, Joseph Ingraham made a drawing of three villages on Masset Inlet (Holm 1982:233). Probably the one closest to the spit on the east side of the inlet is Masset, the one to the south on the same shore is Kayung and the third village on the western shore is Yan.

The hill at Masset was being used as a fort when Lieutenant Camille de Roquefeuil of France explored the inlet in September 1817 (1823:87–88):

PLATE 133

The remains of Goose House at Kayung village. The frontal pole, which illustrates the myth of the lazy son-in-law, is now in the British Museum. *Photograph by Richard Maynard, 1884.*

There is something picturesque in the whole appearance of this large village. It is particularly remarkable for the monstrous and colossal figures which decorate the houses of the principal inhabitants, the wide gaping mouths of which serve as a door . . . Ascending the arm of the sea, there is, on the north side, above the largest village, a fort, the parapet of which is covered with beautiful turf, and surrounded by a palisade in good condition.

From the mid-1830s on, the people of Masset and surrounding villages made annual trading voyages to the Hudson's Bay Company post at Fort Simpson on the mainland to sell the quantities of potatoes they grew. Reverend Jonathan Green saw potatoes growing at villages on North Island in 1829 and thought that the Haida had been cultivating them for a long time before his visit (1915:61). In 1839, another visitor to Haida Gwaii, John Dunn, also noted the Haida trade in potatoes (1844:294): "I have known from five to eight hundred bushels traded in one season from these Indians at Fort Simpson." Each spring, large fleets of canoes left Masset to trade at Fort Simpson and to take part in the eulachon fishery at the mouth of the Nass River. The Haida often fought with the Tsimshian on these occasions, as noted in the Hudson's Bay Company journal entry for September 14, 1837.

The first fur trading post on Haida Gwaii was privately established at Masset in 1853, but it was taken over by the Hudson's Bay Company under Alexander McKenzie in 1869. His account of Masset covers nearly a decade and provides many interesting descriptions of Haida activities (McKenzie 1891). The active trade with Europeans and Americans from the late eighteenth century until the arrival of missionaries at Masset in 1873 did little to change Haida beliefs or their symbolic and artistic expressions (PLATE 2). In many ways, they were enriched by new forms of wealth to which they had ready access, and slavery continued here well after it ended elsewhere in Canada and the United States. Around 1850 Chief Albert Edward Edenshaw owned twelve slaves and brought some of them to Masset when he moved there in 1883. George M. Dawson (1880:132B) notes that chiefs in Masset still had slaves at the time of his visit in 1878.

In June 1876, Reverend William H. Collison became the first missionary to take up residence on Haida Gwaii, and his description of arriving at Masset is memorable (in Lillard 1981:86–88):

We landed in front of the large lodge of the leading chief, Wiah, who was the head of the bear clan at Masset. This numbered among its members the majority of the Masset tribe. The entrance to this lodge was a small oval doorway cut through the base of a large totem, which compelled those entering to bend in order to pass through it. On entering we found ourselves on a tier or gallery of some five or six feet [1.5 or 1.8 m] in width, which formed the uppermost of several similar platforms rising one above the other from the ground floor below, and running all round the house. A stairway led down from this upper platform to the basement or floor. This was the plan on which all the houses were built, the object being defence in case of attack. The small doorway prevented a surprise or rush of an enemy, while

PLATE 134

This view of Masset was taken in 1878 before any European-style houses were built. Within a decade, most of these dwellings had been torn down and the totem poles chopped up for firewood. *Photograph by George M. Dawson. National Archives of Canada 259*

PLATE 135

A model by Charles Edenshaw
of Monster House (Na Yuans),
owned by Wiah, the town
chief of Masset. The actual
house was the largest ever built
by the Haida. *Collected before
1914 by Thomas Deasey, the
Indian agent at Masset.* CMC
VII-B-1166 (s85-3285)

PLATE 136

The scale of Monster House
can be measured by the
number of people standing in
front of it and by the height of
the bottom figure of a Bear on
its frontal pole. *Photograph by
O. C. Hastings, 1879.* CMC
100456

when bullets were flying and crashing through the walls from without, those within remained in safety in the excavated space on the ground floor, in the centre of which was the fireplace.

. . . Around the fire a number of Haida were seated, many of whom, both men and women, had their faces painted in red or black, while some were besmeared with both colours. The chief sat in a peculiarly shaped seat carved out of one piece of wood, a section of a tree, and placed on the first tier or platform, whilst around the fire a number of his slaves were engaged in preparing food.

Chief Wiah welcomed Reverend Collison to his house (PLATES 86, 135, 136, 137) primarily because of the missionary's friendship with Chief Stiltla, Wiah's nearby neighbour, but also because the Haida felt they were losing out to the Tsimshian, who had established a model Christian community under Reverend William Duncan at Metlakatla. Nevertheless, Chief Wiah's greeting was cautious (Collison in Lillard 1981:67–68):

"Your words are good," he replied. "They are wise words. We have heard of the white man's wisdom. We have heard that he possesses the secret of life. He has heard the words of the Chief above. We have seen the change made in the Tsimshian. But why did you not come before? Why did the Iron People not send us the news when it was sent to the Tsimshian? The smallpox which came upon us many years ago killed many of our people. It came first from the north land, from the Iron People who came from the land where the sun sets. Again it came not many years ago, when I was a young man. It came then from the land of the Iron People where the sun rises. Our people are brave in warfare and never turn their backs on their foes, but this foe we could not see and we could not fight. Our medicine men are wise, but they could not drive away the evil spirit, and why? Because it was the sickness of the Iron People. It came from them. You have visited our camps, and you have seen many of the lodges empty. In them the campfires once burned brightly, and around them the hunters and warriors told of their deeds in the past. Now the fires have gone out and the brave men have fallen before the Iron Man's sickness. You have come too late for them!"

He paused, and again his advisers prompted him in low tones, after which he resumed: "And now another enemy has arisen. It is the spirit of the firewater. Our people have learned how to make it, and it has turned friends to foes. This also has come from the land where the sun rises. It is the bad medicine of the *Yetz haada*. It has weakened the hands of our hunters. They cannot shoot as their fathers did. Their eyes are not so clear. Our fathers' eyes were like the eagle's. The firewater has dimmed our sight. It came from your people. If your people had the good news of the Great Chief, the Good Spirit, why did they not send it to us first and not these evil spirits? You have come too late." With these words he sat down.

A few days after arriving in Masset, Collison wrote down an eye-witness account of an important event, a peace ceremony (in Lillard 1981:70):

The following day Edenshaw, an influential chief, arrived from Virago Sound . . . He and his men were received with honours, and a dance of peace was accorded them. There had been a quarrel between the two tribes, and Edenshaw with his leading men had been invited for the purpose of making peace. As their large canoes approached the shore the occupants chanted the brave deeds of the past, and were answered in a similar strain by the concourse of the shore. The chanting was accompanied by regular and graceful motions of the head and body and waving of the hands. The time was kept by a large drum formed like a chest, and made of red cedar wood, painted with grotesque figures, and covered with skin. This was beaten by a drummer seated in the bow of the leading canoe. Naked slaves with their bodies blackened, each bearing a large copper shield, now rushed into the water and cast the shields into the deep, in front of the canoes of the visitors. As these shields are made of native copper, and inscribed with their crests, they are highly valued among the Indians, consequently this was one of the highest marks of welcome and honour. Not that the copper shields were lost to the owners, as they were recovered afterwards on the ebb of the tide.

PLATE 137

The interior of Chief Wiah's Monster House, showing the two deep housepits. There are sleeping compartments on the upper level (*right*). A doorway (*left*) that is covered with pictures from the *London Illustrated News* leads to Wiah's sleeping compartment, which is built outside the house itself. Most of the furniture is from the captured ship *Susan Sturgis*. *Photograph by Richard Maynard, 1884.*

PLATE 138

Dr. Kudé (*second from left*)
and other shaman of Masset
pose for a photograph. Kudé is
wearing a Chilkat blanket.
The figure on the left wearing
the mask with a crooked
mouth represents the wife of
one of the other masked
figures who was supposed to
be dead; Dr. Kudé has just
restored him to life. The man
on the right displays a Bear
tattoo on his chest and upper
arms, and a Whale tattoo on
his forearm. This is the only
known photo of Haida
shaman wearing masks.
*Photograph by Edward
Dossetter, 1881.*

On landing, the visitors were preceded by a number of dancers, male and female, specially arrayed and with faces painted, who led the way to the lodge prepared for their reception. The central seat was given to Edenshaw, and his leading men were seated around. A messenger now entered to announce the coming of his chief and party to welcome his guests. These at once entered, the chief preceding and followed by the sub-chiefs, and principal men in their dancing attire. The headdress or *shikid* bore the crest of the tribe on the front inlaid with mother-of-pearl, and surmounted by a circlet or crown formed of the bristles of the sea lion, standing closely together so as to form a receptacle. This was filled with swan or eagle's down, very fine and specially prepared. As the procession danced around in front of the guests chanting the song of peace, the chief bowed before each of his visitors. As he did so, a cloud of the swan's-down descended in a shower over his guest. Passing on, this was repeated before each, and thus peace was made and sealed.

The strongest opposition to the missionary came from the shaman, who realized the threat he posed to their traditional practices. Foremost among them was Dr. Kudé (PLATE 138), who was a chief as well as a shaman and who owned a most impressive house in the back row of Masset (MacDonald 1983:plate 202). Dr. Kudé seems to have continued his power struggle with Collison's successor for the Church Missionary Society, for according to Reverend Charles Harrison, who took up his charge in 1882 (in Lillard 1984:168), "he endeavored to persuade the people that the medicine of the Europeans was inevitably fatal to an Indian unless its effect was eradicated by a course of treatment also at his hands." Harrison's description of Kudé (in Lillard 1981:169) agrees with photos of the shaman:

> Kudé, the Masset Shaman, had long tangled hair—it well nigh reached his knees—but when not viably engaged he kept it tied up on top of his head and secured by beautifully carved bone pins. This long hair was believed to assist in his magical power over the evil spirits.

Kudé was finally convinced to cut his hair and become a Christian. He handed over his charms and rattles to Reverend Harrison, who deposited them in the Pitt Rivers Museum at Oxford University.

Albert Edward Edenshaw moved permanently to Masset after old Chief Wiah died in the autumn of 1883. The new chief, Henry Wiah, was neither as wealthy nor as powerful as his predecessor but was well liked by the villagers and welcomed Edenshaw to his town. One of the most significant changes in Masset was the resettlement there of the survivors from all of the other north coast villages after 1883, when Chief Henry Wiah called for old differences to be set aside. People also had a growing desire to live in a community with schools and a mission, as well as a degree of health care (including inoculation against smallpox), which missionaries dispensed along with the gospel.

In 1883, Albert Edward Edenshaw inherited a house at Masset (MacDonald 1983:139, no. 7) from a cousin and, according to Charles F. Newcombe (1898:MS), lived there until his

189

PLATE 139

The central area of Masset,
including the house that
Charles Edenshaw inherited
and later replaced with a
European-style building. He
had already begun to advertise
his artwork when this
photograph was taken.
*Photograph by Stephen Allen
Spencer, circa 1880.*

PLATE 140

At Hiellan village, this frontal
pole in a very archaic style was
created before 1840 by the same
carver from Tsal village on
Langara Island who made the
Kiusta triple-mortuary for the
Edenshaws. This pole stood
before House for a Large Crowd
of People, which belonged to
the town chief. Albert Edward
Edenshaw lived there when he
was young and inherited it later.
After moving to Masset, he
continued to use it for feasts to
avoid criticism from the
missionaries and Indian agents.
*Photograph by Harlan I. Smith,
1919.* CMC 46,694

death. A memorial pole that appears to have been erected shortly after he moved into the
house has his crests of the Raven and Beaver. The central interior pole also displays his crests,
the Raven with frogs in its ears on a Bear, but it may have been installed by his cousin when
the house was built; it is now in the Field Museum in Chicago.

Albert Edward Edenshaw appears in almost every traveller's account until his death in
1894. Although he had been suspected of complicity in old Chief Wiah's capture of the *Susan
Sturgis* in 1852, Edenshaw's decisive action was acknowledged by the captain with saving his
and the crew's lives. Edenshaw successfully negotiated their release in return for a ransom
from the Hudson's Bay Company at Fort Simpson, and a marble memorial to this feat was
erected in front of Henry Edenshaw's Property House in the middle of Masset. Albert
Edward also owned a house at Klinkwan village in Alaska, and his house in Masset had a fine
frontal pole and a memorial post topped with a huge figure of a Bear, similar to the figure of
a Bear in Kiusta. His nephew Charles Edenshaw, the famous carver, later resided in this
house and may have placed the name board "Edenshaw" over the door to advertise his art
works for sale to travellers (PLATE 139). In the late 1890s, the dwelling was replaced by the
modest frame house where Charles Edenshaw lived until his death in 1924.

Hiellan

Hiellan was a town of some importance in the early nineteenth century, and an impressive fort stood on the opposite side of the mouth of the Hiellan River on Graham Island. Both Haida and Tsimshian myths include accounts of its tricky defences and the battles fought there. Hiellan belonged to two branches of Eagles. The leading Eagle chief, Sqilao, was closely related to the first known Chief Edenshaw who was the uncle of Albert Edward Edenshaw and for whom the triple mortuary at Kiusta was erected.

The only surviving house frontal pole at Hiellan was photographed by Harlan I. Smith of the Canadian Museum of Civilization in 1919 (PLATE 140). It had stood there for over a century before it was transported in 1947 to Prince Rupert, where it was placed by the road into town to welcome visitors. After a short sojourn in Victoria at the Royal British Columbia Museum, the pole was returned to Masset. The shed in which the pole was stored collapsed under the snow load in the winter of 1993, and it was moved into Haida artist Jim Hart's carving shed, where it awaits replication.

This pole and the triple mortuary at Kiusta were both carved around 1820 by Sqiltcange, who came from Tsal village. Both monuments emphasize large Bear figures with a myriad of small figures emerging from their joints and orifices. The poles are unique in providing examples of the archaic style of Haida art similar to that seen by the first Europeans to visit Haida Gwaii.

At least fifty years before Europeans first made contact with the Haida, some Haida families had reacted to growing pressures on the population of the villages around North Island by beginning to move to the islands of what is now the Prince of Wales archipelago in southeast Alaska. Another reason for the move may have been to position themselves closer to the Russian trading posts at Wrangell and Sitka that supplied important materials as well as new objects of wealth.

According to traders' accounts of the late eighteenth century, the families of Dadens village on Haida Gwaii were actively relocating to southeast Alaska to the extent that it was virtually abandoned as a permanent village by the early nineteenth century. Slowly, the Haida replaced the Tlingit-speaking people who had occupied the area for thousands of years; however, the original Tlingit place names survive, at least in part, in many Kaigani Haida village names. Eventually, the Haida towns and camps included Kaigani itself, a camp that waned as initial immigrants moved on to other settlements, including the larger more permanent villages of Klinkwan, Sukkwan, Howkan and Kasaan.

Klinkwan

Klinkwan is the Haida version of a Tlingit name meaning Shellfish Town. The village stretched around several bays and contained upwards of twenty houses, though John R. Swanton's informants (1905:294) remembered the names of only thirteen of them. John Work (in Dawson 1880:173B), who compiled a population estimate between 1836 and 1841, identifies it as Clickass in reference to the nearby river and assigns it a total of 417 inhabitants. All the families belonged to the Raven moiety.

One prominent resident of Klinkwan was Albert Edward Edenshaw's son Henry, whose house expressed true opulence in Haida terms. This was the only house interior on the entire Northwest Coast that was a rival to the grand interior of the Whale House of the Tlingit at Klinkwan (Emmons 1916), but unfortunately, not one interior element of Edenshaw's house survives: only a photograph bears witness to its grandeur (PLATE 142). In the adjacent house, which belonged to Henry's father-in-law, all three exterior poles display the Dragonfly crest: the central pole was by far the tallest in the village, and both front corner posts are elaborately carved. The large central pole has a Beaver at its base, with a small Beaver between its paws and frogs emerging from its ears. Above them, a Bear holds an insect in its mouth. Next is a *tcamaos* (a supernatural snag that devoured canoes), a Crane with a long beak, and nine potlatch rings. The Raven sits on top.

The left corner post portrays the Bear Mother story, originally a Tsimshian myth in which a berry picker slips on the dung of a grizzly bear and curses her luck. She is abducted by bears and becomes the wife of the Chief of the Bears; their two offspring can appear as human children or bear cubs. She and her children are eventually rescued by her brothers,

PLATE 141

The house of Henry Edenshaw's father-in-law at Klinkwan rivalled that of Chief Wiah of Masset in the elaborately sculptured posts of its facade. *Photograph from Alaska-Yukon-Pacific Expedition, circa 1888–89.* CMC 72-9544

194

PLATE 142 (facing page)

The interior of Henry Edenshaw's house at Klinkwan village, Alaska. The interior pole has a Thunderbird (missing its beak). Henry Edenshaw's father, Albert Edward Edenshaw, probably carved and decorated the house. On the walls of the housepit, carved and painted storage box fronts alternate with images of coppers, providing a lavish appearance. *Photograph by Charles F. Newcombe.* CMC 71-4705

PLATE 143

In 1901, a potlatch was staged in order to mark the move from Klinkwan village to Hydaburg, Alaska, as well as the abandonment of ceremonial regalia. Participants include (*left to right*): Robert Edenshaw (with drum), Matthew Collison (kneeling as Grizzly Bear-of-the-Sea), an unknown man wearing a Chilkat blanket, Eddie Scott, Eddie Cojo, Donald Mikatla, Antkleg (Mike George), Ben Duncan and Nasank (Adam Spoon's son). *Photograph by Winter and Pond, 1901.* CMC J2822

who kill her husband. At the base of the pole is a Bear eating a man, another Bear with an insect in its mouth, and a Hawk.

The right corner post has at its base a Bear holding an insect (a reference to the Bear Mother story), another Bear holding the berry picker from the Bear Mother story between its paws, and a human holding the baby Raven in a moon. The portrayal of the berry picker's long hair and breasts are unusually naturalistic for Haida art.

In Henry Edenshaw's house, the interior post depicts an insect between the arms of a Bear with humanlike hands. These figures sit between the ears of the Thunderbird, whose once prominent beak has fallen off, leaving only a mortise joint. A small arched doorway through the breast of the Thunderbird is symbolic only and leads to a compartment at the back of the house. The planks that formed the wall of this compartment are missing but were undoubtedly highly decorated.

The housepit walls were also elaborately carved and painted (PLATE 142). In fact, there were two sets of walls, each supporting two steps down to the firepit. The walls of the terraces were composed of huge hewn planks some 10 cm (4 inches) thick and about a metre (3 feet) wide. The top row consisted of carved and painted chests alternating with elaborately decorated copper shields; there were six coppers and five storage boxes on each side, for a total of twenty-four coppers and twenty carved and painted boxes. The lower terrace was bounded by two coppers (in a diagonal position) and three chests, for a total of eight coppers and twelve chests. In all, sixty-four symbols of great wealth surrounded the house pit.

The last potlatch held in Klinkwan in 1901, before the Haida left the village and moved to Hydaburg, was the subject of a famous photograph (PLATE 143). All the participants are costumed in their treasures, including Chilkat blankets, painted leather capes, bearskin robes and trade blankets adorned with crests outlined in dentalium shells. They wear frontlets and peaked shaman's hats as well as carved wooden crest helmets (PLATE 144). Masks, cedar bark neckrings of the secret societies, Raven rattles and drums complete the tableau immortalized forever in silver nitrate. This potlatch marked a shift in the cultural paradigm, as proud lineage heads, each with their own links to the supernatural, became colonized wage earners and sold their treasures (PLATE 145). Ronald Weber (1985), an anthropologist at the Field Museum in Chicago (which now possesses much of this regalia), has identified most of the people and items in the photograph.

The house that formed the backdrop of this potlatch was called House Standing Up. The building belonged to the town chief whose name meant "one unable to buy," since he once had owned a copper that a rival chief was unable to afford. It was a suitable setting for the final ceremony.

PLATE 144

On this Sculpin crest helmet, the nine finely woven rings mark the number of feasts that the owner has hosted.

Collected at Klinkwan village in Alaska before 1901 by George T. Emmons for the Lord Bossom collection. CMC VII-B-1437 (S92-4303)

197

Sukkwan

Sukkwan is the Haida version of a Tlingit name meaning Town on the Fine Underwater Grass, a reference to the edible seaweed that grows there. John Work (in Dawson 1880:173B) claimed it had a population of 229 people in the period between 1836 and 1841, including both Ravens and Eagles. Sukkwan was situated on a point of land, with five houses on the south side of the point and seven on the north. John R. Swanton (1905:294) recorded the names of seven houses, including Grizzly Bear House, Cedarbark Skin House, and Clay House (because it was painted with clay). Another was called Watery House after the name of a house at Kiusta, the town from which the people of Sukkwan came.

The pole of the middle house on the north side has a most unusual figure of the lazy son-in-law holding a small Whale in each hand (PLATE 146). He wears a tall chief's hat with three potlatch rings, around which a strange creature is wrapped. It may be a Bullhead, judging by its prominent ribs at the back and its pointed horns, which are firmly grasped by the watchman figure on the top. The son-in-law stands on a Wasgo (or Sea Wolf), which has the small figure of a chief crouched between its ears; inside the ears are curved hornlike devices. The Wasgo also holds an insect in its mouth and has a small human between its knees. Sukkwan was abandoned in the late 1890s, and this pole was taken to the totem park at Hydaburg during a reclamation project in the 1930s.

Howkan

Howkan is first mentioned by John Work (in Dawson 1880:173B) as being a sizable town of 458 inhabitants. The name is a Tlingit one. Ensign Albert P. Niblack (1890:386), who explored the coast of Alaska for the U.S. Navy, claims that the original inhabitants of the camp called Kaigani moved their winter residence to Howkan. Some remained at the small village of Koianglas just below Howkan but were in the process of amalgamating with Howkan when he observed them. Niblack (1890:385) claims that in 1886 Howkan was thriving and had a winter population of about three hundred.

During the last twenty years of the previous century, photographs recorded rapid changes in the houses and poles throughout the village. Perhaps the most radical change, but one that took place in stages, can be seen in Chief Skowl's house. He was town chief of both Howkan and Kasaan. His house in Howkan sat near the centre of town. After he died in the winter of 1882–83, his successor lost no time in adding a second storey to the house by putting joists through the roof and building a European-style cottage on top, complete with a balcony and gingerbread trim. He also added milled lumber and five windows to the facade of the old house.

The pole in front of Chief Skowl's house has a naturalistic American eagle on the top, flanked by two traditional watchmen. Below that is a figure of the Czar of Russia with flowing locks and a beard. He wears a coat with epaulets and stands between the ears of the

PLATE 145
This memorial pole from Howkan village in Alaska tells the myth of Qingi and the flood. When the Great Flood came, all of the villagers had to climb up on the chief's hat to avoid drowning. This pole was displayed at the Century of Progress World's Fair in London, England, in 1951. It is shown here in the rotunda of the old Canadian Museum of Civilization in Ottawa. *Acquired before 1901 by George T. Emmons for the Lord Bossom collection.* CMC VII-B-1557 (S80-254)

The frontal pole *(left)* of this house at Sukkwan portrays the lazy son-in-law holding two Whales and standing on a Wasgo (Sea Wolf). The figure at the top on which the human figure rides is either a Bullhead or a *tcamaos* (supernatural snag). In the centre, a very old mortuary provides the Raven with a spruce sapling for a headdress. *Photograph by W. T. Lopp, circa 1890.* CMC 99400

PLATE 147

This memorial pole *(centre)* from Howkan village in Alaska is arguably the finest Haida carving ever done. The strong diagonal lines help to interlock the multitude of figures, and the deep carving and rich detailing enhance the overall effect. The central portion of the pole illustrates the myth about the lazy son-in-law. It is tempting to think this was the pole at Howkan that Albert Edward Edenshaw carved after he had a dream about what to put on it. The pole was erected in a public park in Indianapolis and later destroyed. A replica of it was erected in Indianapolis in 1996. *Photograph by Julius Sternberg, 1922.*

PLATE 148

Monuments in a newly cleared cemetery thought to have been next to Howkan, but recently determined to have been next to Ketchikan village, Alaska. The Sea Grizzly has two dorsal fins, and shreds of a cloth blanket are attached to its mouth. In the background, the boards of an old painted housefront have been hastily assembled in incorrect sequence on the grave of a chief. *Photograph by Winter and Pond, circa 1890.* CMC VII-B-866 (71-6022)

PLATE 149

Carved and painted screens such as this one were used to separate the chief's compartment from the rest of the household. The circular doorway is between the legs of an ancestor, protected by the Raven in human form. Above him is the Raven in two profiles. The Eagles stand on a large rock that is depicted as a living creature with a mouth and eye. This is the only surviving Haida interior screen. *Acquired in Howkan village, Alaska, by George T. Emmons for the Lord Bossom collection.* CMC VII-B-1527 (s86-21)

Thunderbird that sports an incredible display of plumage on its head, wings, breast, tail and even its feet. At the base, a standing Bear holds an insect in its mouth.

Another remarkable pole was erected next door to Chief Skowl's house in about 1885. A photo of the pole, taken much later, depicts its intricately detailed interlocking figures (PLATE 147).

The graveyard at Howkan is perhaps the most elaborate of any Haida village and included full-sized totem poles that were erected as memorials to the deceased, as well as a large figure of a Killer Whale with a very tall dorsal fin, a full-scale replica of which flanks the entrance to the Burke Museum in Seattle. At Howkan, George T. Emmons acquired a memorial pole, two Sea Lion house posts (PLATE 85) and the remarkable interior house screen (PLATE 149) that once stood between them for the collection of Lord Bossom in London; they were repatriated to the Canadian Museum of Civilization in the 1960s after Lord Bossom's death.

Kasaan

Kasaan is originally a Tlingit word meaning Beautiful Town. The town chief, named Skowl, had a large house situated towards the north end of the settlement. When George T. Emmons first visited the village in 1885, he took a photo of old Chief Skowl's house after it had been freshly clad with milled siding (PLATE 150). Chief Skowl also owned a second house in the village that had an unusual frontal pole (PLATE 151).

Albert P. Niblack witnessed the funeral ceremonies for old Chief Skowl (PLATE 152), who died in the winter of 1882–83 (1890:plate LXVII caption):

> According to the custom of the region, his body was first displayed in state dressed in the ceremonial robes of a chief. Later it was enclosed in a casket and deposited, as shown, on a pile of boxes containing his clothing and ceremonial dance paraphernalia.

The second house belonging to Chief Skowl was also an impressive building; it was the last one at the north end of the second row. The frontal pole incorporates more non-Haida motifs and styles than any other piece; in fact, the only traditional element is the Eagle on top. Another Eagle with its head to one side is clearly an American eagle copied from a coin or a ship's figurehead. The figures on the pole include three Russians and one angel. The Russians are priests dressed in large flowing robes, hands crossed on their breasts—or pointing to heaven, as in the figure at the top. The angel, whose face is surrounded on three sides by feather designs, is a particular delight. Other spaces, usually filled on traditional Haida poles by diminutive animal figures emerging from the orifices of larger figures, are decorated here with tendril and leaf patterns copied from the stylized ship carvings common at the time. This pole was transported to Ketchikan, where it was placed in the midst of traffic beside a tunnel.

PLATE 150

Kasaan village in Alaska, with the house of Chief Skowl, who died in 1882–83, at the right. By the time this photograph was taken, his successor had added milled siding and windows to the house. The Raven stealing the sun poles of both the old and new chief flank the stairway that leads up from the beach. *Photograph by George T. Emmons.* CMC 71-4709

PLATE 151

This pole, in front of a second house in Kasaan belonging to Chief Skowl, depicts priests, an angel and Eagles. Rather than celebrating the arrival of the Russian Orthodox Church in Alaska, however, it ridicules the fact that young men from the villages wanted to train for the priesthood and abandon the old ways. *Photograph by A. Bergstresser, circa 1900.* CMC 71-4707

PLATE 152

For nearly two years after his death, the body of Chief Skowl lay in state inside his house at Kasaan, Alaska. The burial chest, draped with a button blanket, is surrounded by storage chests filled with his regalia; beside the burial chest are his eight copper shields. The people in the photo are his slaves, who were displayed as part of his wealth. *Photograph by Albert P. Niblack, 1883*

S.J. 9.   3880

Another leading chief of Kasaan was Soni-hat, whose name appears frequently in the Hudson's Bay Company journals for Fort Simpson for three decades beginning in the 1870s. He appears in a formal family portrait inside Whale House at Kasaan just before the turn of the century. In addition to the three generations of his relatives arranged around him, he displays all of his chiefly possessions: frontlets, a Chilkat blanket and leggings, a painted leather cape, two copper shields, a talking stick and piles of chests filled with other prerogatives of power. An exquisitely carved interior house post peeks out from behind this display of opulence.

Chief Soni-hat also owned a house in the second row at the south end of Kasaan, called Eagle House. Each of the interior house posts depicts a human figure with large bear's ears. The asymmetrical hand positions and the bear ears indicate a shaman figure, but it is not known why he chose a shaman motif for these posts. Soni-hat donated the carvings from this house as the first chief to answer a plea from Governor Brady of Alaska (1897–1906) for poles to be preserved in a park in Sitka.

The first Soni-hat pole has a large standing Bear, on top of which stood another Bear with its hands in an asymmetrical position grasping an otter by the tail (another reference to shamanic powers). Above that is a third standing Bear holding a small human figure (from the Bear Mother myth) and standing on two animal heads. Next is the Raven with a turned-down beak (from the Raven and the halibut fisherman myth), and above that is a Whale holding a human figure and a Frog, then a Bear holding its extended tongue. At the top are two watchmen looking in opposite directions.

A later but equally remarkable house at Kasaan was also named Eagle House. Its frontal pole stood for many years before the Heye Foundation Headquarters and Museum at 155th Street and Broadway in New York City, the only major outdoor Northwest Coast monument in that metropolis. This pole had a Raven sitting on top of four potlatch rings, emerging from the head of another Raven in reference to the myth of the halibut fisherman. The feathers of the Raven's wings hang below his arms. The figure below is from the Bear Mother story; the Bear is devouring the brother of the Bear Mother who tried to rescue her. Next is a Bear with frogs on its forehead and in its ears, holding a Raven. The bottom figure is a Beaver holding a smaller Beaver behind its tail.

The interior posts of this house were equally interesting. One pair portrayed the Raven with the moon in its beak. Inside the moon disk is the baby Raven, in reference to the story of how the Raven stole the sun, moon and stars while disguised as the infant of the Sky Chief's daughter. The other pair of posts depicted a large standing Bear Mother figure with a cub between her legs and a Frog emerging between her ears. From her lip hangs an engraved labret, and below her is the Raven with a broken beak (from the halibut fisherman myth).

Standing in front of Eagle House are two very old poles, carved in the 1850s by the noted Tlingit artist Kadjis-du-axtc (Herem 1990:54), whose main work is found much further north around Sitka and Klukwan (including the Whale House rear posts). A magnificent crest helmet depicting a Sculpin is on display in an old photo (Royal British Columbia

Museum, PN316), taken in front of Eagle House by Charles F. Newcombe in 1902 just before it was collected by George T. Emmons for Lord Bossom. The helmet sits on a huge mask that is 1.2 m (4 feet) tall and that has mechanical shutters over its eyes. It is tempting to think that this large mask is the one described by Reverend Jonathan Green (1915:66) on his visit to Kasaan in 1829. At that time the mask was being used to cover a mortuary figure which held the remains of Chief Cunnyha, the same chief who had met Captain George Dixon in 1787 at Kiusta. He lived to a venerable age and died in Kasaan about 1820.

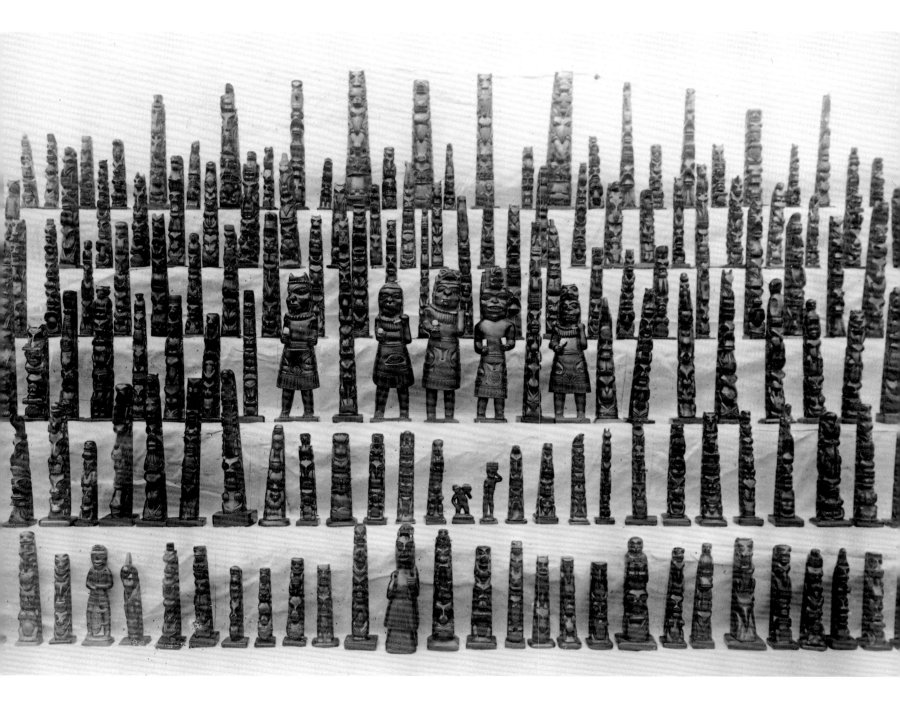

ARTISTS OF THE GOLDEN AGE | Chapter Seven

The golden age of Haida art lasted half a century, beginning in the 1850s when new markets opened in Victoria and elsewhere that stimulated both greater production and the development of new art forms, until the collapse of the Haida population at the beginning of the twentieth century. During this period, large objects were replaced by smaller replicas that could easily be taken home by tourists as mementoes of their visits to the Northwest Coast (PLATES 76, 153). It was a golden age because there was not only a great number of Haida artists who were well trained in their traditional style yet felt free to innovate and create new expressions of their rich heritage but also because there was a large and eager market for their work.

Many Haida artists successfully made the transition to creating pieces for another cultural milieu where having an identifiable style was essential in the marketplace. Even so, signing their work was not an accepted practice, and many artists resisted it, preferring to express themselves through subtle variations on traditional style (Wright 1985). This has resulted in endless speculation among scholars who pen articles with titles like "Will the Real Charles Edenshaw Please Stand Up?" (Holm 1981:75). At least one thesis (Davidson 1967) and several articles have been written on Charles Edenshaw, of which the best are by Bill Holm (1981) and Alan Hoover (1983, 1995). The work of carver Tom Price (PLATES 103, 154) also has been the subject of study (Gessler 1971:245–52 and Holm 1981:193–97). Bill Holm (1981:176–77) originally defined one body of work as that of the Masset artist Gwaitilth, but later found evidence that it was by another Masset artist named Simeon Stiltla (RAIN 1980). Marius Barbeau (1953, 1957) published short studies of many Masset and Skidegate artists of a later period.

ALBERT EDWARD EDENSHAW

Albert Edward Edenshaw was a living link between the traditional world of the Haida, uninterrupted for centuries, and the chaotic world of the historical era (PLATE 155). His achievements as a chief are recorded in the histories of many north coast villages including Kiusta, Dadens, Kung, Yatze, Hiellan and Masset. He has taken on legendary significance, partly because of the numerous if brief references to him in the logs and journals of ships' captains, traders and missionaries throughout much of the nineteenth century. His undisputed contribution was in laying the groundwork for his successors to nurture the fundamentals of Haida culture and assure its survival.

PLATE 153
The personal collection of model argillite pole carvings amassed by Thomas Deasey, the Indian agent at Masset early in this century. The artists represented include Charles Edenshaw. The collection is now at the Florida State Museum, Gainesville. *Photograph by Harlan I. Smith, 1919.* CMC 46701

PLATE 154

An oval argillite platter with a very compact design of a Wasgo, or Sea Wolf. It has both legs and fins, and a long wolflike tail curves over its back. The inverted crescent-shaped slits in the eye forms and other details identify it as the work of the Skidegate carver Tom Price (Chief Ninstints). *Acquired before 1899 for the A. Aaronson collection.* CMC VII-B-760 (S82-265)

PLATE 155

Chief Albert Edward Edenshaw dressed in naval uniform at about eighty years of age. After a long career of warfare, slave trading, art, gold prospecting and possible piracy, he appointed his nephew Charles Edenshaw as his successor and settled down to be a strong supporter of the Methodist Church. His life spanned the era in which the Haida went from being feared as the Vikings of the Pacific to near extinction. *Photograph by Robert Reford, circa 1890. National Archives of Canada* C60824

Albert Edward Edenshaw, who was born in 1812 south of Rose Spit, inherited the title of Chief Edenshaw about 1832 upon the death of his uncle, the first Chief Edenshaw of Dadens. By this time, Dadens had been abandoned as a permanent village. He moved to Kiusta and built Story House, the decorations for which had come to him in a dream (Swanton 1905:125–26, plate IV). It is then that he probably honed his own skills as a canoe maker and especially as a craftsman in copper and steel (PLATE 156). One of his specialties was elaborately decorated steel war daggers.

In 1853, Albert Edward moved to Kung, where he built House That Can Hold a Great Crowd of People (PLATE 128). At the top of the house's frontal pole is a Bear holding two figures: one is a human riding on the back of a Dragonfly. This may represent the vision that he had received in the 1830s when he married a Kaigani Haida woman from Klinkwan, and the town chief asked him to carve a totem pole, an event that launched his career in woodcarving. Alfred Adams, a Masset chief, describes the effect of this early commission (in Barbeau, no date:file 253.3):

> He got inspiration drinking medicine and he would fast and get his imagination and his conception of different stories and legends. His [son] (Henry) told me that his father never was a carver when young, not a public carver. But once he was visiting in Howkan (Prince of Wales Island) and was hired to make a carving there of a big totem pole . . . When he got to the big tree he visualized then what he was to put on. That is how he started but he had not done very much of this before.

Edenshaw and his clansmen regularly participated in the sea otter and fur seal hunt that yearly took them back to Dadens. The single pole that stood there was carved by Edenshaw and raised in the late nineteenth century next to the house he built there for his second wife, Amy (MacDonald 1983:plate 263). At the top is a Bear on a stack of seven potlatch cylinders, and below that is the Raven from the story about the halibut fisherman. The next figure is characteristic of his work; it represents the berry picker that the Haida see in the dark pattern of the moon and relates to a myth associated with his wife Amy's lineage. The small Frog hanging below the moon disk is another favourite of the artist and appears on his poles at Kung and elsewhere. Towards the base is a Grizzly Bear with two cubs, one in its mouth and the other between its legs. Another small human figure is crouched between the Bear's knees and stands on the lowest figure, probably a Whale.

The two human figures are exceptionally well carved, more graceful and animated than most Haida depictions of humans. The figure of a woman with long hair on the right-hand post of the house at Klinkwan (PLATE 141) that belonged to Henry's father-in-law, is a strong indication that Albert Edward carved the whole sculptured facade. The elaborate interior carvings inside Henry's house may also be his work (PLATE 142), since his characteristic Dragonfly is on the left corner post. The house was probably built in the 1870s.

Some time after 1883, Albert Edward moved to Masset. A pair of memorial poles at the

PLATE 156

This very large copper shield, 117 cm (46 inches) high, once belonged to Albert Edward Edenshaw. He was a talented shield engraver and sold his decorated coppers as far south as the Fraser River. This copper portrays his female Grizzly Bear crest. *Purchased from Mary Yaltatse of Masset in 1970.* CMC VII-B-1595 (S92-4312)

northern corner of his house there displayed three important crests. The first pole had a Beaver at the top and the Raven below. The second memorial pole had a standing Frog with potlatch cylinders at the top and a standing Beaver at the base (MacDonald 1983:plate 178). It is not known whether or not these two poles were carved by either Albert Edward or Charles Edenshaw, or by both.

According to tradition, Albert Edward chose Charles Edenshaw, the son of his sister Qwa'Kuna, to be his successor. When Albert Edward passed away in 1894, Charles not only took over the mantle of Chief Edenshaw but raised the artistic heritage of his famous uncle to new heights.

JOHN ROBSON

Little is known about John Robson until the late 1860s when he succeeded his uncle as Chief Giatlins, a Raven lineage chief in Skidegate (PLATE 103); at the same time he inherited Grizzly Bear's Mouth House, one of the most splendid buildings in the village (PLATE 122). Robson was a noted carver of totem poles from the late 1860s until the custom of raising large poles fell into disfavour around 1885. He also produced many house models and works in argillite (PLATES 83, 157).

Robson married Qwa'Kuna, the widowed mother of Charles Edenshaw. Robson taught his stepson many carving skills and worked on a number of poles with him, which explains the points of similarity in their styles.

One fine example of the artistic collaboration between Charles Edenshaw and John Robson is an elaborately carved memorial pole in front of House Upon Which Storm Clouds Make a Noise in Skidegate. The top figure of a Whale is similar to the one on Chief Skidegate's interior pole. John Robson later made a model of it for John R. Swanton (1905:plate VIII-4). The two carvers may also have worked together on a large mortuary post raised in 1879–80 by Chief Skidegate and his wife in honour of Chief Skedans.

PLATE 157

On this argillite platter made by John Robson of Skidegate is a design of a Wasgo, or Sea Wolf, in bas-relief, and a Devilfish in full sculpture. The rim is inlaid with fish made of white bone. *A gift from Mrs. T. Wallwork to the Canadian Museum of Civilization in 1954.* CMC VII-B-1420 (S94-6821)

216

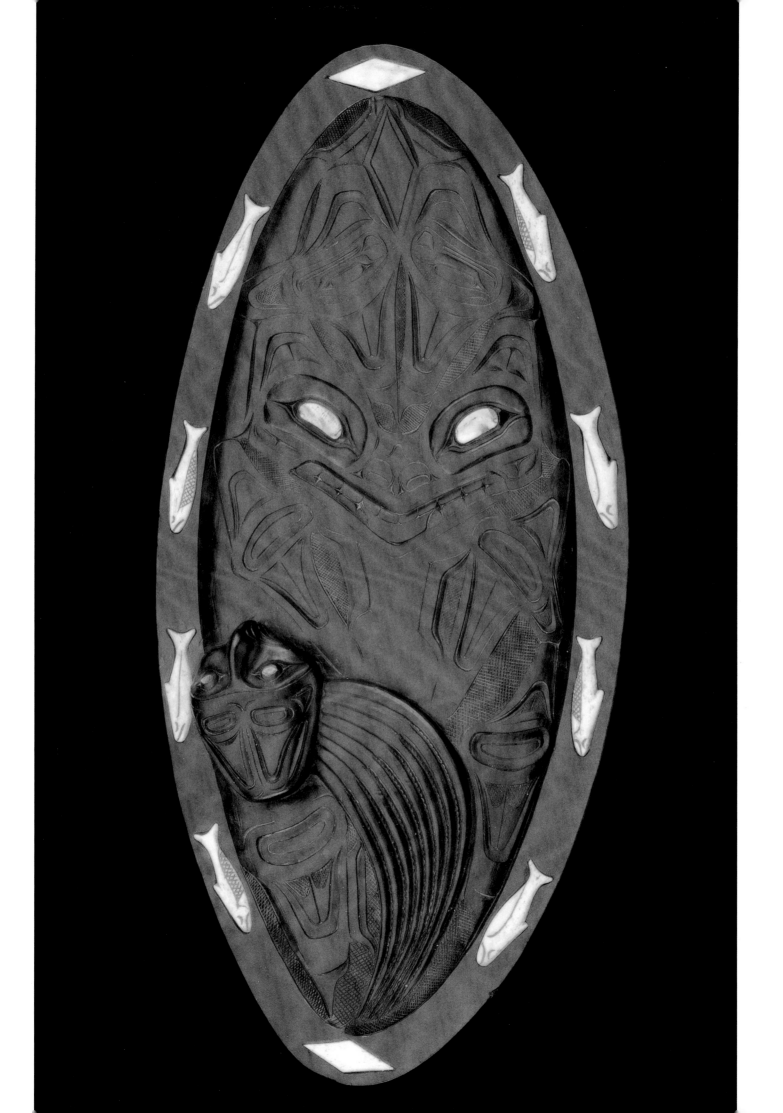

Charles Edenshaw, or Tahayren, was born in 1839 to Albert Edward Edenshaw's only sister, Qwa'Kuna. According to Charles's daughter Florence Edenshaw Davidson (in Blackman 1982:72), her father started carving argillite when he was fourteen and had to stay in bed sick.

Between 1878 and 1881, John Robson raised a memorial pole to Qwa'Kuna, carved by Charles, with the Raven, Beaver and Eagle perched on top (MacDonald 1983:plates 36, 39). The Raven on it is similar to the one on which the figure of Governor James Douglas stands on Albert Edward Edenshaw's "friendship" pole at Kung. Charles may have been an apprentice carver to his uncle on the Kung pole. In his mid-teens, Charles joined his uncle at Kung every summer, and the time he spent there is evident in the exquisite detail of the house model he created of Albert Edward's Story House. After reaching maturity, Charles moved to Masset to apprentice further with his uncle. According to Alfred Adams (in Barbeau, no date:file 251.14):

> While training in his uncle's workshop, Charles perfected his knowledge of ancient traditions, perfected his technique and learned to observe nature . . . To mark his acquiring the master craftsman's position in the community, he gave a potlatch, or feast for the village, in his uncle's home.

Charles married Isabella K'woiyang, whose Aunt Amy was the second wife of Albert Edward. In the 1870s, he carved two poles for Chief Skidegate. The first was an interior house post of a Whale, a Frog and the Raven with a long beak (MacDonald 1983:plate 46). The second, which he may have worked on with John Robson, was a mortuary pole for one of Chief Skidegate's wives, erected in 1879–80. The human figure on it was said to represent the lazy son-in-law story in which a youth killed a Wasgo (or Sea Wolf) in the lake behind Skidegate (MacDonald 1983:plate 146). The face on the pole is a *tcamaos* (supernatural snag).

Charles's skills and repertoire expanded gradually to include work in wood, argillite and precious metals (PLATES 79, 96, 99, 135, 158). In the 1890s, his artistry and traditional knowledge came to the attention of anthropologists and museum collectors engaged in the frantic effort to record and collect Haida art and culture before it died, including Charles F. Newcombe, Franz Boas and especially John R. Swanton. The Indian agent at Masset, Thomas Deasey, also kept him busy with orders for model argillite poles (PLATE 153).

Charles and Isabella had five daughters but only two sons, both of whom died young. To ease his loss, Charles began teaching many young carvers Haida myths and the techniques of carving in a range of materials. Among those he taught were John Marks, Isaac (Ben) Chapman and Daniel Stanley (Skilgoldzo), the grandson of renowned Masset artist Simeon Stiltla.

PLATE 158

A charming example of an argillite platter by Charles Edenshaw with a classic Thunderbird and Whale design. The double outline of formlines and changes of texture in background areas mark this piece as his, although neither he nor other carvers of that time signed their work. *Acquired at Masset before 1899 for the A. Aaronson collection.* CMC VII-B-824 (S94-6817)

Charles Edenshaw's style is very distinctive, with very bold formlines. For Haida clients, he made pieces for personal adornment or practical use. Silver and gold jewellery, including earrings and finger rings, brooches and bracelets were in demand by both Haida and tourists (PLATE 159). His wife, Isabella, wove baskets and hats that he painted with designs, mostly for sale to tourists (PLATES 16, 17). Argillite carvings for tourists represented most of his output, including inkstands, model houses, lidded chests and large platters (PLATE 158). One of his major works, a traditional Haida burial chest, is in the Canadian Museum of Civilization (PLATE 96).

Charles Edenshaw died in Masset in 1924, leaving his tools to his nephew Charles Gladstone, a carver in Skidegate and the grandfather of noted artist Bill Reid.

The momentum of the golden age of Haida art came to an end as lineage groups broke down into separate family units and Christianization turned Haida myths into the equivalent of fairy tales. Argillite carvings continued to be sold through intermediaries to tourist shops in Victoria and Vancouver, but as tourist values took over the market, argillite poles were priced by the inch, and the pride of individual craftsmanship virtually disappeared.

After the last two artists of the golden age died, Charles Edenshaw in 1924 and John Cross in 1939, Rufus Moody and a number of others did what they could to bridge the gap until a new generation of sophisticated artists, many of them trained in art schools, rekindled the flame that led to the renaissance of Haida art beginning in the 1950s and 1960s.

PLATE 159
Charles Edenshaw carving a silver bracelet amidst examples of his argillite model poles and a box. The damage to his left eye from a revolver accident bothered him as he got older but did not affect the exquisite sense of balance and symmetry in his carving. *Photographer unknown, circa 1880.* CMC 88926

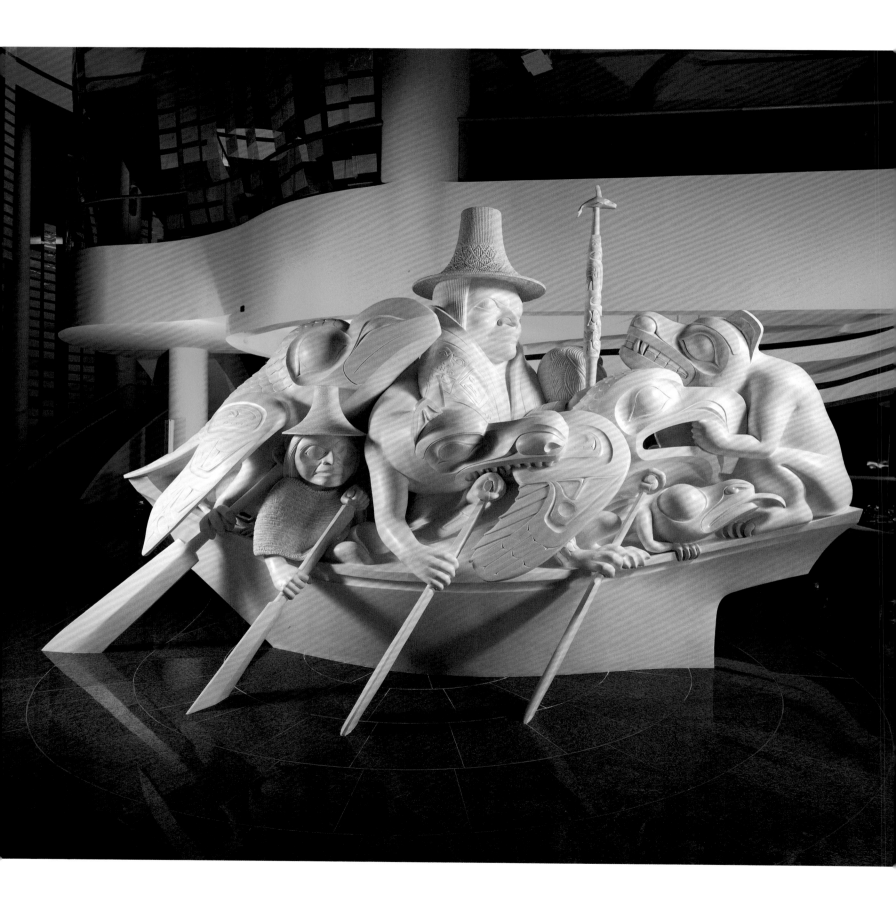

DEATH AND REBIRTH OF THE RAVEN | Chapter Eight

The world is highly sensible of the loss incurred when a species of bird or fish is lost to extinction, yet we are less concerned with the loss of a unique culture. Perhaps, like the survivors of the Black Plague, we celebrate our own survival while ignoring the destruction of others. The age of colonization was just such a plague in the cultural history of humankind. Countless thousands of cultures that had survived and thrived for millennia in various pockets of the earth's habitats suddenly were swamped by warfare and pestilence such as they had never known before. The Haida stand as an example of that physical and cultural decimation.

When the first European sailor spotted the shores of Haida Gwaii in 1774, the Haida population stood at close to twelve thousand, counting both the Prince of Wales archipelago and Haida Gwaii (the Queen Charlotte Islands). By the turn of the century, that population had been dramatically reduced to less than five hundred. Most indigenous peoples in the New World lost 90 per cent of their population to their collision with Europeans. The Haida lost more than 95 per cent.

When I began research on Haida Gwaii in 1966, the number of fluent Haida speakers was estimated at less than forty. Today, programs in the schools have helped those figures to begin to grow, but it still remains to be seen if the Haida can achieve what the Maori of New Zealand have done with their concept of "language nests" (interactive groups) as brooders of indigenous language. The isolation of the Maori from other large populations and their current position as more than 10 per cent of the population of New Zealand provide safer ground for optimism than for the Haida, overwhelmed as they are by English speakers. Even on their own islands they are a minority of the population, although this may change in the next few decades.

The renaissance of Haida culture, however, is attributable to a growing number of artists (PLATE 160). Bill Holm (1990:606–7) notes that the formline style of Northwest Coast art is calligraphic in principle: that is, there is an implicit grammar at play in each work that determines the message of the piece. In a wonderful interplay between anthropologists, art historians and the new generation of Haida artists, this grammar has been revived and extended.

PLATE 160

The original plaster pattern for Bill Reid's bronze sculpture *The Spirit of Haida Gwaii*, now in the Canadian Museum of Civilization. The first bronze cast (called *The Black Canoe*) stands before the Canadian Embassy in Washington, D.C., and the second one (called *The Jade Canoe*) is the centrepiece of the Vancouver airport. CMC (S92-9152)

The renaissance of Haida art begins with a story that has become apocryphal. One fateful day in 1956, Bill Reid, whose mother was a Haida from Skidegate and whose father was a German American, was reading the news as an announcer for CBC Radio in Vancouver: the news item that changed his life was about a grant to recreate the totem poles and houses of a Haida village on the campus of the University of British Columbia (PLATE 161). Reid says that he turned off his microphone right after the newscast and phoned the university's Museum of Anthropology to offer his assistance in pursuing this goal. It proved to be his apprenticeship in rediscovering Haida art and led to almost a half century of pioneering work in cultural reconstruction.

Bill Reid honed his skills over many years through replicating works created by his forebears, especially his great, great uncle, Charles Edenshaw. He studied the several hundred pieces of gold and silver jewellery by Charles Edenshaw in museums and copied images from John R. Swanton's *Contributions to the Ethnography of the Haida,* from Franz Boas's *Primitive Art* and from books by Marius Barbeau on Haida myths and argillite carvings.

This apprenticeship period led to a mature artistry in gold and silver jewellery that set new standards of value among eager collectors and has been well documented (Shadbolt 1986). Eventually, Reid undertook a series of public sculptures, each of which took the art world by surprise because of its increasing innovativeness, not to mention ever-growing scale. These completely new works went far beyond traditional prototypes and brought an indigenous style for the first time to the national level in Canada. Ultimately, Reid's work was recognized on the international level with exhibits in Paris, Budapest, Tokyo and Washington.

Beginning with his large cedar sculpture titled *The Raven and the First Men,* commissioned in 1980 by Dr. Walter Koerner for the Museum of Anthropology at the University of British Columbia, Reid pushed Haida art into a format well beyond the house frontal pole or mortuary post. His second work on a large scale, the bronze *Killer Whale* for the Vancouver Aquarium in 1984, is closely related to Charles Edenshaw's compotes or fruit dishes that featured pivotal figures of Haida cosmology as the handle of the lid (PLATE 163). A prototype for this sculpture was the gold box he made for the Royal British Columbia Museum in 1971, on which the tightly arched Whale forms the handle of the lid. This Whale is all of 7.6 cm (3 inches) high while the monumental bronze version is 5.5 m (18 feet) high. His next large piece, in 1984–85, was a bronze relief mural, *Mythic Messengers,* for Teleglobe Canada's headquarters in Burnaby, near Vancouver (PLATE 162).

Expo 86 in Vancouver coincided with an obsession Bill Reid had developed for understanding the Haida canoe as a paradigm of Haida culture. Its pivotal role was recognized by the Reverend William Collison, who titled his reminiscences of the first mission to the Haida *In the Wake of the War Canoe* (see Lillard 1981). Reid was commissioned to carve and paint a 15-m (50-foot) war canoe from a red cedar log for the world's fair. He agreed to recreate this

PLATE 161

A portion of the Haida village reconstruction created by Bill Reid for the University of British Columbia Museum of Anthropology in Vancouver. *Photograph by George MacDonald, 1968. Author's collection*

PLATE 162

Mythic Messengers is the title given by Bill Reid to his high relief bronze sculpture that combines figures from such classic Haida myths as the Bear Mother, the Dogfish Woman, the Eagle Prince and others. This version was donated to the Canadian Museum of Civilization by Teleglobe Canada. CMC (s89-4183)

PLATE 163 (facing page)

This gold saltbox portraying the Bear Mother myth was commissioned by the Canadian Museum of Civilization from Bill Reid in 1972. The Bear who abducted and married the woman is depicted on the box, while she suckles her two cubs on the lid. CMC IV-B-1574 (s83-368)

canoe, which he named *Lootas* (or *Wave Eater*), for the Canadian Museum of Civilization in fibreglass to permit its outdoor display. Each new canoe was to be the alter ego of the other: one was to have primary formlines in black, the other in red. Consequently, one canoe became known as *Black Eagle* while the other was known as *Red Raven*.

The pièce de résistance of Bill Reid's work is surely *The Spirit of Haida Gwaii,* commissioned by the firm of R. J. Reynolds for the new Canadian Embassy in Washington, D.C. This massive sculpture, which took more than three years to execute and resulted in a price tag of $1.8 million, was unveiled in 1992. The plaster pattern for the bronze cast was a perfect complement to the baroque plaster interiors that architect Douglas Cardinal had created for the new Canadian Museum of Civilization (PLATE 160). Long before the completion and opening of the museum in 1989, I had suggested to Maury and Mary Young of Vancouver, the eventual donors, that *The Spirit of Haida Gwaii* would be the crowning piece in the Grand Hall, signalling that Northwest Coast native culture was not extinct but was, shaman-like, rising from the ashes.

ROBERT DAVIDSON

The next generation of Haida artists is represented by Robert Davidson. In 1966, Bill Reid introduced himself to the young Robert Davidson, who was conducting a carving demonstration at a department store in Vancouver. At the age of twenty, Davidson began an eighteen-month apprenticeship with Reid, then continued his education at the Emily Carr College of Art and Design. A few years later, he was already distinguishing himself as a thoughtful and talented artist. Much has been written about his maturation as one of the new master artists of the Haida tradition (Halpin 1979, Stewart 1979, Thom 1993, Steltzer and Davidson 1994).

PLATE 164

The housefront carved and painted by Robert Davidson for the National Historic Sites and Monuments Board of Canada and the Old Masset Village Council in memory of the great artist Charles Edenshaw (Tahayren). The Frog design is based on a chief's seat carved by Charles Edenshaw. *Photograph by George MacDonald, 1978. Author's collection*

PLATE 165

Robert Davidson's gilded bronze sculpture representing Raven (in bas-relief on the rim) bringing light to humankind. The work was commissioned by Dr. Margaret Hess of Calgary for the Grand Hall of the Canadian Museum of Civilization. CMC VII-B-1822 (S89-1738)

One of the early features of Robert Davidson's work was the fact that he was rooted in the Haida community of Masset where he had spent his early years. Through his grandmother Florence Edenshaw Davidson, he was linked to artists Charles Edenshaw and Albert Edward Edenshaw. His grandfather Robert Davidson Sr. was a carver and a hereditary chief of the town of Kayung, and his father, Claude Davidson, was a carver who inspired his sons Robert and Reg (who is an artist in his own right) to express their heritage through art and other cultural activities, including dancing.

Robert Davidson's period of apprenticeship was brief, and he mastered much of the sophistication of Haida art in his twenties. He carved a totem pole for the village of Masset and, encouraged and aided by his family, raised it with appropriate ceremonies in 1969. A series of exquisite prints in the 1970s expanded his reputation, and in 1978 he completed a commission from the National Historic Sites and Monuments Board of Canada to create a distinctive memorial to Charles Edenshaw, who had been declared an artist of national significance (PLATE 164). Unfortunately, the traditional Haida house with its carved and painted memorial housefront burned to the ground a year later.

A commission in 1984 from the Maclean Hunter Company for its new headquarters in Toronto resulted in possibly the oddest pole raising on record. The triple *Three Watchmen* pole was lowered into place in an atrium by a 15-storey crane from the sky world (Steltzer and Davidson 1994:80). In 1986, the Pepsi-Cola company commissioned a set of three poles called *Three Variations on Killer Whale Myths* for its international sculpture park outside New York City (Steltzer and Davidson:83–84).

The apogee of Robert Davidson's art is possibly the large gilded bronze sculpture *Raven Bringing Light to the World*—over a metre (3 feet) in diameter—commissioned by Dr. Margaret Hess of Calgary in honour of the dedication of the Grand Hall at the Canadian Museum of Civilization in 1986. In this piece, the humanlike face that simultaneously represents the sun, the moon and the stars contrasts effectively with the encircling bas-relief design of the Raven with his all-devouring beak holding the combined celestial bodies (PLATE 165).

In 1994, the Canadian Museum of Civilization co-sponsored a retrospective exhibit, "Eagle of the Dawn," that brought together three decades of Robert Davidson's work and filled 930 m² (10,000 square feet) of exhibition space. He continues to work in gold and silver, as well as creating masks and prints and undertaking commissions for monumental sculptures. The fact that Robert Davidson is only slighter older now than Bill Reid was when he began to create art in the Haida style suggests that Davidson has many further contributions to make.

JIM HART

The youngest of the Haida carvers to show great promise is Jim Hart, who in 1988 supervised the construction of the Haida house in the Grand Hall of the Canadian Museum of Civilization (PLATE 86). He was born in Masset and is a descendant of the famous shaman Dr. Kudé. Jim Hart apprenticed with Bill Reid on the monumental sculpture *The Raven and the First Men.* Previously, he had worked with Robert Davidson on the Charles Edenshaw Memorial Longhouse.

During his early years as an artist, Jim Hart exercised his skills in many media, including silver and gold jewellery, and prints that explore the range of supernatural and human beings that are appropriate to his family. He also carved a replica of a pole that once stood at Masset in the last century and that now graces the outdoor Haida village at the Museum of Anthropology at the University of British Columbia. A bronze miniature of this pole stands as a tribute to the pioneer ethnologist Marius Barbeau in the salon named after him at the Canadian Museum of Civilization.

In 1993, the Canadian Museum of Civilization commissioned Jim Hart to create a *manda'a* figure, whose traditional purpose was to support the coffin of a Haida chief (PLATE 166). This sculpture takes its inspiration from a piece collected from Skedans by Charles F. Newcombe for the Field Museum, but Hart has embellished it with his own distinctive designs on the tail. The idea for this commission rose from the popularity of the *manda'a* figure of a Wasgo (or Sea Wolf) that Bill Reid carved for the Museum of Anthropology in 1964, based on a nineteenth-century one by Charles Edenshaw at the Royal British Columbia Museum.

Another challenge undertaken by Jim Hart was recreating on a monumental scale a small shamanic piece depicting a man and woman straddling a huge Frog carved by an unnamed master of Haida art, probably in the 1870s. This unknown artist is probably the author of a piece acquired by the Glenbow Museum from a New York collection in 1975, depicting a Chinese immigrant with a prominent queue and typical costume of the period, as well as a secret society headpiece (VII-B-110) in the collections of the Canadian Museum of Civilization. Jim Hart finished the tribute to the unknown artist early in 1995.

At an impressive potlatch held in Masset in 1995, the current Chief Edenshaw (Morris White) designated Jim Hart as his heir to his title.

THE NEXT GENERATION

The Haida now regard their future with hope, bolstered by recent developments that hold great potential for reinforcing their cultural revival. The first is the declaration of the islands of the South Moresby group of the Queen Charlotte Islands (Haida Gwaii) as a National Park focussed on the three ancient villages of Skedans, Tanu and Skungwai (Ninstints). Skungwai has in fact been recognized as a place of premier importance to the history of

Realidades 2

 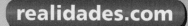

Digital Edition

Peggy Palo Boyles
OKLAHOMA CITY, OK

Myriam Met
ROCKVILLE, MD

Richard S. Sayers
LONGMONT, CO

Carol Eubanks Wargin

PEARSON

Boston, Massachusetts | Chandler, Arizona
Glenview, Illinois | Upper Saddle River, New Jersey

WE DEDICATE THIS BOOK TO THE
MEMORY OF OUR ESTEEMED COLLEAGUE,

Carol Eubanks Wargin.

Front cover, left: Teen girl in airport
Center left: Sentry post on city wall, Old San Juan, San Juan, Puerto Rico
Center right: Young women dancers at street festival, Cartagena, Colombia
Right: Ceramic plate of Moorish design handmade in Andalusia, Spain

Acknowledgments appear on pages 559–561, which constitute an extension of this copyright page.

Copyright © 2014 Pearson Education, Inc., or its affiliates. All Rights Reserved. Printed in the United States of America. This publication is protected by copyright, and permission should be obtained from the publisher prior to any prohibited reproduction, storage in a retrieval system, or transmission in any form or by any means, electronic, mechanical, photocopying, recording, or likewise. For information regarding permissions, write to Rights Management & Contracts, Pearson Education, Inc., One Lake Street, Upper Saddle River, New Jersey 07458.

Pearson, Prentice Hall, and Pearson Prentice Hall are trademarks, in the U.S. and/or other countries, of Pearson Education, Inc., or its affiliates.

ISBN-13:   978-0-13-319966-6
ISBN-10:   0-13-319966-5

PEARSON

8 9 10   V011   16 15

Realidades 2

realidades.com

Digital Edition

Realidades Authors

Peggy Palo Boyles

During her foreign language career of over thirty years, Peggy Palo Boyles has taught elementary, secondary, and university students in both private and public schools. She is currently an independent consultant who provides assistance to schools, districts, universities, state departments of education, and other organizations of foreign language education in the areas of curriculum, assessment, cultural instruction, professional development and program evaluation. She was a member of the ACTFL Performance Guidelines for the K–12 Learners task force and served as a Senior Editor for the project. She currently serves on the Advisory Committee for the ACTFL Assessment for Performance and Proficiency of Languages (AAPPL). Peggy is a Past-President of the National Association of District Supervisors of Foreign Language (nadsfl) and was a recipient of ACTFL's K–12 Steiner Award for Leadership in K–12 Foreign Language Education. Peggy lives in Oklahoma City, OK with her husband, Del. Their son, Ryan, works at the University of Texas at Arlington.

Myriam Met

For most of her professional life, Myriam (Mimi) Met has worked in the public schools, first as a high school teacher in New York, then as K–12 supervisor of language programs in the Cincinnati Public Schools, and finally as a Coordinator of Foreign Language in Montgomery County (MD) Public Schools. She is currently a Senior Research Associate at the National Foreign Language Center, University of Maryland, where she works on K–12 language policy and infrastructure development. Mimi Met has served on the Advisory Board for the National Standards for Foreign Language Learning, on the Executive Council of ACTFL, and as President of the National Association of District Supervisors of Foreign Languages (NADSFL). She has been honored by ACTFL with the Steiner Award for Leadership in K–12 Foreign Language Education and the Papalia Award for Excellence in Teacher Education.

Richard S. Sayers

Rich Sayers has been an educator in world languages since 1978. He taught Spanish at Niwot High School in Longmont, CO for 18 years, where he taught levels 1 through AP Spanish. While at Niwot High School, Rich served as department chair, district foreign language coordinator, and board member of the Colorado Congress of Foreign Language Teachers. Rich has also served on the Board of the Southwest Conference on Language Teaching. In 1991, Rich was selected as one of the Disney Company's Foreign Language Teacher Honorees for the American Teacher Awards. Rich has served as a world languages consultant for Pearson since 1996. He is currently the Curriculum Specialist Manager for Pearson in the Mountain Region.

Carol Eubanks Wargin

Carol Eubanks Wargin taught Spanish for 20 years at Glen Crest Middle School, Glen Ellyn, IL, and also served as Foreign Languages department chair. In 1997, Ms. Wargin's presentation "From Text to Test: How to Land Where You Planned" was honored as the best presentation at the Illinois Conference on the Teaching of Foreign Languages (ICTFL) and at the Central States Conference on the Teaching of Foreign Languages (CSC). She was twice named Outstanding Young Educator by the Jaycees. Ms. Wargin passed away in 2004.

Contributing Writers

Sheree Altmann
Lassiter High School
Marietta, GA

Madela Ezcurra
New York, NY

Thomasina Pagán Hannum
Albuquerque, NM

Norah L. Jones
Gladys, VA

Mary A. Mosley, Ph.D.
Fulton, MO

Craig Reubelt
The University of Chicago Laboratory Schools
Chicago, IL

National Consultants

María R. Hubbard
Braintree, MA

Patrick T. Raven
Milwaukee, WI

¡Bienvenidos!

Welcome back to **Realidades 2!** You've already begun to understand, speak, read, and write in Spanish. You've also explored many different Spanish-speaking countries and their cultures. Because learning language is a process in which you build upon what you already know, in **Realidades 2** you'll be using and building on what you learned in your first year of study.

Tips for Reviewing

Here are some ways you can review.

• **Para empezar Realidades 2** begins with a review chapter that focuses on the basics from first year: talking about yourself, friends, and activities. It is likely that you'll remember this vocabulary and grammar. If not, use the textbook activities and **realidades.com** for extra practice.

• **A ver si recuerdas** Prior to each theme and some chapters, you'll find this section, the title of which means "Let's see if you remember." It contains a quick summary of vocabulary and grammar from first-year Spanish that connects to the upcoming theme or chapter.

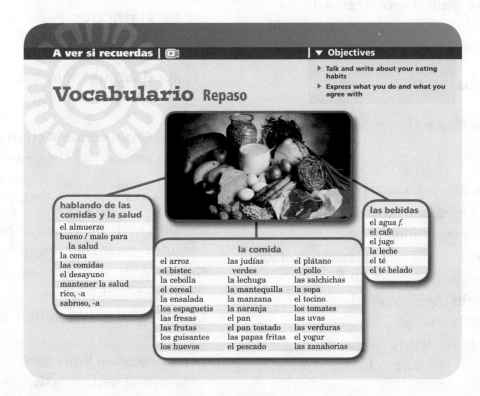

A ver si recuerdas | ▶️

▼ Objectives
▶ Talk and write about your eating habits
▶ Express what you do and what you agree with

Vocabulario Repaso

hablando de las comidas y la salud
el almuerzo
bueno / malo para la salud
la cena
las comidas
el desayuno
mantener la salud
rico, -a
sabroso, -a

la comida

el arroz	las judías verdes	el plátano
el bistec		el pollo
la cebolla	la lechuga	las salchichas
el cereal	la mantequilla	la sopa
la ensalada	la manzana	el tocino
los espaguetis	la naranja	los tomates
las fresas	el pan	las uvas
las frutas	el pan tostado	las verduras
los guisantes	las papas fritas	el yogur
los huevos	el pescado	las zanahorias

las bebidas
el agua f.
el café
el jugo
la leche
el té
el té helado

• **Grammar Summary and Glossaries** At the end of the book, you'll find grammar and vocabulary references from both first- and second-year Spanish.

• **realidades.com** Be sure to use the online activities as a review. These will provide further practice in grammar, reading, and writing. You will also find some fun activities to help you practice even more!

Online Resources with realidades.com

REALIDADES includes lots of online resources to help you learn Spanish! You can easily link to all of them when you log on to your Home Page within realidades.com. Your teacher will assign some activities, such as the ones in the workbooks. Others you can access on your own.

You'll find these resources highlighted on the pages of your print or online Student Edition with technology icons. Here's a list of the different icons used.

 Bilingual Visual Dictionary Links to additional vocabulary words presented visually

Reference Atlas Quick links to the countries in the online atlas

 Mapa global interactivo Links to GIS showing locations across the Spanish-speaking world

 Videos

Videocultura Cultural overview of each theme

Videohistoria Vocabulary video to help present the new vocabulary

GramActiva Grammar explanations to help present the new grammar

Grammar Tutorials Clear explanations of grammar with comparison to English

Animated Verbs Animations that highlight verb conjugations

En busca de la verdad A 10-episode mystery video starting in *Capítulo 3A*

Modelo *Videomodelos* Video models of speaking activities

 Audio Audio files for vocabulary, listening practice, and pronunciation

 Canciones de hip hop Songs to help practice new vocabulary and grammar

 Flashcards Practice for the new vocabulary

 RealTalk! Speak-and-record tool for speaking activities

 GramActiva Activity Extra practice for the *GramActiva* video

Más práctica GO **Online practice**

Instant Check Short activities that check your progress right away

Guided Workbook Step-by-step vocabulary and grammar practice

Core Workbook Vocabulary and grammar exercises

Communication Workbook Listening, video, and writing activities

Cultural Reading Activity Questions for the *Lectura* reading

Actividades Questions for the *Videomisterio*

Puzzles End-of-chapter games

Getting Started on realidades.com

At the beginning of the year, you'll want to get registered on realidades.com. Your teacher will help you get started. If you log on to realidades.com using a non-school computer, be sure to check out the System Requirements to make sure you are using compatible browsers and have the needed software.

realidades.com Home Page

After you register, you'll land on your realidades.com Home Page. Here you'll be able to access assignments, grades, and study resources. You'll also be able to communicate with your teacher.

 You'll find everything that's in the book online as eText.

RealTalk!

You'll be able to record many of your speaking activities using RealTalk! You can use the microphone in your computer or a headset with microphone. If you want, you can download and save your recording.

Mapa global interactivo

Build your geography skills and learn about more locations throughout the Spanish-speaking world. You can download .kmz files from realidades.com and link to sites using Google Earth™ or other geographic information systems.

Tabla de materias

Tema 1 Tu día escolar

Tema 2 Un evento especial

Tema 3 Tú y tu comunidad

Tema 4 **Recuerdos del pasado**

Tema 5 En las noticias

Tema 6 La televisión y el cine

Tema 7 Buen provecho

Tema 8 Cómo ser un buen turista

Tema 9 ¿Cómo será el futuro?

México

La Pirámide del Sol, Teotihuacán, México

Día de la Independencia, México

México

Capital: México, D.F.

Población: 113.7 millones

Área: 761,606 mi cuadradas / 1,972,550 km cuadrados

Lenguas: español (oficial), náhuatl, lenguas maya, y otras lenguas indígenas

Religiones: católica romana, protestante

Gobierno: república federal

Moneda: peso mexicano

Exportaciones: productos manufacturados, petróleo y sus derivados, plata, café, algodón

ESTADOS UNIDOS

realidades.com **GO**

🌐 *Mapa global interactivo*

📖 Reference Atlas

Tijuana

Ciudad Juárez

30° N

Río Bravo del Norte

Chihuahua

SIERRA MADRE OCCIDENTAL

Baja California

Golfo de California (Mar de Cortés)

Río Grande

Nuevo Laredo

SIERRA MADRE ORIENTAL

Monterrey

Golfo de México

Trópico de Cáncer

LEYENDA
Elevación

Metros	Pies
3,000	9,840
2,000	6,560
1,000	3,280
500	1,640
200	656

— Frontera nacional
⊛ Capital
● Ciudad
▲ Volcán o montaña

0   200 Millas
0   200 Kilómetros
Proyección cónica conforme de Lambert

Guadalajara

20° N

Querétaro

Mérida

Península de Yucatán

Paracutín ▲

Ciudad de México ⊛

Iztaccíhuatl ▲
▲ ● Puebla
Popocatépetl

Veracruz

N
O   E
S

SIERRA MADRE DEL SUR

Oaxaca

ISTMO DE TEHUANTEPEC

BELICE

Acapulco

OCÉANO PACÍFICO

GUATEMALA

EL SALVADOR

110° O

100° O

Arquitectura colonial, Guanajuato, México

América Central

Guatemala

Capital: Ciudad de Guatemala

Población: 13.8 millones

Área: 42,043 mi cuadradas / 108,890 km cuadrados

Lenguas: español (oficial), quiché, cakchiquel, kekchi, mam, garifuna, xinca, y otras lenguas indígenas

Religiones: católica romana, protestante, creencias tradicionales mayas

Gobierno: república democrática constitucional

Moneda: quetzal, dólar

Exportaciones: combustibles, maquinaria y equipos de transporte, materiales para construcción, granos

Honduras

Capital: Tegucigalpa

Población: 8.1 millones

Área: 43,278 mi cuadradas / 112,090 km cuadrados

Lenguas: español (oficial), lenguas indígenas

Religiones: católica romana, protestante

Gobierno: república constitucional democrática

Moneda: lempira

Exportaciones: café, plátano, camarón, langosta, carne, cinc, madera

El Salvador

Capital: San Salvador

Población: 6.1 millones

Área: 8,124 mi cuadradas / 21,040 km cuadrados

Lenguas: español (oficial), nahua

Religiones: católica romana, protestante

Gobierno: república

Moneda: colón salvadoreño, dólar

Exportaciones: elaboración de productos con materiales fabricados en el extranjero, equipos, café, azúcar, camarón, textiles, productos químicos, electricidad

Piscinas termales, cerca del Volcán Arenal, Costa Rica

realidades.com **GO**

🌐 *Mapa global interactivo*

📖 Reference Atlas

JAMAICA

MÉXICO

Parque
Nacional
Tikal ▪

Lago
Petén
Itzá

BELICE

Golfo de
Honduras

Lago de
Izabal

GUATEMALA

Quetzaltenango

San Pedro Sula

Copán

HONDURAS

Ciudad de
✪ Guatemala • Santa Rosa de Copán

Antigua ✪

*Mar
Caribe*

Cerro El Pital ▲

Volcán de
Santa Ana ▲ Santa Ana

✪ Tegucigalpa

San
Salvador

Santa Rosa
de Lima

La Libertad •

CORDILLERA
ISABELIA

EL SALVADOR

Golfo de
Fonseca

Lago de
Managua

NICARAGUA

CORDILLERA CHONTALEÑA

Managua ✪ • Masaya

Granada

Lago de
Nicaragua

Los Chiles •

COSTA RICA

San José ✪ • Puerto Limón

Canal de
Panamá

Colón •

Ciudad de
Panamá

Golfo de
Nicoya

PANAMÁ

OCÉANO PACÍFICO

Golfo
Dulce

Golfo de
Panamá

Parque
Nacional
Darién ▪

COLOMBIA

LEYENDA
Elevación

Metros	Pies
3,000	9,840
2,000	6,560
1,000	3,280
500	1,640
200	656

—— Frontera nacional
✪ Capital
• Ciudad
▲ Volcán o montaña
▪ Zona arqueológica

0 _____ 100 Millas
0 _____ 100 Kilómetros
Proyección azimutal
equivalente de Lambert

16° N

12° N

92° O

84° O

80° O

Nicaragua

Capital: Managua

Población: 5.7 millones

Área: 49,998 mi cuadradas / 129,494 km cuadrados

Lenguas: español (oficial), inglés, miskito, otras lenguas indígenas

Religiones: católica romana, protestante

Gobierno: república

Moneda: córdoba oro

Exportaciones: café, camarón, langosta, algodón, tabaco, carne, azúcar, plátano, oro

Costa Rica

Capital: San José

Población: 4.6 millones

Área: 19,730 mi cuadradas / 51,100 km cuadrados

Lenguas: español (oficial), inglés

Religiones: católica romana, protestante

Gobierno: república democrática

Moneda: colón de Costa Rica

Exportaciones: café, plátano, azúcar, textiles, componentes electrónicos

Panamá

Capital: Ciudad de Panamá

Población: 3.5 millones

Área: 30,193 mi cuadradas / 78,200 km cuadrados

Lenguas: español (oficial), inglés

Religiones: católica romana, protesta

Gobierno: democracia constitucional

Moneda: balboa, dólar

Exportaciones: plátano, azúcar, camarón, café

El Caribe

El Capitolio, La Habana, Cuba

El Yunque, Puerto Rico

ESTADOS
UNIDOS

*Golfo de
México*

ISLAS BAHAMAS

N
O E
S

realidades.com GO

🌐 *Mapa global interactivo*

DK Reference Atlas

Estrecho de la Florida

⊛ La Habana

24° N

Trópico de Cáncer

OCÉANO
ATLÁNTICO

CUBA

*Isla de la
Juventud*

Santiago
de Cuba ● Guantánamo

REPÚBLICA
DOMINICANA

*Bahía de
Samaná*

20° N

PUERTO
RICO
(E.E.U.U.)

San Juan ★

▲ VIEQUES

HAITÍ

⊛ Santo
Domingo

Ponce ●

El Yunque

JAMAICA

LEYENDA
Elevación

Metros   Pies
3,000   9,840
2,000   6,560
1,000   3,280
500   1,640
200   656

── Frontera nacional
⊛ Capital
● Ciudad
▲ Volcán o montaña

0   100 Millas
0   100 Kilómetros

*Proyección azimutal
equivalente de Lambert*

16° N

Mar Caribe

80° O

68° O

12° N

República Dominicana

Capital: Santo Domingo

Población: 10 millones

Área: 18,815 mi cuadradas / 48,730 km cuadrados

Lenguas: español (oficial)

Religiones: católica romana, protestante

Gobierno: democracia representativa

Moneda: peso dominicano

Exportaciones: ferroníquel, azúcar, oro, plata, cacao, tabaco, carne

Puerto Rico

Capital: San Juan

Población: 4 millones

Área: 3,515 mi cuadradas / 9,104 km cuadrados

Lenguas: español e inglés (lenguas oficiales)

Religiones: católica romana, protestante

Gobierno: estado libre asociado de los Estados Unidos

Moneda: dólar estadounidense

Exportaciones: productos manufacturados, petróleo y productos derivados, plata, café, algodón

Cuba

Capital: La Habana

Población: 11.1 millones

Área: 42,803 mi cuadradas / 110,860 km cuadrados

Lenguas: español (oficial)

Religiones: católica romana, protestante, y otras religiones

Gobierno: estado comunista

Moneda: peso cubano

Exportaciones: azúcar, níquel, tabaco, mariscos, productos médicos, cítricos, café

América del Sur
(Parte norte)

Colombia

Capital: Bogotá

Población: 44.7 millones

Área: 439,736 mi cuadradas / 1,138,910 km cuadrados

Lenguas: español (oficial)

Religiones: católica romana

Gobierno: república

Moneda: peso colombiano

Exportaciones: textiles, petróleo y productos derivados, café, oro, esmeraldas, plátano, tabaco, algodón, madera, energía hidroeléctrica

Ecuador

Capital: Quito

Población: 15 millones

Área: 109,483 mi cuadradas / 283,560 km cuadrados

Lenguas: español (oficial), quechua, otras lenguas indígenas

Religiones: católica romana

Gobierno: república

Moneda: dólar

Exportaciones: petróleo, textiles, plátano, camarón, cacao, azúcar, carne

Perú

Capital: Lima

Población: 29.2 millones

Área: 496,226 mi cuadradas / 1,285,220 km cuadrados

Lenguas: español (oficial), quechua (oficial), aymara, y otras lenguas indígenas

Religiones: católica romana

Gobierno: república constitucional

Moneda: nuevo sol

Exportaciones: oro, cinc, cobre, pescado y productos de pescado, textiles

Volcán Cotopaxi, Ecuador

Mapa

80° O
60° O
40° O

Mar Caribe

Cartagena ●
Maracaíbo ●
☆ Caracas

Río Orinoco

VENEZUELA

Medellín ●
Río Magdalena

Cali ●
☆ Bogotá
COLOMBIA

ECUADOR

Ecuador ————— *Ecuador* —— 0°

Quito ☆
Chimborazo ▲
Guayaquil ●

ISLAS GALÁPAGOS *(Ecuador)*

Golfo de Guayaquil

PERÚ

BRASIL

Huascarán ▲

Callao ●
Lima ☆

Machu Picchu ▪
● Cuzco

BOLIVIA

OCÉANO PACÍFICO

☆ La Paz
● Cochabamba

Titicaca

ALTIPLANO

Nevado Sajama ▲
☆ Sucre
● Potosí

PARAGUAY

20° S

CHILE

———— *Trópico de Capricornio*

N
O — E
S

ARGENTINA

URUGUAY

OCÉANO ATLÁNTICO

40° S

LEYENDA
Elevación

Metros	Pies
3,000	9,840
2,000	6,560
1,000	3,280
500	1,640
200	656

— Frontera nacional
☆ Capital
● Ciudad
▲ Volcán o montaña
▪ Zona arqueológica

0   400 Millas
0   400 Kilómetros

Proyección azimutal
equivalente de Lambert

realidades.com   GO
🌐 *Mapa global interactivo*
📖 **Reference Atlas**

Venezuela

Capital: Caracas

Población: 27.6 millones

Área: 352,144 mi cuadradas / 912,050 km cuadrados

Lenguas: español (oficial), varias lenguas indígenas

Religiones: católica romana, protestante

Gobierno: república federal

Moneda: bolívar fuerte

Exportaciones: petróleo y productos derivados, azúcar, plátano, acero, aluminio, energía hidroeléctrica

Bolivia

Capital: La Paz, Sucre

Población: 10.1 millones

Área: 424,164 mi cuadradas / 1,098,580 km cuadrados

Lenguas: español, quechua, aymara (todas lenguas oficiales)

Religiones: católica romana, protestante

Gobierno: república

Moneda: boliviano

Exportaciones: soja, gas natural, cinc, madera, oro

América del Sur
(Parte sur)

Puerto de Ushuaia, Tierra del Fuego, Argentina

Paraguay

Capital: Asunción

Población: 6.5 millones

Área: 157,047 mi cuadradas / 406,750 km cuadrados

Lenguas: español y guaraní (lenguas oficiales)

Religiones: católica romana, protestante

Gobierno: república constitucional

Moneda: guaraní

Exportaciones: azúcar, carne, tapioca, energía hidroeléctrica

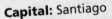

Chile

Capital: Santiago

Población: 16.9 millones

Área: 292,260 mi cuadradas / 756,950 km cuadrados

Lenguas: español (oficial)

Religiones: católica romana, protestante

Gobierno: república

Moneda: peso chileno

Exportaciones: cobre, pescado, equipos de transporte, fruta, papel y pulpa, productos químicos, energía hidroeléctrica

Argentina

Capital: Buenos Aires

Población: 41.8 millones

Área: 1,068,302 mi cuadradas / 2,766,890 km cuadrados

Lenguas: español (oficial), inglés, francés, italiano, alemán

Religiones: católica romana, protestante, judía

Gobierno: república

Moneda: peso argentino

Exportaciones: carne, aceites comestibles, combustibles y energía, cereales, forraje, vehículos automotores

LEYENDA

Elevación

Metros	Pies
3,000	9,840
2,000	6,560
1,000	3,280
500	1,640
200	656

—— Frontera nacional

☆ Capital

● Ciudad

▲ Volcán o montaña

0   400 Millas

0   400 Kilómetros

Proyección azimutal
equivalente de Lambert

Uruguay

Capital: Montevideo

Población: 3.3 millones

Área: 68,039 mi cuadradas / 176,220 km cuadrados

Lenguas: español (oficial), portuñol/brasilero

Religiones: católica romana, protestante y otras religiones

Gobierno: república constitucional

Moneda: peso uruguayo

Exportaciones: alimentos, vehículos, carne, arroz, maderas

España
Guinea Ecuatorial

España

Capital: Madrid

Población: 46.8 millones

Área: 194,897 mi cuadradas / 504,782 km cuadrados

Lenguas: castellano (oficial); catalán, gallego, vasco (oficiales regionalmente)

Religiones: católica romana

Gobierno: monarquía parlamentaria

Moneda: euro

Exportaciones: alimentos, maquinaria, vehículos automotores

Un molino en Castilla-La Mancha, España

La Sagrada Familia, Barcelona, España

Golfo de Vizcaya

FRANCIA

PIRINEOS

Asturias
Cantabria
Santiago de Compostela
Bilbao
País Vasco
Pamplona
Navarra
Galicia
La Rioja
Castilla y León
Zaragoza
Cataluña
Valladolid
Aragón
Barcelona

OCÉANO ATLÁNTICO

Río Duero

ESPAÑA

PORTUGAL

Madrid

Mar Mediterráneo

Menorca
40° N

Mallorca

Río Tajo

Valencia

Baleares

Extremadura
Castilla-La Mancha
Valencia

ISLAS BALEARES

Ibiza
Río Guadiana
Mérida

38° N

SIERRA MORENA

Alicante

Córdoba
Murcia

Río Guadalquivir

Sevilla
Andalucía
Granada

Málaga

0   100 Millas

0   100 Kilómetros

Proyección azimutal equivalente de Lambert

Estrecho de Gibraltar
Ceuta

Melilla

LEYENDA
Elevación

Metros	Pies
3,000	9,840
2,000	6,560
1,000	3,280
500	1,640
200	656

—— Frontera nacional
✪ Capital
● Ciudad

ISLAS CANARIAS

La Palma
Lanzarote
Tenerife
Fuerteventura
Gomera
Gran Canaria
Hierro
28° N

OCÉANO ATLÁNTICO
18° O   16° O

0   50 mi
0   50 km

Malabo

Isla Bioko

0   50 Millas
0   50 Kilómetros

Proyección azimutal equivalente de Lambert

Golfo de Guinea

GUINEA ECUATORIAL

CAMERÚN

CAMERÚN

Isla Bioko

GUINEA ECUATORIAL

Ebebiyin
2° N

Bata
Río Muni

Mbini

GABÓN

Isla Annobón

PARQUE NACIONAL MONTE ALEN

GABÓN

OCÉANO ATLÁNTICO

8° E   10° E   12° E

Guinea Ecuatorial

Capital: Malabo

Población: 668,225

Área: 10,831 mi cuadradas / 28,051 km cuadrados

Lenguas: español y francés (lenguas oficiales), fang, bubi, ibo, inglés pidgin

Religiones: católica romana, religiones africanas tradicionales y otras religiones

Gobierno: república

Moneda: franco CFA

Exportaciones: petróleo, maderas, cacao, café

Un grupo de niños, Guinea Ecuatorial

Estados Unidos

Estados Unidos

Capital: Washington, D.C.

Población: 313.2 millones

Área: 3,717,813 mi cuadradas / 9,631,418 km cuadrados

Lenguas: inglés, español, otras lenguas indoeuropeas, lenguas asiáticas y del Pacífico, otras lenguas

Religiones: protestante, católica romana, judía, musulmana y otras religiones

Gobierno: república federal

Moneda: dólar estadounidense

Exportaciones: vehículos automotores, aviones, medicinas, telecomunicaciones, equipos electrónicos, productos químicos, soja, fruta, trigo, maíz

Ruinas de Square Tower House, Mesa Verde, CO

Un chilenoamericano con la bandera de los Estados Unidos

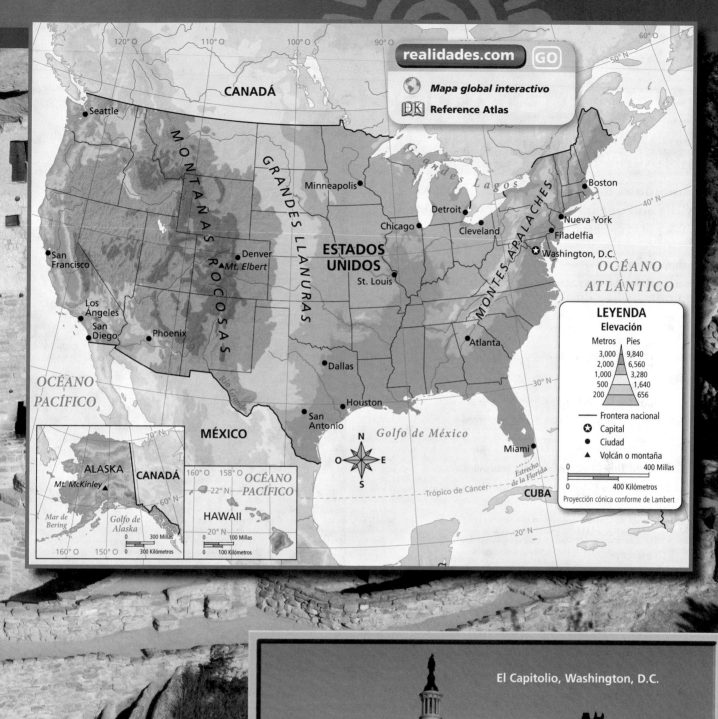

realidades.com GO

🌐 *Mapa global interactivo*

📖 Reference Atlas

CANADÁ

Seattle

MONTAÑAS ROCOSAS

GRANDES LLANURAS

Minneapolis

Grandes Lagos

Detroit

Boston

Chicago

Cleveland

Nueva York

Filadelfia

MONTES APALACHES

San Francisco

Denver

Mt. Elbert

ESTADOS UNIDOS

St. Louis

Washington, D.C.

OCÉANO ATLÁNTICO

Los Ángeles

San Diego

Phoenix

Atlanta

OCÉANO PACÍFICO

Dallas

Río Grande

Houston

San Antonio

MÉXICO

Golfo de México

Miami

Estrecho de la Florida

Trópico de Cáncer

CUBA

LEYENDA
Elevación

Metros	Pies
3,000	9,840
2,000	6,560
1,000	3,280
500	1,640
200	656

— Frontera nacional

✪ Capital

● Ciudad

▲ Volcán o montaña

0 ——— 400 Millas

0 ——— 400 Kilómetros

Proyección cónica conforme de Lambert

ALASKA

CANADÁ

Mt. McKinley

Mar de Bering

Golfo de Alaska

0 — 300 Millas
0 — 300 Kilómetros

OCÉANO PACÍFICO

HAWAII

0 — 100 Millas
0 — 100 Kilómetros

N O E S

El Capitolio, Washington, D.C.

Para empezar

▼ **Chapter Objectives**

Communication

By the end of *Para empezar* you will be able to:

- Talk and write about yourself and your friends
- Listen and read about what people are like and the things they do

You will demonstrate what you know and can do:

- Presentación escrita, p. 13

You will also learn to:

1 ¿Cómo eres tú?

- Talk about what you and other people are like
- Tell where you and other people are from

2 ¿Qué haces?

- Talk about things you and other people do
- Talk about how often you do certain things

realidades.com (GO)

 Reference Atlas

 Mapa global interactivo

Estudiantes de una escuela
secundaria en Texas

Arte y cultura | El mundo hispano

El primer día de clases En los países hispanohablantes, los estudiantes regresan a las clases en diferentes meses. Por ejemplo, en Uruguay y Chile los estudiantes regresan en marzo porque las vacaciones de verano son de noviembre a febrero. En Colombia, hay tres calendarios para las escuelas. Unas escuelas van de enero a noviembre, el horario tradicional, y otras van de agosto a junio. El tercer calendario va de septiembre a junio, que es igual a los calendarios de los Estados Unidos y de México.

• ¿En qué mes regresas a la escuela después de las vacaciones de verano?

El primer día de clases en el Perú

▼ **Objectives**
▶ Talk about what you and other people are like
▶ Tell where you and other people are from

1 ¿Cómo eres tú?

Gloria

Enrique

Sonia

Alicia

Felipe

—Oye, Enrique, ¿eres artístico?

—Sí, según mis amigos soy muy artístico y estudioso. También dicen que soy reservado. Y Gloria, ¿cómo eres tú?

—Bueno . . . mis amigos dicen que soy paciente y trabajadora. Pero según mi hermanito, ¡soy impaciente y perezosa!

—¡Hola, Sonia y Alicia! ¡Uy! ¡Qué deportistas son Uds.!

—Sí, somos muy deportistas y también muy talentosas. ¿Te gusta practicar deportes, Felipe?

—Pues, no. No soy nada deportista, pero me gusta pasar tiempo con mis amigos. Soy sociable y muy simpático.

▼1 Los chicos

Leer • Escribir • Hablar

Los chicos de las fotos de arriba hablan de cómo son. Usa las fotos y las conversaciones para contestar las preguntas.

1. ¿Cómo es Enrique?

2. Según sus amigos, ¿cómo es Gloria? ¿Y según su hermanito?

3. ¿Cómo son Sonia y Alicia?

4. ¿Quién es sociable?

¿Recuerdas?

Here are some question words that are often used with *ser:*

• ¿Quién(es)?

• ¿Cómo?

• ¿De dónde?

Gramática Repaso

Adjectives

Remember that adjectives describe people, places, and things. In Spanish, adjectives have the same number and gender as the nouns they describe and they usually come after the noun.

Masculine		Feminine	
Singular	Plural	Singular	Plural
serio	serios	seria	serias
deportista	deportistas	deportista	deportistas
trabajador	trabajadores	trabajadora	trabajadoras
paciente	pacientes	paciente	pacientes
joven	jóvenes*	joven	jóvenes

*Note that *jóvenes* needs an accent mark in the plural form.

▼2 Y tú, ¿cómo eres?

Escribir • Hablar

1. Según tus amigos, ¿cómo eres tú? ¿Artístico(a)? ¿Talentoso(a)? ¿Simpático(a)?

2. ¿Eres paciente o impaciente? ¿Eres trabajador(a) o perezoso(a)?

3. ¿Cómo es tu mejor amigo(a)?

¿Recuerdas?

You already know these words to describe what you and your friends are like:

alto, -a	impaciente
atrevido, -a	inteligente
bajo, -a	ordenado, -a
desordenado, -a	reservado, -a
estudioso, -a	sociable
gracioso, -a	viejo, -a
guapo, -a	

▼3 ¿Cómo son?

Escribir

Trabajen en grupos para hacer una lista de ocho personas famosas. Luego usen los adjetivos de la *Gramática* y de *¿Recuerdas?* y escriban una frase para describir a estas personas.

Modelo

Marc Anthony
Marc Anthony es talentoso y muy guapo.

El cantante Marc Anthony en concierto

▼4 Dos jóvenes | 🔊

Leer • Escuchar

Lee esta descripción de dos chicas latinoamericanas. Luego escribe los números del 1 al 6 en una hoja de papel. Escucha las frases y escribe *C* si la información es cierta y *F* si es falsa.

Nombres: Alicia Menéndez García y Carmen Díaz Ortiz

Edades: Tienen 18 años.

Residencia: Viven en Santiago de los Caballeros, República Dominicana, con sus familias.

Cómo son: Alicia es una poeta joven. Lee sus poemas en público. Ella es muy inteligente y artística. Carmen no es artística pero le gusta escuchar los poemas de Alicia. Carmen es muy sociable y deportista. Las dos jóvenes son amigas inseparables.

Amigos: "Nuestros amigos son graciosos y simpáticos", dicen Alicia y Carmen. "No tenemos tiempo para las personas negativas".

▼5 ¿Y cómo son tú y tus amigos?

Escribir

Ahora escribe una descripción de tu mejor amigo(a) y de ti. Usa la información de la descripción en la Actividad 4: nombres, edades, residencia y cómo son.

▼6 Amigos y primos

Leer • Escribir • Hablar

Lee la conversación entre los dos chicos del dibujo. Imagina lo que dicen las chicas sobre los chicos. Escribe la conversación de las chicas usando la conversación de los chicos como modelo. Presenta la conversación a la clase.

Esas chicas son muy bonitas. ¿Sabes cómo se llaman, Carlos?

Sí, hombre. Se llaman Dolores y Marisa. Son de Buenos Aires.

¿Cómo son?

Las dos son simpáticas. Dolores es seria y reservada. Le gusta leer. Marisa es graciosa y muy sociable. Le gusta pasar tiempo con sus amigos.

¿Uds. son muy buenos amigos?

Pues, sí, pero también somos primos.

Más práctica (GO)	realidades.com | print
Guided WB pp. 1–6	✔ ✔
Core WB p. 1	✔ ✔
Comm. WB pp. 1, 3	✔ ✔
Hispanohablantes **WB** pp. 2–3	✔

Gramática Repaso

The verb *ser*

You have learned to use the verb *ser* with adjectives to tell what someone is like.

Esas chicas **son bonitas**.

You have also learned to use *ser* with *de* to tell where someone is from.

Son de Buenos Aires.

Remember that *ser* is irregular. Here are its present-tense forms:

(yo)	soy	(nosotros) (nosotras)	somos
(tú)	eres	(vosotros) (vosotras)	sois
Ud. (él) (ella)	es	Uds. (ellos) (ellas)	son

▼7 Así son los compañeros de Alejandro

Leer • Escribir

Escribe la forma correcta del verbo *ser* para completar lo que Alejandro escribe sobre los estudiantes en su clase de español.

Así son los estudiantes en mi clase de español. Ana María __1.__ estudiosa y le gusta mucho leer. Manuel y Marianela practican muchos deportes y __2.__ deportistas. A José Luis le gusta nadar en la piscina grande en el gimnasio; él __3.__ atrevido. A mi compañero Juanito y a mí nos gusta ir a la escuela porque nosotros __4.__ trabajadores. Pero a Mercedes y a Eduardo no les gusta ir a la escuela porque __5.__ perezosos. Carolina dibuja bien y __6.__ muy artística. Manolito y Victoria tocan la guitarra y __7.__ muy talentosos. A mi compañero Ignacio y a mí nos gusta mucho hablar por teléfono y pasar tiempo con amigos porque __8.__ sociables. Pero a mí no me gusta ir al gimnasio porque no __9.__ deportista. Y tú, ¿cómo __10.__ ?

Más práctica **GO**

realidades.com | print

Guided WB p. 7 ✔ ✔
Core WB p. 2 ✔ ✔
Comm. WB p. 4 ✔ ✔
Hispanohablantes **WB** p. 4 ✔

▼8 ¿Y cómo son tus compañeros?

Escribir

¿Cómo son los estudiantes en tu clase de español? Usa la descripción de Alejandro como modelo y escribe cinco o seis frases para describir a tus compañeros.

▼9 Juego | 👥

Escribir • Hablar

Tu profesor(a) te va a dar una tarjeta con el nombre de otro(a) estudiante de la clase. Escribe una descripción de esta persona en la tarjeta. Luego vas a leer la descripción y tus compañeros tienen que adivinar (*guess*) quién es.

Modelo

Es seria y trabajadora, pero muy simpática. Le gusta la música. Ella e Isabel son buenas amigas. ¿Quién es?

Nationalities

You have already learned many adjectives of nationality. The Spanish words for these nationalities are based on the country name. Review the chart to see how each nationality relates to the country of origin. Remember that since the nationalities are adjectives, they agree in gender and number with the nouns they describe. They are usually used with the verb *ser*.

País	Nacionalidad	País	Nacionalidad	País	Nacionalidad
Argentina	argentino, -a	El Salvador	salvadoreño, -a	Paraguay	paraguayo, -a
Bolivia	boliviano, -a	España	español, española	Perú	peruano, -a
Chile	chileno, -a	Guatemala	guatemalteco, -a	Puerto Rico	puertorriqueño, -a
Colombia	colombiano, -a	Honduras	hondureño, -a	República Dominicana	dominicano, -a
Costa Rica	costarricense	México	mexicano, -a		
Cuba	cubano, -a	Nicaragua	nicaragüense	Uruguay	uruguayo, -a
Ecuador	ecuatoriano, -a	Panamá	panameño, -a	Venezuela	venezolano, -a

▼10 Una población diversa

Leer • Escribir

Los Estados Unidos es un país de inmigrantes, donde hay gente de todas partes del mundo. Un grupo importante de los inmigrantes está formado por hispanohablantes. La población hispana representa más de 50 millones de personas, o el 16 por ciento *(percent)* de la población total. Es muy diversa porque hay hispanohablantes de muchos países hispanos. Lee la gráfica sobre esta población y escribe un resumen.

Modelo

El grupo más grande de hispanohablantes en los Estados Unidos es el grupo de México. Los mexicanos son el 63 por ciento . . .

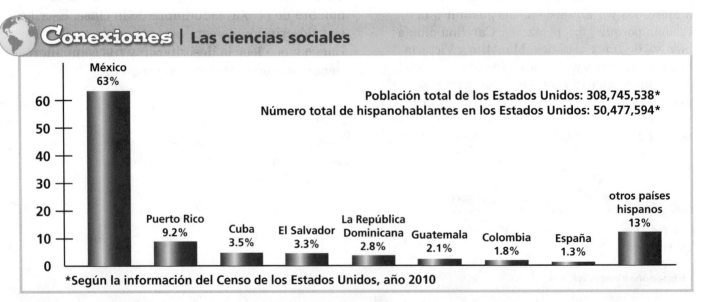

Conexiones | Las ciencias sociales

México 63%

Población total de los Estados Unidos: 308,745,538*
Número total de hispanohablantes en los Estados Unidos: 50,477,594*

Puerto Rico 9.2%
Cuba 3.5%
El Salvador 3.3%
La República Dominicana 2.8%
Guatemala 2.1%
Colombia 1.8%
España 1.3%
otros países hispanos 13%

*Según la información del Censo de los Estados Unidos, año 2010

▼11 ¿De dónde son?

Hablar

Estos estudiantes le escriben a tu clase por correo electrónico. Trabaja con otro(a) estudiante y pregúntale de dónde es cada estudiante y de qué nacionalidad. Después de hablar de estos chicos, pregunta a tu compañero(a) de dónde es.

▶ **Modelo**

A —¿De dónde es <u>Teresa</u>?

B —Es de <u>Asunción</u>. Es <u>paraguaya</u>.

Para decir más . . .

estadounidense   U.S. citizen

norteamericano, -a   North American (including Canada, Mexico, and the United States)

canadiense   Canadian

Estados Unidos

Juanita, La Habana

México   Cuba

José, Tegucigalpa

Ricardo, Santo Domingo

República Dominicana

Puerto Rico

Guatemala   Honduras
El Salvador   Nicaragua

Costa Rica

Panamá   Venezuela

Colombia

Ecuador

Linda, Caracas

Mercedes, La Ciudad de Panamá

Perú

Bolivia

Chile

Paraguay

Teresa, Asunción

Esteban, Lima

Uruguay

Argentina

Benjamín, Montevideo

Sergio, Madrid

España

María José, Madrid

▼12 ¿Y de dónde eres tú?

Hablar

Imagina que eres de uno de los países hispanohablantes que está en el mapa de la Actividad 11. Con otro(a) estudiante, pregunta y contesta según el modelo.

▶ **Modelo**

A —¿De dónde eres tú?

B —Soy de San Juan.

A —Ah, eres puertorriqueño(a).

Más práctica	GO	
	**realidades.com	print**	
Instant Check	✔	
Core WB p. 3	✔	✔
Comm. WB p. 1	✔	✔
Hispanohablantes **WB** pp. 1, 5		✔

2 ¿Qué haces?

Pepe

Paula

—¡Uy! No me gusta nada el invierno. Paula, ¿qué te gusta hacer en el invierno?

—Pues, paso tiempo con mis amigos: escuchamos música, tocamos la guitarra y por la noche bailamos. Lo que más me gusta hacer es practicar deportes.

—¿Qué deportes practicas?

—Monto en bicicleta o corro todos los días para hacer ejercicio. Practico deportes todo el año. ¿Y tú, Pepe?

—No soy muy deportista. A veces nado, por eso me encanta el verano. Generalmente tomo el sol y leo. También escribo canciones. ¿Qué haces en tus vacaciones de verano?

—En el verano a veces patino y también monto en monopatín con mis amigos.

▼13 Paula y Pepe

Escuchar

Divide una hoja de papel en dos columnas. En la primera columna escribe *Paula,* y en la segunda escribe *Pepe.* Escucha una lista de actividades. Si Paula hace la actividad, escribe el número de la actividad debajo de *Paula.* Si Pepe la hace, escribe el número debajo de *Pepe.* Usa los dibujos para ayudarte.

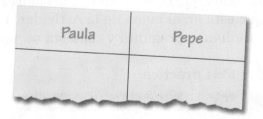

Paula	Pepe

Gramática Repaso

Present tense of regular verbs

Remember that in Spanish there are three groups of regular verbs. Their infinitives end in *-ar, -er,* or *-ir.* To form the present tense of a regular verb, you drop the *-ar, -er,* or *-ir* ending from the infinitive and add the appropriate present-tense ending. Use the present tense to talk about what someone is doing or what someone does.

comer

(yo)	**como**	(nosotros) (nosotras)	**comemos**
(tú)	**comes**	(vosotros) (vosotras)	**coméis**
Ud. (él) (ella)	**come**	Uds. (ellos) (ellas)	**comen**

hablar

(yo)	**hablo**	(nosotros) (nosotras)	**hablamos**
(tú)	**hablas**	(vosotros) (vosotras)	**habláis**
Ud. (él) (ella)	**habla**	Uds. (ellos) (ellas)	**hablan**

vivir

(yo)	**vivo**	(nosotros) (nosotras)	**vivimos**
(tú)	**vives**	(vosotros) (vosotras)	**vivís**
Ud. (él) (ella)	**vive**	Uds. (ellos) (ellas)	**viven**

▼14 ¿Qué hace Claudia los fines de semana?

Leer • Escribir

A Claudia le gusta pasar tiempo con sus amigos. Lee la descripción y completa su historia con la forma apropiada de cada verbo.

Me gusta pasar tiempo con mis amigos los fines de semana. Los viernes generalmente vamos al cine. (Nosotros) __1.__ *(vivir)* cerca de un cine donde dan muchas películas. Por lo general, los sábados por la mañana, (yo) __2.__ *(correr)* por una hora y luego __3.__ *(montar)* en bicicleta. Mis amigos, Carlos y Mario, generalmente __4.__ *(montar)* en monopatín y en el invierno __5.__ *(esquiar).* Los domingos generalmente (yo) __6.__ *(leer)* un libro y hago la tarea para el lunes.

¿Recuerdas?

You can talk about leisure activities using these regular verbs and expressions:

bailar	montar en bicicleta
caminar	montar en monopatín
cantar	nadar
comer	pasar tiempo
correr	patinar
dibujar	practicar deportes
escribir cuentos	tocar la guitarra
escuchar música	tomar el sol
esquiar*	usar la computadora
leer revistas	

*In the present tense, *esquiar* has an accent on the *i* in all forms except *nosotros* and *vosotros*: *esquío, esquías, esquía, esquiamos, esquiáis, esquían.*

▼15 Unas preguntas

Escribir

Vas a contestar unas preguntas, pero primero
tienes que completarlas. En una hoja de papel,
escribe los números del 1 al 7. Luego escribe la
palabra apropiada para completar cada pregunta.

1. ¿Con ___ pasas tiempo los fines de semana?
2. ¿ ___ vas al cine, los viernes, los sábados o los
   domingos?
3. ¿ ___ vives? ¿Está cerca de la escuela?
4. ¿ ___ deportes practicas?
5. ¿ ___ es tu restaurante favorito?
6. ¿ ___ usas la computadora, después de las
   clases o por la noche?
7. ¿ ___ veces vas a la biblioteca durante la
   semana?

> ### ¿Recuerdas?
>
> Here are the question words you already know:
>
> | | | |
> |---|---|---|
> | ¿Adónde? | ¿Cuánto, -a? | ¿Por qué? |
> | ¿Cómo? | ¿Cuántos, -as? | ¿Qué? |
> | ¿Cuál(es)? | ¿De dónde? | ¿Quién(es)? |
> | ¿Cuándo? | ¿Dónde? | |
>
> And here are words you can use to talk about how
> often you do an activity:
>
> | | | |
> |---|---|---|
> | a menudo | el (los) fin(es) | siempre |
> | a veces | de semana | todos los días |
> | después de | nunca | |

▼16 ¿A menudo o nunca? |

Hablar • Escribir

Usa las preguntas de la Actividad 15 para hacer una
conversación con otro(a) estudiante. Pregúntale con qué
frecuencia hace estas actividades. Escribe las respuestas
de tu compañero(a) y úsalas para escribir un párrafo.

Modelo

*A veces paso los fines de semana con
mis amigos. Siempre vamos al cine
los sábados . . .*

▼17 Dos preguntas, por favor |

Escribir • Hablar

❶ Van a trabajar en grupos de tres. Cada
estudiante debe escribir en una hoja de
papel una actividad que hace.

Modelo

Monto en bicicleta.

❷ Pasen la hoja de papel a la persona a la
izquierda. Esta persona va a escribir una
pregunta usando la información de la
primera frase y una palabra interrogativa.

Modelo

¿Cuándo montas en bicicleta?

❸ Pasen la hoja de papel a la persona a la
izquierda que va a escribir otra pregunta
usando la información de la primera frase
y otra palabra interrogativa.

Modelo

¿Dónde montas en bicicleta?

❹ Pasen la hoja a la persona que escribió la
primera frase. Esta persona tiene que leer
las preguntas y contestarlas.

Modelo

*Monto en bicicleta a menudo. Monto
en bicicleta en el parque.*

▼18 Tu tiempo libre |

Hablar

Trabaja con otro(a) estudiante y pregúntale adónde va en su tiempo libre. Tu compañero(a) te va a contestar y va a decir con qué frecuencia va.

▶ **Modelo**

A —*¿Adónde vas en el verano?*
B —*En el verano voy a la piscina todos los días.*

Estudiante A

1. en el invierno
2. los fines de semana
3. después de las clases
4. en la primavera
5. en el otoño
6. de vacaciones

Estudiante B

¿Dónde?	¿Cuándo?
la piscina	todos los días
el centro comercial	siempre
la playa	a veces
el parque	nunca
el gimnasio	a menudo
¡Respuesta personal!	¡Respuesta personal!

▼19 ¡Enrique!

Leer • Escribir

Lee este artículo de una revista sobre el cantante Enrique Iglesias. Luego contesta las preguntas.

Enrique Iglesias

El cantante Enrique Iglesias es de España pero ahora vive en Miami. Su padre es el famosísimo cantante Julio Iglesias, pero los jóvenes de todo el mundo conocen a Enrique por sus canciones populares como "Cuando me enamoro", "I Like It" y "Do You Know?". Por primera vez en la historia de la música latina, recibe el premio Grammy como Mejor Artista Latino con su primer disco; y en 2011 recibe el premio al Álbum del año en los premios Billboard de la Música Latina, entre muchos más. Enrique dice que la inspiración de su música viene de la música rock norteamericana y de las influencias latinas, caribeñas y europeas. Dice que "Soy y voy a ser siempre latino, pero mi música no lo es". Cuando no está escribiendo música o cantando en conciertos, le gusta practicar deportes acuáticos, pasar tiempo con sus perros, Lucas y Grammy, y ver la tele, especialmente los programas musicales. Sus amigos dicen que es gracioso, independiente, romántico y optimista.

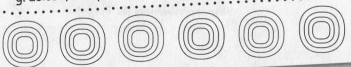

1. ¿Cómo se llama el padre de Enrique?
2. ¿De dónde es Enrique?
3. ¿Dónde vive ahora?
4. ¿Cuándo recibe el premio Billboard?
5. ¿Qué tipo de música le inspira a Enrique?
6. ¿Quién es Grammy?
7. ¿Quién es tu cantante favorito(a)? ¿Por qué te gusta?

▼20 Juego | 👥

Pensar • Escribir • Hablar

1 Escribe palabras que puedes usar para hablar de los tres dibujos. No tienes que escribir frases completas. Piensa en estas preguntas:

¿Qué hacen los jóvenes?

¿Dónde están?

¿Cuándo es?

¿Cómo se llaman ellos?

¿Cómo son ellos?

2 Formen grupos de tres. Decidan quién va a empezar *(start)*. La primera persona habla del primer dibujo por 20 segundos. Su profesor(a) va a decirles cuándo se termina el tiempo. La segunda persona habla del mismo dibujo por 15 segundos sin repetir nada. Su profesor(a) va a decirles cuándo se termina el tiempo. Luego la tercera persona habla del mismo dibujo por diez segundos.

3 Ahora repitan el Paso 2, pero describan el segundo dibujo. Luego repitan lo mismo, pero con el tercer dibujo.

▼21 Y tú, ¿qué dices? | 💬

Escribir • Hablar

1. ¿Qué haces los fines de semana?
2. ¿Cuándo vas al gimnasio: nunca, a veces o todos los días? ¿Por qué?
3. ¿Qué hace tu familia en el verano?

Más práctica	GO	
	realidades.com	**print**
Instant Check	✔	
Guided WB pp. 8–14	✔	✔
Core WB p. 4	✔	✔
Comm. WB pp. 2, 5, 210	✔	✔
Hispanohablantes **WB** pp. 6–8		✔

Presentación escrita

Poemas en diamante

Task
Write a diamond-shaped poem that describes you.

1 Prewrite Use these steps to write your poem:

1. Escribe tu nombre.
2. Escribe dos adjetivos que no te describen.
3. Escribe tres adjetivos que te describen.
4. Escribe cuatro actividades que haces todos los días.
5. Escribe tres actividades que tus amigos y tú hacen en el verano.
6. Escribe dos actividades que nunca haces.
7. Escribe "¡Así soy yo!"

2 Draft Write your poem in the shape of a diamond.

3 Revise Show your poem to a partner, who will check:

- Did you include all the information from Step 1?
- Are the adjectives and verb forms correct?
- Is there anything you should add or change?

Rewrite your draft, making any necessary changes.

4 Publish Put your poem on a sheet of paper or poster board. Decorate it with images that are representative of you.

5 Evaluation The following rubric will be used to grade your presentation.

Estrategia

Organizing your thoughts
Follow the guidelines of a graphic organizer in a diamond shape as you write your poem. This will help you organize your ideas and improve your writing.

Rubric	Score 1	Score 3	Score 5
Completeness of your task	You provide some of the information required.	You provide most of the information required.	You provide all of the information required.
Your use of adjectives and verbs	You use adjectives and verbs with many grammatical errors.	You use adjectives and verbs with occasional grammatical errors.	You use adjectives and verbs with very few grammatical errors.
Neatness and attractiveness of your presentation	You provide no visuals and your poster contains visible error corrections and smudges.	You provide few visuals and your poster contains visible error corrections and smudges.	You provide several visuals, have no error corrections and smudges, and your poster is attractive.

Me llamo Linda.

No soy ni seria ni vieja.

Soy alta, sociable, estudiosa.

Todos los días yo escucho música, leo, corro, uso la computadora.

En el verano mis amigos y yo nadamos, cantamos, bailamos.

Nunca patino ni monto en bicicleta.

¡Así soy yo!

Vocabulario Repaso

las clases

el arte
las ciencias naturales
las ciencias sociales
la educación física
el español
el inglés
las matemáticas
la tecnología

descripciones de las clases

aburrido, -a
difícil
divertido, -a
fácil
interesante
práctico, -a

en mi mochila

un bolígrafo
una calculadora
una carpeta
una carpeta de argollas
un cuaderno
un diccionario
una hoja de papel
un lápiz
un libro
la tarea

mi horario

primera hora
segunda hora
tercera hora
cuarta hora
quinta hora
sexta hora
séptima hora
octava hora
novena hora
décima hora

en la sala de clases

una bandera
un cartel
un escritorio
una mesa
la papelera
la puerta
un pupitre
un reloj
un sacapuntas
una silla
la ventana

▼1 Tu escuela

Hablar • Escribir

Un estudiante de América Central estudia en tu escuela este año.
Usa la información del organizador gráfico y dile *(tell him):*

- una clase que tienes   *Tengo . . .*
- el nombre del profesor / de la profesora
  El (La) profesor(a) se llama . . .
- cómo es la clase   *La clase es . . .*

- las cosas que traes a la clase todos los días
  Todos los días traigo . . .
- a qué hora tienes la clase   *Tengo la clase a las . . .*
- si te gusta o no te gusta la clase y por qué
  Me gusta / No me gusta la clase porque . . .

Gramática Repaso

The verb *tener*

Use the verb *tener* to show relationship, possession, or age, or in other expressions such as *tener hambre / sueño / sed*.

(yo)	tengo	(nosotros) (nosotras)	tenemos
(tú)	tienes	(vosotros) (vosotras)	tenéis
Ud. (él) (ella)	tiene	Uds. (ellos) (ellas)	tienen

Use *tener que* + infinitive to say that something has to be done.

Tenemos que escribir mucho en la clase de inglés.

Verbs with irregular *yo* forms

Some verbs are irregular in the *yo* form only.

hacer *(to do, to make)*	poner *(to put)*	traer *(to bring)*
hago	pongo	traigo

Hago la tarea de español todos los días.
Pongo los libros en el escritorio.
Traigo una carpeta a la clase.

▼2 ¿Qué tienen que hacer?

Escribir

¿Qué tienen que hacer estas personas en sus clases? Escribe frases con una actividad diferente para cada persona.

Modelo

mi amiga (nombre)
Mi amiga Gloria tiene que usar la computadora.

1. yo
2. mi amigo *(nombre)*
3. nosotros
4. mis amigos
5. la profesora
6. tú

Más práctica GO

realidades.com | print

A ver si recuerdas with Study Plan ✔
Guided WB pp. 15–16 ✔ ✔
Core WB pp. 5–6 ✔ ✔
Hispanohablantes **WB** p. 10 ✔

▼3 ¿Cómo son las clases?

Leer • Escribir

Completa la siguiente conversación con la forma correcta del verbo apropiado. Luego escribe un párrafo para describir tus clases.

A —¿Qué __1.__ *(traer / hacer)* Uds. en la clase de ciencias?

B —Nosotros __2.__ *(tener / hacer)* muchas cosas diferentes. Estudiamos plantas y animales. A veces el profesor __3.__ *(poner / hacer)* un experimento y nosotros __4.__ *(tener / traer)* que escribir nuestras observaciones.

A —¿El profesor __5.__ *(traer / hacer)* animales o insectos a la clase para estudiar?

B —Sí, él __6.__ *(poner / hacer)* un animal sobre la mesa y nosotros lo describimos. A veces los estudiantes __7.__ *(poner / traer)* una planta o una piedra interesante a la clase también.

A —¿ __8.__ *(Traer / Tener)* Uds. mucha tarea en la clase?

B —Sí. Leemos mucho y __9.__ *(traer / hacer)* una prueba cada semana. Yo siempre __10.__ *(poner / hacer)* mi libro de ciencias en mi mochila porque hay tarea todos los días.

Capítulo 1A ¿Qué haces en la escuela?

Estudiantes en Cartagena, Colombia

▼ Chapter Objectives

Communication

By the end of this chapter you will be able to:

- Listen and read about classes and classroom rules
- Talk and write about classroom activities and schoolwork
- Exchange information about what you do in class

Culture

You will also be able to:

- Understand the meaning and role of coats of arms in the Spanish-speaking world
- Compare school rules and customs in the Spanish-speaking world and the U.S.

You will demonstrate what you know and can do:

- Presentación oral, p. 37
- Preparación para el examen, p. 41

You will use:

Vocabulary
- School activities and rules
- Items you need for class

Grammar
- Stem-changing verbs
- Affirmative and negative words

Exploración del mundo hispano

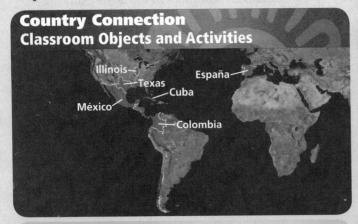

Country Connection
Classroom Objects and Activities

Illinois
Texas
México
Cuba
España
Colombia

realidades.com (GO)

 Reference Atlas

 Videocultura y actividad

🌎 **Mapa global interactivo**

Arte y cultura | México

Diego Rivera El artista mexicano Diego Rivera (1886–1957) pintó cuadros y también murales en edificios importantes de México y de los Estados Unidos. Durante cuatro años, Rivera pintó murales por todo el interior del edificio de la Secretaría de Educación Pública en la Ciudad de México. *Alfabetización* muestra la importancia de la educación pública gratis *(free)* en México.

• En tu opinión, ¿es necesaria la educación pública gratis? ¿Por qué?

"Alfabetización. Aprendiendo a leer." (1923–1928), Diego Rivera ▶

| ▼ **Objectives**

Read, listen to, and understand information about
▶ school activities and rules
▶ items you need for class

Vocabulario en contexto

❝ ¡Hola! Me llamo Miguel. En mi escuela siempre estamos muy ocupados. Vamos a ver **lo que** hacemos en las clases ❞.

Estos estudiantes **discuten** la tarea en **el laboratorio**.

Estos estudiantes hacen **un proyecto de arte**.

sacar una buena nota

Marcos escribe **un informe sobre** la música latinoamericana.

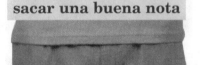

Victoria **repite** las palabras nuevas para **aprender de memoria** el vocabulario.

La profesora le **explica** a Elena cómo usar la computadora.

La profesora de español de la Escuela Benito Juárez prepara un cartel con **las reglas** de la escuela. ¿Cuáles son las reglas?

Más vocabulario

alguien someone, anyone
ningún, ninguno, -a no, none
prestar atención to pay attention
respetar to respect

Hay que . . .

• Hay que llevar el carnet de identidad.

• Hay que entregar la tarea a tiempo.

hacer una pregunta

contestar

• Hay que pedir ayuda si no entiendes.

la cinta adhesiva

las tijeras

• Hay que traer los materiales a clase.

la grapadora

• Hay que estar en el asiento cuando la clase empieza.

Se prohíbe . . .

• Se prohíbe ir al armario durante las clases.

• Se prohíbe almorzar en la sala de clases.

▼1 ¿Qué hacen en la escuela?

Escuchar

Escucha lo que estos estudiantes hacen en la escuela y señala el dibujo apropiado.

▼2 ¿Qué reglas tienes?

Escuchar

Escucha estas seis reglas. Si tienes la misma regla en tu clase de español, levanta una mano. Si no tienes la regla, levanta las dos manos.

Más práctica (GO)   realidades.com | print

Instant Check	✔	
Guided WB pp. 17–22	✔	✔
Core WB pp. 7–8	✔	✔
Comm. WB p. 12	✔	✔
Hispanohablantes WB p. 12		✔

La clase de Esteban

¿Qué pasa con Esteban el primer día de clases? Lee la historia.

Estrategia

Making inferences
As you read the story, think about why such strange things are happening to Esteban.

• Why is Esteban acting like the teacher?
• Why is his mother in the class?

1

Esteban: Bienvenidos a la clase de historia. **Algunos** de Uds. me **conocen** como Esteban. Pero hoy soy el profesor.

Pedro: Esteban piensa que es el profesor. ¡Qué divertido!

Pedro · Esteban · Angélica · Mamá · Lisa

5

Esteban: ¡No! ¡Se prohíbe ir al armario durante la clase! **Nadie** tiene el libro. Es el primer día de clases.

6

Esteban: Mamá, ¿por qué estás aquí en la clase?

Mamá: No tengo idea. ¿Y qué vas a enseñar hoy?

7

Mamá: ¿Por qué no empiezas?

Esteban: Es la clase de historia. Pienso **dar un discurso** sobre algunos de los presidentes de los Estados Unidos . . . El primer presidente fue George Washington . . .

Esteban: Señoritas, ¿saben qué hora es?

Angélica: Hola, Esteban. Son las nueve y seis.

Esteban: Y la clase empieza a las nueve y cinco. ¿Por qué **llegan tarde** Uds.?

Lisa: Pero, ¿por qué estás tú delante de la clase? ¿Dónde está la profesora?

Esteban: Yo soy el profesor. ¡Y hay que estar en el asiento cuando la clase empieza!

Lisa: Profesor . . . necesito ir al armario. No tengo el libro.

Mamá: Esteban. Esteban. ¡Ya es tarde!

Esteban: ¿Qué pasa? ¿Dónde estoy? ¡Ay! El primer día de clases . . .

▼**3** **¿Comprendiste?**

Escuchar • Hablar

1. ¿Quién es el profesor de la clase?
2. ¿Quiénes llegan tarde a la clase?
3. ¿Adónde necesita ir Lisa? ¿Por qué?
4. ¿Qué enseña Esteban?
5. ¿Sobre qué da un discurso Esteban?
6. ¿Cuáles son las reglas en la clase de Esteban?

Más práctica GO

realidades.com | print

Instant Check	✔	
Guided WB pp. 23–26	✔	✔
Core WB pp. 9–10	✔	✔
Comm. WB pp. 6–8, 9	✔	✔
Hispanohablantes **WB** p. 13		✔

▼ **Objectives**

▶ Talk about what you and others do at school
▶ Discuss classroom activities and rules
▶ Write about your classes

Vocabulario en uso

▼4 ¿Qué tienen que hacer?

Escribir • Hablar

1 Estudia los dibujos y escribe frases para describir las actividades que estos estudiantes tienen que hacer en cada clase.

Gloria

Modelo
Gloria tiene que dar un discurso en la clase de historia.

1. Isabel

2. Luis

3. Victoria

4. Marta y Eva

5. David y Clara

6. Mercedes y Ana

2 Habla con otro(a) estudiante sobre lo que ustedes tienen que hacer en sus clases.

 Modelo

A —*¿En qué clase tienes que dar un discurso?*

B —*Tengo que dar un discurso en la clase de literatura.*

Para decir más . . .

el álgebra *(f.)* algebra	**la historia** history
la biología biology	**la literatura** literature
la física physics	**la química** chemistry
la geografía geography	*Para más clases, mira la página 14.*
la geometría geometry	

▼5 ¡Tantas actividades! |

Hablar

Con otro(a) estudiante, habla de lo que hacen estos estudiantes en su escuela.

▶ **Modelo**

A —¿Qué hace Lisa en la clase de español?
B —*Repite las palabras para aprender de memoria el vocabulario.*

▼6 Tus clases |

Escribir • Hablar

① Haz una lista de cinco clases que tienes. Escribe una frase para describir lo que pasa en cada clase. Usa las expresiones del recuadro.

hacer proyectos	dar discursos
hacer preguntas	escribir informes
aprender de memoria	trabajar en el laboratorio

Modelo

En la clase de inglés, la profesora da muchos discursos.

② Trabaja con otro(a) estudiante y comparen lo que hacen en diferentes clases.

▶ **Modelo**

A —*En la clase de inglés, la profesora da muchos discursos.*
B —*En la clase de inglés, la profesora nunca da discursos.*
o: —*No tengo una clase de inglés.*

▼7 Para ser un(a) buen(a) estudiante |

Escribir • Hablar

Completa las frases. Después compara tus opiniones con las de otro(a) estudiante.

Modelo

Para sacar una buena nota, . . .
Para sacar una buena nota, hay que estudiar mucho.

1. Para aprender de memoria el vocabulario, . . .

2. Para entender mejor la tarea, . . .

3. Para leer mejor en español, . . .

4. Para hacer un proyecto de arte, . . .

5. Para ir a la universidad, . . .

6. Para un examen, . . .

> **¿Recuerdas?**
>
> *Para* has a number of different meanings. Here are some you've seen:
>
> • *in order to*
> Estudio **para** sacar buenas notas.
>
> • *intended for*
> Estos materiales son **para** el proyecto.
>
> • *in (my) opinion*
> **Para** mí, las reglas son muy buenas.

▼8 ¿Qué hago? | 🗨️ 👥

Hablar

Habla de los problemas que tienes en la escuela. Tu compañero(a) va a decirte lo que debes hacer.

▶ Modelo

sacar malas notas

A —*Saco malas notas en la clase de inglés.*

B —*Tienes que pedir ayuda.*

o: —*Hay que pedirle ayuda a la profesora.*

Estudiante A

1. tener hambre
2. no traer ni tijeras, ni grapadora ni cinta adhesiva
3. no tener la tarea de . . .
4. no entender la tarea
5. no saber las reglas
6. muchas veces llegar tarde
7. hablar mal de los profesores

Estudiante B

saber las reglas
almorzar
entregar la tarea a tiempo
llegar a tiempo
pedir ayuda

traer los materiales a clase
respetar a los demás
prestar atención

Estos estudiantes mexicanos están tomando apuntes *(taking notes)* en clase.

▼9 ¿Qué aprendes de memoria?

Leer • Escribir • Hablar

En la escuela debes aprender muchas palabras y fechas de memoria. En casa, aprendes números de teléfono y fechas de cumpleaños. Si te gusta la música, también aprendes canciones de memoria. Aquí hay parte de un poema muy famoso, *Versos sencillos*. Lee el poema y busca los cognados para ayudarte a entenderlo mejor. Luego contesta las preguntas.

1. ¿Cuáles son los cognados que te ayudan a entender el poema?
2. ¿Qué le da el poeta a un buen amigo? ¿Y al cruel?
3. ¿Qué palabras riman *(rhyme)* en el poema?
4. ¿Te gusta el poema? ¿Por qué?

Conexiones | La literatura

Versos sencillos[1]
José Martí

Cultivo una rosa blanca,
en julio como en enero,
para el amigo sincero
que me da su mano franca.

Y para el cruel que me arranca[2]
el corazón[3] con que vivo,
cardo[4] ni ortiga[5] cultivo:
cultivo una rosa blanca.

* * *

[1]simple [2]pulls out [3]heart [4]thistle
[5]nettle *(a thorny plant)*

▼10 ¡Aprende el poema!

Leer • Hablar

Lee el poema *Versos sencillos* varias veces. Luego practica con otro(a) estudiante sin mirar las palabras. Tu compañero(a) te puede ayudar. Recita el poema en grupos pequeños o para la clase. Hay que:

• hablar claramente
• expresar emoción
• comunicar los sentimientos del poeta

Estrategia

Memorizing
Repeating out loud is a good strategy for memorizing any text, such as this poem. It will also help you to remember new vocabulary and verbs.

 Fondo Cultural | Cuba

José Martí (1853–1895) fue un poeta y patriota cubano muy famoso. Él es un símbolo de la independencia de Cuba de los españoles. Los versos que acabas de leer son sólo una pequeña parte del poema *Versos sencillos*, en el que el poeta describe su poesía y la vida *(life)* con palabras sencillas y sinceras. Muchas personas creen que este poema es lo mejor de su trabajo literario. Las palabras de la canción "Guantanamera" son de estos versos.

• ¿Qué poema o poeta es famoso por ser símbolo de la independencia de los Estados Unidos?

Una estatua de José Martí en la ciudad de Nueva York

▼11 Las reglas de mis clases |

Escribir • Hablar

Copia esta tabla. En la tabla, escribe todas tus clases, las horas y las reglas. Luego escribe una descripción.

Trabaja con otro(a) estudiante y habla de las reglas en las clases. ¿Tienen las mismas reglas en las mismas clases? ¿Qué piensa tu compañero(a) de estas reglas?

Clase / Hora	Hay que...	Se prohíbe...
matemáticas /segunda	usar una calculadora	hablar con los amigos

▶️ Modelo

A —*En la clase de educación física, hay que llevar uniformes. Se prohíbe tomar refrescos. ¿Qué piensas?*

B —*En mi clase también hay que llevar uniformes y no debes tomar refrescos. ¡Estoy de acuerdo! Son buenas reglas porque . . .*

o: —*¡No estoy de acuerdo! No debemos llevar uniformes y me gustaría tomar refrescos.*

▼12 Y tú, ¿qué dices? | 🗨️

Escribir • Hablar

1. ¿Qué actividades te gusta hacer en tus clases? ¿Cuáles no te gusta hacer?

2. ¿Qué proyectos haces en tus clases?

3. Piensa en las reglas de tus clases. ¿Qué regla(s) no te gusta(n)? ¿Por qué?

4. ¿Cuál es tu clase favorita este año? ¿Qué tienes que hacer en esta clase? ¿Qué se prohíbe?

5. ¿Siempre entiendes todo en tus clases? ¿Qué haces si no entiendes algo?

▼13 Citas sobre la educación

Leer • Escribir

Lee las citas *(quotes)* sobre la educación. ¿Qué quiere decir cada persona? ¿Piensan que la educación es importante? Escoge dos citas y escribe un párrafo para compararlas. Explica lo que las citas quieren decir y da tu opinión.

"El fundamento verdadero de la felicidad: la educación". —Simón Bolívar (1783–1830), militar y político venezolano

Modelo

Las palabras de Gabriela Mistral quieren decir que hay una conexión importante entre la educación y el país. Yo estoy de acuerdo porque . . .

"Según como sea¹ la escuela, así será² la nación entera". —Gabriela Mistral (1889–1957), poeta y educadora chilena

"Todos los problemas son problemas de educación". —Domingo Faustino Sarmiento (1811–1888), escritor, educador y político argentino

¹is ²shall be

Gramática Repaso

Stem-changing verbs

The stem of a verb is the part of the infinitive that is left after you drop the endings *-ar, -er,* or *-ir*. For example, the stem of *empezar* is *empez-*. Stem-changing verbs have a spelling change in their stem in all forms of the present tense except the *nosotros(as)* and *vosotros(as)* forms.

There are three kinds of stem-changing verbs that you have learned. To review them, here are the present-tense forms of *poder (o → ue), empezar (e → ie),* and *pedir (e → i).*

—Si no **puedes** contestar una pregunta, ¿qué haces?
—Generalmente le **pido** ayuda a otro estudiante o al profesor.

poder (o → ue)

(yo)	**pued**o	(nosotros) (nosotras)	**pod**emos
(tú)	**pued**es	(vosotros) (vosotras)	**pod**éis
Ud. (él) (ella)	**pued**e	Uds. (ellos) (ellas)	**pued**en

empezar (e → ie)

(yo)	**empiez**o	(nosotros) (nosotras)	**empez**amos
(tú)	**empiez**as	(vosotros) (vosotras)	**empez**áis
Ud. (él) (ella)	**empiez**a	Uds. (ellos) (ellas)	**empiez**an

pedir (e → i)

(yo)	**pid**o	(nosotros) (nosotras)	**ped**imos
(tú)	**pid**es	(vosotros) (vosotras)	**ped**ís
Ud. (él) (ella)	**pid**e	Uds. (ellos) (ellas)	**pid**en

Más ayuda	realidades.com

 GramActiva Video
Tutorial: Conjugation of stem-changing verbs
Animated Verbs

 Canción de hip hop: ¿Cómo aprendes tú?

 GramActiva Activity

▼14 Mi clase favorita

Leer • Escribir

Completa las frases con la forma correcta del verbo apropiado.

> **¿Recuerdas?**
>
> Here are more stem-changing verbs that follow the patterns above.
>
> | o → ue | u → ue | e → ie | e → i |
> |---|---|---|---|
> | almorzar | jugar | entender | servir |
> | costar | | pensar | repetir |
> | dormir | | preferir | |
> | | | querer | |

Es increíble pero mi clase favorita __1.__ *(empezar / entender)* a las siete y media de la mañana. El profesor, el Sr. Díaz, es muy simpático y él __2.__ *(pedir / entender)* que todos tenemos mucho sueño en la mañana. Ningún estudiante __3.__ *(dormir / querer)* en esta clase porque siempre estamos muy activos. Yo creo que los estudiantes __4.__ *(preferir / poder)* las clases que tienen más actividades. Generalmente el Sr. Díaz __5.__ *(repetir / querer)* las instrucciones para las actividades dos o tres veces. A veces nosotros no __6.__ *(entender / servir)* los ejercicios en el libro y __7.__ *(pensar / pedir)* ayuda. El Sr. Díaz siempre __8.__ *(jugar / poder)* ayudarnos.

▼15 Juego | | ♻

Hablar • GramActiva

Con otros(as) tres estudiantes, van a hacer dos cubos para su grupo con el modelo que les da su profesor(a).

Escriban un pronombre *(yo, tú, él, ella, nosotros, nosotras, Uds., ellos, ellas)* diferente en cada cara *(side)* del cubo 1. Escriban también un número diferente del 1 al 6 en cada cara.

Escriban un infinitivo diferente en cada cara del cubo 2. Escojan entre los verbos que ves aquí. Escriban también un número diferente del 1 al 6 en cada cara.

almorzar	jugar	preferir
dormir	pedir	querer
empezar	pensar	repetir
entender	poder	servir

Tiren *(Roll)* los dos cubos y, según el resultado, formen una frase. Si la frase es lógica y correcta, reciben los puntos que indican los números en los cubos, pero si la frase no es ni lógica ni correcta, no reciben nada. El grupo con más puntos gana *(wins)*.

Modelo

yo (= 6 puntos)   preferir (= 2 puntos)
Yo prefiero estudiar español y ciencias sociales. (= 8 puntos)

▼16 Un día típico | 💬👥

Escribir • Hablar

¿Puedes describir tu día típico en la escuela? Usa las palabras y expresiones en el recuadro y escribe un párrafo sobre tus clases, tus compañeros, los profesores y lo que haces durante el día.

yo ✓	almorzar	durante la clase de . . .
mi amigo(a)	empezar ✓	en la cafetería
el (la) profesor(a)	(no) dormir	en la clase de . . .
nosotros	(no) entender	muy temprano
las clases	preferir	sacar buenas / malas notas
mis amigos	querer	

Ahora compara tus descripciones con las de otro(a) estudiante. Hablen de las diferencias y las semejanzas *(similarities)* en el día de cada uno de ustedes.

Estos estudiantes argentinos almuerzan en la cafetería de su escuela.

▼17 Tu proyecto favorito . . .

Escribir • Hablar

Contesta las siguientes preguntas. Compara tus respuestas con las de otro(a) estudiante.

1. ¿En qué clases haces muchos proyectos?
2. ¿Prefieres hacer proyectos o tomar exámenes? ¿Por qué?
3. ¿Quieres hacer un proyecto en tu clase de español? ¿Qué tipo de proyecto?
4. ¿Pides ayuda cuando tienes que hacer un proyecto? ¿A quién?
5. Cuando haces un proyecto, ¿qué materiales usas?

Unos estudiantes pintan un mural en el barrio de Pilsen, Chicago, Illinois.

▼ Pronunciación | 🔊 | 💬

The letters *b*, *v*, and *d*

The letters *b* and *v* are both pronounced the same. When the *b* or *v* is the first letter of a word or follows an *m* or *n*, it is pronounced like the English letter *b*. Listen to and say these words:

> **b**ien **v**ecinos tam**b**ién in**v**ierno

In all other positions, the letters *b* and *v* have a softer "b" sound. To produce it, put your lips close together (but not touching) and push the air through them. Listen to and say these words and sentences:

> gusta**b**a jó**v**enes ár**b**ol de**v**ol**v**er
>
> **B**enito **V**ásquez era un hom**b**re que viaja**b**a en **B**rasil.
>
> Mi novio vi**v**ía en el Cari**b**e pero ahora vi**v**e en **B**uenos Aires.

Like the *b* and *v*, the Spanish *d* can have a hard or a soft sound. The *d* is hard at the beginning of a word or after *n* or *l*, like the *d* in the English word *dough*. Listen to and say these words:

> donde desfile falda cuando aprender

Otherwise the *d* is soft like the English *th* in the English word *though*. Listen to the soft *d* in these words and repeat them:

> ciudad moderno cuñado boda ayudar

Repeat the following *refranes*. What do you think they mean?

> **Un hombre que sabe dos lenguas vale por dos.**
>
> **Quien mucho vive, mucho ve.**

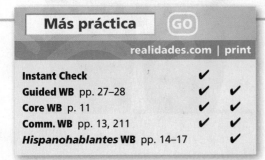

"GOOD MORNING." "BUENOS DÍAS."

Más práctica	(GO)	
realidades.com	print	
Instant Check	✔	
Guided WB pp. 27–28	✔	✔
Core WB p. 11	✔	✔
Comm. WB pp. 13, 211	✔	✔
Hispanohablantes WB pp. 14–17		✔

▼18 ¿Sacas buenas notas?

Leer • Escribir • Hablar

Mira las notas de Nora, una estudiante de Zacatecas, México. Observa cómo son las notas en la escuela de Nora. Observa también el número de asignaturas *(subjects)* que ella estudia.

1. ¿Cuál es la nota más alta de Nora? ¿Y la más baja?
2. ¿Cuántas asignaturas estudia Nora?
3. ¿Qué asignatura(s) estudia Nora que tú no estudias?
4. ¿Para qué semestre son las calificaciones?

▼Fondo Cultural | México

Las notas El sistema de notas, o calificaciones, en México va del 1 (que es la nota más baja) al 10 (que, lógicamente, es la nota más alta). ¡Pero no todas estas notas son buenas! Para aprobar *(pass)* una asignatura necesitas una nota mínima de 6. Notas de 6 y 7 son equivalentes a una nota de "C" en los Estados Unidos. Notas de 8 son equivalentes a una "B" y las de 9 y 10 son como una "A".

• ¿Cómo son tus notas según el sistema de México?

Gobierno del Estado de Zacatecas
Secretaría de Educación y Cultura
Dirección de Educación Media Superior y Superior

José Rodríguez Elías

La dirección de la escuela preparatoria *Ing.* _____ certifica que, según constancias¹ que están en el archivo de e: con clave ___32EBH0007Y___ escuela el (la) alumno(a) Nora Ramírez Valenzuela con clave única de registro de población (CURP) __RAVN850303MZSMLR__ cursó las asignaturas del primer semestre del plan de estudi: bachillerato del período escolar ___2001–2002___ que a continuación se detallan:

ASIGNATURAS	CLASES POR SEMANA	CALIFICACIÓN FINAL	
		CIFRA	LETRA
Matemáticas	4	8	OCHO
Física I	4	9	NUEVE
Inglés I	3	10	DIEZ
Biología I	4	9	NUEVE
Química I	4	10	DIEZ
Etimologías latinas	3	8	OCHO
Metodología de la ciencia I	4	7	SIETE
Introducción a las ciencias sociales I	4	9	NUEVE
Informática I	2	8	OCHO
Orientación vocacional I	1	ACREDITADA	
Educación física I	1	ACREDITADA	

OBSERVACIONES
1. El plan de estudios está integrado en cursos semestrales.
2. El año escolar comprende² 40 semanas.
3. La escala⁴ oficial de calificaciones es numérica del 5 al 10.

Gramática

Affirmative and negative words

By now you know many affirmative and negative words.

Affirmative		Negative	
alguien	someone, anyone	**nadie**	no one, nobody
algo	something	**nada**	nothing
algún, alguno(s), alguna(s)	some, any	**ningún, ninguno, ninguna**	no, none, not any
siempre	always	**nunca**	never
también	also, too	**tampoco**	neither, either

¿Recuerdas?

To make a sentence negative, you usually put *no* in front of the verb.

• **No** sacamos buenas notas en la clase de álgebra.

Sometimes you can also use a negative word after the verb.

• **No** estudiamos **nunca** el sábado por la noche.

Alguno, alguna, algunos, algunas, and *ninguno, ninguna* match the number (singular or plural) and gender (masculine or feminine) of the noun to which they refer.

—¿Uds. van al laboratorio de computadoras en **algunas** clases?

—No, no vamos al laboratorio en **ninguna** clase.

When *alguno* and *ninguno* come before a masculine singular noun, they change to *algún* and *ningún*.

—¿Vas a dar **algún** discurso en la clase de inglés?

—No, no voy a dar **ningún** discurso.

Más ayuda **realidades.com**

▶ *GramActiva* Video
Tutorial: Indefinite and negative expressions

GramActiva Activity

▼19 Los profesores muy estrictos

Leer • Escribir

Los profesores de la escuela de Hugo son muy estrictos. Completa las descripciones con la palabra apropiada.

¡La profesora de álgebra es la más estricta de la escuela! __1.__ (*Ninguno/Ningún*) estudiante quiere estudiar con ella. Hay muchas reglas en la clase __2.__ (*también/tampoco*). En la clase de historia, tenemos __3.__ (*ninguna/algunas*) reglas, y son muy estrictas. En nuestra escuela __4.__ (*nunca/siempre*) podemos comer __5.__ (*nada/algo*) en clase. __6.__ (*También/Tampoco*) podemos beber. En la clase de ciencias puedo trabajar con __7.__ (*nadie/alguien*) para hacer la tarea. Pero, para la clase de inglés, no podemos trabajar con __8.__ (*nadie/alguien*). En la clase de español __9.__ (*siempre/nunca*) trabajamos en parejas o en grupos para hacer proyectos. No conozco __10.__ (*ninguna/alguna*) escuela con tantas reglas. ¡Esta escuela tiene __11.__ (*algunos/algunas*) de los profesores más estrictos!

▼20 ¿Qué conoces y a quién conoces? |

Hablar

Trabaja con otro(a) estudiante y habla de algunas personas y cosas que conoces en tu escuela.

> **¿Recuerdas?**
>
> *Conocer* means "to know" or "to be familiar with" a person, place, or thing. It is a regular *-er* verb except in the *yo* form: *conozco*. When you say that you know a person, use *a* after the verb.
>
> - **Conozco a** Estela, la amiga de Juan.
> - **¿Conoces** la escuela Benito Juárez?
>
> When using *conocer* with *alguien* or *nadie*, use *a* after the verb, since both words refer to a person.
>
> - **¿Conoces a** alguien en esta escuela?
> - No, no **conozco a** nadie.

▶ Modelo

estudiantes trabajadores

A —¿Conoces a *algunos estudiantes trabajadores*?

B —*No, no conozco a ningún estudiante trabajador.*

o: *Sí, conozco a algunos. Enrique y Sara son muy trabajadores.*

1. profesores graciosos
2. estudiantes reservados
3. clase aburrida
4. chica estudiosa
5. libro interesante en la biblioteca
6. buenos lugares para estudiar
7. secretarias de la escuela

▼21 ¿Y en tu escuela? |

Hablar

Haz las siguientes preguntas a otros(as) dos estudiantes. Comparen sus experiencias en diferentes clases.

1. ¿En qué clases puedes comer? ¿En cuáles puedes beber?
2. ¿Cuándo vienes a clases los fines de semana?
3. ¿Cuándo llegas temprano a la escuela? ¿Cuándo llegas tarde a casa?
4. ¿A veces puedes trabajar con alguien en algún proyecto o alguna tarea? ¿En cuál(es)?
5. ¿Cuáles son algunas de las reglas de tu clase de español? ¿Cuáles son algunas de las reglas de tus otras clases?

▼ Fondo Cultural | El mundo hispano

¿Más estrictos? En muchos países hispanohablantes *(Spanish-speaking)*, las relaciones entre *(between)* los profesores y los estudiantes son más formales que en los Estados Unidos. En muchas escuelas, los estudiantes se levantan *(stand up)* cuando los profesores llegan a la sala de clases. Los estudiantes usan "usted" cuando hablan con un(a) profesor(a), y muchas veces los llaman "profesor" o "profesora" sin decir el apellido *(last name)*.

- Piensa en cómo te comunicas con tus profesores. ¿En qué sentido *(way)* es similar o diferente a cómo se comunican en los países hispanohablantes? ¿Cómo afecta las relaciones entre los profesores y los estudiantes?

▼22 En la sala de clases

Escribir • Hablar

Imagina que tu clase está en un país hispanohablante. Las relaciones entre los estudiantes y los profesores son más formales. En grupos de cuatro, escriban un guión *(script)* sobre diferentes situaciones en la clase. Luego actúen su drama para la clase. Una persona es profesor(a) y los otros son estudiantes.

Modelo

La profesora entra en la sala de clases. Los estudiantes están de pie.
Clase: *Buenos días, profesora.*
La profesora: *Buenos días.*

▼23 Y tú, ¿qué dices?

Leer • Escribir

Lee lo que Joaquín te escribe por correo electrónico desde México. Luego escríbele una carta a Joaquín para contestar sus preguntas.

¡Hola!

¿Cómo estás? Yo estoy bien, pero tengo muchísima tarea. Tengo que escribir un informe para la clase de inglés. Quiero comparar las clases aquí en México con las clases de los Estados Unidos. ¿Me puedes ayudar? ¿Cuáles son las reglas de tus clases? ¿Qué cosas debes hacer? ¿Hay que llevar el carnet de identidad? ¿Qué se prohíbe? ¿Puedes llegar tarde a las clases? ¿Qué es lo que hay que hacer para sacar buenas notas en tus clases? Por favor, contesta mis preguntas. ¡Gracias!

Joaquín

El español en el mundo del trabajo

El profesor de español, Craig Reubelt, enseña en la *Laboratory Schools* de la Universidad de Chicago. Empezó a estudiar español a los 13 años y vivió en México por dos años. Tiene una maestría *(master's degree)* en Literatura de la Universidad de Chicago. En los veranos, el profesor Reubelt siempre viaja a un país hispanohablante.

- ¿Qué es lo que hay que hacer para ser un(a) buen(a) profesor(a)? ¿Quieres ser profesor(a) de español?

"Me encanta enseñar español y explicar cosas sobre las culturas hispanas".

Más práctica | GO

realidades.com | print

Instant Check	✔	
Guided WB pp. 29–30	✔	✔
Core WB pp. 12–13	✔	✔
Comm. WB pp. 11, 14	✔	✔
Hispanohablantes **WB** pp. 18–21		✔

▼ **Objectives**

▶ Read about good study habits
▶ Use heads and subheads to predict reading content
▶ Compare and contrast teen magazines

Lectura
Para estudiar mejor...

Para comprender bien tus clases y sacar buenas notas, es importante estudiar bien. Pero hay muchos estudiantes que no saben estudiar. A veces no prestan atención y otras veces no piden ayuda cuando no entienden algo. Lee estos consejos *(advice)* para estudiar mejor de la revista española *Okapi*.

Estrategia

Using heads and subheads
Reading the heads and subheads in an article will often help you anticipate the material being presented. Before you read the magazine article below, try reading the head and subheads. What kinds of advice do you think will be in the article?

¡ENTRE NOSOTROS!
REGLAS DE ORO¹
PARA ESTUDIAR MEJOR

Silvia López, fiel lectora² de *Okapi*, nos da estas interesantes técnicas de estudio para los exámenes. Queremos repetirlas aquí para todos ustedes.

¹gold ²faithful reader

¿Comprendiste?

1. ¿Cierto o falso? No es necesario estudiar a la misma hora todos los días.
2. Según el artículo, ¿es importante ser una persona organizada?
3. ¿Qué consejos del artículo ya *(already)* practicas?
4. ¿Qué piensas de estos consejos? ¿Son fáciles de seguir *(to follow)* en tu casa?
5. ¿Qué otros consejos para estudiar mejor les puedes dar a tus compañeros?

Más práctica	GO

realidades.com | print

Guided WB p. 31	✔	✔
Comm. WB pp. 15, 212	✔	✔
Hispanohablantes WB pp. 22–23		✔
Cultural Reading Activity	✔	

▼ **Fondo Cultural** | El mundo hispano

Revistas para jóvenes Hay muchas revistas para jóvenes en español. Por ejemplo, la revista española *Okapi* tiene artículos sobre temas como los estudios, la vida social, la música y la escuela. Hay secciones dedicadas a las ciencias, los deportes, la historia, la tecnología, los libros y mucho más.

- ¿Lees una revista similar a *Okapi*? ¿Qué tipos de revistas puedes identificar en esta foto?

¿Qué debes hacer a la hora de estudiar?

Para estudiar mejor necesitas una buena organización de trabajo y unos hábitos saludables. Siempre debes ser positivo. Repite frases como "yo puedo hacerlo" o "soy capaz[3]". Cuida[4] tus libros y otros materiales. Generalmente una persona constante, organizada y trabajadora tiene buenos resultados en los estudios.

¿Cómo puedes organizarte para estudiar?

Establece un horario fijo para estudiar y planifica tu tiempo. Tienes que pasar suficiente tiempo para llegar al punto de máxima concentración. También debes planear unos pequeños descansos de 5 a 10 minutos. Y si no entiendes algo, pide ayuda: ¡Tus padres o tus hermanos mayores te pueden ayudar!

¿Cómo puedes estudiar mejor y sacar buenas notas?

Tienes que cuidarte. Debes comer bien y dormir lo suficiente. Por ejemplo, no es bueno estudiar muy tarde por la noche antes de un examen. Debes estar tranquilo, sin estar ni nervioso ni ansioso. La tranquilidad emocional te ayuda a pensar mejor. También tienes que cuidar tu vista[5]: cuando lees, el libro debe estar a 35–40 cm de distancia de tus ojos y siempre debes usar una buena lámpara.

[3]capable   [4]Take care of   [5]vision

La cultura en vivo

Un nuevo escudo de armas

Los escudos de armas[1] son una manera antigua de identificar a las familias importantes o a los reyes[2]. Los escudos tienen símbolos, animales y colores que representan a la familia. Hoy, muchas familias continúan usando los escudos de armas. Muchas compañías, universidades y escuelas también usan escudos de armas que son una versión moderna de esta manera de identificación.

Figura 1 Éste es el escudo del Reino de España. En la parte de arriba está la corona *(crown)* de los reyes.

¡Compruébalo! ¿Tiene tu escuela un escudo de armas? Investiga si tu escuela tiene uno y cuál es su significado.

Objetivo

Haz un escudo de armas para tu escuela. Si tu escuela tiene uno, haz otro nuevo.

Materiales

• hojas grandes de papel
• lápices de colores

Instrucciones

Trabaja con un grupo de tres o cuatro estudiantes.

1 Piensen en los símbolos de su escuela. ¿Cómo pueden usar estos símbolos en su nuevo escudo?

2 Dibujen la forma de un escudo o hagan una copia del escudo en la Figura 2.

3 Escojan tres o más símbolos.

4 Escojan tres o más colores.

5 Escojan un lema[3] en español para la escuela, por ejemplo, *Siempre listos* o *Salud, trabajo y bienestar.*

6 Dibujen el escudo y preséntenlo a la clase.

¹coats of arms ²kings ³slogan

Figura 2

Presentación oral

Director(a) por un día

Task

As principal for a day, your first task is to create new school rules and display them on a poster. You will present your poster to the class.

❶ Prepare List six new school rules to create a supportive environment where people will learn better. Include three things students must do and three that are not allowed. Illustrate your rules with a poster.

❷ Practice Using your poster, go through your presentation several times. You can use your notes when you practice, but not when you present. Be sure to:

- include three things that students must do and three that are not allowed
- use complete sentences
- speak clearly

Modelo

Éstas son mis reglas nuevas: Todos los estudiantes deben hacer preguntas si no entienden algo. Y hay que . . . ¡Se prohíbe hablar inglés en la clase de español! Y tampoco deben . . .

❸ Present Explain your new school rules, using your poster.

❹ Evaluation The following rubric will be used to grade your presentation.

Directora

Rubric	Score 1	Score 3	Score 5
Completeness of your task	You provide some of the information required.	You provide most of the information required.	You provide all of the information required.
How easily you are understood	You are difficult to understand and have many grammatical errors.	You are fairly easy to understand and have occasional grammatical errors.	You are easy to understand and have very few grammatical errors.
How clearly your visuals match your rules	You provide four visuals that clearly match your rules.	You provide five visuals that clearly match your rules.	You provide six visuals that clearly match your rules.

Estrategia

Brainstorming
Before you prepare a presentation, think of all the possible ideas for your project. List *all* your ideas, without judging whether they are good or bad. Then go back and review your list. Pick the best ones for your presentation.

Preparación para . . .

En busca de la verdad

Las *estudiantinas* de Guanajuato son grupos de jóvenes que pasean cantando y caminando por las calles. Llevan trajes de diferentes colores y tocan instrumentos musicales.

Guanajuato

Bienvenidos a Guanajuato, lugar principal del *Videomisterio*. A unos 450 kilómetros al noroeste de la Ciudad de México, Guanajuato tiene una población de más de 141,000 habitantes y es una ciudad con mucha historia. En los dos primeros Temas, van a conocer algunos lugares que tienen importancia en el video *En busca de la verdad*. Van a empezar a ver el video con el Tema 3.

Esta bella ciudad tiene una hermosa arquitectura del período colonial (siglos[1] XVI a XVIII). Esto fue posible gracias a la riqueza[2] de sus minas durante la colonización española de México. Estas minas hicieron de Guanajuato una ciudad muy importante, con costumbres y tradiciones españolas.

Hoy en día, Guanajuato todavía es una de las ciudades mexicanas más importantes en la producción de plata[3]. Sus minas, tal como la *Bocamina de la Valenciana,* son lugares de mucho valor histórico y cultural. ▶

Guanajuato es famosa por sus grandes héroes y batallas de la independencia mexicana (1810–1821). "El Pípila" es un monumento en homenaje al minero Juan José de los Reyes Martínez. En 1810 él se convirtió en héroe cuando le prendió fuego[4] a la puerta de la fortificación española, llamada *Alhóndiga de Granaditas.* ▶

[1]centuries [2]riches [3]silver [4]set fire

Guanajuato es famosa por sus estrechas y empedradas[5] calles, llamadas *callejones*. También es un gran centro artístico, intelectual y cultural. Aquí nació el muralista Diego Rivera. Hay una respetada universidad en el centro. También hay una gran cantidad de museos, algunos artísticos, como el *Museo Iconográfico del Quixote,* y otros raros[6], como el *Museo de las Momias.*

Guanajuato celebra cada octubre el *Festival Cervantino.* Es en honor al escritor español Miguel de Cervantes y llegan personas de todo el mundo.

¿Sabes que . . . ?

Guanajuato tiene muchas calles subterráneas. Las calles son productos de las viejas minas y antiguos ríos. Éstas permiten que los coches pasen por la ciudad sin afectar la arquitectura colonial y el estilo de vida guanajuatense.

Para pensar

La belleza colonial y la vida cultural de Guanajuato atraen a visitantes de todo el mundo. ¿Qué ciudad estadounidense conoces que hace lo mismo?

[5]narrow and cobblestoned   [6]strange

Repaso del capítulo

Vocabulario y gramática

to talk about what you do in class

aprender de memoria	to memorize
contestar	to answer
dar un discurso	to give a speech
discutir	to discuss
explicar	to explain
hacer una pregunta	to ask a question
el informe	report
el laboratorio	laboratory
la palabra	word
pedir (e → i) ayuda	to ask for help
el proyecto	project
sacar una buena nota	to get a good grade

to talk about classroom rules

a tiempo	on time
entregar	to turn in
llegar tarde	to arrive late
prestar atención	to pay attention
la regla	rule
respetar	to respect
se prohíbe . . .	it's forbidden . . .

to name school objects

el armario	locker
el asiento	seat
el carnet de identidad	I.D. card
la cinta adhesiva	transparent tape
la grapadora	stapler
los materiales	supplies, materials
las tijeras	scissors

For *Vocabulario adicional*, see pp. 498–499.

negative and affirmative words

alguien	someone, anyone
algún, alguna, algunos, -as	some, any
nadie	no one, nobody
ningún, ninguno, -a	no, none, not any

(See p. 31 for a complete chart.)

other useful words

conocer (c → zc)	to know
lo que	what
sobre	on, about

almorzar (o → ue) *to have lunch*

almuerzo	almorzamos
almuerzas	almorzáis
almuerza	almuerzan

empezar (e → ie) *to start, to begin*

empiezo	empezamos
empiezas	empezáis
empieza	empiezan

entender (e → ie) *to understand*

entiendo	entendemos
entiendes	entendéis
entiende	entienden

repetir (e → i) *to repeat*

repito	repetimos
repites	repetís
repite	repiten

Más repaso GO realidades.com | print

Instant Check	✔	
Puzzles	✔	
Core WB pp. 14–15		✔
Comm. WB p. 213	✔	✔

Preparación para el examen

On the exam you will be asked to . . .	Here are practice tasks similar to those you will find on the exam . . .	For review go to your print or digital textbook . . .

Interpretive

 1 Escuchar Listen to and understand how students describe what they must do and what they cannot do in class

Listen as two students compare their Spanish classes. (a) What are two things that students do in both classes? (b) What are two things that are different? (c) Which class would you prefer? Why?

pp. 18–21 *Vocabulario en contexto*

Interpersonal

 2 Hablar Ask and respond to statements made about classroom activities

Your teacher has asked you and a partner to see which classroom activities are the most common. Each of you will make a chart with a list of your classes across the top. Then think of five or six classroom activities and write them down the side of your chart. Write an *X* next to the activities that you do in each class. Then describe how often you do these activities.

Doy discursos en las clases de historia, español e inglés. Hablo sólo español en la clase de español todos los días.

p. 22 Actividad 4
p. 23 Actividades 5–6
p. 24 Actividad 7
p. 28 Actividades 15–16
p. 29 Actividad 17
p. 32 Actividad 21

Interpretive

 3 Leer Read and understand a list of typical classroom rules

Read the rules below. Write the numbers 1–5 and then write a *P* for those statements that you think were the idea of *un(a) profesor(a)* or an *E* for those you think were written by *un(a) estudiante.*

1. Se prohíbe hacer la tarea a tiempo.
2. Hay que pedir ayuda si no entiendes.
3. Hay que prestar atención.
4. Se prohíbe traer libros a la clase de literatura.
5. Hay que dormir en las clases.

p. 31 Actividad 19
p. 33 Actividad 23
p. 37 *Presentación oral*

Presentational

 4 Escribir Write a paragraph about your favorite class

In a short paragraph, describe your favorite class. Include: (a) what you do in the class; (b) the kind of homework you have.

p. 26 Actividad 12
p. 27 Actividad 14
p. 29 Actividad 17

Cultures

 5 Pensar Demonstrate an understanding of coats of arms

You are researching *los escudos* before creating one for an assignment. A list of Web sites gives historical examples from Spanish-speaking countries. Based on what you have learned, what types of decoration would you expect to find on them? Where would they be displayed?

p. 36 *La cultura en vivo*

▼ Objectives
▶ Talk and write about places and leisure activities
▶ Express where you and others go and what you do there

Vocabulario Repaso

los lugares

el café
el centro comercial
el cine
el gimnasio
el parque
el restaurante
el trabajo
la biblioteca
la casa
la iglesia, la mezquita,
  el templo, la sinagoga
la piscina

las actividades

caminar
dormir
escuchar música
hablar por teléfono
ir a la lección de
  (piano)
ir de compras
jugar videojuegos
leer
pasar tiempo con
  amigos
tocar (la guitarra)
trabajar
hacer trabajo
  voluntario
usar la computadora

los deportes

correr
hacer ejercicio
ir al partido
jugar al (básquetbol,
  béisbol, fútbol, golf,
  tenis, vóleibol)
levantar pesas

▼1 ¿Qué haces?

Escribir • Hablar

❶ En una hoja de papel, dibuja una tabla como la que está aquí. Escoge cinco lugares de la lista de vocabulario y escríbelos en la primera columna de la tabla. Entrevista a dos compañeros(as) de clase. Pregúntales si van a los lugares de la tabla. Ellos deben contestar según el modelo, usando *todos los días, a veces* o *nunca*. Después pregúntales qué hacen en los lugares.

▶ **Modelo**
A —*¿Vas al gimnasio después de las clases?*
B —*Sí, a veces voy al gimnasio.*
A —*¿Qué haces allí?*
B —*Levanto pesas y juego al básquetbol.*

❷ Ahora completa la tabla con información personal. Después de hacerlo, compara tu tabla con las de tus compañeros. Guarda *(Keep)* tu tabla para la Actividad 2.

nombre:			
lugares	todos los días	a veces	nunca
el gimnasio			

Gramática Repaso

The verb *ir*

Use *ir* to say where someone is going.

(yo)	voy	(nosotros) (nosotras)	vamos
(tú)	vas	(vosotros) (vosotras)	vais
Ud. (él) (ella)	va	Uds. (ellos) (ellas)	van

> **¿Recuerdas?**
>
> Spanish has two contractions:
>
> *a* + *el* = *al*
>
> *de* + *el* = *del*
>
> • Mis amigos y yo vamos **al** café después de las clases.
>
> • El nombre **del** café es Café Sol.

ir + *a* + infinitive

Use *ir* + *a* + infinitive to tell what someone is going to do.

Vamos a hablar por teléfono después de las clases.

▼2 ¿Adónde vamos?

Escribir

Usa la información de la Actividad 1 para escribir frases que dicen adónde van tus compañeros y tú y qué hacen allí.

Modelo

otro(a) estudiante y tú
Después de las clases Lisa y yo vamos a casa.
Usamos la computadora todos los días.

1. otros dos estudiantes
2. un(a) estudiante y tú
3. un(a) estudiante
4. otros dos estudiantes y tú
5. tú

> **Más práctica** (GO)
>
> realidades.com | print
>
> *A ver si recuerdas* with Study Plan ✔
> **Guided WB** p. 33 ✔ ✔
> **Core WB** pp. 16–17 ✔ ✔
> *Hispanohablantes* WB p. 30 ✔

▼3 ¿Qué vas a hacer?

Escribir

Di qué va a hacer cada una de estas personas. Usa los verbos del recuadro para contestar las preguntas.

Modelo

¿Qué va a hacer Jorge en el gimnasio?
Él va a jugar al vóleibol.

beber	estudiar	leer
comprar	jugar	nadar

1. ¿Qué van a hacer Uds. en el centro comercial?
2. ¿Qué van a hacer tus hermanos en la piscina?
3. ¿Qué va a hacer Mario en el parque?
4. ¿Qué va a hacer Verónica en la biblioteca?
5. ¿Qué voy a hacer en casa?

Capítulo 1B

¿Qué haces después de las clases?

▼ Chapter Objectives

Communication

By the end of this chapter you will be able to:

- Listen and read about students' after-school activities
- Talk and write about your extracurricular activities
- Exchange information about what you do after school

Culture

You will also be able to:

- Understand the differences between schools in the United States and Spain
- Compare extracurricular activities, sports, and dance in the United States and Latin America

You will demonstrate what you know and can do:

- Presentación escrita, p. 65
- Preparación para el examen, p. 69

You will use:

Vocabulary

- Extracurricular activities
- Sports
- Music and drama

Grammar

- Making comparisons
- The verbs *saber* and *conocer*
- *Hace* + time expressions

Exploración del mundo hispano

Country Connection
Extracurricular Activities

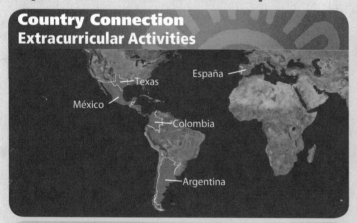

España
Texas
México
Colombia
Argentina

 realidades.com **GO**

 Reference Atlas

▶ **Videocultura y actividad**

 Mapa global interactivo

Jugadores de fútbol mexicanos

Arte y cultura | Argentina

Antonio Berni (1905–1981) nació en Rosario, Argentina, y fue uno de los artistas más importantes de Argentina y de América Latina. A veces Berni pintó *(painted)* cuadros con temas populares como éste que muestra *(shows)* el equipo de fútbol del barrio. Este cuadro es un buen ejemplo del estilo realista de Berni y vemos cómo pintó a cada uno de los jugadores como individuo.

• ¿Qué importancia tiene el fútbol en la cultura latinoamericana? ¿Qué actividades extracurriculares tienen importancia en tu comunidad? ¿Por qué?

"Club Atlético Nueva Chicago" (1937), Antonio Berni

Oil on canvas, 6'¾ x 9' 10¼". Inter-American fund (645.1942). The Museum of Modern Art/Licensed by Scala-Art Resource, NY. Digital Image © 2004 Museum of Modern Art, New York.

Vocabulario en contexto

—En mi escuela los estudiantes **participan** en muchas **actividades extracurriculares.** Les gusta practicar deportes o son **miembros** de algún **club,** como el club de computadoras. Éstas son algunas de las actividades más populares **entre los jóvenes.**

—¿Tienes tú **la oportunidad** de participar en muchas actividades? ¿Tiene tu escuela **tantas** actividades **como** mi escuela? ¿Cuánto tiempo **hace que** participas?

el ajedrez

jugar a los bolos

la animadora

el animador

el músico

la música

la banda

el equipo

Tienes que ir a **los ensayos** de la banda o a **las prácticas** del equipo de básquetbol para participar.

grabar una canción

la orquesta

la cantante

el coro

el cantante

El coro y la orquesta están grabando una canción.

el bailarín

la fotógrafa

la bailarina

el fotógrafo

Los dos fotógrafos son miembros del club de **fotografía. Hace dos años que son** miembros del club.

¡Bienvenidos!

... navegar en la Red.

BIENVENIDOS
a la página de Ramón

... crear una página Web **99**.

66 Conozco a varios miembros del club de computadoras. Creo que este club es **tan** interesante **como** los otros clubes. En el club puedo . . .

¡Encuéntralo aquí!

... hacer una búsqueda.

Ramón está en línea. Le gusta visitar salones de chat.

66 Me gusta ir al **club atlético 99**.

las artes marciales

el hockey

hacer gimnasia

la natación

> **Más vocabulario**
> ganar   to win, to earn
> el pasatiempo   pastime

▼1 Unos estudiantes muy ocupados | 🔊

Escuchar

Escucha a un estudiante que describe las actividades en su escuela. Señala cada actividad que él describe.

▼2 ¿Sí o no? | 🔊

Escuchar

Escucha las frases. Si lo que escuchas es lógico, señala con el pulgar hacia arriba (*thumbs-up*). Si la respuesta no es lógica, señala con el pulgar hacia abajo (*thumbs-down*).

Más práctica GO	realidades.com | print	
Instant Check	✔	
Guided WB pp. 34–40	✔	✔
Core WB pp. 18–19	✔	✔
Comm. WB p. 21	✔	✔
Hispanohablantes **WB** p. 32		✔

Después de las clases

¿En qué actividades extracurriculares participan Esteban y sus amigos? Vamos a ver.

Estrategia

Using visuals
Using the photographs that accompany the dialogue can help you understand what is being said.

1

Angélica: Hola, todos. Otro año nuevo. ¡Me encanta el primer día de clases! Hola, Lisa.

Lisa: Hola, Angélica. Esteban, ¿cómo estás?

Esteban: Estoy cansado. No dormí bien anoche.

Lisa: Lo siento. Siéntense.

Pedro Lisa Angélica Esteban

5

Angélica: Prefiero los deportes. Voy a ser miembro* del equipo de fútbol en la primavera. También soy animadora.

6

Pedro: Yo prefiero trabajar porque me gusta ganar dinero. También **tomo lecciones** de artes marciales en un club atlético. Me gusta mucho el karate.

7

Angélica: ¿Practicas mucho las artes marciales?

Pedro: Participo en algunas competiciones.

Lisa: ¿Ganas a veces?

Esteban: Pedro gana más que "a veces". Él tiene el cinturón negro. ¿Qué piensas de él ahora?

*The word *miembro* is used for both male and female students.

Lisa: ¿Tienen **interés** en participar en actividades extracurriculares este año?

Esteban: Hace dos años que soy miembro del club de computadoras. ¿A alguien le interesa **asistir a la reunión** conmigo esta tarde?

Lisa: Soy miembro de la banda y de la orquesta.

Angélica: ¿Vas a cantar en el coro también? Tienes **una voz** bonita.

Lisa: Sí, gracias. ¿Y tú? ¿Por qué no cantas en el coro? Vamos a **ensayar** hoy.

Angélica: Pedro, eres muy talentoso.

Pedro: Gracias.

Lisa: Pedro, ¡eres tan misterioso! ¿Tienes más secretos?

Angélica: Bueno, hay que **volver** a clases. ¡Hasta luego!

▼3 ¿Comprendiste?

Escribir • Hablar

1. ¿Dónde están los estudiantes? ¿De qué hablan?
2. ¿En qué actividad participa Esteban? ¿Cuánto tiempo hace que es miembro?
3. ¿Cuáles son las actividades extracurriculares de Lisa?
4. ¿Qué prefiere hacer Angélica?
5. ¿Por qué trabaja Pedro?
6. ¿Qué lecciones toma Pedro? ¿Dónde? ¿Es bueno?

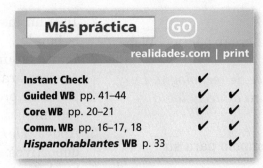

Más práctica	GO	
realidades.com	print	
Instant Check	✔	
Guided WB pp. 41–44	✔	✔
Core WB pp. 20–21	✔	✔
Comm. WB pp. 16–17, 18	✔	✔
Hispanohablantes WB p. 33	✔	

Vocabulario en uso

▼4 Las actividades de mis amigos

Leer • Escribir

Completa las frases con la palabra apropiada.

Mis amigos y yo __1.__ *(participamos / volvemos)* en muchas actividades extracurriculares. Mi amiga Raquel tiene una buena __2.__ *(voz / reunión)*. Por eso, canta en __3.__ *(el coro / el ensayo)*. A mi amiga Gloria le encanta el español. Ella es __4.__ *(miembro / reunión)* del club de español. Raquel y Gloria también tocan un instrumento en la orquesta. Tienen __5.__ *(un ensayo / el interés)* todas las tardes. María es muy deportista. __6.__ *(Hace gimnasia / Estudia)* en el gimnasio y también es __7.__ *(animadora / bailarina)* para el equipo de fútbol de la escuela. A mí me gustan los deportes. Por la tarde __8.__ *(practico / asisto)* las artes marciales. Tengo el cinturón amarillo. También me gustan las computadoras. Con mi amigo Pedro, visitamos __9.__ *(salones de chat / la práctica)*. Somos __10.__ *(miembros / jóvenes)* del club de computadoras. Cuando no estamos ocupados con nuestras actividades, nos gusta ir al cine o tomar un refresco en un café.

> **También se dice . . .**
>
> **el animador, la animadora** = el/la porrista *(México, Colombia)*
>
> **jugar a los bolos** = jugar al boliche *(Costa Rica, México)*

Rubén Blades es un cantante y actor panameño muy popular.

▼5 ¿Quién es? | ♻

Leer • Escribir

Lee estas descripciones. Para cada una, escribe la palabra que corresponde a la descripción. Después escribe una frase sobre alguien que tú conoces (una persona de tu comunidad o una persona famosa) usando la palabra.

Modelo

Enseña a los estudiantes a crear páginas Web y a hacer búsquedas en la Red.
Es una profesora de la clase de tecnología. La Sra. Ramos es una profesora de tecnología fantástica.

1. Saca fotos como pasatiempo o para su trabajo.

2. Toca un instrumento en la orquesta o en la banda.

3. Canta en un coro o en otro grupo musical. A veces graba canciones también.

4. Baila en programas de la escuela o de la comunidad.

5. Apoya *(He / She supports)* a los equipos deportivos. A veces baila y hace gimnasia también.

▼6 En tu escuela |

Hablar

¿A quién conoces en tu escuela que participa en actividades extracurriculares? Habla con otro(a) estudiante de estas personas.

▶ Modelo

A —¿Conoces a un miembro de <u>la banda</u>?

B —Sí, conozco a Ryan Johnston. Es un miembro de la banda. Asiste a <u>los ensayos todos los días.</u>

o: No, no conozco a ningún miembro de la banda.

o: No tenemos banda.

Estudiante A

1. el club de
2. el equipo de
3.
4. el equipo de
5. el club de
6.

Estudiante B

las reuniones	todos los días
las prácticas	a menudo
los ensayos	a veces

¡Respuesta personal!

▼7 Escucha y escribe | 🔊

Escuchar • Escribir

Escucha lo que dice una estudiante de Managua, Nicaragua, sobre las actividades extracurriculares allí. Escribe los números del 1 al 5 en una hoja de papel y escribe lo que escuchas. Después indica si estas actividades son populares entre los jóvenes de tu comunidad también.

▼ Fondo Cultural | El mundo hispano

Las actividades extracurriculares En América Latina, generalmente no hay oportunidades en las escuelas para participar en un coro, equipo deportivo, lecciones de artes marciales u otras actividades después de las clases. Los estudiantes que tienen interés en aprender algún pasatiempo como la fotografía, la música o el baile, van a centros culturales o talleres *(workshops)* en su comunidad.

• ¿Hay centros culturales en tu comunidad? ¿Qué actividades hay allí?

▼8 Las actividades populares | | ♻

Escribir • Hablar

❶ Escribe tres frases para describir qué actividades haces después de las clases. Usa las actividades del recuadro.

Modelo
Después de las clases yo voy a casa y navego en la Red. También tomo lecciones de piano. A veces voy a un club atlético.

las artes marciales	la orquesta
el hockey	el béisbol
la natación	la música
la fotografía	los videojuegos
la banda	el ajedrez
el coro	

❷ Habla con tres estudiantes para saber qué hacen después de las clases. Escribe los nombres de los estudiantes y las actividades que hacen ellos.

 Modelo
A —¿*En qué actividades extracurriculares participas después de las clases?*
B —*Ensayo con la orquesta y después voy al club atlético. También tomo clases de artes marciales.*

❸ Escribe cinco frases sobre las actividades que hacen tus compañeros y tú.

Modelo
Pablo ensaya con la orquesta. Marisa va a casa y navega en la Red.

Unos amigos juegan a los bolos, Colombia

▼9 Y tú, ¿qué dices? | Talk!

Escribir • Hablar

1. ¿Qué te gusta más, ser miembro de un club o participar en un deporte? ¿Por qué?

2. ¿Usas la computadora mucho o poco en tu tiempo libre? ¿Para qué usas más la computadora? ¿Cuánto tiempo pasas en línea cada día?

3. ¿Cuáles son las actividades más populares en tu escuela? Describe por qué son populares.

4. ¿Hay suficientes actividades para jóvenes en tu comunidad? ¿Qué otras actividades debe ofrecer (*offer*)?

Gramática

Making comparisons

To compare people or things that are equal to one another, you use:

tan + *adjective* + como	*as + adjective + as*

En mi club, levantar pesas es **tan** popular **como** correr.

To say that things are *not* equal, you can use the negative.

En el club atlético, levantar pesas **no** es **tan** popular **como** correr.

To say "as much as" or "as many as," you use:

tanto, -a + *noun* + como	*as much + noun + as*
tantos, -as + *noun* + como	*as many + noun + as*

Note that *tanto* agrees in gender and number with what is being compared.

Hay **tantas** actrices en el ensayo **como** actores.

¿Recuerdas?

You already know several ways to compare things and people.

más + *adjective* + que

menos + *adjective* + que

mayor que / menor que

mejor que / peor que

You also know how to say that someone or something is "the most" or "the least":

el / la / los / las + *noun* + más / menos + *adjective* + de

el / la / los / las + mejor(es) / peor(es) + *noun* + de

• Cecilia cree que hacer gimnasia es **la actividad más divertida de** la escuela.

Más ayuda | realidades.com

 GramActiva Video

GramActiva Activity

▼10 Comparaciones

Leer • Escribir

Estás hablando de personas de tu escuela. Completa las siguientes frases con la palabra apropiada.

1. La canción de Mercedes es _____ (tan / tanta) buena como la de Enrique.

2. Elena no es _____ (tanta / tan) deportista como Angélica.

3. La voz de Catalina es _____ (tan / tanto) bonita como la voz de Victoria.

4. En la banda no hay _____ (tantos / tan) músicos como en la orquesta.

▼11 En la escuela

Leer • Escribir

Todos hacemos comparaciones. Ahora es tu turno. Completa las siguientes frases y usa la forma apropiada de *tanto*.

1. yo / (no) tener / amigos(as) / como Luz

2. este año nosotros / (no) tener / profesores interesantes / como el año pasado

3. el equipo de fútbol americano / (no) tener / partidos / como el equipo de básquetbol

4. los chicos / (no) tener / oportunidades para hacer gimnasia / como las chicas

5. (no) hay / interés en el club de ajedrez / como en el club de ciencias

▼12 ¿Qué piensas de . . . ? | | ♻

Hablar

Habla con otro(a) estudiante sobre lo que Uds. piensan de los siguientes temas. Usen la expresión *tan . . . como* y un adjetivo apropiado. Si prefieren, pueden usar también expresiones como *más . . . que* y *menos . . . que* para expresar sus opiniones.

▶ Modelo

A —¿Qué piensas de *la clase de matemáticas y la clase de ciencias?*
B —*Pienso que* la clase de matemáticas es tan *difícil* como la clase de ciencias. ¿Y tú?
A —*Pienso que* la clase de matemáticas es *más interesante* que la clase de ciencias.

Estudiante A

1. la música clásica / la música rock
2. el fútbol americano / el fútbol
3. jugar a los bolos / jugar al ajedrez
4. los deportes de verano / los deportes de invierno
5. hacer gimnasia / practicar las artes marciales
6. practicar la fotografía / crear una página Web

Estudiante B

bonito, -a	fácil
emocionante	interesante
difícil	aburrido, -a

¡Respuesta personal!

▼13 Las actividades más populares | 👥 | ♻

Escribir • Hablar

1 Trabaja con otro(a) estudiante. Escriban tres preguntas que pueden hacerles a los otros estudiantes de la clase sobre diferentes categorías de actividades, pasatiempos, deportes y personas.

Modelo

Para ti, ¿cuál es la actividad extracurricular más importante?
En tu opinión, ¿quién es el (la) cantante más talentoso(a) de la escuela?

2 Cada estudiante debe hablar con otros(as) dos compañeros(as) y hacerles las preguntas. Escribe sus respuestas. Con tu compañero(a), comparen las respuestas a sus preguntas.

3 Hagan una presentación sobre las opiniones de sus compañeros de clase.

Modelo

Muchos estudiantes piensan que la actividad extracurricular más importante es el deporte en equipos. Otros estudiantes dicen que el coro y la banda son tan importantes como los deportes.

🌐 Fondo Cultural | El mundo hispano

Los deportes más populares El fútbol es el deporte preferido entre muchos jóvenes hispanohablantes. En la República Dominicana, Puerto Rico, Cuba, Venezuela y otros países, el béisbol es tan popular como el fútbol y muchas veces es el deporte más popular.

• ¿Cuáles son los deportes más populares en tu ciudad? Compara estos deportes con los de los jóvenes hispanohablantes. En tu opinión, ¿qué deporte es el mejor? ¿Por qué?

▼14 Los músicos | 👥

Escribir • Hablar

Mira estos dos cuadros del gran artista colombiano Fernando Botero. ¿En qué sentido *(way)* son similares? ¿En qué sentido son diferentes?

"Los músicos" (1979), Fernando Botero
Oil on canvas, 74(1).75 x 85.5 in. © Fernando Botero courtesy of the Marlborough Gallery, NY.

"Tres músicos" (1983), Fernando Botero
Oil on canvas, 64.5 x 48.5 in. © Fernando Botero courtesy of the Marlborough Gallery, NY.

1 Copia el diagrama de Venn y escribe Cuadro 1 y Cuadro 2 encima de los círculos según el modelo. Escribe las características diferentes de cada cuadro en el círculo apropiado y las características similares en la intersección de los círculos. Luego escribe tres frases comparando los cuadros.

Modelo

Cuadro 1   Los dos   Cuadro 2

nueve músicos   músicos grandes   tres músicos

Los músicos en el primer cuadro son tan grandes como los músicos en el segundo cuadro.

2 Trabaja con un grupo de tres. Lee una de tus frases. En grupo, escriban una comparación de los dos cuadros. Usen las ideas de todos los miembros del grupo. Presenten su comparación a la clase.

Modelo

Hay más músicos en el primer cuadro que en el segundo cuadro.

🌐 Fondo Cultural | Colombia

Fernando Botero es conocido por su estilo de arte único *(unique)*. Es famoso tanto por sus cuadros como por sus esculturas. Esta escultura de un pájaro sufrió daños *(was damaged)* durante una explosión en 1995. Con el material dañado, Botero hizo una nueva escultura y la dedicó a la paz.

• Compara esta escultura con los cuadros de Botero. También compara la escultura con las esculturas en tu comunidad. ¿En qué sentido son similares y en qué sentido son diferentes?

"El Pájaro" (Little Bird or The Sparrow) (1988), Fernando Botero. Medium series, bronze sculpture. Courtesy of Jeremy Horner. © 2003 Corbis.

Más práctica (GO)

realidades.com | print

Instant Check	✔	
Guided WB pp. 45–46	✔	✔
Core WB p. 22	✔	✔
Comm. WB pp. 19, 22	✔	✔
Hispanohablantes **WB** pp. 34–37		✔

Gramática Repaso

The verbs *saber* and *conocer*

You already know the present-tense forms of *saber* and *conocer*. *Saber* and *conocer* both follow the pattern of regular *-er* verbs in the present tense, but each has an irregular *yo* form.

¿Recuerdas?

Use the *a personal* when you use *conocer* to say you know a person.

- Guillermo **conoce a** mi primo Tomás.

(yo)	sé	(nosotros) (nosotras)	sabemos
(tú)	sabes	(vosotros) (vosotras)	sabéis
Ud. (él) (ella)	sabe	Uds. (ellos) (ellas)	saben

(yo)	conozco	(nosotros) (nosotras)	conocemos
(tú)	conoces	(vosotros) (vosotras)	conocéis
Ud. (él) (ella)	conoce	Uds. (ellos) (ellas)	conocen

- *Saber* means to know facts and information. You can also use *saber* with the infinitive of another verb to say that you know how to do something.

  ¿Sabes si tenemos tarea para mañana?

  ¿Sabes quién es el director de la banda?

  Sé jugar al ajedrez.

- *Conocer* means to know a person or to be familiar with a place or thing.

  ¿Conoces al profesor de esta clase?
  No, no lo conozco.

  ¿Conoces el club atlético de la calle Ocho?

Más ayuda   realidades.com

- **GramActiva Video**
  Tutorial: *Saber* and *conocer*
  Animated Verbs

- **GramActiva Activity**

▼15 Tu profesor(a) quiere saber

Escuchar • GramActiva

En una hoja de papel, escribe *No lo conozco* por un lado y *No lo sé* por el otro. Tu profesor(a) quiere saber lo que sabes y lo que conoces. Escucha sus frases y contesta cada una en el negativo. Muestra el lado apropiado del papel según lo que dice.

No lo conozco.

No lo sé.

▼16 ¡Qué emocionante!

Leer • Escribir

❶ Imagina que un estudiante de intercambio *(exchange student)* viene a tu escuela. Completa las frases de su correo electrónico con las formas apropiadas de los verbos *saber* y *conocer*.

❷ Escríbele una carta por correo electrónico a este estudiante y contesta sus preguntas.

¡Hola!

Voy a ser un nuevo estudiante en tu escuela y tengo muchas preguntas. ¿Puedes ayudarme? Yo no __1.__ nada de tu escuela. ¿Es grande? ¿ __2.__ tú cuántos estudiantes hay? ¿ __3.__ tú a muchos estudiantes? ¿Cómo son? ¿ __4.__ al director de la escuela? ¿Es muy estricto? ¿ __5.__ si tiene muchas reglas? ¿ __6.__ qué tipo de actividades extracurriculares hay en la escuela o comunidad? Soy miembro de una banda en mi comunidad. Toco la trompeta. ¿ __7.__ tocar algún instrumento musical? Me gusta salir con mis amigos después de las clases. ¿ __8.__ muchos lugares bonitos adonde ir? Quiero __9.__ toda la ciudad donde vives.

Escríbeme pronto.

Rogelio

▼17 ¿Conoces a tu compañero(a)? |

Hablar • Escribir

❶ Habla con otro(a) estudiante para conocerlo(la) mejor. Usa el verbo *saber* o *conocer* y hazle preguntas. Escribe sus respuestas.

▶ Modelo

A — *¿Conoces la música de Rubén Blades?*
B — *Sí, la conozco.*
A — *¿Sabes jugar al vóleibol?*
B — *No, no sé jugar al vóleibol, pero sé jugar al fútbol.*

Estudiante A

muchos estudiantes de esta escuela
un buen club atlético
un buen salón de chat para visitar
navegar en la Red

otras ciudades
crear una página Web

¡Respuesta personal!

Estudiante B

¡Respuesta personal!

❷ Usa las respuestas de tu compañero(a) y escribe un párrafo sobre él (ella).

Modelo

Mario es un chico muy talentoso. Sabe jugar al fútbol y al béisbol y sabe usar la computadora. Sabe crear páginas Web y conoce muchos salones de chat . . .

En Malinalco, México

Más práctica [GO]

realidades.com | print

Instant Check	✔	
Guided WB pp. 47–48	✔	✔
Core WB p. 23	✔	✔
Comm. WB pp. 19, 23	✔	✔
Hispanohablantes WB pp. 38–39	✔	

Gramática

| ▼ Objectives

▶ Talk and write about how long people have been doing things
▶ Exchange information about how long you have done certain activities

Hace + time expressions

To ask how long something has been going on, use:

¿Cuánto tiempo + hace que + present-tense verb?

¿Cuánto tiempo hace que eres miembro del club atlético?

How long have you been a member of the athletic club?

¿Cuánto tiempo hace que Uds. practican con el equipo de básquetbol?

How long have you been practicing with the basketball team?

To tell how long something has been going on, use:

Hace + period of time + que + present-tense verb

Hace más de dos años que soy miembro del club atlético.

I've been a member of the athletic club for more than two years.

Hace tres semanas que practicamos con el equipo de básquetbol.

We've been practicing with the basketball team for three weeks.

| **Más ayuda** | **realidades.com** |

 Canción de hip hop: ¿Qué haces después de las clases?

▼18 Hace mucho tiempo que . . . |

Escribir • Hablar

❶ Escribe seis frases para decir cuánto tiempo hace que estos estudiantes hacen diferentes actividades.

Modelo

dos años / Esteban / ser miembro del club
Hace dos años que Esteban es miembro del club de computadoras.

1. diez meses / Pedro / tomar lecciones

2. muchos años / Lisa / hacer

3. un año y medio / Juan y Alberto / participar

4. dos años / yo / ser miembro del club

5. un año / Marta / ser

6. seis años / tú y yo / jugar

❷ Trabaja con otro(a) estudiante. Pregunta y contesta sobre las actividades de los estudiantes.

▶ **Modelo**

A —¿*Cuánto tiempo hace que Esteban es miembro del club de computadoras?*
B —*Hace dos años que es miembro del club.*

▼19 Una entrevista | ♻

Escribir • Hablar

❶ Escribe cinco frases sobre tus actividades favoritas y tus pasatiempos.

❷ Entrevista a otro(a) estudiante para saber en qué actividades participa y cuándo empezó a practicarlas. Escribe las respuestas de tu compañero(a).

▶ Modelo

A —¿En qué actividades participas?
B —Me encanta esquiar en el invierno.
A —¿Cuánto tiempo hace que esquías?
B —Hace diez años que esquío.

▼20 Juego | ♟ | ♻

Escribir • Leer • Escuchar

Usa la información de la Actividad 19 y escribe una descripción de tu compañero(a). No debes incluir el nombre de tu compañero(a) en la descripción. Pon la descripción en una bolsa. Otro(a) estudiante toma una descripción y la lee delante de la clase. La clase tiene que identificar a quién describe.

Modelo

A esta persona le gusta practicar deportes. Hace diez años que . . .

▼21 Una cantante famosa | ♟

Leer • Hablar

Lee esta descripción de una cantante famosa. Después trabaja con otro(a) estudiante para contestar las preguntas.

Celia Cruz

Reina[1] de la salsa

Hace más de 50 años que el mundo[2] conoce y admira a Celia Cruz. Esta cantante y actriz cubana vivió en los Estados Unidos desde[3] los años 60 hasta[4] su muerte, en 2003. Todos la conocen por su música de "salsa". Celia grabó[5] más de 70 discos y recibió 18 nominaciones al Grammy. Recibió su primer Grammy en el año 1989. También conocemos a Celia por sus películas, como *The Mambo Kings*, una película con Antonio Banderas y Armand Assante. Ella es tan famosa que hay una estrella[6] en el Boulevard de Hollywood con su nombre. Otra cantante famosa, Gloria Estefan, dice que "Celia ejemplifica la energía y el espíritu de la música cubana y latina".

[1]Queen [2]world [3]since [4]until [5]recorded [6]star

1. ¿Por qué conoce el mundo a Celia Cruz?

2. ¿Hace cuántos años el mundo conoce a Celia Cruz?

3. ¿De dónde es Celia? ¿Cuánto tiempo hace que ella recibió su primer Grammy?

4. ¿Cómo sabemos que Celia es muy famosa?

Más práctica GO

realidades.com | print

Instant Check	✔	
Guided WB pp. 49–50	✔	✔
Core WB p. 24	✔	✔
Comm. WB pp. 20, 214	✔	✔
***Hispanohablantes* WB** p. 40		✔

▼22 Dibuja una página Web | 👥

Leer • Hablar • Escribir • Dibujar

Trabaja con otro(a) estudiante y dibujen una página Web sobre una actividad extracurricular favorita.

Conexiones | Las computación

Para crear una página Web, pueden empezar a trabajar sin usar una computadora. Dibujen un tablero *(storyboard)* para la página principal. Decidan cómo van a ilustrar la página y qué enlaces *(links)* van a tener. Preparen una presentación de su página Web. Usen la página Web del Club de fotografía de la Escuela Secundaria Vallejo como modelo.

*Equipment

Trabaja con tu compañero(a) y comparen la página Web que Uds. dibujaron con una verdadera página Web de deportes. Luego contesta las siguientes preguntas.

1. ¿Qué información tienen las dos páginas? ¿Qué otra información tiene la verdadera página Web?

2. ¿Qué información no tiene tu página Web?

3. ¿Qué puedes cambiar para dibujar una página Web mejor?

▼ Exploración del lenguaje

Nouns and verbs

In Spanish, you can turn some verbs into nouns by dropping the final *r* of the infinitive and adding *-ción*. The *-ción* ending is equivalent to the *-tion* ending in English. The nouns formed in this way are feminine:

decorar → la decoración

preparar → la preparación

¡Compruébalo! What are the corresponding nouns for each of the following verbs?

celebrar   explicar   observar   participar

And what are the corresponding verbs for these nouns?

comunicación   presentación

graduación   repetición

Refrán

Primero la obligación y entonces la celebración.

▼23 Un anuncio |

Leer • Escribir • Hablar

Lee el folleto *(brochure)* del Club Deportivo Acuasol. Luego contesta las preguntas con otro(a) estudiante.

Bienvenidos

¡Club Deportivo Acuasol!

Deporte

Un estilo de vida

En el Club Deportivo Acuasol, tenemos una misión: dar a nuestra comunidad un lugar agradable para el ejercicio personal y la integración de la familia, a través del* deporte, la recreación y la cultura, con el fin de ofrecer bienestar y calidad de vida. En el Club Deportivo Acuasol hay una variedad de cursos tanto culturales como deportivos, en diferentes horarios y días de la semana.

La mayor parte de nuestras actividades se ofrece sin costo adicional. También tenemos **parqueadero,** **cafetería** y **servicio médico.**

Por eso, empieza desde hoy a cuidar tu salud y a ampliar tus horizontes culturales y sociales aquí en el . . .

¡Club Deportivo Acuasol!

Ofrecemos:

Aeróbicos

Ballet

Cultura

Básquetbol

Danza regional

Jazz

Gimnasia reductiva

Natación

Tae Kwon Do

Tai Chi Chuan

Tenis

Recreación

Yoga

Taller de teatro

Squash

Coro

*through

1. ¿Para qué es este folleto?
2. ¿Qué servicios hay en el Club Deportivo Acuasol?
3. ¿Te gustaría ser miembro de este club? ¿Por qué?
4. ¿Conoces un club atlético en tu comunidad? ¿Tiene ese club tantos servicios diferentes como el Club Deportivo Acuasol? Compara los dos clubes.
5. ¿Eres miembro de algún club? ¿Cómo se llama? ¿Cuánto tiempo hace que eres miembro del club?

El español en la comunidad

La salsa es uno de los bailes más populares entre los hispanohablantes. Hoy en día, muchas veces uno puede encontrar *(find)* clases que enseñan este baile en varios lugares dentro de la comunidad. Busca en el periódico o en tu comunidad o en una comunidad cerca lugares que ofrecen clases de salsa.

• ¿Te gustaría aprender a bailar salsa como actividad extracurricular? ¿Por qué?

▼ **Objectives**

▶ **Read about a dance school**
▶ **Make predictions about reading content**
▶ **Compare and contrast dance in the Spanish-speaking world with that in your community**

Lectura

¡A bailar!

¿Te gusta bailar pero eres un poco tímido? ¿Piensas que bailas muy mal? ¿Necesitas aprender a bailar en seguida? ¡Haz tus sueños realidad hoy mismo! Lee la página Web de la Escuela Internacional de Baile.

Estrategia

Predicting
You are going to read a page from the Web site of a dance school. What kind of information do you expect to see on the page?

Archivo Editar Ver Ir a Favoritos Ayuda

Regresar Siguiente Inicio Recargar Buscar Detener Favoritos

La Escuela Internacional de Baile

● **TANGO**

● **MERENGUE**

● **FLAMENCO**

● **SWING**

te ofrece una gran variedad de clases de bailes tradicionales y contemporáneos.

Razones para hacerse[1] miembro hoy mismo:
• Puedes participar en una actividad sana y deportiva que te ayuda a entender las ricas tradiciones y costumbres de varios países hispanohablantes.
• Si no tienes pareja para bailar, ¡no te preocupes! Puedes conocer a otros jóvenes simpáticos de varias escuelas que vienen a aprender estos bailes.
• Puedes ir a competiciones internacionales en Francia, los Estados Unidos y el Japón, y hasta ganar muchos premios.

[1]Reasons to become

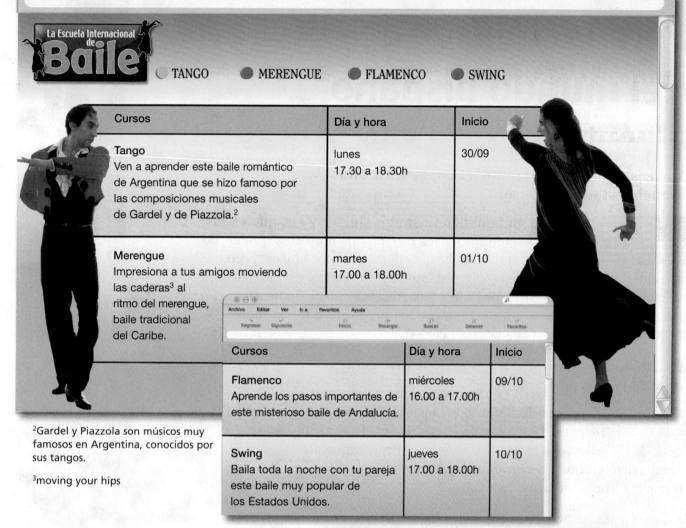

La Escuela Internacional de Baile

○ TANGO ● MERENGUE ● FLAMENCO ○ SWING

Cursos	Día y hora	Inicio
Tango Ven a aprender este baile romántico de Argentina que se hizo famoso por las composiciones musicales de Gardel y de Piazzola.[2]	lunes 17.30 a 18.30h	30/09
Merengue Impresiona a tus amigos moviendo las caderas[3] al ritmo del merengue, baile tradicional del Caribe.	martes 17.00 a 18.00h	01/10

Archivo   Editar   Ver   Ir a   Favoritos   Ayuda

Regresar   Siguiente   Inicio   Recargar   Buscar   Detener   Favoritos

Cursos	Día y hora	Inicio
Flamenco Aprende los pasos importantes de este misterioso baile de Andalucía.	miércoles 16.00 a 17.00h	09/10
Swing Baila toda la noche con tu pareja este baile muy popular de los Estados Unidos.	jueves 17.00 a 18.00h	10/10

[2]Gardel y Piazzola son músicos muy famosos en Argentina, conocidos por sus tangos.

[3]moving your hips

¿Comprendiste?

1. ¿Qué clases puedes tomar en la Escuela Internacional de Baile?
2. ¿Qué razones da la página Web para ser miembro de la escuela?
3. ¿Cuál de los bailes te interesa más? ¿Por qué?
4. ¿Te gustaría tomar una clase en esta escuela? ¿Por qué?

Más práctica   GO

realidades.com | print

Guided WB p. 51	✔	✔
Comm. WB pp. 24, 215	✔	✔
Hispanohablantes WB pp. 42–43		✔
Cultural Reading Activity	✔	

▼ Fondo Cultural | México

El ballet El ballet clásico y el ballet folklórico tienen una larga historia en varios países hispanohablantes. Muchos países tienen un ballet nacional, como el Ballet Nacional de España o el Ballet Folklórico de México. El ballet folklórico se inspira en el folklore, la danza popular y los bailes tradicionales de un país, e interpreta estas tradiciones con técnicas de la danza clásica y moderna. Muchas compañías de ballet también tienen escuelas de baile.

El Ballet Folklórico de México

• ¿El ballet es popular donde vives? ¿Hay algún baile folklórico en tu región? ¿Hay una compañía de ballet en tu ciudad?

Perspectivas del mundo hispano

¡Cuántos libros y cuadernos!

Marcos, un estudiante mexicano, está en una escuela estadounidense.

 "Vivo con mi familia en Estados Unidos y veo que en las escuelas estadounidenses hay menos materias que en las escuelas de mi país. Aquí tenemos menos clases, pero hay más actividades extracurriculares. No usamos tantos libros y cuadernos, pero necesitamos muchas cosas para los deportes, las clases de música y las visitas a lugares interesantes. Siempre les pregunto a mis amigos: "¿Quién me ayuda con todas estas cosas?".

Latifa, una estudiante norteamericana, está en una escuela española.

 "Aquí en España todos los estudiantes tienen muchas clases, 11 ó 12 cada curso. Todos los días hay que llevar a la escuela muchos libros y muchos cuadernos, y también el almuerzo. A veces, ¡no puedo poner todos los libros en la mochila!".

En los países hispanohablantes, los planes de estudio de la educación secundaria y el bachillerato tienen muchas asignaturas[1]. Cada plan de estudio tiene de 10 a 12 asignaturas. En los primeros años, las asignaturas son obligatorias. En los últimos años, puedes escoger[2] algunas de las asignaturas.

¡Compruébalo! Compara tus asignaturas con la lista de asignaturas de la escuela secundaria de España. ¿Qué clases tienes en común con las de este país? ¿Hay clases en España que no tiene tu escuela?

¿Qué te parece? ¿Tienes que llevar muchos libros y cuadernos a clase? ¿Qué otras cosas tienes que llevar? ¿Qué prefieres: tener más asignaturas y menos actividades extracurriculares o menos asignaturas y más actividades?

[1]courses [2]choose

Asignaturas de la escuela secundaria

España

Lengua y literatura castellana

Lengua y literatura de las comunidades autónomas

Lengua extranjera

Matemáticas

Ciencias sociales, Geografía e Historia

Educación física

Ciencias de la naturaleza

Educación plástica y visual

Tecnología

Música

Presentación escrita

Mis actividades extracurriculares

Task
Your teacher wants to learn more about you and has asked you to write about your extracurricular activities and tell why you chose them.

❶ **Prewrite** List your activities and tell why you find them interesting or challenging. Also note how long you have participated in them.

❷ **Draft** Use your list and notes to write a first draft of your paragraph. Try to personalize it as much as possible.

❸ **Revise** Read through your paragraph and check:

- spelling
- verb forms
- use of *hace* + time expressions

> **Estrategia**
>
> **Personalizing**
> To personalize your writing, think about why you enjoy certain activities and what attracts you to them.

Share your paragraph with a partner, who will check:

- Is your paragraph easy to understand?
- Does it give information about you and your activities?
- Is there anything you should add or change?
- Are there any errors?

Rewrite your paragraph, making any necessary changes. You may want to add a personal photo or drawings of the activities.

❹ **Publish** Make a final copy of your paragraph to give to your teacher or to add to your portfolio.

❺ **Evaluation** The following rubric will be used to grade your presentation.

Rubric	Score 1	Score 3	Score 5
How much information you communicate	You provide one activity with explanation.	You provide two activities with explanations.	You provide three or more activities with explanations.
Your use of vocabulary and grammar	You use very little variation of vocabulary and have frequent usage errors.	You use limited vocabulary and have some usage errors.	You use an extended variety of vocabulary and have very few usage errors.
Your use of the writing process	You turn in only the prewrite notes.	You turn in prewrite notes and a rough draft.	You turn in prewrite notes, a rough draft, and a final product.

Preparación para . . .

En busca de la verdad

San Miguel de Allende

Bienvenidos a San Miguel de Allende, una ciudad visitada en el videomisterio. San Miguel de Allende está a unos 92 kilómetros al sudeste de Guanajuato y tiene una población de más de 134,000 habitantes. Fue fundada por Fray Juan de San Miguel en 1542, y a él debe parte de su nombre.

El clima primaveral[1] de San Miguel de Allende la hace una de las ciudades de México más populares para visitar. La ciudad tiene un ambiente[2] cultural y artístico de muchísima variedad. Es famosa por sus restaurantes. También es un refugio para artistas y artesanos. ▶

Según la historia, San Miguel de Allende creció alrededor de un manantial[3] de agua llamado El Chorro. Este famoso manantial que da agua todo el año puede verse en el Paseo del Chorro, un parque popular al sur de la ciudad.

▲ La Plaza Allende es el corazón de la ciudad y uno de los sitios más visitados, especialmente los domingos. Tiene un quiosco y muchos jardines con flores, principalmente rosas. Desde este jardín también puedes ver la Presidencia Municipal[4], casas históricas e iglesias importantes.

[1]spring-like   [2]atmosphere   [3]spring

[4]Town Hall

En esta casa nació Ignacio Allende, uno de los líderes de la independencia mexicana. La estatua es una representación de este gran hombre.

¿Sabes que . . . ?

Ignacio Allende estudió en el colegio de San Francisco de Sales, en San Miguel de Allende. Fue aquí donde recibió la educación que lo inspiró para luchar contra[5] los españoles por la independencia. Después la ciudad tomó el apellido de este héroe.

Para pensar

San Miguel de Allende, igual que Guanajuato, se ha convertido[6] en un centro cultural e intelectual internacional sin perder su ambiente de pueblo tranquilo. ¿En Estados Unidos hay ciudades con las mismas características de San Miguel de Allende? ¿Cuáles son?

[5]to fight against   [6]has been changed

Repaso del capítulo

Vocabulario y gramática

to talk about extracurricular activities

las actividades extracurriculares	extracurricular activities
el ajedrez	chess
el club, pl. los clubes	club
el club atlético	athletic club
el equipo	team
la fotografía	photography
el fotógrafo, la fotógrafa	photographer
los jóvenes	young people
el miembro ser miembro	member to be a member
el pasatiempo	pastime
la práctica	practice
la reunión, pl. las reuniones	meeting

to talk about athletic activities

el animador, la animadora	cheerleader
las artes marciales	martial arts
hacer gimnasia	to do gymnastics
el hockey	hockey
jugar a los bolos	to bowl
la natación	swimming

to talk about music and drama

la banda	band
el bailarín, la bailarina	dancer
la canción, pl. las canciones	song
el (la) cantante	singer
el coro	chorus, choir
ensayar	to rehearse
el ensayo	rehearsal
el músico, la música	musician
la orquesta	orchestra
la voz, pl. las voces	voice

to talk about actions with activities

asistir a	to attend
ganar	to win, to earn
grabar	to record
participar (en)	to participate (in)
tomar lecciones	to take lessons
volver (o → ue)	to return

to talk about and describe Internet activities

crear una página Web	to create a Web page
estar en línea	to be online
hacer una búsqueda	to do a search
navegar en la Red	to surf the Web
visitar salones de chat	to visit chat rooms

other useful words

entre	among, between
el interés	interest
la oportunidad, pl. las oportunidades	opportunity

to tell how long something has been going on

¿Cuánto tiempo hace que . . . ?	How long . . . ?
Hace + time + que . . .	It has been . . .

to make comparisons

tan + adj. + como	as + adj. + as
tantos(as) + noun + como	as much / many + noun + as

saber to know (how)

sé	sabemos
sabes	sabéis
sabe	saben

conocer to know, to be acquainted with

conozco	conocemos
conoces	conocéis
conoce	conocen

For *Vocabulario adicional*, see pp. 498–499.

Más repaso (GO)	realidades.com	print
Instant Check	✔
Puzzles	✔
Core WB pp. 25–26	✔
Comm. WB pp. 216, 217–219	✔ ✔

Preparación para el examen

On the exam you will be asked to . . .	Here are practice tasks similar to those you will find on the exam . . .	For review go to your print or digital textbook . . .

Interpretive

 1 Escuchar Listen and understand as teenagers talk about what they do after school

Listen as two teenagers describe what they do after school. See if you can understand: (a) what they like to do; (b) why they like to do it; (c) how long they have been participating in that particular activity.

pp. 46–49 *Vocabulario en contexto*
p. 51 Actividad 7
p. 57 Actividad 17
p. 59 Actividad 20

Interpersonal

 2 Hablar Talk about the extracurricular activities that you are interested in doing after school and how long you have been doing these activities

Imagine that you meet a new classmate from Venezuela who is going to your school. Since you both seem to like the same types of things: (a) tell him about some of the things you do after school that you think would interest him; (b) ask him to go with you to one of your activities.

p. 51 Actividad 6
p. 52 Actividad 8
p. 54 Actividad 13
p. 58 Actividad 18
pp. 59 Actividades 19–20

Interpretive

 3 Leer Read and understand a letter making comparisons

Read the following letter to an advice columnist. What problem is the writer describing? How does he compare himself to his brother?

Mi hermano mayor es muy estudioso y deportista. Pero yo . . . ¡no! A mí me interesa visitar a mis amigos en los salones de chat en la Red. Según mis amigos, soy increíble con mi computadora. ¡El problema es que todos mis profesores piensan que soy tan estudioso y deportista como mi hermano! Mis padres dicen que debo ser como mi hermano. No me gusta.

—Frustrado

p. 53 Actividad 11
p. 57 Actividad 16
pp. 62–63 *Lectura*

Presentational

 4 Escribir Write briefly about your extracurricular activities

You're trying to get an after-school job. Most of the applications you have picked up ask the same questions: *¿En qué actividades extracurriculares participas? ¿Cómo te van a ayudar estas actividades en este trabajo?* Write a brief paragraph describing your extracurricular activities and mention why you like these activities.

p. 50 Actividad 4
p. 52 Actividades 8–9
p. 57 Actividad 16
p. 59 Actividad 19
p. 65 *Presentación escrita*

Cultures

 5 Pensar Demonstrate an understanding of the differences between schools in the United States and Spain

Your friend's father is being transferred to Spain for one year, so your friend will be attending school in Madrid. Based on this chapter, what could you tell him about the differences that he will probably find in his new school there?

p. 64 *Perspectivas del mundo hispano*

Vocabulario Repaso

Parte superior del cuerpo

el abrigo
los anteojos de sol
la blusa
la camisa
la camiseta
la chaqueta
la corbata
la gorra
los guantes
la sudadera
el suéter
el traje
el traje de baño
el vestido

Parte inferior del cuerpo

las botas
los calcetines
la falda
los jeans
los pantalones
los pantalones cortos
los zapatos

▼1 ¿Qué llevas?

Escribir • Hablar

Completa las frases con la ropa que llevas en las siguientes ocasiones. Después compara tus respuestas con las de otro(a) estudiante. Habla de la ropa que los dos usan.

Modelo
Cuando hace frío, *llevo un suéter y guantes.*

1. Cuando voy a la piscina, . . .
2. Cuando voy a un partido de fútbol, . . .
3. Cuando estoy en casa, . . .
4. Cuando voy al cine, . . .
5. Cuando voy a un baile elegante, . . .
6. Cuando llueve, . . .

▼2 Juego

Escuchar

Tu profesor(a) va a ser Simón y te va a decir que toques *(touch)* una parte de tu cuerpo. Por ejemplo, si escuchas, "Simón dice . . . 'tócate la cabeza'", tienes que tocarte la cabeza. Si no escuchas "Simón dice . . ." y te tocas esa parte del cuerpo, ¡pierdes *(you lose)*!

Gramática Repaso

Verbs and expressions that use the infinitive

When you use two verbs together in Spanish, the second one is usually the infinitive.

Óscar **prefiere llevar** jeans los fines de semana.
¿**Vas a llevar** un suéter esta noche?

- Here are some verbs and expressions that you have used that are often followed by an infinitive:

me gusta / gustaría	I like / would like	querer (e → ie)	to want
me encanta	I love	pensar (e → ie)	to plan
poder (o → ue)	to be able	necesitar	to need
deber	ought to, should	tener que	to have to
preferir (e → ie)	to prefer	ir a	to be going to

You can use the present tense of the verb *acabar* followed by *de* + the infinitive to indicate that something has just happened:

Nosotros **acabamos de escuchar** esa canción.

*We **just listened to** that song.*

▼3 Un mensaje electrónico

Leer • Escribir

Recibes este mensaje por correo electrónico. Lee las actividades que recomienda Carlos y contéstale. Usa una combinación de dos verbos para decirle lo que te interesa hacer y lo que no te interesa hacer.

¡Hola!

¿Qué quieres hacer este fin de semana? ¿Comer en un restaurante? Todos dicen que el restaurante Las Pampas tiene comida argentina fabulosa. ¿Prefieres ir a un concierto? Hay una banda que toca música de los Andes en la plaza. ¿Jugar al tenis? Dicen que va a hacer buen tiempo todo el fin de semana. Escríbeme.

Carlos

▼4 ¿Qué quieres hacer?

Hablar

Pregúntale a otro(a) estudiante si quiere hacer algo este fin de semana.

▶ Modelo

A —*¿Quieres ir al parque conmigo?*
B —*Sí, me gustaría ir al parque pero acabo de caminar con mi amiga.*
o:—*No, gracias. No puedo ir porque mi primo acaba de llegar.*

1. ir al cine
2. estudiar español
3. tomar un refresco
4. jugar al béisbol
5. venir a mi casa
6. escuchar música
7. ¡Respuesta personal!

Más práctica GO	realidades.com | print
A ver si recuerdas **with Study Plan**	✔
Guided WB pp. 53–54	✔ ✔
Core WB pp. 27–28	✔ ✔
Hispanohablantes **WB** p. 50	✔

2A ¿Cómo te preparas?

▼ **Chapter Objectives**

Communication

By the end of this chapter you will be able to:

- Listen and read about daily routines
- Talk and write about your daily routine and getting ready for a special event
- Exchange information about your typical morning routine

Culture

You will also be able to:

- Understand why *ponchos* are worn in the Andes
- Compare parties and special events in the Spanish-speaking world with those in the U.S.

You will demonstrate what you know and can do:

- Presentación oral, p. 93
- Preparación para el examen, p. 97

You will use:

Vocabulary
- Getting ready for an event
- Daily routines

Grammar
- Reflexive verbs
- *Ser* and *estar*
- Possessive adjectives

Exploración del mundo hispano

Country Connection
Getting Ready for an Event and Daily Routines

Nueva York
Florida
México
Costa Rica
Perú
Bolivia
Argentina

 realidades.com GO

DK **Reference Atlas**

▶ *Videocultura y actividad*

🌐 **Mapa global interactivo**

Participantes en una celebración de quinceañera, Ciudad Juárez, México

Arte y cultura | México

Bailes tradicionales En "Baile en Tehuantepec" vemos la ropa típica de los bailes de esta región de México. Las mujeres se visten con blusas y faldas tradicionales. El uso del sombrero es tradicional para los hombres del campo, no sólo en México, sino en otros países hispanohablantes como el Perú y el Ecuador.

• Compara a las personas de este cuadro con las jóvenes de la foto. ¿Qué ropa llevas cuando vas a un baile especial?

"Baile en Tehuantepec" (1935), Diego Rivera ▶

Charcoal and watercolor, 18 15/16 x 23 7/8 inches. Los Angeles County Museum of Art, gift of Mr. and Mrs. Milton W. Lipper, from the Milton W. Lipper Estate. © 2009 Banco de México Diego Rivera & Frida Kahlo Museums Trust, México, D.F./Artists Rights Society (ARS), New York. Photo: © Museum Associates/LACMA.

▼ Objectives

Read, listen to, and understand information about
▶ getting ready for an event
▶ daily routines

Vocabulario en contexto

❝¡Hola! Me llamo Antonio. ¿Qué hago yo **antes de** ir a **un evento especial?** Siempre **me despierto** temprano y **me levanto** de la cama. Primero **me ducho** lentamente. Generalmente estoy en la ducha unos 20 minutos.

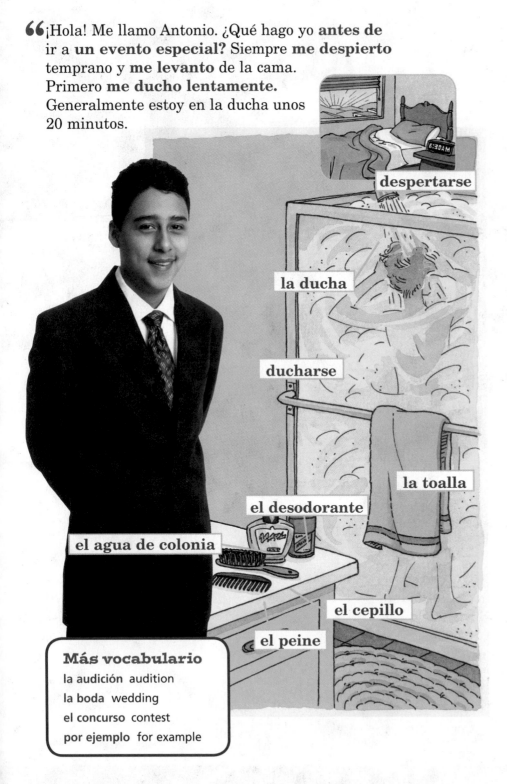

despertarse

la ducha

ducharse

la toalla

el desodorante

el agua de colonia

el cepillo

el peine

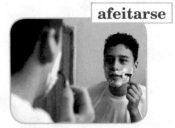

afeitarse

Después de ducharme, **me afeito** . . .

cepillarse los dientes

. . . y **me cepillo** los dientes.

arreglarse el pelo

secarse

el secador

Luego me seco el pelo con el secador y **me arreglo** el pelo con el peine.

ponerse

vestirse

Después **me pongo** el desodorante y el agua de colonia y **me visto**❞.

Más vocabulario

la audición audition
la boda wedding
el concurso contest
por ejemplo for example

—Tengo **una cita** con Rafael. ¡Vamos a un baile **elegante!**

—Debes estar muy **entusiasmada.** ¿Qué vas a hacer para **prepararte?**

—Primero **me baño,** . . .

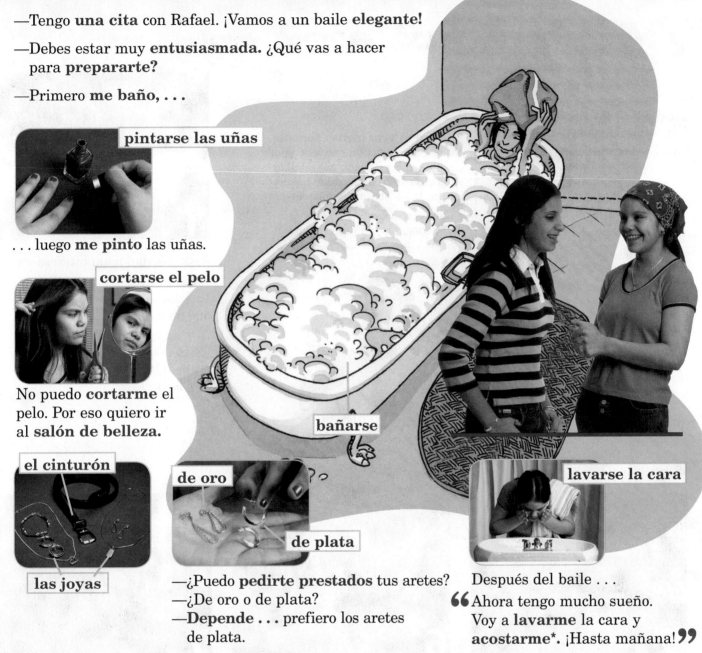

pintarse las uñas

. . . luego **me pinto** las uñas.

cortarse el pelo

No puedo **cortarme** el pelo. Por eso quiero ir al **salón de belleza.**

bañarse

el cinturón

de oro

de plata

las joyas

lavarse la cara

Después del baile . . .

66 Ahora tengo mucho sueño. Voy a **lavarme** la cara y **acostarme*.** ¡Hasta mañana! 99

—¿Puedo **pedirte prestados** tus aretes?
—¿De oro o de plata?
—**Depende** . . . prefiero los aretes de plata.

▼1 ¿Qué haces por | ◀)) la mañana?

Escuchar

Vas a escuchar siete frases que describen qué hace alguien por la mañana. Representa (*Act out*) cada una de estas acciones sin hablar.

Más práctica (GO)	realidades.com | print	
Instant Check	✔	
Guided WB pp. 55–60	✔	✔
Core WB pp. 29–30	✔	✔
Comm. WB p. 31	✔	✔
Hispanohablantes WB p. 52		✔

▼2 ¿Lógica o no? | ◀))

Escuchar

Vas a escuchar siete frases. Algunas son lógicas y otras no. Señala con el pulgar hacia arriba si la frase es lógica y con el pulgar hacia abajo si no es lógica.

*The verb *acostarse* has an *o* → *ue* stem change.

¿Más maquillaje?

¿Qué emergencia tiene Gloria? ¿Cómo se arreglan Raúl y Tomás? Lee la historia para saber.

Estrategia

Relating to your own experience
Making a connection between your own life and what you are reading will help you to understand a story better. Think about the following:

• Have you ever done a favor for someone, only to regret it later?

1

Raúl: No dan nada interesante hoy.

Tomás: Tienes razón. ¿Por qué no tomamos un refresco?

Gloria: *(al teléfono)* ¡Ay, no! ¿Estás seguro? ¿Qué podemos hacer? Un momento, tengo una idea.

Gloria

Tomás

Raúl

5

Raúl: ¡Qué idea! Mira dónde estamos.

Gloria: Primero, no es idea **mía** . . . ¡**Tranquilos**! No deben estar tan **nerviosos.**

Raúl: No estamos nerviosos. Pero no me gusta vestirme a lo ridículo.

6

Tomás: ¿Es necesario pintarse **los labios?**

Raúl: ¿Tanto **gel?** ¿Por qué tiene que ponerme tanto **maquillaje?** Dos horas así. No va a ser muy **cómodo.**

7

Tomás: Tienes razón. Pero te ves muy bien.

Raúl: ¿Tú crees? Y mira tus zapatos. ¡Qué grandes son!

Gloria: ¿Les gustaría participar en una obra de teatro? Es una emergencia. Necesitamos a dos personas y tienen que venir **rápidamente.**

Raúl: ¿En qué? ¡No!

Tomás: Pero, ¿por qué no? Puede ser interesante.

Gloria: ¡Fantástico! Les va a gustar mucho.

Tomás: ¿Cómo me preparo? ¿Me arreglo el pelo?

Gloria: Tomás, **te ves** bien. Pero Raúl . . .

Raúl: Sí, voy a cepillarme los dientes, lavarme el pelo . . .

Gloria: Tienen 30 minutos.

Raúl: ¡Esto va a ser un desastre!

▼3 ¿Comprendiste?

Leer • Escribir

Indica si las siguientes frases son *(C)* ciertas o *(F)* falsas. Si la frase es falsa, escribe la información correcta.

1. Tomás y Raúl miran un programa de televisión muy interesante.

2. Tomás quiere ayudar a Gloria con una obra de teatro.

3. Raúl no quiere ayudar a Gloria.

4. Raúl va a cepillarse los dientes y lavarse el pelo.

5. A Raúl le gusta vestirse a lo ridículo.

6. A Raúl no le gusta el maquillaje porque no es cómodo.

7. Tomás se pone zapatos muy grandes para la obra de teatro.

8. Raúl cree que todo va a ser muy divertido.

Más práctica	GO	
realidades.com	print	
Instant Check	✔	
Guided WB pp. 61–64	✔	✔
Core WB pp. 31–32	✔	✔
Comm. WB pp. 25–27, 28	✔	✔
Hispanohablantes WB p. 53	✔	

Vocabulario en uso

▼4 ¿Cómo se prepara Margarita?

Escribir

Hoy Margarita va a la boda de su prima. Mira el dibujo y escribe una lista de las cosas que necesita para prepararse. Si puedes, también escribe para qué se usa cada cosa.

Modelo

un peine
Margarita necesita un peine para arreglarse el pelo.

▼5 ¿Ropa elegante o ropa cómoda? | 🗨️👥 | ♻️

Escribir • Hablar

① ¿Qué clase de ropa llevas en estas ocasiones? Haz una tabla como la que ves aquí. Escribe los eventos de la lista en la primera columna. Decide si llevas ropa elegante o ropa cómoda en esta ocasión y escribe qué llevas en la columna apropiada.

1. una boda
2. un baile elegante
3. un concurso
4. una cita para ir al cine
5. un partido de hockey
6. una fiesta en la casa de un(a) amigo(a)
7. una audición
8. ¡Respuesta personal!

Ocasión	Ropa elegante	Ropa cómoda
la escuela		unos jeans y una camiseta
el cumpleaños de mi abuela	un traje o un vestido elegante	

② Con otro(a) estudiante, habla de la ropa que Uds. llevan en las ocasiones del Paso 1.

▶️ Modelo

A —*¿Qué llevas para el cumpleaños de tu abuela?*
B —*Para el cumpleaños de mi abuela llevo ropa elegante. Llevo una falda elegante y una blusa blanca.*

▼6 ¿Por la mañana o por la noche?

Escribir

Copia el diagrama de Venn. Luego mira los dibujos y decide si haces la actividad por la mañana o por la noche. Escribe la acción en el círculo apropiado del diagrama. Si haces la actividad por la mañana *y* por la noche, escribe tu respuesta en la intersección de los círculos.

Modelo

Me ducho.

1.

2.

3.

4.

5.

6.

7.

8.

▼7 ¿Rápidamente o lentamente? | Talk!

Hablar

¿Te preparas rápidamente para ir a la escuela? Habla con otro(a) estudiante sobre cuánto tiempo crees que es necesario para hacer las cosas de la Actividad 6.

▶ Modelo

A —*¿Cuánto tiempo necesitas para ducharte?*
B —*Me ducho rápidamente. Necesito sólo dos minutos.*
o: —*Me ducho lentamente. Necesito 20 minutos.*

¿Recuerdas?

You use adverbs to tell how you do an action. In English they often end in *-ly*. To form adverbs in Spanish, you can often add *-mente* to the feminine form of the adjective.

general → generalmente

rápida → rápidamente

▼ Fondo Cultural | El mundo hispano

La ropa de fiesta En los países hispanohablantes, los jóvenes llevan ropa cómoda pero elegante a las fiestas entre amigos o para citas con amigos. Los jeans son muy populares, pero llevan jeans con camisas o blusas buenas, nunca con camisetas viejas o rotas *(torn)*. Muchos jóvenes prefieren llevar pantalones o vestidos de moda en vez de *(instead of)* jeans.

• ¿Qué llevas cuando asistes a una fiesta entre amigos?

| ▼ Objectives

▶ Talk and write about daily routines and getting ready for special events
▶ Exchange information about what you do on an ideal day

Gramática

Reflexive verbs

To say that people do something to or for themselves, you use reflexive verbs. For example, washing one's hands and brushing one's hair are reflexive actions because the person doing the action also receives the action.

> Antes de una cita, (yo) me ducho y me arreglo el pelo.

You know that a verb is reflexive if its infinitive form ends with the letters *se*.

> ducharse

The reflexive pronouns in Spanish are *me, te, se, nos,* and *os.* Each pronoun corresponds to a different subject. Here are the present-tense forms of the reflexive verb *secarse:*

(yo)	me seco	(nosotros) (nosotras)	nos secamos
(tú)	te secas	(vosotros) (vosotras)	os secáis
Ud. (él) (ella)	se seca	Uds. (ellos) (ellas)	se secan

Some verbs have both reflexive and non-reflexive forms and usages. A verb is used in its non-reflexive form if the action is being done to someone or something else.

Lavo el coche a menudo. *I wash the car often.*
Me lavo el pelo todos los días. *I wash my hair every day.*

When you use a reflexive verb with parts of the body or clothing, use the definite article.

¿Siempre te pintas las uñas? *Do you always polish your nails?*
Felipe se pone los zapatos. *Felipe puts on his shoes.*

You can put reflexive pronouns before the conjugated verb or you can attach them to the infinitive.

Me voy a duchar.
Voy a ducharme.
Te tienes que vestir para la fiesta.
Tienes que vestirte para la fiesta.

Más ayuda **realidades.com**

▶ **GramActiva Video**
Tutorials: Reflexive pronouns, Reflexive/non-reflexive actions
Animated Verbs

🔊 *Canción de hip hop:* ¿A qué hora te despiertas?

✎ **GramActiva Activity**

▼8 Nos preparamos para la fiesta

Leer • Escribir

Isabel y Elena se preparan para ir a una fiesta de quinceañera. En una hoja de papel, escribe el pronombre reflexivo correcto para cada número para completar la historia.

Isabel y Elena son dos hermanas que __1.__ preparan para una fiesta de quinceañera. "Debemos acostar __2.__ temprano esta noche", dice Isabel. "Sí, y mañana yo __3.__ baño primero. Después __4.__ maquillo y __5.__ pinto las uñas. Me gusta preparar __6.__ lentamente", dice Elena. "Es verdad", dice Isabel. "Siempre __7.__ preparas más lentamente que yo". La noche de la fiesta Elena __8.__ arregla el pelo primero y luego ayuda a Isabel. Las dos __9.__ visten y salen para la fiesta a las seis y media.

▼9 Una rutina lógica |

Escribir • Hablar

¿Eres una persona lógica? Usa *antes de* o *después de* para escribir frases lógicas.

1. lavarse las manos / comer
2. despertarse / levantarse
3. vestirse / ponerse desodorante
4. acostarse / bañarse
5. ducharse / vestirse
6. cepillarse los dientes / comer

Modelo
lavarse la cara / acostarse
Me lavo la cara antes de acostarme.

> **Nota**
> Note that in Spanish you use the infinitive after a preposition even if an infinitive is not used in English.
> • Generalmente me pongo loción en la cara **después de afeitarme.** *I usually put lotion on my face **after shaving.***

▼10 Preparaciones

Escribir • Hablar

Imagina que tú y tu hermanito están preparándose para un evento especial y tienes que ayudarlo. Describe tu día según los dibujos. Usa la forma reflexiva del verbo en tu descripción si es necesario.

Modelo
Me despierto a las siete de la mañana.

Modelo
Despierto a mi hermanito a las siete y cinco.

1.

2.

3.

4.

5.
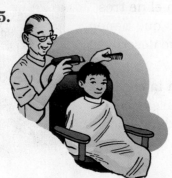

6.

▼11 Tu horario

Escribir

¿Cómo es tu horario típico? Piensa en tu horario para un día de escuela. En general, ¿a qué hora haces las siguientes acciones? Usa una tabla para organizar tus respuestas.

1. levantarse
2. bañarse o ducharse
3. cepillarse los dientes
4. arreglarse el pelo
5. vestirse
6. acostarse temprano / tarde

Mi rutina	La hora
me despierto	a las 6:30

▼12 Compara horarios |

Hablar

Ahora compara tu horario de la Actividad 11 con el de otro(a) estudiante. Hablen de las diferencias en sus rutinas.

▶️ **Modelo**

A —¿A qué hora te despiertas por la mañana?

B —Me despierto a las seis y media. ¿Y tú?

A —Yo me despierto a las siete. ¿Qué haces después de levantarte?

B —Siempre me ducho primero y me lavo el pelo. Y tú, ¿qué haces luego?

> . . . a la(s) (siete) . . .
> Primero . . .
> Luego . . .
> . . . después de . . .
> . . . antes de . . .

▼13 Mi día ideal |

Escribir • Hablar

❶ Describe tu día ideal en cinco frases. Usa expresiones que necesitan un infinitivo en cada frase. También usa los verbos reflexivos.

❷ Ahora compara tu día ideal con el de tres estudiantes. De todas las frases que tienen, escojan (choose) cinco frases que describen el día ideal para todo el grupo.

❸ Cada grupo debe compartir con la clase su descripción del día ideal. La clase debe votar por la mejor descripción del día ideal.

Modelo

En mi día ideal puedo levantarme muy tarde.
En mi día ideal no tengo que ir a la escuela.

▼14 ¡Quiero dormir más!

Leer • Pensar • Escribir • Hablar

¿Es difícil despertarte temprano todas las mañanas? ¿Te gustaría
dormir más? Lee el siguiente informe sobre la cantidad *(amount)* de
sueño que necesita cada joven. Luego contesta las preguntas.

Conexiones | La salud

¿Necesitas dormir más?

*M*uchos jóvenes no pueden levantarse
temprano a la hora de ir a la escuela
y el 20 por ciento de ellos se duermen[1]
en las clases. Nuevos estudios revelan que
los jóvenes de 13 a 18 años de edad
necesitan dormir 9.25 horas cada noche.
Esto es 1.25 horas más que un adulto.
La realidad es que muchos jóvenes
duermen sólo seis o siete horas cada
noche. Si un joven no duerme suficiente,
puede tener problemas de concentración
y de control de sus emociones.

¿Cuál es la respuesta a este problema? Pues,
acuéstate temprano y sigue una rutina cada noche.
Otros consejos para dormir mejor son:

➤ Toma sólo bebidas sin cafeína después de
las cinco de la tarde.

➤ Evita[2] programas de televisión o películas
violentas antes de acostarte. También evita
usar la computadora o jugar videojuegos
antes de dormir.

➤ Un baño o una ducha antes de acostarte puede ayudarte a dormir.

➤ Haz ejercicio todos los días pero no antes de acostarte.

➤ Debes acostarte y levantarte cada día a la misma hora. Si quieres acostarte
tarde durante el fin de semana, es mejor no hacerlo dos noches seguidas.

[1]fall asleep   [2]Avoid

1. ¿Cuántas horas duermes cada noche?

2. ¿Cuántas horas crees que debes dormir cada noche?

3. ¿Crees que estos consejos son buenos? ¿Por qué?

▼15 ¡Un día loco! | 👥

Escribir • Hablar

Con otro(a) estudiante, van a crear una rutina
loca. Usen las ideas de abajo o piensen en
otras. Luego lean su rutina a la clase. ¡La
pareja con la rutina más loca gana!

 Modelo

A —*Primero nos levantamos a las tres
de la mañana.*

B —*Después nos ponemos una camisa
elegante y unos pantalones cortos.*

Estudiante B

Estudiante A

acostarse	afeitarse
cepillarse los dientes	vestirse
peinarse	despertarse
arreglarse el pelo	lavarse

¡Respuesta personal!

¡Respuesta personal!

▼16 Juego | 👥

Escribir • Hablar

¿Cómo te preparas para la escuela o para una fiesta? Vas a presentar tu rutina sin hablar.

❶ Primero cada estudiante va a escribir una lista corta de lo que hace alguien cuando se prepara para salir.

❷ En grupos o equipos, cada persona tiene que representar sus acciones sin hablar. Cuando "el actor" está actuando, cada miembro del grupo debe adivinar cuáles son las actividades y debe escribirlas en una hoja de papel. Después cada estudiante lee su lista. El actor o la actriz decide si la lista tiene las acciones correctas y si están en orden.

Modelo

Primero, Marta se levanta. Luego, ella . . . Después . . .

Los resultados:

3 puntos	en orden con todos los verbos correctos
2 puntos	en orden con la mitad *(half)* de los verbos correctos
0 puntos	ni en orden ni con todos los verbos correctos

▼17 Y tú, ¿qué dices? |

Escribir • Hablar

1. ¿Te gusta levantarte temprano o tarde? ¿A qué hora te acuestas generalmente? ¿A qué hora te levantas? ¿Siempre te cepillas los dientes después de comer o sólo antes de acostarte?

2. ¿Cómo te preparas para un evento especial? ¿Qué haces primero? ¿Vas al salón de belleza o te arreglas el pelo? ¿Cuánto tiempo necesitas para prepararte?

3. ¿Qué ropa u otros accesorios te pones para ir a una fiesta o un baile?

Más práctica	GO
	realidades.com | print

Instant Check	✔	
Guided WB pp. 65–66	✔	✔
Core WB p. 33	✔	✔
Comm. WB pp. 29, 32, 220	✔	✔
Hispanohablantes WB pp. 54–57	✔	

▼ Fondo Cultural | El mundo hispano

La familia y los eventos especiales En los países hispanohablantes, los primeros invitados a un evento especial generalmente son los miembros de la familia. Los cumpleaños, el día del santo y otros días especiales se celebran con la familia y los amigos.

• ¿Invitas a tíos y a primos a todos tus cumpleaños? ¿A quiénes invitas a tus fiestas? ¿Por qué?

Una familia de San Miguel de Allende, México, celebra un cumpleaños.

▼18 Corte de pelo con estilo

Leer • Escribir • Hablar

Lee el anuncio sobre la máquina para cortar el pelo "Cortapelo" que tú puedes usar en casa. Luego contesta las preguntas.

1. ¿Por qué da un buen corte el "Cortapelo"?

2. ¿Por qué puedes crear estilos diferentes?

3. ¿Crees que es bueno pagar dinero por un corte de pelo?

4. ¿Vas a un salón de belleza o te cortas el pelo en casa? ¿Por qué?

> **También se dice . . .**
>
> **el salón de belleza** = la peluquería *(muchos países)*
> **el pelo** = el cabello *(muchos países)*

Con el revolucionario **Cortapelo** puedes cortarte el pelo sin salir de casa

La profesionalidad de un buen corte de pelo

Con su exclusivo sistema puedes cortarte el pelo sin errores ya que* su peine pivotante se adapta perfectamente a la forma de tu cabeza. Su sistema de dos peines corta con precisión el corte que deseas.

Quedas siempre perfecto y con un corte de pelo verdaderamente profesional.

Cortapelo

¡Es muy fácil y muy cómodo!

*since

El español en la comunidad

En muchas regiones de los Estados Unidos donde hay una concentración de personas hispanohablantes, hay eventos especiales para la comunidad hispana. Estas comunidades se preparan durante meses para las celebraciones. Preparan comida típica, música, bailes y desfiles. La celebración puede ser internacional o de un solo país, como el festival puertorriqueño en Nueva York. Lo que estos eventos tienen en común es que siempre participan personas de todos los grupos hispanos.

• Busca un calendario de los eventos especiales de tu comunidad para saber si hay un evento hispano o internacional. Estos eventos se celebran generalmente en el verano, cuando es posible organizarlos en parques.

El Desfile (*Parade*) Nacional Puertorriqueño en Nueva York

Festival de la calle Ocho, Miami, la Florida

Gramática Repaso

The verbs *ser* and *estar*

You know that both *ser* and *estar* mean "to be." You have seen that their uses, however, are different.

(yo)	soy	(nosotros) (nosotras)	somos
(tú)	eres	(vosotros) (vosotras)	sois
Ud. (él) (ella)	es	Uds. (ellos) (ellas)	son

(yo)	estoy	(nosotros) (nosotras)	estamos
(tú)	estás	(vosotros) (vosotras)	estáis
Ud. (él) (ella)	está	Uds. (ellos) (ellas)	están

Use *ser* to talk about:
- what a person or thing is
- what a person or thing is like
- where a person or thing is from
- what a thing is made of
- to whom something belongs

Ricardo y Lola **son** actores.
Son muy simpáticos.
Son de Nicaragua.
Este anillo **es** de plata.
Es el anillo de Juana.

Use *estar* to talk about:
- how a person or thing is at the moment
- how someone feels
- where a person or thing is located

Mi hermana **está** muy cansada.
Alicia y Carlos **están** entusiasmados.
Alonso **está** en el baño.

Más ayuda **realidades.com**

▶ *GramActiva* **Video**

✎ *GramActiva* **Activity**

▼19 Ellos quieren ser músicos

Leer • Escribir

Alfredo y Juan tocan en la banda y van a entrar en un concurso. Escoge el verbo correcto para completar su conversación.

Alfredo y Juan __1.__ *(son/están)* chicos talentosos. __2.__ *(Son/Están)* miembros de la banda de su escuela. Ahora los chicos __3.__ *(son/están)* en casa de Juan y se preparan para ir a un concurso de la banda.

—¿ __4.__ *(Eres/Estás)* nervioso, Juan?
—Sí, un poco. Todo mi familia va a __5.__ *(ser/estar)* allí. Mis padres, mis abuelos . . .
—¿Tu novia?
—No, hombre. Ella __6.__ *(es/está)* enferma y no puede ir. ¿Y tú, Alfredo?
—Nervioso no. Yo __7.__ *(soy/estoy)* entusiasmado. Yo sé que __8.__ *(somos /estamos)* los mejores.

▼20 ¿Cómo estás?

Leer • Escribir

¿Cómo están tú y las otras personas en estas situaciones? Usa adjetivos de la lista para formar frases.

1. Elena y María van a participar en un concurso.

2. Vas a un baile con el (la) chico(a) más popular de la escuela.

3. Tienes mucha tarea y también tienes que lavar el coche, cortar el césped y limpiar tu dormitorio.

4. Tu hermano va a un concierto para escuchar una banda nueva.

5. Uds. están en una clase que no les interesa y la profesora habla lentamente.

6. Tu mejor amigo(a) tiene que dar un discurso para los padres de los estudiantes de tu escuela.

Modelo

Carlos toma el sol en la playa.
Carlos está muy contento.

aburrido, -a	nervioso, -a
cansado, -a	ocupado, -a
contento, -a	tranquilo, -a
entusiasmado, -a	

▼21 El dormitorio de Ramona

Hablar • Escribir

❶ Ramona tiene muchas cosas en su dormitorio. ¿Es el dormitorio típico de una chica de 16 años? Mira el dibujo y habla de Ramona y su dormitorio con otro(a) estudiante.

▶ Modelo

A —*¿Dónde están las joyas de Ramona?*
B —*Están encima del escritorio.*
A —*¿De qué son las joyas?*
B —*Son de oro.*

❷ Ahora piensa en tu dormitorio. ¿Es como el dormitorio de Ramona? Describe dónde están y cómo son las cosas en tu dormitorio.

Más práctica GO   realidades.com | print

Instant Check	✔	
Guided WB p. 67	✔	✔
Core WB p. 34	✔	✔
Comm. WB p. 33	✔	✔
Hispanohablantes **WB** pp. 58–59		✔

Gramática

Possessive adjectives

Spanish possessive adjectives have a long form that comes after the noun. These forms are often used for emphasis.

mío / mía míos / mías	nuestro / nuestra nuestros / nuestras
tuyo / tuya tuyos / tuyas	vuestro / vuestra vuestros / vuestras
suyo / suya suyos / suyas	suyo / suya suyos / suyas

Voy al partido con un amigo **mío**.
*I'm going to the game with a friend **of mine**.*

¿Vas al baile con unas amigas **tuyas**?
*Are you going to the dance with some friends **of yours**?*

¿Recuerdas?

You already know a different form of possessive adjectives. They agree in gender and number with the nouns they describe and always go in front of the noun. They include *mi(s), tu(s), su(s), nuestro(a), nuestros(as), vuestro(a),* and *vuestros(as).*

• **Tus** joyas de plata son muy bonitas.

These possessive adjectives may be used without the noun.

¿Estas chaquetas son **suyas**?
*Are these jackets **yours**?*

Sí, son **nuestras**.
*Yes, they are **ours**.*

To clarify or emphasize possession, you can use *de* + a noun or pronoun instead of a form of *suyo.*

Aquí está un collar **suyo**.
= un collar **de Ud. / él / ella / Uds. / ellos / ellas.**
*Here is a necklace of **yours / his / hers / theirs**.*

▼22 ¿Son suyos?

Leer • Escribir

¿De quiénes son estas cosas? Escoge la mejor respuesta.

1. ¿De quién son esos zapatos elegantes? ¿De Ud.?
   a. Sí, son míos.   **b.** Sí, son mías.

2. ¿De quiénes son esos globos? ¿De los niños?
   a. Sí, son suyas.   **b.** Sí, son suyos.

3. ¿De quién es esa toalla? ¿De Uds.?
   a. Sí, es nuestra.   **b.** Sí, es mía.

4. ¿De quién son estas joyas? ¿De tu prima?
   a. Sí, son suyas.   **b.** Sí, son tuyas.

5. ¿De quién es este secador? ¿De Laura?
   a. Sí, es tuyo.   **b.** Sí, es suyo.

6. ¿De quién es esta corbata? ¿De tu hermano?
   a. Sí, es suya.   **b.** Sí, es mía.

▼23 Escucha y escribe | 🔊

Escuchar • Escribir

Hoy muchos clientes están en el salón de belleza. Escucha y escribe lo que dice Felipe mientras organiza el salón.

Un salón de belleza en la Argentina

▼24 ¿De quién es? |

Leer • Hablar

Tu hermana está arreglando su cuarto y preguntando de quién son las cosas que ella encuentra *(finds)*. Contesta sus preguntas, diciendo de quién es cada cosa.

▶ **Modelo**

A —*¿Es tu agua de colonia?*
B —*Sí, el agua de colonia es mía.*
o: —*No, el agua de colonia no es mía.*

1. ¿Son sus toallas? (de ellos)
2. ¿Es mi peine?
3. ¿Es su gel? (de ella)
4. ¿Son nuestras joyas?
5. ¿Es tu maquillaje?
6. ¿Es su desodorante? (de él)

▼25 ¿Es tuyo? |

Hablar

¿A quién le gusta pedir prestada la ropa? Pregúntale a otro(a) estudiante sobre la ropa y los accesorios que lleva. ¿Todo es de él/ella?

▶ **Modelo**

A —*Me gustan las joyas que llevas. ¿Son tuyas?*
B —*Sí, son mías.*
o: —*No, son de mi hermana, pero me gustan mucho.*

Más práctica	GO	
	realidades.com	print	
Instant Check	✔	
Guided WB p. 68	✔	✔
Core WB p. 35	✔	✔
Comm. WB p. 30	✔	✔
Hispanohablantes WB p. 57	✔	

▼ Pronunciación | 🔊 | 💬

Consonants that change their sounds

In Spanish, when the letter *c* combines with *a, o,* or *u* ("strong" vowels) it makes the sound of the letter *k*. Listen to and say these words:

expli**c**a bus**co** **cu**chillo ¿**Có**mo? ¿**Cuá**ndo?

When *c* combines with *e* or *i* ("weak" vowels) it makes the sound of the letter *s*. Listen to and say these words:*

cepillo **ci**encias cono**ces** **ce**ntro de reci**c**laje

Practice saying these sentences:

Para mi cita con Carmen, voy a ponerme una corbata y un cinturón.

A Celia le gusta comer cacahuates cuando va al cine.

In Spanish, the letter *g* combined with *a, o,* or *u* ("strong" vowels) makes a hard *g* sound. Listen to and say these words:

ganga lue**go** al**gún** al**go**dón yo**gur**

In words with the letters *e* or *i* ("weak" vowels), you need to add a *u* after the *g* to keep the hard *g* sound.

Listen to and say these words:

espa**gue**tis pa**gué** **gui**sante hambur**gue**sa

Practice saying these sentences:

Gasté mucho dinero en las gangas y pagué con cheque.

Compré un regalo para Guillermo: unos guantes de algodón.

Can you figure out the meaning of the following *refranes?*

Lo barato es caro cuando no es necesario.

Peseta guardada, dos veces ganada.

*In some parts of Spain, *c* before *e* and *i* is pronounced like the *th* in *think*.

This is discussed further in *Tema 6, Capítulo 6A, Pronunciación.*

Lectura

Asistir al teatro siempre es un evento especial. Y estar en una producción puede ser aun más especial. Vamos a ver lo que dice un joven cantante.

Estrategia

Identifying the writer's attitude
As you read the *Lectura*, look for phrases that help you understand how the writer feels about the event.

El Teatro Colón: Entre bambalinas[1]

Pasar una noche en el Teatro Colón de Buenos Aires siempre es un evento especial y hoy es muy especial para mí. Vamos a presentar la ópera "La Traviata" y voy a cantar en el coro por primera vez. ¡Estoy muy nervioso! Pero, ¿qué me dices? ¿No conoces el Teatro Colón? Pues, es el teatro más importante de toda Argentina, quizás de toda América del Sur. Lleva más de 150 años ofreciendo espectáculos de ópera al público argentino y "La Traviata" fue la ópera que se presentó en la inauguración del teatro el 27 de abril de 1857. Por eso estamos todos muy entusiasmados.

[1]Behind the scenes

AUDICIONES

para jóvenes de 15 a 25 años de edad.

Si quieres ser músico, cantante o bailarín, tienes talento, eres joven y vives en Buenos Aires, tienes la oportunidad de hacer tus sueños realidad. Preséntate en el Teatro Colón para la siguiente audición. Los interesados pueden presentarse el jueves, 22 de agosto a las 10:00 de la mañana.

Bajo el auspicio del Gobierno de la Ciudad de Buenos Aires

¿Te gustaría saber cómo ser miembro de los grupos que se presentan aquí? La mejor manera es presentarte a una audición para la escuela del teatro. Se llama el Instituto Superior de Arte y funciona dentro del teatro. En el Instituto puedes estudiar canto, danza, dirección de orquesta y otras especialidades para la ópera. Si estudias en el Instituto, puedes llegar a ser miembro del coro o del cuerpo de baile. Para músicos con talento también está la Orquesta

Académica del Teatro Colón. Esta orquesta está formada por jóvenes entre 15 y 25 años de edad. La orquesta hace sus presentaciones en el teatro o en las principales ciudades del país. Aquí en el teatro siempre buscan jóvenes con talento.

Si no te gusta actuar ni cantar, pero te encanta el teatro, puedes estudiar otra especialidad. Por ejemplo, si te gusta el arte, puedes aprender a hacer los escenarios. O si te interesa la tecnología, puedes estudiar la grabación o el video. En el teatro hay talleres[2] para todos los elementos de una presentación. Hay talleres para los decorados,[3] la ropa, los efectos especiales electromecánicos, la grabación y el video. Bueno, tengo que irme. ¡Ahora mismo empieza el "show" y tengo

que ponerme el maquillaje! ¡Nos vemos!

[2]workshops   [3]scenery

Fondo Cultural | El mundo hispano

Los grandes teatros son parte de la cultura de muchas ciudades hispanohablantes: el Teatro Real de Madrid (1850), el Palacio de Bellas Artes de México, D.F. (1934), el Teatro Municipal de Santiago, Chile (1857), el Teatro Nacional de San José, Costa Rica (1897). Como el Teatro Colón de Buenos Aires, ofrecen al público conciertos, óperas, ballet y otros programas culturales.

• ¿Hay un teatro o institución en tu comunidad que da programas culturales? ¿Qué tipo de programas dan?

¿Comprendiste?

1. Según la información, ¿qué talento debes tener para participar en las audiciones? ¿Cuántos años debes tener?

2. ¿Por qué es importante el Teatro Colón?

3. Si tocas la trompeta, ¿en qué puedes participar en el Instituto?

4. Si no te gusta ni bailar ni cantar, ¿qué otras actividades puedes hacer en el teatro?

5. ¿Te gustaría ver una ópera? ¿Por qué?

6. ¿Hay presentaciones de teatro o de orquesta en tu escuela? ¿Participas en las presentaciones o te gusta verlas? ¿Por qué?

Más práctica GO

realidades.com | print

Guided WB p. 69   ✔ ✔
Comm. WB pp. 34, 221   ✔ ✔
Hispanohablantes **WB** pp. 62–63   ✔
Cultural Reading Activity   ✔

La cultura en vivo

Cómo hacer un poncho

El poncho es ropa típica del altiplano, una zona elevada y fría, situada entre Bolivia y el Perú. El poncho también se usa en la Argentina, Chile, Colombia, el Ecuador, Guatemala y México. Estos países tienen regiones montañosas y frías. El poncho protege[1] contra el frío y está hecho de materiales como lana de llama o de oveja, que son animales de estos países.

En general hay dos clases de ponchos: los ponchos de trabajo que se llevan todos los días, y los ponchos de fiesta, que se llevan en las celebraciones y los eventos especiales. Los ponchos de fiesta tienen diseños[2] más complejos y, a veces, son de colores.

Dos indígenas peruanos del Cuzco con ponchos

Objetivo

Hacer un poncho

Materiales

- una tela[3] como cobija[4] de aproximadamente 90 cm* por 120 cm
- tijeras
- hilo[5] y aguja de coser[6]
- pintura[7] para tela
- un pincel[8]

Un indígena boliviano en un festival de agricultores

Instrucciones

1 Para hacer la parte principal del poncho, dobla la tela en diagonal como en el dibujo para hacer un cuadrado. Corta la tela que no necesitas y guárdala. *(Figura 1)*

Figura 1

2 Haz un corte de unos 30 cm de largo para la cabeza. *(Figura 2)*

3 Corta un pedazo de la tela que no usaste, y cósela al poncho para hacer un bolsillo.[9] *(Figura 3)*

Figura 2

4 Decora el poncho con los colores, la mascota o el escudo de tu escuela. Si necesitas ideas, busca ejemplos de ponchos que usan los habitantes de los Andes.

*2.54 cm = 1 in

[1] protects [2] designs [3] cloth [4] blanket [5] thread [6] sewing needle [7] paint
[8] paintbrush [9] pocket

Figura 3

Presentación oral (Talk!)

Un evento especial

Task

You are an exchange student in Mexico. Your host family wants to know about special events in which you participate in your community. Show them photos of a typical special event you or your friends might attend.

❶ **Prepare** Bring a personal photo or magazine picture of a special event that teens might attend. Think about getting ready for this event. Answer these questions for yourself or for others:

- ¿Qué tipo de evento es? ¿Qué ropa llevas?
- ¿Qué haces para prepararte?
- ¿Cómo estás? ¿Entusiasmado(a)? ¿Nervioso(a)? ¿Contento(a)?

You can use notes to help you remember what you want to say.

❷ **Practice** Go through your presentation several times. Try to:

- provide as much information as you can
- use complete sentences
- speak clearly

Estrategia

Taking notes
When preparing for a presentation, it is often helpful to take notes. These notes can help you organize your thoughts. Using index cards with your notes can help keep you on track while giving your presentation.

Modelo

Cuando voy a un concierto, llevo ropa nueva . . . Para prepararme, me ducho, me peino . . . Mis amigos y yo siempre estamos entusiasmados porque . . .

❸ **Present** Show your photo and give the information about the event.

❹ **Evaluation** The following rubric will be used to grade your presentation.

Rubric	Score 1	Score 3	Score 5
Completeness of your preparation	You provide one of the following: photos, answers to questions, index cards.	You provide two of the following: photos, answers to questions, index cards.	You provide three of the following: photos, answers to questions, index cards.
How much information you communicate	You respond to only one of the questions.	You respond to two of the questions.	You respond to all the questions.
How easily you are understood	You are difficult to understand and have many grammatical errors.	You are fairly easy to understand and have occasional grammatical errors.	You are easy to understand and have very few grammatical errors.

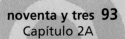

Preparación para . . .

En busca de la verdad

El Jardín de la Independencia es un lugar de gran atractivo en la ciudad de Dolores Hidalgo. El monumento principal de esta plaza es la estatua del famoso padre Hidalgo. En el jardín puedes disfrutar de[3] un agradable descanso. Si quieres, puedes probar[4] los helados tradicionales que se venden en el jardín, helados de variados y exóticos sabores como queso, aguacate, maíz y más.

Dolores Hidalgo

Bienvenidos a Dolores Hidalgo, otra ciudad visitada en el videomisterio. Está a unos 22 kilómetros al noreste de Guanajuato y tiene una población de 129,000 habitantes. Es una ciudad prominente porque allí, en la medianoche del 15 de septiembre del año 1810, el padre[1] Miguel Hidalgo y Costilla gritó:[2] "¡Viva México!". Con este histórico "Grito de la independencia", o "Grito de Dolores", empezó la independencia de México.

◀ Este monumento honra a los héroes de la Guerra de la Independencia (1810–1821). Aproximadamente 600,000 personas murieron durante los 11 años de lucha contra España.

[1]priest   [2]shouted

[3]enjoy   [4]taste

▲ La cerámica de Talavera
es típica de Dolores Hidalgo.
Muchas personas llegan a la
ciudad para comprar esta
cerámica de diseños originales y
colores diferentes. En muchas
casas de Dolores Hidalgo puedes
ver a los artesanos trabajando
con la cerámica en sus talleres[5].

¿Sabes que . . . ?

Cada año, el 15 y 16 de septiembre, los mexicanos
celebran su independencia. En memoria del primer
grito de Dolores, el presidente del país se para en el
balcón del Palacio Nacional en la ciudad de México
y grita tres veces "¡Viva México!".

Para pensar

Generalmente hay ciudades, como Dolores Hidalgo,
que tienen una importancia histórica por los hechos
que pasaron allí. ¿Qué ciudad o ciudades de los
Estados Unidos tienen importancia histórica por su
participación en la independencia? ¿Qué pasó en
estas ciudades?

[5]workshops

Repaso del capítulo

Vocabulario y gramática

to talk about getting ready

acostarse (o → ue)	to go to bed
afeitarse	to shave
arreglarse (el pelo)	to fix (one's hair)
bañarse	to take a bath
cepillarse (los dientes)	to brush (one's teeth)
cortarse el pelo	to cut one's hair
despertarse (e → ie)	to wake up
ducharse	to take a shower
levantarse	to get up
lavarse (la cara)	to wash (one's face)
pedir prestado, -a (a)	to borrow (from)
pintarse (las uñas)	to paint, to polish (one's nails)
ponerse	to put on
prepararse	to get ready
secarse	to dry
vestirse (e → i)	to get dressed

to talk about things you need to get ready

el agua de colonia	cologne
el cepillo	brush
el cinturón, pl. los cinturones	belt
el desodorante	deodorant
la ducha	shower
el gel	gel
las joyas (de oro, de plata)	(gold, silver) jewelry
los labios	lips
el maquillaje	make-up
el peine	comb
el pelo	hair
el salón de belleza, pl. los salones de belleza	beauty salon
el secador	blow dryer
la toalla	towel
las uñas	nails

For *Vocabulario adicional,* see pp. 498–499.

to talk about a special event

la audición, pl. las audiciones	audition
la boda	wedding
la cita	date
el concurso	contest
un evento especial	special event

to talk about how you feel

entusiasmado, -a	excited
nervioso, -a	nervous
tranquilo, -a	calm

other useful words and expressions

antes de	before
cómodo, -a	comfortable
depende	it depends
elegante	elegant
lentamente	slowly
luego	then
por ejemplo	for example
rápidamente	quickly
te ves (bien)	you look (good)

reflexive verbs

me acuesto	nos acostamos
te acuestas	os acostáis
se acuesta	se acuestan

ser *to be*

soy	somos
eres	sois
es	son

estar *to be*

estoy	estamos
estás	estáis
está	están

possessive adjectives

mío, -a, -os, -as	nuestro, -a, -os, -as
tuyo, -a, -os, -as	vuestro, -a, -os, -as
suyo, -a, -os, -as	suyo, -a, -os, -as

Repaso

Más repaso GO realidades.com | print

Instant Check ✔
Puzzles ✔
Core WB pp. 36–37 ✔
Comm. WB p. 222 ✔ ✔

Preparación para el examen

On the exam you will be asked to . . .	Here are practice tasks similar to those you will find on the exam . . .	For review go to your print or digital textbook . . .

Interpretive

 1 Escuchar Listen and understand as teenagers talk about what they do on the weekend versus during the school week

Everyone does things a little differently on the weekend. Most people sleep later, dress more casually, and do things they don't have time to do during the week. As you listen to each person, decide whether you think they are talking about the weekend or a weekday. Be prepared to explain why you made your choice.

pp. 74–77 *Vocabulario en contexto*
p. 78 Actividad 5
p. 82 Actividad 12

Interpersonal

 2 Hablar Talk about your daily routine

Your parents have given you permission to go on the Spanish Club trip to Mexico this summer in which the boys share rooms and the girls share rooms. You want to share a room with a friend who wants to know if you have the same morning routine. Describe your typical routine to your friend.

p. 78 Actividad 5
p. 79 Actividad 7
p. 82 Actividades 12–13
p. 83 Actividad 15
p. 84 Actividades 16–17

Interpretive

 3 Leer Read and understand statements people make about typical and "not-so-typical" daily routines

Read the following statements from an online survey about people's morning routines. In your opinion, which ones would describe a typical daily routine? Which ones would be very unusual?

(a) Antes de bañarme, me pongo el maquillaje.
(b) Después de ponerme el desodorante, me ducho.
(c) Antes de lavarme el pelo, me seco con una toalla.
(d) Antes de arreglarme el pelo, me ducho.

pp. 74–77 *Vocabulario en contexto*
p. 80 Actividad 8
p. 83 Actividad 14
p. 85 Actividad 18
pp. 90–91 *Lectura*

Presentational

 4 Escribir Write briefly about a special event that you look forward to each year

Everyone looks forward to special events during the year. Your teacher asks you to write about one of them. After writing a brief description, exchange your paragraph with a partner to see if he or she can guess what type of event it is. You might include: (a) the time of year that the event occurs; (b) how you usually feel the days before the event; (c) how you usually dress for the event. Give as many clues as you can.

p. 78 Actividades 4–5
p. 84 Actividad 17
p. 86 Actividad 19

Cultures

 5 Pensar Demonstrate an understanding of the living conditions of the indigenous people of the *altiplano* in the Andes

You may have worn a *poncho* during a rainy football game or while camping. Explain where *ponchos* originated, how they are made, and why they are necessary for the people of that region.

p. 92 *La cultura en vivo*

Vocabulario Repaso

¿De qué color es?
amarillo, -a
anaranjado, -a
azul
blanco, -a
gris
marrón, *pl.* marrones
morado, -a
negro, -a
rojo, -a
rosado, -a
verde

¿Qué vas a hacer?
buscar
comprar
ir de compras
pagar
vender

¿Adónde vas?
el almacén,
   pl. los almacenes
el centro comercial
la joyería
la librería
la tienda de descuentos
la tienda de
   electrodomésticos
la tienda de ropa
la zapatería

¿Qué vas a comprar?
unos anteojos de sol
un bolso
una cartera
un disco compacto
un llavero
un regalo
el software
un videojuego

¿Cómo es?
barato, -a
bonito, -a
caro, -a
feo, -a
grande
nuevo, -a
pequeño, -a
viejo, -a

▼1 ¿Qué compras?

Escribir • Hablar

❶ Escribe tres frases para decir a qué tienda vas y qué compras. Incluye dos adjetivos para describir las cosas que compras.

Modelo
Voy a la joyería para comprar unos aretes rojos muy elegantes.

❷ Usa las frases del Paso 1. Habla con otro(a) estudiante y trata de adivinar *(try to guess)* qué va a comprar.

▶️ **Modelo**
A —*¿Adónde vas de compras?*
B —*Voy a la joyería.*
A —*¿Qué vas a comprar?*
B —*Algo rojo y elegante.*
A —*¿Compras un collar?*
B —*No, compro unos aretes.*

Gramática Repaso

Cardinal numbers

10 diez	90 noventa	800 ochocientos, -as
20 veinte	100 ciento (cien)	900 novecientos, -as
30 treinta	200 doscientos, -as	1,000 mil
40 cuarenta	300 trescientos, -as	2,000 dos mil
50 cincuenta	400 cuatrocientos, -as	100,000 cien mil
60 sesenta	500 quinientos, -as	200,000 doscientos, -as mil
70 setenta	600 seiscientos, -as	
80 ochenta	700 setecientos, -as	

Un is not used before *cien, ciento,* and *mil.*

cien personas	**a hundred** people
mil pesos	**one thousand** pesos

Un/una and numbers ending in *-cientos /-cientas* agree in gender with the nouns that follow them.

Hay **treinta y un** videojuegos en la mesa.
Esta librería tiene más de **quinientas** revistas.

- To give the date in Spanish, use:

el + *cardinal number* + **de** + *month*

el veinte **de** enero

- The year is always given using complete numbers:

mil novecientos ochenta y cuatro

▼2 ¿Cuánto cuestan? |

Hablar

Tienes que hacer un proyecto para tu clase de economía. Con otro(a) estudiante, habla de cuántos pesos cuesta cada producto en un centro comercial en la Ciudad de México.

1. un bolso de cuero (515)
2. una cartera (325)
3. unos pantalones (250)
4. un disco compacto (179)
5. una camisa de seda (399)
6. un collar de oro (1,200)
7. una revista (35)

Más práctica GO

realidades.com | print

A ver si recuerdas with **Study Plan** ✔
Guided WB p. 71 ✔ ✔
Core WB pp. 38–39 ✔ ✔
Hispanohablantes **WB** p. 70 ✔

▼3 ¿Cuándo fue? |

Hablar

Pregunta a otro(a) estudiante cuándo ocurrieron los siguientes eventos importantes.

▶️ **Modelo**

el Día de la Independencia en los Estados Unidos

A —¿Cuándo fue el Día de la Independencia en los Estados Unidos?

B —Fue el cuatro de julio de mil setecientos setenta y seis.

1. el primer día de clases este año
2. el año del primer viaje de Cristóbal Colón
3. el año del viaje de los peregrinos (Pilgrims)
4. el año del primer viaje a la Luna
5. el fin de la Segunda Guerra Mundial

▼ Chapter Objectives

Communication

By the end of this chapter you will be able to:

- Listen and read about clothing people bought
- Talk and write about shopping trips
- Exchange information about when and where you bought what you are wearing

Culture

You will also be able to:

- Understand *la parranda* in Spanish-speaking countries
- Compare shopping in Spain and the United States

You will demonstrate what you know and can do:

- Presentación escrita, p. 121
- Preparación para el examen, p. 125

You will use:

Vocabulary	Grammar
• Shopping	• Preterite of regular verbs
• Clothing	• Demonstrative adjectives
	• Using adjectives as nouns

Exploración del mundo hispano

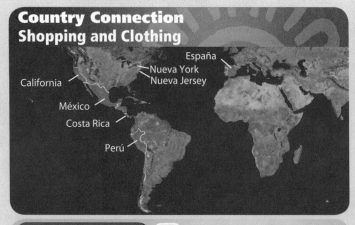

Country Connection
Shopping and Clothing

España
Nueva York
Nueva Jersey
California
México
Costa Rica
Perú

realidades.com (GO)

 Reference Atlas

▶ *Videocultura y actividad*

Mapa global interactivo

De compras en Barcelona, España

OFERTA
ANTES 29,90 €
AHORA 24,90 €

Arte y cultura | España

La Infanta Margarita de Austria Los reyes de España prometieron en matrimonio *(promised in marriage)* a su hija, Margarita, a su primo Leopoldo, quien luego fue emperador de Austria. Como *(Since)* Margarita y su primo no vivían *(lived)* en la misma ciudad, los reyes mandaron muchos cuadros de ella a la corte de Viena para que la familia real pudiera verla *(could see her)*. En este cuadro, Margarita tiene aproximadamente nueve años.

• ¿Qué tipo de ropa llevas tú para fotos importantes? ¿Y a quién envías estas fotos?

"La Infanta Margarita Teresa" (1659), Diego Velázquez ▶

Oil on canvas, 120.5 x 94.5. Kunsthistorisches Museum, Vienna, Austria. Courtesy The Bridgeman Art Library International Ltd.

Vocabulario en contexto

la entrada

la salida

ENTRADA

SALIDA

ZAPATOS

LIQUIDACIÓN de verano ¡Descuento del 70%!

LIQUIDACIÓN de verano ¡Descuento del 50%!

los colores **vivos**

los colores **pastel**

azul **oscuro**

azul **claro**

—Mira, Lupita. **Aquellas** blusas tienen un descuento del 50 por ciento. ¡Me encanta ir de compras cuando hay **una liquidación**!

—¡Es **una ganga**! Pero no me gustan los colores **tan** vivos.

—¡No importa! **Están de moda**. Con **precios** tan **bajos**, voy a **probarme** dos o tres.

—Y mira **aquellos** bolsos en la mesa. **El letrero anuncia** un descuento del 70 por ciento. ¡Vamos!

Más vocabulario

el cheque de viajero traveler's check
el cupón de regalo gift certificate
la lana wool
el número shoe size
la seda silk

la caja

la cajera

—Es una buena **marca**. Y **encontré** mi **talla, mediana**.

—**En realidad,** no necesito estos bolsos. Pero me gusta **el estilo** y no cuestan mucho.

—Tienes razón. Y pueden ser regalos para tus amigas. Vamos a la caja para pagar.

—¿Por qué siempre pagas **en efectivo?**

—Porque no me gusta usar ni mi **tarjeta de crédito** ni **un cheque personal**.

—Yo estoy contenta. No **gasté** mucho. Con esta liquidación los precios no están muy **altos**. Compré esta blusa pero, ¿no piensas que es un poco **exagerada? ¿Qué te parece?**

—**Me parece** muy bien. Y pagaste muy poco por todas las blusas.

▼1 ¿Dónde está? | 🔊

Escuchar

Imagina que estás en la tienda de las páginas 102–103. Mira los dibujos y escucha las siguientes frases. Señala lo que escuchas.

▼2 ¿Cierto o falso? | 🔊

Escuchar

Escucha las siguientes frases que describen a Lupita y a su amiga. Si la frase es cierta, señala con el pulgar hacia arriba y si la frase es falsa, señala con el pulgar hacia abajo.

Más práctica (GO)

realidades.com | print

Instant Check	✔	
Guided WB pp. 72–78	✔	✔
Core WB pp. 40–41	✔	✔
Comm. WB p. 42	✔	✔
Hispanohablantes WB p. 72		✔

Buscando una ganga

¿Qué pasó cuando Gloria fue de compras con Raúl y Tomás?

Estrategia

Scanning
By scanning the photos from the *Videohistoria* and the accompanying text, can you figure out who buys what?

1

Gloria: ¡Mira **aquel** letrero!

Tomás: A ver . . . ¿qué anuncia?

Gloria: ¡Una liquidación fabulosa! ¿Qué les parece? ¿Vamos a ver qué tienen?

Raúl: No **me importa,** pero creo que los precios aquí siempre son altos.

Tomás

Gloria

Raúl

5

Gloria: Aquí, encontré mi talla.

Tomás: ¿Usas mediana? Es bonita. **¿De qué está hecha?**

Gloria: **Está hecha de algodón.** ¿Qué te parece?

Raúl: No me parece mal. Y el algodón es mejor que **las telas sintéticas.**

6

Gloria: ¿Cuál **escojo?** ¿Ésta o la blusa **de sólo un color?**

Raúl: No me importa. Compra algo **inmediatamente** y ¡vamos!

Gloria: ¡Qué impaciente eres! ¿Por qué no van a mirar otras cosas mientras yo me pruebo las blusas?

7

Gloria: Quiero comprarme esta blusa.

La dependienta: Muy bien, señorita. ¿Cómo va a pagar?

Gloria: En efectivo. Aquí está.

Gloria: Compré esta blusa aquí **recientemente**. Me gusta porque me queda un poco **floja**. No me gusta la ropa **apretada**.

Raúl: Mira, no tengo dinero. ¿Cuánto tiempo pasamos aquí?

Gloria: No importa. Yo tengo dinero.

Tomás: ¿Hay **un mercado** cerca de aquí? Me gustaría visitar uno.

Raúl: Siempre hay buenas gangas aquí en el mercado.

Tomás: Sí, hay mucho que puedes comprar aquí. Por eso me gusta ir de compras en el mercado.

Gloria: ¡Mira aquellas blusas! ¡Qué estilo tan bonito tienen! ¡Y los colores son tan vivos!

Raúl: Gloria, por favor, ¿otra blusa?

Raúl: Estas chaquetas **de cuero** son fabulosas. ¿Cuál te gusta más?

Tomás: Te ves muy bien.

Gloria: ¿Y no tienes dinero?

▼3 ¿Comprendiste?

Escribir • Hablar

1. ¿Qué anuncia el letrero que ve Gloria?
2. ¿Por qué no quiere Raúl pasar mucho tiempo en la tienda?
3. ¿Adónde van los tres jóvenes para buscar gangas?
4. ¿Qué encuentra Gloria en el mercado?
5. ¿Cómo es la ropa que compra Gloria?
6. ¿Cómo paga Gloria?
7. ¿Qué tipo de ropa se prueba Raúl?

Más práctica	GO	
	realidades.com	print	
Instant Check	✔	
Guided WB pp. 79–82	✔	✔
Core WB pp. 42–43	✔	✔
Comm. WB pp. 35–37, 38	✔	✔
Hispanohablantes WB p. 73		✔

▶ **Talk about clothing preferences**
▶ **Listen to and write about comments on clothes and fashion**
▶ **Write about clothes shopping**
▶ **Discuss how people pay for their purchases**

Vocabulario en uso

▼4 ¿Quién es? | _____

Escuchar • Escribir • Hablar

1 En una hoja de papel, escribe los números del 1 al 5. Después escucha los comentarios sobre la ropa y la moda. Escribe las frases que oyes.

2 Ahora lee los comentarios que escribiste y, según el dibujo, decide si habla Santiago o Timoteo. Escribe *Santiago* o *Timoteo* en tu papel.

3 Lee otra vez las frases sobre Timoteo y Santiago. Escoge tres y da tus opiniones. Explica por qué estás de acuerdo o no. Lee tus frases a otro(a) estudiante.

Modelo

No me importan los precios altos si la ropa está de moda.
Estoy de acuerdo. Para mí, la marca de la ropa es más importante que el precio.

▼5 ¿Cierta o falsa? | _____

Escribir • Hablar

Escribe seis frases para describir lo que hacen Santiago y Timoteo. Usa las palabras del recuadro. Algunas frases deben ser ciertas y otras, falsas. Lee tus frases a otro(a) estudiante. Tu compañero(a) va a decir si la frase es cierta o falsa y cambiarla si es falsa para dar la información correcta.

▶ Modelo

A —*Timoteo lleva ropa a la caja.*
B —*Falso. Santiago lleva ropa a la caja.*

color oscuro	el cajero
color claro	la talla
la salida	el descuento
la caja	la entrada

▼6 Muchos descuentos _____

Leer • Escribir

Lee el mensaje electrónico que Dolores le escribe a su amiga Marta sobre una oportunidad fantástica. Escribe la palabra apropiada para completar cada frase.

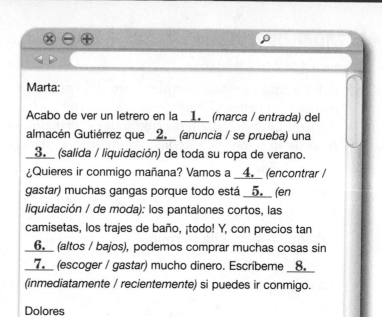

Marta:

Acabo de ver un letrero en la __1.__ *(marca / entrada)* del almacén Gutiérrez que __2.__ *(anuncia / se prueba)* una __3.__ *(salida / liquidación)* de toda su ropa de verano. ¿Quieres ir conmigo mañana? Vamos a __4.__ *(encontrar / gastar)* muchas gangas porque todo está __5.__ *(en liquidación / de moda):* los pantalones cortos, las camisetas, los trajes de baño, ¡todo! Y, con precios tan __6.__ *(altos / bajos),* podemos comprar muchas cosas sin __7.__ *(escoger / gastar)* mucho dinero. Escríbeme __8.__ *(inmediatamente / recientemente)* si puedes ir conmigo.

Dolores

▼7 ¿Qué compran y cómo pagan? | | ♻ _____

Escribir • Hablar

❶ Copia y completa la tabla para indicar qué compran las diferentes personas que conoces y cómo pagan.

¿Quién?	¿Qué?	¿Cómo?
mis hermanos	discos compactos	tarjeta de crédito
mi mamá (o papá)		
yo		
mis amigos		
(nombre) y yo		
mi mejor amigo(a)		

❷ Trabaja con otro(a) estudiante y describe lo que compra alguien de tu tabla. Tu compañero(a) debe tratar de adivinar *(try to guess)* cómo paga la persona.

 Modelo

A —*Mis hermanos compran discos compactos.*

B —*¿Pagan ellos en efectivo?*

A —*No, pagan con una tarjeta de crédito.*

▼8 Muchos detalles | 👥 | ♻

Dibujar • Escribir • Hablar

❶ Dibuja una persona completa con diferentes prendas *(articles)* de ropa. Usa diferentes colores en tu dibujo. En una hoja de papel, escribe una descripción de la ropa de la persona. Puedes incluir información sobre:

- los colores
- el estilo
- la talla y el número
- de qué está hecha la ropa
- dónde lo compró

Tu descripción debe tener un mínimo de cuatro frases.

Modelo

Esta persona usa ropa bastante exagerada. Sus pantalones son flojos y su camiseta de seda es de un color verde vivo. Su gorra roja está hecha de lana. Lleva zapatos rojos del número 11.

❷ Trabaja con un grupo de tres estudiantes. Lee tu descripción dos veces en voz alta *(aloud)*. Tus compañeros tienen que dibujar una persona según tu descripción. Deben recordar los detalles *(remember the details)* de tu descripción sin escribir lo que dices. Después van a repetir la descripción completa.

▼9 La moda | 💬👥

Hablar

Con otro(a) estudiante, habla de las chaquetas de la foto.

1. ¿Cómo es el estilo de estas chaquetas? ¿De qué color son las chaquetas? ¿Son de color oscuro, claro o vivo?

2. ¿De qué están hechas las chaquetas? ¿Cuánto cuestan? ¿Es un buen precio?

3. ¿Crees que las chaquetas son para llevar a eventos especiales o para todos los días? Imagina que compraste una de estas chaquetas. ¿Adónde y cuándo vas a llevarla?

ÚLTIMA MODA

CHAQUETAS PARA HOMBRE

CHAQUETAS PARA MUJER

$199

$199

Visítenos
de lunes a viernes, 9 A.M. – 6 P.M.
Rt. 28 (al lado del Videocentro) Lawrence, MA

▼ Fondo Cultural | El mundo hispano

¡No sé qué talla uso! Si algún día vas de compras en un país hispanohablante, debes saber que tanto la ropa como los zapatos tienen diferentes tallas y números. Un vestido de la talla 12, por ejemplo, puede ser 46 en España. Además, entre países, a veces los números son diferentes. Por ejemplo, un zapato de hombres de $9\frac{1}{2}$ es aproximadamente el 43 en España y el 27 en México. Hay sitios Web que dan las conversiones y algunas tiendas también ofrecen tablas de conversión. En España, para calcular el número de zapatos de mujer, generalmente añades *(you add)* 30, y para los de hombres añades 33.5.

• ¿Aproximadamente, qué número de zapato calzas *(do you wear)* en España?

▼10 ¿En qué puedo servirle? |

Hablar

Estás de compras en una zapatería en España. Necesitas comprar un par de zapatos para llevar a un evento especial y otro para usar todos los días. Pídale al dependiente (a la dependienta) lo que prefieres, indicando tu número y el color de los zapatos. Trabaja con otro(a) estudiante.

▶ **Modelo**

A —¿En qué puedo servirle?

B —Necesito comprar un par de zapatos para una fiesta.

A —¿De qué número y color?

B —Soy del número . . . y prefiero zapatos de color . . .

▼11 Juego | 👥

Hablar

Describe a otro(a) estudiante la ropa de cinco estudiantes de tu clase sin decir los nombres. Menciona el color, el estilo y de qué material está hecha toda la ropa que llevan los chicos. Tu compañero(a) tiene que adivinar *(guess)* a quién describes. Por cada persona que tu compañero(a) adivina correctamente, tú recibes un punto.

Modelo

Lleva una camisa azul de tela sintética y unos pantalones cortos blancos de algodón. ¿Quién es?

▼12 Y tú, ¿qué dices? | 🗨

Escribir • Hablar

1. ¿Qué colores de ropa te gusta usar? ¿Prefieres los colores claros o los oscuros? ¿Generalmente usas ropa de colores pastel o colores vivos?

2. ¿Qué ropa está de moda ahora? ¿Los estilos que están de moda te parecen exagerados o sencillos? ¿Qué marcas son más populares entre los jóvenes?

3. ¿En qué almacén o tienda puedes encontrar gangas? ¿Los precios allí siempre son bajos o sólo cuando hay una liquidación?

4. ¿Vas mucho de compras? ¿Qué compras? ¿Cómo pagas generalmente?

Gramática Repaso

Preterite of regular verbs

To talk about actions that were completed in the past, use the preterite tense. To form the preterite tense of a regular verb, add the preterite endings to the stem of the verb.

(yo)	miré aprendí escribí	(nosotros) (nosotras)	miramos aprendimos escribimos
(tú)	miraste aprendiste escribiste	(vosotros) (vosotras)	mirasteis aprendisteis escribisteis
Ud. (él) (ella)	miró aprendió escribió	Uds. (ellos) (ellas)	miraron aprendieron escribieron

Note that -ar and -er verbs that have a stem change in the present tense do not have a stem change in the preterite.

Generalmente **me pruebo** la ropa antes de comprarla, pero ayer no **me probé** los pantalones que compré.

Ver has regular preterite endings, but unlike those of other verbs, they have no written accent marks.

Anoche, David **vio** una camisa que le gustó mucho.

• Verbs that end in *-car*, *-gar*, and *-zar* have a spelling change in the *yo* form of the preterite.

buscar	c → qu	yo busqué
pagar	g → gu	yo pagué
almorzar	z → c	yo almorcé

¿**Pagaste** mucho por tu suéter nuevo?

No, no **pagué** mucho. Lo encontré en una liquidación.

Más ayuda   realidades.com

▶ *GramActiva* Video
Tutorials: Preterite, Regular verbs in the preterite

◀))) *Canción de hip hop:* ¿Qué compraste?

✍ *GramActiva* Activity

▼13 ¡Gracias por el regalo!

Leer • Escribir

Elena está escribiendo una carta a su abuela. Escribe la forma apropiada del pretérito del verbo entre paréntesis para cada frase.

Cupón de regalo

0123475

Querida abuelita:

Hace tres días, yo __1.__ (recibir) el cupón de regalo que tú me __2.__ (enviar). ¡Muchas gracias! Yo __3.__ (decidir) comprarme ropa nueva. Fui de compras con mis amigas al centro comercial, pero nosotras no __4.__ (encontrar) buenas gangas. Por eso, __5.__ (tomar) el autobús al mercado. Allí, yo __6.__ (escoger) unos pantalones de cuero. ¡Están muy de moda! Mi amiga Sonia __7.__ (comprar) unos aretes que __8.__ (ver) porque le __9.__ (gustar) mucho. Cuando yo __10.__ (llegar) a casa, me __11.__ (probar) los pantalones. Son perfectos. ¡Muchísimas gracias, abuelita!

Besitos,

Elena

▼14 ¿Qué compraron? |

Hablar

Habla con otro(a) estudiante de lo que hicieron estas personas en el almacén.

▶ Modelo

tú / encontrar

A —¿Qué encontraste en el almacén?

B —Encontré un suéter de color oscuro.

Estudiante A

1. las chicas / probarse
2. tú / comprar
3. Uds. / ver
4. Felipe / buscar
5. la madre de la novia / mirar
6. Marta / usar para pagar
7. Pedro y Félix / escoger

Estudiante B

▼15 La última vez |

Escribir • Hablar

❶ ¿Cuándo fue la última vez *(last time)* que alguien que tú conoces hizo estas actividades? Puede ser tú, alguien de tu familia, un(a) amigo(a) o tú y tus amigos. Usa las expresiones del recuadro para contestar. Escribe tus respuestas.

esta mañana	el mes pasado
anoche	el año pasado
ayer	hace + dos semanas,
la semana pasada	un mes . . .

❷ Ahora habla con otro(a) estudiante para comparar tu lista con su lista.

❸ Escribe cuatro frases para comparar lo que dijeron *(said)* los (las) dos.

Modelo

comer en un restaurante

Anoche mis amigos y yo comimos en un restaurante.

1. comprar un regalo
2. preparar la comida
3. ver una película a las dos de la tarde
4. escribir una carta por correo electrónico
5. decorar para una fiesta
6. beber un refresco
7. salir para una fiesta
8. despertarse a las diez de la mañana

Modelo

Anoche comí en un restaurante, pero Jorge comió en casa.

16 Muchas actividades |

Escribir • Hablar

Escribe una frase para indicar si hiciste o no cada una de las actividades de la lista. Después habla con otro(a) estudiante para saber si hizo estas actividades recientemente.

Modelo
practicar deportes
A —*¿Practicaste deportes hoy?*
B —*Sí, practiqué deportes hoy.*
o: —*No, no practiqué deportes hoy.*

1. llegar temprano a la escuela
2. tocar un instrumento musical
3. empezar a leer una novela
4. almorzar con tu mejor amigo(a)
5. jugar al ajedrez o practicar un deporte
6. navegar en la Red
7. buscar un regalo para alguien

17 ¿Qué llevaste? |

Hablar

Trae una foto en que estás vestido(a) para un evento especial, o una foto de un(a) modelo de una revista. Con otro(a) estudiante, describe la ropa de la foto. Incluye el color, la tela y el estilo. Explica cuándo y dónde compraste la ropa, cómo pagaste y adónde fuiste vestido(a) así. Si traes una foto de una revista, usa tu imaginación para contestar las preguntas.

▶ Modelo

A —*Estoy vestido(a) para una fiesta. Llevo una camisa amarilla y pantalones marrones. La camisa está hecha de algodón y los pantalones están hechos de lana.*
B —*¿Dónde compraste la ropa?*
A —*La compré en . . . y pagué con . . .*

18 Los textiles y el cuero

Leer • Pensar • Escribir • Hablar

La lana, el algodón y el cuero son productos que los indígenas de las Américas usaban *(used)* antes de la llegada de los españoles. Lee la línea cronológica *(timeline)* sobre estos productos y contesta las preguntas.

Conexiones | La historia

1000
En las Américas, los indígenas precolombinos usan el telar[1]. Usan algodón y otras fibras para hacer sus telas y vestidos.

1638
Se establece la primera fábrica[4] de tela en Lowell, Massachusetts.

1500
Los españoles traen caballos a las Américas. Luego traen ovejas[2] y vacas[3]. Los indígenas incorporan la lana de oveja en sus telas tradicionales.

[1]loom   [2]sheep   [3]cows   [4]factory

Exploración del lenguaje

Origins of words from Arabic

In Spanish, words that came from Arabic often begin with the letters *al.* In Arabic, *al* means "the." Translate the following sentences, noting the words in bold borrowed from Arabic.

1. Cuando voy al **almacén** voy a comprar una **alfombra** de **algodón**.

2. También voy a comprar **azúcar**, **naranjas** y **aceitunas**.

El Patio de los Leones de La Alhambra, en Granada, España

Más práctica (GO)

realidades.com | print

Instant Check	✔	
Guided WB pp. 83–84	✔	✔
Core WB p. 44	✔	✔
Comm. WB pp. 39, 43, 223	✔	✔
Hispanohablantes WB pp. 74–75	✔	

1793
Whitney inventa la desmotadora de algodón[6] y revoluciona la industria del algodón en los Estados Unidos.

1760–1815
Los avances mecánicos e inventos de la Revolución Industrial aumentan[5] la producción y bajan los precios.

1900
Argentina y Brasil son grandes productores mundiales[7] de textiles y cuero.

Siglo XX
Los métodos científicos, la electrónica y las computadoras permiten el desarrollo[8] de las telas sintéticas.

1. ¿Qué cosa usaron los indígenas precolombinos para hacer sus telas? ¿De qué estaban (*were*) hechas?

2. ¿Cuándo empezaron a usar los indígenas la lana de oveja en sus telas tradicionales? ¿De dónde vino esta lana?

3. ¿Quién inventó la desmotadora de algodón? ¿Cómo cambió (*changed*) esta invención la industria del algodón?

[5]increase [6]cotton gin [7]worldwide [8]development

Gramática

▼ **Objectives**
▶ **Point out items of clothing and other objects**
▶ **Listen to and write about the relative location of objects**

Demonstrative adjectives

To point out something or someone that is far from both you and the person you are speaking to, you use a form of *aquel,* which means "that one over there."

¿Recuerdas?

Do you remember this rhyme about the two demonstrative adjectives *este* and *ese?*

This and *these* both have *t's.* *That* and *those* don't.

Here's a chart that compares the three demonstrative adjectives and their meanings.

Singular		Plural	
este, esta	*this*	estos, estas	*these*
ese, esa	*that*	esos, esas	*those*
aquel, aquella	*that one over there*	aquellos, aquellas	*those over there*

All demonstrative adjectives come before the noun and agree with the noun in gender (masculine or feminine) and number (singular or plural).

Más ayuda   **realidades.com**

▶ *GramActiva* **Video**
Tutorial: Demonstrative adjectives

✎ *GramActiva* **Activity**

▼19 ¿Esta corbata o aquella corbata?

Leer • Escribir

Marta y su hermano, Asís, necesitan comprar un regalo para su padre, pero nunca están de acuerdo. Completa su conversación con la forma apropiada de *aquel.*

Marta: A mí me gusta __1.__ gorra roja.
Asís: A mí no. Prefiero comprarle __2.__ disco compacto de Shakira.
Marta: ¡Asís! ¡El regalo es para papá! ¿Qué te parece __3.__ camisa azul?
Asís: Quizás, pero me gusta más __4.__ camisa roja.
Marta: ¿Qué piensas de __5.__ pantalones amarillos?
Asís: ¿Estás loca? Nuestro padre no juega al golf.
Marta: Bueno, ¿y __6.__ corbatas? Desde aquí veo dos que combinan con la camisa roja.
Asís: ¡Perfecto! Las compramos.

▼20 Escucha y escribe |

Escuchar • Escribir

En una hoja de papel, escribe los números del 1 al 8. Escucha y escribe las frases. Luego indica si el objeto de la frase está al lado de, cerca de o lejos de la persona que habla.

▼21 ¿Qué te parece? |

Hablar

Imagina que estás en el mercado de Pisac, en Perú. Habla con otro(a) estudiante de las cosas que venden. ¿Qué te gustaría comprar?

▶ Modelo

A —*¿Qué te parece esta cartera de colores vivos?*
B —*Esa cartera es muy bonita. Me gusta.*

o:

A —*¿Te gustan estos bolsos de colores vivos?*
B —*No, prefiero aquellos bolsos de sólo un color.*

El mercado de Pisac, en Perú

▼22 Juego |

Hablar

❶ Busca cinco objetos en la sala de clases. Unos deben estar cerca de ti, otros deben estar más lejos. Piensa en cómo puedes describirlos sin mencionar su nombre.

❷ Ahora, con un grupo de tres o cuatro, describe tus objetos. Las otras personas del grupo tienen que adivinar el objeto que estás describiendo. La primera persona que identifica correctamente el objeto, y que usa el adjetivo demostrativo apropiado, recibe un punto.

▶ Modelo

A —*Es azul y negro. Es muy importante llevarlo a la clase. Lo usas para escribir.*
B —*Este bolígrafo.*
A —*No. Casi. Está lejos de mí.*
B —*Es aquel bolígrafo de Laura.*
A —*Sí. Recibes un punto.*

El español en el mundo del trabajo

Hoy en día, los negocios *(businesses)* quieren atraer *(attract)* a más clientes hispanohablantes, porque es el sector más creciente *(growing)* de la población. Para los hispanohablantes es importante poder comunicarse en español cuando hacen compras o abren cuentas en un banco. Por eso, las tiendas, los bancos y otros negocios emplean a personas bilingües que hablan español e inglés.

* ¿Cuáles son las tiendas o negocios en tu comunidad con empleados bilingües? ¿Por qué es importante tener empleados bilingües?

Más práctica	GO
realidades.com	print

Instant Check	✔	
Guided WB pp. 85–86	✔	✔
Core WB p. 45	✔	✔
Comm. WB p. 44	✔	✔
Hispanohablantes WB pp. 78–79		✔

Gramática

Using adjectives as nouns

When you are comparing two similar things, you can avoid repetition by dropping the noun and using an article with an adjective:

¿Cuál prefieres, la sudadera apretada o la floja?

Which do you prefer, the tight sweatshirt or **the loose one?**

Prefiero la floja.

I prefer **the loose one.**

You can also do this with expressions that use *de:*

¿Compraste una chaqueta de lana o **una de cuero?**

Did you buy a wool jacket or *a leather one?*

¿Prefieres el abrigo de Paco o **el de Juan?**

Do you prefer Paco's coat or **Juan's?**

▼23 ¿Qué te parece?

Hablar

Vas de compras con tu mejor amigo(a) que siempre tiene una opinión. Él / Ella te dice lo que prefiere.

Nota

Me parece(n) functions like *me gusta(n)* with singular and plural objects.

• **El** roj**o** me parec**e** bonit**o.**
• **Los** azul**es** me parec**en** fe**os.**

▶ Modelo

A —*¿Prefieres el vestido rojo o el azul?*
B —*El rojo me parece feo. Prefiero el azul.*

Estudiante A

Estudiante B

Me parece(n) . . .
Prefiero . . .

¡Respuesta personal!

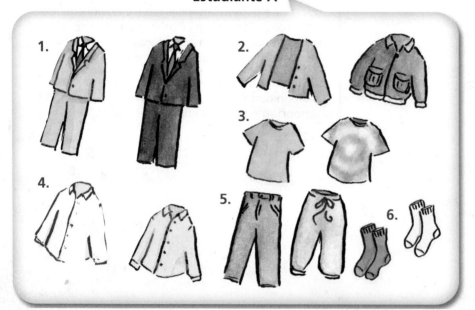

▼24 Un desfile de modas | 👥

Pensar • Hablar • Escribir

❶ Vas a participar en un desfile de moda *(fashion show)* en tu clase. Con un grupo, tienen que decidir qué ropa va a llevar cada persona. Escriban una lista de posibilidades. Usen una tabla como ésta para organizar sus ideas:

Para un *evento especial*	Para *todos los días*
un vestido o traje elegante, color blanco	unos jeans con una sudadera roja

Un conjunto del diseñador Narciso Rodríguez

❷ Usen la tabla y escriban una descripción de la ropa que va a presentar cada "modelo" en su grupo. Pueden incluir el lugar donde venden la ropa y los precios. Mientras los modelos desfilan *(model)* la ropa, un miembro del grupo va a describirla a la clase.

Modelo

Hoy Elena lleva una camisa elegante y una falda de cuero. Esta ropa es perfecta para un evento muy especial. Los colores negro y blanco siempre están de moda. Ustedes pueden comprar esta camisa por sólo 75 dólares.

❸ Después del desfile de moda, vas a tener la oportunidad de "comprar" uno de los conjuntos *(outfits)* que viste. Describe el conjunto a la clase y di cómo vas a pagar.

Modelo

Yo quiero comprar la ropa de Enrique. Me gustó mucho porque es perfecta para llevar a un partido de fútbol. Él llevó unos jeans con una camiseta azul y una sudadera roja. Puedo pagar en efectivo porque no cuesta mucho: sólo 60 dólares.

▼ Fondo Cultural | Estados Unidos

Narciso Rodríguez nació en Nueva Jersey, de padres cubanos y abuelos españoles. Estudió en la *Parsons School of Design* en Nueva York, y ha trabajado *(has worked)* para los diseñadores Anne Klein, Donna Karan y Calvin Klein. Presentó su primera colección independiente en 1997. Ganó el premio *(award)* del *Council of Fashion Designers of America* al mejor diseñador de ropa femenina en 2002 y 2003. Diseña vestidos para muchas actrices y otras mujeres famosas.

• ¿Te gustaría ser diseñador(a)? ¿Por qué? ¿Qué talentos necesitas para este trabajo y qué debes estudiar?

Más práctica (GO)   realidades.com | print

Instant Check	✔	
Guided WB p. 87	✔	✔
Core WB p. 46	✔	✔
Comm. WB p. 41	✔	✔

Lectura

LOS JEANS:
LOS PANTALONES MÁS POPULARES DEL MUNDO

Probablemente tienes jeans en tu armario. Muchas personas, desde la Argentina hasta el Canadá y desde el Japón hasta España, llevan estos cómodos y prácticos pantalones. Se llevan en el trabajo, en la escuela y para salir de noche. Dicen que los jeans son ropa democrática porque los lleva gente de todas las clases sociales.

Estrategia

Tolerating ambiguity
Often when you read, you will find unfamiliar words. Don't stop, but keep on reading, since the meaning may become clear in context, or you may decide the words might not be necessary to understand the reading.

EL REMACHE

LA ESQUINA DEL BOLSILLO

EL BOLSILLO

UN POCO DE HISTORIA

Levi Strauss, un joven alemán, llegó a los Estados Unidos con su familia en 1847 a la edad de 18 años. Después de trabajar algunos años con su familia, Strauss viajó a California para abrir una tienda de ropa y accesorios. Esta tienda se convirtió en un negocio[1] próspero durante los siguientes 20 años, y Strauss se hizo rico.

En el año 1872, recibió una carta de Jacob Davis, un sastre[2] de Reno, Nevada, en la que le explicó el proceso que él inventó para poner remaches en las esquinas de los

[1]business [2]tailor

bolsillos de los pantalones de hombres. El uso de los remaches resultó en unos pantalones bastante fuertes para aguantar[3] los rigores de un trabajo difícil y en unos bolsillos más resistentes al peso[4] del oro.

Con el dinero de Strauss y la invención de Davis, los dos decidieron pedir la patente para el proceso. En 1873 recibieron la patente para poner los remaches en los pantalones y empezaron a

fabricar "*overalls* a la cintura" o *waist overalls* (el antiguo nombre en inglés de los jeans) en San Francisco. Como dicen, "el resto es historia".

YO DIGO "MAHONES" Y TÚ, ¿QUÉ DICES?

Si tienes amigos que hablan español debes saber que hay varias palabras que se usan para decir "jeans". Por ejemplo, se les llaman "vaqueros"[5] porque los vaqueros del oeste de los Estados Unidos usan este tipo de pantalón. En Cuba les dicen "pitusa" mientras en México les llaman "pantalones de mezclilla". Algunas personas usan las palabras "tejanos" y "mecánicos", pero la palabra más común sigue siendo simplemente "jeans".

[3]stand up to   [4]weight   [5]cowboys

¿Comprendiste?

1. Haz una línea cronológica *(timeline)* con las fechas mencionadas en esta lectura. Incluye las tres fechas y describe lo que pasó en cada una.

2. ¿Por qué escribió Jacob Davis una carta a Levi Strauss en 1872? ¿Qué dijo Davis en la carta?

3. Jacob Davis y Levi Strauss empezaron un nuevo negocio. ¿Qué contribuyó Davis? ¿Y Strauss?

Y tú, ¿qué dices? |

1. ¿Estás de acuerdo con la expresión "los jeans son ropa democrática"? ¿Por qué?

2. ¿Llevas jeans? ¿Por qué?

3. Entre tus amigos, ¿qué ropa y colores están de moda hoy en día?

Más práctica	GO

realidades.com | print

Guided WB p. 88	✔	✔
Comm. WB pp. 45, 224	✔	✔
Hispanohablantes WB pp. 82–83		✔
Cultural Reading Activity		✔

Perspectivas del mundo hispano

La parranda

Un amigo te invita a su casa. Cuando llegas, encuentras a gente de todas las edades, niños y adultos. Se oye música. Alguien te saluda. Otra persona empieza a hablar contigo. Hay varias personas bailando en pareja[1]. No ves a tu amigo. Luego alguien te invita a bailar. ¿Qué está ocurriendo aquí?

Es una parranda. Una *parranda* es una fiesta con comida, refrescos, música y baile. En las casas hispanas se celebran parrandas cuando hay algún evento especial, como una boda o alguna fiesta nacional. En estas fiestas participan los miembros de la familia y los amigos. Todos comen, bailan y se divierten. A veces, hay parranda todo el día.

En general, las casas hispanas tienen un patio y una sala grande. La sala es el cuarto que usa la familia para las grandes ocasiones. Durante las fiestas normalmente hay espacio para bailar. Frecuentemente en vez de[2] discos compactos, hay una orquesta. Muchas veces los miembros de la familia o los amigos componen[3] la orquesta y tocan música para bailar.

¡Compruébalo! Pregúntales a tus compañeros de clase si les gusta hacer fiestas con su familia. Pregúntales si bailan en pareja frecuentemente. Pregúntales cómo debe ser una buena fiesta. Según los resultados, completa las siguientes oraciones.

Modelo

Mis compañeros de clase creen que hacer una fiesta con su familia es buena idea.

1. Mis compañeros de clase creen que hacer una fiesta con su familia es . . .

2. Mis compañeros de clase bailan en pareja . . .

3. Mis compañeros de clase creen que una buena fiesta debe ser . . .

¿Qué te parece? ¿Qué indican las respuestas de tus compañeros sobre las fiestas familiares? En tu opinión, ¿qué debe ocurrir en una buena fiesta? Considera los diferentes tipos de fiestas. ¿Qué hay de bueno en cada una?

[1]in pairs [2]instead of [3]make up

Presentación escrita

Encontré unas gangas

Task
You received $200 for your birthday and bought some clothing. Write an e-mail to a friend describing your shopping trip.

① **Prewrite** Think about your trip. Copy and fill in this chart.

¿Qué compraste?	¿Dónde . . . ?	¿Cuánto pagaste?	¿Por qué te gusta(n)?

② **Draft** Use the chart to write a first draft. You may begin with:

¡Hola! Para mi cumpleaños recibí . . . Decidí ir al centro comercial porque . . . Encontré . . . Compré . . .

③ **Revise** Check your e-mail for spelling, accents, forms of the preterite, and agreement. Share it with a partner, who will check:

- Is the e-mail easy to understand?
- Does it include all the information from your chart?
- Is there anything you should add or change?
- Are there any errors?

④ **Publish** Rewrite the e-mail, making any necessary changes or corrections. Send it to your teacher or your friend, or print it out and add it to your portfolio.

⑤ **Evaluation** The following rubric will be used to grade your presentation.

> ### Estrategia
>
> **Using a chart**
> When writing, it is helpful to have a way to organize your thoughts. A chart or a graphic organizer is a good way to do this.

Rubric	Score 1	Score 3	Score 5
How easily your message is understood	You are difficult to understand and have many grammatical errors.	You are fairly easy to understand and have occasional grammatical errors.	You are easy to understand and have very few grammatical errors.
Completeness of your information	You provide some of the information required.	You provide most of the information required.	You provide all of the information required.
Your use of accurate spelling and grammar	You have many misspellings and grammatical errors.	You have several misspellings and grammatical errors.	You have very few misspellings and grammatical errors.

Preparación para . . .

En busca de la verdad

La participación hispana en la Segunda Guerra Mundial

La Segunda Guerra Mundial (1939–1945) cambió el destino de los hispanohablantes en los Estados Unidos. A partir de[1] diciembre de 1941, muchos estadounidenses dejaron sus trabajos para ir a luchar[2] en la guerra. Por eso, muchos mexicanos llegaron a trabajar en los Estados Unidos. En el videomisterio vas a ver algo relacionado con este tema.

En 1942, los gobiernos[3] de los Estados Unidos y de México firmaron el acuerdo[4] del programa de "braceros", que les permitió a trabajadores agrícolas mexicanos trabajar en los Estados Unidos. La mayoría de los mexicanos llegaron a trabajar en el campo y usaron sus brazos (por eso se llamaron "braceros").

Algunos braceros se enlistaron[5] en el ejército[6] de los Estados Unidos. Después de su servicio militar, ganaban la ciudadanía[7] estadounidense.

Se calcula que entre 250,000 y 500,000 hispanoamericanos sirvieron en las fuerzas armadas[8] durante la Segunda Guerra Mundial. Esto representa entre el 2.5 por ciento y el 5 por ciento de todas las personas que participaron en la guerra.

COMO UN SOLO HOMBRE

▲ Braceros mostrando el signo de la victoria en 1944

[1]From [2]to fight [3]governments
[4]pact, agreement [5]enlisted [6]army [7]citizenship

[8]armed forces

Este monumento en Los Ángeles, California, conmemora a todos los soldados del ejército de los Estados Unidos que han sido condecorados[9] por el Congreso con la Medalla de Honor.[10] Está especialmente dedicado a los 39 hispanoamericanos que han ganado ese honor. En la Segunda Guerra Mundial, doce mexicoamericanos y un cubano recibieron la medalla.

▲ Algunos países hispanohablantes también participaron en la Segunda Guerra Mundial. Por ejemplo, México envió un escuadrón[11] aéreo mexicano llamado la Unidad de Caza 201. El escuadrón, llamado "Águilas Aztecas", luchó en las Filipinas y tuvo la reputación de ser feroz[12].

¿Sabes que . . . ?

La Medalla de Honor del Congreso es una condecoración que les dan a los soldados del ejército norteamericano por su admirable participación en la guerra. Es el honor más prestigioso que puede recibir un soldado. Más de 3,400 medallas han sido entregadas a lo largo de la historia de los Estados Unidos.

Para pensar

Aunque en las guerras siempre necesitan la colaboración de muchas personas, éstas no sólo tienen que ser soldados. ¿Qué otras personas crees que son necesarias en tiempo de guerra? ¿Para qué crees que pueden ser necesarias?

[9]decorated with honors   [10]Congressional Medal of Honor
[11]squadron   [12]had the reputation of being ferocious

Repaso del capítulo

Vocabulario y gramática

to talk about shopping

la entrada	entrance
la ganga	bargain
el letrero	sign
la liquidación, *pl.* las liquidaciones	sale
el mercado	market
la salida	exit

to talk about colors

claro, -a	light
de sólo un color	solid-colored
oscuro, -a	dark
pastel	pastel
vivo, -a	bright

to describe what clothing is made of

¿De qué está hecho, -a?	What is it made of?
Está hecho, -a de ...	It is made of ...
algodón	cotton
cuero	leather
lana	wool
seda	silk
tela sintética	synthetic fabric

to discuss paying for purchases

alto, -a	high
bajo, -a	low
la caja	cash register
el cajero, la cajera	cashier
el cheque (personal)	(personal) check
el cheque de viajero	traveler's check
el cupón de regalo, *pl.* los cupones de regalo	gift certificate
en efectivo	cash
gastar	to spend
el precio	price
tan + *adjective*	so
la tarjeta de crédito	credit card

For *Vocabulario adicional*, see pp. 498–499.

to discuss clothing purchases

apretado, -a	tight
escoger (*g → j*)	to choose
estar de moda	to be in fashion
el estilo	style
exagerado, -a	outrageous
flojo, -a	loose
la marca	brand
mediano, -a	medium
el número	shoe size
probarse (*o → ue*)	to try on
la talla	size

other useful words and expressions

anunciar	to announce
encontrar (*o → ue*)	to find
en realidad	really
me / te importa(n)	it matters (it's important) / they matter to me / to you
inmediatamente	immediately
me parece	it seems to me
¿Qué te parece?	What do you think? / How does it seem to you?
recientemente	recently

preterite of regular verbs

miré aprendí escribí	miramos aprendimos escribimos
miraste aprendiste escribiste	mirasteis aprendisteis escribisteis
miró aprendió escribió	miraron aprendieron escribieron

demonstrative adjectives

Singular		Plural	
este, esta	this	estos, estas	these
ese, esa	that	esos, esas	those
aquel, aquella that one over there		aquellos, aquellas those over there	

Más repaso GO realidades.com | print

Instant Check ✔
Puzzles ✔
Core WB pp. 47–48 ✔
Comm. WB pp. 225, 226–228 ✔ ✔

Preparación para el examen

On the exam you will be asked to . . .	Here are practice tasks similar to those you will find on the exam . . .	For review go to your print or digital textbook . . .

Interpretive

 1 Escuchar Listen and understand as people talk about why they purchased a clothing item

Listen as María explains why she bought her outfit. Was it because: (a) it was a bargain; (b) it was a good brand name; (c) it fit well; or (d) it was very "in style."

pp. 102–105 *Vocabulario en contexto*
p. 103 Actividad 2
p. 106 Actividad 4

Interpersonal

 2 Hablar Talk about when and where you bought the clothing you are wearing today

Your partner really likes your outfit. Tell him or her: (a) where you bought it; (b) how long ago you bought it; (c) if it was very expensive or a bargain; (d) the brand, if you know it. Then reverse roles.

p. 107 Actividad 7
p. 108 Actividades 8–9
p. 109 Actividades 10–11
p. 111 Actividad 14
p. 112 Actividad 17
p. 115 Actividad 21
p. 116 Actividad 23
p. 117 Actividad 24

Interpretive

 3 Leer Read and understand a thank-you note for a recently received gift certificate

Your Spanish class recently sent last year's exchange student from Argentina a gift certificate for her birthday. Read her note about what she bought and what she thought about her purchases.

> ¡Hola! Muchas gracias por el cupón de regalo para el Almacén Palete. Compré una blusa de colores pastel que me gusta mucho y está muy de moda. También encontré un cinturón de cuero muy bonito para llevar con mis pantalones favoritos. Aquí tienen mi foto. ¿Qué les parece mi nuevo estilo?
>
> Besos, Susi

p. 107 Actividad 6
p. 110 Actividad 13
p. 114 Actividad 19
pp. 118–119 *Lectura*

Presentational

 4 Escribir Write a short description of your most recent shopping trip for clothes, including what you bought, the brand, and how you paid for the items

Your grandmother sent you a check for your birthday and wants to know what you bought. Describe the vacation clothes that you bought and where you bought them. Include as many details as possible. You might begin by writing:

> Querida abuelita:
> Muchas gracias por el cheque que me enviaste para mi cumpleaños. Decidí comprarme ropa para las vacaciones . . .

p. 107 Actividades 6–7
p. 109 Actividades 10–11
p. 110 Actividad 13
p. 112 Actividad 16
p. 121 *Presentación escrita*

Cultures

 5 Pensar Demonstrate an understanding of *la parranda* in Spanish-speaking countries

When you ask your parents if you can go to a *parranda* at the home of a Spanish-speaking friend, they have no idea what you are talking about. Explain it to them. What would you compare it to?

p. 120 *Perspectivas del mundo hispano*

Vocabulario Repaso

en el dormitorio
arreglar el cuarto
hacer la cama

en la cocina
cocinar
dar de comer al
  perro/gato
lavar los platos
poner la mesa
separar (botellas,
  latas, vidrio,
  periódicos, cartón)

en otros cuartos
ayudar
lavar la ropa
limpiar el baño
pasar la aspiradora
quitar el polvo

fuera de la casa
cortar el césped
lavar el coche
sacar la basura
trabajar en el jardín

For additional
vocabulary for
the city, see *A
ver si recuerdas*
1B, p. 42.

los lugares
el barrio
la calle
el cine
la comunidad
el estadio
el hospital
el monumento
el museo
el teatro

▼1 Los quehaceres

Escribir • Hablar

¿Quién en tu familia hizo estos quehaceres?
¿Cuándo los hizo?

Modelo

cortar el césped
*El verano pasado mi hermano y yo cortamos el
césped cada semana.*

1. lavar los platos
2. arreglar el cuarto
3. cocinar pollo
4. limpiar el baño
5. sacar la basura
6. pasar la aspiradora
7. lavar la ropa

▼2 ¿Qué hay en tu comunidad?

Escribir

Imagina que alguien visita tu comunidad por
primera vez. Escríbele una breve descripción.
Incluye los lugares de interés y cómo son.

Modelo

*Si visitas mi comunidad, vas a ver muchas
casas con jardines y césped. En el centro hay
tiendas y restaurantes, pero no hay un cine . . .*

Gramática Repaso

Telling time

To ask about and tell the time of day, you usually say:

¿Qué hora es? **Es** la una.
Son las cinco.

When you tell at what time something happens, you use *a*.

¿**A** qué hora es el concierto? **A** las ocho.

When talking about time after the hour, use *y* to express the time.

1:10	Es la una y diez.
3:15	Son las tres y cuarto.
	o: Son las tres y quince.
6:25	La clase empieza a las seis y veinticinco.
10:30	Generalmente me acuesto a las diez y media.

When talking about time before the hour, there are several expressions commonly used.

Son las diez **menos** veinte.
Son las nueve y cuarenta. — *It's 9:40.*
Faltan veinte **para** las diez.

You know several words and expressions for talking about the time of day.

de la mañana	*in the morning,* A.M.
de la tarde	*in the afternoon,* P.M.
de la noche	*in the evening,* P.M.
temprano	*early*
tarde	*late*
a tiempo	*on time*

▼3 ¿A qué hora?

Escribir

Escribe frases para decir a qué hora . . .

Modelo
. . . te levantas durante la semana.
Me levanto a las seis.

1. . . . te acuestas los fines de semana.
2. . . . te despiertas los fines de semana.
3. . . . almuerzas durante la semana.
4. . . . regresas a casa después de las clases.
5. . . . empieza tu clase favorita.
6. . . . empieza tu programa de televisión favorito.

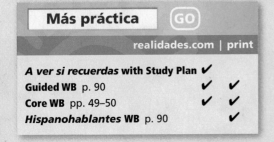

| **Más práctica** | **GO** |

realidades.com | print

A ver si recuerdas with Study Plan ✔
Guided WB p. 90 ✔ ✔
Core WB pp. 49–50 ✔ ✔
Hispanohablantes **WB** p. 90 ✔

▼4 ¿Quién lo hace?

Hablar

Trabajen en grupos de cuatro y hagan preguntas a sus compañeros para saber quiénes del grupo hacen las siguientes actividades.

▶ **Modelo**
. . . se levanta temprano todos los días
A —*Ariana, ¿te levantas temprano todos los días?*
B —*Sí, me levanto muy temprano. Me levanto a las seis de la mañana.*

¿Quién en el grupo . . .
. . . se levanta temprano los fines de semana?
. . . se levanta tarde los fines de semana?
. . . siempre llega a tiempo a la escuela?
. . . siempre llega temprano para ver a sus amigos?
. . . hace la cama antes de ir a la escuela?
. . . se acuesta antes de las diez de la noche?
. . . almuerza después de las dos de la tarde?

3A ¿Qué hiciste ayer?

▼ Chapter Objectives

Communication

By the end of this chapter you will be able to:

- Listen and read about where people went, what they did, and what they received as gifts
- Talk and write about whether you fulfilled certain obligations and what you bought in the past
- Exchange information about whether you did certain things you had to do

Culture

You will also be able to:

- Understand the popularity of open-air markets in the Spanish-speaking world
- Compare famous buildings and neighborhoods in Spanish-speaking countries with those in the U.S.

You will demonstrate what you know and can do:

- **Presentación oral, p. 149**
- **Preparación para el examen, p. 153**

You will use:

Vocabulary

- Running errands around town
- Where people go and what they buy

Grammar

- Direct object pronouns
- Irregular preterite verbs: *ir, ser*
- Irregular preterite verbs: *hacer, tener, estar, poder*

Exploración del mundo hispano

Country Connection
Errands and Places in Town

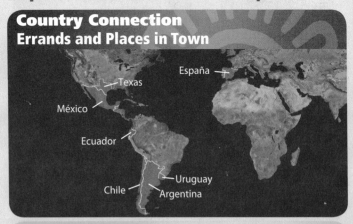

España
Texas
México
Ecuador
Uruguay
Chile
Argentina

realidades.com [GO]

 Reference Atlas

 Videocultura y actividad

 Mapa global interactivo

Avenida Portal de l'Angel,
Barcelona, España

🌎 **Arte y cultura** | Argentina | Uruguay

Buenos Aires Esta imagen moderna de Buenos Aires
es del pintor uruguayo Julio Alpuy. Nació en 1919 y su
pintura y escultura son del estilo constructivo, un estilo
que se basa en las formas geométricas y el espacio.
Buenos Aires es una ciudad muy "internacional". Entre los
años 1850 y 1945 muchos inmigrantes de Europa (Italia,
Alemania, España, Francia y otros países) llegaron a vivir
en Buenos Aires.

• En el cuadro, ¿cómo es Buenos Aires? Compara este
  cuadro con la foto de Barcelona. ¿En qué sentido (*way*)
  son similares? ¿En qué sentido son diferentes?

"Buenos Aires" (1957), Julio Alpuy ▶
Courtesy of Cecilia de Torres, Ltd.

| ▼ Objectives

Read, listen to, and understand information about
- ▶ running errands around town
- ▶ where people go and what they buy

Vocabulario en contexto

el centro

el champú

el jabón

el cepillo de dientes

la pasta dental

LIQUIDACIÓN de equipo deportivo

Farmacia ORTIZ

la farmacia

Supermercado Carranza

EQUIPO DEPORTIVO

el supermercado

EL CORREO

la tienda de equipo deportivo

tomates 2X10

el correo

la raqueta de tenis

los patines

la pelota

echar una carta

el buzón

el palo de golf

el sello

la tarjeta

la carta

—¿A qué hora **se abre** el correo en el centro? Quiero comprar unos sellos y **enviar*** una carta.

—Se abre a las nueve de la mañana y **se cierra** a las ocho de la noche.

▼1 ¿Lógica o no? | 🔊

Escuchar

Escucha las frases y señala con el pulgar hacia arriba si la frase es lógica y con el pulgar hacia abajo si no es lógica.

*Enviar has an accent mark on the *i* in all present-tense forms except *nosotros* and *vosotros*.

el consultorio

CONSULTORIO

DR. VICENTE ROJAS CAMACHO DENTISTA

DRA. MARÍA ELENA VIVAS BLANCO MÉDICA

el médico, la médica

el dentista, la dentista

Biblioteca

sacar un libro

devolver un libro

el banco

BANCO NACIONAL

cobrar un cheque

▼2 ¿Cómo van? 🔊))

Escuchar • Escribir

Escribe en una hoja de papel los números del 1 al 4. Escucha los diálogos y escribe la letra de la respuesta apropiada.

1. ¿Qué tiene que comprar en la farmacia?
   a. jabón y pasta dental
   b. un cepillo de dientes y champú

2. ¿Adónde va después de ir al banco?
   a. al consultorio
   b. al supermercado

3. ¿Qué necesita comprar?
   a. una tarjeta
   b. unos sellos

4. ¿Cómo van a la biblioteca?
   a. Van en coche.
   b. Van a pie.

Más práctica (GO)

realidades.com | print

Instant Check	✔	
Guided WB pp. 91–96	✔	✔
Core WB pp. 51–52	✔	✔
Comm. WB p. 52	✔	✔
Hispanohablantes **WB** p. 92		✔

cuidar a los niños

"Ayer cuidé a Carlota y a Paco **por** cinco horas. **Fuimos a pie** al zoológico.

Nos quedamos allí **hasta** la una. Fue muy divertido.

Luego regresamos a casa. Sus padres me pagaron por cuidarlos. Me gusta cuidar niños porque puedo ganar dinero. Es importante tener mi propio dinero".

¿Qué hiciste esta mañana?

Estrategia

Using visuals to predict
Scan the pictures to predict what will happen in the *Videohistoria*. Can you tell where the characters went and what they did there?

1

Teresa: Hola, Claudia. ¿Cómo estás?

Claudia: Bien, Teresa. ¿Y tú? Oye, tenemos que darnos prisa.[1] Manolo y Ramón nos esperan[2] a las dos para ir al cine, ¿verdad?

Teresa: Sí, pero tengo que comprar **varias** cosas aquí en la farmacia. ¿Vamos a entrar?

[1]to hurry   [2]are expecting

Ramón

Manolo

Claudia

Teresa

5

Ramón: Primero fuimos a una tienda de equipo deportivo. Me compré una camiseta del Cruz Azul.

Claudia: ¡Genial! Es uno de mis equipos favoritos. Y después, ¿qué hicieron?

6

Ramón: Fuimos a **la estación de servicio** a comprar **gasolina.**

Manolo: Buenos días, señor. ¿Puede **llenar el tanque,** por favor?

Asistente: Sí señor. **En seguida.**

7

Teresa: ¡Ay, **caramba,** se me olvidó!

Claudia: ¿Ahora qué, Teresa?

Teresa: Mañana es el cumpleaños de mi abuela. Tengo que comprarle algo.

Claudia: Estamos cerca del Bazar San Ángel. ¿Por qué no vamos allí?

Claudia: ¿Por qué no fuiste a la farmacia ayer?

Teresa: No **pude. Tuve** que ir a la biblioteca a devolver un libro. No **estuve** allí por mucho tiempo pero tuve que hacer otras cosas también.

Teresa: Ay, **casi se me olvidó.** Tengo que enviar esta carta. Pero necesito comprar sellos . . .

Claudia: Vamos, vamos. Ramón y Manolo ya deben estar en el cine. La película empieza a las dos y media.

Teresa: Tranquila, Claudia. **Todavía** tenemos tiempo. Regreso en un momento.

Claudia: Hola, Ramón. Aquí Claudia.

Ramón: Hola, Claudia. ¿Qué tal?

Claudia: Muy bien. **Tuvimos** que ir a varios sitios, pero **pronto** vamos a ir al cine. Ya casi terminamos. Y Uds., ¿qué hicieron esta mañana?

Claudia: Ramón, vamos al Bazar San Ángel. Tenemos que comprar un regalo. ¿Por qué no nos vemos allí? Vamos al cine después.

Ramón: ¡Cómo no! Nos vemos allí.

Claudia: Adiós. **Hasta pronto.**

▼3 ¿Comprendiste?

Hablar • Escribir

1. Los cuatro jóvenes tienen planes para la tarde. ¿Adónde piensan ir?

2. Antes de ver a Ramón y Manolo, ¿cuáles son las tres cosas que Teresa tuvo que hacer?

3. ¿Por qué entró Teresa en el correo?

4. ¿Qué se le olvidó a Teresa?

5. ¿Adónde fueron Ramón y Manolo por la mañana?

6. ¿Adónde decidieron ir antes de ir al cine?

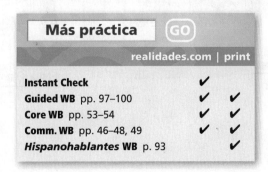

Más práctica	GO
realidades.com	print	
Instant Check	✔
Guided WB pp. 97–100	✔ ✔
Core WB pp. 53–54	✔ ✔
Comm. WB pp. 46–48, 49	✔ ✔
Hispanohablantes WB p. 93	✔

| ▼ **Objectives**

▸ Talk about places in your community
▸ Discuss what you had to do and what you couldn't do last weekend
▸ Listen to a list of errands and chores
▸ Write about places and the errands you do there

Vocabulario en uso

▼4 Muchas cosas que hacer | ♻

Escribir

En una hoja de papel, escribe los lugares que ves en los dibujos. Escribe una cosa que tienes que hacer en cada lugar. Vas a usar la información para la Actividad 5.

Lugares	Tengo que . . .
el supermercado	comprar leche

▼5 ¿A qué hora se abre? | | ♻

Hablar

Trabaja con otro(a) estudiante. Explícale lo que tienes que hacer y hablen de los horarios de cada lugar. Usen la información de la tabla de la Actividad 4.

▶ **Modelo**

A —*Tengo que comprar cereal. ¿A qué hora se abre el supermercado?*
B —*Se abre a las ocho de la mañana.*
A —*¿Y a qué hora se cierra?*
B —*Creo que se cierra a las once de la noche.*

▼6 Escucha y escribe |

Escuchar • Escribir • Hablar

1 Tu mamá necesita tu ayuda para hacer todos los quehaceres. Escucha lo que ella dice y escribe las seis frases.

2 Escoge una expresión del recuadro y escribe respuestas a las preguntas de tu mamá. Después trabaja con otro(a) estudiante y lee las conversaciones entre ustedes.

¡Caramba!	lo siento
casi	no puedo
¡Cómo no!	pronto
en seguida	se me olvidó
ir a pie	todavía

▼7 ¿Adónde fuiste? |

Hablar

El fin de semana pasado tus padres te dieron varios mandados (*errands*) que hacer. Ahora quieren saber si los hiciste. Diles adónde fuiste y cuándo hiciste todo.

▶ Modelo

A —¿*Compraste los sellos?*
B —*Sí, fui al correo esta mañana.*

Estudiante A

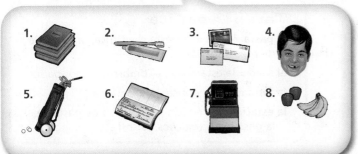

1. 2. 3. 4.
5. 6. 7. 8.

Estudiante B

esta mañana
ayer
anoche
hace . . . días
¡Respuesta personal!

🌎 Fondo Cultural | México

El Palacio de Correos de la Ciudad de México, fue construido entre 1902 y 1907. Diseñado por el arquitecto italiano Adamo Boari, el Palacio de Correos es uno de los edificios (*buildings*) más famosos de la ciudad.

• El Palacio de Correos es un edificio muy conocido en México. ¿Cuáles son algunos edificios famosos de los Estados Unidos? ¿Por qué son famosos?

Interior del Palacio de Correos, Ciudad de México

▼8 Un fin de semana muy aburrido |

Hablar

No pudiste hacer muchas cosas divertidas el fin de semana pasado. Trabaja con otro(a) estudiante y habla de las cosas que tuviste que hacer.

▶ **Modelo**

A —¿*Fuiste al centro el fin de semana pasado?*

B —*No, no pude. Tuve que cuidar a mis hermanitos.*

Estudiante A

1.
2.
3.
4.
5.
6.

Estudiante B

No, no pude.

Tuve que . . .

Estuve en . . . por . . . horas.

Estuve en . . . hasta las . . .

Tuve que esperar . . .

Me quedé en . . .

¡Respuesta personal!

También se dice . . .

la pasta dental = la pasta dentífrica, la pasta de dientes *(España)*

el sello = la estampilla, el timbre *(muchos países)*

la farmacia = la botica, la droguería

la estación de servicio = la bomba de gasolina, la gasolinera *(muchos países)*

▼9 Para unos dientes más blancos . . .

Leer • Escribir

Lee el anuncio del periódico y contesta las preguntas.

1. ¿Cómo se llama el producto del anuncio? ¿Para qué puedes usarlo?

2. ¿Con qué frecuencia debes usar el producto, todos los días o una vez a la semana?

3. ¿Qué garantiza el producto? ¿Por qué?

4. ¿Dónde puedes comprar el producto?

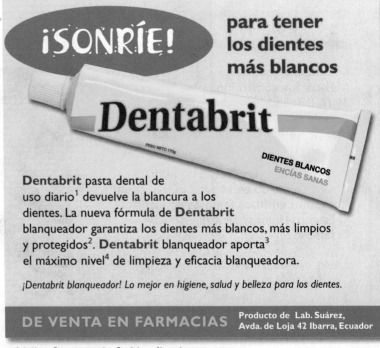

¡SONRÍE! para tener los dientes más blancos

Dentabrit

PESO NETO 170g

DIENTES BLANCOS
ENCÍAS SANAS

Dentabrit pasta dental de uso diario[1] devuelve la blancura a los dientes. La nueva fórmula de **Dentabrit** blanqueador garantiza los dientes más blancos, más limpios y protegidos[2]. **Dentabrit** blanqueador aporta[3] el máximo nivel[4] de limpieza y eficacia blanqueadora.

¡Dentabrit blanqueador! Lo mejor en higiene, salud y belleza para los dientes.

DE VENTA EN FARMACIAS Producto de Lab. Suárez, Avda. de Loja 42 Ibarra, Ecuador

[1]daily [2]protected [3]adds [4]level

▼ Fondo Cultural | El mundo hispano

Las farmacias en los países hispanohablantes frecuentemente venden antibióticos y otras medicinas sin necesidad de receta *(prescription)* y es común consultar a un farmacéutico, y no al médico. Los horarios de servicio varían. En España, hay *Farmacias de guardia* que están abiertas las 24 horas. En otros países, se pueden encontrar *Farmacias de turno* que también dan servicio las 24 horas al día. En las farmacias uno también puede comprar productos de belleza, como perfumes y maquillaje, y de higiene personal, como champú y pasta dental.

• ¿Hay farmacias abiertas las 24 horas al día en tu comunidad? ¿Cómo son y qué productos venden?

Una farmacia en Barcelona, España

▼10 Juego | |

Escribir • Hablar

❶ Vas a jugar con otro(a) estudiante. Tu profesor(a) va a decirles a todos un lugar en la ciudad. Escriban las personas, acciones u otras cosas que se asocian con este lugar. Tu profesor(a) va a indicar cuándo termina el tiempo.

Modelo

restaurante
camarero, mesa, comida, comer, servir, decoraciones, tenedor, cuchillo, . . .

❷ Uds. van a trabajar con otras tres parejas. Lean la lista de palabras para un lugar. Si las otras parejas tienen una de estas palabras, ninguna pareja recibe puntos por ella. Pero si hay palabras que las otras parejas no tienen, Uds. reciben un punto por cada una.

▼11 Y tú, ¿qué dices? |

Escribir • Hablar

1. ¿Qué tipo de tiendas y servicios hay en el centro de tu comunidad? ¿A qué hora se abren? ¿A qué hora se cierran? ¿Se cierran antes o después de las seis de la tarde?

2. Cuando tu familia compra equipo deportivo, ¿dónde lo compra? ¿Y dónde compra cosas como jabón o pasta dental?

3. ¿Te gusta caminar? ¿A qué lugares puedes ir a pie fácilmente en tu comunidad?

4. ¿Qué haces para ganar dinero? ¿Te gusta cuidar a los niños? ¿Por qué?

El español en la comunidad

Hoy en día, en los Estados Unidos, muchas etiquetas *(labels)* de medicinas e instrucciones para otros productos están escritas *(written)* en inglés y en español. Para muchas personas que hablan y leen español, es más fácil y seguro *(safe)* leer las instrucciones en español.

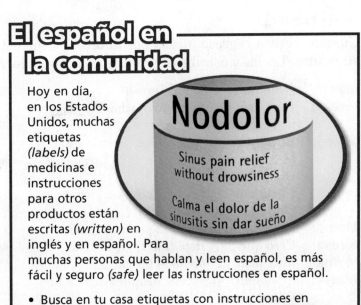

• Busca en tu casa etiquetas con instrucciones en español. ¿Qué parte de las instrucciones entiendes?

Gramática Repaso

Direct object pronouns

A direct object tells who or what receives the action of the verb.

Devolví el libro.   *I returned **the book**. (book is the direct object)*

To avoid repeating a direct object noun, you can replace it with a direct object pronoun. In English, *him, her,* and *it* are examples of direct object pronouns. You have already used the following direct object pronouns in Spanish:

Singular	Plural
lo *it, him, you (masc. formal)*	los *them, you (masc.)*
la *it, her, you (fem. formal)*	las *them, you (fem.)*

Direct object pronouns have the same gender (masculine or feminine) and number (singular or plural) as the nouns they replace. They come right before the conjugated verb.

¿Devolviste los libros a la biblioteca? No, no los devolví.

¿Ayudaste a tu mamá en casa? Sí, la ayudé.

When an infinitive follows a verb, the direct object pronoun can be placed before the conjugated verb or attached to the infinitive.

¿Sacaste el libro sobre Simón Bolívar? No, no lo pude sacar. o: No, no pude sacarlo.

Más ayuda **realidades.com**

***GramActiva* Video**
Tutorial: Direct object pronouns

***GramActiva* Activity**

▼12 ¡A lavar!

Leer • Escribir

Cuando Teresa regresa a casa por la tarde, tiene esta conversación con su madre. Léela, y escribe el pronombre apropiado: *lo, la, los* o *las*.

Mamá: ¿Qué tal la película, Teresa?

Teresa: Bien, mamá. Me gustó mucho. Tú **1.** viste anoche, ¿no?

Mamá: Sí, pero no me gustó. Oye, ¿dónde están las cosas que compraste en la farmacia? No **2.** veo.

Teresa: El champú está sobre la mesa. ¿No **3.** ves?

Mamá: Ah, sí, aquí está. ¿Y la pasta dental?

Teresa: Creo que **4.** dejé *(I left)* en el baño.

Mamá: Muy bien. ¿Y enviaste las cartas?

Teresa: Sí, mamá, **5.** envié después de ir a la farmacia.

Mamá: Gracias, hija. Ah, ¿compraste un regalo para tu abuela?

Teresa: ¡Sí, mamá! Le compré un collar muy bonito. ¿ **6.** quieres ver?

Mamá: Sí, pero más tarde. Ahora tenemos que limpiar la cocina. Tú puedes lavar los platos.

Teresa: ¡Ay! No puedo lavar **7.** , mamá . . . ¡Se me olvidó comprar el detergente!

Mamá: No importa, Teresa. ¡Yo **8.** compré ayer! Y ahora, ¡a lavar!

▼**13 De compras** |

Hablar

Tu compañero(a) quiere saber por qué tienes varias cosas contigo. Explícale por qué las tienes.

▶ **Modelo**

A —¿*Por qué tienes los palos de golf?*
B —*Los tengo porque quiero jugar al golf esta tarde.*

Estudiante A

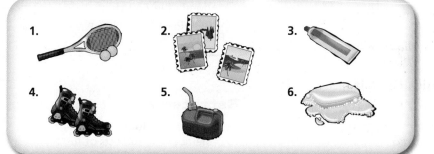

1.
2.
3.
4.
5.
6.

Estudiante B

quiero . . .
necesito . . .
voy a . . .
tengo que . . .
¡Respuesta personal!

▼**14 ¿Todavía lo usas?** |

Escribir • Hablar

A veces compramos o recibimos algo y después no lo usamos mucho.

❶ Escribe cinco frases para decir qué cosas compraste tú o qué cosas te compraron otras personas.

❷ Lee tus frases a tu compañero(a). Tu compañero(a) te va a preguntar si todavía tienes, usas o llevas esa cosa.

▶ **Modelo**

A —*Hace dos años mis padres me compraron unos palos de golf.*
B —*¿Todavía los usas?*
A —*Sí, los uso porque juego al golf mucho.*
o: —*No, no los uso porque no tengo tiempo para jugar al golf.*

Estudiante A

Hace . . . me compraron . . .   Un día compré . . .
Hace . . . compré   **¡Respuesta personal!**

Estudiante B

¿ . . . llevas?
¿ . . . tienes?
¿ . . . usas?
¡Respuesta personal!

Más práctica | GO

realidades.com | print

Instant Check ✔
Guided WB pp. 101–102 ✔ ✔
Core WB p. 55 ✔ ✔
Comm. WB pp. 50, 53 ✔ ✔
Hispanohablantes WB pp. 94–97, 101 ✔

Gramática

Irregular preterite verbs: *ir, ser*

In the preterite, the forms of *ser* are the same as the forms of *ir.* The context makes the meaning clear.

El cantante Jon Secada **fue** a vivir a Miami, Florida, en 1970.
*The singer Jon Secada **went** to live in Miami, Florida, in 1970.*

Después **fue** estudiante en la Universidad de Miami.
*Later he **was** a student at the University of Miami.*

(yo)	fui	(nosotros) (nosotras)	fuimos
(tú)	fuiste	(vosotros) (vosotras)	fuisteis
Ud. (él) (ella)	fue	Uds. (ellos) (ellas)	fueron

- Notice that these irregular preterite forms do not have any accents.

¿Recuerdas?

You already know the verb *ir* in the preterite.

- ¿Adónde **fueron** Uds. el verano pasado? **Fuimos** a Puerto Rico.

Estrategia

Using memory clues
To remember the subjects of *fui* and *fue*, remember that *fui*, the *yo* form, ends in *i*, while *fue*, the *él / ella* form, ends in *e*.

Más ayuda **realidades.com**

▶ **Tutorial:** Preterite forms *ser* and *ir*

▼15 El día de Simón y sus amigos

Leer • Escribir

Lee lo que hicieron Simón y sus amigos ayer. Escribe la forma correcta del verbo *ir* o *ser*. Luego contesta la pregunta sobre el día que ellos pasaron.

Ayer __1.__ un día bastante bueno para nosotros. Primero yo __2.__ a la estación de servicio para llenar el tanque con gasolina. Luego Fernando y yo __3.__ a la tienda de equipo deportivo para mirar patines. Nuestras amigas Teresa y Patricia __4.__ al almacén. Después Teresa __5.__ al correo y Patricia __6.__ al banco. En la noche todos nosotros __7.__ al cine. La película __8.__ muy cómica pero no sé quiénes __9.__ los actores principales.

En tu opinión, ¿el día de Simón y sus amigos __10.__ divertido? ¿Por qué?

Un día divertido entre amigos

Conexiones | La literatura

Fui tuyo, fuiste mía. ¿Qué más? Juntos[2] hicimos un recodo[3] en la ruta donde el amor pasó.

▼16 Un poema de amor

Leer • Escribir

Pablo Neruda (1904–1973) fue poeta chileno y ganador del Premio Nobel de Literatura en 1971. En muchos de sus poemas, Neruda escribió sobre el amor.[1] Estos versos son de su primer libro de poemas *Crepusculario,* que él publicó a los 19 años de edad. Lee los versos.

1. ¿Está el poeta todavía con "su amor"? ¿Cómo lo sabes?
2. En tu opinión, ¿qué quiere decir el poeta en estos versos?

[1]love [2]together [3]turn

▼17 Juego |

Escribir • Hablar • GramActiva

❶ Trabaja con un grupo de tres para escribir preguntas sobre personas famosas del pasado. Pueden usar las ideas del recuadro o sus propias ideas. También tienen que escribir las respuestas a sus preguntas.

> el presidente en el año . . .
>
> los cantantes de la canción . . .
>
> los actores en la película . . .
>
> la persona que escribió el poema / libro . . .
>
> los campeones *(champions)* . . .
>
> **¡Respuesta personal!**

❷ Su profesor(a) va a formar dos grupos grandes en la clase. Un grupo lee una pregunta. Si el otro grupo contesta correctamente, recibe un punto. El grupo con más puntos al final gana.

 Modelo

A —*¿Quién fue el poeta que escribió* Crepusculario?

B —*El poeta fue Pablo Neruda.*

▼18 Y tú, ¿qué dices? |

Escribir • Hablar

1. ¿Cuál fue tu día más divertido del mes pasado? ¿Por qué? ¿Adónde fuiste? ¿Con quiénes?
2. ¿Cuál fue tu viaje más interesante? ¿Adónde y con quiénes fuiste? ¿Cuáles fueron algunos de los lugares que visitaron o las actividades que hicieron?
3. ¿Cuál fue tu mejor o peor cumpleaños? ¿Por qué fue tan bueno o malo?

Más práctica (GO)

realidades.com | print

Instant Check	✔	
Guided WB pp. 103–104	✔	✔
Core WB p. 56	✔	✔
Comm. WB pp. 51, 54, 229	✔	✔
Hispanohablantes **WB** pp. 97–99, 101	✔	

Gramática

Irregular preterite verbs: *hacer, tener, estar, poder*

The preterite forms of *tener*, *estar*, and *poder* follow a pattern similar to that of the verb *hacer*. Like *hacer*, these verbs do not have any accent marks in the preterite.

(yo)	hice tuve estuve pude	(nosotros) (nosotras)	hicimos tuvimos estuvimos pudimos
(tú)	hiciste tuviste estuviste pudiste	(vosotros) (vosotras)	hicisteis tuvisteis estuvisteis pudisteis
Ud. (él) (ella)	hizo tuvo estuvo pudo	Uds. (ellos) (ellas)	hicieron tuvieron estuvieron pudieron

¿Recuerdas?

Dar is also irregular in the preterite tense: *di, diste, dio, dimos, disteis, dieron.*

Más ayuda **realidades.com**

▶ *GramActiva* **Video**
Tutorial: Preterite forms of *estar* and *tener*
Animated Verbs

◀))) *Canción de hip hop:* ¿Qué hiciste ayer?

📝 *GramActiva* **Activity**

▼19 ¡Nadie pudo venir!

Leer • Escribir

Rosalinda invitó a varios amigos a ver una película en su casa a las cinco, pero nadie llegó. Completa cada frase con la forma apropiada del verbo *estar, tener* o *poder* para explicar por qué no llegaron.

Fernando __1.__ en la biblioteca por tres horas. __2.__ que escribir un informe muy largo. Jorge y Pati no __3.__ venir porque __4.__ en el banco donde trabajan hasta las ocho. Yo no __5.__ ir a su casa tampoco porque __6.__ que cuidar a mi hermanito. ¡Pobre Rosalinda! Todos nosotros __7.__ que hacer otras cosas y no __8.__ ir a su casa y ella __9.__ allí sola toda la tarde.

▼20 ¿Por qué no hicieron sus quehaceres? | | ♻

Hablar

Cuando tus padres vuelven a casa después de un viaje, no entienden por qué tus hermanos y tú no hicieron los quehaceres. Trabaja con otro(a) estudiante para preguntar y contestar.

▶ Modelo

no comprar pan
A —¿Por qué no compraron pan?
B —Porque no pudimos ir al supermercado.

Estudiante A

1. no dar de comer al perro
2. no hacer las camas
3. no ir a la farmacia para comprar champú y jabón
4. no devolver los libros a la biblioteca
5. no enviar las cartas
6. no ir al dentista

Estudiante B

tener que quedarnos en casa con el perro
no poder ir al supermercado
no tener tiempo por la mañana
no poder encontrar su comida
tener que leerlos otra vez
tener que hacer tantos quehaceres
no poder encontrar el buzón

▼21 Una raqueta de tenis nueva | ♻ | 🔊

Leer • Escuchar • Escribir

Santiago acaba de comprar una raqueta de tenis. Primero lee las preguntas. Después escucha la descripción dos veces y escribe respuestas a las preguntas.

1. ¿Cómo pudo tener Santiago suficiente dinero para comprar una raqueta de tenis?
2. ¿Cuándo fueron a la tienda de equipo deportivo Santiago y Héctor?
3. Para Santiago, ¿cómo fue la experiencia de buscar una raqueta nueva?
4. ¿Miraron sólo una raqueta o varias?
5. ¿Estuvieron en la tienda por mucho o por poco tiempo?
6. ¿Cuándo escogió Santiago su raqueta nueva?

▼22 Y tú, ¿qué dices? | 🗨 | ♻

Escribir

Escribe un párrafo en que describes cuando tú fuiste de compras. Usa las ideas de la experiencia de Santiago en la Actividad 21 como modelo. Puedes incluir:

• cómo conseguiste (*you obtained*) dinero para comprar algo
• si fuiste solo(a) o con otra persona
• adónde fuiste
• si tuviste que ir a diferentes tiendas
• si pudiste decidir inmediatamente
• por cuánto tiempo estuviste en la tienda
• si te gusta lo que compraste

Más práctica GO

realidades.com | print

Instant Check	✔	
Guided WB pp. 104–105	✔	✔
Core WB p. 57	✔	✔
Comm. WB p. 51	✔	✔
Hispanohablantes WB pp. 98–100		✔

▼ Pronunciación | 🔊 | 💬

The written accent

You already know the standard rules for stress and accent in Spanish.

- When words end in a vowel, *n,* or *s,* the stress is on the next-to-last syllable.

- When words end in a consonant (except *n* or *s*), the stress is on the last syllable.

- Words that do not follow these patterns must have a written accent (called *acento ortográfico* or *tilde*). The accent indicates that you should place the stress on this syllable as you pronounce the word.

Listen to and say these examples:

champú	olvidó	cómodo	médico
película	patín	jabón	adiós
demás	césped	fútbol	lápiz

¡Compruébalo! Here are some new words that all require accent marks. Copy the words and, as you hear them pronounced, write the accent mark over the correct vowel.

antropologo	cajon	carcel	ejercito	fosforo
lucho	nilon	util	tipico	lider

Listen to and say the following *refrán:*

Del árbol caído, todos hacen leña.

🌐 Fondo Cultural | España

Los barrios Hay barrios *(neighborhoods)* famosos en las ciudades grandes de España y América Latina que tienen su propia identidad. Por ejemplo, el Barrio de Santa Cruz, en Sevilla, España, es el más antiguo de la ciudad y originalmente fue un barrio judío *(Jewish)*. En este barrio, las calles son muy estrechas *(narrow)* y hay monumentos históricos, como la Catedral. Las personas que viven allí se sienten muy orgullosas *(proud)* de las tradiciones, la arquitectura y la historia que existen en su barrio.

- ¿Cuáles son las características de los barrios en general? ¿Hay algún barrio famoso en tu ciudad? ¿Cómo es?

El Barrio de Santa Cruz, en Sevilla, España

▼23 ¿Por cuánto tiempo? | 👥

Pensar • Hablar • Escribir

Es difícil encontrar el tiempo suficiente para hacer todos los quehaceres necesarios. A veces es necesario estar muy consciente del tiempo que requiere cada actividad que vas a hacer. Con otro(a) estudiante, lee y resuelve *(solve)* este problema matemático.

Conexiones | Las matemáticas

1 Ayer Ángela salió de la escuela y fue a la farmacia para comprar champú y jabón. Estuvo allí por 13 minutos.

2 Después caminó al correo en diez minutos. Se quedó allí por 45 minutos mirando y comprando unos sellos bonitos e interesantes.

3 Caminó del correo a su casa en 15 minutos. Llegó a su casa a las 4:40 de la tarde.

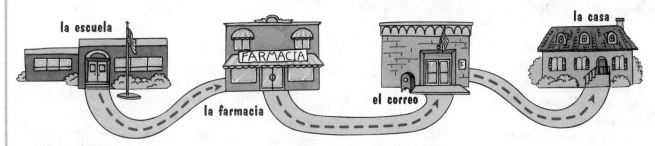

la escuela

la farmacia

el correo

la casa

4 Si la farmacia está a dos minutos de la escuela, ¿a qué hora salió Ángela de la escuela?

5 Escribe una frase para indicar a qué hora llegó y salió Ángela de cada lugar.

▼24 Te toca a ti | 👥

Hablar • Escribir

Con otro(a) estudiante, escriban un problema original similar al problema matemático de la Actividad 23. Pueden incluir una ilustración. Después cambien *(exchange)* su problema con otro grupo e intenten *(try)* resolverlo.

▼ Fondo Cultural | España

Los sellos, la tradición y la comunidad El tema de esta antigua serie de sellos de España son los trajes tradicionales de las comunidades españolas. Durante los festivales anuales de un pueblo o ciudad, los bailadores llevan trajes tradicionales. Los bailes, o danzas, y los trajes de cada comunidad son diferentes.

• ¿Conoces alguna serie de sellos que recuerda tradiciones regionales en los Estados Unidos? ¿Qué otros tipos de series de sellos tenemos en los Estados Unidos?

Trajes tradicionales de las regiones de España: Coruña, Córdoba, Granada, Huelva y Sevilla

Lectura
La unidad en la comunidad internacional

Estrategia

Using the structure of a text
Sometimes the way the text is structured will help you understand the main idea. Look at this brochure and read only the headings. What do you think it is about?

Ciudades Hermanas
Internacional

El programa de "Ciudades Hermanas Internacional" fue creado por el presidente de los Estados Unidos, Dwight D. Eisenhower, en el año 1956. La misión de este programa es promover¹ el intercambio y la cooperación entre los habitantes de ciudades en diferentes países. Hoy en día, más de 1,200 ciudades en los Estados Unidos tienen una ciudad hermana en casi 137 países. A través de² la cooperación económica, cultural y educativa, el programa de Ciudades Hermanas construye puentes³ entre las personas y ayuda a la comprensión entre diferentes culturas.

¡Quiero tener una ciudad hermana!

Cualquier⁴ ciudad de los Estados Unidos puede tener una ciudad hermana. Primero es necesario encontrar otra ciudad extranjera.⁵ Esta ciudad puede tener alguna relación con la ciudad original. Por ejemplo, ciudades que tienen el mismo nombre, como Toledo,

Ohio, y Toledo, España, pueden asociarse. También las ciudades que celebran el mismo festival pueden formar relaciones de hermandad. Para tener una relación oficial, hay que llenar un formulario en la comisión del programa para las Ciudades Hermanas. La organización tiene que aprobar⁶ la petición.

Intercambio económico

El programa de Ciudades Hermanas ayuda a establecer una cooperación económica entre los países. Por ejemplo, varios productos de Toledo, España, se venden en algunas tiendas en Toledo, Ohio. Las ciudades de Atlanta, Georgia, y de Salcedo, República Dominicana, también exploran varias posibilidades para intercambiar productos. El intercambio profesional y técnico es importante, como aprendieron los bomberos⁷ y policías de la ciudad de Phoenix, Arizona, cuando tomaron clases de español en Sonora, México.

¹to promote   ²Through   ³bridges   ⁴Any   ⁵foreign   ⁶approve   ⁷firefighters

·REGLAS·
para los jóvenes embajadores

Los jóvenes embajadores tienen que:

- obedecer las leyes[8] del país de la ciudad hermana

- respetar las costumbres del país

- ayudar a la familia con las tareas domésticas

- participar en muchas actividades para aprender sobre la cultura del país

- tratar de[9] hablar un poco en el idioma[10] del país

Intercambio cultural

Hay diferentes posibilidades para un intercambio cultural. Los proyectos posibles incluyen:

- un festival con bailes y comida en honor a su ciudad hermana.
- una exposición de arte. Por ejemplo, la ciudad de Phoenix, Arizona, dio una exposición de arte en Sonora, México.
- el intercambio de música, grabaciones o dramas.

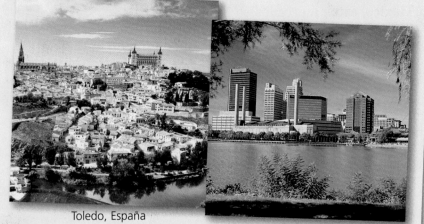

Toledo, España

Intercambio educativo

En programas de intercambio educativo, los jóvenes son embajadores[11] en ciudades hermanas. Representan a los Estados Unidos en su viaje a otra ciudad. Se quedan con familias y así aprenden mucho sobre la cultura de ese país. Luego un embajador del país extranjero viene a los Estados Unidos y se queda con la familia del estudiante estadounidense.

Toledo, Ohio

A primera vista, las ciudades hermanas de Toledo, España y Toledo, Ohio no tienen mucho en común. En una ciudad se habla español, en la otra inglés; un lugar es antiguo y el otro, moderno. Pero en verdad lo que une a las dos Toledos es el gran intercambio artístico, cultural y económico.

[8] laws   [9] try to   [10] language   [11] ambassadors

¿Comprendiste?

1. ¿Por qué es importante el programa de las Ciudades Hermanas Internacional?

2. ¿Qué es necesario para tener una ciudad hermana?

3. ¿Por qué es importante el intercambio económico? ¿El intercambio cultural?

4. Si tu ciudad tiene una ciudad hermana, ¿qué puedes hacer como joven embajador?

5. ¿Cuál es la ciudad hermana de Phoenix, Arizona? ¿De Atlanta, Georgia? ¿De Toledo, Ohio?

6. En tu opinión, ¿cuál es la regla más importante para los jóvenes embajadores?

Y tú, ¿qué dices?

Imagina que los estudiantes de una clase de tu ciudad hermana vienen a tu escuela. Prepara un horario de lo que pueden hacer y ver en tu escuela y en tu comunidad.

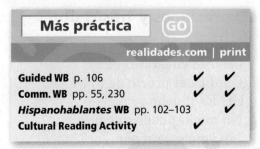

Más práctica   GO

realidades.com | print

Guided WB p. 106	✔	✔
Comm. WB pp. 55, 230	✔	✔
Hispanohablantes WB pp. 102–103		✔
Cultural Reading Activity	✔	

La cultura en vivo

Los mercados al aire libre

En los países hispanohablantes, los mercados al aire libre son muy populares. Son lugares para comprar y vender toda clase de cosas, como comida, productos del campo, artesanías y ropa. Los vendedores ponen sus tiendas en la calle y la gente mira los productos. Estos mercados son buenos lugares para ver a los amigos, comer algo o pasear.

En México, estos mercados se llaman *tianguis,* una palabra que en náhuatl significa "el lugar del mercado". El *tianguis,* o mercado al aire libre, es una tradición antigua que viene de los aztecas.

Pero no hay mercados sólo en México. En Ecuador, el mercado de Otavalo es muy conocido por sus artesanías. En La Paz, Bolivia, un mercado popular es el mercado de las Brujas. En Madrid, España, los domingos se abre el mercado de El Rastro. Cuando los compradores pasan por las calles, los vendedores los invitan a comprar y les preguntan, *¿Qué va a llevar?*

El Rastro, en Madrid, España

Mercado en Zumbagua, Ecuador

Objetivo

Preparar un día de mercado en tu clase

Procedimiento

Los estudiantes deben formar dos grupos. Los estudiantes en Grupo 1 (los vendedores) deben traer algo a la clase para vender y decidir el precio del objeto o producto. Los estudiantes en Grupo 2 (los compradores) deben visitar a los vendedores y, si quieren, comprar su mercancía. Pueden regatear *(bargain)* para bajar el precio. ¡Buena suerte!

Expresiones y frases útiles

Comprador

¿Cuánto cuesta(n) . . . ?

¿Cuál es el precio de . . . ?

¡Uf! Es mucho . . .

¿No me lo puede dar por . . . ?

¿Me vende esto por . . . ?

Es un buen precio. Muy bien.

Vendedor

¿Qué va a llevar?

¿Qué desea Ud.?

¡Cómprame algo!

Cuesta . . . / El precio es . . .

¡Lo siento!

Presentación oral (Talk!)

Preparándose para un viaje

Task

You are going to visit a friend in Mérida, Mexico, where summers are hot and humid. Your friend has made plans to visit Mayan ruins, spend time with friends, and go to the beach in Cancún. Explain what you did to prepare for the trip.

① Prepare Copy this chart and list ten items you need to bring. Do you already have them, or do you need to buy them? If so, where?

Cosas que necesito	¿Ya lo / la compré?	¿Dónde?
sombrero para el sol	sí, lo compré	el almacén

② Practice Go through your presentation several times. You can use your notes in practice, but not when you present. Try to:

• talk about all your preparations for the trip

• use complete sentences   • speak clearly

Modelo

Para visitar a mi amigo en Mérida, necesito . . . No tuve que comprar . . . Pero tuve que comprar . . . También tuve que ir al banco para . . .

③ Present Talk about your preparation for the trip. You might want to bring in props to show some of your preparations.

④ Evaluation The following rubric will be used to grade your presentation.

Rubric	Score 1	Score 3	Score 5
Completeness of your task	You provide some of the information required.	You provide most of the information required.	You provide all of the information required.
Talking about things you need for the trip	You include up to five items.	You include up to eight items.	You include ten or more items.
How easily you are understood	You are difficult to understand and have many grammatical errors.	You are fairly easy to understand and have occasional grammatical errors.	You are easy to understand and have very few grammatical errors.

Estrategia

Using charts
Create a chart to help you think through the key information you will want to talk about. This will help you speak more effectively.

Una bella playa de Cancún, México

En busca de la verdad

Episodio 1

"Esa noche, mi mamá, mi papá, mi hermano y yo nos reunimos y hablamos sobre el viaje".

Antes de ver el video

"Hay una escuela en Guanajuato muy interesada en un intercambio".

Nota cultural En Guanajuato, muchas haciendas* antiguas ahora son hoteles para turistas. También hay hoteles nuevos que conservan el estilo colonial de México. Casi todos tienen verdes jardines con árboles y flores, fuentes de agua y patios con pisos de piedra. ¡Es como volver 300 años atrás en el tiempo!

*ranches

Resumen del episodio

La historia empieza en San Antonio, Texas. Allí vive y estudia en una escuela bilingüe Linda Toledo. Carmen, la mamá de Linda, es maestra en la misma escuela y quiere establecer un programa de intercambio con una escuela mexicana. Carmen decide visitar una escuela en Guanajuato y va con Linda a una agencia de viajes para hacer los planes del viaje. Al final del episodio Linda recuerda a su abuelo en el hospital.

Palabras para comprender

intercambio exchange
próximo next
Segunda Guerra Mundial
World War II
soldado soldier
ciudadano citizen
querido, -a dear

"¿En qué puedo servirles?"

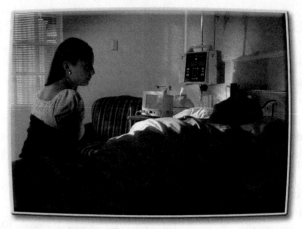

"¿Cómo estás, abuelito?"

Después de ver el video

¿Comprendiste?

A. Lee las siguientes frases y escribe quién dijo cada una: Linda, Carmen, el Sr. Balzar, el director, Berta o el abuelo.

1. "Hay una escuela en Guanajuato muy interesada en un intercambio".

2. "¿Qué le parece si me acompaña mi hija Linda?"

3. "Hay un vuelo que sale a las diez de la mañana y otro, a las seis de la tarde".

4. "Así llegamos un poco más temprano".

5. "¿Y ya tienen reservaciones de hotel en Guanajuato?"

6. "Voy a reservarles un buen hotel".

7. "Pero, ¿qué familia, abuelo?"

8. "Siempre recuerdo a mi querida familia mexicana".

B. Termina las siguientes frases explicando lo que sucede en el videomisterio:

1. El Sr. Balzar es _____.

2. Carmen y Linda quieren _____.

3. El Sr. Balzar llama a Berta Toledo en Guanajuato para _____.

4. Linda recuerda a su abuelo cuando _____.

5. El abuelo de Linda le dice que hablen otro día porque _____.

C. Mira la escena de la primera foto en la página anterior. Son el director y Carmen. Escribe un resumen de lo que hablaron.

Más práctica	GO
realidades.com | print	
Actividades	✔

Repaso del capítulo
Vocabulario y gramática

to talk about places in a community

el banco	bank
el centro	downtown
el consultorio	doctor's / dentist's office
la estación de servicio, *pl.* las estaciones de servicio	service station
la farmacia	pharmacy
el supermercado	supermarket

to talk about mail

el buzón, *pl.* los buzones	mailbox
la carta	letter
echar una carta	to mail a letter
el correo	post office
enviar *(i → i)*	to send
el sello	stamp
la tarjeta	card

to talk about items in a sporting-goods store

el equipo deportivo	sports equipment
el palo de golf	golf club
los patines	skates
la pelota	ball
la raqueta de tenis	tennis racket

to talk about pharmacy products

el cepillo de dientes	toothbrush
el champú	shampoo
el jabón	soap
la pasta dental	toothpaste

to make excuses

se me olvidó	I forgot

For *Vocabulario adicional*, see pp. 498–499.

to talk about errands

cerrar *(e → ie)*	to close
cobrar un cheque	to cash a check
cuidar a	to take care of
el dentista, la dentista	dentist
devolver *(o → ue)* (un libro)	to return (a book)
la gasolina	gasoline
ir a pie	to go on foot
llenar (el tanque)	to fill (the tank)
el médico, la médica	doctor
sacar (un libro)	to take out, to check out (a book)
se abre	opens
se cierra	closes

other useful words and expressions

caramba	good gracious
casi	almost
¡Cómo no!	Of course!
en seguida	right away
hasta	until
por	for (how long)
pronto Hasta pronto.	soon See you soon.
quedarse	to stay
todavía	still
varios, -as	various, several

preterite of *ir (to go)* and *ser (to be)*

fui	fuimos
fuiste	fuisteis
fue	fueron

preterite of *tener, estar,* and *poder*

tuve estuve pude	tuvimos estuvimos pudimos
tuviste estuviste pudiste	tuvisteis estuvisteis pudisteis
tuvo estuvo pudo	tuvieron estuvieron pudieron

direct object pronouns: *lo, la, los, las*

Más repaso GO   realidades.com | print

Instant Check   ✔
Puzzles   ✔
Core WB pp. 58–59   ✔
Comm. WB p. 231   ✔   ✔

Preparación para el examen

On the exam you will be asked to . . .	Here are practice tasks similar to those you will find on the exam . . .	For review go to your print or digital textbook . . .

Interpretive

1 Escuchar Listen and understand as people tell where they went and what they did there

As sponsor for the school's summer trip to Mexico, the Spanish teacher has heard many excuses about why students don't return to the bus in time to depart for the next stop. Listen to the excuses to determine where the students went and why they were late.

pp. 130–133 *Vocabulario en contexto*

p. 135 Actividad 6

p. 136 Actividad 8

p. 143 Actividad 21

Interpersonal

2 Hablar Ask and respond to questions about whether you did certain things that you had to do

To avoid any delays for the next day's tour, the sponsor for the Mexico City summer trip asked each student if he or she prepared the night before. She wants you to help her next time. How would you ask someone if he or she did the following: (a) cashed a check; (b) bought stamps; (c) sent postcards to friends; (d) went to the pharmacy to buy soap and toothpaste? With a partner, practice asking and answering these questions.

p. 134 Actividad 5

p. 135 Actividad 7

p. 136 Actividad 8

p. 143 Actividad 20

p. 149 *Presentación oral*

Interpretive

3 Leer Read and understand what people say they received as gifts in the past

You're helping your classmate read the answers to a survey he is conducting for his Spanish project. The survey question was: *¿Cuál es el regalo más loco que recibiste este año?* Look at the first response. Can you identify what the gift was and why the person thought it was silly?

Recibí un cupón (coupon) para llenar el tanque de mi coche, pero no tengo coche. Tuve que venderlo el mes pasado.

pp. 132–133 *Videohistoria*

pp. 146–147 *Lectura*

Presentational

4 Escribir Write responses to questions about things you have bought in the past

You decided to answer some of the other questions on your friend's survey. What would you write for the following question: *¿Qué hiciste para ganar dinero el verano pasado y qué compraste con el dinero?*

p. 137 Actividad 11

p. 139 Actividad 14

p. 143 Actividad 22

Cultures

5 Pensar Demonstrate an understanding of the popularity of outdoor markets in Spanish-speaking countries

Vendors and buyers enjoy the open-air markets so popular in Spanish-speaking countries. How would both of them spend their day at the market? What might they sell and buy?

p. 148 *La cultura en vivo*

Vocabulario Repaso

las preposiciones

a la derecha de
a la izquierda de
al lado de
cerca de
debajo de
delante de
detrás de
encima de
entre
lejos de

los medios de transporte

el autobús, *pl.* los autobuses
el avión, *pl.* los aviones
el barco
la bicicleta
el coche
el taxi
el tren

▼1 ¿Dónde está? |

Escribir • Hablar

Escribe cinco frases para describir la ciudad del dibujo. Incluye cinco preposiciones y cinco medios de transporte en tu descripción. Escribe tres frases ciertas y dos falsas según el dibujo. Luego lee tus frases a otro(a) estudiante que va a repetir las frases ciertas y cambiar las frases falsas.

📹 Modelo

A —*Hay una chica en bicicleta. Ella está a la derecha del monumento.*

B —*Sí, hay una chica en bicicleta, pero ella no está a la derecha del monumento, está a la izquierda.*

▼2 Completa la frase |

Dibujar • Hablar

❶ Trabaja con un grupo de tres o cuatro estudiantes. Cada grupo necesita siete tarjetas. En cada tarjeta dibujen uno de los medios de transporte de la lista. Un(a) estudiante escoge una tarjeta y empieza a decir una frase.

Modelo

Muchas personas van en autobús . . .

❷ El estudiante le da la tarjeta a la persona a su izquierda, que repite la frase y la completa. Si el grupo cree que la frase es correcta, el (la) estudiante que la completó escoge otra tarjeta para empezar una frase nueva.

Modelo

Muchas personas van en autobús al partido.

Gramática Repaso

The verbs *salir*, *decir*, and *venir*

Salir "to leave, to go out," *decir* "to say, to tell," and *venir* "to come" are irregular *-ir* verbs. They also have a *yo* form that ends in *-go*.

(yo)	salgo digo vengo	(nosotros) (nosotras)	salimos decimos venimos
(tú)	sales dices vienes	(vosotros) (vosotras)	salís decís venís
Ud. (él) (ella)	sale dice viene	Uds. (ellos) (ellas)	salen dicen vienen

¿Recuerdas?

You already know four *-er* verbs that have a *yo* form that ends in *-go*.

tener: yo tengo   **poner:** yo pongo

hacer: yo hago   **traer:** yo traigo

Note that *salir* is irregular only in the *yo* form; *decir* follows a pattern similar to that of *e* → *i* stem-changing verbs; and *venir* follows a pattern similar to that of *e* → *ie* stem-changing verbs.

▼3 En la ciudad

Leer • Escribir

Enrique describe lo que pasa en la ciudad. Escribe la forma apropiada del verbo correcto para completar las frases.

Muchas personas __1.__ *(poner / venir)* a la ciudad en autobús o en tren. Ellos __2.__ *(decir / salir)* que es mejor que ir en coche. Mi primo es muy deportista. Él siempre __3.__ *(decir / venir)* a la ciudad en bicicleta y __4.__ *(traer / salir)* todas sus cosas en una mochila. __5.__ *(Salir / Hacer)* de casa muy temprano porque vive bastante lejos de la ciudad. Él __6.__ *(decir / traer)* que es mejor montar en bicicleta porque __7.__ *(salir / hacer)* ejercicio al mismo tiempo. Mis hermanos y yo __8.__ *(hacer / venir)* en autobús o a veces en el coche de papá. __9.__ *(Poner / Traer)* el almuerzo porque no regresamos a casa para almorzar.

Más práctica

GO

realidades.com | print

A ver si recuerdas with Study Plan ✔

Guided WB p. 108   ✔ ✔

Core WB pp. 60–61   ✔ ✔

Hispanohablantes WB p. 110   ✔

▼4 ¿Con qué frecuencia?

Escribir • Hablar

Escribe seis frases para decir con qué frecuencia haces las actividades del recuadro. Luego lee tus frases a otro(a) estudiante para ver si hace las mismas cosas que tú.

> venir a la escuela en autobús
>
> decir la verdad
>
> traer un cuaderno a clase
>
> salir de casa antes de las siete de la mañana
>
> poner los libros en una mochila
>
> hacer la tarea en casa

▶ Modelo

salir con los amigos

A —*Siempre salgo con mis amigos los fines de semana. ¿Y tú?*

B —*Pues, salgo con ellos a veces.*

3B ¿Cómo se va . . . ?

▼ Chapter Objectives

Communication

By the end of this chapter you will be able to:

- Listen and read about driving advice
- Talk and write about giving directions and driving
- Exchange information about how to get to places near your school

Culture

You will also be able to:

- Understand the importance of one's neighborhood in Spanish-speaking communities
- Compare driving requirements in the Spanish-speaking world and the U.S.

You will demonstrate what you know and can do:

- Presentación escrita, p. 177
- Preparación para el examen, p. 181

You will use:

Vocabulary

- Driving
- Giving and receiving driving advice
- Asking for and giving directions

Grammar

- Direct object pronouns: *me, te, nos*
- Irregular affirmative *tú* commands
- Present progressive: irregular forms

Exploración del mundo hispano

Country Connection
Getting Around Town

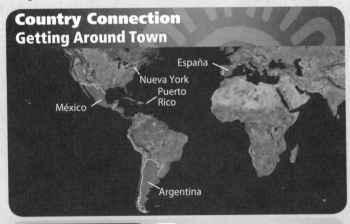

España
Nueva York
Puerto Rico
México
Argentina

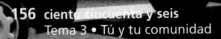
realidades.com **GO**

 Reference Atlas

 Videocultura y actividad

 Mapa global interactivo

Cerca de la Plaza de Mayo en
Buenos Aires, Argentina

Arte y cultura | Estados Unidos | México

Diego Rivera (1886–1957) pintó este mural
en el Instituto de Arte de San Francisco en
sólo cinco semanas. El artista está sentado
en el centro, con sus asistentes alrededor.
El mural representa la construcción de una
moderna ciudad industrial e indica el
entusiasmo de Rivera por el desarrollo
industrial de la década de 1930.

• Compara el entusiasmo de Rivera por el
  desarrollo industrial con el interés que
  tiene la gente hoy en día en la tecnología.

"La elaboración de un fresco" (1931), Diego Rivera ▶

271 x 357 inches, The San Francisco Art Institute, California. © 2009 Banco de México
Diego Rivera & Frida Kahlo Museums Trust, México, D.F./Artists Rights Society (ARS),
New York. Photo: Museum Associates/LACMA.

▼ Objectives

Read, listen to, and understand information about
▶ places in a city or town
▶ driving and transportation

Vocabulario en contexto

"Hola, me llamo Miguel. Hoy estoy en el centro y necesito ir al Banco Nacional. Voy a preguntarle a este policía **cómo se va** al banco".

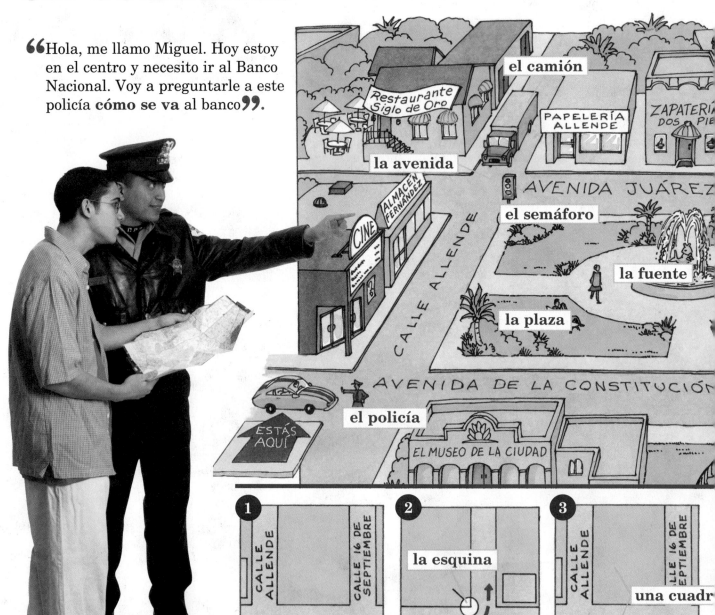

el camión

la avenida

el semáforo

la fuente

la plaza

el policía

AVENIDA JUÁREZ

AVENIDA DE LA CONSTITUCIÓN

EL MUSEO DE LA CIUDAD

ESTÁS AQUÍ

Restaurante Siglo de Oro

PAPELERÍA ALLENDE

ZAPATERÍA DOS PIE

CINE

ALMACÉN FERNÁNDEZ

CALLE ALLENDE

1 CALLE ALLENDE — CALLE 16 DE SEPTIEMBRE

2 la esquina

3 CALLE ALLENDE — LLE 16 DE EPTIEMBRE — una cuadr

—Señor policía, ¿cómo se va al Banco Nacional?

—Es muy fácil.

—**Cruza** esta calle y **sigue derecho** hasta llegar a la señal de parada.

. . . Allí, **dobla** a la izquierda.

. . . Después de **manejar por** una cuadra, dobla a la derecha. El banco **queda** a mano izquierda **en medio de** la avenida Juárez.

el puente

estrecho, -a

ancho, -a

la carretera

Más vocabulario

hasta as far as, up to

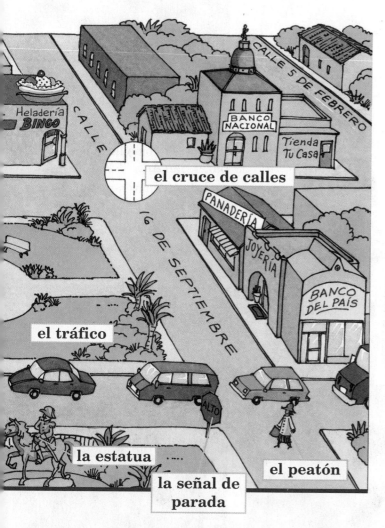

CALLE 5 DE FEBRERO

Heladería BINGO

BANCO NACIONAL

Tienda Tu Casa

CALLE

el cruce de calles

16 DE SEPTIEMBRE

PANADERÍA

JOYERÍA

BANCO DEL PAÍS

el tráfico

ALTO

la estatua

la señal de parada

el peatón

—Miguel, **ten cuidado.** Es un poco **peligroso** por aquí. La carretera es ancha pero vamos a **pasar por** un puente que es bastante estrecho.

—**¡Basta! Ya** sé manejar.

el permiso de manejar

poner una multa

el conductor

—¡Hombre! **Ve** más **despacio.** La policía te va a poner una multa y a veces te **quitan** el permiso de manejar.

—**Me estás poniendo nervioso. Déjame en paz** por un momento.

▼1 ¿Qué es y dónde queda? | 🔊

Escuchar

Escucha las descripciones y busca la palabra o expresión apropiada del vocabulario en el mapa de las páginas 158–159. Señala la palabra o expresión y dila en voz alta *(say it aloud)* para indicar que la encontraste.

▼2 ¿Dónde estoy ahora? | 🔊

Escuchar

Escucha las direcciones y síguelas en el mapa de las páginas 158–159. Empieza cada vez en las palabras *Estás aquí.* Indica adónde llegas y contesta con *Estoy delante de . . .*

Más práctica GO	realidades.com | print	
Instant Check	✔	
Guided WB pp. 109–114	✔	✔
Core WB pp. 62–63	✔	✔
Comm. WB p. 63	✔	✔
Hispanohablantes WB p. 112		✔

¿Cómo llegamos a la plaza?

¿Cómo van los cuatro amigos al Bazar San Ángel? Lee la historia.

Estrategia

Reading for key information
Reading the questions at the end of the *Videohistoria* will help you focus on key information.

1

Teresa: ¿Y cómo llegamos al Bazar San Ángel?

Claudia: Vamos a tomar **el metro desde** aquí.

Teresa: Está bien. Vamos.

Manolo

Teresa

Ramón

Claudia

5

Ramón: Ahora, ¿adónde?
Manolo: Espera. Esto es **complicado.** Vamos a doblar a la derecha. No, mejor, vamos a seguir por aquí.

Ramón: ¿Estás seguro?

Manolo: Sí, sí. Yo sé por dónde vamos. Me estás poniendo nervioso.

6

Teresa: Ya son las dos y cuarto. ¿Dónde están Ramón y Manolo?

Claudia: Estoy segura que no saben dónde está . . .

7

Ramón: ¡Basta! Vamos a preguntarle a alguien. Señor, ¿cómo se va al Bazar San Ángel?

Señor: Pues, miren. En este cruce de calles van a doblar a la izquierda.

Ramón: Gracias. Vamos, rápido.

Ramón: Claudia y Teresa nos van a **esperar** en el Bazar San Ángel. Mira, aquí hay un banco. **¿Tienes prisa?**

Manolo: No, no tengo prisa. Tenemos tiempo. ¿Por qué?

Ramón: ¿Puedes **parar** por un momento, por favor? Tengo que sacar dinero.

Ramón: Doscientos pesos. Ahora, vamos a ver a Claudia y a Teresa.

Manolo: Sí. Pero no vamos a manejar el coche. Vamos a **dejarlo** en casa para ir a pie. El Bazar San Ángel queda **aproximadamente** a veinte minutos de mi casa.

Ramón: Vamos.

Manolo: De acuerdo.

Ramón: ¿Y cómo es el Bazar?

Manolo: Hace mucho tiempo que no voy por allí. Pero te va a gustar. Es muy popular.

Ramón: ¿Y **estás seguro** que sabes cómo llegar allí?

Manolo: Sí, claro. Está a* unas siete cuadras de aquí.

*Estar a is used to indicate distance.

Manolo: ¡Claudia, Teresa, aquí estamos!

▼3 ¿Comprendiste?

Escribir • Hablar

1. ¿Cómo van a ir Claudia y Teresa al Bazar San Ángel?
2. Antes de ir al Bazar, ¿qué tiene que hacer Ramón?
3. ¿Cómo van a llegar Ramón y Manolo a San Ángel? ¿Por qué?
4. ¿Sabe Manolo llegar al Bazar? Según Manolo, ¿por qué?
5. ¿Tienen problemas los dos chicos en llegar al Bazar San Ángel? ¿Qué les pasa?
6. ¿Quiénes están esperándolos cuando llegan al Bazar?

Más práctica	GO

realidades.com | print

Instant Check	✔	
Guided WB pp. 115–118	✔	✔
Core WB pp. 64–65	✔	✔
Comm. WB pp. 56–58, 59	✔	✔
Hispanohablantes **WB** p. 113		✔

| ▼ **Objectives**

▶ **Talk about driving**
▶ **Discuss how to get around Old San Juan**
▶ **Listen to driving advice and directions**
▶ **Write about driving habits**

Vocabulario en uso

▼4 Las glorietas

Leer • Escribir

Lee este párrafo sobre las glorietas *(traffic circles)* y escribe las palabras correctas para completarlo.

Hace muchos años, en Europa y en América Latina, encontraron una solución al problema de accidentes en los **1.** *(cruces de calles / peatones):* la glorieta. Las glorietas reducen el número de accidentes porque los conductores no pueden **2.** *(tener prisa / doblar)* a la izquierda. En muchos casos, los cruces de calles con glorietas son menos **3.** *(anchos / peligrosos)* que los que tienen semáforos. En muchas ciudades, las glorietas también son lugares de mucho interés turístico, porque hay grandes **4.** *(fuentes / esquinas),* monumentos o **5.** *(carreteras / estatuas)* en el centro. Frecuentemente hay muchos coches, taxis, **6.** *(camiones / avenidas)* y autobuses que pasan por estas glorietas y es necesario tener un **7.** *(puente / policía)* allí para ayudar a controlar el **8.** *(tráfico / metro).* En algunas partes de los Estados Unidos, como en Nueva Jersey, también es común ver glorietas en las calles.

Glorieta de la Plaza de Cánovas del Castillo, Madrid

▼5 Y tú, ¿qué dices? |

Escribir • Hablar

1. ¿Hay una glorieta en una comunidad que tú conoces? ¿Cómo es? ¿Hay una fuente, estatua o monumento allí?

2. Para algunos conductores las glorietas parecen complicadas. ¿Qué piensas? ¿Las glorietas te parecen más o menos peligrosas que los cruces de calles con semáforos o señales de parada? ¿Por qué?

3. ¿Cómo manejan los conductores en las glorietas, despacio o con mucha prisa?

4. En tu comunidad, ¿hay mucho tráfico en los cruces de calles? ¿Los policías ayudan a controlar el tráfico? ¿Qué hacen los policías si alguien no respeta las reglas de tráfico?

También se dice . . .

el cruce de calles = la intersección *(Colombia, Ecuador)*

manejar = conducir *(España, Puerto Rico)*

doblar = dar la vuelta *(Colombia)*

la carretera = la autopista *(Colombia)*

la cuadra = la manzana *(España, Colombia)*

el permiso de manejar = la licencia de conducir *(México);* el carnet de conducir *(España)*

derecho = recto *(Ecuador, Guatemala)*

el tráfico = la circulación *(España, Uruguay, Venezuela, México);* el tránsito *(España)*

▼6 ¿Qué hay en el mapa? | 💬 👥 | ♻

Escribir • Hablar

Haz una lista de ocho cosas que puedes ver en el centro de una ciudad. Trabaja con otro(a) estudiante y pregúntale si ve estas cosas en el mapa de las páginas 158–159. Si necesitas ayuda con las preposiciones ve *A ver si recuerdas* en la página 154.

> ▶ **Modelo**
> **A** —¿*Hay una fuente?*
> **B** —*Sí. Está en medio de la plaza.*

▼7 Escucha y escribe | 🔊

Escuchar • Escribir

Tus parientes *(relatives)* saben que estás aprendiendo a manejar y todos tienen consejos *(advice)*. Pero algunas de sus ideas no son muy lógicas. Escucha lo que dicen y escribe las frases. Después escribe *L* si es una idea lógica o *I* si es una idea ilógica.

▼8 ¡Me estás poniendo nervioso! | 💬 👥

Leer • Hablar

Tu compañero(a) y tú están en el coche. Tú estás manejando, pero tu compañero(a) ve las señales de tráfico y te está poniendo nervioso(a) con todo lo que te dice. Hagan una conversación lógica usando las señales y frases de abajo. Las señales indican el orden de las frases que debes usar en la conversación.

> ▶ **Modelo**
> **A** —*Ten cuidado. Hay una zona de construcción por aquí.*
> **B** —*Por favor. ¡Ya sé manejar!*

1. 　　2. 　　3. 　　4.

5. **ALTO**　　6. 　　7. 　　8.

Estudiante A

¡Espera! Se prohíbe entrar. No puedes seguir derecho.

Debes parar en la señal de parada.

Cuidado. Este cruce de trenes es bastante peligroso.

Si no respetas la velocidad máxima *(speed limit)*, el policía te pone una multa.

¿Estás seguro(a) que podemos cruzar este puente estrecho?

Ve más despacio. Hay muchos peatones en el cruce de calles.

En esta avenida no puedes doblar a la derecha.

Ve despacio en esta zona escolar.

Estudiante B

De acuerdo. Voy a . . .

Déjame en paz.

Ya sé manejar.

Me estás poniendo nervioso(a).

¡Basta!

Gracias, pero no necesito tu ayuda.

Escuchar

Estás de vacaciones con tu familia en el Viejo San Juan, Puerto Rico. Empiezas tu excursión hoy en el Parque de las Palomas. (Mira ⭐ en el mapa.) Escucha las direcciones que te dan tres personas y síguelas en el mapa. Escribe el nombre de cada lugar adonde llegas.

Empezaron a construir el sistema de defensas para la ciudad de San Juan en el siglo *(century)* XVI con murallas *(walls)* grandes como ésta y el famoso Castillo El Morro.

La Puerta de San Juan es la entrada a la antigua ciudad del mar.

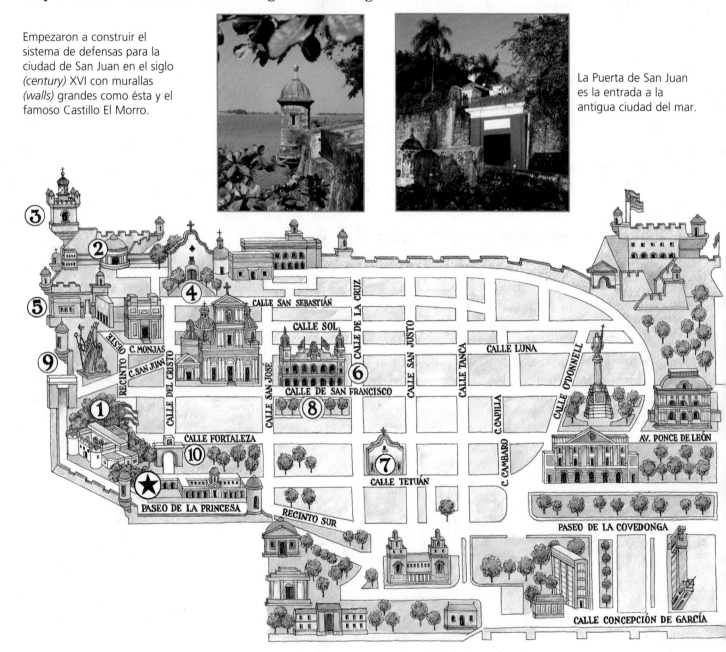

Leyenda

1. La Fortaleza	6. la Alcaldía
2. el Museo de las Américas	7. la Iglesia de Santa Ana
3. el Castillo El Morro	8. la Plaza de Armas
4. la Plaza Quinto Centenario	9. la Puerta de San Juan
5. la Casa Blanca	10. la Capilla del Cristo

▼10 Puntos de interés |

Hablar

Hoy quieres visitar otros puntos de interés en el Viejo San Juan. Empiezas tu excursión otra vez en el Parque de las Palomas. Con otro(a) estudiante, habla de cómo se va a los lugares que ven en el mapa de la página 164.

▶ Modelo

A —*Por favor, ayúdame. ¿Cómo se va del Parque de las Palomas a la Catedral?*

B —*Camina dos cuadras por la Calle del Cristo. Queda a la derecha.*

Estudiante A

1. La Fortaleza
2. el Museo de las Américas
3. el Castillo El Morro
4. la Plaza Quinto Centenario
5. la Casa Blanca
6. la Alcaldía

Estudiante B

Camina (por) . . .   Cruza . . .
Toma . . .   Pasa (por) . . .
Ve . . .   Dobla . . .
Sigue (derecho) . . .   Para . . .

▼11 Y tú, ¿qué dices? |

Escribir • Hablar

1. En tu comunidad, ¿cómo son las calles? ¿Es fácil o es complicado ir de un lugar a otro?

2. ¿Ya tienes tu permiso de manejar? Si no, ¿cuándo lo vas a obtener? ¿Qué haces (hiciste) para aprender las reglas y señales de tráfico?

3. En una encuesta *(survey)*, les preguntaron a unos jóvenes españoles con qué frecuencia usan su coche para salir de la ciudad. Los jóvenes contestaron:

Casi todos los días	48%
Sólo el fin de semana	7%
Tres o cuatro veces a la semana	5%
Casi nunca	11%
No tengo coche	29%

¿Crees que contestarían *(would answer)* los jóvenes de tu comunidad estas preguntas de una forma similar? ¿Por qué?

Fondo Cultural | El mundo hispano

La Plaza Mayor En las antiguas ciudades de España y las ciudades coloniales de América Latina, la plaza era *(was)* el centro de la ciudad. Hoy las plazas son lugares populares para pasar tiempo con los amigos. La Plaza Mayor de Madrid es una de las más bonitas de España. El Zócalo, en la Ciudad de México, es una de las más grandes del mundo.

• ¿Hay algo similar a una plaza mayor en tu comunidad? ¿Qué es? ¿Adónde vas tú para pasar tiempo con amigos?

El Zócalo, Ciudad de México

Plaza Mayor de Madrid, España

Gramática Repaso

Direct object pronouns: *me, te, nos*

You know that direct object pronouns replace direct object nouns. The direct object pronouns *lo, la, los,* and *las* can refer to both objects and people. The pronouns *me, te, nos,* and *os* refer only to people. Here are all the direct object pronouns:

Singular		Plural	
me	me	nos	us
te	you *(familiar)*	os	you *(familiar)*
lo	him, it, you *(formal)*	los	them, you
la	her, it, you *(formal)*	las	

Remember that the subject and the verb ending tell who does the action and the direct object pronoun indicates who receives the action.

¿Me ayudas, por favor?

Direct object pronouns usually come right before the conjugated verb. When an infinitive follows a conjugated verb, the pronoun can be placed before the first verb or attached to the infinitive.

¡No te entiendo!

Quieren llevarnos al centro.

Más ayuda **realidades.com**

▶ **Tutorial:** Direct object pronouns

▼12 Tarde otra vez

Leer • Escribir

Hoy Manolo llegó tarde a la escuela. Completa la conversación entre él y Ramón con *me, te* o *nos.*

Ramón: Oye, Manolo, ¿por qué no tomaste el autobús a la escuela esta mañana? __1.__ esperamos en la esquina de tu calle por diez minutos.

Manolo: Lo siento. Mi padre no __2.__ despertó a tiempo.

Ramón: ¿Y cómo llegaste a la escuela? ¿Tu hermana __3.__ llevó en su coche?

Manolo: Sí, ella __4.__ llevó a la escuela.

Ramón: ¿Ya sabes que repasamos en la primera hora para el examen de mañana?

Manolo: Sí, lo sé y no entiendo la materia. ¿__5.__ ayudas a estudiar esta noche?

Ramón: Lo siento, amigo, pero no __6.__ puedo ayudar. Mi familia y yo vamos a la casa de mis tíos. Ellos __7.__ invitaron a cenar esta noche.

Manolo: Pues, entonces __8.__ veo mañana. Tengo que hablar con Claudia y Teresa. Estoy seguro que ellas __9.__ pueden ayudar.

"Perdón, señora. Nos puede decir cómo llegar a . . . ?"

▼13 Una foto y una voz | 👥 | ♻️

Leer • Hablar

Lee el anuncio a la derecha y, con otro(a) estudiante, contesta las preguntas.

1. ¿Qué hace el navegador GPS de este teléfono?

2. Si tienes este nuevo teléfono celular, ¿cuál es la ventaja *(advantage)* para tus amigos?

3. ¿Te gustaría tener un teléfono celular como éste? ¿Por qué?

SI NO SABES DÓNDE ESTÁS

Con el nuevo teléfono celular MX P-45, puedes salir tranquilo de tu casa. El navegador GPS integrado en este celular te dice dónde estás y cómo llegar a tu tienda o restaurante favorito. También, te informa sobre el tráfico, y así puedes llamar a tus amigos si vas a llegar tarde.

¡TU TELÉFONO TE ENCUENTRA!

▼14 Una fiesta en el centro | ♻️

Escribir

Hoy es la fiesta de cumpleaños de la abuela de Teresa. La familia decidió celebrar en un restaurante del centro. Escribe lo que hicieron Teresa, su familia y los invitados *(guests)*.

Modelo

Teresa / invitar a la fiesta de su abuela: a nosotros
Teresa nos invitó a la fiesta de su abuela.

1. Teresa / llamar anoche: a ti

2. mis padres / ayudar a comprar un regalo: a mí

3. mi padre / llevar en su coche a la fiesta: a mí

4. Teresa y su madre / ver: a nosotros

5. la abuela de Teresa / conocer: a ti

6. mis padres / llevar a casa a las diez: a nosotros

▼15 Tus relaciones con otras personas | 🗨️👥 | ♻️

Hablar

Habla con otro(a) estudiante sobre las relaciones que tienes con otras personas.

▶️ **Modelo**

llevar a la escuela por la mañana
A —*¿Quién te lleva a la escuela por la mañana?*
B —*Mis padres me llevan a la escuela.*
o: —*Nadie me lleva a la escuela. Voy a pie.*

Estudiante A

1. invitar a su casa a menudo
2. comprender casi siempre
3. ayudar con las tareas
4. recoger de la escuela por la tarde
5. esperar mucho
6. despertar por la mañana

Estudiante B

mi mamá (papá)
mis padres
mi hermano(a)
mi mejor amigo(a)

mis amigos

¡Respuesta personal!

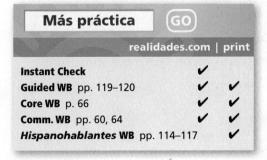

Más práctica	GO

realidades.com | print

Instant Check	✔	
Guided WB pp. 119–120	✔	✔
Core WB p. 66	✔	✔
Comm. WB pp. 60, 64	✔	✔
Hispanohablantes WB pp. 114–117	✔	

Gramática

Irregular affirmative *tú* commands

Some verbs have irregular affirmative *tú* commands. To form many of these commands, take the *yo* form of the present tense and drop the *-go*:

Infinitive	yo form	command
poner	pongo	pon
tener	tengo	ten
decir	digo	di
salir	salgo	sal
venir	vengo	ven

Hacer, ser, and *ir* have irregular *tú* command forms that must be memorized.

hacer	haz
ser	sé
ir	ve

—¿Cómo se va a la carretera?

—**Sal** de aquí y sigue derecho hasta el tercer semáforo.

¿Recuerdas?

To give someone an affirmative *tú* command, use the *Ud. / él / ella* form of the verb.

• Elena, ¡**maneja** con cuidado!

If you use a direct object pronoun with an affirmative command, attach the pronoun to the command. When a pronoun is added to a command of two or more syllables, a written accent mark is needed over the stressed vowel.

Josefina, ¡**hazlo** ahora mismo!

Martín, **ayúdame**.

Más ayuda realidades.com

▶ *GramActiva* Video
Tutorial: Formation of irregular *tú* commands

◀)) *Canción de hip hop: ¿Cómo se va?*

✎ *GramActiva* Activity

▼16 Los consejos de una amiga

Leer • Escribir

Joaquín visita por primera vez Caracas, Venezuela, y quiere manejar al centro. Lee los consejos que le da una amiga venezolana. Empareja *(Match)* la información de las dos columnas y escribe los mandatos apropiados que ella le dice.

Modelo
(ir) al banco primero
Ve al banco primero si no tienes mucho dinero.

1. *(poner)* el permiso de manejar
2. *(salir)* temprano para no encontrar
3. *(ser)* un(a) buen(a) conductor(a) para
4. *(tener)* cuidado cuando pasas por
5. *(ir)* despacio por
6. *(hacer)* una pregunta
7. *(decir)* la verdad (¡que no sabes!)
8. *(venir)* directamente a casa

a. una zona de construcción
b. si no sabes dónde queda algo
c. en tu cartera antes de salir
d. a las cuatro de la tarde
e. no recibir multas de la policía
f. si alguien te pregunta cómo se va a algún lugar
g. las calles estrechas
h. mucho tráfico

▼17 ¡Toma el metro! | Talk!

Hablar

Mira el mapa del metro de la Ciudad de México. Habla con otro(a) estudiante sobre la mejor forma de ir de un lugar a otro usando el metro.

> **Para decir más . . .**
> **bajar**   to get off
> **cambiar**   to change
> **hacia**   toward

▶ **Modelo**

A —¿Cómo se va en el metro del Hospital General al Zócalo?

B —Pues, desde el Hospital General toma la línea 3 y ve hacia Indios Verdes. Baja en Hidalgo y cambia a la línea 2. Ten cuidado. Ve hacia Villa de Cortés y baja en la estación Zócalo. Sal del metro y estás en el Zócalo.

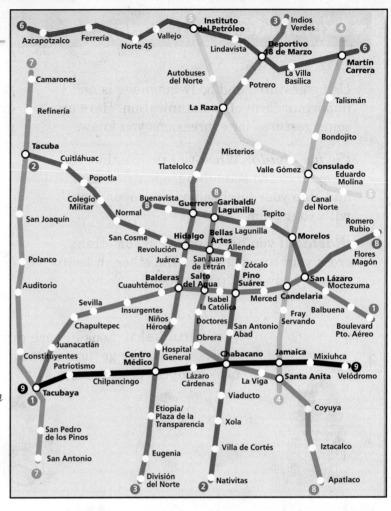

¿Cómo se va . . .

1. . . . del parque Chapultepec al Zócalo?

2. . . . de Santa Anita a Lázaro Cárdenas?

3. . . . del Palacio de Bellas Artes a la estación Autobuses del Norte?

4. . . . de Chabacano a San Juan de Letrán?

5. . . . de Tlatelolco a Garibaldi?

6. . . . del Colegio Militar a Insurgentes?

▼ Fondo Cultural | México

El Metro de la Ciudad de México 3.9 millones de personas usan diariamente las 11 líneas del metro en la Ciudad de México. Es económico viajar por metro. Un viaje cuesta tres pesos. Si usas mucho el metro, puedes comprar boletos con descuento. Durante las horas pico (*rush hour*) hay tantas personas que hay unos vagones (*subway cars*) sólo para hombres y otros vagones para mujeres y niños.

• ¿Por qué crees que el metro es un sistema de transporte tan popular en la ciudad?

La estación de metro Chapultepec, Ciudad de México

▼ Exploración del lenguaje

Los gestos

Using gestures and body language is an important form of communication. Here are some gestures for expressions you know.

¡Se me olvidó! When you realize that you have forgotten something, open your mouth and slap your forehead or your open mouth with your palm.

¡Basta! If you have enough of something, cross your arms one over the other, in front of your body, with palms down.

¡Vete! If you want someone to go away, extend one arm toward the person with the palm of the open hand, as if to make a stop sign. Move the hand near and far, as if pushing something.

¡Ven aquí! If you want someone to come closer, turn the palm of your hand up and fold your fingers toward you, into your palm.

¡Sigue derecho! To help a person find the way, extend your arm ahead. Move your arm forward and back, indicating the way to go with your hand.

¡Compruébalo! Look at each drawing and write the appropriate expression for the gesture shown. Then work with a partner and use one of the gestures in a skit.

▼18 Ayúdame, por favor

Leer • Escribir • Hablar

Anita está en casa con su hermano mayor y quiere ir al centro comercial. Primero escribe los mandatos que completan la conversación entre ellos. ¡Ojo! Si añades un pronombre a un verbo que tiene más de una sílaba, tienes que escribir un acento. Después lee la conversación con otro(a) estudiante.

ayudarme	escucharme	llevarme	ser
decirme	esperarme	preguntarme	venir

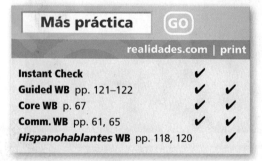

Más práctica (GO)

realidades.com | print

Instant Check	✔	
Guided WB pp. 121–122	✔	✔
Core WB p. 67	✔	✔
Comm. WB pp. 61, 65	✔	✔
Hispanohablantes WB pp. 118, 120		✔

Anita: Roberto, quiero ir al centro comercial pero queda bastante lejos. __1.__ muy simpático y __2.__ en tu coche, por favor.

Roberto: No puedo. Tengo mucho que hacer. Pero __3.__ aquí un minuto. Tengo un mapa en mi coche. Estoy seguro que lo puedes encontrar. Si no entiendes algo, __4.__ .

Anita: Todavía parece complicado. __5.__ con el mapa, Roberto. O mejor, __6.__ conmigo.

Roberto: Yo sé que lo puedes hacer sola. __7.__ con atención y te explico las direcciones otra vez.

Anita: Pues, __8.__ , ¿no hay una tienda cerca de nuestra casa? Prefiero quedarme por aquí.

Gramática

Present progressive: irregular forms

Some verbs have irregular present participle forms.

To form the present participle of *-ir* stem-changing verbs, the *e* in the infinitive form changes to *i*, and the *o* in the infinitive form changes to *u*:

decir: **diciendo**   servir: **sirviendo**
pedir: **pidiendo**   vestir: **vistiendo**
repetir: **repitiendo**   dormir: **durmiendo**
seguir: **siguiendo**

In the following *-er* verbs, the *i* of *-iendo* changes to *y*.

creer: **creyendo**
leer: **leyendo**
traer: **trayendo**

When you use object pronouns with the present progressive, you can put them before the conjugated form of *estar* or attach them to the present participle.

Notice that if a pronoun is attached to the present participle, an accent mark is needed. Write the accent mark over the vowel that is normally stressed in the present participle.

—¿Están Uds. esperando el autobús?

—Sí, **lo** estamos esperando.

o: Sí, estamos esperándo**lo**.

¿Recuerdas?

To say that an action is happening right now, use the present progressive. To form the present progressive, use the present tense of *estar* + the present participle (*-ando* or *-iendo*).

doblar → doblando
• Ella **está doblando** a la izquierda.

aprender → aprendiendo
• **Estamos aprendiendo** a manejar.

escribir → escribiendo
• **Están escribiendo** una carta.

Más ayuda **realidades.com**

▶ *GramActiva* Video
Animated Verbs

GramActiva Activity

▼19 En la calle |

Escribir • Hablar

Examina el cuadro del pintor español Juan Ferrer y Miró. Escribe cinco frases para decir lo que están haciendo las personas que ves. Después trabaja con otro(a) estudiante y pregúntale qué están haciendo las diferentes personas.

"Exposición de pintura" (siglo XIX), Juan Ferrer y Miró
Photo courtesy of SuperStock. © 2004 Artists Rights Society, ARS, NY.

▶ Modelo

A —¿Qué está haciendo el perro?
B —El perro está esperando al niño.

▼20 Un(a) instructor(a) nervioso(a) | 🗣👥

Hablar

Imagina que eres un(a) estudiante que está aprendiendo a manejar. Estás poniendo nervioso(a) a tu instructor(a) porque estás mirando a la gente en vez de *(instead of)* mirar la calle. Con otro(a) estudiante que hace el papel *(plays the role)* del (de la) instructor(a), hagan una conversación.

▶ **Modelo**

esa señora / pedirle ayuda al policía mirar / el semáforo / cambiar de verde a amarillo

A —*Esa señora está pidiéndole ayuda al policía.*

B —*Mira, Catalina. El semáforo está cambiando de verde a amarillo.*

Estudiante A

1. ese señor / leer un mapa de la ciudad
2. esos niños / decirle algo a su mamá
3. esos jóvenes / dormir debajo de un árbol
4. ese perro / seguir a los niños
5. esa camarera / servirles bebidas a los clientes
6. esa policía / ponerle una multa a ese conductor

Estudiante B

a. parar / esos peatones / cruzar la calle
b. mirar / ese camión / parar
c. ir más despacio / nosotros / entrar en la plaza
d. tener cuidado / los niños / correr hacia la calle
e. esperar / ese conductor / doblar a la izquierda
f. volver a la escuela / tú / ponerme muy nervioso(a)

▼ Fondo Cultural | El mundo hispano

Permiso de manejar En los países hispanohablantes hay diferentes requisitos *(requirements)* para conseguir el permiso de manejar. En todos los países hay que presentar documentos de identidad y un certificado médico que declara que tienes buena salud física y mental. También hay que aprobar un examen. En muchos países los exámenes son de teoría (escrito) y de práctica (manejo). En Argentina puedes manejar un ciclomotor *(moped)* a los 16 años y un coche a los 17. En España puedes manejar un ciclomotor sin llevar pasajeros a los 14 años, llevar pasajeros a los 16 y manejar un coche a los 18.

• ¿Cuáles son los requisitos en tu estado para conseguir el permiso de manejar? ¿Son más fáciles o más difíciles que en los países hispanohablantes?

Una escuela para aprender a manejar en Argentina

Más práctica	**GO**

realidades.com | print

Instant Check	✔	
Guided WB pp. 123–124	✔	✔
Core WB p. 68	✔	✔
Comm. WB pp. 62, 232	✔	✔
Hispanohablantes **WB** pp. 119, 121	✔	

▼21 El camión | 👥

Observar • Hablar

La artista mexicana Frida Kahlo pintó muchos autorretratos, pero también pintó imágenes que representan la cultura popular de su país. Pintó una colorida imagen de un autobús mexicano en *El camión* (1929), que es la palabra que se usa en México para decir *el autobús*. En los viejos tiempos, los autobuses en la Ciudad de México estaban hechos de caoba *(mahogany)* por adentro. Hoy en día este estilo ya no existe.

Conexiones | El arte

"El camión" (1929), Frida Kahlo.

1. Con otro(a) estudiante, describe a las personas que viajan en el autobús del cuadro. ¿Qué tienen en común? ¿En qué sentido son diferentes? ¿Qué están haciendo?

2. ¿Las personas del cuadro parecen ser realistas? ¿Por qué?

3. Digan cinco mandatos que la madre puede decirle al niño o al bebé.

▼22 En mi comunidad | 👥

Dibujar • Escribir • Hablar

Tienes un(a) amigo(a) que acaba de llegar a tu comunidad y quiere saber adónde ir para hacer sus quehaceres. Dibuja un mapa de tu comunidad con ocho lugares importantes. Marca dónde debe empezar con *Estás aquí*. Escribe tres series de instrucciones para ir de un lugar a otro. Muestra *(Show)* tu mapa a otro(a) estudiante y dile cómo se va a los diferentes lugares. Luego mira el mapa de tu compañero(a) y sigue sus instrucciones para ir de un lugar a otro en su comunidad.

El español en el mundo del trabajo

Para atraer a los turistas hispanohablantes en los Estados Unidos, es importante tener empleados *(employees)* hispanohablantes en los centros de información turística. Así pueden contestar preguntas o dar información o instrucciones a las personas hispanohablantes.

• ¿Vives en una comunidad donde llegan muchos turistas? ¿Cuáles son los lugares de interés turístico populares en tu comunidad?

▼ **Objectives**

▷ **Read about safe driving practices**
▷ **Use context to help you understand unfamiliar words**
▷ **Understand the importance of the Pan-American Highway**

Lectura

Lee esta sección de una guía del conductor que explica reglas para manejar con precaución.

Estrategia

Context clues
In this reading you may come across words you don't know. Use the context in which they are found to help you guess their meanings.

GUÍA DEL BUEN CONDUCTOR

Un buen conductor siempre debe estar alerta para evitar[1] accidentes. No es difícil; simplemente tienes que estar atento[2], respetar las señales y observar la forma de manejar de los demás.

Notas importantes:

- Ten cuidado con los conductores agresivos.
- Usa las luces de tu coche de manera apropiada.
- Cuando llueve o nieva, tienes que estar mucho más atento al tráfico.
- Maneja por calles y carreteras en buenas condiciones.
- Presta atención al 100%.

Conductores agresivos

Muchos conductores no respetan la velocidad máxima, no paran en la señal de parada o pasan muy cerca de tu coche. Tienes que actuar con tranquilidad, no discutir y mantenerte lejos de ese vehículo.

Si el conductor es muy agresivo, puedes reportarlo con la policía.

Luces y señales

Por la noche debes manejar con luces. Así puedes ver tu camino[3], y los otros conductores y peatones te pueden ver a ti.

¡Importante! Usa siempre la luz direccional[4] para doblar a la izquierda o la derecha.

Manejar con lluvia

Cuando llueve o nieva, siempre debes usar luces y manejar más despacio, aproximadamente un 50% menos que la velocidad usual.

¡Cuidado! Cuando llueve o nieva, el coche requiere más tiempo para parar.

Rutas

Debes evitar calles y carreteras en malas condiciones, en construcción o con muchos camiones. Es más probable tener un accidente en un camino con mucho tráfico.

Descansos

Es importante descansar. Si manejas en la ciudad, cada vez que paras en un semáforo en rojo, quita la vista del camino por unos segundos. Así puedes relajar los ojos.

Cuando haces viajes largos por la carretera, para cada 100 millas para tomar un refresco y mover las piernas.

8

[1]avoid   [2]attentive   [3]way   [4]turn signal

Atención al 100%

Es fácil distraerse[5] al manejar; para evitarlo sigue estos consejos:

- no quitar los ojos del camino
- mantener la distancia con el vehículo de adelante
- observar los espejos continuamente
- no leer periódicos
- no escuchar la radio con el volumen alto
- no hablar por teléfono
- no enviar mensajes de texto

Puedes manejar con amigos y hablar con ellos tranquilamente, pero no los debes mirar. Un segundo sin mirar el camino puede causar un accidente serio.

Manejar muy cerca de otro coche es peligroso. Si el otro coche para de repente[6], tú no tienes suficiente tiempo para parar.

¡No mires hacia atrás[7]! Usa los espejos. Así puedes observar los vehículos de atrás y de adelante.

10

La música a un volumen alto no permite escuchar lo que ocurre en la calle: otro coche, un peatón, una ambulancia o un policía. Escucha música con volumen moderado.

¡**ALERTA!** El teléfono celular es muy popular pero también muy peligroso. Incluso si utilizas un sistema de manos libres, causa mucha distracción. Si tienes que usar el teléfono con urgencia, para el coche y habla o envía un mensaje de texto con tranquilidad.

Éstas fueron las reglas de oro para el buen conductor. Síguelas y disfruta de[8] tu viaje.

11

---

[5]to get distracted   [6]suddenly   [7]Don't look behind you!   [8]enjoy

¿Comprendiste?

1. ¿Cuáles son las tres reglas básicas para ser un buen conductor?

2. ¿Qué puedes hacer si ves a un conductor agresivo?

3. ¿En qué momento es muy importante usar las luces?

4. ¿Por qué es importante quitar la vista del camino cuando estamos parados en un semáforo?

5. ¿Qué dice esta guía sobre el teléfono celular?

Y tú, ¿qué dices? | (Talk!)

1. ¿Cuál es la velocidad máxima para manejar en la carretera de tu ciudad? ¿Te da miedo viajar en coche cuando llueve o nieva?

2. ¿Tus amigos y familiares hablan por teléfono celular cuando manejan? ¿Crees que es absolutamente necesario?

3. ¿Crees que es buena idea tomar un curso en una escuela de manejar? ¿Por qué?

Fondo Cultural | **El mundo hispano**

La Carretera Panamericana es una carretera que une *(links)* los países de América del Norte, América Central y América del Sur. La construcción de la carretera empezó en 1936, y hoy en día tiene aproximadamente 16,000 millas (25,750 km) de extensión.

- ¿Por dónde pasa la Carretera Panamericana en los Estados Unidos? ¿Por qué es importante en la economía del hemisferio occidental?

Más práctica GO

realidades.com | print

Guided WB p. 125	✔	✔
Comm. WB pp. 66, 233	✔	✔
Hispanohablantes **WB** pp. 122–123	✔	
Cultural Reading Activity	✔	

Perspectivas del mundo hispano

El barrio

Imagina que llegas a casa y no puedes abrir la puerta. No hay nadie en casa y no puedes entrar. Mañana tienes un examen y los libros están en la casa. No tienes dinero. No puedes llamar por teléfono. Tienes hambre y no puedes comprar comida. ¿Qué puedes hacer?

Un barrio típico de Guanajuato, México

Esto no es un gran problema si vives en un barrio de un país hispanohablante. Aquí los vecinos[1] se conocen[2] bien. Son simpáticos y se ayudan. Cuando te olvidas las llaves puedes ir a casa de tus vecinos. Si pueden, ellos te ayudan a entrar en tu casa. Si tienes hambre, te dan algo de comer. Te dejan llamar por teléfono.

El Museo del Barrio en la ciudad de Nueva York. En él se pueden ver trabajos artísticos de la comunidad hispanohablante.

En los países hispanohablantes, el barrio es una institución. Las casas del barrio están cerca unas de otras y frecuentemente están cerca de una plaza. Normalmente en el barrio hay un mercado, un cine y pequeñas tiendas para comprar comida, ropa o materiales para la escuela. El barrio es como una extensión del hogar[3]—un buen lugar para la familia, donde los niños y los mayores pueden jugar y pasear.

¡Compruébalo! Compara las calles que hay cerca de tu casa con los barrios de los países hispanohablantes. ¿Conoces a los vecinos de tu comunidad? ¿Hay pequeñas tiendas familiares?[4] ¿Hay una plaza?

¿Qué te parece? ¿Cuáles son los aspectos de la organización de un barrio que más te interesan? ¿Crees que el barrio es una buena manera de organizar una comunidad? ¿Por qué?

[1]neighbors [2]know one another [3]home [4]family-run

Uno de los muchos barrios que se encuentran en Sevilla, España

Presentación escrita

Maneja con cuidado

Task
Make a poster that can be displayed in the classroom that reminds everyone of safe driving practices and special traffic signs you need to recognize.

❶ **Prewrite** Use these questions to help you organize your ideas for your poster.
- ¿Qué señales son importantes y qué información dan?
- ¿Qué forma tienen? (cuadrados, rectángulos, triángulos, círculos, octágonos o diamantes)? ¿De qué color son? Dibújalas.
- ¿Cuáles son algunas de las zonas especiales en tu comunidad?
- ¿Cuál es la velocidad máxima en estas zonas?
- ¿Cómo maneja un(a) buen(a) conductor(a)? ¿Qué debes recordar *(remember)* cuando manejas un coche?

❷ **Draft** Reread your answers from Step 1 and decide what points you want to emphasize. Draw a first draft of your poster.

❸ **Revise** Check your first draft for spelling, verb forms, and agreement. Is it arranged clearly and logically? Share the poster with a partner, who will check:
- Is the information important and accurate?
- Is the visual presentation clear and easy to understand?
- Is there anything you should add, change, or correct?

❹ **Publish** Prepare a final copy of your poster. Make any necessary changes or additions. Add designs or illustrations to make the poster attractive. Display it in your classroom, the school library, or your portfolio.

❺ **Evaluation** The following rubric will be used to grade your presentation.

> **Estrategia**
>
> **Using illustrations**
> Photographs, designs, and colors help to draw the eye to important information.

Rubric	Score 1	Score 3	Score 5
Your completeness and accuracy of information	You provide some of the information required with many factual errors.	You provide most of the information required with some factual errors.	You provide all of the information required with very few factual errors.
Neatness and attractiveness of your presentation	You provide no visuals and your poster contains visible error corrections and smudges.	You provide a few visuals and your poster contains visible error corrections and smudges.	You provide several visuals, have no error corrections and smudges, and your poster is attractive.
How easily you are understood	You are difficult to understand and have many errors.	You are fairly easy to understand and have occasional errors.	You are easy to understand and have very few errors.

En busca de la verdad

Episodio 2

Antes de ver el video

"Volveremos en una hora, Sra. Toledo".

"Sra. Toledo . . . , y Srta. Toledo . . . Nosotros también somos Toledo".

Resumen del episodio

Carmen y Linda llegan a Guanajuato y van directo a la agencia de viajes "Ultramar". Allí conocen a Berta Toledo, Roberto, Daniela y Julio. Al día siguiente Daniela lleva a Carmen y a Linda a la escuela.

Nota cultural En México, una *escuela* también es un "colegio" o un "instituto". A veces las escuelas tienen el nombre de personas importantes como, por ejemplo, Escuela Josefa Ortiz, Colegio Benito Juárez o Instituto Miguel Hidalgo. Los mexicanos también demuestran su admiración por personas de otros países. Algunas escuelas tienen nombres como Escuela Winston Churchill, Escuela John F. Kennedy o Escuela Abraham Lincoln.

Palabras para comprender

para nada not at all
apellido last name
acompañar to go with
mostrar to show
el idioma language

Después de ver el video

¿Comprendiste?

A. Decide cuáles de las siguientes frases son ciertas y cuáles son falsas:

1. Carmen y Linda llegan en avión a San Antonio.

2. Berta Toledo trabaja en una agencia de viajes.

3. La escuela Benito Juárez está muy lejos del hotel de Carmen y Linda.

4. Julio le dice a Carmen: "Mamá, necesito usar el coche".

5. Carmen y Linda van al hotel San Diego.

6. El apellido de Julio es Lobero.

7. Roberto lleva la maleta de Linda.

8. Daniela le muestra la escuela a Linda.

9. A Julio le gusta jugar al fútbol.

B. Las siguientes frases del videomisterio están incompletas. Complétalas con la palabra o palabras correctas de la lista.

ir allí	San Antonio
servirles	acompañar
aquí en Guanajuato	escuela
en común	la escuela

1. Buenas tardes. ¿En qué puedo _____?

2. Mañana tengo que _____.

3. Las señoras son de _____.

4. ¿Es el apellido de todos _____?

5. Mañana van a visitar tu _____.

6. Discúlpenme, pero no los puedo _____.

7. Daniela va a mostrarme _____.

8. Nuestras escuelas tienen mucho _____.

"Mira, allí está Julio".

Más práctica GO

realidades.com | print

Actividades ✔

Repaso del capítulo
Vocabulario y gramática

to talk about driving

la avenida	avenue
el camión, *pl.* los camiones	truck
la carretera	highway
el conductor, la conductora	driver
el cruce de calles	intersection
la cuadra	block
la esquina	corner
la estatua	statue
la fuente	fountain
el peatón, *pl.* los peatones	pedestrian
el permiso de manejar	driver's license
la plaza	plaza
el policía, la policía	police officer
poner una multa	to give a ticket
el puente	bridge
el semáforo	stoplight
la señal de parada	stop sign
el tráfico	traffic

to give and receive driving advice

ancho, -a	wide
¡Basta!	Enough!
De acuerdo.	OK. Agreed.
dejar	to leave, to let
Déjame en paz.	Leave me alone.
despacio	slowly
esperar	to wait
estar seguro, -a	to be sure
estrecho, -a	narrow
Me estás poniendo nervioso, -a.	You are making me nervous.
peligroso, -a	dangerous
quitar	to take away, to remove
tener cuidado	to be careful
ya	already

For *Vocabulario adicional,* see pp. 498–499.

to ask for and give directions

aproximadamente	approximately
¿Cómo se va . . . ?	How do you go to . . . ?
complicado, -a	complicated
cruzar	to cross
derecho	straight
desde	from, since
doblar	to turn
en medio de	in the middle of
hasta	as far as, up to
manejar	to drive
el metro	subway
parar	to stop
pasar	to pass, to go
por	for, by, around, along, through
quedar	to be located
seguir (*e → i*)	to follow, to continue
tener prisa	to be in a hurry

present progressive: irregular forms

decir:	diciendo	vestir:	vistiendo
pedir:	pidiendo	dormir:	durmiendo
repetir:	repitiendo	creer:	creyendo
seguir:	siguiendo	leer:	leyendo
servir:	sirviendo	traer:	trayendo

irregular affirmative *tú* commands

hacer:	haz
ir:	ve
ser:	sé

See p. 168 for a more complete chart.

direct object pronouns

	Singular		Plural
me	me	nos	us
te	you (fam.)	os	you (fam.)
lo, la	him, her, it, you	los, las	them, you

| **Más repaso** GO | realidades.com | print |

Instant Check ✔
Puzzles ✔
Core WB pp. 69–70 ✔
Comm. WB pp. 234, 235–237 ✔ ✔

Preparación para el examen

On the exam you will be asked to . . .	Here are practice tasks similar to those you will find on the exam . . .	For review go to your print or digital textbook . . .

Interpretive

 1 Escuchar Listen to and understand driving advice

Gabriel's father is teaching him to drive. Listen as he cautions Gabriel about what to do. (a) Do you think they're driving on a highway or just around town? (b) Give at least two reasons why you think so.

pp. 158–161 *Vocabulario en contexto*
p. 163 Actividades 7–8

Interpersonal

 2 Hablar Tell someone how to get from your school to a particular location near your school

You volunteered to host a student from Costa Rica who wants to see what's near your school. Can you explain to him how to get to several places? Practice by giving your partner the directions. You could begin by saying: *Sal de la escuela y toma la calle _____.*

pp. 158–161 *Vocabulario en contexto*
p. 165 Actividad 10
p. 169 Actividad 17
p. 173 Actividad 22

Interpretive

 3 Leer Read and understand advice for establishing good driving habits

Take a look at some driving rules on a Web site from Mexico:

1. Ve muy despacio en una zona escolar.
2. Sigue detrás de otro coche aproximadamente el largo (length) de dos coches.
3. Entra con precaución a un cruce de calles con un semáforo amarillo.

Which of the following was NOT mentioned: (a) driving through a red light; (b) driving in a school zone; or (c) being cautious at a yellow light?

pp. 158–161 *Vocabulario en contexto*
p. 168 Actividad 16
pp. 174–175 *Lectura*

Presentational

 4 Escribir Write about things that might happen as you drive that would make you nervous

Everyone occasionally gets nervous about something. What's making you nervous today? Write down at least two things for your journal entry. You could start by writing: _____ *me está poniendo nervioso(a) porque siempre está _____ . . .*

p. 162 Actividad 5
p. 163 Actividad 8
pp. 174–175 *Lectura*

Cultures

 5 Pensar Demonstrate an understanding of the importance of one's neighborhood in Spanish-speaking communities

Your friend is going to Mexico City this summer to study Spanish and will be living with a Mexican family. What could you tell her about neighborhoods in Spanish-speaking countries? What might be different from the neighborhood she lives in now? What might be similar?

p. 176 *Perspectivas del mundo hispano*

▼ Objectives
▸ Talk and write about parties and celebrations
▸ Express degrees of size, intensity, or affection

Vocabulario Repaso

las personas

los abuelos
la familia
los hermanos
los padres
los primos
los tíos

las decoraciones

decorar
la flor, *pl.* las flores
el globo
la luz, *pl.* las luces
el papel picado

la comida

las bebidas
la galleta
la hamburguesa
el helado
el jamón
la limonada
los pasteles
el perrito caliente
la pizza
el postre
el queso
el refresco
el sándwich

la mesa

el azúcar
la cuchara
el cuchillo
la pimienta
el plato
la sal
la servilleta
el tenedor
el vaso

las actividades

abrir los regalos
la celebración, *pl.* las celebraciones
celebrar
compartir
el cumpleaños
la fiesta
hacer un video
preparar
la quinceañera
romper la piñata
sacar fotos

▼1 Voy a dar una fiesta |

Hablar • Escribir • Leer • Escuchar

❶ Con otro(a) estudiante, hagan planes para dar una fiesta. Escriban una lista de:

1. las personas que van a invitar

2. la comida

3. lo que van a hacer

4. lo que van a poner en la mesa

5. las decoraciones que van a usar

❷ Usen la lista y escriban una descripción de cómo va a ser la fiesta.

❸ Lean sus descripciones a otros grupos. Deben decir por qué (o por qué no) les gustaría ir a las fiestas de los demás.

Modelo
Nos gustaría ir a su fiesta porque Uds. . . .

▼2 Me gustan las piñatas |

Escribir • Hablar

Escribe cuatro frases sobre una celebración o fiesta que ya pasó. Tres de las frases deben ser ciertas y una debe ser falsa. Trabaja con un grupo de tres personas. Lee tus frases. Las otras personas del grupo tienen que decir cuál de las frases no es cierta.

▶ Modelo

A —*Muchas personas fueron a la fiesta en el parque. Rompimos una piñata grande. Mis tíos hicieron un video de la fiesta. Comimos hamburguesas y perritos calientes.*

B —*¡No es cierto! Uds. no rompieron una piñata grande.*

A —*Correcto. No rompimos una piñata grande.*

o: —*Sí, es cierto. Rompimos una piñata grande.*

Gramática Repaso

-ito

Add the suffix -*ito*(-*a, -os, -as*) to the end of nouns to mean "small" or "little." It can also be used to show affection.

- Mis primos acaban de comprar un **perrito** nuevo.

-ísimo

Add the suffix -*ísimo*(-*a, -os, -as*) to the end of adjectives to say that someone or something is "very . . ." or "extremely . . .".

- Esta película es **interesantísima**.

Here are a few patterns you already know:

hermano → hermanito
poco → poquito
ricas → riquísimas
popular → popularísimo

▼3 Nuevas frases

Escribir

Escribe otra forma de las palabras subrayadas (*underlined*) usando -*ito(a)* o -*ísimo(a)*. Después escribe una frase usando la nueva palabra.

Modelo

Mis tíos tienen una <u>casa pequeña</u> en las montañas.
casita   Me gusta mucho ir a su casita.

Mi mamá compró un vestido <u>muy elegante</u> ayer.
elegantísimo   Va a llevar su vestido elegantísimo a la fiesta.

1. El sábado es el cumpleaños de mi <u>abuela</u>.
2. Dame un <u>plato pequeño</u>, por favor.
3. Los pasteles de ese café son <u>muy ricos</u>.
4. Quiero comprar <u>un regalo pequeño</u> para mi amiga.
5. Las fotos de la fiesta son <u>muy graciosas</u>.
6. La piñata es <u>muy grande</u>.
7. Mi <u>hermano menor</u> y yo siempre compartimos la comida.

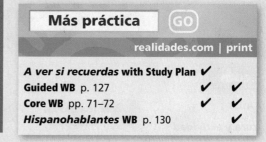

Más práctica (GO)

realidades.com | print

A ver si recuerdas with Study Plan ✔
Guided WB p. 127   ✔   ✔
Core WB pp. 71–72   ✔   ✔
Hispanohablantes WB p. 130   ✔

Un grupo de niños en Xochimilco en la Ciudad de México

▼ Chapter Objectives

Communication

By the end of this chapter you will be able to:

- Listen and read about favorite childhood toys and elementary school experiences
- Talk and write about what you were like as a child and your experiences in elementary school
- Exchange information about what you were like as a child

Culture

You will also be able to:

- Understand favorite nursery rhymes and songs from Spanish-speaking countries
- Compare the role of pets in Spanish-speaking countries and the U.S.

You will demonstrate what you know and can do:

- Presentación oral, p. 205
- Preparación para el examen, p. 209

You will use:

Vocabulary

- Toys
- Playing with other children

Grammar

- The imperfect tense: regular verbs
- The imperfect tense: irregular verbs
- Indirect object pronouns

Exploración del mundo hispano

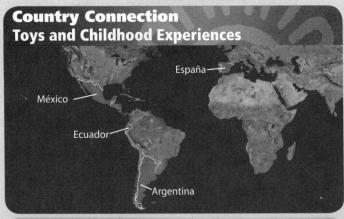

Country Connection
Toys and Childhood Experiences

España

México

Ecuador

Argentina

 realidades.com (GO)

Reference Atlas

Videocultura y actividad

Mapa global interactivo

Arte y cultura | España

Pablo Picasso (1881–1973) era uno de los mejores artistas españoles del siglo XX. En este cuadro, como en muchas de sus obras, Picasso usó formas abstractas para ilustrar las dos figuras. Pintó la figura de la niña mucho más grande en proporción que la figura de la mujer y pintó las caras muy serias.

• ¿Por qué crees que pintó Picasso la figura de la niña tan grande? ¿Cómo captas tú los momentos más importantes de tu familia?

"Primeros pasos" (1943), Pablo Picasso ▶

Oil on canvas 130.2 x 97.1 cm (51 1/4 x 38 1/4 in.) Yale University Art Gallery, gift of Stephen Carlton Clark, B.A. 1903 © 2009 Estate of Pablo Picasso/Artists Rights Society (ARS), New York.

▼ Objectives

Read, listen to, and understand information about
▶ toys
▶ playing with other children

Vocabulario en contexto

EL MUNDO de Juguetes

San Andrés, 18
San Juan
Horas: de 10:00 A.M.
a 8:00 P.M.
318-43-72

Descuentos del 10% este sábado

$27.00	**$18.00**	**$37.00**
el tren eléctrico	la muñeca	el triciclo
$15.00	**$9.00**	**$7.00**
el oso de peluche	los bloques	el dinosaurio
$3.00	**$6.00**	**$9.00**
el pez	los peces	la tortuga

Llámanos o visita nuestro sitio Web:
www.mundodejuguetes.com

—¿Con qué **jugabas de pequeña?**

—**Tenía** una muñeca favorita que se llamaba Pepita. **Era** muy bonita y rubia. ¿Y tú?

—Me gustaba montar en triciclo y **coleccionar** osos de peluche. Tenía más de 30 en mi **colección.**

Más vocabulario

la moneda coin

el mundo world

el vecino, la vecina neighbor

la guardería infantil

Los Angelitos

el muñeco

—¡Raúl! ¡Miguelito! ¡Basta! Los muñecos no deben **pelearse** así.

el patio de recreo

la cuerda

saltar a la cuerda

—Inés, ¿por qué no les **ofreces*** a los otros un poco de tu pastel? Debes ser **generosa** y compartir con **todo el mundo.**

—Margarita, no debes **molestar** a Juanito. ¡Estás muy **traviesa** hoy! No **permitimos** esto aquí.

*The verbs *ofrecer* and *obedecer* have an irregular *yo* form in the present tense: *ofrezco, obedezco.*

▼1 Los juguetes favoritos | 🔊

Escuchar

Escucha mientras (*while*) unos chicos describen sus juguetes favoritos. Señala con tu dedo el juguete apropiado en la página 186.

Más práctica	GO	
realidades.com	print	
Instant Check	✔	
Guided WB pp. 128–132	✔	✔
Core WB pp. 73–74	✔	✔
Comm. WB p. 74	✔	✔
Hispanohablantes WB p. 132		✔

▼2 ¿Cierta o falsa? | 🔊

Escuchar

Divide una hoja de papel en dos columnas. Escribe *Cierta* en una columna y *Falsa* en la otra. Escucha las siete descripciones de los niños en la guardería infantil y compáralas con el dibujo de arriba. Escribe el número de cada descripción en la columna apropiada para indicar si es cierta o falsa.

¿Cómo era de niña?

¿Cómo se portaba Ana de niña? ¿Qué le gustaba a ella?

Estrategia

Looking ahead
It is often helpful to look ahead to the questions at the end of a reading. This helps you to focus on the key information you will need to understand the reading.

Ignacio: Hola. ¿Qué hacéis?*

Elena: Hacemos árboles genealógicos para una clase.

Ana: Mira. Ésta soy yo, **de niña.**

Ignacio: **¿Cómo eras? ¿Obediente** o **desobediente?**

Ana: Por lo general, muy obediente y muy **tímida.**

Elena Ana Mamá Ignacio

1

5

Ana: Mamá tiene razón. Me encantaba mi oso de peluche. Era mi juguete favorito.

6

Ignacio: ¿También jugabas con muñecas?

Ana: Sí, y también tenía una colección de animales de peluche.

7

Ignacio: **¡Tenías** tantos juguetes! Eras muy **consentida.**

Ana: Sí, un poco. ¿Y tú? ¿Cómo eras?

Ignacio: Yo era muy **bien educado** y siempre obedecía.

Elena: ¿Tú? Nunca.

---

* Remember that in Spain, the *vosotros(as)* form of verbs is used when speaking to a group of people you would address individually with *tú*.

Mamá: Aquí tenéis* algo para comer.

Ana: Gracias, mamá. ¿No es verdad que siempre **obedecía**?

Mamá: **De vez en cuando.** ¿Siempre? ¡No!

Ignacio: ¿Y quién es?

Ana: Es mi abuela. Siempre **iba** a visitarla en su casa.

Mamá: Aquí tengo el video de cuando eras pequeña.

Ana: ¡Ay, no, mamá!

Ignacio: ¡Vamos a verlo!

Elena: Sí. Ana, tienes que **portarte** muy **bien** mientras vemos el video. Ni una palabra.

Mamá: Ana era un poco tímida. Y en sus pijamas, era preciosa. Le gustaba dormir con su oso de peluche y se levantaba muy temprano.

Ignacio: Y ahora siempre llegas tarde a clase.

Ana: ¡Ignacio, **mientes**! Nunca dices **la verdad.** Yo llego a tiempo.

Ignacio: De vez en cuando.

Ana: ¡Siempre!

Ana: ¡No! No podemos ver más.

Ignacio: ¿Por qué no?

Ana: Nadie va a ver esto nunca.

▼3 ¿Comprendiste?

Escribir • Hablar

1. ¿Qué hacen Elena y Ana para una de sus clases?
2. En la opinión de Ana, ¿cómo era ella de niña?
3. ¿Qué deciden ver los jóvenes?
4. Según su mamá, ¿cómo era Ana de niña?
5. Según Ignacio, ¿llega Ana a clase a tiempo o tarde?
6. ¿Cuáles eran los juguetes favoritos de Ana?
7. ¿Qué coleccionaba Ana?
8. ¿Cómo era Ignacio de niño?

Más práctica	GO

realidades.com | print

Instant Check	✔	
Guided WB pp. 133–136	✔	✔
Core WB pp. 75–76	✔	✔
Comm. WB pp. 67–69, 70	✔	✔
Hispanohablantes WB p. 133		✔

| ▼ **Objectives**

▶ Talk about childhood pets and toys
▶ Listen to a description of a childhood pet
▶ Discuss past activities
▶ Write about what you were like as a child

Vocabulario en uso

▼4 ¿Qué juguetes tenías?

Escribir

Escribe frases para decir qué juguetes y
animales tenías cuando eras niño(a).

Modelo

Tenía un gato cuando era niño(a).
o: *Tenía muchos gatos cuando era niño(a).*
o: *No tenía un gato cuando era niño(a),
pero sí tenía un perro.*

> **También se dice . . .**
>
> **los bloques** = los cubos (*muchos
> países*)
>
> **consentido, -a** = mimado, -a (*muchos
> países*)
>
> **montar en triciclo** = andar en triciclo
> (*España*)
>
> **saltar** = brincar (*muchos países*)

1.

2.

3.

4.

5.

6.

▼5 ¿Tenías lo mismo? | 🗨️👥

Hablar

Lee tus frases de la Actividad 4 a otro(a)
estudiante para ver si Uds. tenían las mismas
cosas cuando eran niños.

 Modelo

A —*Yo tenía <u>un gato</u> cuando era niño(a).
Y tú, ¿tenías <u>un gato</u>?*
B —*Sí, yo tenía <u>un gato</u> también.*
o: —*No, yo no tenía <u>un gato</u>.*

▼6 Escucha y escribe | 🔊

Escuchar • Escribir

Víctor describe un animal
que tenía cuando era
niño. Escucha las cinco
frases y escríbelas
en una hoja de
papel.

▼ Fondo Cultural | El mundo hispano

Las mascotas Generalmente en los países hispanohablantes el papel *(role)* de las mascotas *(pets)* es más que sólo ser "otro miembro de la familia". Por ejemplo, un perro protege *(protects)* la casa en la ciudad o ayuda en el campo. Por lo general, los conejillos de Indias *(Guinea pigs)* o los ratoncitos no son mascotas comunes.

• Compara el papel de las mascotas en los Estados Unidos con su papel en los países hispanohablantes.

El perro ayuda mucho a este gaucho argentino.

▼7 ¿Con qué jugabas de niño(a)? |

Hablar

Pregunta a otro(a) estudiante con qué juguetes jugaba de niño(a).

▶ **Modelo**

A —¿Jugabas con <u>muñecas</u> de niño(a)?

B —Sí, por lo general jugaba con <u>muñecas</u> de niño(a).

o: —No, <u>nunca</u> jugaba con <u>muñecas</u> de niño(a).

Estudiante A

Estudiante B

nunca	a menudo
a veces	por lo general
siempre	de vez en cuando

▼8 ¿Qué te gustaba hacer de pequeño(a)? |

Escribir • Hablar

Escribe una lista de seis actividades que son populares entre los niños. Después pregunta a otro(a) estudiante si le gustaba hacer estas actividades de pequeño(a).

▶ **Modelo**

coleccionar tarjetas de *Star Wars*

A —De pequeño(a), ¿te gustaba <u>coleccionar</u> <u>tarjetas de</u> Star Wars?

B —Sí, me gustaba <u>coleccionar tarjetas de</u> Star Wars.

o: —No, no me gustaba nada <u>coleccionar</u> <u>tarjetas de</u> Star Wars.

9 Las analogías | ♻

Leer • Pensar • Escribir

Hay pruebas de vocabulario sobre las relaciones entre palabras, o "las analogías". Completa cada analogía según el modelo.

Modelo

los jóvenes : la escuela :: los niños : la guardería infantil

Se lee: "Los jóvenes son a la escuela como los niños son a la guardería infantil".

1. levantarse : acostarse :: decir la verdad : _____
2. montar : el triciclo :: saltar : _____
3. la piscina : nadar :: el patio de recreo : _____
4. generoso : ofrecer :: travieso : _____
5. el pájaro : el árbol :: el pez : _____
6. obedecer : obediente :: pelearse : _____
7. no : sí :: prohibir : _____
8. la blusa : la ropa :: la moneda : _____

10 La guardería infantil

Leer • Escribir

Lee las descripciones de los niños en la guardería infantil y luego decide qué adjetivo del recuadro describe a cada uno. Escribe las descripciones de los niños en una hoja de papel.

bien educado, -a	generoso, -a
desobediente	tímido, -a
obediente	travieso, -a

Modelo

Los padres de Carlota le compran cada juguete que pide.
Carlota es consentida.

1. Antonio tiene miedo de hablar con otras personas.
2. Julio se porta mal y molesta a todo el mundo.
3. Eugenia no miente porque sus padres dicen que es muy malo mentir.
4. Ricardo siempre dice "gracias" y "por favor" y no se pelea con nadie.
5. Ana comparte sus juguetes con los otros niños.

11 Y tú, ¿qué dices? | (Talk!)

Escribir • Hablar

1. ¿Con qué juguetes te gustaba jugar de pequeño(a)?
2. De niño(a), ¿cómo eras? ¿Bien educado(a) o travieso(a)? ¿Sociable o tímido(a)?
3. De niño(a), ¿qué te gustaba coleccionar? ¿Monedas? ¿Tarjetas de algún deporte? ¿Todavía tienes tu colección?
4. De niño(a), ¿obedecías a tus padres siempre, a menudo o a veces? Y ahora, ¿los obedeces siempre? ¿Obedeces las reglas de tu escuela siempre?

▼ Fondo Cultural | El mundo hispano

Las guarderías infantiles En los países hispanohablantes hay una variedad de opciones de guarderías infantiles. Unas guarderías son del gobierno municipal *(city government)* o provincial *(provincial)*. Algunas compañías ofrecen servicio de guardería infantil para las personas que trabajan allí. También hay guarderías privadas.

• De niño(a), ¿ibas a una guardería infantil? En tu opinión, ¿cuál es la mejor opción para cuidar a los niños? ¿Por qué?

▼12 ¿Cómo cuidar al niño?

Leer • Escribir • Hablar

Lee este anuncio de la guardería infantil Rincón del niño en Guadalajara, México, y contesta las preguntas.

Estrategia
Using context
Use the context of words you don't know to guess their meaning in this reading.

Guardería infantil Rincón del niño
Excelencia personal y escolar

Nuestros maestros tienen preparación profesional y comprenden las necesidades del niño según su edad. Ofrecemos instrucción bilingüe y varias actividades usando música y juegos.

Recibimos niños desde los 13 meses hasta los cinco años de edad. Tenemos ya 25 años de experiencia.

Cuidar a sus niños es nuestra pasión. Trabajamos todos los días para desarrollar[1] en sus niños la capacidad de:
• trabajar en grupo
• mantener una actitud positiva
• tener éxito[2] en actividades académicas
• desarrollar hábitos higiénicos y cuidados personales

Favor de llamarnos al 515-34-98
Avenida Guerrero, 48

1. Lee la lista de características que la guardería infantil quiere desarrollar en los niños. En tu opinión, ¿cuáles son las dos más importantes? ¿Por qué?

2. ¿Esta guardería infantil es similar a las guarderías infantiles donde tú vives? ¿En qué sentido *(way)* es similar? ¿En qué sentido es diferente?

3. ¿Te gustaría trabajar en una guardería infantil como Rincón del niño? ¿Por qué?

4. En tu opinión, ¿cómo debe ser una persona que trabaja en una guardería infantil?

[1]develop   [2]to be successful

▼ Pronunciación | 🔊 | 💬

The letters *r* and *rr*

Except at the beginning of a word or after *l* or *n*, the sound of the letter *r* is made as you raise the tip of your tongue and tap the roof of your mouth. The position of your tongue is similar to the position when you pronounce the *d* in the English word *Daddy*. The sound of the *rr* is made as you raise the tip of your tongue and tap the roof of your mouth several times very quickly. Listen to and say these pairs of words:

| pero | ahora | moro | caro |
| perro | ahorra | morro | carro |

When *r* is the first letter of a word or comes after *l* or *n*, it is pronounced like the *rr*.

¡Compruébalo! Listen to these two verses of a popular Spanish lullaby, then try to repeat them.

A la rorro[1] niño
a la rorro ya,
duérmete mi niño,
duérmete mi amor.

Señora Santa Ana,
Señor San Joaquín
Arrullen[2] al niño
que se va a dormir.

[1]sound to quiet a baby
[2]Whisper, Lull

Gramática

The imperfect tense: regular verbs

Another way to talk about the past is with the imperfect tense. Use the imperfect tense to talk about actions that happened repeatedly in the past.

Rafael **patinaba** y Mónica **corría**.

*Rafael **used to skate** and Monica **used to run**.*

Here are the regular forms of -*ar*, -*er*, and -*ir* verbs in the imperfect tense. Notice the accent mark on the *nosotros* form of *jugar*:

(yo)	jug**aba**	(nosotros) (nosotras)	jug**ábamos**
(tú)	jug**abas**	(vosotros) (vosotras)	jug**abais**
Ud. (él) (ella)	jug**aba**	Uds. (ellos) (ellas)	jug**aban**

Note that -*er* and -*ir* verbs, such as *hacer* and *vivir*, have the same endings:

(yo)	hac**ía** viv**ía**	(nosotros) (nosotras)	hac**íamos** viv**íamos**
(tú)	hac**ías** viv**ías**	(vosotros) (vosotras)	hac**íais** viv**íais**
Ud. (él) (ella)	hac**ía** viv**ía**	Uds. (ellos) (ellas)	hac**ían** viv**ían**

Notice the accent mark on each ending.

¿Recuerdas?

You have already learned to talk about completed actions in the past using the preterite tense.

• Ayer Rafael **patinó** y Mónica **corrió** en el parque.

• As you know, in Spanish you can often omit the subject of a verb because the subject is made clear in the verb ending:

Vivo en Chicago. (The subject, *yo*, is included in the verb ending.)

However, since the *yo* and *Ud.* / *él* / *ella* forms are the same in the imperfect for -*ar*, -*er*, and -*ir* verbs, speakers often use the subject pronouns to avoid confusion.

Patricia **tenía** un triciclo rojo pero **yo tenía** uno azul.

• Expressions such as *generalmente, por lo general, a menudo, muchas veces, de vez en cuando, todos los días,* and *nunca* can cue you to use the imperfect because they imply that something happened repeatedly in the past.

Más ayuda	**realidades.com**

▶ **Tutorial:** Imperfect of regular verbs
Animated Verbs

▼13 Escucha y escribe | ◀))

Escuchar • Escribir

Lola y Lulú eran vecinas y muy buenas amigas, pero eran muy diferentes. Lola era muy bien educada, pero Lulú era desobediente. Escucha las seis descripciones de las niñas y escribe las frases. Indica si la descripción es de Lola, de Lulú o de las dos.

Dos amigas de México

▼14 En la casa de nuestros abuelos |

Leer • Escribir

Margarita recuerda cómo, de niña, pasaba tiempo en la casa de sus abuelos. Escribe la forma apropiada del imperfecto de los verbos.

Cuando era niña mis hermanos y yo __1.__ *(pasar/pensar)* tiempo en la casa de nuestros abuelos de vez en cuando. Mi abuela __2.__ *(preparar/participar)* galletas muy ricas y nosotros las __3.__ *(correr/comer)* en el patio. Ella siempre nos __4.__ *(ofrecer/obedecer)* más galletas. Mi abuelo nos __5.__ *(estudiar/leer)* cuentos y a veces él nos __6.__ *(hacer/escribir)* pequeños juguetes de madera *(wood)*. Mis abuelos no __7.__ *(trabajar/limpiar)* y __8.__ *(decir/tener)* mucho tiempo para pasar con nosotros. Mis hermanos y yo siempre __9.__ *(regresar/bailar)* a casa muy contentos después de estar con nuestros abuelos.

Dos niños ecuatorianos

▼15 Tus amigos y tú |

Hablar

Trabaja con otro(a) estudiante para hablar de lo que hacían tus amigos y tú cuando eran niños.

▶ Modelo

jugar con los vecinos
A —*¿Jugaban Uds. con los vecinos?*
B —*No, nunca jugábamos con los vecinos.*
o:—*Sí, jugábamos con los vecinos de vez en cuando.*

Estudiante A

1. montar en triciclo
2. saltar a la cuerda
3. correr en el parque
4. escuchar cuentos
5. coleccionar cosas
6. compartir los juguetes

Estudiante B

No, nunca . . .
Sí, siempre . . .
De vez en cuando . . .

Más práctica GO		
realidades.com	print		
Instant Check	✔	
Guided WB pp. 137–138	✔	✔
Core WB p. 77	✔	✔
Comm. WB pp. 71, 75, 238	✔	✔
Hispanohablantes **WB** pp. 134–137, 140		✔

Gramática

The imperfect tense: irregular verbs

There are only three irregular verbs in the imperfect tense: *ir*, *ser*, and *ver*. Here are all the forms:

ir

(yo)	iba	(nosotros) (nosotras)	íbamos
(tú)	ibas	(vosotros) (vosotras)	ibais
Ud. (él) (ella)	iba	Uds. (ellos) (ellas)	iban

ser

(yo)	era	(nosotros) (nosotras)	éramos
(tú)	eras	(vosotros) (vosotras)	erais
Ud. (él) (ella)	era	Uds. (ellos) (ellas)	eran

• Notice the accent mark on the *nosotros* form for the verbs *ir* and *ser*.

ver

(yo)	veía	(nosotros) (nosotras)	veíamos
(tú)	veías	(vosotros) (vosotras)	veíais
Ud. (él) (ella)	veía	Uds. (ellos) (ellas)	veían

• Notice the accent mark on each form of *ver*.

Más ayuda | **realidades.com**

▶ *GramActiva* Video
Tutorial: Imperfect of irregular verbs

))) *Canción de hip hop:* ¿Cómo eras de niño?

📖 *GramActiva* Activity

▼16 Los veranos en Boston | ♻

Leer • Escribir

Ana María recuerda los veranos que pasaba en Boston. Completa su descripción con las formas apropiadas del imperfecto de los verbos *ir, ser* y *ver*.

Cuando __1.__ pequeña, me encantaban los veranos. Vivíamos en Boston donde mi papá y yo __2.__ al famoso estadio de béisbol de las Medias Rojas, Fenway Park. Cada verano nosotros __3.__ a nuestros jugadores favoritos, como Pedro Martínez. Mi papá __4.__ originalmente de la República Dominicana y por eso él __5.__ todos los partidos cuando Pedro jugaba allí. También yo siempre __6.__ a la playa con mi familia. ¿Qué más? También nosotros __7.__ al cine donde comíamos palomitas y __8.__ las películas más populares. Los veranos en Boston __9.__ fantásticos y los recuerdo muy bien.

Pedro Martínez, cuando jugaba para las Medias Rojas

▼**17** Un niño inteligente | ♻

Leer • Escribir

Completa esta descripción de Isaac Newton, un famoso científico inglés, con la forma correcta del imperfecto del verbo apropiado.

Conexiones | Las ciencias

De niño

tener, ser, decir, ir

Isaac Newton nació en 1642. __1.__ un bebé tan pequeño y débil[1] que los médicos __2.__ que él no __3.__ a tener capacidad mental para hacer cosas importantes durante su vida.

En la escuela primaria

querer, ser, hacer, ver, creer

__4.__ un estudiante inteligente que nunca __5.__ sus tareas porque no le interesaba mucho lo que los profesores __6.__ enseñarle. Su madre tampoco __7.__ que era muy inteligente.

En la universidad

leer, ir, poder, trabajar

Como estudiante universitario, Newton siempre __8.__ y estaba muy metido[2] en sus experimentos físicos. No __9.__ a los restaurantes elegantes y tampoco salía con los amigos. __10.__ siempre en alguna investigación y por eso inventó el análisis matemático y descubrió que la luz blanca tiene colores.

Su fama

poder, consistir, estar, ver

Un día Newton __11.__ en casa de su madre pensando en cómo la Luna[3] __12.__ dar vueltas alrededor de[4] la Tierra,[5] cuando le cayó[6] una manzana en la cabeza. Newton empezó a pensar y recordó un juego de niños que __13.__ en llenar con agua una cubeta[7] y darle vueltas rápidamente por encima de la cabeza sin permitir caer el agua. Así se le ocurrió a Newton la idea de la gravedad y la velocidad.

[1]weak [2]involved [3]moon [4]spin around [5]Earth [6]fell [7]bucket

▼**18** Y tú, ¿qué dices? |

Escribir • Hablar

1. En la escuela primaria, ¿cómo eras? ¿Qué clases te interesaban más? Y ahora, ¿qué clases te interesan?

2. De pequeño(a), ¿te gustaban las ciencias? ¿Qué experimentos hacían tus compañeros de clase y tú en la escuela? Y ahora, ¿qué experimentos hacen en sus clases de ciencias?

3. De niño(a), ¿en qué pensabas más: los estudios, los libros, los deportes o los juguetes? Y ahora, ¿en qué piensas más?

▼19 Cómo era de niño(a) | 👥 | ♻

Escribir • Hablar

Escribe frases para hablar de tu niñez *(childhood)* usando las formas apropiadas del imperfecto de los verbos y tus propias ideas. Después trabaja con otro(a) estudiante y lean sus frases. ¿Eran similares o diferentes sus experiencias de niñez?

1. Cuando yo *(ser)* niño(a), *(ser)* muy . . .
2. Mis amigos *(ser)* . . .
3. De vez en cuando mi familia y yo *(ir)* . . .
4. A menudo yo *(ir)* a la casa de . . .
5. Mis hermanos (o amigos) y yo *(jugar)* . . .
6. Por lo general yo *(ver)* a mis primos . . .

▼20 El (La) estudiante | 👥 | ♻ modelo

Escribir • Hablar

❶ En una hoja de papel, escribe cuatro descripciones de cómo eras y qué hacías en la escuela primaria.

Modelo

Era muy obediente. Siempre obedecía las reglas de la escuela.

❷ Trabaja con un grupo de tres. Lean sus descripciones de cómo eran en la escuela primaria. Apunten en una hoja de papel cómo responden los tres. Después escriban un resumen *(summary)* de cómo eran.

Modelo

María y yo éramos muy buenos estudiantes y siempre escuchábamos a los profesores. Antonio era un poco desobediente y nunca escuchaba a los profesores.

▼21 Juego | 👥 | ♻

Escribir • Hablar

❶ Trabaja con otro(a) estudiante. Escriban una descripción del punto de vista de una persona del pasado que muchos estudiantes conocen. La descripción debe ser de cómo era, de dónde era, qué hacía para ser famoso(a), dónde vivía la persona y más.

❷ Lean su descripción a otras parejas de estudiantes. Si los otros estudiantes identifican a la persona, reciben cinco puntos. Si ellos no pueden identificar a la persona, Uds. reciben cinco puntos.

Frida Kahlo

▶ Modelo

A —*Era de México. De niña a menudo estaba enferma. Cuando era mayor, era artista y pintaba mucho. Diego Rivera era mi esposo. Yo no tenía una vida muy sencilla ni feliz. ¿Quién soy yo?*

B —*Tú eres Frida Kahlo.* (Correcto. Cinco puntos para la pareja B)

Más práctica	GO
realidades.com | print	
Instant Check	✔
Guided WB pp. 139–140	✔ ✔
Core WB p. 78	✔ ✔
Comm. WB pp. 72, 76	✔ ✔
Hispanohablantes WB pp. 138–139, 141	✔

▼ **Objectives**
▶ Talk and write about what people used to do for others
▶ Exchange information about what you were allowed to do in elementary school

Gramática Repaso

Indirect object pronouns

Remember that an indirect object tells to whom or for whom an action is performed. Indirect object pronouns are used to replace or accompany an indirect object noun.

Nuestros profesores no **nos** permitían beber refrescos en clase.

Sus abuelos siempre **les** daban regalos a los niños.

Singular		Plural	
me	(to / for) me	nos	(to / for) us
te	(to / for) you *(familiar)*	os	(to / for) you *(familiar)*
le	(to / for) him, her, you *(formal)*	les	(to / for) them, you *(formal)*

- Because *le* and *les* have more than one meaning, you can make the meaning clear by adding *a* + name, noun, or pronoun.

  Lolita siempre **les** decía la verdad a **sus padres.**

  Lolita siempre **les** decía la verdad a **ellos.**

- Like direct object pronouns and reflexive pronouns, indirect object pronouns are placed right before the verb or attached to the infinitive.

  Siempre **le** quería comprar dulces a su hija.

  Siempre quería comprar**le** dulces a su hija.

Más ayuda **realidades.com**

GramActiva Video
Tutorial: Indirect objects

GramActiva Activity

▼22 Una tía muy generosa | ♻

Escribir

Mi tía era muy generosa, pero siempre nos compraba los mismos regalos. Escribe frases para decir lo que compraba ella.

mi padre

Modelo
Por lo general ella le compraba una corbata a mi padre.

1.

mi madre

2.

mis hermanitas

3.

yo

4.

su esposo

5.

mis primos

6.

nosotros

▼23 ¿Qué les permitían hacer? | 👥

Hablar

Trabaja con otro(a) estudiante para hablar de lo que les permitían hacer en la escuela primaria.

1. comer y beber en la sala de clases
2. tener animales en la escuela
3. jugar en el patio de recreo
4. ver películas en clase

¡Respuesta personal!

▶ **Modelo**

A —¿*Les permitían llevar gorras en la escuela primaria?*

B —*No, no nos permitían llevar gorras.*

o: —*Sí, nos permitían llevar gorras, pero sólo en los días especiales.*

▼ Fondo Cultural | El mundo hispano

Juguetes mayas Los mayas no usaban la rueda (*wheel*) para el trabajo, pero crearon juguetes de niños en forma de animales (reales e inventados), con ruedas. Estos juguetes eran similares al *pull-toy* que se usa hoy.

- ¿Son similares los juguetes de los mayas a los juguetes con los que tú jugabas de niño(a), o son diferentes? ¿En qué sentido?

▼24 Jugando con los amigos | 👥

Leer • Escribir • Hablar

Estudia el cuadro, lee el párrafo y luego contesta las preguntas.

1. ¿Quiénes crees que son las personas mayores del cuadro?
2. Con otro(a) estudiante, imaginen que Uds. eran unos niños del cuadro y que ya son mayores. Hablen de los juguetes que tenían cuando eran niños(as).
3. Ahora imaginen que Uds. tienen sesenta años. Piensen en los juguetes que les gustaban de niños(as). Descríbanlos para las personas que no los conocen. ¿Estos juguetes son populares hoy?

"Los niños del futuro" (1998)

© Lorenzo Armendariz/Latin Focus.com.

Leovigildo Martínez (1959–) nació en Oaxaca, México. Este cuadro es parte de un mural que pintó para el hospital que lo atendió (*treated*) cuando era niño. En el cuadro ves los juguetes tradicionales de la región.

▼25 ¿Quiénes te compraban regalos? |

Hablar

Habla con otro(a) estudiante sobre quiénes hacían estas cosas para ti cuando eras niño(a).

▶ **Modelo**

A —¿Quiénes te compraban regalos?
B —Mis padres me compraban regalos de vez en cuando.

1. leer cuentos
2. preparar galletas
3. enviar tarjetas de cumpleaños
4. dar dinero para comprar cosas
5. prestar (lend) juguetes
6. cantar canciones de cuna (lullabies)

▼26 Los retratos

Leer • Pensar • Escribir • Hablar

Mira el retrato (portrait) del niño y lee el párrafo debajo del retrato. Luego contesta las preguntas.

1. ¿Qué mascotas tenías cuando eras niño(a)? ¿Cómo se llamaban?

2. Cuando te sacan fotos, ¿qué ropa te gusta llevar?

3. Hace muchos años, los artistas pintaban retratos porque las personas no tenían cámaras para sacar fotos de su familia. Compara el retrato de este niño con una foto tuya cuando eras niño(a). ¿En qué sentido son similares? ¿En qué sentido son diferentes?

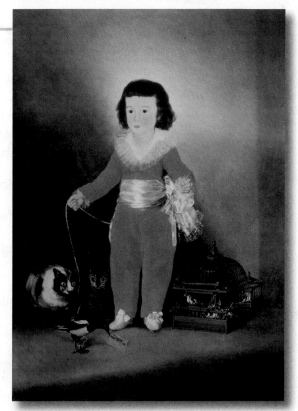

"Don Manuel Osorio Manrique de Zúñiga" (1788)

Oil on canvas, 127 x 101. Metropolitan Museum of Art, New York, USA / Bridgeman Art Library

Francisco de Goya (1746–1828) era uno de los pintores más importantes de España. Por la ropa elegante que el niño lleva en este retrato, sabemos que es de una familia aristocrática. Goya pintó al niño con sus mascotas: gatos y unos pájaros.

El español en la comunidad

Es importante aprender otro idioma (language) a una edad muy joven. Muchas guarderías infantiles, escuelas preescolares y escuelas primarias dan clases en español o en francés. Busca en tu comunidad una guardería o escuela que enseña español. ¡Puedes visitarla para observar o para enseñarles a los niños un poco de español!

• ¿Crees que es fácil o difícil aprender otro idioma de pequeño(a)? ¿Por qué?

el pato

Más práctica	GO

realidades.com | print

Instant Check	✔	
Guided WB pp. 141–142	✔	✔
Core WB p. 79	✔	✔
Comm. WB pp. 73, 77	✔	✔
Hispanohablantes WB pp. 139, 141	✔	

Lectura
El grillo y el jaguar
Una fábula mexicana

Estrategia

Using background knowledge
Think of fables you read as a child. Write down what you think might happen in this encounter between a cricket and a jaguar. When you finish reading, check to see how close your prediction was to the real story.

Hace ya muchísimos años, sólo vivían por el mundo los animales. Y el rey de todos era el jaguar.

Un día el jaguar salió de su casa rugiendo[1] y empezó a correr al lago porque tenía sed. Como todos los animales le tenían miedo[2], se escondieron[3]. Todos menos el grillo, que no lo oyó[4] porque cantaba muy contento en su jardín.

El jaguar se sorprendió[5] cuando no vio a nadie, pero oyó la canción del grillo.

—¿Quién canta esa canción tan fea? —se preguntó el jaguar.

Cuando el jaguar vio al grillo, le rugió: —¡Qué mal educado eres, grillo! ¿Por qué no me saludas[6]?

—¡Ay, don Jaguar! Lo siento. ¿Me perdona?

—Sólo si eres obediente —le contestó el jaguar.

—¿Y qué tengo que hacer, don Jaguar?

—Vamos a hacer una carrera[7] hasta aquella roca enorme que está por donde empiezan las montañas. Si llegas primero, te perdono todo y puedes seguir cantando, pero si llego primero yo, te prohíbo cantar.

[1]roaring   [2]were afraid   [3]they hid   [4]didn't hear him   [5]was surprised   [6]greet me   [7]race

El grillo no contestó inmediatamente, pero por fin dijo:
—Bien. ¿Cuándo corremos?

—¡Ahora mismo! —respondió el jaguar.

Al oír "ahora mismo" el grillo saltó a la cola[8] del jaguar y muy despacito iba saltando hasta llegar a su cabeza. Así llegaron los dos a la roca enorme. Pero en ese momento (y antes de que el jaguar lo viera[9]), el grillo saltó de la cabeza del jaguar a la roca y dijo: —¡Hola, don Jaguar! Estaba esperándolo.

El jaguar no sabía qué decir, pero perdonó al grillo, y el grillo empezó a cantar otra vez.

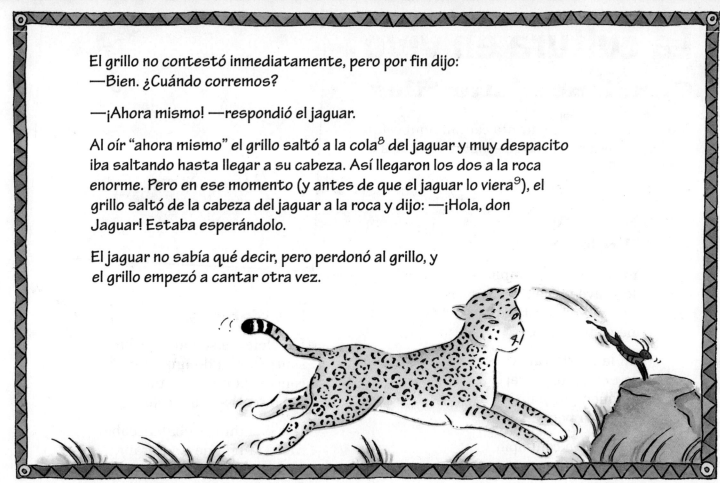

[8]tail [9]could see

¿Comprendiste?

1. Según esta leyenda, ¿quiénes vivían por el mundo hace muchos años?

2. ¿Por qué se escondieron todos los animales?

3. ¿Por qué el grillo no oyó al jaguar?

4. Según el jaguar, ¿cómo era la canción del grillo?

5. ¿Qué hizo el grillo para llegar primero a la roca?

6. Al fin, ¿quién era más inteligente, el jaguar o el grillo?

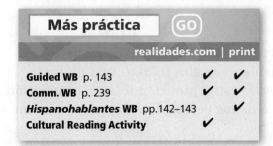

Más práctica	GO
	realidades.com | print
Guided WB p. 143	✔ ✔
Comm. WB p. 239	✔ ✔
Hispanohablantes WB pp.142–143	✔
Cultural Reading Activity	✔

Y tú, ¿qué dices?

Hace muchísimos años que las fábulas son importantes en muchas culturas para enseñarles a los niños y a los adultos lecciones sobre la vida. En muchas fábulas los personajes son animales. Trabaja con otro(a) estudiante. Piensa en unas fábulas y describe a los animales en esas fábulas.

Modelo

La tortuga caminaba muy lentamente y era muy trabajadora.

Para decir más . . .
el conejo rabbit
la gallina, el gallo hen, rooster
el león lion
el zorro fox

La cultura en vivo 🔊

Canciones infantiles

A todos los niños les encanta cantar. Aquí están dos canciones populares que cantan los niños en algunos países hispanohablantes mientras *(while)* juegan con sus amigos.

El columpio

Yo tengo un columpio[1]
de suave vaivén[2]
y en él muy contento
me vengo a mecer[3].

En la fuerte rama[4]
de un fuerte laurel[5],
mi buen papacito
lo vino a poner.

Qué suave columpio
qué rico vaivén
¿muchachos, no quieren
venirse a mecer?

[1]swing   [2]swaying motion   [3]to swing
[4]branch   [5]laurel tree

Los elefantes

Un elefante se balanceaba
sobre la tela de una araña[6]
como veía que resistía
fue a buscar a otro elefante.

Dos elefantes se balanceaban
sobre la tela de una araña
como veían que resistía
fueron a buscar a otro elefante.

Tres elefantes se balanceaban . . .
Cuatro elefantes se balanceaban . . .
Cinco elefantes se balanceaban . . .
Seis elefantes se balanceaban . . .
Siete elefantes se balanceaban . . .
Ocho elefantes se balanceaban . . .
Nueve elefantes se balanceaban . . .

Diez elefantes se balanceaban
sobre la tela de una araña,
como veían que se rompía,
fueron a dejar a un elefante.

Nueve elefantes se balanceaban . . .

[6]spider web

¡Compruébalo! En grupos de cuatro, practiquen en voz alta *(aloud)* una de las canciones. Presten atención a la pronunciación y al ritmo de los versos. Presenten su canción a la clase.

Presentación oral

▼ **Objectives** | **Aplicación**
▶ Talk about what you were like and what you used to do as a child
▶ Use visuals to help you organize your thoughts

¿Cómo eras de niño(a)?

Task
You have a summer job at a *guardería infantil.* Create a series of pictures to show the children what you were like when you were young.

① Prepare Think about your childhood. Create a chart like this one and provide at least two pieces of information for each column.

¿Cómo era?	Jugaba con ...	Me gustaba más ...	Tenía que ...	No me permitían ...
tímido(a)	mi oso de peluche	jugar con mis amigos	hacer mi cama	pelearme con mis hermanos

Create a series of drawings or photos that illustrate all of the information on your chart. Be sure they are easy to understand and represent you when you were young.

② Practice Go through your presentation several times. You can use your chart to practice, but not when you present. Use your drawings and photos when you practice to help you recall what you want to say. Try to:

• provide as much information as possible

• use complete sentences

• speak clearly

③ Present Talk about what you were like as a child. Be sure to use your drawings during your presentation.

④ Evaluation The following rubric will be used to grade your presentation.

> **Estrategia**
>
> **Using visuals**
> Using visuals during an oral presentation helps organize your thinking.

Rubric	Score 1	Score 3	Score 5
How much information you communicate	You provide only one piece of information in each category.	You provide two pieces of information in each category.	You provide three or more pieces of information in each category.
How easily you are understood	You are difficult to understand and have many grammatical errors.	You are fairly easy to understand and have occasional grammatical errors.	You are easy to understand and have very few grammatical errors.
Quality of your visuals	You provide only one visual and it contains visible error corrections and smudges.	You provide only two visuals and they contain visible error corrections and smudges.	You provide several visuals and they contain no visible error corrections and smudges.

En busca de la verdad

Episodio 3

"Tu abuelo se llamaba Federico Toledo. Es todo lo que puedo decirte".

Antes de ver el video

"Vamos a ver . . . ¿Qué hay de nuevo en el correo electrónico?"

 Nota cultural El mercado es el lugar donde la gente va a comprar comida fresca. En Guanajuato está el famoso Mercado Hidalgo, donde venden frutas, verduras, carnes y muchas cosas más.

Resumen del episodio

En este episodio van a conocer a Nela, la abuela de Roberto. Él hace planes para visitarla al día siguiente. La familia Toledo almuerza en casa. Después de comer, Roberto le pregunta a su papá sobre su abuelo.

Palabras para comprender

catrina artistic rendering of a skull

una cosa más one more thing

carpintero carpenter

conocerse mejor to know each other better

a propósito by the way

Después de ver el video

¿Comprendiste?

A. Escoge la palabra correcta de las tres que están entre paréntesis.

1. "Me parece estupendo. Saben que ustedes siempre son (esperados/bienvenidos/queridos) en esta casa".

2. "Su mamá está aquí arreglando un programa de (juegos/televisión/intercambio) con nuestra escuela".

3. "Mañana viene el carpintero a reparar algunas (cosas/plantas/mesas) en mi casa".

4. "Hoy hablé con la maestra Toledo. Ella dice que todo está (caminando/progresando/funcionando) muy bien para el intercambio".

5. "Bueno, tengo que volver a la (escuela/clínica/casa). ¡Mis pacientes me esperan!"

6. "Dani, tengo un (mensaje/regalo/pastel) para la abuela".

7. "Ella sabe más que yo. Ahora, tengo que (vestirme/irme/dormirme)".

B. ¿Por qué crees que Roberto empieza a pensar en su abuelo con la llegada de Linda? Escribe lo que piensas.

C. Mira las fotos de Roberto y su abuela mientras hablan por teléfono. Escribe un resumen de la conversación.

Más práctica GO

realidades.com | print

Actividades ✔

Repaso del capítulo

Vocabulario y gramática

to name toys

los bloques	blocks
la colección, *pl.* las colecciones	collection
la cuerda	rope
el dinosaurio	dinosaur
la muñeca	doll
el muñeco	action figure
el oso de peluche	teddy bear
el tren eléctrico	electric train
el triciclo	tricycle

to name animals

el pez, *pl.* los peces	fish
la tortuga	turtle

to discuss things you used to do

coleccionar	to collect
molestar	to bother
pelearse	to fight
saltar (a la cuerda)	to jump (rope)

to name places

la guardería infantil	daycare center
el patio de recreo	playground

to explain your actions

de niño, -a	as a child
de pequeño, -a	as a child
de vez en cuando	once in a while
mentir *(e → ie)*	to lie
obedecer *(c → zc)*	to obey
ofrecer *(c → zc)*	to offer
permitir	to permit, to allow
por lo general	in general
portarse bien / mal	to behave well / badly
todo el mundo	everyone
el vecino, la vecina	neighbor
la verdad	truth

to describe what someone was like

bien educado, -a	well-behaved
consentido, -a	spoiled
desobediente	disobedient
generoso, -a	generous
obediente	obedient
tímido, -a	timid
travieso, -a	naughty, mischievous

other useful words

la moneda	coin
el mundo	world

imperfect of *ir*

iba	íbamos
ibas	ibais
iba	iban

imperfect of *jugar*

jugaba	jugábamos
jugabas	jugabais
jugaba	jugaban

imperfect of *ser*

era	éramos
eras	erais
era	eran

imperfect of *ver*

veía	veíamos
veías	veíais
veía	veían

indirect object pronouns

me	(to / for) me	nos	(to / for) us
te	(to / for) you	os	(to / for) you
le	(to / for) him, her, you *(formal)*	les	(to / for) them, you *(formal)*

For *Vocabulario adicional,* see pp. 498–499.

Más repaso **GO** realidades.com | print

Instant Check	✔
Puzzles	✔
Core WB pp. 80–81	✔
Comm. WB p. 240	✔ ✔

Preparación para el examen

On the exam you will be asked to . . .	Here are practice tasks similar to those you will find on the exam . . .	For review go to your print or digital textbook . . .

Interpretive

 1 Escuchar Listen and understand as people describe their favorite childhood toy

You volunteer after school at the Youth Center. To get to know your kids better, you ask them about their favorite toys when they were younger. See if you can understand: (a) what the toy was; (b) how old the child was when he or she used to play with it; (c) where he or she used to play with it.

pp. 186–189 *Vocabulario en contexto*
p. 190 Actividad 6

Interpersonal

 2 Hablar Talk about what you were like as a child

Now your group at the Youth Center wants to know what you were like as a child! What could you tell them? You could start by telling them: (a) what you liked to do; (b) what your favorite toy was; (c) how you used to behave.

pp. 188–189 *Videohistoria*
p. 190 Actividad 5
p. 191 Actividades 7–8
p. 192 Actividad 11
p. 195 Actividad 15
p. 200 Actividad 23
p. 205 *Presentación oral*

Interpretive

 3 Leer Read someone's recollections about their elementary school experience

Read an entry in Armando's journal about his elementary school years. As you read, see if you can determine: (a) whether he liked or disliked elementary school and (b) why or why not?

p. 195 Actividad 14
p. 196 Actividad 16
p. 197 Actividad 17

De vez en cuando yo pienso en mis amigos de la escuela primaria. ¡Ay! Jorge siempre se peleaba conmigo y Carlos me molestaba. Yo era muy tímido y no me levantaba a tiempo para la escuela porque no quería jugar con ellos.

Presentational

 4 Escribir Write about some of your experiences in elementary school

After reading Armando's recollection, you begin to think about your days in elementary school. What are some of the things you remember? Write a few sentences, describing what your best friend was like and what you used to do together at recess.

p. 190 Actividad 4
p. 191 Actividad 8
p. 197 Actividad 18
p. 198 Actividades 19–20

Cultures

 5 Pensar Demonstrate an understanding of favorite nursery rhymes and songs from Spanish-speaking countries

Children around the world love songs that are easy to remember and fun to sing. Think about the songs on p. 204. Which song do you think a child would like best? Why? Does either of them remind you of songs you sang as a child? Which ones?

p. 193 *Pronunciación*
p. 204 *La cultura en vivo*

4B Celebrando los días festivos

▼ Chapter Objectives

Communication

By the end of this chapter you will be able to:

- Listen and read about family celebrations
- Talk and write about how your family used to celebrate holidays and your best birthday
- Exchange information about where, with whom, and how you used to celebrate holidays as a child

Culture

You will also be able to:

- Understand how some Hispanic families celebrate special days and holidays
- Compare holidays and celebrations in Mexico and the U.S.

You will demonstrate what you know and can do:

- Presentación escrita, p. 231
- Preparación para el examen, p. 235

You will use:

Vocabulary

- Common etiquette
- Holiday celebrations

Grammar

- Preterite and imperfect: describing a situation
- Reciprocal actions

Exploración del mundo hispano

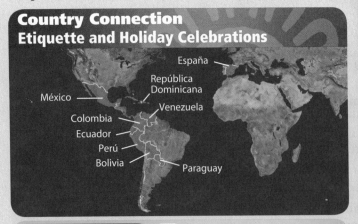

Country Connection
Etiquette and Holiday Celebrations

España
República
Dominicana
México
Venezuela
Colombia
Ecuador
Perú
Bolivia
Paraguay

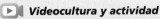 realidades.com GO

 DK Reference Atlas

 Videocultura y actividad

 Mapa global interactivo

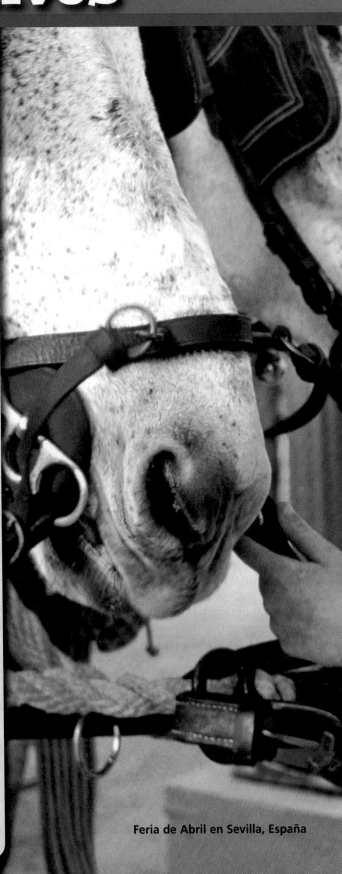

Feria de Abril en Sevilla, España

Arte y cultura | México

Antonio M. Ruiz (1897–1964) pintó en este cuadro la celebración del Día de la Independencia en un pueblo de México. Es el día festivo más importante del país y todo el mundo participa. Aquí ves un desfile de estudiantes. El desfile pasa por la plaza de un pueblo mexicano. Todos los niños llevan en la mano banderas de color verde, rojo y blanco, que son los colores de la bandera mexicana. Estos colores también se ven en el centro de la plaza. Los mayores escuchan a un hombre que les habla.

- ¿Qué piensas que está diciendo el señor del cuadro? Compara este desfile con las celebraciones del Día de la Independencia en tu comunidad.

"Desfile cívico escolar" (1936), Antonio M. Ruiz ▶

Vocabulario en contexto

Recuerdos del pasado
Los buenos modales

sonreír

❝Mis papás me enseñaron la importancia de los buenos **modales.** Es importante ser sociable y sonreír cuando **te reúnes*** con las personas.

dar(se) la mano

Cuando **saludas** o **te despides** es **costumbre** siempre dar la mano.

Para saludar a los amigos, puedes decir '¡Hola!,' '¿Qué tal?' o '¿Cómo estás?'

los mayores

Debes saludar a los mayores con una expresión como 'Buenos días, señora' o '¿Cómo está Ud.?'

besar(se)

Cuando dos personas se conocen muy bien, generalmente se besan para **saludarse** y despedirse.

Mi papá me dijo que una persona siempre debe saludar a todas las personas en **una reunión** o una fiesta. Cuando sales, debes **despedirte de** cada persona también❞.

*Reunirse has an accent on the *u* in all present-tense forms except *nosotros* and *vosotros:* reúne, reúnes, reúne, . . . reúnen.

abrazar(se)

Muchos hombres se abrazan cuando se saludan en la calle o cuando se despiden.

Cómo celebrábamos los días festivos

"El 10 de agosto fue el cumpleaños de mi papá. Celebramos con **una fiesta de sorpresa. Cumplió** 46 **años.** Durante la fiesta, mi abuela habló de cuando él **nació** y ella empezó a **llorar.** Dijo que era **un bebé** grande y guapito. ¡Mi familia y yo le **regalamos** una cámara digital!

¡Felicidades!

Mis abuelos celebraron su **aniversario** el 23 de octubre. **Se casaron** hace 50 años. Todos nuestros **parientes** (mis tíos y primos) y muchos amigos asistieron para **felicitarlos.** Todos cantamos: ¡Felicidades! Les regalamos un reloj **antiguo** muy bonito. Durante la fiesta los niños no se pelearon; todos **se llevaban bien** porque era un día muy especial.

los fuegos artificiales

Frecuentemente, durante los veranos, nosotros íbamos a un parque **enorme** donde **hacíamos un picnic. Mientras** los mayores **charlaban,** nosotros jugábamos. Mi tío, que es muy cómico, siempre nos **contaba chistes** y todos **nos reíamos** mucho. Para días muy especiales, como el Día de la Independencia, **había** fuegos artificiales por la noche. Todas las personas **alrededor del** parque **se divertían**".

▼1 Los buenos modales | 🔊 | 👥

Escuchar

Trabaja con otro(a) estudiante. Van a escuchar ocho frases sobre los buenos modales. Tienen que representar (act out) en pareja cada una de estas acciones.

Más práctica	GO
realidades.com	print	
Instant Check	✔
Guided WB pp. 145–148	✔ ✔
Core WB pp. 82–83	✔ ✔
Comm. WB p. 84	✔ ✔
Hispanohablantes WB p. 152	✔

▼2 Vamos a celebrar | 🔊

Escuchar

Escribe en una hoja de papel los números del 1 al 8. Vas a escuchar ocho frases. Escribe la letra *a, b* o *c* para indicar cuándo ocurrió cada actividad.

a. durante la fiesta de cumpleaños

b. durante la fiesta de aniversario

c. durante la celebración del Día de la Independencia

La fiesta de San Pedro

¿Por qué es especial la fiesta de San Pedro?

Estrategia

Using visuals
Ignacio is describing a celebration in the Basque town of Alsasua that he visited as a child. Look at the different visuals in the *Videohistoria*. For each picture, write what you think he might say.

Ignacio   Javier

1

Javier: ¿Adónde vas, Ignacio?

Ignacio: A Alsasua para la fiesta de San Pedro. Se celebra el 29 de junio. Es **un día festivo.** De niño iba allí con mi familia todos los veranos.

5

Ignacio: Luego íbamos a la iglesia. Recuerdo que a veces hablaban en vasco.

Javier: ¿Sabes hablar vasco?

Ignacio: No, yo no. Mis abuelos lo hablaban.

6

Ignacio: Y la comida era fantástica. Comíamos paella y salchichas que se llaman en vasco *txistorra*. ¡Qué ricas!

Javier: ¡Mmm! Ya tengo hambre.

7

Ignacio: Después de comer, la gente charlaba, contaba chistes y se reía.

Javier: ¿Y los jóvenes?

Ignacio: Los jóvenes seguían bailando.

Javier: ¿Cómo es la fiesta?

Ignacio: Muy divertida. **Recuerdo** que empezaba con **un desfile** por la mañana.

Ignacio: Había bailes día y noche. Los músicos tocaban instrumentos antiguos como el *txistu* y el tamboril.[1]

Javier: ¿El *txistu*? ¿Qué es eso?

[1] El *txistu* es el instrumento característico de la música vasca. Es una flauta de madera y metal. Se usa en procesiones, serenatas y danzas. El tamboril es un tambor pequeño.

Ignacio: Éste es un *txistu*. Es una palabra vasca.

Javier: ¿Sabes tocarlo?

Ignacio: Sí, un poco. Mi abuelo me enseñó hace años. ¡Ay!

Javier: Aquí estoy. Son las siete.

Ignacio: En Alsasua tenemos que comprarte una boina[2].

Javier: Tienes razón.

Ignacio: Bueno. Vamos a la estación.

[2] beret

▼3 ¿Comprendiste?

Leer • Escribir

1. ¿Por qué conocía Ignacio este día festivo?
2. ¿Cómo empezaba el día?
3. ¿Qué tipo de instrumentos tocaban los músicos?
4. ¿Adónde iba Ignacio después del desfile?
5. ¿Qué otros idiomas *(languages)* hablan en Alsasua?
6. ¿Qué es la *txistorra*?
7. ¿Qué hacía la gente después de comer?
8. Según las fotos, ¿cómo se viste Ignacio para ir a la celebración?
9. ¿Qué le falta a Javier?

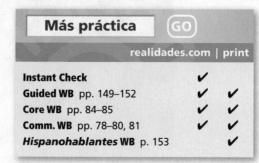

Más práctica GO

realidades.com | print

Instant Check	✔	
Guided WB pp. 149–152	✔	✔
Core WB pp. 84–85	✔	✔
Comm. WB pp. 78–80, 81	✔	✔
Hispanohablantes WB p. 153		✔

Vocabulario en uso

▼4 El intruso

Leer • Escribir

Identifica en cada grupo de palabras "el intruso", es decir, la palabra que no va con las otras tres. Luego escribe una frase completa con la forma apropiada del intruso.

Modelo

fiesta de sorpresa   regalo   cumplo años me despido
Cuando me despido de mis padres, generalmente los abrazo.

1. saludo   recuerdo   le doy la mano   abrazo
2. contamos chistes   nos divertimos hacemos un picnic   nos reímos
3. desfile   nací   día festivo   fuegos artificiales
4. los mayores   felicitan   se casan   ¡Felicidades!
5. se llevan mal   se pelean   lloran   sonríen

> **Nota**
>
> In the present tense, these verbs have stem changes:
>
> **recordar, contar** *(o → ue)*
>
> **divertirse** *(e → ie)*
>
> **despedirse, reírse, sonreír** *(e → i)*
>
> In addition, *reírse* and *sonreír* have accent marks on the *i* in all present-tense forms.

▼5 Escucha y escribe | 🔊

Escuchar • Escribir

Escucha las descripciones de diferentes personas que están presentes en la boda. Escribe las frases. Después indica si las personas tienen buenos o malos modales. *(Nota:* A las personas que acaban de casarse también se les llama "los novios").

Fondo Cultural | España

Euskadi Las diferentes regiones de España tienen su propia identidad, su comida, sus costumbres y a veces su idioma *(language)*. En el País Vasco, situado en el norte de España, se habla euskera (vasco, en español), un idioma que no tiene ninguna relación con el español. En euskera, el nombre de esta región es Euskadi. Una tradición de San Sebastián (o Donostia), una de las ciudades más grandes de Euskadi, es la Tamborrada, que se celebra el 20 de enero. Ese día, hombres tocan el tambor mientras caminan por las calles de la ciudad.

- ¿Qué diferencias de identidad hay entre las regiones de los Estados Unidos?

La Tamborrada de San Sebastián

▼6 Una costumbre de mi familia |

Leer • Escribir

Lee la historia de lo que hacía la familia de Alejandra cuando ella era niña. Completa la historia con las palabras apropiadas.

alrededor de	había
contaban chistes	mientras
frecuentemente	nos divertíamos

antigua   costumbre   enorme   reunirse

Recuerdo muy bien los días festivos que celebrábamos cuando era niña. Era nuestra __1.__ ir a la casa de nuestros abuelos en el campo. Ellos no vivían en una casa moderna como las casas en la ciudad. Su casa era __2.__ pero también __3.__. ¡Todos mis parientes podían __4.__ allí al mismo tiempo!

__5.__ que los adultos charlaban o __6.__, nosotros jugábamos en el jardín que estaba __7.__ la casa. __8.__ muchos árboles en el jardín y __9.__ hacíamos un picnic debajo de ellos. Siempre __10.__ mucho en los días festivos en la casa de nuestros abuelos.

▼7 Costumbres sociales |

Hablar • Escribir

❶ ¿Cómo saludas y te despides de las personas? Habla con otro(a) estudiante y escriban sus respuestas.

▶ Modelo

saludar a tus primos
A —*Generalmente, ¿cómo saludas a tus primos?*
B —*Por lo general los abrazo. ¿Y tú?*
A —*No tengo primos.*

Estudiante A

1. saludar a tus profesores
2. despedirse de tus abuelos (o tíos)
3. despedirse de los padres de tus amigos
4. saludar a tu papá (o mamá)
5. despedirse de tu mejor amigo(a)
6. saludar a un(a) amigo(a) que no has visto *(haven't seen)* recientemente

Estudiante B

❷ Escribe cinco frases para decir si lo que Uds. hacen es similar o es diferente.

Modelo

Por lo general yo abrazo a mis primos cuando los saludo. Enrique no tiene primos, pero siempre abraza a sus abuelos cuando los saluda.

▼8 ¿Qué hacían Uds.? |  | ♻

Hablar

Habla con otro(a) estudiante sobre cómo celebraban diferentes ocasiones sociales cuando eran pequeños(as). Digan dos costumbres que tenían Uds. en cada ocasión.

▶ Modelo

celebrar un aniversario

A —*¿Qué hacía tu familia cuando alguien celebraba un aniversario?*

B —*Hacíamos una fiesta y les regalábamos cosas muy bonitas.*

o: —*No recuerdo lo que hacíamos.*

Estudiante A

1. cumplir años
2. hacer un largo viaje
3. comprar un coche nuevo
4. celebrar un día festivo

Estudiante B

felicitar a . . .
reunirse en . . .
hacer una fiesta (de sorpresa)
hacer un picnic
comprar . . .

regalarle(s) . . .
invitar a . . .
no hacer nada
hacer una reunión de familia
despedirse

▼9 Y tú, ¿qué dices? |

Escribir • Hablar

1. Por lo general, ¿qué les dices a los padres de un bebé que nació recientemente? ¿Qué les regalas?

2. En tu comunidad, ¿en qué días festivos hay fuegos artificiales? ¿En qué días hay desfiles?

3. ¿Cuándo te reúnes con tus parientes? ¿Dónde se reúnen Uds. generalmente? ¿Con quién charlas? ¿Se llevan todos bien o a veces se llevan mal?

▼ Fondo Cultural | El mundo hispano

El Día de la Raza Muchos jóvenes participan en los desfiles del Día de la Raza en el mundo hispano. Este día festivo conmemora la llegada de Cristóbal Colón a las Américas. En Costa Rica el nombre oficial es "el Día de las Culturas" para celebrar también las contribuciones culturales de los pueblos indígenas, asiáticos y africanos del país.

• ¿Cuál de estos dos nombres prefieres tú? ¿Por qué?

Celebración del Día de la Raza en Puebla, México

Gramática

Preterite and imperfect: describing a situation

In addition to saying what someone used to do, the imperfect tense is used:

- to describe people, places, and situations in the past

  La casa de mis abuelos **era** enorme. **Tenía** cinco dormitorios.

- to talk about a past action or situation when no beginning or end is specified

  Había mucha gente en la casa para el aniversario.

- to describe the situation or background information when something else happened or interrupted the ongoing action.

  Todos mis parientes **bailaban** cuando **llegamos**.
  *All my relatives **were dancing** when **we arrived**.*

Note that the imperfect tense is used to tell what someone **was doing** when something **happened** (preterite).

> ### ¿Recuerdas?
> Use the preterite tense to describe completed actions or events.
>
> - Mis abuelos **se casaron** hace 50 años.
>
> - **Celebramos** su aniversario el mes pasado.

> **Más ayuda**   **realidades.com**
>
> ▶ *GramActiva* Video
> **Tutorials:** Summary of uses of preterite and imperfect, Use of the imperfect
>
> *GramActiva* Activity

▼ 10 La Semana Santa | ♻

Leer • Escribir

Patricia, una estudiante norteamericana que está pasando un año en España, les escribe a sus padres sobre una experiencia fantástica que tuvo. Completa su descripción con las formas apropiadas del pretérito o del imperfecto.

el 30 de abril
Sevilla, España

Queridos padres:

Acabo de pasar unos días increíbles. Mi familia española __1.__ (decidir) ir a Sevilla para celebrar la Semana Santa. Nosotros __2.__ (llegar) el martes por la noche y las calles ya __3.__ (estar) llenas de personas. Había un desfile que en la Semana Santa se llama procesión. En la procesión, __4.__ (ver) pasos[1] muy grandes con flores y estatuas enormes (que se llaman *imágenes*) de las iglesias. Las imágenes __5.__ (ser) antiguas y muy impresionantes. Había bandas y otras personas que tocaban música durante las procesiones. Y luego ocurrió algo fantástico. Una mujer __6.__ (salir) a un balcón y __7.__ (empezar) a cantar una saeta. Una saeta es una canción del estilo flamenco que cantan aquí en Sevilla. Todas las personas en la calle escucharon con atención mientras ella cantaba. Por fin,[2] el paso __8.__ (llegar) a la entrada de la catedral y entró, como es la costumbre durante la Semana Santa. ¡Qué experiencia maravillosa!

Besos y abrazos,

Patricia

[1]floats (during Holy Week)   [2]At last

▼11 Un pariente favorito |

Hablar

Trabaja con otro(a) estudiante para describir a un pariente favorito que recuerdas de tu niñez. Usen el imperfecto en sus preguntas y respuestas.

⏵ **Modelo**

¿Quién (ser) tu pariente favorito?
A —¿Quién era tu pariente favorito?
B —Mi pariente favorito era mi abuelo.

Estudiante A

1. ¿Quién (ser) tu pariente favorito?
2. ¿Cómo (llamarse)?
3. ¿Cómo (ser)?
4. ¿Dónde (vivir)?
5. ¿Qué le (gustar) hacer?
6. ¿Qué (hacer) tu pariente contigo?

Estudiante B

Mi pariente favorito era . . .
Se llamaba . . .
Era . . .
Vivía en . . .

🌎 Fondo Cultural | México

El Día de los Muertos En México y en otros países hispanohablantes celebran el Día de los Muertos *(Day of the Dead)* el 2 de noviembre. Preparan el "pan de muertos", un pan en forma de muñecos, y dulces en forma de esqueletos y calaveras *(skulls).* La gente hace altares en sus casas en honor a los parientes muertos. Los altares tienen fotos de los parientes muertos, flores, frutas, pan y la comida favorita del muerto. Algunas familias hacen un picnic en el cementerio donde están sus parientes muertos. Estas costumbres les permiten a las familias recordar a los parientes que ya no viven.

• Compara lo que hacen en México para recordar a los muertos con lo que hace tu familia.

El pan de muertos

Celebración del Día de los Muertos, en México

▼12 ¿Cuántos años tenías? | | ♻

Hablar

Pregunta a otro(a) estudiante cuántos años tenía cuando hizo estas actividades por primera vez.

▶ **Modelo**

recibir tu propia bicicleta

A —*¿Cuántos años tenías cuando recibiste tu propia bicicleta?*

B —*Yo tenía seis años cuando recibí mi propia bicicleta.*

Estudiante A

1. aprender a caminar
2. asistir a la escuela por primera vez
3. ir a tu primer baile
4. leer tu primer libro
5. ir al cine sin tus padres
6. ver un desfile por primera vez

Estudiante B

Yo tenía . . .

▼ Exploración del lenguaje

Prefixes

Think about the meaning of the following Spanish words. What pattern do you notice?

obediente → desobediente
posible → imposible
formal → informal
regular → irregular

Like English, Spanish uses prefixes to extend and change the meanings of words—in this case to create a word with the opposite meaning.

¡Compruébalo! Copy the following words on a sheet of paper. Underline the prefix in each word. Then determine which word (with or without the prefix) is needed to complete the sentences about Mariana and Julieta.

desordenado   impaciente
injusto   irresponsable

Mariana   Julieta

1. A Mariana no le gusta esperar a los demás. Es muy ____.

2. A Julieta le gusta tener su cuarto limpio y ____.

3. Julieta cree que es importante conservar agua. Cree que es ____ no hacerlo.

4. Julieta y Mariana piensan que es ____ tener que dormirse temprano.

▼13 Escucha y escribe |  | 🔊

Escuchar • Escribir

En el cuadro "Tamalada", la niña que está en la puerta recuerda el día, hace muchos años, cuando entró en la cocina con su padre y vio esta escena. ¿Recuerda ella la escena correctamente? Escucha las seis descripciones y escríbelas. Después, si la información es falsa, escribe la información correcta.

"Tamalada / Making tamales" (1988), Carmen Lomas Garza

Oil on linen mounted on wood, 24" x 32". © 1988 Carmen Lomas Garza. Photo credit: M. Lee Featherree. Collection of Paula Macie-Benecke and Norbert Benecke, Aptos, CA.

▼14 ¿Qué había en la pared? | 💬 | ♻

Escribir • Hablar

Usa el imperfecto y escribe tres preguntas sobre la escena que recuerda la niña del cuadro "Tamalada". Después haz tus preguntas a otro(a) estudiante y contesta las preguntas de él (ella).

> **Para decir más . . .**
> **la estufa**   stove
> **el horno**   oven
> **las ollas**   pans
> **el suelo**   floor

> ▶ **Modelo**
> A —¿*Qué había en la pared?*
> B —*Había un cuadro de una pareja bailando flamenco en la pared.*

> **Nota**
> You know that *hay* means "there is, there are." In the imperfect tense, *había* means "there was, there were." *Hay* and *había* are forms of *haber.*

▼15 Y tú, ¿qué dices? | 💬

Escribir • Hablar

1. ¿Siempre has vivido *(have you lived)* en la misma casa? Si no, ¿dónde vivías antes? ¿Era una casa antigua?

2. Cuando tú eras niño(a), ¿te divertías con tus amigos? ¿Charlaban? ¿Hacían picnics? ¿Contaban chistes?

3. ¿Cuántos años tenías cuando aprendiste a caminar?

4. ¿Qué te regalaban tus abuelos o tus tíos cuando eras niño(a)?

Más práctica	**GO**	
realidades.com | print		
Instant Check	✔	
Guided WB pp. 153–157	✔	✔
Core WB p. 86	✔	✔
Comm. WB pp. 82, 85	✔	✔
***Hispanohablantes* WB**		
pp. 154–157, 160		✔

▼16 El Día de la Independencia

Leer • Escribir

En muchos países del mundo, la gente celebra un día para conmemorar la independencia de su país con desfiles, fuegos artificiales y bailes. Lee esta información sobre los días de la independencia en diferentes países. Luego haz una línea cronológica con las fechas de la independencia de los países mencionados abajo.

Conexiones | La historia

Fechas importantes

Los Estados Unidos

El 4 de julio es el Día de la Independencia en los Estados Unidos. Es el aniversario de la Declaración de la Independencia, que firmó[1] el Segundo Congreso Continental en 1776. Luego, los Estados Unidos obtuvieron[2] su independencia de Gran Bretaña.

La Revolución Francesa

Los franceses obtuvieron su independencia de la monarquía el 14 de julio de 1789. Pelearon bajo el lema[3] "Libertad, igualdad y fraternidad".

España

Los franceses invadieron España en el año 1808 y los españoles pelearon contra ellos durante la Guerra[4] de la Independencia. En 1814, los españoles obtuvieron su independencia de los franceses.

México

La independencia de los Estados Unidos y la de Francia fueron grandes ejemplos para los países de América Latina. Unos años después, el 16 de septiembre de 1810, Miguel Hidalgo comenzó la guerra de la independencia contra los españoles, que ocupaban México.

Colombia, Venezuela, Perú, Ecuador y Bolivia

Simón Bolívar comenzó el movimiento de independencia de España en muchos países hispanoamericanos. Ayudó a establecer la independencia de cinco países: Colombia (el 20 de julio de 1810), Venezuela (el 5 de julio de 1811), Perú (el 28 de julio de 1821), Ecuador (el 10 de agosto de 1809 y el 13 de mayo de 1830) y Bolivia (el 6 de agosto de 1825).

Firmando la Declaración de la Independencia

The Declaration of Independence, 4 July 1776, John Trumbull (American, 1756–1843) 1786–1820. Oil on canvas, 53 x 78.7 cm (20-7/8 x 31 in). © Corbis Bettmann.

José Gil de Castro. Courtesy of Corbis Bettmann.

Simón Bolívar, El Libertador

[1]signed [2]gained [3]motto [4]War

Gramática

Reciprocal actions

Sometimes the reflexive pronouns *se* and *nos* are used to express the idea "(to) each other." These are called reciprocal actions.

> Los novios **se abrazaban** y **se besaban**.
> *The bride and groom **were hugging each other** and **kissing each other**.*

> Por lo general **nos saludábamos** con un abrazo. También **nos dábamos** la mano.
> *We usually **greeted each other** with a hug. **We** also **would shake hands**.*

¿Recuerdas?

You already know that *Nos vemos* means "We'll see each other later."

Más ayuda — **realidades.com**

 GramActiva Video Tutorial: Reciprocal actions

 Canción de hip hop: *¿Cómo celebraban ustedes?*

GramActiva Activity

▼**17 Los buenos amigos** | | ♻

Hablar

Habla con otro(a) estudiante sobre lo que hacen tus mejores amigos y tú.

▶ **Modelo**

verse frecuentemente
A —¿*Uds. se ven frecuentemente?*
B —*Sí, nos vemos todos los días.*
o: —*No, no nos vemos frecuentemente.*

Unos amigos en Loma Plata, Paraguay

Estudiante A

1. llevarse bien siempre
2. ayudarse con la tarea de vez en cuando
3. escribirse por correo electrónico a menudo
4. hablarse por teléfono todos los días
5. respetarse mucho
6. comprenderse generalmente

Estudiante B

Sí, nos . . .

No, no nos . . .

▼18 Durante la boda |

Hablar

Durante la boda de Carmen y Alfonso algunos de los invitados *(guests)* se portaban mal. Usa el imperfecto para describir lo que hacían todos mientras los novios se casaban.

▶️ Modelo

Pati y Juanito

A —¿Qué hacían Pati y Juanito mientras Carmen y Alfonso se casaban?

B —Pati y Juanito se peleaban.

Roberto y Belita

el Sr. Vásquez

el Sr. García y el Sr. Ramírez

Pati y Juanito

Carmen y Alfonso

el Sr. Medina

las tías

la Sra. Fernández y la Sra. Peña

los padres de Carmen

Estudiante A

1. las tías
2. el Sr. García y el Sr. Ramírez
3. la Sra. Fernández y la Sra. Peña
4. el Sr. Vásquez y el Sr. Medina
5. Roberto y Belita
6. los padres de Carmen

Estudiante B

besar(se)   llevarse mal
charlar   hablar por
contar(se) chistes   teléfono
pelear(se)   prestar atención

▼ Fondo Cultural | México

La ceremonia del lazo En México, la ceremonia del lazo es parte de la boda y simboliza la unión entre los novios. Es cuando dicen sus promesas matrimoniales y luego el sacerdote *(priest)* les pone en el cuello *(neck)* una cuerda en forma de ocho. La expresión "atar el nudo" *(to tie the knot)* viene de esta tradición mexicana.

• ¿Qué piensas que significa el acto de "atar el nudo" durante la ceremonia? ¿Hay tradiciones similares en los Estados Unidos? ¿Cuáles son?

Una boda mexicana

El carnaval es una de las celebraciones más alegres *(happy)* y animadas de América Latina. Por lo general se celebra durante tres días. Casi siempre hay desfiles de carrozas *(floats)*, grupos de personas con máscaras, bailarines y músicos. En los desfiles de la República Dominicana las personas se disfrazan *(wear costumes)* con máscaras que representan a diferentes personajes reales o imaginarios. En el Uruguay los desfiles son con música, sobre todo de tambores, llamada *candombe*. Las personas siguen a los músicos, todos bailan y algunos se disfrazan. En el Ecuador y en Venezuela no hay desfiles. La tradición es tirar *(to throw)* agua a los peatones que pasan por la calle, o entre los vecinos y miembros de la familia.

Una celebración en Venezuela

• En tu comunidad, ¿en qué festividades o celebraciones hay desfiles? ¿Participas en los desfiles? ¿Te gusta ver los desfiles?

▼**19 Una celebración** | |

Hablar • Escribir

Habla con otro(a) estudiante sobre cómo celebraba un día festivo cuando era niño(a).

❶ Pregunta a tu compañero(a) qué día festivo le gustaba celebrar.

> ▶ **Modelo**
>
> **A** —*¿Qué día festivo era tu favorito cuando eras niño(a)?*
> **B** —*Me encantaba Halloween.*

❷ Escribe cinco preguntas que puedes hacerle a tu compañero(a) usando el imperfecto. Hazle las preguntas y escribe sus respuestas.

❸ Escribe un párrafo de por lo menos *(at least)* cinco frases sobre cómo tu compañero(a) celebraba el día festivo.

> **Modelo**
>
> *A Carmen le encantaba Halloween cuando era niña. Siempre se vestía de princesa. Todos decían que ella era muy bonita. Iba a las casas de sus parientes y ellos le daban muchos dulces. Después se comía todos los dulces.*

Para decir más . . .

El Día de San Valentín   Valentine's Day
El Día de San Patricio   St. Patrick's Day
El Día de Acción de Gracias   Thanksgiving Day

Más práctica	GO	
realidades.com	print	
Instant Check	✔	
Guided WB p. 158	✔	✔
Core WB pp. 87–88	✔	✔
Comm. WB pp. 82–83, 86, 241	✔	✔
Hispanohablantes **WB** pp. 158–159, 161		✔

▼20 Las Fallas de Valencia | ♻ | 🌐

Leer • Escribir

Lee el artículo sobre Las Fallas de Valencia, una de las fiestas más divertidas de España, y luego contesta las preguntas.

Las Fallas tienen origen en la celebración de San José, el santo de los carpinteros, y los valencianos conservan esta tradición tan interesante. En tiempos antiguos, los carpinteros celebraban el día de San José y la llegada de la primavera quemando[1] la madera[2] que ya no necesitaban. Hoy en día, durante unos seis meses, varias organizaciones en Valencia construyen unos 350 **ninots,** grandes estatuas de madera, *papier-mâché* y cartón. Estas estatuas representan los eventos del año o a personas famosas, generalmente de una forma muy cómica. Cada año escogen un ninot por voto popular y lo ponen en el Museo del Ninot. La *Cremá* (el 19 de marzo) es la última noche de la celebración, cuando ponen fuegos artificiales dentro de los otros ninots y a la medianoche los queman todos.

Un ninot en Valencia

[1]burning   [2]wood

1. ¿Cuándo y por qué quemaban la madera en tiempos antiguos?

2. ¿Qué hacen con los ninots que construyen hoy en día?

3. ¿Te gustaría estar en Valencia la noche del 19 de marzo? ¿Por qué?

▼21 El mejor ninot | 👥 | ♻

Dibujar • Escribir • Hablar

Con otro(a) estudiante, dibujen un ninot en color. Describan el ninot en tres o cuatro frases y expliquen por qué lo hicieron. Presenten los ninots a la clase y pongan los dibujos en la pared. Voten por el mejor ninot.

Modelo

Nuestro ninot es un jugador de básquetbol. Tiene las manos muy grandes y las piernas muy largas. Usamos los colores de la escuela en su uniforme. Hicimos este ninot porque nuestro equipo de básquetbol ganó todos los partidos el mes pasado.

El español en el mundo del trabajo

En el mercado de decoraciones y ornamentos de los Estados Unidos, los hispanohablantes ocupan un lugar importante. En el pasado se importaban de países hispanohablantes las decoraciones para días festivos pero hoy en día se hacen en los Estados Unidos. Por ejemplo, en Lynn, Massachusetts, se fabrican *(they make)* ornamentos hechos de masa de pan *(dough ornaments)* para la Navidad. En San Antonio, Texas, se hacen *cascarones,* que son las cáscaras de huevos rellenos de confeti *(confetti-filled eggshells)*. En la "Fiesta" de abril, las personas rompen los cascarones en las cabezas de sus amigos.

• ¿Se usa en tu comunidad alguna decoración u ornamento en los días festivos? ¿Cómo es? ¿Dónde se fabrica? ¿Es un ornamento que se usa en otro país o región?

Lectura
El seis de enero

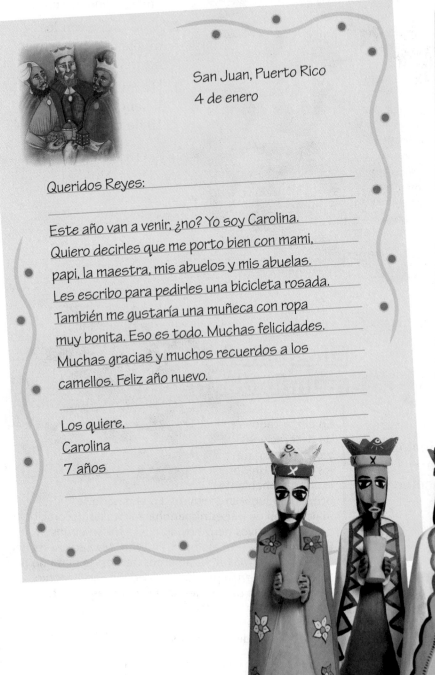

San Juan, Puerto Rico
4 de enero

Queridos Reyes:

Este año van a venir, ¿no? Yo soy Carolina.
Quiero decirles que me porto bien con mami,
papi, la maestra, mis abuelos y mis abuelas.
Les escribo para pedirles una bicicleta rosada.
También me gustaría una muñeca con ropa
muy bonita. Eso es todo. Muchas felicidades.
Muchas gracias y muchos recuerdos a los
camellos. Feliz año nuevo.

Los quiere,
Carolina
7 años

Estrategia

Using background knowledge
Using your own experience can help you predict the types of information you may find in a reading. Make a list of three types of information you might find in a letter to Santa Claus or some other fictional character. When you have finished the reading, see if what you predicted was mentioned.

Uno de los días más anticipados y felices para los niños del mundo hispano es el seis de enero, el Día de los Reyes Magos. Según la tradición, los tres Reyes Magos: Melchor, Gaspar y Baltasar, vienen montados en sus camellos[1] durante la noche y les traen regalos a todos los niños. La noche del cinco, las familias van al centro de la ciudad para ver un desfile de carrozas[2] con luces y flores y, por supuesto, los Reyes Magos. Después, los niños reúnen hierba o paja[3] para los camellos y la ponen en una caja cerca de sus zapatos. La mañana del seis, los niños se despiertan para ver qué les regalaron los Reyes Magos.

[1]camels   [2]carriages   [3]straw

Queridos Reyes Magos:

Me llamo José Alejandro y les escribo esta carta con mi mamá para decirles los regalos que quiero para mí y para mi hermanito, Jorge Andrés. Nos portamos bien. Yo saco muy buenas notas en la escuela y hago toda mi tarea. Yo quiero un carrito de control remoto y un videojuego de fútbol para mi computadora. Mi hermanito quiere un juguete o cualquier cosa que ustedes puedan. Gracias, y recuerden llevarles juguetes a los niños pobres y traernos paz y amor.

Los quieren,
José Alejandro y Jorge Andrés
7 y 2 años
Argentina

Antes del seis de enero, los niños les escriben cartas a los Reyes Magos pidiendo sus regalos. A veces también visitan a los Reyes Magos en los almacenes de las ciudades grandes. Antes era costumbre poner las cartas al lado de los zapatos, pero luego comenzaron a enviarlas por correo postal y hoy en día las envían por correo electrónico.

Niña con un Rey Mago, Madrid, España

Niños vestidos de Reyes Magos, en la República Dominicana

¿Comprendiste?

1. ¿Por qué es el Día de los Reyes Magos feliz para los niños?
2. ¿Qué hacen los niños antes del seis de enero?
3. ¿Qué hacen los niños el día del seis?
4. En los Estados Unidos, muchos niños creen en Santa Claus. ¿En qué sentido son similares las tradiciones de Santa Claus y de los Reyes Magos? ¿En qué sentido son diferentes?

Y tú, ¿qué dices?

Escribe una carta a los Reyes Magos. Usa una de las cartas escritas por niños del mundo hispano como modelo.

Más práctica   GO

realidades.com | print

Guided WB p. 159	✔	✔
Comm. WB pp. 87, 242	✔	✔
Hispanohablantes **WB** pp. 162-163		✔
Culture Reading Activity		✔

Perspectivas del mundo hispano

El Roscón de Reyes

Es el Día de los Reyes Magos, el seis de enero, y mientras los niños juegan con sus regalos, los mayores preparan la merienda[1] de Reyes para sus amigos y familia. Esta merienda incluye un postre especial que se llama el roscón (o en México, la rosca) de Reyes. Cuando es la hora de comer el roscón, todo el mundo se acerca a la mesa y una persona empieza a cortarlo. Cada persona corta una rebanada[2] del roscón. Todos comen su porción cuando una persona grita, "¡Lo tengo!"

¿Qué es lo que tiene? Pues, dentro del roscón hay un muñequito de plástico. Según la tradición la persona que encuentra el muñequito debe pagar por la cena u otro roscón. Según otra tradición, la persona que encuentra el muñequito es el rey o la reina[3] de la fiesta.

El roscón es dulce, parecido a un pan dulce o a una torta, que se hace y se come sólo una vez al año. Está hecho con harina,[4] huevos, azúcar, mantequilla y frutas confitadas.[5] Como toda comida tradicional, la receta puede variar según la familia o la región. En ciertos países, el roscón se acompaña[6] con una taza de chocolate caliente.

Un roscón de Reyes

¡Compruébalo! ¿Hay una tradición o celebración de tu familia en la que comen algo especial? ¿Qué es? ¿Cómo se prepara? ¿Hay algo especial que hacen mientras la preparan?

¿Qué te parece? ¿Crees que es importante mantener la tradición de preparar una comida especial? ¿Por qué?

Un vendedor de roscas de Reyes en México

[1]snack [2]slice [3]king or queen [4]flour
[5]candied [6]is accompanied

Presentación escrita

Mi celebración favorita

Task
Write an e-mail to a friend describing a favorite holiday or celebration from your childhood.

① Prewrite Think of an event you used to celebrate. Copy this chart and fill it in with words or expressions related to your topic.

¿Qué hacían?	¿Dónde se reunían?	¿Cómo era?	¿Quiénes estaban?	¿Por qué te gustaba?

② Draft Use the ideas from the chart to write a first draft.
Modelo
Mi celebración favorita era el Día de la Madre. Celebrábamos este día con toda la familia y, claro, con mi mamá. Íbamos a . . . Siempre le regalábamos . . . Ella siempre lloraba porque . . .

③ Revise Check your e-mail for correct spelling and use of vocabulary and the imperfect tense. Share the e-mail with a partner, who should check:

- Is the e-mail easy to read and understand?
- Does it provide an interesting description of the event?
- Is there anything you should add?
- Are there any errors?

④ Publish Rewrite the e-mail, making any necessary changes. Make a copy for your teacher or add it to your portfolio.

⑤ Evaluation The following rubric will be used to grade your presentation.

Estrategia

Using a chart
Thinking through categories and writing down key words and expressions will give you more ideas for writing.

Rubric	Score 1	Score 3	Score 5
Amount of information you provide	You respond to only two questions.	You respond to only three questions.	You respond to all five questions.
Your accuracy in describing events in the past	You use three verbs in the past with grammatical errors.	You use four verbs in the past with some grammatical errors.	You use five or more verbs in the past with very few grammatical errors.
Your use of vocabulary and grammar	You use very little variation of vocabulary and have frequent usage errors.	You use limited vocabulary and have some usage errors.	You use an extended variety of vocabulary and have very few usage errors.

En busca de la verdad

Episodio 4

"¡Federico! Pero, ¿dónde estás?"

Antes de ver el video

"Mira, éste es tu abuelo".

Nota cultural El mole es una típica salsa mexicana. Hay muchos tipos de moles, pues en cada región de México se preparan diferentes salsas. Hay algunos moles que se hacen con unos veinte ingredientes distintos . . . ¡y a veces más de veinte! En la Ciudad de México hay una Feria Nacional del Mole todos los años en octubre. Gente de todo el país llega a la capital para participar en esta festividad.

Resumen del episodio

Linda, Roberto y Daniela van a San Miguel de Allende a visitar a Nela. Ella está contenta de conocer a Linda pero no quiere hablar de su esposo Federico. Roberto le pregunta sobre su abuelo y ella le muestra una foto antigua. Esa foto contiene la primera pista para Roberto. Al final del episodio Nela se queda sola frente a la computadora y se lleva una gran sorpresa.

Palabras para comprender

pista hint

¿Será posible? Is it possible?

No te preocupes. Don't worry.

Cuídate mucho. Take care of yourself.

Volveré lo más pronto posible. I will return as soon as possible.

No tardes. Don't be late.

apellido de soltera maiden name

Después de ver el video

¿Comprendiste?

A. Escribe la respuesta correcta.

1. ¿Quiénes viajan en coche a San Miguel de Allende?
2. ¿Con quién habla Linda por el teléfono celular?
3. ¿Adónde invita Julio a Linda?
4. ¿Qué preparó Nela para el almuerzo?
5. ¿Cuáles fueron las últimas palabras del esposo de Nela antes de irse?

B. Contesta las siguientes preguntas.

1. ¿Qué pista obtiene *(obtains)* Roberto en este episodio?
2. ¿Cómo reacciona Roberto cuando Linda habla con Julio por teléfono? ¿Por qué?
3. ¿Por qué Roberto le pregunta a su abuela sobre el apellido de Linda?
4. En 1941, ¿con quién se fue Federico Toledo? ¿Adónde fue?

"Cuando mi esposo y yo llegamos aquí, San Miguel era un pueblo muy pequeño y muy lindo".

"Aquí estamos con la abuela".

Más práctica GO

realidades.com | print

Actividades ✔

Repaso | 🔊 | ▶ | ▭

| ▼ **Objectives**
▸ Review the vocabulary and grammar
▸ Demonstrate you can perform the tasks on p. 235

Repaso del capítulo

Vocabulario y gramática

to talk about manners and customs

abrazar(se)	to hug
besar(se)	to kiss
dar(se) la mano	to shake hands
despedirse *(e → i)*(de)	to say good-bye (to)
los modales	manners
saludar(se)	to greet
sonreír *(e → i)*	to smile

to talk about people

el bebé, la bebé	baby
contar *(o → ue)* (chistes)	to tell (jokes)
llevarse bien / mal	to get along well / badly
llorar	to cry
los mayores	grown-ups
los parientes	relatives
reírse *(e → i)*	to laugh
reunirse *(u → ú)*	to meet

to talk about special events

alrededor de	around
el aniversario	anniversary
casarse (con)	to get married (to)
charlar	to chat
la costumbre	custom
cumplir años	to have a birthday
el desfile	parade
el día festivo	holiday
divertirse *(e → ie)*	to have fun
enorme	enormous
¡Felicidades!	Congratulations!
felicitar	to congratulate
la fiesta de sorpresa	surprise party
los fuegos artificiales	fireworks
hacer un picnic	to have a picnic
nacer	to be born
regalar	to give (a gift)
la reunión, *pl.* las reuniones	gathering

For *Vocabulario adicional,* see pp. 498–499.

to discuss the past

antiguo, -a	old, antique
frecuentemente	frequently
había	there was / there were
mientras (que)	while
recordar *(o → ue)*	to remember

using the preterite and imperfect to describe a situation

Use the imperfect to describe people, places, and situations:

La casa donde **vivía estaba** al lado de un lago.

Use the imperfect to describe an action or situation with no specific beginning or end:

Había mucha gente en la fiesta de sorpresa.

The imperfect tense is used to tell what someone was doing when something happened:

Mis padres me **felicitaban** cuando **llegó** mi tía.

Mis tíos **se saludaban** cuando **empezaron** los fuegos artifciales.

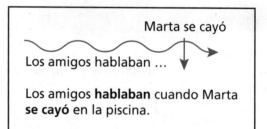

Marta se cayó

Los amigos hablaban …

Los amigos **hablaban** cuando Marta **se cayó** en la piscina.

reciprocal actions

Los estudiantes **se saludaban** todos los días.

Nos veíamos frecuentemente cuando éramos niños.

Se escribían por correo electrónico de vez en cuando.

Más repaso (GO) realidades.com | print

Instant Check ✔
Puzzles ✔
Core WB pp. 89–90 ✔
Comm. WB pp. 243, 244–246 ✔ ✔

Preparación para el examen

On the exam you will be asked to . . .	Here are practice tasks similar to those you will find on the exam . . .	For review go to your print or digital textbook . . .

Interpretive

1 Escuchar Listen and understand as people talk about their childhood memories of family celebrations

To celebrate "Grandparents' Day," your teacher invited Spanish-speakers from the community to talk about their favorite childhood memories. Listen as one of them describes one of their favorite family celebrations. See if you understand: (a) the reason for the gathering; (b) who was there; (c) what people used to do at the celebration.

pp. 212–215 *Vocabulario en contexto*

p. 218 Actividad 8

p. 222 Actividad 13

Interpersonal

2 Hablar Talk about how your family used to celebrate holidays when you were a child

You have been invited to an elementary Spanish classroom to talk to the children about how you used to celebrate holidays when you were their age. What could you say? Try to include: (a) where you used to celebrate most holidays; (b) what you used to do; (c) who got together to celebrate with you.

p. 218 Actividad 8

p. 222 Actividad 14

p. 226 Actividad 19

Interpretive

3 Leer Read and understand a description of activities at a special event

Read part of the notes that Miguel wrote for the wedding reception video he just finished filming for his friend, Mauricio, the groom, and the bride, Luisa. Can you determine who was having a good time and who was not without seeing the video?

Cuando Mauricio besó a Luisa, la madre de Luisa lloraba y el padre de ella sonreía. Los sobrinos pequeños se reían y jugaban con sus juguetes.

p. 219 Actividad 10

p. 227 Actividad 20

pp. 228–229 *Lectura*

Presentational

4 Escribir Write about your best birthday

A local Spanish-language radio station is asking people to send e-mails or faxes describing their best birthday. You might begin by writing: *Yo recuerdo bien mi cumpleaños de trece años* . . . Describe people who were there, where it was held, and what happened.

p. 226 Actividad 19

p. 231 *Presentación escrita*

Cultures

5 Pensar Demonstrate an understanding of how some Hispanic families celebrate special days and holidays

Describe a holiday, such as *Las Fallas* or *Carnaval,* that is of special interest to you. How is this holiday similar to one that you celebrate in your community?

p. 210 *Fondo cultural*

p. 214–215 *Videohistoria*

p. 220 *Fondo cultural*

p. 226 *Fondo cultural*

p. 227 Actividad 20

p. 230 *Perspectivas del mundo hispano*

Vocabulario Repaso

¿Qué tiempo hace?

Hace calor.
Hace frío.
Hace sol.
Hace viento.
Llueve. (llover)*
Nieva. (nevar)*

los cuartos de la casa

el baño	el patio
la cocina	la planta baja
el comedor	el primer piso
el dormitorio	la sala
el garaje	el segundo piso
el jardín, *pl.* los jardines	el sótano
la oficina	

en los cuartos

la alfombra
la cama
la cómoda
las cortinas
el cuadro
el disco compacto
el equipo de sonido
el espejo
el estante
la lámpara
la mesita
la pared
el televisor
el video

*The verbs *llover* ("to rain") and *nevar* ("to snow") are stem-changing verbs in the present tense. The third-person singular form is the only form used.

▼1 ¿Cómo son las casas?

Escribir • Hablar

Un estudiante de intercambio va a vivir con tu familia. Te escribe por correo electrónico con algunas preguntas. Contesta las preguntas.

1. ¿Qué tiempo hace ahora allí?

2. En mi dormitorio hay muchos carteles, unos cuadros y fotos, y un espejo en las paredes. ¿Qué tienes tú?

3. Las casas en mi país generalmente son de un piso. ¿Y allí?

4. Tenemos una cocina bastante grande, pero comemos en el comedor. ¿Y Uds.?

5. Mi familia pasa mucho tiempo en la sala. ¿Dónde pasan tiempo Uds.?

▼2 En mi casa | 👥

Dibujar • Escribir • Hablar

❶ Dibuja una casa. Incluye en la casa algunas de las cosas de la lista "en los cuartos". Escribe cinco frases que describen la casa. Algunas de las frases deben ser ciertas y otras deben ser falsas.

❷ Muestra *(Show)* tu dibujo a otro(a) estudiante y lee tus frases. Tu compañero(a) tiene que decir si las frases son ciertas o falsas y escribir la información correcta para las frases falsas.

Gramática Repaso

Expressions using *tener*

In many expressions, *tener* is used to express the verb "to be." See how many of these expressions you remember:

tener . . .

. . . años	miedo
calor	prisa
cuidado	razón
frío	sed
hambre	sueño

Tengo sed porque hace mucho calor.

Vamos rápido porque **tenemos prisa**.

The use of *¡Qué . . . !* in exclamations

Qué is used in exclamations of emotion or feeling.

Use *¡Qué . . . !* with adverbs and adjectives to mean "How . . . !"

¡Qué **rápido** corren ellos!

¡Qué **triste**!

Use *¡Qué . . . !* with nouns to mean "What (a) . . . !"

No puedo jugar porque me duele el estómago. ¡Qué **pena**!

No comí ni el desayuno ni el almuerzo. ¡Qué **hambre** tengo!

▼3 ¿Qué tiene?

Escribir • Hablar

Completa estas frases con una expresión con *tener*.

Modelo

Si dices que la capital de Nicaragua es San José, *no tienes razón*.

1. Si acabo de correr y necesito agua, ___.
2. Si estás buscando tu suéter, ___.
3. Si vas a acostarte, ___.
4. Si no quieren llegar tarde a la escuela, ___.
5. Si comemos cinco tacos, ___.
6. Si hace muchísimo calor en la clase, ___.
7. Si decimos que Bolivia queda al norte de Argentina, ___.
8. Si tu hermanito dice que no le gustan nada las películas de horror, ___.

▼4 ¡Qué fiesta!

Escribir • Hablar

Estás en una fiesta y observas las siguientes cosas. Da una exclamación para cada una, usando las palabras entre paréntesis.

Modelo

A todos les encantan las decoraciones. (bonito)
¡Qué bonitas son las decoraciones!

1. Todos comen los sándwiches. (sabroso)
2. Ese chico tiene sólo nueve años, pero ya sabe álgebra. (inteligente)
3. María Teresa baila muy bien. (bailarina)
4. ¿Quieres bailar? (buena idea)
5. El pastel es para 100 personas. (grande)

Más práctica GO   realidades.com | print

A ver si recuerdas with Study Plan	✔	
Guided WB pp. 161–162	✔	✔
Core WB pp. 91–92	✔	✔
Hispanohablantes WB p. 170		✔

5A Un acto heroico

▼ Chapter Objectives

Communication

By the end of this chapter you will be able to:

- Listen to and read about disasters and rescues
- Talk and write about how things were during your day and about disaster movies
- Exchange information about newsworthy events

Culture

You will also be able to:

- Understand volcano names and legends that are related to them
- Compare natural disasters in the Spanish-speaking world with those in your community

You will demonstrate what you know and can do:

- Presentación oral, p. 259
- Preparación para el examen, p. 263

You will use:

Vocabulary

- Natural disasters, weather extremes, and fires
- The news and rescues

Grammar

- Preterite and imperfect: other uses
- The preterite of the verbs *oír, leer, creer,* and *destruir*

Exploración del mundo hispano

Country Connection
Disasters, Emergencies, and Rescues

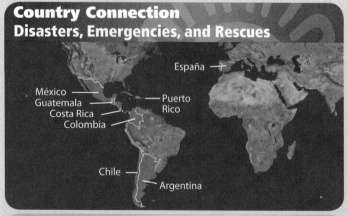

España
México
Guatemala
Costa Rica
Colombia
Puerto Rico
Chile
Argentina

realidades.com GO

 Reference Atlas

 Videocultura y actividad

 Mapa global interactivo

Rescate de los mineros de la mina San José, Atacama, Chile

Arte y cultura | El mundo hispano

Zulia Gotay de Anderson nació en Ponce, Puerto Rico, y ahora vive en Port Aransas, Texas. Este cuadro ilustra un cuento de pescadores *(fishermen)* volviendo a casa durante un huracán. Sus esposas tienen miedo porque piensan que los pescadores no van a poder regresar. En 1998, más de diez mil personas murieron *(died)* en el huracán Mitch. Para reducir los efectos devastadores de los huracanes en el futuro, varios grupos trabajan en Honduras y Guatemala para mejorar los métodos de informar a la gente cuando venga *(comes)* otro huracán.

• Cuando hay un desastre en tu comunidad, por ejemplo un incendio *(fire)* o una inundación *(flood)*, ¿ayudan unas personas a otras? ¿Cómo se ayudan?

"The Storm / La tempestad" (2002),
Zulia Gotay de Anderson ▶

Oil on masonite, 24 x 30 in.

Vocabulario en contexto

❝Hoy **hubo** un incendio que **destruyó** unos apartamentos. No sabemos **la causa** del incendio, pero se cree que **comenzó** a causa de **una explosión.** Un vecino **valiente** ayudó a una señora a salir de su apartamento. **Afortunadamente,** no había más gente en el edificio. Llegaron los bomberos y **apagaron** el incendio después de unas horas. En otras noticias . . .

TELE 5

el noticiero

la locutora

el edificio de apartamentos

quemarse

el incendio

los bomberos

la escalera

el humo

Hubo **un terremoto** en el sur de México. Dicen que más de 100 personas **se murieron** en este desastre.

Ayer **el huracán** Gabriel llegó a la costa de Honduras cerca del pueblo de La Ceiba. **Llovió** por 12 horas.

Hubo muchas **inundaciones** en Honduras a causa de **las tormentas de lluvia,** pero dicen que todos los habitantes están **vivos.**

En Chile, **nevó** durante tres días y las carreteras están cerradas❞.

Más vocabulario
a causa de because of
de prisa in a hurry
de repente suddenly

La Prensa

Un héroe local | el artículo

Carlos Arroyo Medina es un héroe según sus vecinos porque le salvó la vida a una señora de 82 años. Ayer ocurrió un incendio en su edificio de apartamentos. El Sr. Arroyo le cuenta a nuestra reportera lo que pasó.

" Estaba delante del edificio y vi el humo. Pensé inmediatamente en la Sra. Hurtado, que vive en el segundo piso. Tiene 82 años y yo sabía que no podía **escaparse**. Un vecino mío llamó por teléfono para pedir ayuda.

Entré corriendo y **subí** la escalera hasta llegar a su apartamento. **Traté de abrir** la puerta pero no pude. **Creí** que la Sra. Hurtado estaba **dormida** o, peor, **muerta**.

Pero ella **se escondía** entre **los muebles** de su apartamento y **gritaba** '¡Socorro!'. De repente pude abrir la puerta y entré en el apartamento.

Bajamos de prisa la escalera y nos escapamos del incendio. Lo que hice no fue un acto heroico. Ayudé a mi vecina, nada más. Ella también es **heroína** "

▼1 ¿Quién es? | ◀))

Escuchar

Vas a escuchar las noticias. Señala la noticia que se describe en la página 240.

Más práctica	GO

realidades.com | print

Instant Check	✔	
Guided WB pp. 163–170	✔	✔
Core WB pp. 93–94	✔	✔
Comm. WB p. 94	✔	✔
Hispanohablantes WB p. 172		✔

▼2 El noticiero de San José | ◀))

Escuchar

Escucha las noticias y escoge la respuesta correcta.

Noticia 1

1. a. muchas personas
   b. nadie

2. a. una escuela
   b. una tienda

Noticia 2

1. a. un bombero
   b. un policía

2. a. un incendio
   b. un terremoto

Noticia 3

1. a. un incendio
   b. un huracán

2. a. más de 40
   b. más de 50

En el noticiero

¿Qué hay en las noticias cuando Tomás y Raúl ven la televisión?

Estrategia

Scanning for key information
News reports provide important facts. Look through the dialogue before reading to find out what event happened and what connection it has with Tomás and Raúl.

1

Raúl: ¡Mira! Anoche hubo un incendio en una casa. ¡Caramba!

Tomás: ¿Y ahora qué?

Raúl: ¡Está a dos calles de aquí! ¡Tenemos que ir a verla! Quiero saber qué pasó.

Tomás: ¿Por qué? Yo no quiero salir ahora.

el bombero

Tomás

Raúl

la reportera

5

Bombero: Un vecino vio humo. Vinieron **los paramédicos.** Afortunadamente, los pudimos **rescatar** a todos.

6

Reportera: Y ustedes, ¿cómo se llaman?

Raúl: Pues, Raúl Padilla Salazar.

Tomás: Tomás.

Reportera: ¿Viven cerca de aquí?

Raúl: Más o menos.

7

Reportera: ¿Oyeron el incendio? ¿O vieron el humo?

Tomás: Pues, estábamos viendo la televisión en casa cuando vimos el noticiero . . .

Reportera: Entonces, ¿no saben nada del incendio?

Raúl: Pues, la verdad, no.

Raúl: Mira, allí está **la reportera.** Está hablando con un bombero.

Tomás: ¿Qué ocurrió?

Raúl: No sé. Vamos a **investigar.**

Reportera: ¿A qué hora comenzó el incendio?

Bombero: No estamos seguros. Sobre las dos de la mañana.

Reportera: ¿Cómo comenzó?

Bombero: Pensamos que hubo una explosión. Estamos investigando la causa.

Reportera: ¿Había personas en la casa?

Bombero: Sí. Una familia de seis personas.

Reportera: ¿Hubo algún **herido?**

Bombero: Afortunadamente, no estaban **heridos.** Pero, **sin duda,** estaban un poco **asustados.**

Reportera: Esto es todo por ahora. Laura Martínez desde Calle 21 para el canal cinco.

▼3 ¿Comprendiste?

Escribir • Hablar

1. ¿Qué ven Tomás y Raúl en la televisión? ¿Qué pasó?

2. ¿Adónde quiere ir Raúl? ¿Quiere ir Tomás también?

3. ¿A quiénes ven Tomás y Raúl cuando llegan a la casa? ¿Qué hacen ellos?

4. ¿A qué hora comenzó el incendio? ¿Qué lo causó?

5. ¿Había gente en la casa? ¿Cómo estaba?

6. ¿Por qué habla la reportera con Tomás y Raúl? ¿Qué le dicen los chicos?

Más práctica	GO	
realidades.com	print	
Instant Check	✔	
Guided WB pp. 171–174	✔	✔
Core WB pp. 95–96	✔	✔
Comm. WB pp. 88–90, 91	✔	✔
Hispanohablantes WB p. 173	✔	

| ▼ **Objectives**

▸ Talk about natural disasters
▸ Discuss a fire and rescue
▸ Listen to a radio announcer's description of a fire
▸ Write about natural disasters, emergencies, rescues, and heroic acts

Vocabulario en uso

▼4 El incendio

Leer • Escribir

Escribe frases completas para explicar lo que ocurrió ayer en un barrio de la ciudad.

Modelo

 sacó fotos del

El fotógrafo sacó fotos del incendio.

Una señora vio __1.__ y llamó por teléfono a __2.__ . __3.__  investigó

la causa de __4.__ en el apartamento. El incendio destruyó todos __5.__ en el

apartamento. __6.__ llevó al señor que estaba __7.__ a la ambulancia.

__8.__ rescató a una perra del __9.__ . __10.__ valiente subió

__11.__ y apagó __12.__ .

▼5 Escucha y escribe | 👥 | 🔊

Escuchar • Escribir • Hablar

Escucha las seis frases de un locutor que da las noticias del incendio que se describe en la Actividad 4. Escribe las frases. Después, con otro(a) estudiante, pongan en orden estas frases siguiendo el orden de la Actividad 4 para contar lo que ocurrió.

▼6 El artículo de la reportera

Leer • Escribir

Una reportera, Alicia Fernández, habló con el Sr. Osorio. Lee otra vez la información del incendio en las Actividades 4 y 5. Escoge las palabras del recuadro y completa las notas de Alicia en preparación para escribir el artículo para el periódico.

El Sr. Osorio estaba __1.__ en su cama cuando, __2.__ , su perra Blanca __3.__ a ladrar *(bark)*. El señor salió de su cama muy __4.__ y llamó a los bomberos. __5.__ llegar a la puerta del apartamento pero no pudo.

Afortunadamente el señor y su perra __6.__ y están __7.__ . Muchos dicen que Blanca es una verdadera __8.__ . __9.__ , Blanca ayudó a salvarle __10.__ al Sr. Osorio.

comenzó	heroína	sin duda
de prisa	muertos	trató de
de repente	se escaparon	la vida
dormido	se escondió	vivos

▼7 Profesiones para nuestros compañeros | 🗨️Talk! 👥 | ♻️

Escribir • Hablar

❶ Escribe verbos y adjetivos que asocias con estas personas.

Modelo

profesor, -a
ayudar, enseñar, explicar, inteligente, simpático

1. bombero, -a
2. paramédico, -a
3. reportero, -a
4. locutor, -a
5. policía

❷ Trabaja con otro(a) estudiante. Habla de las personas en tu escuela que deben tener estas profesiones.

📹 **Modelo**

A —*¿Quién debe ser profesor(a)?*
B —*Martín Echevarría debe ser profesor de español. Es inteligente y muy simpático. Le gusta ayudar a otras personas. Explica muy bien los verbos y puede enseñar a la clase si es necesario.*

▼ Fondo Cultural | Chile

Los bomberos chilenos ¿Sabes que todos los bomberos en Chile son voluntarios? Para ser bombero, uno tiene que llenar una solicitud *(application)* en una estación de bomberos y aprobar *(pass)* un examen físico y mental. Los bomberos no tienen horarios fijos *(fixed)*. Van a la estación cuando pueden y todos tienen radios para saber cuándo los necesitan. Sirven durante el día y también durante la "guardia nocturna". Para comprar el equipo necesario, los voluntarios tienen que pagar dinero todos los meses para servir a la comunidad.

• ¿Crees que los voluntarios deben pagar sus propios gastos *(expenses)*? ¿Por qué?

Un bombero voluntario, Chile

▼8 Antónimos

Leer • Escribir

Lee las frases y complétalas con el antónimo de la palabra señalada. Escoge el antónimo del recuadro y escríbelo en la forma correcta según la frase.

Estrategia

Using antonyms
Learning vocabulary through antonyms, or words of opposite meaning, can be helpful, especially in recalling the meanings of words.

comenzar	muerto
de prisa	se murieron
dormido	subir

1. Sus peces no están *vivos,* están ___.
2. ¿Qué vas a hacer, ___ o *bajar* la escalera?

3. No puede *terminar* el trabajo porque primero tiene que ___ el trabajo.
4. Los gatos no están *despiertos.* Están ___.
5. La señorita no está caminando *lentamente.* Está caminando ___.
6. En el artículo dice que tres personas *nacieron* y tres personas ___ en el hospital ayer.

▼9 Los desastres naturales | |

Escribir • Hablar

❶ Mira los dibujos de los desastres naturales. Copia la tabla, escribe el nombre de los desastres y completa la información en las otras columnas. Puedes buscar información en la Red o usar tu imaginación.

Un incendio en España

Desastre	Lugar	Destrucción	Cuándo ocurrió
los incendios forestales	Colorado	árboles, animales, casas	hace dos años

1.  **2.** **3.**  **4.**

❷ Usa la tabla para hablar con otro(a) estudiante sobre los desastres naturales.

▶ **Modelo**

A — *¿Dónde ocurren frecuentemente los incendios forestales?*
B — *Creo que ocurren en Colorado.*
A — *¿Los incendios forestales destruyen* mucho?*
B — *Sí, desafortunadamente destruyen árboles, animales y a veces casas. Hace dos años hubo incendios forestales grandes en Colorado.*

*In the present tense, *destruir* adds y to all forms except *nosotros* and *vosotros: destruyo, destruyes, destruye, destruimos, destruís, destruyen.*

▼10 Juego |

Escribir • Hablar • GramActiva

❶ Escoge verbos del recuadro u otros verbos y escribe tres series de acciones en orden lógico, diciendo qué ocurrió primero y qué ocurrió después.

apagar	gritar	rescatar
bajar	investigar	salvar
comenzar (a)	ocurrir	subir
escaparse	quemarse	tratar de

❷ Trabaja con tres estudiantes. Lee la primera frase de una de las series. Los estudiantes tienen que adivinar *(guess)* lo que pasó después. Si la primera persona adivina lo que pasó, gana cinco puntos. Si no puede, le toca el turno a la segunda persona. Si esta persona adivina correctamente, gana tres puntos. Si la tercera persona adivina correctamente, gana sólo un punto. Si nadie adivina correctamente, la persona que escribió la serie gana cinco puntos.

Estrategia

Sequencing of events
Putting events in a sequence helps others to understand what happened. Common expressions used to order events are *primero*, *luego*, and *después*.

Modelo

Primero los bomberos subieron la escalera. Luego entraron por la ventana de la casa.

▶ **Modelo**

A — *Primero los bomberos subieron la escalera. ¿Qué ocurrió luego?*

B — *¿Los bomberos apagaron el incendio?*

A — *No. Lo siento. María, ¿qué ocurrió luego?*

C — *¿Entraron por la ventana?*

A — *Sí. Muy bien. Tres puntos para ti.*

▼11 Y tú, ¿qué dices? |

Escribir • Hablar

1. Para ti, ¿quién es un héroe o una heroína? ¿Cómo es esta persona? ¿Qué hace o hizo?

2. Mira un periódico de tu comunidad. ¿Hay información sobre algún incendio o explosión? Descríbelo.

3. ¿Qué tipo de desastres naturales afecta tu comunidad o región? ¿Qué hacen Uds. para protegerse *(protect yourselves)*?

🌎 Fondo Cultural | El mundo hispano

Los volcanes representan una amenaza *(threat)* para muchas comunidades de América Latina y el Caribe. En el siglo XX, de todas las personas que murieron a causa de erupciones volcánicas, el 76 por ciento murieron en esta región. En los Andes hay mucha actividad volcánica. El volcán Puyehue, en Chile, entró en erupción el 3 de junio de 2011. Las cenizas *(ashes)* llegaron hasta 39,000 pies de altura y afectaron a todo el hemisferio sur. Otros volcanes activos de la región son Tungurahua en Ecuador (2010) y Galeras en Colombia (2010).

• ¿Hay volcanes activos o dormidos cerca de tu comunidad? ¿Qué desastres naturales afectan a tu comunidad de la misma manera *(in the same way)* que la explosión del Puyehue afectó al hemisferio sur? Descríbelos.

Limpiando la ciudad de Bariloche, Argentina, después de la erupción del volcán Puyehue, en Chile

| ▼ **Objectives**

▶ Write about states of being, weather, and time in the past

▶ Exchange information about time and physical and mental states in the past

Gramática

Preterite and imperfect: other uses

Había and *hubo* are forms of *haber* and both mean "there was, there were." *Había* is used to describe a situation that existed in the past, while *hubo* is used to say that an event took place.

Había mucho humo en el apartamento.

Hubo un terremoto ayer a las seis de la mañana.

The preterite and imperfect tenses may both be used in a single sentence.

<table>
<tr><td>Use the imperfect:</td><td>Use the preterite:</td></tr>
<tr><td>• to tell what day or time it was
Eran las cinco de la mañana cuando…</td><td>• when something happened
…empezó a llover.</td></tr>
<tr><td>• to tell what the weather was like
Llovía mucho cuando…</td><td>• for actions completed in the past
…salimos de la fiesta.</td></tr>
<tr><td>• to describe the physical, mental, and emotional states of a person or thing
Mucha gente quería ayudar cuando…</td><td>• to talk about an event
…el incendio destruyó la casa.</td></tr>
</table>

These verbs are often used in the imperfect to describe states of being:

estar (triste, contento, cansado)	pensar
parecer (cansado, mal)	querer
sentirse (bien, enfermo)	saber
tener (calor, frío, hambre, sed, sueño)	

¿Recuerdas?

You already know how to use the imperfect tense together with the preterite to describe a situation that existed when something else happened.

• Nadie **estaba** en la casa cuando los bomberos **entraron**.

Más ayuda   **realidades.com**

 GramActiva Video

 GramActiva Activity

▼**12 ¿Qué hora era?** | |

Hablar

¿Qué hora era cuando estas condiciones ocurrieron?

También se dice . . .

el terremoto = el sismo (muchos países)

4:00 P.M.

▶ **Modelo**

A —¿Qué hora era cuando comenzó la tormenta de nieve?
B —Eran las cuatro de la tarde cuando comenzó.

6:00 P.M.

1.

4:30 P.M.

2.

2:15 P.M.

3.

1:00 P.M.

4.

7:45 P.M.

5.

10:50 P.M.

6.

sus primos, Anita y Pepe

¡FELIZ CUMPLEAÑOS!

sus tíos

Isabel

su mamá

6:30

su papá

su hermana, Alejandra

su abuela

su primo, Federico

▼13 El cumpleaños desastroso | |

Observar • Hablar • Escribir

Los padres de Isabel planearon una fiesta de
sorpresa para su cumpleaños, pero ella llegó tarde.
Con otro(a) estudiante, describan la situación usando
el imperfecto de las expresiones del recuadro.

Modelo

*Era el cumpleaños de Isabel. Cuando ella llegó
a casa, sus parientes ya estaban allí.*

estar dormido	pensar que
estar furioso	querer salir
haber	tener hambre
ir a	tener sed
llegar	tener sueño
llover	**¡Respuesta**
parecer cansado	**personal!**

▼14 Y tú, ¿qué dices? | |

Escribir • Hablar

1. ¿Qué hora era cuando te despertaste hoy?
   ¿Tenías mucho sueño cuando te levantaste?

2. ¿Qué tiempo hacía cuando saliste de casa?
   ¿Alguien estaba todavía en tu casa cuando
   saliste?

3. ¿Qué hora era cuando llegaste a la escuela?
   ¿Ya había muchos estudiantes en la escuela?

4. ¿Cómo estabas cuando comenzaste a
   estudiar o a trabajar en tu primera clase?

Más práctica GO

realidades.com | print

Instant Check	✔	
Guided WB pp. 175–177	✔	✔
Core WB p. 97	✔	✔
Comm. WB pp. 92, 95	✔	✔
Hispanohablantes WB pp. 174–177, 180	✔	

Gramática

The preterite of the verbs *oír*, *leer*, *creer*, and *destruir*

In the preterite forms of *oír*, the *i* changes to *y* in the *Ud./él/ella* and *Uds./ellos/ellas* forms. There is also an accent mark over the *i* in all other forms. Here are the present and preterite forms of *oír*:

Present tense		Preterite tense	
oigo	oímos	oí	oímos
oyes	oís	oíste	oísteis
oye	oyen	oyó	oyeron

Creer and *leer* follow the same pattern in the preterite.

creer		leer	
creí	creímos	leí	leímos
creíste	creísteis	leíste	leísteis
creyó	creyeron	leyó	leyeron

—¿Leíste el artículo sobre el incendio en el periódico?

—No, oí el noticiero en la televisión.

¿Recuerdas?

You know the expression ¡*Oye!* ("Hey!"), which is used to get someone's attention. *Oye* is the affirmative *tú* command form of *oír*. It is formed from the present-tense *Ud. / él / ella* form of the verb.

• *Destruir* is conjugated like *oír*, *creer*, and *leer* in the preterite except that the *tú*, *nosotros*, and *vosotros* forms do not have accent marks.

¿**Destruiste** la carta que le mandó Raúl?

El incendio **destruyó** todos los muebles de la casa.

Más ayuda 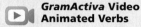 realidades.com

▶ *GramActiva* Video
Animated Verbs

◀)) *Canción de hip hop:*
Un acto heroico

📝 *GramActiva* Activity

▼15 Escucha y escribe | ◀))

Escuchar • Escribir

1 En una hoja de papel, escribe los números del 1 al 4. Vas a oír una conversación sobre un desastre. Mientras la escuchas, escribe las frases.

2 Usa la conversación que escribiste en el Paso 1 y contesta las siguientes preguntas con frases completas.

1. ¿Dónde ocurrió la explosión? ¿Qué destruyó?

2. ¿Quién oyó de la explosión en la radio?

3. ¿Pablo leyó sobre la explosión en la Red o en el periódico?

4. ¿Los dos jóvenes creyeron la noticia fácilmente?

▼16 ¿Lo oíste?

Leer • Escribir

La Reina Sofía de España visitó Guatemala después del huracán. Para saber lo que José y Marcos dicen sobre el evento, completa la conversación con la forma apropiada del verbo *oír*.

José: Hoy **1.** a la locutora del canal 5 decir que la Reina Sofía era muy simpática cuando visitó.

Marcos: Julieta, Liliana y yo también **2.** lo mismo.

José: Recuerdo la visita muy bien. Yo **3.** a muchas personas gritar: "¡Bienvenida!" Mamá y papá estaban con mi tío Juan y **4.** a la reina decir cosas simpáticas.

Marcos: Mi tía Rocío **5.** al presidente cuando le dijo a la Reina que el pueblo guatemalteco la saludaba.

José: Pero, ¿ **6.** tú lo que dijo mi hermanito?

Marcos: Sí, **7.** a tu hermanito cuando dijo que quería mucho a la Reina Sofía. ¡Qué gracioso tu hermanito!

La Reina Sofía de España en Guatemala después del huracán Stan. Es una de las muchas oportunidades que tiene España para mantener un fuerte lazo de unión con las Américas.

▼17 ¿Qué leíste recientemente? | |

Escribir • Hablar

Habla con los estudiantes en tu clase sobre lo que leyeron recientemente.

❶ En una hoja de papel, copia la tabla. En la primera línea, escribe lo que leíste tú, cuándo y cómo era.

❷ Trabaja con tres estudiantes. Pregúntale a un(a) estudiante sobre lo que leyó. Este(a) estudiante contesta y los otros también deben decir lo que leyeron. Deben escribir toda la información en la tabla.

❸ Cada estudiante debe usar la información en la tabla para escribir cinco frases sobre lo que leyeron los miembros del grupo y cómo eran las cosas que leyeron.

Persona	Lo que leyó	Cuándo	Descripción
yo	una revista sobre la moda	la semana pasada	fantástica

▶ **Modelo**

A —*Elena, ¿qué leíste tú?*

B —*Leí una revista sobre la moda la semana pasada. Era fantástica.*

▼18 El terremoto en Popayán |

Leer • Escribir

Completa la descripción de lo que ocurrió en 1983 en Popayán, Colombia, usando las formas apropiadas del pretérito o del imperfecto.

__1.__ *(Ser)* un día de primavera muy bonito en Popayán. __2.__ *(Haber)* muchísimas personas en la ciudad porque __3.__ *(ser)* Semana Santa.[1] Todos __4.__ *(estar)* muy alegres. De repente, __5.__ *(haber)* un terremoto de una magnitud de 5.5 en la Escala Richter que __6.__ *(sacudir)*[2] la ciudad entera.[3] El terremoto __7.__ *(destruir)* el centro histórico de Popayán, donde __8.__ *(haber)* muchos edificios, iglesias y casas de arquitectura colonial. Muchas personas __9.__ *(tratar de)* salir del centro pero no __10.__ *(escaparse)*. Después __11.__ *(haber)* tres incendios a causa del terremoto y una gran parte de la ciudad __12.__ *(quemarse)*. Finalmente, los oficiales de la ciudad __13.__ *(tener)* que ordenar la evacuación de muchas familias. Por lo menos 120 personas se murieron en el desastre y __14.__ *(haber)* más de 1,000 personas heridas.

Una catedral destruida por el terremoto en Popayán, Colombia

[1] Holy Week, the week between Palm Sunday and Easter [2] to shake [3] whole

▼19 Un desastre natural | 💬👥 _____

Hablar

Con otro(a) estudiante, mira el cuadro de Botero, la foto de Popayán y la descripción del terremoto en la Actividad 18. Hablen de lo que ocurrió en Popayán y cómo la descripción, la foto y el cuadro enseñan la historia.

Modelo

En la descripción aprendemos que antes del terremoto había muchas personas en la ciudad . . . .
En la foto vemos que el terremoto destruyó . . . .
En el cuadro de Botero, vemos que eran las tres cuando . . . .

El pintor colombiano Fernando Botero pintó este cuadro, *"Terremoto en Popayán"*, en 1999, 16 años después del terremoto.

Oil on canvas, 173 x 112 c. Museo Botero, Banco de la República de Colombia. Marlborough Gallery.

▼20 En caso de un incendio . . . | 👥 _____

Leer • Hablar

Un hotel de México da información a las personas que pasan tiempo con ellos sobre cómo sobrevivir (*survive*) un incendio que puede ocurrir en el hotel. Lee la información y contesta las preguntas con otro(a) estudiante.

Estrategia

Anticipating text
Many times you can predict the kind of information you will find in a piece of text. What information would you expect to find in your hotel about how to survive a fire? Think about Spanish words that are likely to be used.

CÓMO SOBREVIVIR UN INCENDIO EN EL HOTEL

Cuando entre en el hotel, Ud. debe . . .

- **encontrar las salidas** del hotel.
- **buscar las salidas** y escaleras para incendios en el piso donde está su cuarto.
- **mirar las ventanas** de su cuarto. ¿Se abren? ¿Es posible escaparse por la ventana?

Si el incendio comienza en su cuarto, Ud. debe . . .

080

- **llamar** inmediatamente a la operadora de teléfono.
- **tratar de apagarlo.** Si no lo puede hacer, debe salir de su cuarto, cerrar la puerta y sonar[1] la alarma.

Si Ud. está en su cuarto y oye la alarma, debe . . .

- **tocar[2] la puerta** de su cuarto. Si no está caliente,[3] la puede abrir muy despacio, salir y cerrar la puerta. Si la puerta está caliente, no debe abrirla. Si es posible, debe salir por la ventana.

- **caminar a la salida** que está más cerca. Si hay mucho humo, debe gatear[4] por el corredor.[5] Si el humo está denso en los pisos de abajo, debe subir a un piso más alto o al techo.[6] Es importante recordar que NUNCA se debe usar el elevador cuando hay un incendio.

Ud. debe recordar que muy pocas personas se queman en los incendios. La mayoría[7] de los problemas ocurren a causa del humo y del pánico. El pánico es usualmente el resultado de no saber qué hacer.

[1]sound [2]touch [3]hot [4]crawl [5]hallway [6]roof [7]majority

1. ¿Qué debes hacer primero cuando entras en el hotel?

2. ¿Debes usar el elevador o las escaleras en caso de un incendio?

3. ¿Cuáles son las cosas más importantes que debes hacer si hay un incendio en tu cuarto?

4. ¿Qué debes hacer si estás en tu cuarto y oyes la alarma?

5. ¿Cuándo es importante gatear por el corredor o por el cuarto?

6. ¿Cuáles son las causas de la mayoría de las muertes en un incendio?

▼21 Y tú, ¿qué dices? | _____

Escribir • Hablar

¿Oíste o leíste algo recientemente sobre un incendio, una explosión o un desastre natural? Escribe un párrafo para describirlo.

- ¿Cómo lo oíste o leíste?
- ¿Qué día / hora era cuando ocurrió / comenzó?
- ¿Dónde estabas tú cuando ocurrió?
- ¿Había personas allí cuando ocurrió?
- ¿Destruyó muchos edificios y otras cosas?
- ¿Alguien trató de ayudar en la situación?

Accent marks to separate diphthongs

Remember that a single syllable called a diphthong occurs when *i* or *u* appear together or in combination with *a, e,* or *o.* Listen to and say these words:

ca**u**sa	val**ie**nte	**oi**go
destr**ui**r	m**ue**rto	hac**ia**

We use a written accent when the vowels that form what would otherwise be a diphthong need to be pronounced separately. Listen to and say these words:

o**í**	le**í**ste	cre**í**mos
sab**í**a	pa**í**s	env**í**o

Refrán

Explica lo que quiere decir este refrán.

Consejo* no pedido, consejo mal oído.

*advice

▼22 Las tempestades

Pensar • Leer • Escribir • Hablar

Conexiones | La geografía

Hay tempestades[1] violentas de lluvia y vientos fuertes en varias regiones del mundo. Estas tempestades salen de un sistema de baja presión que se encuentra encima de aguas tropicales donde hay una tempestad y vientos fuertes en forma de torbellino.[2] Las tempestades con vientos de más de 39 millas por hora se llaman tormentas tropicales. Cuando los vientos superan[3] 74 millas por hora, se llaman huracán, tifón o ciclón, según la región geográfica.

[1]storms [2]whirlwind [3]exceed

1. ¿En qué parte del mundo hay huracanes? ¿Dónde hay tifones y ciclones? ¿Qué tienen en común estas regiones?

2. ¿En qué región geográfica ocurren los huracanes en los Estados Unidos? ¿Qué estados son afectados? Compara su posición geográfica con la de las tempestades en el mapa.

▼23 Un bombero valiente | 👥

Observar • Hablar • Escribir

Mira la serie de dibujos. Trabaja con otro(a) estudiante para hablar de esta situación.

❶ Primero hagan una lista de todas las partes del cuento que van a escribir usando el imperfecto. Luego hagan una lista de las acciones que van a escribir usando el pretérito.

imperfecto	pretérito
el gatito estaba en el árbol	los bomberos llegaron en su camión

❷ Escriban lo que ocurrió. Usen su imaginación e incluyan detalles adicionales para hacer su cuento más interesante.

Más práctica	GO

realidades.com	print
Instant Check	✔	
Guided WB p. 178	✔	✔
Core WB pp. 98–99	✔	✔
Comm. WB pp. 93, 96, 247	✔	✔
Hispanohablantes WB		
pp. 178–179, 181		✔

El español en la comunidad

Hay muchas oportunidades para ayudar a los demás en tu comunidad o en otros países. Un año después del huracán Stan, muchas personas que habían perdido *(had lost)* sus casas y todas sus cosas seguían sin hogar *(home)*. MayaWorks, un grupo sin fines de lucro *(nonprofit)* en Chicago que ayuda a artesanos indígenas en Guatemala a vender sus productos en el mercado estadounidense, decidió ayudar. Les compró tierra *(land)* a diez familias indígenas y así éstas pudieron construir nuevas casas y continuar con sus artesanías.

• ¿Conoces a alguien que haya ayudado *(has helped)* en un esfuerzo humanitario? ¿Hay oportunidades en tu comunidad para ayudar a personas después de algún desastre?

Lectura 🌐

▼ **Objectives**

▶ Read about an earthquake in Chile
▶ Use prior knowledge to predict reading content
▶ Compare emergency planning in Chilean schools with that of your school

Estrategia

Using prior knowledge
Think about articles you've read about earthquakes and natural disasters. Make a list of four pieces of information you might find. After you've read the article below, refer to your list to see if the information was there.

Después del terremoto, Valdivia, Chile

Desastre en Valdivia, Chile

Tres desastres:
Dos terremotos y después un tsunami

VALDIVIA, Chile A las seis y dos minutos de la mañana, el 21 de mayo de 1960, una gran parte del país sintió el primer terremoto. El próximo día, el 22 de mayo a las tres y diez de la tarde, otro terremoto más intenso, con epicentro cerca de la ciudad de Valdivia, ocurrió. El segundo y más famoso de los terremotos registró un récord de 9.5 en la Escala Richter. Simplemente fue el terremoto de más intensidad jamás[1] registrado.

- Aproximadamente 2,000 personas murieron (de 4,000 a 5,000 en toda la región); 3,000 resultaron heridas y 2,000,000 perdieron[2] sus hogares.[3]

- Los ríos cambiaron[4] su curso. Nuevos lagos nacieron. Las montañas se movieron. La geografía cambió visiblemente.

LA ESCALA RICHTER	
Representa la energía sísmica liberada en cada terremoto y se basa en el registro sismográfico.	
MAGNITUD EN LA ESCALA RICHTER	EFECTOS DEL TERREMOTO
Menos de 3.5	Generalmente no se siente, pero es registrado.
3.5–5.4	A menudo se siente, pero sólo causa daños[5] menores.
5.5–6.0	Ocasiona daños a edificios.
6.1–6.9	Puede ocasionar daños graves en áreas donde vive mucha gente.
7.0–7.9	Terremoto mayor. Causa graves daños.
8 o mayor	Gran terremoto. Destrucción total de comunidades cercanas.

[1]ever [2]lost [3]homes [4]changed [5]damages

Revisando los daños, Valdivia, Chile

Unos minutos después del desastroso terremoto, llegó un tsunami que destruyó lo poco que quedaba en la ciudad y en las pequeñas comunidades. La gran ola[6] de agua se levantó destruyendo a su paso casas, animales, puentes, botes y, por supuesto, muchas vidas humanas. Algunos barcos fueron a quedar a kilómetros del mar, río arriba. Como consecuencia del sismo, se originaron tsunamis que llegaron a las costas del Japón, Hawai, las Islas Filipinas y la costa oeste de los Estados Unidos.

EL TSUNAMI

Un tsunami es una ola o serie de olas de agua producida después de ser empujada[7] violentamente. Los terremotos pueden causar tsunamis. Estos tsunamis ocurren de 10 a 20 minutos después del terremoto. El 26 de diciembre de 2004, un terremoto de magnitud 9.0, en Sumatra, causó un tsunami en Indonesia y Tailandia. La destrucción fue terrible. Hubo más de 250,000 víctimas.

¿Qué debes hacer durante un terremoto?

Dentro de un edificio

- Mantener la calma y calmar a los demás
- Mantenerse lejos de ventanas, cristales, cuadros, chimeneas y objetos que puedan caerse[8]
- Protegerse[9] debajo de los dinteles de las puertas[10] o de algún mueble sólido, como mesas, escritorios o camas; cualquier protección es mejor que ninguna
- No utilizar los elevadores

Fuera de un edificio

- Mantenerse lejos de los edificios altos, postes de energía eléctrica y otros objetos que puedan derrumbarse[11]
- Ir a un lugar abierto

En un coche

- Parar el coche y quedarse dentro del vehículo, lejos de puentes, postes de energía eléctrica y edificios dañados o zonas de desprendimientos[12]

---

[6]wave   [7]pushed   [8]fall   [9]Protect yourself   [10]door jams   [11]collapse   [12]landslides

¿Comprendiste?

1. Pon en orden de ocurrencia los tres desastres que sufrió Valdivia, Chile.
2. ¿Qué importancia tiene el segundo terremoto en los estudios sismográficos?
3. Si se registra un terremoto de 6.5 en la Escala Richter, ¿qué daños van a ocurrir?
4. ¿Cuál es una causa de los tsunamis?
5. ¿Qué debes hacer si ocurre un terremoto y estás en un coche?

Más práctica   GO

realidades.com | print

Guided WB p. 179	✔	✔
Comm. WB pp. 97, 248	✔	✔
Hispanohablantes WB pp. 182–183	✔	
Cultural Reading Activity	✔	

▼ Fondo Cultural | Chile

En caso de terremoto En Chile hay un Plan Integral de Seguridad Escolar para responder ante emergencias como terremotos, incendios, inundaciones o accidentes. Este plan nacional se aplica a todas las escuelas del país. Cada escuela tiene que crear un plan que incluye a los profesores, estudiantes y trabajadores del colegio. También debe incorporar a personal especializado en emergencias como los bomberos, la Guardia Civil y la Cruz Roja. Este plan se implementó durante el terremoto del 27 de febrero del 2010, que tuvo una magnitud de 8.8.

- Piensa en tu escuela. ¿Hay un plan para emergencias? ¿Qué hacen en caso de incendios, huracanes o tornados?

La cultura en vivo 🌎

Las leyendas

Las leyendas muchas veces personifican a los fenómenos naturales o tratan de resolver misterios de fenómenos naturales. De tal manera hay muchos volcanes en México, América Central y América del Sur que llevan nombres y características humanas. Los habitantes que vivían a su alrededor contaban leyendas para explicar el origen de estos volcanes y la relación que éstos tenían con el pueblo[1].

En Chile, el volcán Parinacota lanza humo cuando trata de comunicarse con Pomerape. Según la leyenda, los novios volcanes lloran y hablan con fuego y ceniza.

También hay leyendas universales que se cuentan en muchos lugares del mundo. Por ejemplo, en México hay una famosa leyenda sobre los volcanes Popocatépetl e Iztaccíhuatl que dice que eran dos enamorados, pero su amor fue prohibido. La misma leyenda también existe en Chile sobre los volcanes Parinacota y Pomerape. Según la leyenda había un príncipe y una princesa de diferentes tribus y se enamoraron. Pero su matrimonio fue prohibido y para evitar su unión, las dos tribus mataron a los novios. Esto entristeció[2] a la Naturaleza[3] que, como castigo[4], causó una inundación que destruyó a los dos pueblos. De la inundación se formaron dos lagos, el Chungará y el Cota-Cotani. Los dos novios fueron transformados en dos hermosos volcanes cercanos, Parinacota y Pomerape. Así, siempre están juntos.

¡Compruébalo! Escoge algún lugar cerca de tu comunidad como una montaña, un lago o una formación de rocas. Escribe un cuento que explica el origen de este lugar.

[1]people, village [2]saddened [3]Nature [4]punishment

Presentación oral

Y ahora, un reportaje especial . . .

Task
You are the anchor for a local television station and your partner is a reporter at the scene of a fire. You will interview him or her about what happened.

❶ Prepare You will role-play this conversation with a partner. Be sure to prepare for both roles. Here's how to prepare:

Locutor(a): Make a list of questions to ask the reporter, such as "who," "what," "when," "where," and "why." You might ask how many people were injured or died.

Reportero(a): Be prepared to report on the fire. Think of the information you'll provide based on the anchor's questions.

❷ Practice Work in groups of four, with two reporters and two news anchors. Practice different questions and different responses. Here's how you might start the report:

Locutor(a): *Buenos días, Juan. ¿Qué pasó?*

Reportero(a): *Hubo un incendio en un edificio de apartamentos. Cinco personas se murieron y había . . .*

Continue the conversation using your notes. Be sure to speak clearly and make your interview sound natural.

❸ Present You will be paired with another student, and your teacher will tell you which role to play. The news anchor begins the conversation. Listen to your partner's questions or responses and keep the report going.

❹ Evaluation The following rubric will be used to grade your presentation.

Estrategia

Speaking from notes
When doing an interview or reporting back as a news reporter, it is important to have thought through important questions or have notes to provide accurate answers.

Rubric	Score 1	Score 3	Score 5
Completeness of your task	You discuss up to two facts about the event.	You discuss up to four facts about the event.	You discuss six or more facts about the event.
How easily you are understood	You are difficult to understand and have many grammatical errors.	You are fairly easy to understand and have occasional grammatical errors.	You are easy to understand and have very few grammatical errors.
Ability to keep conversation going	You do not provide a conversational response or follow-up to what your partner says.	You provide frequent responses or follow-ups to what your partner says.	You always respond to your partner, listen and ask follow-up questions or volunteer additional information.

En busca de la verdad

Episodio 5

Antes de ver el video

"Según la leyenda del Callejón del Beso, ella vivía en una casa con balcón que estaba tan cerca que podían besarse".

"¡Amigo, qué coincidencia!"

Nota cultural Este callejón es famoso por ser tan estrecho que una persona, asomada a la ventana de un lado, puede tocar con la mano la pared de enfrente. También es famoso por la leyenda de una bella señorita que se enamoró de un joven. Al padre de ella no le gustó nada y prohibió que su hija lo viera. Pero ella no lo obedeció y siguió viendo al joven. Un día el padre los vio besándose, el joven desde la ventana de un lado y su hija desde la otra. Se puso furioso y mató a su hija con una daga *(dagger)*. El joven le dio a su enamorada el último beso en la mano, cada vez más fría. Por eso se llama El Callejón del Beso.

Resumen del episodio

Julio invita a Linda a comer. Luego llega Roberto y los tres van a pasear por Guanajuato. Van al Callejón del Beso. Al día siguiente, Roberto empieza a seguir la pista que tiene.

Palabras para comprender

amable kind

un poco antes a little earlier

dar una vuelta take a tour

la crema de elote corn soup

el pozole thick soup made with corn, meat, and vegetables

las enchiladas mineras enchiladas unique to Guanajuato, made with cheese and onion

las flautas de pollo fried tortilla dish

averiguar find out about

Después de ver el video

¿Comprendiste?

A. ¿Quién dijo cada una de las siguientes frases?
(Carmen/Julio/Linda/Roberto)

1. "Pues, en la Plaza San Fernando hay un buen café, la Oreja de Van Gogh".

2. "Oye, ¿te gustaría dar una vuelta por Guanajuato?"

3. "Quiero descansar hoy. Tengo que hacer varias llamadas".

4. "Ay, no sé qué pedir. Todo parece delicioso".

5. "La comida aquí es muy buena. Aquí están los platos del día".

6. "Mejor . . . así tengo dos guías".

7. "¿Por qué no vamos al Callejón del Beso?"

B. Trabaja con otro(a) estudiante para escribir la conversación entre Linda y Julio. Luego presenten su conversación a la clase.

Más práctica (GO)

realidades.com | print

Actividades ✔

Repaso del capítulo

Vocabulario y gramática

to talk about natural disasters and weather extremes

el huracán, *pl.* los huracanes	hurricane
la inundación, *pl.* las inundaciones	flood
llover *(o →ue)*	to rain
la lluvia	rain
nevar *(e →ie)*	to snow
el terremoto	earthquake
la tormenta	storm

to discuss the news

el artículo	article
investigar	to investigate
el locutor, la locutora	announcer
el noticiero	newscast
ocurrir	to occur
el reportero, la reportera	reporter
tratar de	to try to

to talk about fires

apagar	to put out (fire)
bajar	to go down
el bombero, la bombera	firefighter
comenzar *(e →ie)*	to start
destruir *(i →y)*	to destroy
dormido, -a	asleep
el edificio de apartamentos	apartment building
la escalera	ladder
escaparse	to escape
esconder(se)	to hide (oneself)
la explosión, *pl.* las explosiones	explosion
el humo	smoke
el incendio	fire
los muebles	furniture
muerto, -a	dead
el paramédico, la paramédica	paramedic
quemar(se)	to burn (oneself), to burn up
se murieron	they died
subir	to go up

to discuss rescues

herido, -a	injured
el herido, la herida	injured person
el héroe	hero
la heroína	heroine
rescatar	to rescue
salvar	to save
valiente	brave
la vida	life
vivo, -a	living, alive

to tell a story

a causa de	because of
afortunadamente	fortunately
asustado, -a	frightened
la causa	cause
de prisa	in a hurry
de repente	suddenly
gritar	to scream
hubo	there was
llamar (por teléfono)	to call (on the phone)
oír	to hear
sin duda	without a doubt
¡Socorro!	Help!

present of *oír*

oigo	oímos
oyes	oís
oye	oyen

preterite of *oír*

oí	oímos
oíste	oísteis
oyó	oyeron

preterite of *creer*

creí	creímos
creíste	creísteis
creyó	creyeron

preterite of *leer*

leí	leímos
leíste	leísteis
leyó	leyeron

preterite of *destruir*

destruí	destruimos
destruiste	destruisteis
destruyó	destruyeron

For *Vocabulario adicional,* see pp. 498–499.

Más repaso GO **realidades.com | print**

Instant Check ✔
Puzzles ✔
Core WB pp. 100–101 ✔
Comm. WB p. 249 ✔ ✔

Preparación para el examen

| On the exam you will be asked to . . . | Here are practice tasks similar to those you will find on the exam . . . | For review go to your print or digital textbook . . . |

Interpretive

1 Escuchar Listen and understand as someone talks about her experience during a tragic event

Listen as a talk-show host interviews a young woman who recently escaped from a dangerous situation. See if you can understand: (a) what happened; (b) what time it was; (c) what she was doing at the time; and (d) who she considered to be the hero of the day.

pp. 240–243 *Vocabulario en contexto*
p. 244 Actividad 5
p. 250 Actividad 15

Interpersonal

2 Hablar Talk about and describe how things were during certain times of the day

As part of your school's community service project, you visit an elderly man in an assisted living center. He is from Mexico and speaks little English, but he enjoys hearing about your day. Tell him what the weather was like when you woke up, how you were feeling, and what time it was when you left for school.

p. 248 Actividad 12
p. 249 Actividades 13–14

Interpretive

3 Leer Read and understand newspaper headlines

Even though you may not be able to understand an entire newspaper article in Spanish, you can get the idea by reading headlines. Read the following headline and see if you can determine if it refers to: (a) a fire; (b) a flood; or (c) an explosion.

Los bomberos salvaron a 200 personas anoche; más de 100 casas dañadas por el agua.

p. 241 *Vocabulario en contexto*
p. 244 Actividad 4
p. 245 Actividad 6
p. 252 Actividad 18
pp. 256–257 *Lectura*

Presentational

4 Escribir Write about a "disaster movie"

Write a few sentences about your favorite or least favorite "disaster movie." Be sure to mention what type of disaster it was, where it took place, what people were doing before the disaster struck, and any other details that would help your classmates guess which movie it was.

p. 246 Actividad 9
p. 247 Actividad 11
p. 250 Actividad 15
p. 253 Actividad 21

Cultures

5 Pensar Demonstrate an understanding of volcano names and legends that are related to them

Your friend is going sight-seeing in Chile. While there, she is going to visit the Parinacota and Pomerape volcanoes. What can you tell her about the legend behind these volcanoes? Do you know any legends about places in your community?

p. 258 *La cultura en vivo*

▼ **Chapter Objectives**

Communication

By the end of this chapter you will be able to:

- Listen and read about accidents
- Talk and write about injuries and medical treatments
- Exchange information about how someone was injured

Culture

You will also be able to:

- Understand emergency medical services in Spanish-speaking countries
- Compare health services in Spain, Colombia, and your community

You will demonstrate what you know and can do:

- Presentación escrita, p. 285
- Preparación para el examen, p. 289

You will use:

Vocabulary

- Medical treatments
- Accidents
- Parts of the body

Grammar

- Irregular preterites: *venir, poner, decir,* and *traer*
- Imperfect progressive and preterite

Exploración del mundo hispano

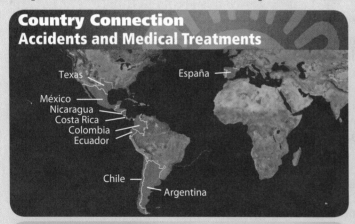

Country Connection
Accidents and Medical Treatments

Texas
España
México
Nicaragua
Costa Rica
Colombia
Ecuador
Chile
Argentina

realidades.com **GO**

 Reference Atlas

 Videocultura y actividad

 Mapa global interactivo

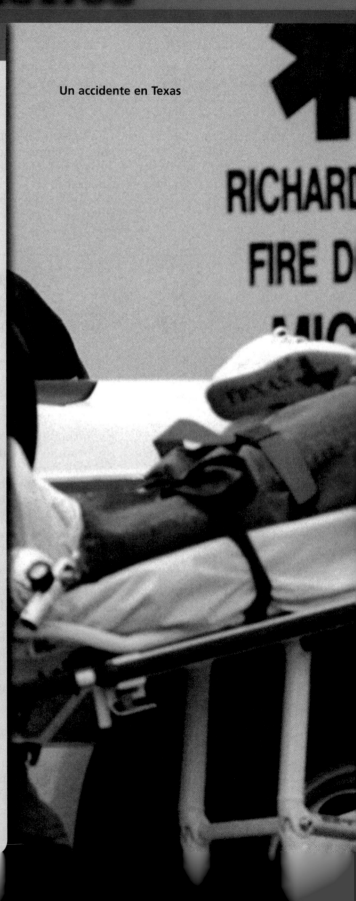

Un accidente en Texas

RICHARD

FIRE D

MI

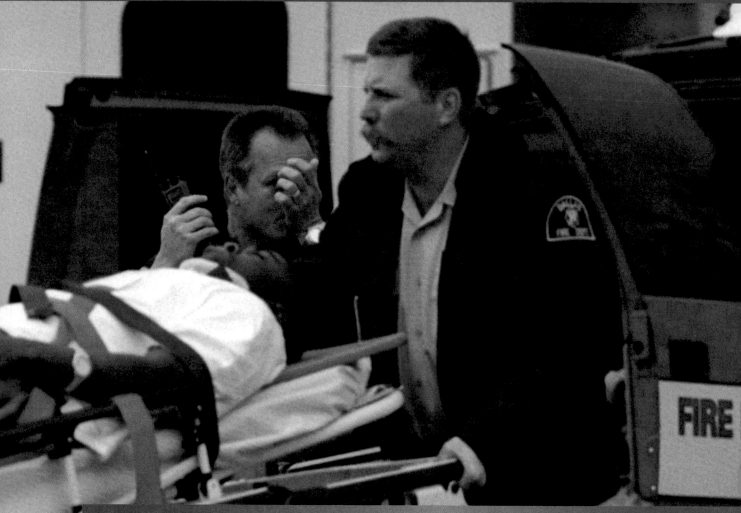

Arte y cultura | México

Diego Rivera (1886–1957) fue uno de los mejores artistas del siglo XX. Nació en Guanajuato, México, y cuando era niño se mudó *(he moved)* con su familia a la Ciudad de México. Rivera pintó muchos murales de temas sociales. Este mural representa el estado de los servicios médicos de México en esa época. Nota las expresiones de las caras de las personas esperando al médico.

• ¿Qué piensas de las expresiones de las personas en este mural? ¿Por qué crees que tienen esas expresiones?

"La medicina antigua y la moderna (1953)", Diego Rivera ▲

Fresco, approx. 7.4 x 10.8 m. Hospital de la Raza, Mexico City, D.F., Mexico. Photo: Art Resource, NY. © 2009 Banco de México Diego Rivera & Frida Kahlo Museums Trust, México, D.F./Artists Rights Society (ARS).

▼ **Objectives**

Read, listen to, and understand information about
▶ parts of the body
▶ accidents
▶ what happens in an emergency room

Vocabulario en contexto

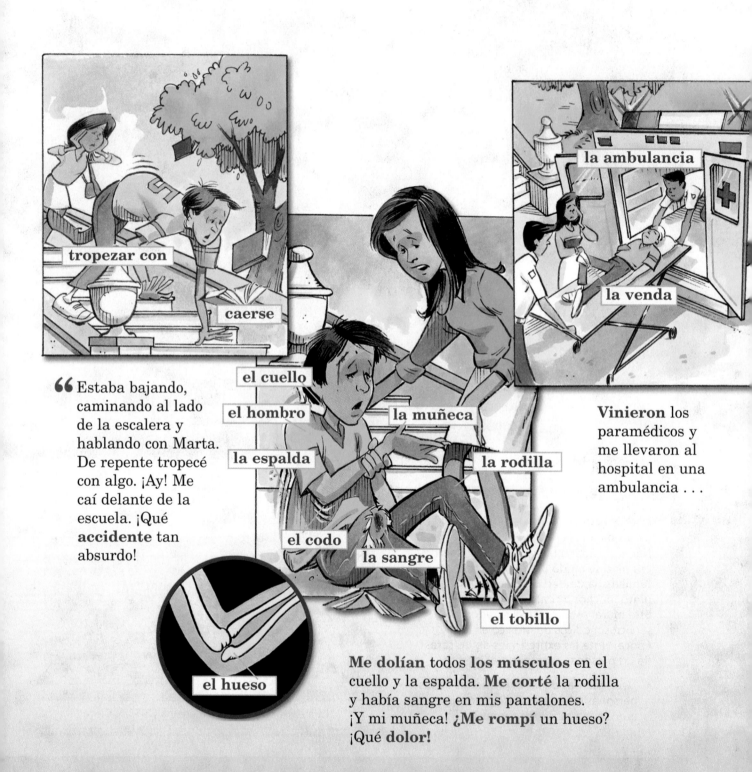

tropezar con

caerse

la ambulancia

la venda

el cuello

el hombro

la muñeca

la espalda

la rodilla

el codo

la sangre

el tobillo

el hueso

❝ Estaba bajando, caminando al lado de la escalera y hablando con Marta. De repente tropecé con algo. ¡Ay! Me caí delante de la escuela. ¡Qué **accidente** tan absurdo!

Vinieron los paramédicos y me llevaron al hospital en una ambulancia . . .

Me dolían todos **los músculos** en el cuello y la espalda. **Me corté** la rodilla y había sangre en mis pantalones. ¡Y mi muñeca! ¿**Me rompí** un hueso? ¡Qué **dolor**!

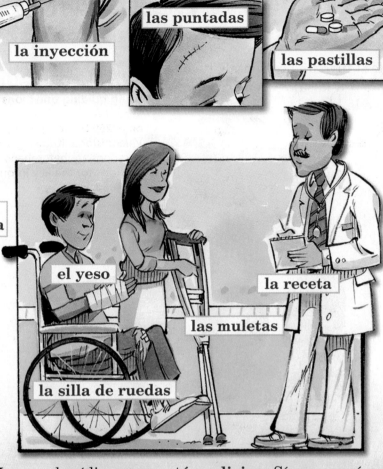

la inyección

las puntadas

las pastillas

SALA DE EMERGENCIA

examinar

la radiografía

el enfermero

la enfermera

sacar una radiografía

dar puntadas

poner una inyección

el yeso

las muletas

la receta

la silla de ruedas

Cuando entré en **la sala de emergencia,** el enfermero sacó una radiografía de mi muñeca. La enfermera me **puso** una inyección y el médico me dio puntadas.

Luego, el médico me **recetó medicina.** Sí, me rompí un hueso en la muñeca y ahora necesito llevar un yeso por unas seis semanas. Si **me siento** muy mal, el médico me dijo que puedo tomar una pastilla cada ocho horas. ¡Qué día horrible! 𝟿𝟿

▼1 ¡Acción! | 🔊

Escuchar

Escucha estas frases sobre varias partes del cuerpo y problemas médicos. Representa (*Act out*) la acción para indicar que comprendiste la frase.

▼2 La sala de emergencia | 🔊

Escuchar

Escucha las frases. Si la frase que escuchas es lógica, señala con el pulgar hacia arriba. Si la frase no es lógica, señala con el pulgar hacia abajo.

Más práctica	GO	
realidades.com	print	
Instant Check	✔	
Guided WB pp. 181–186	✔	✔
Core WB pp. 102–103	✔	✔
Comm. WB p. 103	✔	✔
Hispanohablantes WB p. 192		✔

¡El pobrecito soy yo!

Raúl tuvo un accidente y tuvo que ir a la sala de emergencia. Lee la historia para saber qué le pasó.

Estrategia

Using guiding questions
Read the comprehension questions on p. 269 before starting the *Videohistoria*. Knowing what the questions are beforehand can help you look for the key information as you read.

1

Gloria: ¡Raúl! ¿Qué te pasó?
Raúl: Pues, tuve un accidente anoche.
Gloria: Dime todo.

Gloria

Tomás

Raúl

5

Raúl: Me sentía muy mal y me dolía mucho la muñeca. Mamá y papá me **pusieron** una venda en la muñeca y me llevaron al hospital.

6

Raúl: Entramos en la sala de emergencia. Me **trajeron** una silla de ruedas. Luego me dieron cinco puntadas. Me **dijeron** que no tenía el brazo **roto.**

7

Raúl: El médico me recetó estas pastillas para el dolor.
Gloria: ¡Qué lástima! ¿Ves, Raúl? ¡No debes despertarte tan temprano!
Raúl: Gracias.

Raúl: Estaba durmiendo cuando de repente oí el despertador. Eran las tres. Traté de despertar a Tomás, pero no se despertó. No **se movió.** Tuve que apagar el despertador. Me levanté y empecé a caminar. Estaba muy oscuro.

Raúl: Tropecé con algo y **me torcí** el tobillo.

Raúl: Me caí al suelo. **Choqué con** la mesa y **me lastimé** el brazo. Me corté la muñeca.

Mamá: ¡Pobre Tomás! ¡Nos fuimos al hospital tan de prisa que lo dejamos aquí, solo!

Raúl: ¿Tomás? ¡El **pobrecito** soy yo!

▼3 ¿Comprendiste?

Escribir • Hablar

1. ¿Qué le pregunta Gloria cuando ve a Raúl?
2. ¿Qué oyó Raúl mientras dormía? ¿Qué hizo? ¿Qué hizo Tomás?
3. ¿Qué le pasó luego a Raúl?
4. ¿Cómo se sentía Raúl? ¿Qué le dolía?
5. ¿Qué hicieron los padres de Raúl?
6. ¿Qué le hicieron a Raúl en el hospital?
7. ¿Qué le dio el médico a Raúl? ¿Por qué?

Más práctica	GO

realidades.com | print

Instant Check	✔	
Guided WB pp. 187–190	✔	✔
Core WB pp. 104–105	✔	✔
Comm. WB pp. 98–99, 100, 101	✔	✔
Hispanohablantes **WB** p. 193		✔

| ▼ **Objectives**

▸ Talk about accidents and medical care
▸ Discuss injuries
▸ Listen to descriptions of emergency room visits
▸ Write about injuries and medical treatments

Vocabulario en uso

▼4 En la sala de emergencia

Leer • Escribir

Ana María quiere ser médica. Lee la descripción de su visita a la sala de emergencia. Escoge y escribe la palabra correcta para decir lo que pasó allí.

> **También se dice . . .**
>
> **la radiografía** = los rayos X *(muchos países)*
>
> **las puntadas** = los puntos *(muchos países)*
>
> **dar puntadas** = hacer puntadas, dar puntos *(muchos países)*
>
> **sala de emergencia** = sala de urgencias *(muchos países)*

Ayer visité la sala de emergencia porque algún día quiero ser médica. Ayudé a una **1.** *(receta / enfermera)* todo el día. Vi muchas cosas muy interesantes. Una chica **2.** *(se torció / tropezó)* la rodilla esquiando, y por eso le trajeron unas **3.** *(muletas / puntadas)*. El médico la **4.** *(examinó / chocó)* y le recetó **5.** *(pastillas / muletas)* para el dolor. Otra persona **6.** *(chocó / se rompió)* el tobillo y le sacaron unas **7.** *(radiografías / recetas)* de los huesos. Después le pusieron un **8.** *(cuello / yeso)* porque tenía el hueso **9.** *(roto /*

pobrecito). Unos paramédicos **10.** *(vinieron / dijeron)* a la sala de emergencia en una **11.** *(ambulancia / silla de ruedas)* con un señor que tuvo un accidente de coche. **12.** *(Trajeron / Dijeron)* que tenían que hacerle una operación de emergencia porque estaba perdiendo *(losing)* mucha **13.** *(medicina / sangre)*. A veces, durante mi visita a la sala de emergencia, tenía miedo de todo lo que estaba pasando, pero todavía quiero ser médica para ayudar a la gente.

▼5 Escucha y escribe | 🔊

Escuchar • Escribir

Escucha lo que dicen unas personas que fueron a la sala de emergencia ayer. En una hoja de papel, escribe los números del 1 al 6. Escribe lo que escuchas. Vas a usar las frases para la Actividad 6.

▼6 Los accidentes | 👥

Dibujar • Hablar

Dibuja una de las situaciones de las Actividades 4 ó 5. Muéstrales *(Show)* tu dibujo a otros(as) dos estudiantes. Traten de usar el máximo número de palabras nuevas para describir lo que les pasó a las personas que ven en los dibujos de sus compañeros(as).

SALA DE EMERGENCIA

▼7 Juego | 👥 | ♻

Cantar • Hablar

Tu profesor(a) va a enseñarles una canción infantil que se usa para practicar los nombres de las partes del cuerpo.

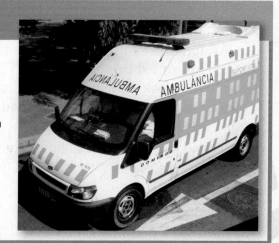

CABEZA, HOMBROS, RODILLAS, PIES
RODILLAS, PIES
RODILLAS, PIES
CABEZA, HOMBROS, RODILLAS, PIES
OJOS, OREJAS, BOCA, NARIZ

① Todos van a levantarse y señalar las partes del cuerpo mientras cantan.

② Pueden cantar la canción otra vez usando diferentes partes del cuerpo. Comiencen con *Espalda, cuello, tobillos, pies* y terminen con *Codos, muñecas, brazos, nariz.*

▼8 En el hospital | 👥

Escribir • Hablar

Piensa en algunas personas que conoces que tuvieron que ir al hospital.

① Escribe cuánto tiempo estuvieron en el hospital. Luego mira los dibujos y escribe una frase para cada uno para decir lo que le hicieron a cada persona.

Modelo

poner

Mi hermano Rafael estuvo en el hospital por tres días. Le pusieron una inyección.

1. dar

2. llevar

3. recetar

4. sacar

5. poner

② Habla con otro(a) estudiante. Describan lo que les hicieron a las personas que Uds. conocen. Escribe cuatro frases para comparar lo que les hicieron.

Modelo

Mi hermano Rafael y el amigo de Carlota estuvieron en el hospital. No les pusieron sangre, pero sí les sacaron radiografías a los dos.

▼ Fondo Cultural | España

La Ambulancia Azul es un servicio de ambulancias en España. Tiene tres niveles *(levels)* de servicio: SVA (Soporte Vital Avanzado) para pacientes en condiciones urgentes; SVB (Soporte Vital Básico) para enfermos que necesitan transporte en ambulancia, pero que no necesitan atención médica urgente; y Colectivo, una ambulancia que comparten varios pacientes.

• ¿Por qué crees que la Ambulancia Azul ofrece tres niveles de servicio? Compara este sistema al servicio de ambulancias en tu comunidad.

9 ¿Por qué no corriste?

Hablar

No hiciste varias actividades la semana pasada porque te dolían diferentes partes del cuerpo. Habla de tus dolores con otro(a) estudiante.

¿Recuerdas?

The imperfect tense is used to describe feelings and ongoing conditions in the past. The preterite expresses the actions that did or did not happen.

▶ Modelo

A —¿Por qué no <u>corriste ayer por la tarde</u>? ¿No te sentías bien?

B —No <u>corrí</u> porque me dolía <u>el tobillo</u>.

correr / ayer
por la tarde

Estudiante A

1. jugar al tenis / el fin de semana pasado
2. esquiar / el sábado pasado
3. hacer gimnasia / ayer
4. levantar pesas / esta mañana
5. patinar / anoche
6. moverse de la cama / el domingo pasado
7. jugar al béisbol / la semana pasada

Estudiante B

1. 2. 3. 4.

5. 6. 7.

▼ Exploración del lenguaje

False cognates

Cognates are words that look alike in both English and Spanish and have the same meaning:

  bank → banco   **photo** → foto

But not all words that look alike in Spanish and English mean the same thing. Certain words are called **false cognates.** These are words that look alike but have different meanings. You have already learned some false cognates. You know that:

  parientes means "relatives," not "parents"
  recordar means "to remember," not "to record"

¡Compruébalo! Complete these sentences about other false cognates you already know:

1. **sopa** means ____, not ____
2. **collar** means ____, not ____
3. **librería** means ____, not ____
4. **carpeta** means ____, not ____
5. **vaso** means ____, not ____

▼10 ¿Cuánto tiempo hace . . . ?

Hablar

Hace mucho tiempo que no ves a un(a) amigo(a) y no sabías que tuvo un accidente. Habla con otro(a) estudiante de lo que le pasó.

tres días

Modelo

A —*Oye, ¿cuánto tiempo hace que <u>estás en el hospital</u>?*

B —*Hace <u>tres días</u>. <u>Me rompí la pierna</u>.*

A —*¡Pobrecita! ¿Qué te pasó?*

B —*Me caí cuando estaba <u>esquiando</u>.*

A —*¡Qué lástima!*

Estudiante A	
estar en	tener
usar	llevar

Estudiante B	
romperse	
torcerse	**¡Respuesta personal!**
lastimarse	
cortarse	

1. seis días

2. cuatro días

3. dos semanas

4. una semana

▼11 Y tú, ¿qué dices?

Escribir • Hablar

1. ¿Te gustaría ser médico(a) o enfermero(a)? ¿Te pone nervioso(a) ver sangre o huesos rotos? ¿Cómo te sientes cuando un(a) enfermero(a) te pone una inyección?

2. Cuando tienes dolor de cabeza, de estómago o de otra parte del cuerpo, ¿qué haces para sentirte mejor?

3. ¿A veces te caes* cuando practicas un deporte u otra actividad? ¿Qué te pasa cuando te caes?

*In the present tense, *caerse* is conjugated like a regular *-er* verb, except in the *yo* form: *me caigo.*

Una médica con una paciente, en México

Gramática

Irregular preterites: *venir, poner, decir,* and *traer*

The verbs *venir, poner, decir,* and *traer* follow a pattern in the preterite that is similar to that of *estar, poder,* and *tener.* All these verbs have irregular stems and use the same unaccented endings.

Infinitive	Stem
decir	dij-
estar	estuv-
poder	pud-
poner	pus-
tener	tuv-
traer	traj-
venir	vin-

Irregular preterite endings	
-e	-imos
-iste	-isteis
-o	-ieron / -eron

puse	pusimos
pusiste	pusisteis
puso	pusieron

Note that verbs like *decir* and *traer,* whose irregular stems end in *j,* drop the *i* in the *Uds./ellos/ellas* form and add only *-eron.*

Me **trajeron** una silla de ruedas y me **dijeron** que no debía tratar de caminar.

Más ayuda | **realidades.com**

▶ *GramActiva* **Video**
Tutorial: Irregular preterite forms

✎ *GramActiva* **Activity**

▼12 Escucha y escribe | |

Escuchar • Escribir • Hablar

❶ Javier fue a esquiar en las montañas. El primer día tuvo un accidente. Escucha su descripción de lo que pasó y escribe las seis frases, pero ten cuidado. Javier no está contando en orden lo que pasó.

❷ Trabaja con otro(a) estudiante para poner en orden lógico el cuento de Javier.

❸ Cuenten otra vez lo que le pasó a Javier, pero imaginen que dos enfermeras y dos médicos lo atendieron. Cambien las formas de los verbos apropiados.

Modelo

Dos enfermeras le trajeron a Javier una silla de ruedas.

Bariloche, Argentina, es un lugar turístico internacional. En el invierno se puede esquiar y en el verano se puede ir de pesca, montar a caballo o escalar las montañas (*go mountain climbing*).

▼13 Mi programa favorito

Leer • Escribir

Anoche Adela vio sólo una parte de su programa de televisión favorito, *Emergencia*. Completa el correo electrónico que ella le escribe a su amiga con las formas apropiadas de los verbos.

Tere: ¿Viste *Emergencia* anoche? Yo lo vi por media hora pero no **_1._** *(poder / venir)* ver más porque **_2._** *(estar / tener)* que llevar a mi hermana a su práctica de gimnasia. Esto es lo que vi. Una señora **_3._** *(decir / venir)* al hospital con mucha sangre en la mano. Ella **_4._** *(decir / poner)* que se cortó la mano cuando estaba cocinando. Una médica le **_5._** *(poner / venir)* una inyección y después le **_6._** *(dar/ poder)* ocho puntadas. Luego los paramédicos **_7._** *(decir / traer)* a un anciano al hospital en una ambulancia. Ellos **_8._** *(decir / venir)* que el anciano **_9._** *(poder / tener)* un accidente en su coche. Los médicos le hicieron una operación de emergencia para salvarle la vida. Pues, dime, Tere, ¿qué **_10._** *(poder / pasar)* al final del programa? ¡Escríbeme pronto y dime todo!

Adela

▼14 Si necesitas ayuda . . .

Leer • Escribir

Lee el siguiente anuncio sobre el servicio de ambulancias que existe para un hospital de Quito, Ecuador. Después contesta las preguntas.

Hospital de Clínicas Pichincha

Ponemos a su disposición dos ambulancias, manejadas por profesionales preparados para el transporte rápido pero seguro.*

Clínicas Pichincha

AMBULANCIA

Ofrecemos:
- ambulancias equipadas para dar atención inmediata
- paramédicos entrenados para atender al paciente críticamente enfermo o herido
- equipo médico moderno
- servicio permanente, sin interrupción (disponible los 365 días del año, las 24 horas del día)
- comunicación directa con el Servicio de Emergencia

El teléfono para acceder a nuestro servicio es el 505-505 (Quito). Vamos a atender a su llamada de inmediato pues, una emergencia no espera.

*safe

1. ¿Por qué puedes tener confianza *(confidence)* en el servicio de estas ambulancias? Menciona tres razones *(reasons)*.

2. ¿A qué horas puede atenderte este servicio?

3. ¿Por qué dice el servicio que va a atender rápidamente a una llamada?

▼15 Necesitabas una ambulancia |

Escribir • Hablar

Imagina que trabajas para el servicio de ambulancias de la Actividad 14 y quieres saber qué tipo de servicio recibieron los pacientes. Con otro(a) estudiante, entrevista *(interview)* a un(a) paciente y pregúntale sobre el servicio que recibió. Usa las siguientes preguntas en la entrevista:

- ¿Qué te dijeron? ¿Qué preguntas te hicieron?
- ¿Cuántos paramédicos vinieron? ¿Vinieron inmediatamente?
- ¿Qué trajeron en la ambulancia?
- ¿Te pusieron una inyección cuando llegaron?

▼16 Una celebración | muy especial

Pensar • Hablar • Escribir

❶ Piensa en una fiesta que muchas personas celebraron en tu casa. Vas a trabajar con otro(a) estudiante para hablar de la fiesta.

❷ Completa las preguntas con los verbos en el pretérito, y hazle estas preguntas a tu compañero(a). Escribe lo que dice.

1. ¿*(Ponerse)* tú ropa elegante o ropa de todos los días para esta fiesta?

2. ¿Quiénes *(venir)* a la fiesta?

3. ¿Quién *(traer)* regalos, comida u otras cosas?

4. ¿Qué *(hacer)* todos durante la fiesta?

5. ¿Por cuánto tiempo *(estar)* las personas allí?

6. ¿*(Poder)* tú hablar con todo el mundo?

❸ Escribe un resumen de la fiesta que te describió tu compañero(a).

Más práctica	GO
realidades.com	print

Instant Check	✔	
Guided WB pp. 191–192	✔	✔
Core WB p. 106	✔	✔
Comm. WB pp. 101, 104	✔	✔
Hispanohablantes **WB** pp. 194–197, 201	✔	

▼17 Juego |

Escribir • Hablar • GramActiva

❶ Trabaja con tres estudiantes. En tarjetas o pequeñas hojas de papel, escriban las raíces *(stems)* de los verbos irregulares en el pretérito de la página 274 y pongan las tarjetas en un grupo boca abajo *(facedown).*

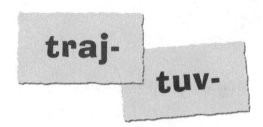

❷ Van a jugar en parejas *(pairs).* La primera pareja escoge una tarjeta y crea una frase en 30 segundos para decir lo que pasó en el hospital o en un accidente. Después leen la frase. La otra pareja tiene que decir si la frase es correcta. La primera pareja recibe un punto por cada palabra correcta en su frase.

Modelo

Anoche hubo un incendio y trajeron a varias personas heridas al hospital en una ambulancia. (15 puntos)

El español en el mundo del trabajo

Los intérpretes y traductores *(translators)* médicos son muy importantes en los hospitales de los Estados Unidos. A veces, cuando una persona que no habla inglés va al hospital, el médico y las enfermeras no pueden entender lo que dice y no pueden ayudarle. Las personas pueden morir si no reciben atención adecuada y a tiempo. Por eso los hospitales contratan a intérpretes y a traductores. Tener intérpretes en los hospitales es una necesidad y también una ley.

• ¿Crees que es importante tener intérpretes y traductores en los hospitales? ¿Hay un servicio de intérpretes en el hospital de tu comunidad?

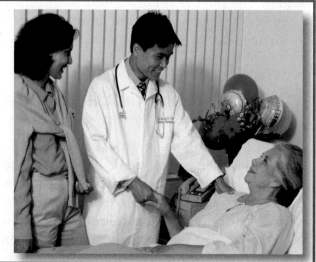

Gramática

Imperfect progressive and preterite

To describe something that was taking place over a period of time in the past, use the imperfect progressive, which uses the imperfect tense of *estar* + the present participle.

Estaba esquiando cuando me caí y me torcí la rodilla.

I was skiing when I fell and sprained my knee.

The present and imperfect progressive tenses use the same present participles. Remember, to form the present participle of *-ir* stem-changing verbs, *e* changes to *i* and *o* changes to *u*:

¿Recuerdas?

When you say that an action is happening right now, you use the present progressive tense. The present progressive uses the present tense of *estar* + the present participle.

• No puedo ir al cine. **Estoy estudiando** para el examen.

For the following *-er* verbs, the *i* of *-iendo* changes to *y*:

e → i		o → u	i → y
decir: diciendo seguir: siguiendo pedir: pidiendo servir: sirviendo repetir: repitiendo vestir: vistiendo		dormir: durmiendo	creer: creyendo leer: leyendo traer: trayendo

• When you use object pronouns with the imperfect progressive, you can put them before *estar* or attach them to the participle.

—¿Qué estabas haciendo cuando te cortaste?

—Estaba afeitándome. **o:** Me estaba afeitando.

• Note that the imperfect progressive describes what was taking place while the preterite tells a specific occurrence in the past or interrupts the action.

Ella estaba corriendo cuando se lastimó el tobillo.

Más ayuda **realidades.com**

▶ *GramActiva* Video

◀))) *Canción de hip hop: Un accidente*

📖 *GramActiva* Activity

▼18 Cuando llegó la ambulancia

Escribir

Mira el dibujo y escribe frases para decir lo que estaban haciendo las personas en la sala de emergencia cuando llegó la ambulancia.

Modelo

el médico

El médico estaba hablando por teléfono.

1. la médica
2. el enfermero
3. la enfermera
4. los jóvenes
5. la niña
6. los ancianos

▼19 Tus pacientes

Escribir

Tú eres enfermero(a) en una sala de emergencia y tienes que escribir una historia médica de tus pacientes. Mira los dibujos y describe qué estaban haciendo las personas y qué les pasó.

Modelo
Laura estaba cocinando cuando se quemó la mano.

Laura

1. Yolanda 2. Héctor 3. Juan y Anita 4. Antonio 5. Rosa

▼20 ¿Quiénes se cayeron?

Escribir • Hablar

Piensa en las personas que tú conoces que se cayeron alguna vez. ¿Quiénes son y cuándo se cayeron? Describe los accidentes de tres personas y describe qué estaban haciendo cuando se cayeron. Luego habla con otro(a) estudiante y compara sus respuestas.

▶ Modelo

A —*Mi hermana se cayó el mes pasado.*
B —*¿Qué estaba haciendo tu hermana cuando se cayó?*
A —*Estaba poniendo carteles en la pared.*

Nota

In the preterite, *caerse* is like *leer,* with forms that change the *i* to *y* in the *Ud./él/ella* and *Uds./ellos/ellas* forms. There is also an accent mark over the *i* in all other forms.

• Cuando estaba bajando la escalera, Enrique **se cayó.**

• Cuando yo estaba subiendo la escalera, **me caí.**

Fondo Cultural | Colombia

La Patrulla Aérea Colombiana (PAC) es un equipo de pilotos y médicos que viaja en avión a pueblos remotos que no tienen ni médicos ni hospitales. La PAC enseña programas de prevención de salud a las comunidades y ofrece servicios médicos básicos y cirugía *(surgery).* Muchos de los pueblos están en los Andes o en las regiones amazónicas y la Patrulla es el único servicio médico que llega a estas comunidades.

• ¿Conoces partes de los Estados Unidos donde no hay ni médicos ni hospitales? ¿Qué soluciones hay para esta situación en los Estados Unidos y en Colombia?

Los pilotos y médicos de la Patrulla Aérea Colombiana

▼21 Las lesiones en los deportes | 👥

Leer • Pensar • Hablar

¿Practicas un deporte o juegas en un equipo? Quizás patinas o montas en monopatín. ¿Sabes cuáles son las lesiones *(injuries)* que te pueden ocurrir cuando practicas deportes? Lee el artículo y luego contesta las preguntas.

Conexiones | La salud

Los dos tipos de lesiones deportivas

Las lesiones en los deportes son las que ocurren típicamente en los deportes organizados, los entrenamientos[1] o las actividades diarias de acondicionamiento.

◉ **Lesión traumática aguda:**[2] causada por un golpe[3] intenso como un choque o una caída. Ejemplos son la fractura de un hueso, una torcedura (se estira[4] o se rompe un músculo o tendón) o una distensión (se estira o se rompe un ligamento). Estas lesiones afectan más las rodillas, los tobillos y las muñecas.

◉ **Lesión crónica:** causada por el uso continuo o excesivo. Es el resultado del entrenamiento repetitivo tal como correr o lanzar[5] una pelota. Ejemplos son las fracturas de un hueso por estrés, la tendinitis (se rompen las fibras del tendón a causa de estiramientos excesivos) o la bursitis (inflamación de la bursa en el hombro, en el codo o en la rodilla).

[1]training sessions   [2]acute traumatic injury   [3]blow   [4]pull   [5]throw

En las siguientes descripciones, ¿tienen los atletas una lesión traumática aguda o crónica? Habla con otro(a) estudiante. Usen la información del artículo y den razones por su diagnóstico.

1. Lisa practicaba el golf todos los días. Siempre sentía un dolor en el codo.

2. En un partido de básquetbol, Kevin chocó con otro jugador. Se torció el tobillo y se cayó.

3. Hugo levantaba pesas todas las tardes en el gimnasio. Quería levantar el máximo de peso. Un día trataba de levantar 300 libras cuando tuvo un dolor agudo en el hombro y no pudo levantar la barra.

4. Sara jugaba al fútbol en el otoño y al básquetbol en el invierno. Sin descansar, empezó a entrenar para el fútbol en la primavera. Le dolía la rodilla después de cada práctica.

▼22 Familias de palabras

Pensar • Escribir

Si reconoces *(you recognize)* familias de palabras, entiendes mejor lo que lees. Mira las palabras de *Conexiones*. Escribe las palabras que ya conoces que te ayudan a entender las siguientes palabras nuevas.

Modelo
el uso
usar

1. una caída
2. una torcedura

3. repetitivo
4. un choque

▼23 Los días más difíciles

Leer • Escribir • Hablar

Lee este artículo sobre un famoso futbolista y contesta las preguntas.

1. ¿Qué le pasó cuando tenía once años?

2. ¿Qué tuvo que hacer en el tratamiento médico?

3. ¿Cuándo se lastimó la pierna derecha?

4. ¿Qué tuvo que hacer para recuperarse?

Fenómeno de perseverancia

Lionel Andrés Messi es un jugador de fútbol argentino muy talentoso. A los once años, los médicos le diagnosticaron un problema de crecimiento[1] hormonal: era tan bajo que a esa edad[2] tenía la estatura de un niño de ocho años. Por eso, se fue a España con su familia para recibir un tratamiento médico. "Durante tres años, tuve que ponerme inyecciones todos los días", dijo Lionel. Por esta enfermedad, Lionel aprendió a jugar al fútbol ágilmente y con gran rapidez. Pero su estilo de juego explosivo le produce lesiones en las piernas con frecuencia. Mientras estaba jugando un partido en un campeonato europeo, Lionel sufrió una lesión en la pierna derecha. Cinco días más tarde, estaba jugando cuando se cayó y sufrió otra lesión más grave en la misma pierna. Como resultado, no pudo jugar el partido final de ese campeonato. Lionel tuvo que operarse y caminar con muletas por tres meses, pero pudo recuperarse[3] completamente. Sin duda, Lionel es un verdadero fenómeno de perseverancia.

[1] growth [2] age [3] recover

▼24 Y tú, ¿qué dices?

Escribir • Hablar

1. Recientemente cuando estabas practicando un deporte o haciendo otra actividad, ¿sentiste* un dolor en algún músculo o hueso? ¿Qué hiciste para el dolor?

2. ¿Te lastimaste alguna vez cuando estabas practicando un deporte? ¿Cómo te lastimaste? ¿Qué deporte estabas practicando?

3. Piensa en alguien que conoces que se rompió un hueso o se torció un tobillo o una rodilla. ¿Qué estaba haciendo cuando ocurrió el accidente? ¿Le sacaron radiografías? ¿Tuvo que llevar un yeso o usar muletas?

* When *sentir* is followed by a noun, the non-reflexive form of the verb is used.

▼ Fondo Cultural | El mundo hispano

El jai alai ¿Sabías que el jai alai es el deporte de pelota más rápido del mundo? En este juego, ¡la pelota llega a alcanzar velocidades de 150 millas por hora! El jai alai se originó en el País Vasco, en el norte de España. Se juega en una cancha *(court)* con tres paredes y los jugadores llevan casco *(helmet)* porque este deporte puede ser peligroso y causar lesiones. Se juega en muchos países y en los Estados Unidos es muy popular en Florida y Connecticut.

• ¿En qué sentido es diferente el jai alai de los juegos que practicas tú?

Jugadores mexicanos de jai alai

▼25 Juego

Escribir • Hablar • GramActiva

❶ Trabaja con otro(a) estudiante. En pequeñas hojas de papel, escriban dos frases que describen lo que estaban haciendo una o dos personas cuando algo ocurrió. Su profesor(a) va a dividir a la clase en dos grupos. Los estudiantes en cada grupo ponen todas sus hojas de papel en una bolsa y le dan la bolsa al otro grupo.

❷ Saca una hoja de papel de la bolsa y lee la frase. No puedes mostrar (*show*) la hoja a tu grupo ni puedes decirles lo que dice. Tienes un minuto para representar la situación para ver si tu grupo puede decir correctamente la frase. Si lo pueden hacer en un minuto o menos, reciben un punto. Si no lo pueden hacer en un minuto, no reciben ningún punto.

> Estabas nadando cuando chocaste con la pared de la piscina.

▼26 Un accidente en la carretera | Talk!

Hablar

❶ Trabaja con dos estudiantes. Uno(a) de Uds. es reportero(a) y está investigando el choque de coches en el dibujo. El (La) reportero(a) está hablando con dos testigos (*witnesses*) que tienen diferentes versiones de lo que pasó en el accidente. En su dramatización, pueden incluir:

- lo que estaban haciendo los testigos cuando ocurrió el accidente
- lo que estaban haciendo los coches y los conductores cuando ocurrió
- qué hora era cuando ocurrió y qué otras condiciones existían
- qué les pasó a las personas en el accidente y si hubo muchos heridos
- quiénes vinieron a ayudar y lo que hicieron
- lo que hicieron todos después del accidente

❷ Preparen su dramatización y preséntenla para la clase entera o para otro grupo.

Más práctica	GO
	realidades.com | print
Instant Check	✔
Guided WB pp. 193–196	✔ ✔
Core WB pp. 107–108	✔ ✔
Comm. WB pp. 102, 105, 250	✔ ✔
Hispanohablantes **WB** pp. 198–201	✔

▼ Objectives

▶ Read about health campaigns
▶ Use cognates to predict reading content
▶ Compare and contrast health campaigns in Spanish-speaking countries and the U.S.

Lectura

Mejorar la salud para todos

Lee sobre estas tres organizaciones que ayudan a mejorar la salud en los países hispanohablantes.

Estrategia

Using cognates
When you encounter a word in Spanish you don't know, see if it resembles a word you know in English. Saying the word aloud can also be helpful. Scan this text for cognates before you read and make a list of the ones you find. Think about their meanings. Then try to link these words together to anticipate what you're about to read.

Organización Panamericana de la Salud

La Organización Panamericana de la Salud (OPS) es una organización internacional de salud pública con más de 100 años de experiencia. La sede[1] de la organización se encuentra en Washington, D.C., y la institución representa 35 países. Los objetivos fundamentales de la OPS son la promoción entre los países de las Américas para:

- combatir las enfermedades
- prolongar la vida
- estimular el bienestar físico y mental de sus habitantes

Voces para la salud

Para promover[2] sus objetivos la OPS produjo[3] una serie de mensajes[4] de interés público sobre la salud, hechos por personalidades conocidas y admiradas del hemisferio. Estos artistas, atletas y actores vienen de diferentes países e informan a los pueblos de las Américas sobre importantes temas de salud.

LUIS ENRIQUE HABLA SOBRE LA PREVENCIÓN DEL USO DE LAS DROGAS

El cantante nicaragüense Luis Enrique, conocido como "el príncipe de la salsa", canta "Date un chance", un himno contra el uso de las drogas. Esa canción es parte de su mensaje para promover la salud en las Américas.

❝La vida nos pone a prueba[5] día a día, con momentos buenos y malos. Es nuestra responsabilidad tomar las decisiones correctas. ¡Dile no a las drogas y dile sí a la vida, siempre!❞

[1]headquarters   [2]promote   [3]produced   [4]messages   [5]test

Más práctica   GO

realidades.com | print

Guided WB p. 197	✔	✔
Comm. WB pp. 106, 251	✔	✔
Hispanohablantes WB pp. 202–203		✔
Cultural Reading Activity	✔	

DON FRANCISCO HABLA SOBRE LA DONACIÓN DE SANGRE SEGURA

Don Francisco, actor de origen chileno, es la personalidad más reconocida del mundo del espectáculo en la televisión en español. Su programa *Sábado Gigante* se ve en las Américas y en otros países del mundo por satélite.

❝Millones de personas necesitan sangre segura[6] para vivir. En América Latina, necesitamos 25 millones de unidades de sangre. Donen su sangre segura; es el mejor regalo❞.

MERCEDES SOSA HABLA SOBRE LA VACUNACIÓN

Mercedes Sosa, cantante de origen argentino, es conocida como "la Voz de América Latina". Una de sus canciones más famosas se llama "Gracias a la vida".

❝*No le falles[7] a tus chicos, llévalos a vacunar.[8] Así pueden estar completamente protegidos y darle ¡Gracias a la vida!*❞

Cuerpo de la Paz[9] y *Medical Aid For Children of Latin America* (MACLA) ayudan a niños que requieren cirugía plástica[10]

MACLA es una organización estadounidense que ayuda a personas con deformidades físicas en la República Dominicana, Bolivia y otros países. El Dr. Thomas Geraghty, un médico de Kansas City, fundó **MACLA** en el año 1985 y hasta la fecha más de 210 médicos, anestesiólogos, enfermeros y enfermeras han donado[11] su tiempo para trabajar como voluntarios en esta institución, la

cual ha realizado más de 6,000 cirugías reconstructivas en la República Dominicana. Un voluntario del Cuerpo de la Paz que ayudó en este proyecto en la República Dominicana declaró: "Traducir[12] y servir como puente entre los pacientes y los profesionales médicos fue una experiencia que me dio mucha satisfacción. Ver la cirugía reconstructiva de los médicos de **MACLA** y los efectos

que tiene en la vida de los pacientes me dio aun más satisfacción. Escuchar los testimonios de los pacientes es una verdadera inspiración".

[6]safe   [7]fail   [8]to be vaccinated   [9]Peace Corps   [10]plastic surgery   [11]have donated   [12]To translate

¿Comprendiste?

1. Según Luis Enrique, ¿qué responsabilidad tiene cada persona?

2. ¿Qué mensaje quiere promover don Francisco?

3. Según Mercedes Sosa, ¿por qué es importante vacunar a los niños?

4. ¿Qué ayuda les da MACLA a los habitantes de la República Dominicana?

5. Según el voluntario del Cuerpo de la Paz, ¿qué le dio mucha satisfacción?

Y tú, ¿qué dices?

1. En tu opinión, ¿crees que los mensajes de interés público son efectivos en motivar al público? ¿Por qué?

2. Compara los mensajes de la OPS con los que ves en la televisión contra las drogas o contra los cigarillos. ¿En qué sentido son diferentes o similares?

Perspectivas del mundo hispano

Seguridad Social y los servicios médicos

En el siglo XX, muchos países de América Latina decidieron crear la Seguridad Social y la medicina socializada para ofrecer servicios médicos a las personas que viven y trabajan en un país. Cuando un(a) trabajador(a) se enferma o tiene un accidente y no puede trabajar, la Seguridad Social le ayuda con los gastos[1] médicos y continúa pagándole parte de su salario[2]. Si la enfermedad es permanente, la Seguridad Social le paga al (a la) trabajador(a) una pensión y los servicios médicos básicos, y si el (la) trabajador(a) muere[3], la Seguridad Social ayuda a la familia. Los servicios de la Seguridad Social también incluyen los hospitales, las medicinas y la ayuda para los ancianos.

En Costa Rica, la Seguridad Social funciona desde hace más de 50 años y hoy ayuda al 98 por ciento de la población. Y en España, funciona desde hace casi 100 años y cubre[4] a toda la población, incluidos los inmigrantes. Las personas que viven en estos dos países tienen muy buenos servicios médicos, gracias a los servicios de la Seguridad Social.

¡Compruébalo! ¿Hay un programa de Seguridad Social en los Estados Unidos? ¿Qué beneficios ofrece?

¿Qué te parece? ¿Te parece importante el sistema de Seguridad Social? ¿Por qué?

[1]expenses [2]salary [3]dies [4]covers

Países miembros de la Organización Iberoamericana de Seguridad Social (OISS)

Argentina Bolivia Brasil Chile
Colombia Costa Rica Cuba Ecuador
El Salvador España Guatemala
Guinea Ecuatorial Honduras México
Nicaragua Panamá Paraguay Perú
Portugal República Dominicana
Uruguay Venezuela

Presentación escrita

Documentar el accidente

Task
You go into the school office to report an accident you saw outside. The secretary asks you to write a summary as documentation for the school.

❶ Prewrite Think about the important details of the accident. Jot down information about these items.

- Nombre(s)
- Descripción del accidente
- ¿Cuándo y dónde ocurrió?
- Descripción de los heridos
- Tipo de ayuda ofrecida
- Otra información

❷ Draft Use the information from step 1 to prepare a report for your school. Decide which information is important and in what order it should be presented.

❸ Revise Check your report for spelling, verb usage, and vocabulary. Share your report with a partner, who will check:

- Is the report easy to understand?
- Is the information retold in a clear, logical order?
- Is there anything that you could add to give more information or change to make it clearer?
- Are there any errors?

❹ Publish Rewrite your report, making any necessary changes. Give a copy to your teacher or put one in your portfolio.

❺ Evaluation The following rubric will be used to grade your presentation.

Estrategia

Taking notes
When you are retelling information for a report, it is helpful to jot down key details to include in the report. When you write the report, you build the narrative around retelling the facts.

Rubric	Score 1	Score 3	Score 5
Amount of information you present	You present three facts about the accident.	You present four facts about the accident.	You present five or more facts about the accident.
Your effective retelling of information	Your facts are not told in a logical sequence, and it is difficult to follow your sequence.	Your facts are told in a somewhat logical sequence, but it is somewhat difficult to follow your sequence.	Your facts are retold in a logical sequence and you include connecting words like *first, second, then,* etc.
Your accuracy in retelling an event in the past	You use three verbs in the past with grammatical errors.	You use four verbs in the past with some grammatical errors.	You use five or more verbs in the past with very few grammatical errors.

En busca de la verdad

Episodio 6

"Déjelo en mis manos. Y no hable con nadie".

Antes de ver el video

"Cuando Federico y yo entramos en el ejército, abrimos cuentas en este banco, el Banco de la Frontera, en San Antonio".

Nota cultural Cada 15 de septiembre, a medianoche, los mexicanos se reúnen en ciudades y pueblos para conmemorar su independencia de España y recordar a sus héroes nacionales. Todos los mexicanos saben de memoria los famosos "vivas": "¡Vivan los héroes que nos dieron Patria y Libertad! ¡Viva Miguel Hidalgo! ¡Viva Allende! ¡Viva la Independencia de México! ¡Viva México! ¡Viva México! ¡Viva México!"

Resumen del episodio

Roberto empieza a buscar la verdad sobre su abuelo. Él y Linda van a Dolores Hidalgo para hablar con Chato Montesinos. Allí descubren otra pista sobre el misterio del abuelo. El episodio termina con una llamada misteriosa.

Palabras para comprender

movimiento movement

Yo he estado varias veces. I have been many times.

nadie ha visto nobody has seen

Se casó. He / She got married.

nieto grandson

desapareció disappeared

ejército army

cuenta de banco bank account

Después de ver el video

¿Comprendiste?

A. Decide cuáles de las siguientes frases son ciertas y cuáles son falsas:

1. Roberto obtiene la dirección de Chato Montesinos en San Miguel de Allende.

2. Linda va con Roberto a Dolores Hidalgo.

3. Cuando llegan a Dolores Hidalgo, Roberto y Linda compran un pastel.

4. Linda no sabe quién era el padre Hidalgo.

5. Roberto conoce bastante bien Dolores Hidalgo.

6. Chato Montesinos sabe dónde está Federico Zúñiga.

7. Después de visitar a Chato Montesinos, Roberto llama a una agencia de viajes en San Antonio.

8. Federico Zúñiga y Chato Montesinos se fueron juntos para México.

9. Roberto llama al Banco de la Frontera para obtener información sobre su abuelo Federico Zúñiga.

B. Contesta las siguientes preguntas.

1. Escribe un resumen de todo lo que Roberto sabe hasta ahora sobre su abuelo.

2. Haz una predicción. ¿Quién es el hombre misterioso? ¿Dónde está? ¿Por qué tiene tanto interés en el abuelo de Roberto? Lee tus predicciones y discútelas con el resto de la clase. Tu profesor(a) va a guardar las predicciones hasta el final del video. Entonces vas a saber si estabas cerca de la verdad.

Más práctica **GO**

realidades.com | print

Actividades ✔

Repaso del capítulo
Vocabulario y gramática

to talk about treatments for medical conditions

doler (o → ue)	to hurt
el dolor	pain
el enfermero, la enfermera	nurse
examinar	to examine, to check
la inyección, pl. las inyecciones	injection, shot
poner una inyección	to give an injection
la medicina	medicine
las muletas	crutches
las pastillas	pills
las puntadas	stitches
dar puntadas	to stitch (surgically)
la radiografía	X-ray
sacar una radiografía	to take an X-ray
la receta	prescription
recetar	to prescribe
roto, -a	broken
la sala de emergencia	emergency room
la sangre	blood
la silla de ruedas	wheelchair
la venda	bandage
el yeso	cast

to explain how an accident occurred

el accidente	accident
la ambulancia	ambulance
caerse	to fall
me caigo	I fall
te caes	you fall
se cayó	he / she fell
se cayeron	they / you fell
chocar con	to crash into, to collide with
cortarse	to cut oneself
lastimarse	to hurt oneself
¿Qué te pasó?	What happened to you?
romperse	to break, to tear
torcerse (o → ue)	to twist, to sprain
tropezar (e → ie) (con)	to trip (over)

to name parts of the body

el codo	elbow
el cuello	neck
la espalda	back
el hombro	shoulder
el hueso	bone
la muñeca	wrist
el músculo	muscle
la rodilla	knee
el tobillo	ankle

other useful words and expressions

moverse (o → ue)	to move
pobrecito, -a	poor thing
¡Qué lástima!	What a shame!
sentirse (e → ie)	to feel

preterite of venir

vine	vinimos
viniste	vinisteis
vino	vinieron

preterite of decir and traer

dije	traje	dijimos	trajimos
dijiste	trajiste	dijisteis	trajisteis
dijo	trajo	dijeron	trajeron

preterite of poner

puse	pusimos
pusiste	pusisteis
puso	pusieron

imperfect progressive tense

Use the imperfect-tense forms of *estar* + the present participle to say that something was taking place over a period of time in the past.

present participles:

-ar	stem + -ando →	caminando
-er	stem + -iendo →	corriendo
-ir	stem + -iendo →	escribiendo

For *Vocabulario adicional,* see pp. 498–499.

Más repaso (GO) realidades.com | print

Instant Check	✔
Puzzles	✔
Core WB pp. 109–110	✔
Comm. WB pp. 252, 253–255	✔ ✔

Preparación para el examen

On the exam you will be asked to . . .	Here are practice tasks similar to those you will find on the exam . . .	For review go to your print or digital textbook . . .

Interpretive

 1 Escuchar Listen and understand as someone talks about what has happened at an accident

Listen as a 911 operator takes a call from someone who is at the scene of an accident. See if you can understand: (a) what the victim was doing before the accident occurred; (b) what caused the accident; and (c) what the injury appears to be.

pp. 266–269 *Vocabulario en contexto*
p. 270 Actividad 5
p. 274 Actividad 12

Interpersonal

 2 Hablar Ask and answer questions about how someone was injured

You would like to get some training in emergency room questioning techniques. With a partner, practice what you learned by role-playing a situation in which one person asks: (a) what time the patient came to the emergency room and how he / she got there; (b) what caused the injury; and (c) what the person was doing at the time of the injury. Then switch roles.

p. 270 Actividad 6
p. 271 Actividad 8
p. 272 Actividad 9
p. 273 Actividad 10
p. 275 Actividad 15
p. 278 Actividad 20
p. 281 Actividad 26

Interpretive

 3 Leer Read and understand an account of an accident

In the newspaper, you see an account of an accident. See if you can understand what happened, as well as what medical treatment the victims received.

Ayer, dos niños se chocaron cuando estaban montando en bicicleta en la calle Suárez. La ambulancia llegó rápidamente para llevarlos a la sala de emergencia. Los paramédicos dijeron que uno de los niños tenía la muñeca rota y el otro necesitaba diez puntadas en la rodilla.

pp. 266–269 *Vocabulario en contexto*
p. 270 Actividad 4
p. 275 Actividad 13
p. 279 Actividad 21
p. 280 Actividad 23
pp. 282–283 *Lectura*

Presentational

 4 Escribir Write an account of what medical treatment was given to injured people

Several children that you were supervising were injured on the playground and you took them to the emergency room. Write a summary, in Spanish, describing the medical treatment each child received.

p. 270 Actividad 4
p. 274 Actividad 12
p. 275 Actividades 13, 15
p. 285 *Presentación escrita*

Cultures

 5 Pensar Demonstrate an understanding of emergency medical services in different countries

Imagine that you've been injured. Where would you go? How would you get there? What type of emergency medical services are available in your community? How are they similar to or different from those in Spanish-speaking countries?

p. 271 *Fondo cultural*
p. 278 *Fondo cultural*
pp. 282–283 *Lectura*
p. 284 *Perspectivas del mundo hispano*

Vocabulario Repaso

la televisión

el canal
la comedia
el drama
el programa de concursos
el programa de dibujos animados
el programa deportivo
el programa educativo
el programa de entrevistas
el programa de la vida real
el programa de noticias
el programa musical
la telenovela
¿Qué clase de . . . ?

el cine

el actor
la actriz, *pl.* las actrices
dar
durar
la película de ciencia ficción
la película de horror
la película policíaca
la película romántica

opiniones

cómico, -a
emocionante
fascinante
infantil
interesante
realista
tonto, -a
triste
violento, -a

▼1 Los programas que te gustan |

Escribir • Hablar

❶ Piensa en cuatro programas de televisión o películas que te gustan. Haz una copia de la tabla en una hoja de papel y úsala para describir los programas.

programa/ película	descripción	canal/cine	actor/ actriz
Planeta de los animales	un programa educativo fascinante	canal 14	Ramón Fernández

❷ Trabaja con otro(a) estudiante. Lee sólo la descripción de un programa o película en tu tabla. Tu compañero(a) va a hacerte dos preguntas para identificarlo.

▶ **Modelo**

A —*Es un programa educativo fascinante.*
B —*¿En qué canal / cine lo (la) dan?*
o:—*¿Quiénes son los actores principales?*

Gramática Repaso

Verbs like *gustar*

You already know several verbs that are always used with indirect objects:

encantar	*to love, to delight*
gustar	*to be pleasing*
importar	*to be important*
interesar	*to interest*

These verbs all use a similar construction: indirect object pronoun + verb + subject.

Me gusta el béisbol.
Literally: *Baseball is pleasing to me.*

The two forms of these verbs that are most commonly used are the *Ud. / él / ella* and *Uds. / ellos / ellas* forms.

¿Te interesan los deportes?
Literally: *Are sports interesting to you?*

Remember that, in the sentences above, the subjects are *béisbol* and *deportes,* and *me* and *te* are indirect object pronouns.

▼2 Tu programa favorito |

Hablar

¿Cuál es tu programa de televisión favorito? Pregúntale a otro(a) estudiante sus opiniones usando las palabras del recuadro.

▶ Modelo

gustar / las telenovelas
A —¿*Te gustan las telenovelas?*
B —*Sí, me encantan.*

encantar	los programas educativos
gustar	
interesar	los programas de la vida real
la comedia	las telenovelas
el drama	
los programas de dibujos animados	

▼3 Expresa tu opinión

Escribir • Hablar

¿Qué piensas del cine? Usa la lista de actividades y el verbo *importar* o *interesar* para expresar tu opinión.

Modelo

las comedias
A mí me interesan las comedias.
o: *No me interesan las comedias; me aburren.*

1. las películas de ciencia ficción
2. las películas de horror
3. las películas policíacas
4. las películas románticas
5. el drama
6. las películas realistas

Más práctica	GO
realidades.com	print	
A ver si recuerdas with Study Plan	✔
Guided WB pp. 199–200	✔ ✔
Core WB pp. 111–112	✔ ✔
Hispanohablantes WB p. 210	✔

Capítulo 6A ¿Viste el partido en la televisión?

▼ Chapter Objectives

Communication

By the end of this chapter you will be able to:

- Listen to and read about TV shows and sporting events
- Talk and write about a TV show and your emotions
- Exchange information about your reaction to a TV program

Culture

You will also be able to:

- Understand television programming on Spanish-language channels
- Compare the popularity of game shows and reality shows in Spain and the U.S.

You will demonstrate what you know and can do:

- Presentación oral, p. 313
- Preparación para el examen, p. 317

You will use:

Vocabulary

- Sporting events and contests
- Emotions

Grammar

- Preterite of -ir stem-changing verbs
- Other reflexive verbs

Exploración del mundo hispano

Country Connection
Sporting Events and Contests

España
Cuba
República Dominicana
Puerto Rico
México
Venezuela
Panamá
Colombia
Ecuador
Bolivia
Argentina

realidades.com **GO**

DK Reference Atlas

▶ Videocultura y actividad

🌐 Mapa global interactivo

Los equipos de Argentina
y México en la Copa
Mundial, 2010

Arte y cultura | España

Salvador Dalí Salvador Felipe Jacinto Dalí
(1904–1989) nació en la provincia de Cataluña,
España, cerca de Barcelona. Dalí estudió pintura
y experimentó con varios estilos. Después de la
Guerra Civil Española *(Spanish Civil War)*, Dalí
vivió en los Estados Unidos por unos años. Este
cuadro es titulado "El futbolista".

• ¿Qué tipo de fútbol crees que juegan en este
cuadro? ¿Por qué? ¿Hay elementos del cuadro
que crees que son típicos de España? ¿En qué
otros países crees que el cuadro puede estar
situado?

"El futbolista" (1973), Salvador Dalí ▶

Lithograph on zinc, 19 x 24 in. © 2009 Salvador Dalí,
Gala-Salvador Dalí Foundation/Artists Rights Society (ARS), New York.

Vocabulario en contexto

los aficionados

el campeón

el tanteo

3 2

TOLUCA PUEBLA

alegre

el jugador

los campeones

el público

MONTERREY 1
PACHUCA 1

el empate

enojada

furioso

el comentario

el entrenador

aburrirse

los atletas

❝ Los aficionados del equipo de Toluca se pusieron **alegres** y muy **emocionados** cuando su equipo ganó **el campeonato** de **la Liga** Mexicana **por tercera vez.** El equipo de Puebla **perdió** el partido final con un tanteo de 3 a 2. **La competencia** entre estos dos equipos siempre **resulta** muy intensa.

El partido entre Monterrey y Pachuca terminó en un empate, 1 a 1. **Al final** del partido el entrenador de Monterrey dijo: 'Pareció que nos aburrimos y **nos dormimos** mientras jugábamos. Tenemos que **competir** con más emoción. También hubo problemas entre **el público.** Los aficionados se pusieron muy **agitados. Se enojaron** y empezaron a pelearse. En mi opinión, pueden **aplaudir** y gritar, pero nunca deben **volverse locos**'❞.

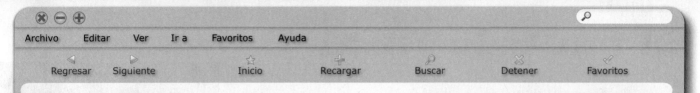

Archivo   Editar   Ver   Ir a   Favoritos   Ayuda

Regresar   Siguiente   Inicio   Recargar   Buscar   Detener   Favoritos

Concurso de Carnaval ayer

FELICIDADES a Rosalinda Pérez Urcillo. Anoche en **el Auditorio** Nacional fue escogida Reina del Carnaval. En **el concurso de belleza** participaron 30 jóvenes talentosas, pero Rosalinda fascinó al público con su presentación de guitarra. **La presentadora** le entregó un cheque para pagar por su primer año de estudios en la universidad.

la reina   la presentadora

Rosalinda Pérez Urcillo, Reina del Carnaval

¡Número uno!

el presentador

¿QUIEN LO SABE?

Cecilia Mendoza, profesora y ganadora

el premio

NUESTRA comunidad tiene una ganadora en la profesora Cecilia Mendoza. La semana pasada participó y ganó en el programa de concursos "¿Quién lo sabe?" Cecilia es profesora de historia en el Colegio Andrés Bello. Como premio, Cecilia recibió un coche nuevo y el presentador del programa le entregó un cheque por **un millón** de pesos.

▼1 ¿Cierta o falsa?

Escuchar

En una hoja de papel, escribe los números del 1 al 8. Escucha las siguientes frases sobre las noticias deportivas de la página 294 y escribe *C* si la frase es cierta o *F* si es falsa.

▼2 ¿Cuál es el concurso?

Escuchar

Vas a escuchar seis frases. Si la frase describe un concurso de belleza, levanta una mano. Si describe un programa de concursos, levanta las dos manos.

Más práctica GO	realidades.com	print
Instant Check	✔	
Guided WB pp. 201–206	✔	✔
Core WB pp. 113–114	✔	✔
Comm. WB p. 112	✔	✔
Hispanohablantes WB p. 212		✔

El partido final

Ramón y Manolo están viendo la entrevista con un jugador de fútbol. ¿Qué sorpresa les da Claudia?

Estrategia

Using visuals
Look at the images as you read to help you understand the story. What do you predict happens at the end of the story? Why?

1

Locutor: ¡Gol! Y con este gol **fenomenal,** el equipo de los Lobos de Madero le ganó a las Águilas del América y llegó al partido final del campeonato mexicano de fútbol.

Ramón   Teresa   Claudia   Manolo

5

Claudia: Oye, Manolo, ¿a quién están entrevistando?

Manolo: Es Luis Campos. Claudia, esta entrevista nos interesa mucho. ¿Por qué no te vas a hablar al otro cuarto?

Claudia: ¡Uy! Manolo está un poco enojado. Sí . . . a ver.

6

Claudia: Oigan, Teresa dice que su tío trabaja en el estadio y que si queremos podemos ir a ver el partido allí.

7

Claudia: Creo que no quieren ir.

Ramón: ¿Ir adónde?

Claudia: Al estadio, a ver el partido allí.

Manolo y Ramón: ¿Qué?

Claudia: Ahora creo que quieren ir. Están gritando. Están muy alegres. **Se mueren** de emoción.

Locutor: Hoy vamos a **entrevistar** al jugador que **metió el gol,** Luis Campos, "la Pantera". Luis, gracias por estar aquí.

Luis: Gracias por invitarme.

Locutor: Este año tuvimos un campeonato muy interesante.

Luis: Así es. Competimos con equipos muy buenos . . .

Claudia: Sí, podemos ir al cine. O de compras . . . ¿Ahora? Estamos viendo la televisión. No sé, parece una **entrevista.**

Locutor: Luis, ¿qué nos puedes decir del **último** partido que ganaron contra las Águilas?

Luis: Bueno, fue un partido muy duro. Ellos metieron el primer gol, pero cinco minutos después nosotros empatamos. Luego, en el segundo tiempo,* metimos dos goles más y ganamos.

*second half

Manolo: ¡No puedo creer que vamos a ver el partido en el estadio!

Ramón: Vamos a divertirnos mucho.

Claudia: ¿Por qué no entramos ahora?

▼3 ¿Comprendiste?

Escribir • Hablar

1. ¿Qué están viendo Ramón y Manolo? ¿Por qué no están contentos?

2. ¿Qué hizo Luis Campos durante el partido?

3. ¿Por qué es importante el partido que los Lobos de Madero van a jugar hoy?

4. ¿A Claudia le interesa la entrevista?

5. ¿Qué quiere preguntarles Teresa?

6. ¿Cuál es la reacción de Ramón y Manolo?

Más práctica GO

realidades.com | print

Instant Check	✔	
Guided WB pp. 207–210	✔	✔
Core WB pp. 115–116	✔	✔
Comm. WB pp. 107–108, 109	✔	✔
Hispanohablantes WB p. 213		✔

| ▼ **Objectives**

▶ **Talk about reactions to TV programs**
▶ **Discuss feelings**
▶ **Listen to people's reactions to TV shows**
▶ **Write about TV programs and sports**

Vocabulario en uso

▼4 Un día malísimo

Leer • Escribir

Lee la conversación entre dos amigos que no están muy contentos con el resultado del campeonato de fútbol. Escribe las palabras apropiadas.

Un partido de fútbol entre Colombia y Bolivia

A —¿Viste el partido ayer en la televisión?

B —Sí, unos amigos míos vinieron a mi casa a verlo. Todos somos __1.__ *(atletas / aficionados)* a los Tigres y por eso __2.__ *(resultó / perdió)* ser un día malísimo.

A —Fue horrible, ¿no te parece? No puedo creer que los Tigres perdieron __3.__ *(el campeonato / el campeón)* por segunda vez.

B —Por unos minutos, pensábamos que el partido iba a terminar en un __4.__ *(empate / tanteo)* pero en los __5.__ *(últimos / primeros)* segundos el jugador de los Osos __6.__ *(metió un gol / compitió)* y ellos ganaron. Al final, el __7.__ *(tanteo / concurso)* fue 4 a 3. ¡Qué horror!

A —Ese jugador es un __8.__ *(atleta / entrenador)* fenomenal. Lo __9.__ *(entrevistaron / empataron)* anoche en la tele después de que le dieron el __10.__ *(tanteo / premio)* por ser el mejor jugador del partido.

B —Sí, vi la entrevista también. Parece ser un hombre muy bueno. Dijo que ganaron a causa de los esfuerzos *(efforts)* de todos los jugadores en el equipo y de sus __11.__ *(entrenadores / presentadores)*. También le dio las gracias a su familia y al __12.__ *(comentario / público)* que siempre lo apoyan *(support)*.

▼5 ¿Quién lo hace?

Leer • Escribir

Escribe la persona, el lugar o la cosa apropiada que corresponde a cada una de estas descripciones.

1. La persona que mete un gol es ____.

2. La persona que da los premios en un programa de concursos es ____.

3. La persona que gana el campeonato es ____.

4. La persona que gana el concurso de belleza es ____.

5. El grupo de personas que ven una competencia o un concurso es ____.

6. La persona que les dice a los jugadores lo que deben hacer es ____.

7. El lugar donde ocurre el concurso de belleza es ____.

8. El grupo de equipos que compiten unos contra otros es ____.

> **También se dice . . .**
>
> **la competencia** = la competición
> *(muchos países)*

▼6 La nueva reina

Leer • Escribir

Lee este artículo de las páginas sociales de un periódico sobre un evento muy especial. Después contesta las preguntas.

Felicitaciones a la Señorita Centroamérica

María Isabel Fernández Melgarejo

Anoche, en todas las ciudades y pueblos de El Salvador, la gente se volvía loca. Por primera vez en la historia de esta pequeña nación, pueden proclamar que la reina del Concurso de belleza, la Señorita Centroamérica, es una joven salvadoreña. La nueva reina es María Isabel Fernández Melgarejo, nativa de Zacatecoluca, Departamento de La Paz. La señorita Melgarejo, una joven talentosa y bonita de 19 años, participó en la competencia de talento con una voz fenomenal, cantando "Mi último recuerdo eres tú". Momentos antes de anunciar a la nueva reina había un silencio increíble en el auditorio. Cuando el presentador Mario Montero anunció el nombre de la joven salvadoreña, el público comenzó a gritar y a aplaudir. Después, en una entrevista, la nueva Señorita Centroamérica habló de sus planes como reina en el año que viene: visitar a personas enfermas y heridas en los hospitales de su país.

1. ¿Qué evento ocurrió anoche? ¿Cómo resultó el evento?

2. ¿Por qué es tan especial el resultado del evento?

3. ¿Qué hizo la nueva reina en la competencia de talento?

4. ¿Quién es Mario Montero y qué hizo en el concurso?

5. ¿El público se puso alegre o agitado cuando oyó el nombre de la nueva reina? ¿Por qué?

6. ¿Qué quiere hacer la nueva reina para ayudar a los demás?

▼7 ¿Qué dices . . . ? |

Escribir • Hablar

Imagina que no leíste bien el artículo de la Actividad 6 sobre la nueva reina. Escribe cuatro frases con información incorrecta sobre lo que ocurrió. Lee tus frases a otro(a) estudiante. Tu compañero(a) tiene que corregir *(correct)* tu información.

▶ Modelo

A —*Es la segunda vez que la reina es de El Salvador, ¿no?*

B —*No, no tienes razón. Es la primera vez que ella es de El Salvador.*

▼8 Escucha y escribe | 👥 | 🔊)))

Escuchar • Escribir • Hablar

❶ Unos jóvenes hablan de cómo se sienten cuando ven diferentes programas de televisión. Escribe las cinco frases que escuchas.

❷ Habla con otro(a) estudiante. ¿Cuál de las reacciones es más similar a la tuya? ¿Cuál es más diferente? ¿Por qué?

▼9 ¿Cuándo te sientes así? |

Escribir • Hablar

Escribe una frase para decir en qué situaciones te sientes así *(this way)*. Lee tus frases a otro(a) estudiante para ver si se siente lo mismo.

1. me aburro

2. me enojo

3. me pongo emocionado, -a

4. me vuelvo loco, -a

5. me pongo agitado, -a

6. me pongo alegre

▶️ Modelo

me pongo furioso, -a

A —*Me pongo furiosa cuando mi hermana usa mis cosas sin mi permiso. ¿Y tú?*

B —*Pues, no tengo hermanos. Pero me pongo furioso cuando un amigo me miente. ¿Y tú?*

A —*Sí, me pongo muy furiosa cuando alguien me miente.*

▼10 Y tú, ¿qué dices? | (Talk!)

Escribir • Hablar

1. ¿Qué clase de programa te gusta ver en la televisión, un programa de premios o un programa de entrevistas? ¿Por qué?

2. ¿Cuál es tu programa de concursos favorito? ¿Quién es el (la) presentador(a)? ¿Qué clase de premios dan?

3. ¿Quién es tu jugador(a) profesional favorito(a)? ¿Compitió recientemente en un campeonato? ¿Ganó o perdió?

4. ¿Conoces a algún (alguna) entrenador(a) profesional o de tu comunidad? ¿Con qué deportes o equipos trabaja él (ella)? ¿Cómo es?

Sergio García, de España, participa en un campeonato de golf.

Rafael Nadal, tenista español

▾11 La Serie del Caribe

Leer • Hablar

¿Eres aficionado(a) al béisbol? Lee la información y contesta las preguntas.

Campeones del Caribe

El equipo de México celebra su victoria en la Serie de Béisbol del Caribe.

Si te gusta el béisbol, la Serie de Béisbol del Caribe es una de las mejores competencias después de la Serie Mundial de las Ligas Mayores.

Equipos de México, Venezuela, la República Dominicana y Puerto Rico participan en esta serie. Cada equipo tiene cientos y hasta miles de aficionados que lo apoyan[1] durante el campeonato. La gente se reúne para disfrutar de[2] una semana del béisbol extraordinaria.

Un ejemplo de la emoción que despierta este evento fue la Serie del Caribe de 2011. En este campeonato se jugaron doce partidos, y cada equipo jugó dos veces contra los otros equipos. Hubo partidos inolvidables y participaciones increíbles de jugadores como Jorge Vázquez, el Jugador Más Valioso (*MVP*). Ese año, los mexicanos terminaron como los campeones de la serie.

La primera batalla[3] comenzó con México y la República Dominicana. Los dos equipos estuvieron empatados 3 a 3 durante seis entradas[4]. En la entrada 15, los mexicanos ganaron 4 a 3. Ese día los aficionados mexicanos celebraron con una gran fiesta. México tuvo otra dramática victoria cuando volvió a ganar el quinto partido contra Venezuela por 7 a 3.

México obtuvo por sexta vez el título de campeón de la serie en 2011. Los aficionados celebraron el resultado de este campeonato con cantos y bailes en las calles. Una vez más, el campeonato de la Serie del Caribe fue un gran éxito[5] y todos los aficionados quedaron contentos por ver jugar a sus equipos.

[1]support [2]enjoy [3]battle [4]innings [5]success

1. ¿Qué países compiten en la serie?
2. ¿Qué equipos jugaron en el primer partido de la serie?
3. ¿Por qué el partido entre México y la República Dominicana fue importante?
4. ¿Cuál fue el tanteo final entre México y Venezuela?
5. ¿Qué hicieron los aficionados después de los partidos?

Fondo Cultural | El mundo hispano

Latinoamericanos en el béisbol Hoy en día hay más de 200 jugadores de América Latina en las Ligas Mayores. Se dice que el béisbol caribeño "empezó" en Cuba en el año 1874, con una competencia entre dos equipos cubanos. Luego la popularidad del deporte pasó a algunos países latinoamericanos. En julio de 1895 se estableció el primer club venezolano, y en 1943 empezó la Federación Mexicana de Béisbol. El club atlético Licey, el club más antiguo de béisbol dominicano, se fundó en 1907.

• ¿Crees que el béisbol es tan popular en América Latina como en los Estados Unidos? Explica.

Carlos González, de los Rockies de Colorado

▼ **Objectives**
▶ Talk and write about what you watched on TV recently
▶ Tell about past televised events

Gramática

Preterite of *-ir* stem-changing verbs

In the preterite, *-ir* verbs like *preferir*, *pedir*, and *dormir* also have stem changes but only in the *Ud. / él / ella* and *Uds. / ellos / ellas* forms. In these forms *e* changes to *i* and *o* changes to *u*.

> Mi mamá se aburrió y **se durmió** durante la película.

> Mis padres **prefirieron** ver el concurso de belleza.

> En la liga **compitieron** los mejores equipos de México.

> **¿Recuerdas?**
>
> You know that stem changes in the present tense take place in all forms except *nosotros* and *vosotros*.
>
> **preferir** (e → ie)
> • **Prefiero** ver programas deportivos.
>
> **pedir** (e → i)
> • **Pedimos** los espaguetis.
>
> **dormir** (o → ue)
> • Los hermanos **duermen** tarde.

preferir (e → i)		pedir (e → i)		dormir (o → u)	
preferí	preferimos	pedí	pedimos	dormí	dormimos
preferiste	preferisteis	pediste	pedisteis	dormiste	dormisteis
prefirió	prefirieron	pidió	pidieron	durmió	durmieron

- Note the special spelling of the preterite forms of *reír: reí, reíste, rió, reímos, reísteis, rieron*

Here are other *-ir* verbs with stem changes in the preterite tense.

- Verbs like *preferir: divertirse, mentir, sentirse*
- Verbs like *pedir: competir, despedirse, repetir, seguir, servir, vestirse*
- Verbs like *dormir: morir*
- Verbs like *reír: sonreír*

Más ayuda | **realidades.com**

 GramActiva Video
Tutorial: Stem-changes in the preterite
Animated Verbs

 GramActiva Activity

▼12 Ayer fue diferente | ♻

Leer • Escribir

La familia Sánchez ve los mismos programas de televisión todos los días y tiene la misma reacción, pero ayer fue diferente. Completa las frases con las formas de los verbos en el presente y en el pretérito.

Modelo

(divertirse) Pablito casi siempre se divierte cuando juega videojuegos en la tele, pero ayer no se divirtió.

1. *(preferir)* Generalmente el Sr. Sánchez ____ ver los partidos en la tele, pero ayer ____ ver un programa de entrevistas.
2. *(sentirse)* Ayer la abuela ____ bastante triste después de ver su telenovela favorita, pero por lo general ella ____ muy entusiasmada después de verla.
3. *(dormirse)* La Sra. Sánchez casi siempre ____ durante uno de los comentarios en la tele, pero ayer no ____. Vio el comentario completo.
4. *(reírse)* A menudo los miembros de la familia ____ cuando escuchan al presentador en el programa de concursos. Ayer no ____ tanto.

▼13 Los Juegos Olímpicos

Escribir

En los Juegos Olímpicos del 2008 en Beijing, China, atletas de varios países hispanohablantes ganaron medallas. Aquí ves a algunos de los campeones y la información sobre el evento y las medallas que ganaron. Forma frases para decir en qué evento compitió cada atleta y qué medalla ganó.

Irving Saladino, de Panamá, gana la primera medalla de oro para Panamá en las Olimpíadas de Beijing en 2008.

Modelo

Irving Saladino, Panamá, salto largo, oro
Irving Saladino compitió en el salto largo y ganó una medalla de oro.

1. Diego Salazar, Colombia, levantamiento de pesas, plata
2. los argentinos, fútbol, oro
3. Yulis Gabriel Mercedes, República Dominicana, taekwondo, plata
4. Osmai Acosta Duarte y Yordenis Ugás, Cuba, boxeo, bronce
5. las argentinas, hockey, bronce
6. Rafael Nadal, España, tenis, oro

Tatiana Ortiz y Paola Espinosa, de México, ganan la medalla de bronce en salto *(diving)* en las Olimpíadas de Beijing en 2008.

▼14 Un camarero distraído | ♻

Leer • Escribir

Ayer Úrsula fue al restaurante Cancún con su mamá, y el camarero no les sirvió lo que pidieron. Lee su diálogo con su amigo Raúl y escribe las formas correctas de los verbos.

Raúl: ¿Cómo fue tu visita al restaurante ayer?
Úrsula: ¡Terrible! El camarero no nos **1.** *(servir)* lo que nosotras **2.** *(pedir).*
Raúl: ¿De veras? ¿Qué **3.** *(pedir)* Uds.?
Úrsula: Primero, yo **4.** *(pedir)* una hamburguesa con queso, pero el camarero me **5.** *(servir)* arroz con pollo.
Raúl: ¿Y qué pasó con tu mamá?
Úrsula: Ella **6.** *(pedir)* una ensalada y una sopa. ¡Luego nuestro camarero y otro camarero también le **7.** *(servir)* bistec con papas fritas! Mi mamá le **8.** *(repetir)* lo que nosotras **9.** *(pedir).*

Raúl: ¿Qué hizo él?
Úrsula: Pues, él **10.** *(sonreír)* y todos nosotros **11.** *(reír)*. Pero, ¿sabes? Quizás él **12.** *(divertirse)* anoche, pero nosotras no **13.** *(divertirse)* mucho. No pensamos regresar a ese restaurante.

▼15 Eventos importantes en la televisión

Leer • Escribir • Hablar

El invento de la televisión trajo muchos eventos importantes al hogar *(home)*.
Lee la información sobre las noticias transmitidas por televisión y contesta
las preguntas.

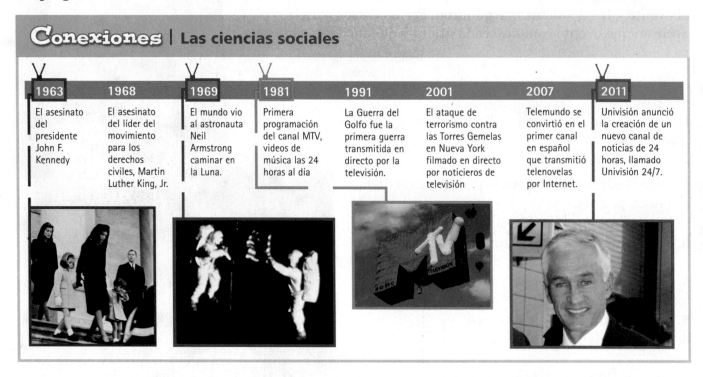

Conexiones | **Las ciencias sociales**

1963	1968	1969	1981	1991	2001	2007	2011
El asesinato del presidente John F. Kennedy	El asesinato del líder del movimiento para los derechos civiles, Martin Luther King, Jr.	El mundo vio al astronauta Neil Armstrong caminar en la Luna.	Primera programación del canal MTV, vídeos de música las 24 horas al día	La Guerra del Golfo fue la primera guerra transmitida en directo por la televisión.	El ataque de terrorismo contra las Torres Gemelas en Nueva York filmado en directo por noticieros de televisión	Telemundo se convirtió en el primer canal en español que transmitió telenovelas por Internet.	Univisión anunció la creación de un nuevo canal de noticias de 24 horas, llamado Univisión 24/7.

1. ¿Cuándo caminó en la Luna Neil Armstrong?

2. ¿Quién se murió en 1968?

3. ¿Qué se vio por primera vez en 1991?

4. ¿Cuál de estos eventos tuvo el mayor impacto en tu vida?

5. Piensa en una noticia importante que viste en la televisión. ¿Cómo te sentiste cuando lo viste?

6. Piensa en algún evento histórico que viste en la televisión con otras personas. ¿Cómo se sintieron?

▼16 Y tú, ¿qué dices?

Escribir • Hablar

1. ¿Qué viste recientemente en la televisión? ¿Los miembros de tu familia también lo vieron o prefirieron ver otro programa?

2. ¿Te dormiste recientemente cuando estabas viendo la tele? ¿Te dormiste porque estabas muy cansado(a) o porque te aburriste mucho?

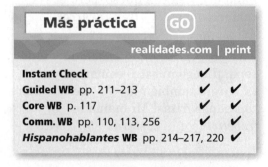

Más práctica	GO	
	**realidades.com	print**	
Instant Check	✔	
Guided WB pp. 211–213	✔	✔
Core WB p. 117	✔	✔
Comm. WB pp. 110, 113, 256	✔	✔
Hispanohablantes **WB** pp. 214–217, 220	✔	

Gramática

Other reflexive verbs

Other reflexive verbs use reflexive pronouns and verb forms but do not have the meaning of a person doing an action to or for himself or herself. These reflexive verbs often describe a change in mental, emotional, or physical state, and can express the idea that someone "gets" or "becomes."

¿Recuerdas?

You know that you use reflexive verbs to say that people do something to or for themselves.

• Felipe **se afeitaba** mientras yo **me cepillaba** los dientes.

Examples of these verbs are:

aburrirse	to get bored	enojarse	to become angry
casarse	to get married	ponerse	to become
divertirse	to have fun	(furioso, -a; alegre; . . .)	(furious, happy, . . .)
dormirse	to fall asleep	volverse loco, -a	to go crazy

Se durmieron durante la película.

Se puso alegre después de ganar.

Más ayuda   **realidades.com**

▶️ *GramActiva* Video

🔊 *Canción de hip hop:* ¿Viste el partido?

📝 *GramActiva* Activity

▼17 En la casa de mi novia | ♻

Leer • Escribir

A Lorenzo le gusta ir a la casa de su novia, pero ¡no es nada divertido ver la tele con sus padres! Completa su descripción con las formas apropiadas de *aburrirse, divertirse, dormirse y ponerse*.

No me gusta ver la tele con los padres de mi novia. Les gusta ver los programas educativos. No me gustan estos programas y __1.__ viéndolos. Y lo malo es que su papá casi siempre __2.__ durante los programas y nunca los ve hasta el final. Pero si yo quiero ver otra cosa y cambio *(I change)* de canales, él siempre se despierta. Entonces __3.__ un poco agitado porque su programa no está en la pantalla. Ellos también __4.__ viendo los programas de concursos que a mí me parecen muy tontos. Su mamá __5.__ emocionada cuando sabe la respuesta correcta o el precio correcto de algún objeto. Me encanta visitar a mi novia pero si veo la tele, __6.__ más cuando estoy en mi propia casa.

"Operación Triunfo", un programa de concursos de España

18 Los programas |

Hablar

¿Cómo te sientes cuando ves cada clase de
programa? Con otro(a) estudiante, pregunta y
contesta según el modelo.

▶ **Modelo**

A —¿Qué piensas de <u>los
programas deportivos</u>?

B —Creo que son muy <u>divertidos</u>.
Me pongo <u>emocionado(a)</u>
cuando los veo.

Estudiante A

1.
2.
3.
4.
5.
6.

Estudiante B

aburrirse   ponerse agitado, -a
divertirse   alegre
dormirse   emocionado, -a
                     enojado, -a
                     furioso, -a

¡Respuesta personal!

19 Un empate |

Hablar • Escribir

¿Qué pasó cuando el partido resultó en un empate? ¿Cómo estuvieron
los aficionados? Trabaja con otro(a) estudiante para describirlos. Usa
los verbos de la Actividad 18. Luego imagina que tú estabas en el
estadio durante el partido. ¿Cómo te sentiste tú cuando el partido
resultó en un empate?

▶ **Modelo**

David

A —¿Cómo estuvo David durante el partido?

B —Se puso agitado.

LOS LEONES **2**
LOS JAGUARES **2**

Guillermo

Pepe y Luisa

José

David

Carlota y Miguel

Paco

Ramón

Juanita y su hija

▼20 Y tú, ¿qué dices? | (Talk!) | ♻️

Escribir • Hablar

Escoge un verbo del recuadro y escribe tres o cuatro frases describiendo cuándo y por qué te sentiste así.

Modelo

Mis amigos y yo queríamos ir al cine el sábado a ver una nueva película. Mi mamá me dijo que tenía que ir con mi familia a la casa de mis tíos. Me puse furioso.

aburrirse	ponerse agitado, -a
divertirse	alegre
enojarse	emocionado, -a
	furioso, -a

¿Recuerdas?

Remember that when telling a story in the past, the preterite tense describes actions that began and ended at a specific time. The imperfect tense, however . . .

• provides background information such as time and weather conditions.

• describes the existing physical, mental, and emotional states of a person or thing.

• says what was happening when something else took place.

▼21 Las pantallas

Escribir • Hablar

Mira el cuadro de Mariano Sapia, un artista argentino. Luego contesta las preguntas.

1. En "Pantallas", ¿dónde está la gente?

2. ¿Qué hace la gente? ¿Qué ve en los televisores? ¿Hay una diferencia entre los televisores y las ventanas de las tiendas?

3. ¿Por qué crees que tanta gente mira la cancha de fútbol donde nadie juega y tan poca gente mira el otro televisor? ¿Cómo piensas que se siente la gente?

"Pantallas" (2002), Mariano Sapia

Oil on canvas, 120 x 170 cm. Photo courtesy of Praxis International Art, New York.

El español en la comunidad

La cadena de televisión número uno en Nueva York, Los Ángeles y Chicago para ver las noticias entre adultos de 18 a 34 años no es ni ABC, ni CBS, ni NBC, ni Fox, ni CNN. Es Univisión, la cadena en español más grande y más vista de los Estados Unidos. Muchos profesores de español en los Estados Unidos recomiendan Univisión para sus estudiantes.

• ¿Tienes canal de Univisión en tu comunidad? ¿Por qué puede ser bueno ver algunos programas en Univisión?

Regional variations of *ll* / *y* and *c* / *z*

The majority of Spanish speakers do not distinguish between *ll* and *y*, pronouncing both like *y* in the English word *yes*. Listen to and say these words and sentences as the majority of Spanish speakers would:

rodilla   joyas   cepillo   rayas

llamar   sellos

Tiene que llevar un yeso.

La calle está cerca de la playa.

Note, however, that the pronunciation of *ll* and *y* varies around the Spanish-speaking world. In Argentina and Uruguay, *ll* and *y* are pronounced like the *s* in the English word *measure*. In other countries, the *ll* is pronounced with a hint of an *l*, much like the English word *million,* but a bit softer.

Listen to and say the words and sentences above again, first as a speaker from Argentina or Uruguay would pronounce them, and then as many other Spanish speakers would.

Enjoy this children's riddle from Mexico:

> A ver tú chiquitillo,
> cara de pillo,
> si sabes contestar.
> Es muy grande y muy feo
> fuerte y fiero
> y vive por el mar.

In Latin America and parts of Spain, *c* before *e* and *i,* and *z* before a vowel are pronounced like the *s* in *sink*. In some parts of Spain, however, these letters are pronounced like the *th* in *think*.

Listen to and say the following words as most Spaniards would pronounce them:

cierto dice bronce ciclismo concierto

belleza abrazo azúcar buzón comenzar

¡Compruébalo! Try this tongue twister about a cat:

> Gato cenizoso,
> sal de ceniza
> descenizósate, gato.

▼ **Fondo Cultural** | **España**

Concursomanía En España, durante los últimos años, se han estrenado *(have premiered)* muchos programas de concursos donde los participantes compiten contestando preguntas de cultura general. Programas como "Pasapalabra" o "Saber y ganar" son divertidos y dan muchos premios como dinero, coches y viajes. Recientemente, los concursos de supervivencia *(survival)* están de moda. Con frecuencia, los concursantes se convierten en personajes muy populares, conocidos en todo el país.

• Compara la popularidad de los programas de concursos y de supervivencia en España y en los Estados Unidos. ¿Son similares estos programas o son diferentes?

▼22 Juego

Escribir • Hablar • GramActiva

1 Trabaja con un grupo de tres. En pequeñas hojas de papel o tarjetas, escriban palabras que conocen de este capítulo y otros capítulos que pueden usar para contar lo que pasó en los dibujos.

2 Pongan todas las tarjetas en un grupo boca abajo *(facedown)*. Un(a) estudiante toma una tarjeta y forma una frase usando la palabra para contar lo que pasó.

Modelo
Los aficionados se pusieron muy alegres.

el tanteo

alegres

los aficionados

▼23 El cuento

Escribir • Hablar

Usen las ideas de la Actividad 22 y preparen el cuento de lo que pasó en las ilustraciones. Vean la nota *¿Recuerdas?* en la página 307 para recordar cómo usar el pretérito y el imperfecto juntos en un cuento. Presenten su cuento a otro grupo, a su profesor(a) o a la clase.

Más práctica GO

realidades.com | print

Instant Check	✔	
Guided WB pp. 214–215	✔	✔
Core WB pp. 118–119	✔	✔
Comm. WB pp. 110–111, 114	✔	✔
Hispanohablantes WB pp. 218–219, 221	✔	

Lectura 🌎

Los Juegos Panamericanos

Estrategia

Using prior knowledge
When reading a text in Spanish, use your knowledge of the subject in English to help you understand the context of the reading. The following piece is about the Pan-American Games, an event similar to the Summer Olympics. What would you expect to find in a reading about a major sporting event?

Atletas en la ceremonia de inauguración en Winnipeg, Canadá

LOS JUEGOS PANAMERICANOS se establecieron para promover la comprensión entre las naciones del continente americano. Los primeros Juegos se inauguraron el 25 de febrero de 1951 en Buenos Aires, con 2,513 atletas de 22 países. El lema[1] de los Juegos —"América, Espírito, Sport, Fraternité"— incorpora cuatro de los idiomas más importantes de las Américas: el español, el portugués, el inglés y el francés. Todos los países de las Américas pueden mandar atletas a competir. Aproximadamente el 80 por ciento de los deportes de los Juegos Panamericanos se juegan en las Olimpíadas. Los Juegos Panamericanos se celebran cada cuatro años durante el verano previo a los Juegos Olímpicos.

EL LOGOTIPO de los Juegos Panamericanos de Guadalajara 2011 es una llama de fuego *(flame)* que representa a las Américas y al deporte olímpico. Tiene cuatro colores: tres corresponden a los colores de los aros *(rings)* olímpicos y el magenta hace referencia a México.

[1] motto

LOGOS Y MASCOTAS

Para conmemorar los Juegos Panamericanos, cada cuatro años el país anfitrión[3] crea una mascota que representa algo histórico o cultural del país.

La Habana, Cuba, 1991
Tocopan—El nombre de la mascota oficial de los Juegos Panamericanos en la Habana proviene de la combinación de la palabra Tocororo (considerado el ave nacional de Cuba por poseer los colores de la bandera nacional) con la palabra *Panamericanos*.

Mar del Plata, Argentina, 1995
Lobi—El león marino es un habitante tradicional del mar cerca de la ciudad de Mar del Plata. Sonriendo con brazos abiertos, Lobi da cordiales saludos de bienvenida a la familia panamericana.

Santo Domingo, República Dominicana, 2003
Tito—El manatí es una especie en peligro de extinción. Tito, la mascota, simboliza el deseo que tienen los dominicanos de proteger su medio ambiente.

Río de Janeiro, Brasil, 2007
Cauê—Ésta no es una mascota típica porque no es un animal. Es un sol que representa el clima tropical de Brasil y la idea de que todos pueden participar en los deportes. Más de un millón de brasileños votaron para seleccionar el nombre "Cauê".

JEFFERSON PÉREZ: UN HÉROE NACIONAL

En el año 1995, el ecuatoriano Jefferson Pérez ganó la medalla de oro en la marcha[4] de 20 km durante los Juegos Panamericanos de Mar del Plata, Argentina. Se convirtió en un héroe nacional de Ecuador cuando ganó otra vez la medalla de oro en 1996, en Atlanta, Estados Unidos, durante los Juegos Olímpicos. Fue la primera vez que un atleta de Ecuador ganó una medalla de oro en las Olimpíadas. Además de esta importante victoria, Pérez ganó tres medallas de oro en los Juegos Panamericanos de Mar del Plata 1995, Santo Domingo 2003 y Río de Janeiro 2007, y una de plata en los Juegos Olímpicos de Beijing 2008. Jefferson Pérez vino de un barrio muy pobre de Cuenca, Ecuador, y llegó a ser un símbolo de lo que uno puede alcanzar[5] con mucho trabajo y esfuerzo.

Jefferson Pérez ganó otra vez la medalla de oro en los Juegos Panamericanos en 2007.

La bandera de Ecuador

[3]host country   [4]speed walking   [5]accomplish

¿Comprendiste?

1. ¿Cómo representan el lema y el símbolo de los Juegos Panamericanos los diferentes países del continente?

2. ¿Por qué son importantes los Juegos Panamericanos para un(a) atleta que quiere competir en las Olimpíadas?

3. ¿Qué representan las mascotas de los Juegos? ¿Qué representa el manatí?

4. ¿Por qué llegó a ser un héroe nacional Jefferson Pérez?

Y tú, ¿qué dices? | (Talk!)

1. ¿Crees que un(a) atleta puede ser un(a) héroe (heroína) nacional? ¿Por qué?

2. Tienes que crear una mascota y un cartel para una celebración para unos juegos deportivos internacionales en tu comunidad. ¿Qué pones en el cartel? ¿Cómo es la mascota?

Más práctica	(GO)

realidades.com | print

Guided WB p. 216	✔	✔
Comm. WB pp. 115, 257	✔	✔
Hispanohablantes WB pp. 222–223		✔
Cultural Reading Activity	✔	

La cultura en vivo

La guía de la tele

¿Sabías que las guías (guides) de televisión se encuentran entre las revistas más leídas en muchos países hispanohablantes? La gente consulta estas guías, tanto las revistas como sus versiones digitales, para informarse de la programación televisiva. Además (Furthermore), muchos periódicos publican la programación en sus ediciones diarias.

Preparar una buena programación no es fácil. La programación debe tener variedad e interés para muchas personas. Tiene que ser divertida, ofrecer noticias informativas y tener programas culturales también.

Objetivo

Hacer una guía de programas de televisión

Materiales

• papel, marcadores y lápices de colores

Instrucciones

Formen grupos de dos o tres estudiantes.

1 Van a planear la programación en un canal para un día de la semana desde las cuatro de la tarde hasta medianoche.

2 Escojan la clase de programas que quieren ofrecer (informativos, culturales, cine, concursos, deportivos y más) y las horas en que se dan. ¡Cuidado! En los países hispanohablantes se usa un horario de programación de 24 horas. ¡No se olviden de dar un nombre a cada programa!

3 Preparen la guía. Usen colores diferentes para las diferentes clases de programas.

4 Al final de la guía, escriban una recomendación para el mejor programa del día.

	Programación de televisión para el martes			
HORA	**Canal 2**	**Canal 3**	**Canal 4**	**Canal 7**
06:30	Noticias	El tiempo	Dibujos animados	Música
07:00	¡Hagamos ejercicio!	Programa escolar	Mundo animal	
07:30	Grandes viajes			Actualidad deportiva
08:00				El tiempo
08:30	La buena cocina	Las aventuras de Simón	Tú y yo	Pueblos de América
09:00	Noticias			
09:30	Cine clásico	Medicina y salud	Fútbol mundial	Película
10:00				
10:30		Siglo XXI		
11:00				Vida en el mar
11:30	Telenovela	Película infantil	Noticias	
12:00				

Presentación oral

Un programa de televisión

Task
Prepare a review of one of your favorite TV shows.

① Prepare Think of a TV show you like to watch and other people might like to watch as well. Make a list of facts needed to persuade others to watch the show, including:

- nombre del programa
- descripción
- día, hora y canal
- para qué edades *(ages)*
- actores / presentadores
- un adjetivo que describe el programa
- lo que ocurrió en un episodio reciente
- cómo te sentiste cuando viste el episodio
- por qué te gustó o no te gustó

② Practice Go through your presentation several times. You can use your notes in practice, but not when you present. Try to:

- present a persuasive and interesting review
- provide all the information on the program
- use complete sentences and speak clearly

Modelo
Mi programa favorito es Modern Family. *Lo dan en el canal . . .*

③ Present Present your review of the TV program.

④ Evaluation The following rubric will be used to grade your presentation.

Rubric	Score 1	Score 3	Score 5
Persuasiveness of your review	You are ineffective in persuading the audience.	You are somewhat effective in persuading the audience.	You are very effective in persuading the audience.
How much information you communicate	You provide up to three facts to your audience.	You provide up to six facts to your audience.	You provide all nine facts to your audience.
How easily you are understood	You are difficult to understand and have many grammatical errors.	You are fairly easy to understand and have occasional grammatical errors.	You are easy to understand and have very few grammatical errors.

Estrategia

Note-taking
Taking notes can help you prepare for an oral or written presentation. As you watch the show you are reviewing, take notes to help you remember details. What do you like about the show? What happens in the particular episode?

En busca de la verdad

Episodio 7

Antes de ver el video

"Señor, no podemos darle tal información".

"Papá, creo que tengo una pista para saber lo que pasó con el abuelo".

Nota cultural La palabra "estudiantina" se usa para hablar de un grupo musical de estudiantes universitarios. Su origen es muy antiguo, y viene de los músicos cantores llamados trovadores. Los trovadores cantaban en las calles, y hoy las estudiantinas cantan en los parques y en las plazas. En México hay más de 200 estudiantinas. Algunas se presentan en Guanajuato durante el festival de teatro que se celebra todos los años.

Resumen del episodio

Roberto, Linda y Julio pasan el día paseando por Guanajuato. Por la tarde, Roberto y Linda van al Jardín de la Unión y escuchan una estudiantina. Al día siguiente, Roberto habla con la familia de lo que sabe sobre el abuelo. El misterioso hombre del episodio anterior llega a Guanajuato.

Palabras para comprender
mensaje message
si me permites if you allow me
a eso de las 9 around 9 o'clock
Están de acuerdo. They agree.
pasado past
pronto soon
pista clue

Después de ver el video

¿Comprendiste?

A. Escoge la palabra correcta entre paréntesis y di quién dice cada frase. (Roberto, Linda, Julio o Tomás Toledo)

a. "No olvides el de Diego Rivera. Fue su _____ casa". (última / primera / bella)

b. "Luego Julio tuvo que _____". (acostarse / irse / salir)

c. "¿Quieres comer o _____ algo mientras esperamos?" (jugar / tomar / ponerte)

d. "El abuelo _____ una cuenta en un banco de los Estados Unidos". (cambió / cerró / abrió)

e. "Por eso en el Banco de San Antonio estaban _____". (confundidos / bravos / asustados)

f. "Hijo, a veces es mejor no tocar el _____". (teléfono / dolor / pasado)

B. Habla de los planes de Roberto. ¿Adónde va a ir para seguir las pistas? ¿Con quién? ¿Qué quiere el hombre misterioso?

Nota cultural El Jardín de la Unión es el parque más importante de Guanajuato. Está sembrado de árboles llamados *Laureles de la India* y tiene la forma de un triángulo. Por eso los habitantes de la ciudad llaman este parque "pedazo de queso". Allí hay un quiosco donde toca la banda del estado. Los parques y las plazas siempre han sido lugares de reunión para los mexicanos. Son espacios públicos que todos pueden disfrutar.

"¡Tú vas con nosotras!"

Más práctica	GO
realidades.com	print
Actividades	✔

Repaso del capítulo

Vocabulario y gramática

to talk about a sporting event

el aficionado	fan
la aficionada	
al final	at the end
aplaudir	to applaud
el / la atleta	athlete
el campeón,	champion
la campeona,	
pl. los campeones	
el campeonato	championship
la competencia	competition
competir (*e → i*)	to compete
el empate	tie
el entrenador,	coach, trainer
la entrenadora	
fenomenal	phenomenal
el jugador,	player
la jugadora	
la liga	league
meter un gol	to score a goal
perder (*e → ie*)	to lose
por . . . vez	for the . . . time
resultar	to result, to turn out
el tanteo	score
último, -a	last, final

to talk about a contest

el auditorio	auditorium
el comentario	commentary
el concurso de belleza	beauty contest
la entrevista	interview
entrevistar	to interview
un millón de /	a million /
millones de	millions of
el premio	prize
el presentador,	presenter
la presentadora	
el público	audience
la reina	queen

For *Vocabulario adicional*, see pp. 498–499.

to talk about how you feel

aburrirse	to get bored
agitado, -a	agitated
alegre	happy
emocionado, -a	excited, emotional
enojado, -a	angry
enojarse	to get angry
furioso, -a	furious
ponerse + *adjective*	to become
volverse (*o → ue*)	to go crazy
loco, -a	

other useful words

dormirse (*o → ue,*	to fall asleep
o → u)	
morirse (*o → ue,*	to die
o → u)	

preterite of -*ir* stem-changing verbs
preferir

preferí	preferimos
preferiste	preferisteis
prefirió	prefirieron

pedir

pedí	pedimos
pediste	pedisteis
pidió	pidieron

dormir

dormí	dormimos
dormiste	dormisteis
durmió	durmieron

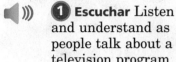

Más repaso GO realidades.com | print

Instant Check ✔
Puzzles ✔
Core WB pp. 120–121 ✔
Comm. WB p. 258 ✔ ✔

Preparación para el examen

On the exam you will be asked to . . .	Here are practice tasks similar to those you will find on the exam . . .	For review go to your print or digital textbook . . .

Interpretive

1 Escuchar Listen and understand as people talk about a television program they saw

Listen as people talk about an awards show they saw on television. Try to identify their reactions to this type of show. Did they become angry? Emotional? Excited? Bored? Nervous?

pp. 294–297 *Vocabulario en contexto*
p. 300 Actividades 8–9

Interpersonal

2 Hablar Talk about a recent television program you saw and describe your reactions to it

As part of a class project, you may be interviewed about a television program you saw. Practice what you might say by telling a partner: (a) what type of program you saw; (b) when you saw it; (c) how you reacted to the program.

p. 300 Actividad 10
p. 304 Actividad 16
p. 306 Actividad 18
p. 313 *Presentación oral*

Interpretive

3 Leer Read and understand a description of a soccer game

Your friend just returned from a trip to Spain. He brought a newspaper clipping from a soccer game he saw. As you read, see if you can understand what happened.

pp. 294–297 *Vocabulario en contexto*
p. 298 Actividad 4
p. 299 Actividad 6
p. 301 Actividad 11
pp. 310–311 *Lectura*

> **MADRID CONOCE A BARCELONA**
> Ayer fue una competencia fenomenal. Millones de madrileños vieron el partido en la tele. En los primeros tres minutos del partido, el Real Madrid metió un gol. Treinta minutos más tarde, Morales de Barcelona también metió un gol. Un empate. Todos los aficionados se pusieron muy alegres durante el partido, pero el público se volvió loco cuando Madrid metió otro gol en los últimos dos minutos. Al final, el tanteo fue Madrid 2 y Barcelona 1.

Presentational

4 Escribir Write about an occasion when you became angry

You may have heard that rather than acting out your anger, it is better to write about it to get it out of your system. Write about a recent event or situation that caused you to feel angry. Describe what happened and why you became angry.

p. 300 Actividad 9
p. 303 Actividad 14
p. 306 Actividad 19
p. 307 Actividad 20

Cultures

5 Pensar Demonstrate an understanding of television shows on Spanish-speaking channels

Think about the popularity of soap operas, game shows, and sporting events on television stations in the United States. Do you think they would be popular choices on Spanish-language television stations too? Give examples from the chapter to support your answer.

p. 308 *Fondo cultural*
p. 312 *La cultura en vivo*

▼ Chapter Objectives

Communication

By the end of this chapter you will be able to:

- Listen and read about movie reviews
- Talk and write about films
- Exchange information about a movie you saw recently

Culture

You will also be able to:

- Understand how movies can reflect the language and culture of the country where they are produced
- Compare movies and movie classification systems in Spanish-speaking countries and the United States

You will demonstrate what you know and can do:

- Presentación escrita, p. 339
- Preparación para el examen, p. 343

You will use:

Vocabulary	Grammar
• Movies • Making a movie	• Verbs that use indirect object pronouns • The present perfect

Exploración del mundo hispano

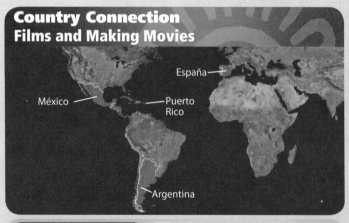

Un cine en Cuernavaca, México

Country Connection
Films and Making Movies

España
México
Puerto Rico
Argentina

 realidades.com **GO**

 Reference Atlas

▶ **Videocultura y actividad**

 **Mapa global interactivo**

Arte y cultura | El mundo hispano

Películas ganadoras del Oscar Los países de habla hispana, particularmente España, Argentina y México, tienen una larga historia de cine. Hasta el año 2010, casi 40 películas de países hispanos recibieron nominaciones al Oscar a la mejor película extranjera. De las seis películas que han ganado *(have won)* el premio, cuatro son de España: *Volver a empezar* (1982), *Belle Époque* (1993), *Todo sobre mi madre* (1999) y *Mar adentro* (2004). Las otras dos son argentinas: *La historia oficial* (1985) y *El secreto de sus ojos* (2009).

- ¿Has visto *(Have you seen)* alguna de estas películas? Si contestas que sí, compárala con las películas de Hollywood que reciben el Oscar. ¿En qué sentido son similares y en qué sentido son diferentes?

▼ Objectives

Read, listen to, and understand information about
▶ movies
▶ making a movie

Vocabulario en contexto

Tu casa - tu cine

PELÍCULAS NUEVAS:
Violencia en la ciudad
El amor eterno

LUNES Y MARTES:
Alquila dos películas por el precio de una.

EL ROBO PERFECTO

robar

la ladrona

el ladrón

el crimen

2050

los efectos especiales

el (la) extraterrestre

VIOLENCIA EN LA CIUDAD

película de acción

el detective

la detective

la víctima*

—¿**Has visto** la película *2050*? **¿Qué tal es?**

—Pues, **me fascinan** las películas de ciencia ficción, pero **no he visto** esa película **todavía. Los críticos** han escrito varios artículos sobre la película y todos la **recomiendan.** Creo que la película **será** muy popular con el público.

—Bueno. ¿Se puede alquilar ya el video o el DVD?

—No. Todavía no.

*Note that *la víctima* is always feminine.

LAS CALLES CRUELES

capturar

arrestar

el criminal

la criminal

el galán

EL AMOR ETERNO

El galán **está enamorado de** la mujer, pero ella no **se enamora de** él hasta el final de la película.

Detrás de *En busca de la verdad*

En busca de la verdad tiene **un argumento** muy básico. Se trata de tres generaciones de una familia mexicana. Roberto le pregunta a su abuela dónde está su abuelo, Federico, pero nadie sabe qué le pasó. Roberto decide buscar la verdad.

los personajes principales

la directora

la escena

Dora Guzmán Trujillo, como directora, está en control de **la dirección** de la película. Roberto Castañeda **hace el papel de** Roberto. Él vive en la ciudad de Querétaro y ha participado en muchas obras de teatro. Elia González hace el papel de Linda. Ella también vive en Querétaro y hace muchos años que es actriz. A los dos jóvenes les gusta **la actuación** y desean tener **papeles** cada vez más importantes en el cine, el teatro y la televisión.

▼1 ¿Qué película es? | 🔊 _____

Escuchar

Mira los carteles de las películas que hay en las páginas 320 y 321. Escucha las frases y señala el cartel de la película que corresponde a cada frase.

Más práctica	GO

realidades.com | print

Instant Check	✔	
Guided WB pp. 218–222	✔	✔
Core WB pp. 122–123	✔	✔
Comm. WB p. 122	✔	✔
Hispanohablantes WB p. 232		✔

▼2 ¿Cuánto sabes de | 🔊 _____ las películas?

Escuchar

Escucha las frases y contesta las preguntas.

1. **a.** el personaje principal
   b. el director

2. **a.** la directora
   b. el actor

3. **a.** los extraterrestres
   b. los efectos especiales

4. **a.** se enamoran de ellos
   b. los capturan

Más vocabulario

la estrella (del cine)   star, (movie) star

tratarse de   to be about

El mosquito

¿Qué pasa en la película que hace Manolo para su clase? ¿Quién es "el mosquito"?

Estrategia

Predicting meaning
The images of a movie can tell a story, even if you don't hear the audio. Look at the images from Manolo's movie. What happens to Ramón? Will he get a good grade on the test?

1

Profesor: Buenos días. ¿Qué película vamos a ver primero? A ver . . . ¿Manolo?

Manolo: Bien. **Está basada en** la historia de un mosquito y un estudiante.

Director: **Manolo**

Estudiante: **Ramón**

El mosquito: **Claudia**

Amiga: **Teresa**

5

Ramón: ¿Lees? ¿Qué dice este libro?

Claudia: Se trata de la historia de los Estados Unidos. Tú puedes dormirte mientras que yo leo el libro. Mañana puedo decirte las respuestas durante el examen.

Ramón: Muy bien. Me voy a dormir.

6

Teresa: ¡Ramón, despiértate! ¿Has estudiado para el examen?

7

Teresa: ¿Qué es esto?

Ramón: ¡Mi libro! ¡Teresa! ¡Déjalo! ¡Lo necesito!

Claudia: ¡NOOOOO!

Ramón: Mañana tengo un examen y no he estudiado. No sé nada. ¿Qué puedo hacer?

Claudia: No vas a **matar**me, ¿verdad? ¡No quiero morirme!

Ramón: ¿Qué has dicho? ¿Tú hablas?

Claudia: Sí. Puedo hablar inglés y español.

Claudia: Yo puedo leer también.

Ramón: ¿Cómo? Yo tengo que estudiar y tú me molestas.

Claudia: ¿Quieres **tener éxito** en el examen? Yo puedo ayudarte a estudiar.

Ramón: ¡Teresa! ¡No! ¿Qué has hecho? Mi libro . . . El examen . . . ¿Qué voy a hacer? ¡Qué **fracaso**!

▼3 ¿Comprendiste?

Leer • Escribir

En una hoja de papel escribe las frases de abajo, poniéndolas en orden cronológico.

1. Los dos deciden que el mosquito va a estudiar para el examen de historia.
2. Ramón le grita y ahora no sabe qué va a hacer.
3. Teresa cierra el libro.
4. Teresa entra en el cuarto para despertar a Ramón.
5. Ramón está nervioso porque tiene un examen y no ha estudiado.
6. El mosquito le dice a Ramón que puede hablar inglés y español.
7. Manolo le va a presentar su película a la clase.
8. Ramón va a matar al mosquito.

Más práctica GO	realidades.com | print	
Instant Check	✔	
Guided WB pp. 223–226	✔	✔
Core WB pp. 124–125	✔	✔
Comm. WB pp. 116–118, 119	✔	✔
Hispanohablantes **WB** p. 233		✔

| ▼ **Objectives**

▸ Talk about movie genres
▸ Discuss the different aspects of a film
▸ Listen to descriptions of movie characters
▸ Write about movies

Vocabulario en uso

▼4 ¿En qué película . . . ?

Hablar

Trabaja con otro(a) estudiante para hablar de las películas en que has visto a estas personas o cosas. ¿Qué clase de película es cada una? Si necesitas repasar *(review)* las diferentes clases de películas, ve las páginas 320 y 321.

▶️ **Modelo**

un criminal

A —*¿En qué película has visto a un criminal?*
B —*He visto a un criminal en El hombre araña. Es una película de acción.*
o: —*No he visto a un criminal en ninguna película.*

1.
2.
3.
4.
5.
6.

▼5 El crítico nos recomienda . . .

Leer • Escribir

Lee el siguiente artículo que escribió el crítico de películas del periódico. Escribe en una hoja de papel la palabra apropiada.

Muchos me preguntan, __1.__ *(¿Qué tal es / ¿Cómo estás)* la nueva película del __2.__ *(director / criminal)* Antonio Sánchez? Pues, en mi opinión, esta película va a ser un(a) __3.__ *(fracaso / escena)* total. __4.__ *(Los efectos especiales / El argumento)* de la película está(n) basado(s) en una novela de amor, pero esta película no es nada romántica: es una película de acción. ¡La película __5.__ *(se trata / hace el papel)* de la violencia, no del amor! En la novela, el personaje principal está __6.__ *(basado / enamorado)* de una joven bonita

pero en la película él sólo trata de arrestar a los criminales. La __7.__ *(actuación / acción)* del actor que hace el papel del galán es terrible también. Y la __8.__ *(actuación / dirección)* del director Sánchez es peor. Por ejemplo, en la escena final, la víctima inocente se muere cuando los criminales la __9.__ *(capturan / fascinan)*. Y el detective no puede __10.__ *(arrestar / robar)* a los criminales. Si no __11.__ *(has visto / he visto)* esta película todavía, ¡no la recomiendo! __12.__ *(Alquila / Roba)* un video y quédate en casa.

▼6 Escucha y escribe | 🔊))

Escuchar • Escribir

Escucha las siguientes descripciones y escríbelas en una hoja de papel. Luego decide quién del recuadro hace cada acción y escribe su nombre al lado de la frase.

También se dice . . .

el (la) extraterrestre = el marciano, la marciana (muchos países)

el ladrón, la ladrona = el bandido, la bandida; el malo, la mala (muchos países)

el (la) criminal	el ladrón, la ladrona
el crítico, la crítica	el director, la directora
el galán	el (la) detective
el (la) extraterrestre	

▼7 Las películas clásicas | 👥

Observar • Leer • Hablar

¿Te gusta ver las películas clásicas? Mira el cartel de cine de una película mexicana. Luego, con otro(a) estudiante, contesta las preguntas.

1. ¿Qué clase de película es?
2. ¿Quién es la estrella de la película? ¿Pueden decir qué papel hace?
3. ¿Cómo se llama el director?
4. Según lo que ves en el cartel, ¿te gustaría ver esta película? ¿Por qué?

El barrendero (1982), director Miguel M. Delgado

▼ Fondo Cultural | México

La época de oro del cine mexicano Entre 1930 y 1950, el cine mexicano tuvo una época de oro, produciendo muchas películas y compitiendo con Hollywood. Uno de los actores más famosos de esta época fue Mario Moreno, mejor conocido como Cantinflas. Cantinflas era un cómico que hizo reír a muchos espectadores desde España hasta Argentina. En los años 60 el cine mexicano no pudo competir con la televisión y la época de oro se terminó.

• ¿Qué películas producidas en otros países conoces? ¿En qué sentido son similares a las películas producidas en los Estados Unidos? ¿En qué sentido son diferentes?

Mario Moreno, famoso actor mexicano

▼8 Los diferentes aspectos de una película |

Escribir • Hablar

Habla con otro(a) estudiante sobre los diferentes aspectos de una película que ayudan a determinar si la película va a tener éxito o si será un fracaso.

❶ Copia la tabla en una hoja de papel. Escribe el título de las películas en que has observado estos aspectos. Escribe una descripción de los aspectos.

la película	la música	los efectos especiales	los personajes	la actuación	el argumento
Avatar	estupenda				

❷ Habla con otro(a) estudiante sobre tus opiniones de diferentes películas usando la tabla que llenaste.

▶ Modelo

la música

A —*La música en la película* Avatar *me pareció estupenda.*

B —*Estoy de acuerdo. Me fascinó la música en esa película.*

o: *No estoy de acuerdo. No me gustó nada la música en esa película.*

o: *¿De veras? No he visto todavía esa película.*

Estudiante A

fantástico, -a   complicado, -a   tonto, -a
tremendo, -a   aburrido, -a   realista
increíble   horrible   **¡Respuesta personal!**
interesante   malo / malísimo, -a

Estudiante B

me fascinó / me fascinaron
me gustó / me gustaron
me encantó / me encantaron

▼ Fondo Cultural | México

Salma Hayek-Jiménez, la primera actriz mexicana en hacerse estrella de Hollywood después de Dolores del Río (1905–1983), nació en el sureste de México el 2 de septiembre de 1966. Empezó su carrera como actriz en las telenovelas mexicanas. En Hollywood tiene mucho éxito como productora; fue productora y también protagonista de *Frida* (2002), sobre la famosa pintora Frida Kahlo. De 2006 a 2010 fue productora ejecutiva de la serie de televisión *Ugly Betty*.

• ¿Crees que es más fácil o más difícil para un actor o actriz hacer el papel de alguien famoso? ¿Por qué?

La actriz mexicana Salma Hayek

▼9 Juego |

Escribir • Hablar

① Usa las palabras del recuadro y trabaja con otro(a) estudiante para escribir cuatro preguntas sobre los actores o las actrices que salieron en diferentes películas. Después compitan contra otro grupo.

hacer el papel de	matar
enamorarse de	morirse
capturar y arrestar	robar
	¡Respuesta personal!

② Hagan sus preguntas para ver si el otro grupo puede identificar al actor o a la actriz. Si pueden, ellos ganan un punto. Si no, Uds. ganan un punto.

 Modelo

A —*¿Quién es el actor que hizo el papel principal en la película* Piratas del Caribe?

B —*Es Johnny Depp.*

▼10 Y tú, ¿qué dices? | (Talk!)

Escribir • Hablar

1. ¿Qué es más importante en una película: mucha acción o personajes interesantes? ¿La actuación o los efectos especiales?

2. ¿Hay demasiada violencia en las películas? ¿Por qué piensas así?

3. ¿Prestas atención a lo que dicen los críticos? Si dicen que una película es un fracaso, ¿la vas a ver? ¿Por qué?

4. ¿Qué película en el cine ahora será un fracaso? ¿Qué película va a tener mucho éxito?

▼ Exploración del lenguaje

The suffixes -oso(a) and -dor(a)

Spanish adjectives that end in -*oso(a)* often have English cognates ending in -*ous*:

fam**oso** → *famous*
nervi**oso** → *nervous*

¡Compruébalo! Write the Spanish adjective for these English words and use the correct form to complete the sentences.

studious   furious   generous

Una chica que estudia mucho es _____.

Él se pone _____ cuando le mentimos.

Ella siempre está dándome regalos. Es _____.

Words ending in -*dor(a)* indicate people who do different actions. Words ending in -*dor(a)* are either nouns or adjectives. Look at these verbs and related nouns and adjectives.

jugar → juga**dor** / juga**dora**
trabajar → trabaja**dor** / trabaja**dora**

Una chica que **anima** a otros durante un partido es una animadora.

Un niño que **habla** mucho es muy hablador.

¡Compruébalo! Look at the drawing and answer the questions.

¿Qué hizo el **ganador?**

¿Qué hizo el **perdedor**?

Gramática Repaso

Verbs that use indirect object pronouns

Here are some verbs that you've already learned that use indirect object pronouns.

aburrir	to bore
doler	to ache
encantar	to love
fascinar	to fascinate
gustar	to like
importar	to matter
interesar	to interest
molestar	to bother
parecer	to seem
quedar	to fit

These verbs all use a similar construction: indirect object pronoun + verb + subject.

Les encantan los efectos especiales en esa película.

Nos aburre mucho esa película.

A + a noun or a pronoun is often used with these verbs for emphasis or clarification. The pronouns agree with and clarify the indirect object pronoun.

(A mí)	me	(A nosotros) (A nosotras)	nos
(A ti)	te	(A vosotros) (A vosotras)	os
(A Ud.) (A él) (A ella)	le	(A Uds.) (A ellos) (A ellas)	les

A mí me importan mucho los efectos especiales en una película.

A Juanita le fascinan las películas de terror.

¿A Uds. les parece realista la película de acción?

Más ayuda realidades.com

▶ *GramActiva* Video
Tutorial: *Gustar* and similar verbs

GramActiva Activity

▼11 Nos gustan las películas

Leer • Escribir

En una hoja de papel, escribe el complemento indirecto *(indirect object pronoun)* apropiado.

A nosotros __1.__ gusta mucho el cine. A mí __2.__ encantan las películas biográficas, como *Selena,* pero a mi novio __3.__ aburren. Esta película __4.__ parece demasiado triste a él. A mis padres __5.__ interesan los dramas o las comedias. A mi mamá __6.__ fascina *Lo que el viento se llevó (Gone with the Wind)* con Clark Gable y Vivien Leigh, porque es muy romántica y a ella __7.__ encantan los vestidos que llevaban las actrices. ¡A mí no __8.__ interesa nada esa clase de película! ¿Qué clase de película __9.__ interesa a ti?

Jennifer López, en el papel de Selena

▼12 ¿Te molesta o te fascina? |

Escribir • Hablar

¿Cuáles son las cosas que te molestan o te fascinan de las películas, del cine o de la televisión? Escribe cuatro frases. Puedes usar las ideas del recuadro o tus propias ideas. Después lee tus frases a otro(a) estudiante para ver si tu compañero(a) reacciona de la misma manera *(in the same way)*.

la actuación

el argumento

los efectos especiales

las películas . . .

los personajes

las personas . . .

las telenovelas

la violencia

▶ **Modelo**

A —*Me fascina un argumento muy complicado en una película. ¿Y a ti?*
B —*No, me gusta más un argumento sencillo.*

Estudiante A

me aburre(n)	me gusta(n) (más)
me encanta(n)	me interesa(n)
me fascina(n)	me molesta(n)

Estudiante B

¡Respuesta personal!

▼13 Una encuesta entre tres | |

Escribir • Hablar

Trabaja con un grupo de tres estudiantes. Primero lee la lista de temas y escribe tus opiniones. Luego cada persona va a expresar su opinión sobre una categoría y preguntarle a otro(a) estudiante su opinión. En una hoja de papel, anoten las opiniones de su grupo para cada categoría en una tabla.

1. las películas de acción
2. las telenovelas
3. la música
4. los deportes
5. los videojuegos
6. la ropa
7. la computadora

▶ **Modelo**

las películas de acción

A —*A mí me encantan las películas de acción. ¿Y a ti, Isabel?*
B —*No me interesan mucho. ¿Y a ti, Roberto?*
C —*A mí también me encantan las películas de acción.*

▼14 ¿Qué les interesa más? |

Escribir

Usa la información de la Actividad 13 y escribe una o dos frases sobre las opiniones de tu grupo para cada categoría.

Modelo

A Roberto y a mí nos encantan las películas de acción, pero a Isabel no le interesan mucho.

▼15 Los anuncios | ♻

Escribir

Trabajas para una compañía de publicidad.
Tienes que escribir un anuncio de radio para
cada producto o lugar que ves abajo.

Modelo

*¿Te fascinan los libros? ¿Te
aburren los programas de
televisión? ¿Por qué no
visitas la Librería Ricardo?
Tenemos miles de libros
para toda la familia.*

1.

2.

3.

4.

▼16 Los premios ALMA

Leer

Lee este artículo sobre los premios ALMA. Después lee las frases que
siguen y decide si cada una es *C (cierta)* o *F (falsa)* según el artículo.
Si la frase es falsa, escribe la información correcta.

En 1995 se establecieron los premios **ALMA**¹ para ayudar
a promover² la representación justa y balanceada de los
latinos en la televisión, el cine y la música. Los premios
reconocen³ a los artistas latinos por sus éxitos y su impacto
positivo en la imagen del latino en los Estados Unidos. En
la categoría del cine, les dan premios a los directores, actores
y actrices latinos que producen películas en inglés para el
público en los Estados Unidos. Hay
premios también para diferentes
clases de programas de televisión
y los actores y actrices que
aparecen en ellos. Otra categoría
es la música: los videos, los
álbumes, los cantantes y los
grupos musicales. Algunas de las
estrellas que han recibido premios
en años recientes son Jimmy Smits,
America Ferrera, Edward James
Olmos, Andy García, Salma Hayek,
Antonio Banderas, Marc Anthony,
Jennifer López, Selena Gómez y
Shakira.

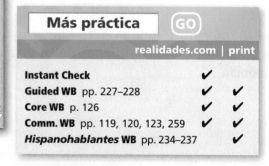

Selena Gómez en los
premios ALMA

1. Un actor latino puede ganar un
   premio ALMA por su papel en un
   programa de televisión dramático.

2. Una cantante que no es latina
   puede ganar un premio ALMA si
   canta en español.

3. Una actriz latina tiene que hablar
   español en la película para recibir
   el premio ALMA.

4. Tratan de usar los premios ALMA
   para dar una imagen positiva de
   los latinos en la televisión, el cine y
   la música.

Más práctica	GO

realidades.com | print

Instant Check	✔	
Guided WB pp. 227–228	✔	✔
Core WB p. 126	✔	✔
Comm. WB pp. 119, 120, 123, 259	✔	✔
***Hispanohablantes* WB** pp. 234–237		✔

¹soul, spirit   ²promote   ³recognize

Gramática

The present perfect

The present perfect tense is used to say what a person *has done*.

> Recientemente **hemos alquilado** muchos videos.
> *Recently **we have rented** a lot of videos.*

To form the present perfect tense, use present-tense forms of *haber* + the past participle.

he alquilado	hemos alquilado
has alquilado	habéis alquilado
ha alquilado	han alquilado

To form the past participle of a verb, drop the ending of the infinitive and add *-ado* for *-ar* verbs and *-ido* for *-er* and *-ir* verbs.

hablar → **hablado**

comer → **comido**

vivir → **vivido**

Most verbs that have two vowels together in the infinitive have a written accent on the *i* of the past participle.

caer → **caído**   oír → **oído**

leer → **leído**   traer → **traído**

Some verbs have irregular past participles.

decir → **dicho**	poner → **puesto**
devolver → **devuelto**	romper → **roto**
escribir → **escrito**	ver → **visto**
hacer → **hecho**	volver → **vuelto**
morir → **muerto**	

When you use object or reflexive pronouns with the present perfect, the pronoun goes immediately before the form of *haber*.

— ¿Has visto la nueva película de Ramón Guevara?

— No, no la he visto.

Más ayuda   **realidades.com**

 GramActiva Video
Tutorials: Formation of present perfect indicative (Spanish tutorial), Formation of present perfect indicative (English tutorial), Formation of the regular past participle
Animated Verbs

 Canción de hip hop: ¿Qué películas has visto?

 GramActiva Activity

▼17 Un informe

Leer • Escribir

En una hoja de papel, escribe la forma correcta del presente perfecto. Después di qué película has visto recientemente.

Sofía: ¿Paco, __1.__ *(oír)* recientemente de algunas películas buenas?

Paco: Pues, no, y tampoco __2.__ *(ir)* al cine, pero __3.__ *(alquilar)* una película aburrida sobre dos personas que __4.__ *(enamorarse)* en un barco en el Atlántico.

Sofía: Sí, sí, la conozco. Entonces, ¿ __5.__ *(escribir)* tu informe para la clase de inglés?

Paco: ¿Qué informe? Yo __6.__ *(estar)* enfermo y todavía no __7.__ *(hacer)* ninguna tarea de ayer.

Sofía: Tenemos que escribir un informe sobre una película que nosotros __8.__ *(ver)* recientemente. La profesora nos __9.__ *(decir)* que no quiere leer sobre ninguna película aburrida.

Paco: Pues, ya __10.__ *(devolver)* esa película aburrida que alquilé. ¡Voy a buscar otra película esta noche!

▼18 Escucha y escribe | | 🔊

Escuchar • Escribir

Tus amigos están viendo una película, pero tú llegaste tarde. Ahora te están diciendo lo que ha pasado. Escribe lo que te dijeron. Después pon las frases en orden según los dibujos.

▼19 ¿Quién lo ha hecho . . . ? |  |

Hablar

Trabaja con otro(a) estudiante. Habla de lo que han hecho las diferentes personas en la película de la Actividad 18.

▶️ **Modelo**

robar las joyas

A —¿Quién ha robado las joyas?

B —Los ladrones las han robado.

Estudiante A

1. tratar de apagar el incendio
2. ver el crimen
3. capturar a los criminales
4. llevar a los heridos al hospital
5. poner una venda en la cabeza de la víctima
6. manejar el coche de los ladrones

Estudiante B

¡Respuesta personal!

▼ Fondo Cultural | El mundo hispano

El cine en el mundo hispano España, México y Argentina tienen industrias cinematográficas importantes, y son los principales productores de películas para el público hispanohablante. Las películas compiten en festivales internacionales como los premios Goya en España, el Festival de Cine de la Habana en Cuba y el Festival de Cine Hispano de Miami. Las películas más populares de estos países se muestran con frecuencia en los Estados Unidos. Además de (Besides) competir en festivales internacionales, muchas películas de América Latina compiten y ganan premios Oscar en los Estados Unidos.

• ¿Por qué crees que las películas del mundo hispano son tan populares aquí?

El actor argentino Ricardo Darín, en una escena de la película *El secreto de sus ojos*

▼20 Preparaciones para el cine | ♻

Escribir

Cristina quiere ir al cine con sus amigos, pero sus padres no están en casa. Di lo que ella ha hecho antes de salir. Escoge los verbos apropiados de la lista y escribe las formas correctas del presente perfecto para completar las frases.

Modelo

___ una película a sus amigos.
Les ha recomendado una película a sus amigos.

cepillarse	decirle	escribirles	hacer
leer	llamarles	pedirle	ponerse

1. ___ todos sus quehaceres.

2. ___ el pelo y los dientes.

3. ___ jeans y su suéter favorito.

4. ___ un comentario sobre la película de un crítico en el periódico.

5. ___ a su hermana mayor adónde va.

6. ___ dinero a su hermana para comprar la entrada al cine.

7. ___ una nota a sus padres diciéndoles cuándo va a regresar.

8. ___ por teléfono a sus amigos para decirles cuándo va a llegar al cine.

▼21 Juego | 👥

Hablar • GramActiva

❶ Van a jugar en dos equipos. Una persona del equipo A escoge una tarjeta del (de la) profesor(a) que tiene el título de una película. Con otro(a) estudiante describan la película a su equipo sin decir el nombre. Pueden indicar:

- si han visto la película y si les ha gustado
- si la película ha tenido éxito o no
- qué papeles han hecho los actores
- cómo ha sido el argumento

❷ Si alguien del equipo A puede adivinar *(guess)* el nombre de la película en menos de un minuto, este equipo gana un punto. Si al final del minuto, el equipo A no ha adivinado el título, el equipo B tiene una sola oportunidad de decirlo. Si lo pueden hacer, ellos ganan el punto. Después los equipos cambian *(change)* de papel. El primer equipo que gana tres puntos gana el juego.

El español en el mundo del trabajo

¿Te interesa una carrera en la industria cinematográfica? Hay muchas compañías en los Estados Unidos que filman películas y videos en los países hispanohablantes. Puedes trabajar con ellos en varios aspectos de la producción de la película: director, asistente del director, técnica de sonido *(sound)*, técnica de luz y otros trabajos. ¿Los requisitos? Talento en filmación, tener una visión del proyecto, capacidad de trabajar en equipo y habilidad de comunicarse en español.

- ¿Por qué crees que es importante poder comunicarse en español durante la filmación en Costa Rica, por ejemplo? ¿En qué aspectos de la producción vas a usar el español?

▼22 Las películas que hemos visto | | ♻

Escribir • Hablar

En grupos de cuatro estudiantes, hagan preguntas sobre las películas que han visto en el último mes.

▶ **Modelo**

A —¿Cuántas películas has visto en el último mes?

B —He visto dos películas.

o:—No he visto ninguna película.

Conexiones | Las matemáticas

❶ Escriban en una tabla el número de películas, la clase de película (acción, comedia, drama) y los lugares donde las vieron (casa, cine o casa de amigos o familiares).

	Total para el grupo	Total para la clase
¿Cuántas películas han visto?		
¿Qué clase de películas?		
¿Dónde las han visto?		

❷ Ahora compartan sus resultados con la clase y sumen el total para el número de películas, la clase de película y los lugares. Hagan dos gráficas circulares como las que se ven aquí para indicar qué clase de películas han visto más todos los estudiantes y dónde las han visto.

Clase de película

comedia 31%
acción 47%
otras 2%
policíaca 6%
de horror 14%

Lugares donde las vieron

su propia casa 58%
cine 35%
casa de amigos o familiares 7%

▼ Fondo Cultural | El mundo hispano

Películas en español Como el mercado hispanohablante es tan grande, las compañías que producen y distibuyen películas ofrecen distintas opciones para alquilar. Además de las tiendas de video tradicionales, en algunas grandes ciudades también existen los videocajeros automáticos de DVDs y el servicio para alquilar DVDs por correo. Las películas extranjeras tienen subtítulos en distintos idiomas o en algunos casos son dobladas (*dubbed*) al español.

• ¿Qué opciones tienes para alquilar películas? ¿Alquilas películas extranjeras con frecuencia? ¿Las prefieres con subtítulos o dobladas?

En una tienda de videos en España

▼23 Una estrella de cine herida | ♻

Leer • Escribir • Hablar

Lee el artículo de una revista sobre una estrella de cine y contesta las preguntas.

1. ¿Qué ha aprendido Chayanne sobre ser estrella del cine?

2. ¿Cómo se ha lastimado el actor durante la filmación de la película?

3. ¿Qué han hecho los médicos? ¿Qué le han dado? ¿Por qué?

4. ¿Qué más le ha pasado al actor?

5. ¿Qué ha hecho el público para decirle a Chayanne que están pensando en él?

6. ¿Se lastimó otra estrella del cine? ¿Qué le ha pasado?

¡Un trabajo peligroso!

El ídolo puertorriqueño Chayanne ha aprendido que puede ser peligroso ser estrella de cine. Recientemente, en la Argentina, el galán se ha caído y se ha lastimado en una escena cuando estaba tratando de salvar a la bellísima actriz Araceli González de una situación peligrosa. Han llevado a Chayanne a un hospital en Buenos Aires, donde lo han examinado. El dolor ha sido tan intenso que el actor ha tenido que usar una silla de ruedas. Además, una inundación ha destruido una parte de su casa en la Argentina. Sus admiradores le han escrito y le han enviado un montón de cartas, tarjetas y mensajes electrónicos.

▼24 En las noticias | 👥 | ♻

Escribir • Hablar

¿Cuáles son las noticias que han ocurrido recientemente en tu comunidad y en el mundo? Trabaja con otro(a) estudiante. Piensen en una noticia que han oído en el noticiero o que han leído en el periódico. Escriban un artículo de cinco frases sobre lo que ha pasado. Usen el modelo y el artículo de la Actividad 23 para escribirlo. Diseñen (Design) su artículo para el periódico, incluyendo una ilustración o foto. Van a usar su artículo para la Actividad 25.

Modelo

La atleta panameña, Yolanda Salazar, ha ganado un premio en la competencia de natación en Costa Rica. Los aficionados y su entrenador se han vuelto locos porque ella ha terminado en primer lugar en este campeonato. Esta competencia ha sido la mejor para Panamá en los últimos años. En una entrevista, Yolanda se ha sentido muy emocionada. Ha dicho que su familia y su público son muy importantes para ella.

▼25 Leyendo las noticias | 👥 | ♻

Leer • Hablar

Lean los artículos que crearon para la Actividad 24 con otros grupos y hablen de ellos.

▶ Modelo

A —*¿Has leído el artículo sobre Yolanda Salazar?*

B —*Sí, dice que ella ha ganado un premio en la competencia de natación en Costa Rica.*

Más práctica (GO)	realidades.com	print
Instant Check	✔	
Guided WB pp. 229–232	✔	✔
Core WB pp. 127–128	✔	✔
Comm. WB pp. 120–121, 124	✔	✔
Hispanohablantes WB pp. 238–241		✔

Lectura
La cartelera del cine

Lee las siguientes críticas de una revista mexicana.
¿Qué película te gustaría ver?

> **Estrategia**
>
> **Reading for details**
> When you read a text for specific information, you may need to read it more than once. First, you might read for the "big picture," and then reread for additional details. Read the text below to find out which film(s) you might be interested in watching.

★ ESTRENOS DE HOY ★

X-MEN: PRIMERA GENERACIÓN
EE.UU., 2011 | Clasificación: PG-13 | Director: Matthew Vaughn |
Actores: James McAvoy, Michael Fassbender, Jennifer Lawrence, Kevin Bacon

Sinopsis
Esta película explica la forma en que Charles Xavier y Eric Lensherr descubren[1] sus poderes sobrenaturales y se convierten en el profesor X y Magneto en los años 60. Junto con otros mutantes, el profesor X y Magneto unen sus fuerzas contra Sebastian Shaw en esta increíble pelea.

Crítica
X-Men: Primera generación tiene mucha acción, buenos efectos especiales y escenas espectaculares. El director Matthew Vaughn hizo un buen trabajo. Las películas sobre los orígenes de personajes famosos están de moda y esta película no es la excepción. Dinámica y entretenida[2], pero a veces incoherente, es importante ver esta película para conocer la historia de Magneto y el profesor X.

Calificación: 6/10

AVATAR
EE.UU., 2009 | Clasificación: PG-13 | Director: James Cameron |
Actores: Sam Worthington, Zoe Saldaña, Sigourney Weaver, Stephen Lang, Michelle Rodríguez

Sinopsis
Es el año 2154. Jake Sully, trabajando para resolver la crisis de energía, debe conseguir un mineral especial que hay en Pandora, donde viven los *na'vi*. El programa Avatar le permite a Jake formar un cuerpo biológico controlado e infiltrarse entre los *na'vi*. Jake tiene que escoger entre el amor y respeto que termina sintiendo por ellos y sus obligaciones al programa Avatar.

Crítica
Hollywood invirtió[3] 300 millones de dólares en una película sensacional. *Avatar* nos habla de la tecnología, los problemas ecológicos y lo que debemos hacer para salvar nuestro planeta. Los efectos especiales nos llevan de viaje por un maravilloso[4] mundo tropical de la ciencia ficción. ¡Excelente!

Calificación: 10/10

[1]discover   [2]entertaining   [3]invested   [4]wondrous

EL CABALLERO OSCURO

EE.UU., 2008 | Clasificación: PG-13 | Director: Christopher Nolan |
Actores: Christian Bale, Heath Ledger, Maggie Gyllenhaal

Sinopsis

Batman regresa una vez más. En esta ocasión, trabaja junto con el teniente[5] Jim Gordon y el Fiscal de Distrito[6] Harvey para luchar contra el crimen de Ciudad Gótica, cuando aparece el Guasón[7] (Heath Ledger). Este temible[8] criminal tiene aterrorizados a todos los residentes de la ciudad y representa para Batman uno de sus mayores desafíos[9]. Para capturarlo, el héroe debe trabajar de manera muy inteligente.

Crítica

El caballero oscuro es genial, con diálogos divertidos y acción sin límites. Hay que mencionar la actuación de Heath Ledger, quien es, sin duda, el protagonista estrella de esta película. De la saga Batman, éste es el mejor trabajo hasta el momento.

Calificación: 10/10

[5]lieutenant [6]District Attorney [7]Joker [8]fearsome [9]challenges

¿Comprendiste?

1. ¿Es muy positiva la crítica de *X-Men: Primera generación*? ¿Qué palabras indican la opinión del crítico?

2. ¿A qué lugar fue Jake Sully? ¿Quiénes viven allí?

3. Según el crítico, ¿qué podemos aprender de la película *Avatar*?

4. Según la crítica de *El caballero oscuro*, ¿quién es más importante, el héroe o el criminal? Escribe su nombre.

5. ¿Crees que estas tres películas son de acción? ¿Por qué?

Y tú, ¿qué dices?

1. ¿Has visto algunas de estas películas? ¿Cuáles? ¿Estás de acuerdo con la crítica que se presenta aquí?

2. ¿Qué prefieres, los efectos especiales o un buen argumento?

Más práctica GO

realidades.com | print

Guided WB p. 233	✔	✔
Comm. WB pp. 125, 260	✔	✔
Hispanohablantes **WB** pp. 242–243		✔
Cultural Reading Activity	✔	

▼ Fondo Cultural | España | Estados Unidos | México

Las clasificaciones de las películas Los sistemas para clasificar las películas varían según el país. En España, por ejemplo, las películas que todos pueden ver son clasificadas TP (todos los públicos). También existe allí la clasificación –7 (los menores de siete años no deben ver esta película). En México, usan las letras *A*, *B* y *C* para clasificar las películas. La letra *A* corresponde a todos los públicos mientras que la *B* es para los mayores de 15 años y la *C* sólo para los mayores de 18 años.

- ¿Qué sistema de clasificación se usa en los Estados Unidos? ¿En qué sentido es diferente del sistema de España o de México?

Película	España	México	Estados Unidos
Carros 2	TP	A	G
Capitán América	–13	B	PG-13
El avispón verde	–13	B	PG-13
El discurso del rey	–18	C	R

Perspectivas del mundo hispano

Películas en otros idiomas

¿Has visto una película de otro país en que los actores hablan un idioma[1] que no es inglés? Por ejemplo, las películas de Francia y México son muy populares en los Estados Unidos. ¡Si no entiendes ni el francés ni el español, son difíciles de comprender!

Pero eso no es un problema. En muchas películas de otros países el diálogo de la película aparece en inglés en la parte de abajo de la pantalla. Con estos subtítulos es más fácil comprender el argumento de la película. Cuando hay subtítulos, es importante concentrarse un poco más y observar las expresiones y movimientos de los actores. Lo bueno es que es más interesante ver la película en versión original con subtítulos.

Otra solución para que el público pueda comprender una película es sustituir el diálogo original por una nueva grabación del diálogo en el idioma del país. Esto se llama doblaje.[2] Por ejemplo, uno puede ver una película italiana en que se oye el diálogo en inglés.

¡Compruébalo! Algunas personas prefieren ver las películas en versión original, con subtítulos, porque comprenden el idioma de la película y pueden escuchar la voz verdadera de los actores y los sonidos de la ambientación. A otras personas les gusta leer los subtítulos porque, cuando los leen, pueden aprender un poco del idioma original de la película. Y otras dicen que no les gusta el doblaje porque pierden el tono de la voz y la entonación de los actores. Si has visto una película de un país extranjero, piensa en lo que prefieres. Pregúntales a otras personas qué prefieren y por qué.

¿Qué te parece? Cuando vemos una película producida en otro país, podemos aprender algo de la cultura y del idioma de ese país. ¿Qué más puedes aprender? ¿Crees que es más fácil aprender de una película con doblaje o con subtítulos? ¿Qué crees que la gente de otros países aprende de nosotros cuando ve las películas de Hollywood?

[1]language [2]dubbing

▶ Write a synopsis of a movie script
▶ Use a storyboard to help illustrate a movie scene

Presentación escrita

Luces, cámara, acción

Task
You are entering a contest for exciting or humorous new movie ideas. You need to submit a brief description of the plot and the main characters and also the details of one scene to provide a preview of your movie.

1 **Prewrite** Use this chart to help you focus on "the big picture." Think about the type of movie you want to write: comedy, science fiction, etc. What is the plot? Who are the main characters? Which scene would provide a good sense of your movie?

Clase de película	Argumento	Actores principales	Escena

2 **Draft** Use your notes to write a short movie synopsis. Then write a script for the scene you chose. Include the dialogue and directions to the actors. You can use the storyboard method to show how the scene progresses.

3 **Revise** Check your work for spelling, agreement, verb usage, and vocabulary. Share your review with a partner, who will check for errors and to see that the synopsis is complete, the story is presented in a logical order, and the scene is easy to understand.

4 **Publish** Rewrite your summary and scene, making any necessary changes or corrections. Give a copy to your teacher or put one in your portfolio.

5 **Evaluation** The following rubric will be used to grade your presentation.

Estrategia

Outlining your ideas
Many filmwriters do extensive outlining of key ideas before they begin to write. They focus on "big picture" vision: type of movie, plot, and description of the characters. This skill will be helpful as you write your contest entry.

Estrategia

Drawing a scene
A common tool in movie writing is to draw the scene. This is called storyboarding. You might sketch the scene you will be writing about.

Rubric	Score 1	Score 3	Score 5
Completeness of your information	You provide two pieces of information in your synopsis.	You provide three pieces of information in your synopsis.	You provide all pieces of information in your synopsis.
Logical presentation of ideas	Your ideas do not have a logical sequence and are difficult to understand.	Your ideas have a somewhat logical sequence and are somewhat understandable.	Your ideas have a logical sequence and are understandable.
Presentation of plot in scene	You present the plot poorly and not all aspects are evident.	You present the plot somewhat clearly and most aspects are evident.	You present the plot clearly and all aspects are evident.

En busca de la verdad

Episodio 8

Antes de ver el video

"Espero que puedas encontrar la respuesta a este misterio de tantos años".

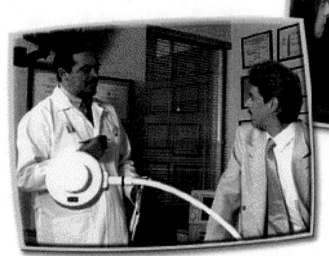

"¿Sabe que por ahí anda un hombre haciendo preguntas sobre Ud.?"

Nota cultural El Mariachi, una tradición típica mexicana, surgió en el estado de Jalisco en el siglo XIX. Es un grupo de músicos vestidos de ropa tradicional de la época de la Revolución Mexicana. Sus instrumentos incluyen el violín, la guitarra, el bajo y la trompeta, y sus canciones tratan de temas como la traición, el amor y la Revolución. Hoy en día se puede oír Mariachi en fiestas, celebraciones y hasta en restaurantes.

Resumen del episodio

El hombre misterioso sigue haciendo preguntas en Guanajuato sobre la familia Toledo. Nadie sabe quién es ni por qué está allí. La familia Toledo invita a Carmen y a Linda a una cena de despedida.

Palabras para comprender

sigue tosiendo keep coughing
cena de despedida farewell dinner
he disfrutado I have enjoyed
agradecer to thank

Después de ver el video

¿Comprendiste?

A. Lee las siguientes frases. Di cuáles son ciertas y cuáles son falsas.

1. El hombre misterioso averigua muchas cosas sobre la familia Toledo.

2. A Tomás no le importa que un hombre extraño pregunte por él.

3. Linda no disfrutó de su viaje a México.

4. Roberto va a viajar a San Antonio para investigar qué pasó con el abuelo.

5. A Berta le gusta la idea del viaje de Roberto a San Antonio.

6. Linda dice que va a regresar a Guanajuato en el invierno.

7. Julio no puede acompañar a Roberto y a Linda porque tiene que ir a ver a Josefina.

B. Imagina que eres un(a) amigo(a) de Roberto. Descríbele todo lo que ha hecho el hombre misterioso en Guanajuato. ¿Con quién habló? ¿Qué quería saber?

Más práctica GO

realidades.com | print

Actividades ✔

Repaso del capítulo
Vocabulario y gramática

to talk about movies

alquilar	to rent
el amor	love
arrestar	to arrest
capturar	to capture
el crimen	crime
el (la) criminal	criminal
el crítico, la crítica	critic
el (la) detective	detective
enamorarse (de)	to fall in love (with)
(estar) enamorado, -a de	(to be) in love with
la estrella (del cine)	(movie) star
el (la) extraterrestre	alien
fascinar	to fascinate
el fracaso	failure
el galán	leading man
he visto	I have seen
has visto	you have seen
el ladrón, la ladrona, *pl.* los ladrones	thief
matar	to kill
la película de acción	action film
¿Qué tal es . . . ?	How is (it) . . . ?
recomendar *(e → ie)*	to recommend
robar	to rob, to steal
será	he / she / it will be
tener éxito	to succeed, to be successful
tratarse de	to be about
la víctima	victim
la violencia	violence

to talk about making movies

la actuación	acting
el argumento	plot
la dirección	direction
el director, la directora	director
los efectos especiales	special effects
la escena	scene
estar basado, -a en	to be based on
el papel	role
hacer el papel de	to play the role of
el personaje principal	main character

other useful words

no . . . todavía	not yet

indirect object pronouns

me	nos
te	os
le	les

present perfect
haber + past participle

he estudiado	hemos estudiado
has estudiado	habéis estudiado
ha estudiado	han estudiado

past participles

hablar → hablado
comer → comido
vivir → vivido

irregular past participles

decir: dicho
devolver: devuelto
escribir: escrito
hacer: hecho
morir: muerto
poner: puesto
romper: roto
ver: visto
volver: vuelto

For *Vocabulario adicional*, see pp. 498–499.

Más repaso	GO	realidades.com	print
Instant Check			✔
Puzzles			✔
Core WB pp. 129–130			✔
Comm. WB pp. 261, 262–264		✔	✔

Preparación para el examen

On the exam you will be asked to . . .	Here are practice tasks similar to those you will find on the exam . . .	For review go to your print or digital textbook . . .

Interpretive

 1 Escuchar Listen and understand as people talk about a movie they have seen

Listen as you hear a film critic interview people as they leave the movie *Mil secretos*. What did they think of: (a) the actors; (b) the director; (c) the special effects; (d) the theme; and (e) future award possibilities.

pp. 320–323 *Vocabulario en contexto*
p. 325 Actividad 6
p. 332 Actividad 18

Interpersonal

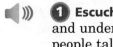 **2 Hablar** Talk about a recent film you have seen at the movies or at home

You discover that you and an exchange student from Spain share a love of movies. What could you say about a recent movie that you saw? Practice the conversation with a classmate and include: (a) the type of film it was; (b) what the movie was about; (c) who the principal actors were; and (d) why you liked or disliked the movie.

p. 324 Actividad 4
p. 325 Actividad 7
p. 326 Actividad 8
p. 329 Actividades 12–13
p. 332 Actividad 19

Interpretive

 3 Leer Read and understand a movie review

Read this review by a popular Spanish movie critic. Do you think he likes the movie? Why or why not?

Esta película, "Nuestra familia", nos cuenta la historia de una "familia" de criminales violentos. ¡Es un producto de Hollywood y nosotros somos las víctimas! Sin duda, la película ha capturado la sociedad mala que nos fascina. Está basada en una familia de la vida real y se trata de la vida diaria de ellos. El actor Ramón Robles hace el papel del galán. Él es un hombre físicamente atractivo y talentoso y sólo su participación vale el precio de la entrada. La película tiene una clasificación de prohibida para menores. ¡Debe ser prohibida para TODOS!

p. 324 Actividad 5
p. 328 Actividad 11
p. 330 Actividad 16
pp. 336–337 *Lectura*

Presentational

 4 Escribir Write about a movie that you would like to produce

While searching the Internet for movie reviews in Spanish, you come upon a survey that you decide to answer. You are asked to write a few sentences about: (a) movies that you have seen within the past month; (b) whether or not you liked them; and (c) what the critics have said about these movies.

p. 326 Actividad 8
p. 327 Actividades 9–10
p. 329 Actividades 12–14
p. 334 Actividad 22
p. 339 *Presentación escrita*

Cultures

 5 Pensar Demonstrate an understanding of how movies can reflect the language and culture of the country where they are produced

Your Spanish teacher assigns a Mexican movie to the class as homework. When you rent the movie at your local video store and bring it home, your family wants to know why it is subtitled or dubbed. How could you explain the process to them? What do you think they would be surprised to learn?

p. 338 *Perspectivas del mundo hispano*

Vocabulario Repaso

hablando de las comidas y la salud

el almuerzo
bueno / malo para
  la salud
la cena
las comidas
el desayuno
mantener la salud
rico, -a
sabroso, -a

la comida

el arroz	las judías	el plátano
el bistec	verdes	el pollo
la cebolla	la lechuga	las salchichas
el cereal	la mantequilla	la sopa
la ensalada	la manzana	el tocino
los espaguetis	la naranja	los tomates
las fresas	el pan	las uvas
las frutas	el pan tostado	las verduras
los guisantes	las papas fritas	el yogur
los huevos	el pescado	las zanahorias

las bebidas

el agua *f.*
el café
el jugo
la leche
el té
el té helado

▼1 ¿Cómo comes? | 👥

Escribir • Hablar

Comer bien para mantener la salud puede ser difícil. ¿Comes tú bien?

1 Piensa en lo que comes en un día típico en el desayuno, en el almuerzo y en la cena. Usa una tabla como ésta para organizar tus ideas.

el desayuno	el almuerzo	la cena
huevos	arroz con pollo	bistec

2 Ahora compara tu tabla con la de otro(a) estudiante. ¿Comen cosas similares? ¿Pueden comer mejor para mantener la salud? Discútelo con tu compañero(a) y escribe unas frases sobre lo que comen y cómo pueden comer mejor.

Modelo

Normalmente en el desayuno como huevos, tocino y salchichas. Carla come cereal y fruta con yogur. Yo debo comer mejor. Por ejemplo, no debo comer salchichas con huevos, pero sí puedo comer fresas o una manzana.

Gramática Repaso

Verbs with irregular *yo* forms

Remember that some verbs are irregular in the *yo* form in the present tense.

Verbs with irregular *-go* forms

caer:	caigo	poner:	pongo
decir:	digo	salir:	salgo
hacer:	hago	tener:	tengo
oír:	oigo	venir:	vengo

Verbs with irregular *-zco* forms

conocer:	conozco
obedecer:	obedezco
ofrecer:	ofrezco
parecer:	parezco

▼2 ¿De acuerdo o no?

Escribir

Lee las siguientes frases y decide si estás de acuerdo o no. Si no estás de acuerdo, explica por qué.

Modelo

Cuando saludas a una persona que no conoces, le dices: ¿Cómo estás tú?
No estoy de acuerdo. Le digo: ¿Cómo está Ud.?

1. Normalmente haces ejercicio a las seis de la mañana.
2. Nunca obedeces a tus padres.
3. Tienes tarea todas las noches.
4. No conoces a muchas personas de tu escuela.
5. Los sábados sales con tus amigos.
6. Cuando uno de tus amigos no tiene el almuerzo, le ofreces parte de tu almuerzo.
7. Eres muy ordenado(a). Siempre pones tus cosas en su lugar.

▼3 No te creo . . .

Escribir • Hablar

1 Escribe cuatro frases usando los verbos con formas irregulares de *-go* y *-zco*. Tres de tus frases deben ser ciertas y una debe ser falsa.

2 Ahora trabaja con un grupo de cuatro estudiantes y lee tus frases al grupo. Los otros tienen que adivinar cuál de tus frases es falsa.

▶ Modelo

A —*Yo siempre salgo de la escuela a las diez de la noche.*
B —*¡No te creo! ¡Nunca sales de la escuela a las diez de la noche!*

Más práctica GO

realidades.com | print

A ver si recuerdas with Study Plan ✔
Guided WB pp. 235–236 ✔ ✔
Core WB pp. 131–132 ✔ ✔
Hispanohablantes **WB** p. 250 ✔

Capítulo 7A

¿Cómo se hace la paella?

▼ Chapter Objectives

Communication

By the end of this chapter you will be able to:

- Listen to and read about cooking instructions and advice
- Talk and write about recipes and kitchen safety
- Exchange information about how to prepare certain dishes

Culture

You will also be able to:

- Understand how foods are incorporated into different cultures
- Compare dishes and foods in Spanish-speaking countries with those found in the U.S.

You will demonstrate what you know and can do:

- Presentación oral, p. 367
- Preparación para el examen, p. 371

You will use:

Vocabulary

- Foods and items in the kitchen
- Recipes and food preparation

Grammar

- Negative *tú* commands
- The impersonal *se*

Exploración del mundo hispano

Country Connection
Food and Recipes

- España
- Florida
- Nuevo México
- República Dominicana
- México
- Puerto Rico
- Costa Rica
- Venezuela
- Bolivia
- Chile
- Argentina

realidades.com **GO**

 Reference Atlas

▶ **Videocultura y actividad**

 Mapa global interactivo

Arte y cultura | España

Luis Egidio Meléndez (1716–1780) es considerado el mejor pintor español de bodegón *(Spanish still life painting)* de su época. En sus obras *(works)*, Meléndez trabajó con los efectos de la luz, los colores y la textura, de manera que objetos muy ordinarios se ven extraordinarios. En este cuadro, observamos pan, unas cajas de dulces y unas jarras típicas de Manises, una ciudad en Valencia que es conocida por su cerámica.

• ¿Qué comidas y artesanías típicas de tu región pintarías *(would you paint)* en un cuadro?

"Bodegón con pan", Luis Egidio Meléndez ▶

Christie's Images, Ltd./Superstock

Una paella de Barcelona, España

A primera vista | 🔊 | 💬

| ▼ Objectives

Read, listen to, and understand
information about
▶ cooking expressions
▶ foods and appliances
▶ following a recipe
▶ giving directions in the kitchen

Vocabulario en contexto

enlatado, -a

congelado, -a

el refrigerador

el microondas

fresco, -a

el horno

probar

el fregadero

al horno

la estufa

la olla

calentar

la sartén

batir

mezclar

pelar

picar

el pedazo

el fuego

frito, -a

añadir

freír

hervir

—¿Qué vamos a preparar?

—**Una receta** que aprendí de mi abuela que vivía en Valencia. Se llama arroz a banda. Es un arroz típico de la provincia de Alicante y ha sido el favorito de mi familia. Aquí está la lista de **los ingredientes** que necesitamos.

el vinagre

el caldo

el ajo

el aceite

la salsa

la cucharada

los camarones

los mariscos

Arroz a banda

Ingredientes (8 personas)

unos 3 litros de caldo de pescado

100 gr de camarones

$\frac{1}{2}$ kg de sepia[1]

1 tomate grande bien cortado

1 cucharada de pimentón dulce[2]

1 kg de arroz

azafrán[3]

aceite de oliva

ajoaceite (una salsa de ajo y aceite)

[1]cuttlefish   [2]paprika   [3]saffron
(Saffron is an expensive spice used for its bright orange-yellow color, intense flavor, and aroma.)

▼1 La cocina típica | ◀)))

Escuchar

¿Qué hay en tu cocina? Escucha mientras Ignacio describe una cocina típica. Mira los dibujos y las fotos, y señala el objeto (o los objetos) que menciona.

▼2 ¿Lógico o no? | ◀)))

Escuchar

¿Sabes cocinar? Levanta una mano si lo que oyes es lógico y levanta las dos manos si no es lógico.

Más práctica (GO)	realidades.com	print	
Instant Check	✔	
Guided WB pp. 237–242	✔	✔
Core WB pp. 133–134	✔	✔
Comm. WB p. 132	✔	✔
Hispanohablantes WB p. 252		✔

¿Cómo se hace la paella?

Estrategia

Using prior experience
What do you know about cooking? Are you "at home" in the kitchen or do you feel uncomfortable? Look at the photos and guess how Javier and Ignacio feel.

Ignacio y Javier van a hacer paella. ¿Qué les pasa en la cocina?

Ignacio: Javier, ¿**cómo se hace** la paella? Quiero preparar una comida especial para Ana.

Javier: Bueno, está bien. Vamos a necesitar camarones y mariscos. No uso ingredientes ni congelados ni enlatados. Queremos todo bien fresco.

Javier: ¡**No tires** el aceite! Y **no añadas** más. Tienes más que suficiente. Primero vamos a freír los ajos.

Javier: ¡No, Ignacio! Tienes que picar los ajos primero.

Ignacio: ¿Picar?

Javier: Sí, cortar los ajos en pedazos muy pequeños.

Ignacio: Voy a encender la cocina . . .

Javier: A ver . . . el aceite tiene que estar bien **caliente.** No, todavía no está . . . Yo preparo los mariscos. Tú, **no te olvides del** aceite. **No dejes** que se caliente demasiado.

También se dice . . .

los camarones = las gambas (*España*)

la estufa = la cocina (*España*)

Ignacio: ¿Con qué se sirve la paella? ¿Con papas fritas?

Javier: No, no, no . . . Se sirve con una ensalada.

Ignacio: Bueno, ¿enciendo el horno ya?

Javier: ¡No! No **se puede** usar el horno para hacer la paella. Se prepara la paella encima de la cocina.

Ignacio: ¿Pongo el aceite en la olla?

Javier: Deja esa olla y escucha bien. Primero tienes que calentar el aceite en una sartén grande.

Javier: ¡Ignacio! ¡**Apaga** la cocina! ¿En qué estabas pensando?

Ignacio: Bueno, en la sorpresa de Ana cuando . . .

Javier: Pues, así, creo que va a recibir una gran sorpresa, pero no va a ser buena . . . Vamos a seguir . . .

▼3 ¿Comprendiste?

Escribir • Hablar

1. ¿Qué le pregunta Ignacio a Javier? ¿Por qué?

2. ¿Qué necesitan los chicos?

3. Según Javier, ¿se puede servir la paella con papas fritas? ¿Con qué se sirve?

4. ¿Qué quiere hacer Ignacio primero en la cocina? ¿Está bien? ¿Qué le dice Javier?

5. ¿Qué quiere hacer Ignacio luego? ¿Qué le dice Javier?

6. ¿Qué le pasó a Ignacio al final? ¿En qué estaba pensando?

Más práctica	GO

realidades.com | print

Instant Check	✔	
Guided WB pp. 243–246	✔	✔
Core WB pp. 135–136	✔	✔
Comm. WB pp. 126–128, 129	✔	✔
Hispanohablantes WB p. 253		✔

▶ Talk about dishes you've tried or would like to try
▶ Discuss food preferences
▶ Listen to where things go in the kitchen
▶ Write about cooking tips

Vocabulario en uso

▼4 ¡Ignacio lo sabe todo!

Escribir • Leer • Hablar

Después de ver a Ignacio en la cocina preparando una paella, ya sabes cómo hacerla. Trabaja con otro(a) estudiante. Completen las preguntas con expresiones y palabras del recuadro y completen las respuestas según los dibujos. Después lean la conversación.

▶ **Modelo**

A —Ignacio, ¿cómo *se llama* lo que vamos a preparar?

B —Es una *paella*. Es un plato tradicional de España.

Estudiante A

| ingredientes | se hace | se puede |
| pedazos | se llama | se sirve |

A —¿Qué __1.__ hay en la paella?

B —Arroz, pollo y __2.__ .

A —¿Cómo __3.__ la paella?

B —Pues, primero hay que calentar __4.__ en una __5.__ .

A —¿ __6.__ usar el microondas para preparar la paella?

B —¡No, en absoluto! Hay que prepararla sobre un __7.__ lento en la estufa.

A —¿Corto la cebolla en __8.__ grandes?

B —No, pica la cebolla y el __9.__ .

A —¿Con qué __10.__ la paella?

B —Con una ensalada de lechuga y tomate con aceite y __11.__ .

Estudiante B

Fondo Cultural | España

La paella es el plato más popular de la cocina española. El nombre *paella* tiene sus orígenes en el latín *patella,* que significa "sartén ancha". Su ingrediente principal es el arroz. La paella tradicional se hace sólo con mariscos, pero también se puede añadir pollo y salchichas. En la costa, ponen los mariscos frescos del día. La paella se come en muchos países. En América Latina preparan platos similares, como el arroz con frijoles y el arroz con pollo.

• Compara la paella con la comida típica que comes. ¿Comes muchas comidas hechas con arroz? ¿Son similares a la paella, o diferentes?

También se dice . . .

el refrigerador = la nevera, el frigorífico *(España, muchos países);* la heladera *(Argentina, Uruguay)*

el fregadero = el lavaplatos *(Colombia);* la pileta *(Argentina)*

▼5 La cocina de mi tía | 👥 | 🔊

Escuchar • Dibujar • Escribir • Hablar

Escucha mientras la tía de Juanita describe su cocina. Dibuja y escribe los nombres de las cosas que menciona. Luego compara tu dibujo con el de otro(a) estudiante.

> **¿Recuerdas?**
>
> Regular affirmative *tú* commands use the present-tense *Ud./él/ella* form of the verb. Some verbs, like *tener* and *poner*, have irregular command forms.

▼6 Los huevos revueltos | ♻

Leer • Escribir

Hoy es sábado y tu madre tiene que trabajar. Ha dejado para ti unas instrucciones para hacer huevos revueltos *(scrambled)*. Usa los verbos en el recuadro y escribe el mandato apropiado para cada número.

Modelo

preparar
Por favor, *prepara* huevos revueltos para la familia.

añadir	hervir *(e → ie)*
apagar	mezclar
batir	poner
dejar	probar
encender	*(o → ue)*
(e → ie)	servir *(e → i)*
freír *(e → i)*	tener

En el desayuno

1. los huevos con un tenedor y 2. sal y pimienta.
3. los huevos con un poquito de leche y queso rallado *(shredded)*.
4. la estufa pero 5. cuidado. No necesitas un fuego muy alto.
6. el tocino.
7. los huevos batidos en una sartén y *cocínalos*.
8. cocinar los huevos por unos minutos.
9. agua para hacer café.
10. los huevos para ver si tienen suficiente sal y pimienta.
11. la estufa y 12. el desayuno.

▼7 ¿Qué has probado? | 🗨👥 | ♻

Leer • Hablar

Lee estas descripciones de unos platos típicos de diferentes países hispanohablantes. Después habla con otro(a) estudiante sobre los platos que han probado y sobre los que les gustaría probar.

 **Modelo**

A —¿Has probado el ceviche?
B —Sí, lo he probado.
(No) Me gusta mucho porque . . .

Camarones al ajillo Fríen los camarones muy frescos con aceite y ajo en una pequeña sartén y los sirven muy calientes.

Pescado frito Fríen el pescado en aceite caliente. Añaden sal, pimienta y otras especias *(spices)*. Es popular en muchos países, desde España hasta Puerto Rico.

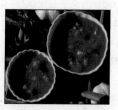

Gazpacho Sirven fría esta sopa de tomate, aceite y ajo que también puede contener verduras como apio *(celery)* y chiles.

Ceviche Mezclan el pescado con tomate, cebolla, vinagre, chile y jugo de limón. Hay diferentes variaciones de ceviche.

▼8 ¿Qué prefieres? |

Hablar

Con otro(a) estudiante, habla de sus preferencias.

▶ **Modelo**

A —¿Qué prefieres, _las papas fritas_ o _las papas al horno_?

B —_Prefiero las papas al horno._

o: —_No me gustan ni las papas fritas ni las papas al horno._

1.  2.   3.

4.   5.

▼9 ¿Dónde los pongo? |

Hablar

Con otro(a) estudiante, habla de dónde se ponen las cosas en la cocina.

▶ **Modelo**

A —¿Dónde pongo _los pedazos de tomate?_

B —_Ponlos en la ensalada._

Estudiante A

  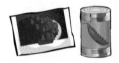

1.   2.   3.

4.   5.   6.

Estudiante B

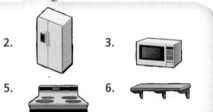

1.   2.   3.

4.   5.   6.

▼10 Recomendaciones para cocinar | |

Leer • Escribir • Escuchar • Hablar

Lee las recomendaciones para cocinar y escoge la mejor palabra o expresión para completar cada una. Luego usa estas frases como modelo y escribe cuatro más con tus propias recomendaciones. Lee tus frases a otro(a) estudiante, quien tiene que completarlas.

1. En una ensalada, las verduras ___ _(frescas / enlatadas)_ son más sabrosas.

2. Mientras fríes algo, ___ _(no tires / prueba)_ el aceite caliente.

3. Es mejor hervir agua para los espaguetis en una ___ _(olla / sartén)._

4. ___ _(Deja / No te olvides de)_ apagar la estufa después de usarla.

5. Usa ___ _(el microondas / el horno)_ para preparar algo rápidamente.

6. Para algunas recetas de arroz necesitas un ___ _(caldo / ajo)_ de pescado o pollo.

▾11 Tostones isleños | 👥

Leer • Escribir • Hablar

Lee este artículo de una revista de cocina. Luego trabaja con otro(a)
estudiante para contestar las preguntas.

TOSTONES

¡No tienes que esperar un viaje a la fantástica isla de Puerto Rico
para disfrutar de[1] este riquísimo plato tropical! Puedes seguir
esta receta fácil y preparar tostones con mojito (¡esa salsa
deliciosa de aceite y ajo!) en tu propia casa.

Ingredientes

Tostones
6 plátanos verdes
agua
sal
aceite

Mojito
8 dientes[2] de ajo
$\frac{1}{2}$ taza de aceite
    de oliva
perejil[3]

Preparación

Tostones
Pela los plátanos y córtalos en pedazos
medianos. Ponlos en una olla con agua y sal
por 15 minutos. Luego ponlos a secar en una
toalla de papel. Calienta aceite en una sartén.
Fríe los plátanos dos minutos por cada lado.
Pon los plátanos sobre una toalla de papel
para escurrirles[4] el aceite y aplasta[5] los
pedazos. Fríelos otra vez. Escúrrelos y añade sal.

Mojito
Pela los dientes de ajo y machácalos[6]. Pica el perejil.
Calienta el aceite de oliva y añade el ajo. Caliéntalo a
fuego lento hasta que el ajo esté dorado[7]. Añade el
perejil picado. Pon la mezcla caliente al lado de los
tostones y sírvelos.

¡Buen provecho!

[1] enjoy [2] cloves [3] parsley [4] drain them [5] flatten [6] crush them [7] is golden

1. En una hoja de papel, hagan dos columnas.
   Escriban las cosas que necesitan para
   preparar los tostones con mojito en una
   columna y escriban para qué las necesitan
   en la otra.

Necesitamos	Para
un cuchillo	pelar el ajo

2. ¿Has probado tostones con mojito? Si ya los
   has probado, ¿te gustaron? Si todavía no los
   has probado, ¿te gustaría probarlos?
3. Dicen que los tostones son similares a las
   papitas *(potato chips)*. ¿En qué sentido son
   similares o diferentes?

▾ Fondo Cultural | El mundo hispano

El plátano es uno de los alimentos más populares de los países tropicales
de América Latina. Se cree que el plátano es originario del sudeste asiático.
Los plátanos amarillos que ves en los supermercados son sólo un tipo de la
gran diversidad de plátanos que hay. Hay pequeños plátanos amarillos y
plátanos grandes, como los verdes y los rojos. Con los plátanos verdes se
preparan los tostones. Otras recetas con plátanos verdes son sopa de
plátano verde y bolas de verde (Ecuador y Colombia).

• ¿Qué relación crees que hay entre la popularidad del plátano como
  comida y su abundancia?

Gramática

Negative *tú* commands

To tell someone what *not* to do, use a negative command. To form negative *tú* commands, drop the *-o* of the present-tense *yo* form and add:

- *-es* for *-ar* verbs.

  usar   uso: **No uses** el microondas.

- *-as* for *-er* and *-ir* verbs.

  encender   enciendo: **No enciendas** el horno.
  añadir   añado: **No añadas** demasiada sal.
  poner   pongo: **No pongas** los camarones en la sartén todavía.

Verbs ending in *-car, -gar,* or *-zar* have spelling changes: *c* changes to *qu, g* changes to *gu,* and *z* changes to *c.*

  picar   pico: **No piques** los tomates.
  pagar   pago: **No pagues** demasiado.
  empezar   empiezo: **No empieces** a cocinar ahora.

These verbs have irregular negative *tú* commands:

dar	no des	ir	no vayas
estar	no estés	ser	no seas

Remember that pronouns are attached to affirmative commands. If the pronoun is added to a command form that has two or more syllables, write an accent mark on the syllable stressed in the present tense.

—¿Pico las cebollas?

—Sí, pícalas.

With negative commands, pronouns always go right before the conjugated verb.

—¿Pico los tomates también?

—No, no los piques.

Más ayuda   **realidades.com**

 ***GramActiva* Video
Tutorial:** Negative *tú* commands

 Canción de hip hop: *¿Cómo se hace la paella?*

***GramActiva* Activity**

▼12 ¡Así no!

Escribir

Tu hermano mayor acaba de limpiar la casa y no quiere limpiarla otra vez. Te escribe una nota diciendo las cosas que no debes hacer. Completa lo que dice él con los mandatos negativos correctos.

Modelo
(picar / tirar) leche en el suelo
No tires leche en el suelo.

1. (*mezclar / dejar*) ollas sucias en el fregadero
2. (*comer / añadir*) en tu cama
3. (*pelar / usar*) la estufa sin limpiarla después
4. (*salir / poner*) pollo frito encima del sofá
5. (*hacer / probar*) espaguetis en el microondas
6. (*dar de comer / ver*) al perro en la sala
7. (*ir / ser*) egoísta*. Piensa en los otros miembros de la familia.

*selfish

▼13 Para tener empanadas exquisitas

Leer • Escribir

❶ A Manolo le gusta hacer las empanadas y ha escrito unas instrucciones para hacerlas. Escoge verbos del recuadro y completa las instrucciones con el mandato negativo.

Modelo
comenzar
___ a cocinar sin leer la receta.
No comiences a cocinar sin leer la receta.

cortar	ir	salir
hacer	mezclar	servir

1. ___ al supermercado por los ingredientes sin llevar una lista.
2. ___ la masa *(dough)* si no te has lavado las manos.
3. ___ las empanadas sin añadir la sal.
4. ___ la carne y las verduras con el mismo cuchillo sin lavarlo.
5. ___ de la cocina cuando las empanadas están en el horno.
6. ___ las empanadas sin probar una primero.

❷ Ayuda a Manolo a escribir cuatro reglas adicionales sobre cómo tener éxito en la cocina. Usa mandatos negativos.

▼14 Un mundo negativo |

Escribir

Imagina que eres el (la) director(a) de la cafetería de tu escuela. Escribe mandatos negativos para dar instrucciones en la cocina.

1. venir a la cocina con las manos sucias
2. tirar el almuerzo a la basura
3. ofrecer demasiado café
4. hacer muchas tortillas
5. ¡Respuesta personal!

Modelo
dejar la sartén en el fuego
No dejes la sartén en el fuego.

Más práctica	GO
	realidades.com	print
Instant Check	✔
Guided WB pp. 247–250	✔ ✔
Core WB p. 137	✔ ✔
Comm. WB pp. 130, 133	✔ ✔
Hispanohablantes **WB**	
pp. 254–257, 260	✔

▼15 ¡No lo hagas todavía! |

Hablar

Imagina que estás en Venezuela y quieres ayudar a la madre (o al padre) de tu familia venezolana en la cocina. Lee la receta para arepas que está abajo. Con otro(a) estudiante, haz preguntas para ver si puedes comenzar a hacer las arepas. Tu compañero(a) no está listo(a) todavía.

▶ Modelo

mezclar el agua con la sal
A —¿Mezclo el agua con la sal ya?
B —No, no las mezcles todavía.

Arepa tradicional venezolana

Ingredientes:
1 taza de harina de maíz[1] precocida[2]
2 tazas de agua
½ cucharadita de sal
½ cucharadita de mantequilla

Preparación:
1. Mezcla las dos tazas de agua con la sal.
2. Añade la harina de maíz poco a poco y amasa[3] hasta tener una masa[4] bien mezclada y sin grumos[5].
3. Añade la mantequilla y forma bolas de masa.
4. Calienta una plancha[6] de cocina, aplasta[7] las bolas de masa un poco y ponlas en la plancha hasta que estén doradas[8] por los dos lados. Si prefieres, puedes ponerlas al horno después para hacerlas más abombadas[9].

Se venden arepas en la playa de Miami, Florida.

[1] corn flour [2] precooked [3] knead [4] dough [5] lumps [6] griddle [7] flatten [8] they are golden [9] dome-shaped

---

▼ Fondo Cultural | Venezuela

La arepa es una comida tradicional que se come casi todos los días en Venezuela. Blancas o amarillas, las arepas siempre han sido el desayuno o la cena perfecta para muchas familias venezolanas. Hay diferentes variedades de arepa: algunas están hechas con papas y otras con queso. En cada región de Venezuela se preparan las arepas de manera diferente. Muchas veces las arepas están rellenas de (filled with) pollo, jamón, huevos y otras cosas.

- ¿Por qué crees que hay tantas variedades de arepas venezolanas? ¿Qué platos de los Estados Unidos se preparan de varias maneras según la región del país?

Haciendo arepas en Mérida, Venezuela

▼16 En la guardería infantil |

Escribir • Dibujar

Una guardería infantil cerca de tu casa necesita personas para trabajar con los niños que sólo hablan español. Otro(a) estudiante y tú van a trabajar allí. Su primera responsabilidad: la comida saludable para los niños.

1 En una hoja de papel, escriban cinco mandatos afirmativos y cinco negativos para los niños, usando la forma *tú*.

Modelo
comer/jugar

Afirmativo	Negativo
come despacio	no juegues con la comida

2 Hagan un cartel usando los mandatos afirmativos y negativos. Hagan dibujos o corten ilustraciones para hacerlo más interesante. Muestren *(Show)* el cartel en la clase.

▼ Pronunciación |

Dividing words into syllables

In Spanish, you divide words into syllables after a vowel sound or between most double consonants. Listen to and say these words:

ca-ma-ro-nes   fres-co   her-vir
ma-ris-cos   en-cien-do   con-ge-la-do

However, you do not separate most combinations of a consonant followed by *l* or *r*. Listen to and say these words:

do-**ble**   in-**gre**-dien-tes   **fre**-ga-de-ro
re-**fres**-cos   vi-na-**gre**   re-**fri**-ge-ra-dor

When two strong vowels *(a, e, o)* appear together, each is pronounced individually, forming two syllables. Listen to and say these words:

pa-**e**-lla   tra-**e**-mos   to-**a**-lla
mi-cro-**o**n-das fe-**o**   hé-ro-**e**

¡Compruébalo! Lee estos versos del poema "Oda a las papas fritas", del famoso poeta chileno, Pablo Neruda (1904–1973), quien ganó el Premio Nobel de Literatura en 1971.

"Oda a las papas fritas"

Chisporrotea[1]
en el aceite
hirviendo
la alegría
del mundo:
las papas
fritas
entran
en la sartén
como nevadas
plumas
de cisne matutino[2]
y salen
semidoradas por el crepitante[3]
ámbar[4] de las olivas.

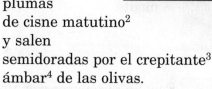

[1] It hisses (or crackles) [2] snowy feathers of a morning swan
[3] crackling [4] amber

Escribe estas palabras del poema y divídelas en sílabas:

chisporrotea   aceite   hirviendo
alegría   sartén   semidoradas

Gramática

The impersonal *se*

In English, you use *they, you, one*, or *people* in an impersonal or indefinite sense to mean "people in general." In Spanish, you use *se* + the *Ud. / él / ella* or *Uds. / ellos / ellas* form of the verb.

A menudo **se sirve** pan con la paella.

*Bread **is** often **served** with paella.*

Se usan otros mariscos también para hacer paella.

***They** also **use** other shellfish to make paella.*

¿Recuerdas?

Remember that you use *se prohíbe* to tell that something is prohibited.

• **Se prohíbe** comer en clase.

Más ayuda   realidades.com

▶ **GramActiva Video**
Tutorial: The impersonal *se*

GramActiva Activity

▼17 Comidas populares

Escribir

Para cada foto, escribe una frase diciendo cuál es una de las comidas populares del país o de la región.

Modelo

España / preparar frecuentemente
En España se prepara frecuentemente la paella.

1.  México / servir a menudo

2.  Puerto Rico / comer con mojito

3.  España / preparar con ajo

4.  Argentina / comer mucho

5.  Bolivia / preparar de maneras diferentes

6.  la República Dominicana / servir bien frescos

7.  Costa Rica / comer con frijoles

8.  Nuevo México / servir con chiles

▼18 ¿Se puede . . . ?

Escribir • Hablar

Imagina que un estudiante nuevo llega a tu comunidad y quiere saber qué se puede hacer en tu escuela.

1 Escribe cinco preguntas sobre las cosas que se pueden, se permiten o se prohíben hacer en tu escuela.

Modelo
En el gimnasio, ¿se puede levantar pesas?

2 Pregúntale a otro(a) estudiante si se pueden hacer las actividades.

▶ **Modelo**
A —*En el gimnasio, ¿se puede levantar pesas?*
B —*Claro, se puede levantar pesas.*

▼19 La dieta ideal

Pensar • Escribir • Hablar

Comer bien es muy importante para todos. ¿Cómo se decide qué comer cada día? Se debe prestar atención a la buena nutrición.

Conexiones | Las ciencias

Lee esta tabla sobre los minerales y las comidas en las que se encuentran.

Mineral	Comidas
Calcio	Leche, queso y verduras
Fósforo	Huevos, pescado, granos integrales (trigo,[1] maíz,[2] arroz, y más), leche, hígado,[3] brócoli y frijoles[4]
Hierro[5]	Hígado, huevos, carnes, verduras, guisantes y melaza[6]
Yodo[7]	Mariscos y sal que contiene yodo

[1] wheat   [2] corn   [3] liver   [4] beans   [5] Iron   [6] molasses   [7] Iodine

1 Trabaja con otro(a) estudiante y busquen en la tabla los minerales que tiene:

1. una paella hecha con arroz, pollo, pescado y mariscos
2. una pizza con salsa de tomate, queso y salchicha

Escriban una lista de los minerales que tienen estas dos comidas. Compárenlas. ¿Cuál de las dos tiene más minerales? ¿Cuál es la comida más saludable?

2 En un grupo de cuatro estudiantes, escojan una comida y busquen en la tabla los minerales que contienen los ingredientes. Lean la descripción de los ingredientes y los minerales a la clase sin decir qué comida es. Los demás deben adivinar la comida.

▼20 ¡Se come bien aquí! 👥

Leer • Hablar

Lee este anuncio sobre un restaurante en Puerto Vallarta, México. Trabaja con otro(a) estudiante y contesta las preguntas.

1. ¿Qué comidas se recomiendan en este restaurante?

2. ¿Qué se puede hacer mientras se cena allí?

3. ¿Qué influencias diferentes se encuentran en la comida mexicana moderna?

4. ¿Cómo se prepara la comida mexicana moderna?

5. ¿Se puede almorzar en este restaurante?

6. ¿Qué se debe hacer si se quiere cenar allí?

7. ¿Te gustaría comer en el Café de los Artistas? ¿Por qué?

▼21 Y tú, ¿qué dices? 🗨Talk!

Escribir • Hablar

1. Piensa en un restaurante donde comes a menudo. ¿Qué comidas se sirven allí? ¿Con qué se sirven estas comidas?

2. ¿Cuál de las comidas de este restaurante es tu favorita? ¿Con qué se hace esta comida?

3. ¿Cuándo se abre el restaurante? ¿Cuándo se cierra? ¿Se recomienda reservar una mesa?

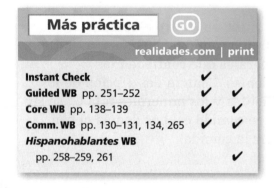

Más práctica	GO
realidades.com | print	

Instant Check	✔	
Guided WB pp. 251–252	✔	✔
Core WB pp. 138–139	✔	✔
Comm. WB pp. 130–131, 134, 265	✔	✔
Hispanohablantes WB pp. 258–259, 261		✔

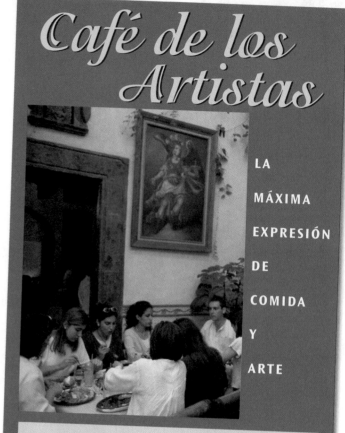

Café de los Artistas

LA

MÁXIMA

EXPRESIÓN

DE

COMIDA

Y

ARTE

Mientras Ud. está en Puerto Vallarta, se le recomienda cenar en el Café de los Artistas. ¡Se come bien aquí! En este restaurante elegante, se puede disfrutar de[1] la mejor comida de la ciudad y al mismo tiempo de las obras de arte regionales más contemporáneas.

En la cena, se deben probar los fresquísimos mariscos y la pesca[2] del día. También se recomienda la comida mexicana moderna, el resultado de las influencias española y francesa con técnicas e ingredientes usados por los pueblos prehispánicos.

Esta comida se caracteriza por sus sopas y guisados[3] cocinados a fuego lento, sus salsas sabrosas y sus ingredientes frescos. Una vez terminada la comida, se quiere prolongar la visita para tomar un café y uno de los riquísimos postres mientras contempla el arte más nuevo y bello de Jalisco.

¡No se pierda[4] la mejor experiencia de comida y arte en Puerto Vallarta! Coma esta noche en el Café de los Artistas.

Se abre diariamente a las 18:00 h.

Se recomienda hacer reservaciones al 225-01-61.
Calle Guerrero 215
Centro

[1] enjoy   [2] catch   [3] stews   [4] Don't miss

▼22 Un anuncio | 👥
para un restaurante

Escribir • Hablar • Dibujar

Trabaja con otro(a) estudiante para crear un anuncio de un restaurante. El restaurante puede ser uno que conocen en su comunidad o en otro lugar, uno que encuentran en la Red o uno que Uds. mismos inventan. Van a crear un cartel o página Web con ilustraciones en las que dan información sobre:

- por qué se debe comer allí
- cómo se preparan diferentes platos
- con qué se sirven estos platos
- qué ingredientes se usan

Incluyan también por lo menos *(at least)* un mandato afirmativo y un mandato negativo en el anuncio. Pueden usar el anuncio de la Actividad 20 como modelo y usar algunas ideas suyas de la Actividad 21 para escribir su anuncio.

El español en la comunidad

En muchas comunidades de los Estados Unidos, en las tiendas, los restaurantes, las bibliotecas y otros lugares públicos, se ven frecuentemente anuncios en español que comienzan con la palabra *se*. Los anuncios más comunes dan información, como "Se habla español"; ofrecen servicios o productos, como "Se alquila . . ." o "Se vende . . ."; anuncian un trabajo o una necesidad, como "Se busca . . .", o "Se necesita . . ." o prohíben algo, como "Se prohíbe . . .".

- ¿Has visto anuncios similares en tu comunidad? ¿Cuáles has visto? ¿Puedes escribir algunos anuncios en español?

▼23 ¡Nos gustaría | 👥
visitar ese restaurante!

Escuchar • Hablar

Presenten su anuncio de la Actividad 22 a otros dos grupos. Luego hablen de por qué les gustaría o no les gustaría visitar los restaurantes que se describen. Pueden hacer preguntas para recibir más información.

Modelo
Nos gustaría visitar ese restaurante porque . . .
¿Se recomienda reservar una mesa?
¿A qué hora se abre?

Un restaurante popular en México

Anuncios para clientes hispanohablantes

Lectura

"ODA AL TOMATE"

La calle
Se llenó de tomates,
mediodía,
verano,
5 la luz
se parte
en dos
mitades
de tomate,
10 corre
por las calles
el jugo.
En diciembre
se desata[1]
15 el tomate,
invade
las cocinas,
entra por los almuerzos,
se sienta
20 reposado[2]
en los aparadores,[3]
entre los vasos,
las mantequilleras,
los saleros[4] azules.
25 Tiene
luz propia,
majestad benigna.[5]

Debemos, por desgracia,[6]
asesinarlo;
30 se hunde[7]
el cuchillo
en su pulpa viviente,
en una roja
víscera,[8]
35 un sol
fresco,
profundo,[9]
inagotable,[10]
llena las ensaladas
40 de Chile,
se casa alegremente
con la clara cebolla,
y para celebrarlo
se deja
45 caer
aceite,
hijo
esencial del olivo,[11]
sobre sus hemisferios
50 entreabiertos[12]
agrega
la pimienta
su fragancia,
la sal su magnetismo (. . .)

Estrategia

Reading and rereading
Poetry is meant to be read several times for a deeper understanding. Remember to pause at the punctuation, not at the end of a line. Read each of Neruda's poems aloud so that you can hear the language. Jot down the descriptive language used to describe the tomato and the onion. Focusing on these words will help you understand the poem better.

[1] is let loose
[2] rested
[3] cupboards
[4] salt shakers
[5] mild
[6] unfortunately
[7] sinks
[8] guts
[9] deep
[10] tireless
[11] olive tree
[12] half-open

**PABLO NERUDA
(1904–1973),**
un poeta chileno, es
considerado uno de los
poetas más importantes del
siglo XX. En 1971 recibió el
Premio Nobel de Literatura y
el Premio Lenin de la Paz.

"Oda a la cebolla"

(. . .) cebolla,

clara como un planeta,

y destinada

a relucir,[1]

constelación constante,

redonda[2] rosa de agua,

sobre la mesa

de las pobres gentes.

[1]shine [2]round

¿Comprendiste?

"Oda al tomate"

1. ¿Por qué crees que Neruda usa el verbo *asesinar?* ¿Qué está describiendo?

2. El poeta no se refiere al tomate como un objeto. ¿Cómo describe el poeta el tomate?

3. ¿Qué quiere decir el poeta con la frase "se casa alegremente con la clara cebolla . . ."?

4. ¿A qué se refiere Neruda con la frase "hijo esencial del olivo"?

5. Lee el poema otra vez. Piensa en cuatro imágenes del poema y dibújalas.

"Oda a la cebolla"

En este poema, Neruda compara la cebolla con varias cosas. ¿Cuáles son?

Y tú, ¿qué dices?

Piensa en algo que comes o bebes, por ejemplo: el pan, el chocolate, las fresas, una tortilla, el cereal o la leche. Escribe un poema de cuatro a seis versos como éstos de Neruda.

Más práctica	GO	
realidades.com	print	
Guided WB p. 253	✔	✔
Comm. WB pp. 135, 266	✔	✔
Hispanohablantes WB pp. 262–263		✔
Cultural Reading Activity	✔	

La cultura en vivo

¡Tortillas y tacos!

La tortilla es la comida fundamental de México y de toda América Central. La tortilla se hace con maíz y también con harina[1]. Los tacos son tortillas con carne o pollo, verduras, queso y chile. El maíz es una planta originaria de las Américas y su nombre azteca fue *toconayao*.

Hoy en día, las tortillas son populares en los Estados Unidos. Las tortillas se pueden comprar frescas o congeladas en los supermercados en casi todas partes del país.

La preparación de los tacos es fácil. Aquí están los ingredientes y la receta.

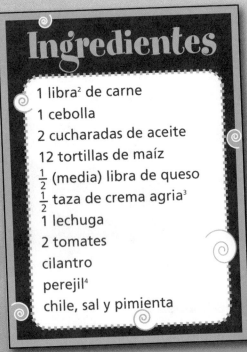

Ingredientes

- 1 libra[2] de carne
- 1 cebolla
- 2 cucharadas de aceite
- 12 tortillas de maíz
- $\frac{1}{2}$ (media) libra de queso
- $\frac{1}{2}$ taza de crema agria[3]
- 1 lechuga
- 2 tomates
- cilantro
- perejil[4]
- chile, sal y pimienta

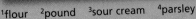

[1]flour   [2]pound   [3]sour cream   [4]parsley

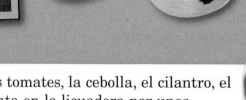

1. Para preparar la salsa: poner los tomates, la cebolla, el cilantro, el perejil, el chile, la sal y la pimienta en la licuadora por unos minutos.

2. Para preparar la carne: freír la carne en aceite con sal y pimienta. Después mezclar un poco de salsa con la carne.

3. Para hacer los tacos: poner una cucharada de carne en cada tortilla.

4. Para hacer más sabrosos los tacos: poner la crema agria primero, y después la salsa, la lechuga y el queso.

▶ Demonstrate how to prepare your favorite dish

▶ Use background knowledge to improve your presentation techniques

Presentación oral (Talk!)

Cómo preparar un plato favorito

Task
You are the guest on a cooking show. Explain how to make your favorite dish: ingredients, main steps for preparing it, and utensils needed.

❶ **Prepare** Bring in samples or pictures of the main ingredients and utensils you need. If possible, bring in the finished product for the class to taste. Make a recipe card like the one shown to help you organize your presentation.

❷ **Practice** Rehearse your presentation. You can use your recipe card only for practice. Try to:

• include the ingredients and utensils needed

• describe and show the preparation in clear steps

• speak clearly

Modelo
Para hacer una quesadilla, se necesitan . . .

❸ **Present** Tell and show the class how to prepare the dish, using the ingredients, utensils, and/or images.

❹ **Evaluation** The following rubric will be used to grade your presentation.

> **Estrategia**
>
> **Using background knowledge**
> Think about cooking shows you have seen. How does the chef present the ingredients? How does he or she explain how to prepare and cook the dish? Use these techniques in your presentation.

> ### Quesadillas
>
> Ingredientes que | Cosas que se usan
> se necesitan | un cuchillo
> tortillas de harina | una sartén
> queso
> frijoles refritos
>
> Preparación
> 1. Primero se extiende $\frac{1}{4}$ taza de frijoles refritos sobre la mitad de cada tortilla.
> 2. Luego se ponen dos cucharadas de queso . . .

Rubric	Score 1	Score 3	Score 5
How complete your preparation is	You provide one of the following: utensils, pictures, recipe card.	You provide two of the following: utensils, pictures, recipe card.	You provide all three of the following: utensils, pictures, recipe card.
Amount of information given	Your presentation includes one of the following: ingredients, utensils, and steps for preparation.	Your presentation includes two of the following: ingredients, utensils, and steps for preparation.	Your presentation includes all three of the following: ingredients, utensils, and steps for preparation.
How easily you are understood	You are difficult to understand and make many errors.	You are fairly easy to understand and make occasional errors.	You are easy to understand and make very few errors.

En busca de la verdad

Episodio 9

Antes de ver el video

"Este archivo contiene las respuestas a todas sus preguntas".

Nota cultural Cuando haces nuevos amigos en México y ellos ya te tienen confianza, es muy común que te digan "Mi casa es tu casa" o "Siéntete como en tu casa". Son expresiones de cortesía.

"Estamos buscando a mi abuelo, Federico Zúñiga. Ésta es su cuenta".

Resumen del episodio

Antes de salir para el aeropuerto, Tomás le da a Roberto unos documentos muy importantes. Carmen, Linda y Roberto llegan a San Antonio. Al día siguiente, Roberto y Linda van al Banco de la Frontera y conocen al Sr. De León. Él les da la última pista para descubrir la verdad sobre el abuelo de Roberto.

Palabras para comprender

certificado de nacimiento birth certificate
tarjeta de estudiante student ID
puede que it may be that
heredero heir
Estoy a cargo del caso. I am in charge of the case.

Después de ver el video

¿Comprendiste?

A. Completa las siguientes frases.

1. Antes de salir para San Antonio, el padre de Roberto le da _____.

2. Enrique es _____.

3. Linda quiere ir primero a su escuela porque _____.

4. Roberto le dice a De León que su familia no usa el apellido Zúñiga porque _____.

5. De León no puede darle a Roberto más información sobre su abuelo porque _____.

6. De León le dice a Roberto que le pueden dar más información en _____.

7. El hombre misterioso viajó a Guanajuato para _____.

8. Roberto descubre que el hombre misterioso es _____.

B. Escribe un resumen de la conversación entre Roberto y De León.

"Buenas tardes, señor. Me llamo Roberto Toledo".

Más práctica GO

realidades.com | print

Actividades ✔

Repaso del capítulo

Vocabulario y gramática

to name foods and items in the kitchen

el aceite	cooking oil
el ajo	garlic
el caldo	broth
el camarón, *pl.* los camarones	shrimp
la estufa	stove
el fregadero	sink
el fuego	fire, heat
el horno	oven
los mariscos	shellfish
el microondas, *pl.* los microondas	microwave
la olla	pot
el pedazo	piece, slice
el refrigerador	refrigerator
la salsa	salsa, sauce
la sartén, *pl.* las sartenes	frying pan
el vinagre	vinegar

to follow a recipe

añadir	to add
no añadas	don't add
batir	to beat
calentar *(e → ie)*	to heat
la cucharada	tablespoon(ful)
freír *(e → i)*	to fry
hervir *(e → ie) (e → i)*	to boil
el ingrediente	ingredient
mezclar	to mix
pelar	to peel
picar	to chop
probar *(o → ue)*	to taste, to try
la receta	recipe

to talk about food preparation

al horno	baked
apagar	to turn off
caliente	hot
¿Cómo se hace . . . ?	How do you make . . . ?
¿Con qué se sirve?	What do you serve it with?
congelado, -a	frozen
dejar	to leave, to let
no dejes	don't leave, don't let
encender *(e → ie)*	to turn on, to light
enlatado, -a	canned
fresco, -a	fresh
frito, -a	fried
olvidarse de	to forget about / to
no te olvides de	don't forget about / to
tirar	to spill, to throw away
no tires	don't spill, don't throw away

another useful expression

se puede	you can

negative *tú* commands

No hables.	Don't speak.
No comas.	Don't eat.
No escribas.	Don't write.

irregular negative *tú* commands

dar	no des
estar	no estés
ir	no vayas
ser	no seas

For *Vocabulario adicional,* see pp. 498–499.

Más repaso (GO) realidades.com | print

Instant Check ✔
Puzzles ✔
Core WB pp. 140–141 ✔
Comm. WB p. 267 ✔ ✔

Preparación para el examen

On the exam you will be asked to . . .	Here are practice tasks similar to those you will find on the exam . . .	For review go to your print or digital textbook . . .

Interpretive

1 Escuchar Listen to and understand someone giving instructions for cooking a meal

Listen as Gabriel's sister Valeria gives him cooking instructions over the phone. See if you can identify: (a) what he wants to cook; (b) what ingredients he still needs to buy; and (c) the first few steps in the recipe.

pp. 348–351 *Vocabulario en contexto*
p. 354 Actividades 9–10
p. 358 Actividad 15

Interpersonal

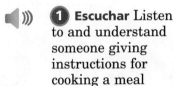

2 Hablar Tell someone the first steps in making a particular recipe

Based on the illustrations below, tell someone the first three steps in preparing paella.

pp. 350–351 *Videohistoria*
p. 355 Actividad 11
p. 358 Actividad 15
p. 367 *Presentación oral*

Interpretive

3 Leer Read and understand as someone gives general advice on cooking

You are reading an article about cooking in a Spanish magazine. Tell which of the following suggestions are focused on: (a) things to do before cooking; (b) things to do while cooking; and (c) things to do after cooking.

1. Apaga el horno cuando terminas de cocinar.
2. Lee primero la receta para saber si tienes todos los ingredientes.
3. No salgas nunca de la cocina mientras algo está hirviendo.

pp. 350–351 *Videohistoria*
p. 353 Actividad 6
p. 354 Actividad 10
p. 357 Actividad 13
pp. 364–365 *Lectura*

Presentational

4 Escribir Write rules to promote safety in the kitchen

The home economics teacher asks you to write down a list of five rules for cooking safely for her Spanish-speaking students. You might begin with something like: *Ten cuidado cuando picas las verduras.*

p. 356 Actividad 12
p. 357 Actividad 13
p. 359 Actividad 16

Cultures

5 Pensar Demonstrate an understanding of how certain foods from one culture are incorporated into another culture

You would like to prepare dinner for your family using some recipes from a Mexican cookbook, but your little brother and sister are very picky eaters. What could you tell them about food(s) from another country that they have eaten before and liked? What might be the best American food or dish to introduce to teenagers from other countries? Why?

p. 366 *La cultura en vivo*

Capítulo 7B
¿Te gusta comer al aire libre?

En el Parque Nacional
Torres del Paine, Chile

▼ Chapter Objectives

Communication
By the end of this chapter you will be able to:
- Listen and read about outdoor cooking and campground signs
- Talk and write about cookouts and outdoor celebrations
- Exchange information about cookout preparations

Culture
You will also be able to:
- Understand outdoor food markets in the Spanish-speaking world
- Compare ways food is prepared in Spanish-speaking countries and in the U.S.

You will demonstrate what you know and can do:
- Presentación escrita, p. 393
- Preparación para el examen, p. 397

You will use:

Vocabulary
- Camping and eating outdoors
- Foods

Grammar
- *Usted* and *ustedes* commands
- Uses of *por*

Exploración del mundo hispano

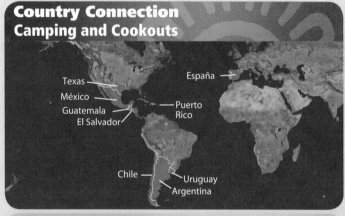

Country Connection
Camping and Cookouts

Texas
México
Guatemala
El Salvador
España
Puerto Rico
Chile
Uruguay
Argentina

realidades.com   GO

 Reference Atlas
 Videocultura y actividad

🌐 *Mapa global interactivo*

Arte y cultura | Estados Unidos

Carmen Lomas Garza nació en Kingsville, Texas, en 1948. Ella empezó a pintar cuando tenía 13 años. Los cuadros de Lomas Garza muestran *(show)* escenas familiares de la vida diaria y fiestas y actividades de la comunidad hispana. En este cuadro, titulado "Sandía", una familia hispana se reúne a comer esa fruta al aire libre.

• ¿Se reúne tu familia o algunos amigos o vecinos en tu casa frecuentemente? ¿En qué sentido *(way)* son similares las reuniones de tu familia a la que se ve en el cuadro? ¿En qué sentido son diferentes?

"Sandía / Watermelon" (1986), Carmen Lomas Garza ▼
Gouache painting on paper, 20 x 28 in. Photo Credit: Wolfgang Dietze Collection of Dudley D. Brooks and Tomas Ybarra-Frausto, New York, NY.

A primera vista | 🔊 | 🗇

▼ Objectives

Read, listen to, and understand information about
▶ camping and cookouts
▶ foods

Vocabulario en contexto

—Voy a encender el fuego ahora. ¿Me puedes dar los fósforos?

—Claro. ¿Qué vamos a comer?

—Carne de res a la parrilla, tortillas de **maíz** y guacamole. También tengo una salsa que está hecha con chiles verdes y es bien **picante.** Y de postre, piña y sandía. Las dos son muy **dulces.**

—¡Fabuloso! Gracias por hacer todas las preparaciones.

—De nada. Me encanta comer **al aire libre.**

hacer una parrillada

el fósforo

el durazno

el melón

el aguacate

las cerezas

la piedra

la sandía

la piña

la cesta

el pollo **asado**

la salsa de tomate

el pavo

la mostaza

la carne de res

la mayonesa

a la parrilla   la chuleta de cerdo   asar

—¡Ay! No me gustan nada los mosquitos. Hay muchos por aquí.

—Sí, y hay moscas y hormigas también. ¡Qué problema!

—Pedro y Roberto, **traigan** más leña para la fogata. Si no, la fogata se va a apagar. **Póngan**la aquí muy cerca.

—Ahora, no. Vamos a dar una caminata por una hora.

—**Tengan** cuidado. Dicen que va a llover.

—Gracias. ¡Hasta pronto!

las nubes · el cielo · dar una caminata · el sendero · la fogata · la leña · la hormiga · la mosca

secos · mojados

Una hora después . . .

—No **entren** en la cabaña.* Están mojados. Aquí, **dentro de** la cabaña, todo está seco. ¡Y dejen las botas sucias **fuera**!

—¿Qué dicen? ¡**Abran** la puerta ahora!

*cabin

▼1 ¿Cierta o falsa? | 🔊

Escuchar

Escucha las siguientes frases. Según la información de la escena de la página 374, indica si son ciertas o falsas. Señala con el pulgar hacia arriba si la frase es cierta y con el pulgar hacia abajo si es falsa.

Más práctica	GO

realidades.com | print

Instant Check	✔	
Guided WB pp. 255–260	✔	✔
Core WB pp. 142–143	✔	✔
Comm. WB p. 142	✔	✔
Hispanohablantes **WB** p. 272		✔

▼2 Al aire libre | 🔊

Escuchar

Escucha las frases y preguntas sobre un día al aire libre. Escoge la respuesta correcta para cada pregunta.

1. **a.** la piedra   **b.** el fósforo
2. **a.** unas nubes   **b.** un pavo
3. **a.** mojada   **b.** seca
4. **a.** la piña   **b.** la chuleta de cerdo
5. **a.** el durazno   **b.** la carne de res
6. **a.** la mostaza   **b.** la sandía

Un día al aire libre

Claudia, Teresa, Manolo y Ramón van a pasar el día en el parque Desierto de los Leones. Todos tienen hambre, pero hay un problema. Lee para saber qué pasa.

Estrategia

Using visuals
Using visuals can help you understand the story. Look at the pictures and write what you think the problem is. Then read to see if your prediction was correct.

Claudia: Me encanta ir al parque y comer al aire libre.

Teresa: A mí también.

Manolo: A mí no me gusta. No me gustan ni las moscas ni los mosquitos.

Ramón   Claudia   Manolo Teresa

Ramón: ¡Uumm, chuletas de cerdo! ¡Qué **olor** tan bueno!

Manolo: Sí. Un poco **grasosas**, pero muy ricas. ¡Ahora tengo sed y hambre!

Teresa: ¿Me pasas las tortillas?

Claudia: Pues, no están aquí. Tampoco está la carne de res. Esta mañana tenía tanta prisa . . . que dejé la comida en la mesa.

Teresa: Pues, ¿qué vamos a comer?

Manolo: Tenemos hambre. ¡Vamos a comer!

Claudia: Tenemos un problema . . . Toda la comida que preparé . . .

Manolo: Bien. Podemos comprar la comida en uno de **los puestos.** Vamos a comer allí.

Teresa: Oye, ¿y qué traes en la cesta?

Claudia: Carne de res, tortillas de **harina, frijoles** y guacamole.

Teresa: ¡Qué rico! Ya tengo mucha hambre.

Teresa: Miren, aquí lo podemos poner.

Claudia: Pero **el suelo** está mojado. Vamos a buscar un lugar seco.

Ramón: Manolo, ¿quieres dar una caminata?

Manolo: ¿Dar una caminata? Tengo sed. Quiero un refresco.

Ramón: Sí, podemos comprar un refresco también. ¿Quieren **acompañar**nos?

Claudia: Gracias, pero vamos a quedarnos aquí, a charlar.

Manolo: ¡Qué bien! Claudia no puede cocinar muy bien. Su comida no tiene mucho **sabor. Será** mucho mejor comer la comida de aquí, del parque.

Claudia: ¿Qué dicen?

Manolo: Nada . . .

▼**3 ¿Comprendiste?**

Escribir • Hablar

1. ¿Adónde van los chicos y qué van a hacer?
2. ¿A Manolo le gusta comer al aire libre? ¿Por qué?
3. ¿Qué dice Claudia que trae en la cesta?
4. ¿Adónde van Manolo y Ramón? ¿Qué ven?
5. ¿Qué le pide Teresa a Claudia? ¿Qué le dice Claudia?
6. ¿Qué deciden hacer los chicos? ¿Qué le dice Manolo a Ramón? ¿Lo oye Claudia?

Más práctica (GO)

realidades.com | print

Instant Check	✔	
Guided WB pp. 261–264	✔	✔
Core WB pp. 144–145	✔	✔
Comm. WB pp. 136–138, 139	✔	✔
Hispanohablantes **WB** p. 273		✔

También se dice . . .

la cesta = la canasta (*muchos países*)

| ▼ **Objectives**

▷ Talk about indoor and outdoor celebrations
▷ Discuss food preferences
▷ Listen to opinions about cookouts
▷ Write about food and cookouts

Vocabulario en uso

▼4 Una parrillada bien organizada

Leer • Escribir

Tú y tus amigos van a hacer una parrillada en el parque. Tus amigos te traen las cosas que necesitan y tú tienes que organizarlas. Lee las listas y escoge cuál de las cosas no debe estar con las demás. Escribe esta palabra y otra palabra que asocias con ella.

Modelo

la parrilla, la leña, el fósforo, el durazno
el durazno, la manzana

1. la carne de res, el pavo, las chuletas de cerdo, el flan

2. la sandía, la harina, la piña, el melón

3. la cereza, la cesta, la leña, la piedra

4. el fósforo, el melón, el maíz, las cerezas

5. los frijoles, el maíz, la piedra, los aguacates

6. la mayonesa, la salsa de tomate, la mostaza, el maíz

▼5 Escucha y escribe | 👥 | 🔊

Escuchar • Escribir

❶ Escribe lo que dicen. Después indica si a la persona le gusta o no le gusta comer al aire libre.

❷ Habla con otro(a) estudiante. ¿Estás de acuerdo con las seis opiniones? ¿Por qué? Escriban tres razones *(reasons)* para comer o no comer al aire libre.

Fondo Cultural | Argentina | Uruguay

La parrillada mixta es una comida típica de la Argentina y el Uruguay. En estos países hay mucho ganado *(cattle)* y se consume mucha carne de res. Las familias se reúnen los domingos para hacer parrilladas mixtas al aire libre. La parrillada mixta puede incluir varios cortes de carne, una variedad de chorizos, salchichas y más.

• ¿Qué tradición en los Estados Unidos es similar a la parrillada? ¿Cuál es el origen de esta tradición? ¿Qué comidas son típicas de esta tradición?

Una parrillada típica de la Argentina y el Uruguay

▼6 Mi hermano Luis | ♻

Leer • Escribir

Lee lo que pasó cuando un joven fue al parque con su hermano.
Completa su historia con las palabras apropiadas del recuadro.

El sábado pasado, fuimos al parque para __1.__ y pasar el día
__2.__ casa. A mí me encanta hacer muchas actividades al aire
libre, pero Luis no quería ir. Mientras __3.__ , él decía que
el __4.__ estaba demasiado mojado y que no quería tener los
zapatos sucios. Luego Luis no podía encontrar un
lugar __5.__ para comer. Pero cuando empezamos a __6.__
las hamburguesas, Luis dijo que le gustaba el olor de la
carne __7.__ y que tenía un __8.__ increíble. ¡Comió cuatro
hamburguesas! Luego él no podía caminar rápidamente
porque no se sentía bien. Creo que si hacemos otra
parrillada, Luis no nos va a __9.__ .

dábamos una caminata	sabor
fuera de	asada
hacer una parrillada	seco
sendero	asar
acompañar	

▼7 ¿Cómo son las comidas? | 👥 | ♻

Escribir • Hablar

❶ Haz una lista de tres comidas para cada una de las
siguientes categorías de comidas: *dulces, grasosas,
picantes*.

❷ Compara tu lista con la de otro(a) estudiante. ¿Cuántas
comidas pueden poner en la lista para cada categoría?

> **También se dice . . .**
>
> **la parrillada** = el asado, la barbacoa
> *(muchos países)*
>
> **el fósforo** = el cerillo *(países andinos,
> México)*; la cerilla *(España)*
>
> **el durazno** = el melocotón *(España)*
>
> **los frijoles** = las habichuelas *(Puerto
> Rico)*; las judías *(España)*; las
> caraotas *(Venezuela)*
>
> **el pavo** = el guajolote *(México)*

▼8 ¿Qué vamos a servir? | 💬👥 | ♻

Hablar

Un(a) amigo(a) y tú quieren decidir qué
comidas van a servir en la parrillada. Hablen
de las comidas que les gustan y de las que no
les gustan. Digan por qué.

 Modelo

A —¿Te gusta *la sandía?*
B —*¡Sí, claro! Me encanta porque es muy dulce.*
o: —*No, no me gusta nada. Es demasiado dulce.*

Estudiante A

1. 2. 3. 4.

5. 6. 7. 8.

Estudiante B

muy	seco, -a
bastante	picante
demasiado	dulce
	grasoso, -a
	sabroso, -a
	delicioso, -a
	riquísimo, -a
	horrible

▼9 No recuerdo la palabra | 👥 | ♻

Escribir • Hablar

No recuerdas o no sabes la palabra en español para una cosa y tienes que usar otras palabras para describirla. Piensa en un objeto o una comida. Escribe tres descripciones. Luego léelas a diferentes miembros de tu clase. Ellos tienen que decir lo que describes.

▶ **Modelo**

sandía

A —*Es una fruta grande. El color de la fruta es verde y rojo. Es muy dulce y la comemos en el verano.*

B —*Es una sandía.*

> **Estrategia**
>
> **Circumlocution**
> When you don't know or can't remember a word, use other words you know to describe what it looks like, is used for, or is similar to.

▼10 La cocina mexicana | ♻

Leer • Escribir

¿Conoces bien la cocina[1] mexicana? Hay muchas variaciones regionales, pero por lo general se usa mucho el ajo, la cebolla, el aceite y el cilantro. Casi todas las comidas se sirven con arroz. Lee las descripciones y complétalas con las palabras apropiadas del recuadro. Se puede usar una palabra más de una vez.

aguacate	maíz
carne de res	queso
frijoles	salsa
harina	

El taco: Es una tortilla de 1. o de 2. . Dentro de la tortilla, hay, por lo general, 3. , pollo o 4. .

El chile relleno: Es un chile, que generalmente está relleno de[2] queso. Se cubre[3] el chile con la parte blanca del huevo y se fríe.

El burrito: Esta comida viene del norte de México y el suroeste de los Estados Unidos. Se hace con una tortilla de 5. . Dentro de la tortilla se pone 6. , pollo o 7. . A veces se sirve con una 8. picante hecha de chiles verdes.

El tamal: Es una masa[4] hecha de harina de maíz rellena de carne de res o cerdo y chiles. Es una comida muy popular para los días festivos, como la Navidad.

La enchilada: Generalmente está hecha de una tortilla de maíz con diferentes ingredientes dentro de la tortilla, como pollo, carne de res o queso. Se sirve con una salsa hecha de chiles rojos o a veces de crema.

El mole: Es una salsa que se hace de chiles rojos y chocolate. Puede ser bastante picante. Muchas veces se come con pollo.

La quesadilla: Es una tortilla de 9. que se fríe. Se usa 10. dentro de o encima de la tortilla. A veces se usan otros ingredientes, como pollo y chiles jalapeños.

El guacamole: Es una comida fresca que se hace con 11. , tomates, ajo y cebolla y se come con muchas otras comidas.

[1]cuisine   [2]stuffed with   [3]Is covered   [4]dough

▼11 ¿Adentro o al aire libre? | 👥 | ♻️

Escribir • Hablar

1 ¿Has ido a una fiesta de familia o de amigos en casa de alguien? ¿Y una fiesta al aire libre? Hay diferencias, ¿verdad? Prepara un diagrama de Venn indicando lo que te gustó de las fiestas dentro de la casa y lo que fue bueno de las fiestas al aire libre. Indica también lo que te gustó hacer adentro y al aire libre. Piensa en los olores, el sabor de la comida, el tiempo que hacía, las personas que vinieron y las actividades que hicieron.

2 Después describe tus experiencias a otro(a) estudiante, comparando lo bueno de las fiestas.

Modelo

adentro | adentro y al aire libre | al aire libre

No había moscas. | Comimos pasteles. | Hicimos una parrillada.

Modelo

Me gustó la fiesta en casa de mi primo porque no había moscas.
o: *Prefiero estar al aire libre. Me encantan las parrilladas.*

▼12 Y tú, ¿qué dices? |

Escribir • Hablar

1. ¿Te gusta la comida picante? ¿Cuáles son algunas comidas picantes que tú u otras personas en tu comunidad comen?

2. ¿Qué comidas son grasosas? ¿Qué comidas son dulces? ¿Comes estas comidas a menudo?

3. ¿Cuándo y dónde hicieron Uds. una parrillada la última vez? ¿Qué asaron a la parrilla? ¿Qué otras cosas comieron? ¿Cómo estuvo la comida?

4. Cuando estás al aire libre, ¿qué te gusta hacer? ¿Dar una caminata? ¿Mirar el cielo y las nubes? ¿Encender una fogata?

5. ¿Cuál fue la última comida que compraste en un puesto? ¿Dónde estaba el puesto? ¿Te gustó la comida? ¿Qué otras cosas vendían?

▼ Fondo Cultural | El mundo hispano

La comida picante Muchas personas creen que todos los platos de la cocina de los países hispanohablantes son picantes. Esto no es cierto. El chile, ají o pimiento picante es originario de las Américas. Se han encontrado semillas *(seeds)* en Perú y Bolivia que tienen más de 7,000 años de antigüedad. En países como Ecuador o México el picante es muy popular, pero en la mayoría de los países hispanohablantes, la gente usa el picante con moderación. Se puede decir que el picante es más popular en las regiones cálidas porque el picante hace sudar *(sweat)* y el sudor refresca la piel. Sin embargo, también hay platos picantes en regiones donde hace frío, como en los Andes, en Bolivia y Perú.

- ¿Conoces un plato picante de los Estados Unidos? ¿Se comen en tu casa platos picantes? ¿Por qué crees que a algunas personas les gusta la comida picante?

▶ **Talk and write about what to do at cookouts**
▶ **Tell people what to do when hiking**

Gramática

Usted and *ustedes* commands

To give an affirmative or negative command in the *Ud.* or *Uds.* form, use the present-tense *yo* form as the stem just as you did for negative *tú* commands.

¿Recuerdas?

You already know how to give negative *tú* commands.

• **No prepares** los frijoles todavía.
• **No enciendas** la fogata.
• **No salgas** de este sendero.

• Add *-e* or *-en* for *-ar* verbs.

| cortar | corto | Señor, **corte** las chuletas de cerdo. |
| probar | pruebo | Señores, **prueben** la carne asada. |

• Add *-a* or *-an* for *-er* and *-ir* verbs.

| perder | pierdo | **No pierdan** Uds. los fósforos. |
| servir | sirvo | Señorita, **sirva** la ensalada. |

Affirmative and negative *Ud.* and *Uds.* commands have the same spelling changes and irregular forms as negative *tú* commands.

The same rules you know for *tú* commands regarding pronouns apply to *Ud.* and *Uds.* commands as well.

Attach pronouns to affirmative commands.

—¿Dónde ponemos la leña?

—Pónganla en un lugar seco.

With negative commands, pronouns go right before the verb.

—¿Encendemos la fogata ahora?

—No, no la enciendan todavía.

negative *tú* command	*Ud.* command	*Uds.* command
no busques	(no) busque	(no) busquen
no hagas	(no) haga	(no) hagan
no des	(no) dé	(no) den
no vayas	(no) vaya	(no) vayan
no seas	(no) sea	(no) sean
no estés	(no) esté	(no) estén

Más ayuda **realidades.com**

 GramActiva Video Tutorials: Formation of formal commands: Spanish version, Commands: English version, Negative formal commands, Attaching object and reflexive pronouns to formal commands

 Canción de hip hop: *Parrillada*

 GramActiva Activity

▼13 ¿Qué hacemos ahora?

Escribir

❶ Pon en orden las cosas que las personas deben hacer para una parrillada. Usa mandatos e incluye expresiones como *primero, segundo, luego, después* y *entonces.*

sacar los fósforos	poner las cestas en el suelo
apagar la fogata	asar la carne
recoger leña y piedras	no dejar la comida al aire libre
encender la fogata	

❷ Luego escribe cada frase del Paso 1 con sólo el pronombre *(pronoun).*

Modelo

buscar un lugar seco
Primero busquen un lugar seco.
Primero búsquenlo.

▼14 La naturaleza muerta |

Observar • Hablar • Escribir

Este cuadro es de la artista mexicana Elena Climent. Sus cuadros representan escenas de la vida diaria. Observa el cuadro con otro(a) estudiante y contesten las preguntas.

Conexiones | El arte

En el estilo de arte que se llama naturaleza muerta *(still life)*, un(a) artista trata de pintar unos objetos como frutas y verduras, con realismo.

◄ "Tienda de legumbres" (1992), Elena Climent

Oil on canvas, 36 x 44-1/8 in. Courtesy of Mary-Anne Martin/Fine Art, New York.

1. ¿Qué objetos se ven?
2. ¿Qué colores ha escogido la artista para representar los objetos? ¿Por qué crees que usó estos colores?
3. ¿Cuál fue la belleza que la artista vio en esta escena? ¿Qué hizo ella para pintar el cuadro con un estilo realista?

▼15 Para ayudar a tu mamá |

Observar • Hablar • Escribir

Imagina que estás en México con un(a) amigo(a) y tu mamá necesita varias cosas de la tienda que se ve en el cuadro de Elena Climent. Trabaja con otro(a) estudiante y escriban mandatos con *Uds.* que ella les puede dar.

Modelo
no comprar
No compren juguetes en la tienda.

1. ir
2. pedir
3. traerme
4. escoger
5. preguntar si
6. tener prisa

▼ Exploración del lenguaje

Compound words

Spanish, like English, sometimes combines two existing words to create new vocabulary. The invention of a new type of oven led to the English "micro" + "wave" and the Spanish *micro + ondas.* Like *el microondas,* compound words formed this way are masculine and singular. In the plural, the noun does not change: *los microondas.*

¡Compruébalo! Create a compound word by combining the action (verb) in the first box with the object (noun) in the second box. Write a command using each compound word.

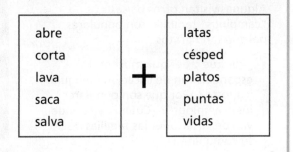

abre	latas
corta	césped
lava	**+** platos
saca	puntas
salva	vidas

Modelo
el microondas
Señor, use el microondas para preparar la comida rápidamente.

▼16 Una nueva vecina | | ♻

Hablar

Con otro(a) estudiante, haz planes para una parrillada. Decide qué comida van a servir y cómo prepararla. Haz preguntas y contéstalas con mandatos con Ud.

 Modelo

asar a la parrilla / carne
A —¿Qué carne aso a la parrilla?
B —Ase el pavo.

Estudiante A

1. comprar / jugo
2. preparar / comida
3. poner / en la ensalada
4. hacer / pastel
5. servir / fruta
6. ¡Respuesta personal!

Estudiante B

1.

2.

3.

4.

5.

6. ¡Respuesta personal!

🌐 Fondo Cultural | España

Las vacaciones de verano La mayoría de las familias españolas van de vacaciones en los meses de julio y agosto. Los lugares favoritos son la playa (40 por ciento) y la montaña (30 por ciento). Muchas familias van de vacaciones a una casa de pueblo, otras alquilan un apartamento y otras van a un hotel o a una pensión (guesthouse). Algunas visitan otros países. Los "campings" también son populares porque son baratos.

• ¿Por qué crees que muchos españoles van de vacaciones en julio y agosto? ¿Por qué son populares los "campings"? ¿Cuándo y adónde van de vacaciones las familias de tu comunidad?

Mallorca, España

▼17 El club de senderismo

Leer • Escribir

A los miembros del club "Aire puro" de Santiago, Chile, les encanta dar caminatas largas por los bosques *(forests)* y por las montañas. Este pasatiempo se llama *senderismo.* Lee el artículo y contesta las preguntas.

Me gusta caminar *con Aire puro*

¿Te gusta dar una larga caminata por un sendero, hacer una buena fogata de leña y dormir bajo las nubes, con el cielo como techo?* El club de senderismo "Aire puro" organiza excursiones al aire libre. Nuestro objetivo es combinar las actividades en la naturaleza con la cultura y el tiempo libre. Escogemos cuidadosamente los lugares de excursión según su belleza, importancia biológica e interés histórico y cultural. No es necesario una preparación o condición física especial y hay muy poco peligro.

Aire puro ¡Es la mejor manera de divertirse en la naturaleza!

*roof

1. ¿Cuál es el objetivo del club "Aire puro"? ¿Qué hace el club?

2. ¿Quién puede dar una caminata en una excursión del club? ¿Se necesita algo especial para participar?

3. ¿De qué cosas puedes disfrutar *(enjoy)* en las excursiones del club?

En los Andes, Chile

▼18 Las reglas de la caminata | Talk! 👥

Hablar

Antes de dar una caminata, los miembros tienen que conocer bien las reglas del senderismo. Trabaja con otro(a) estudiante y dile las reglas que los miembros deben seguir. Tu compañero(a) te va a responder.

1. usar / una mochila para llevar sus cosas

2. no jugar / con los fósforos

3. traer / un mapa de los senderos

4. salir / en grupos, nunca solos

5. no dar caminatas / sin compañero(a)

6. no dejar / la basura en las cestas

▶️ **Modelo**

llevar / zapatos adecuados

A —*Lleven zapatos adecuados.*

B —*Tienes razón. Es difícil caminar por los senderos.*

Más práctica	GO	
realidades.com	print	
Instant Check	✔	
Guided WB pp. 265–267	✔	✔
Core WB p. 146	✔	✔
Comm. WB pp. 140, 143, 268	✔	✔
Hispanohablantes **WB** pp. 274–277, 281		✔

Gramática

▼ **Objectives**
▶ Talk and write about how and why to go to the market
▶ Exchange information about how much time activities take

Uses of *por*

The preposition *por* is used in several ways. You already know many of its uses.

To indicate length of time or distance:

Dejen el pollo en la parrilla **por** unos minutos más.

To indicate movement through, along, or around:

Vamos a dar una caminata **por** ese sendero.

Hay un buen lugar **por allí**.

To indicate an exchange of one thing for another:

No pague Ud. demasiado **por** esos melones.

To indicate reason or motive:

Las chuletas de cerdo no son muy saludables **por** ser bastante grasosas.

¿Recuerdas?

You know several expressions that use *por*. See if you can remember them all.

por ejemplo	por la mañana, tarde, noche
por eso	
por favor	por primera, segunda, . . . vez
por lo general	
	por supuesto

To indicate a substitution or action on someone's behalf:

Felipe y Marcos, traigan esa leña al fuego **por** su papá.

To indicate means of communication or transportation:

Nos hablamos **por** teléfono ayer.

Más ayuda realidades.com

▶ *GramActiva* Video

GramActiva Activity

▼19 Un viaje a Guatemala |

Leer • Escribir

Raquel le está escribiendo una tarjeta postal a su amiga, Anita, en Washington. Lee lo que le dice y escribe las expresiones apropiadas con *por*.

Querida Anita:

¡Qué bonito país es Guatemala! Ayer, _1._ (por lo general / por la mañana), fuimos a la ciudad de Tikal, unas ruinas mayas bellísimas. Tikal está en medio de una selva tropical.* _2._ (Por eso / Por lo general) vimos pájaros en muchos árboles. _3._ (Por supuesto / Por eso) hemos probado la comida guatemalteca. El maíz es importante en la comida aquí. _4._ (Por favor / Por ejemplo), comen tortillas, tamales y enchiladas. También he probado los postres guatemaltecos. Ayer, _5._ (por primera vez / por lo general), comí buñuelos—un tipo de postre frito riquísimo. _6._ (Por lo general / Por favor) los guatemaltecos comen postres _7._ (por la noche / por supuesto). Mañana visitamos Chichicastenango.
Raquel

*rain forest

¡Guatemala!

▼20 ¿Cuál es?

Escribir

Completa las siguientes frases con la expresión correcta de *por*.

1. Fuimos al concierto ___.
2. Omar quiere visitar a su familia en Perú. Va ___.
3. En la ciudad había mucha gente ___.
4. El profesor de español está enfermo hoy. ¿Quién va a enseñar ___?
5. Pagué 200 dólares ___ de avión.

a. por un mes en verano
b. por él
c. por los boletos
d. por la música
e. por todas partes

▼21 Voy al mercado |

Hablar

Imagina que encuentras a un(a) amigo(a) que va a un mercado. Habla con él (ella) sobre qué va a hacer allí.

▶ **Modelo**

A —*¡Hola! ¿Adónde vas?*
B —*Necesito ir al mercado. ¿Quieres ir conmigo?*
A —*¿Por cuánto tiempo vas?*
B —*Voy por una hora, más o menos.*

Estudiante A

¿Cómo vas?

¿Por qué vas?

¿A qué mercado vas?

Estudiante B

la calle principal

duraznos frescos

. . . para no pagar mucho por ellos

¡Respuesta personal!

🌐 Fondo Cultural | El Salvador

El Parque de la Familia se estableció en 1996 a unos 12 kilómetros de San Salvador, la capital de El Salvador. Es el parque de recreo con juegos mecánicos más grande del área. Mucha gente va allí para escapar del ruido *(noise)* de la ciudad. En el parque hay actividades para niños y lugares para practicar deportes. También hay peces y pájaros, un anfiteatro, un mirador panorámico, puestos de artesanías *(handicrafts)*, un área de piñatas, cafetines *(small cafés)* y un parqueadero amplio.

• ¿Hay un parque en tu comunidad similar al Parque de la Familia? ¿En qué sentido es similar? ¿Por qué es tan popular este tipo de parque?

Leyendo en el Parque de la Familia, en El Salvador

▼22 ¿Por cuánto tiempo? |

Hablar

Habla con otro(a) estudiante sobre cuánto tiempo se debe hacer diferentes cosas en la cocina, en los estudios y en los deportes.

▶️ **Modelo**

dejar la leche en el refrigerador

A —*¿Por cuánto tiempo se debe dejar la leche en el refrigerador?*

B —*Por una semana, más o menos.*

1. asar hamburguesas a la parrilla
2. estudiar para un examen de español
3. usar la computadora sin descansar
4. hacer ejercicio sin beber agua
5. dormir un chico de 15 años
6. hablar por teléfono celular con un(a) amigo(a)

▼23 Nuestras | 👥 | ♻️ recomendaciones

Escribir • Dibujar • Hablar

Imagina que un grupo de jóvenes que no conocen la región donde vives vienen a visitarte. Sabes que les encanta hacer actividades al aire libre.

1 Escribe cinco recomendaciones, usando mandatos en la forma *Uds.,* que puedes darles. Puedes incluir:

- adónde deben ir y qué deben hacer al aire libre
- por dónde deben pasar y cuánto tiempo deben pasar en diferentes lugares
- qué cosas y ropa deben llevar
- qué pueden comer y dónde
- reglas que necesitan seguir
- si deben tener cuidado con algo

2 Trabaja con un grupo de tres estudiantes. Hagan un cartel o folleto *(brochure)* usando visuales. Preséntenlo a la clase.

El español en el mundo del trabajo

¿Te gusta trabajar al aire libre? Las agencias federales de los Estados Unidos tienen abundantes bosques *(forests)*, parques y reservas nacionales. El Servicio de Parques Nacionales, formado en 1916, es muy conocido ya que *(since)* administra 58 parques nacionales. El Sistema de Parques Nacionales incluye más de 33 millones de hectáreas y cerca de 400 unidades que incluyen desde Monumentos Nacionales hasta Áreas Nacionales de Recreación. Cada año vienen más turistas hispanohablantes a los Estados Unidos y se necesitan empleados bilingües para ayudarlos. También hay que escribir folletos de turismo, crear programas educativos y escribir información en los sitios Web en español.

- Piensa en un parque nacional o monumento nacional cerca de tu comunidad. ¿Hablan español los empleados del parque? ¿Hay información en español para los visitantes?

▼24 Supermercado El Ranchero | 🔊))

Leer • Escuchar

Lee las preguntas sobre un anuncio. Luego escucha el anuncio para el supermercado El Ranchero. Escribe la letra correcta para cada pregunta.

1. ¿Cuándo empiezan los precios especiales?
   a. mañana por la tarde
   b. mañana por la mañana
   c. hoy por la mañana

2. ¿Qué se vende en la carnicería?
   a. carne de res, pollo y chuletas de cerdo
   b. pescado, chuletas de cerdo y bistec
   c. carne de res, verduras y frutas

3. ¿Cuánto cuesta la carne de res para asar?
   a. $2.99 por libra[1]
   b. $3.49 por libra
   c. $2.49 por libra

Un supermercado en Uruguay

4. ¿Qué ofrecen en la taquería?
   a. carne de res con arroz
   b. pedazos de pollo con tortillas
   c. un pollo gratis[2] si compra un pollo entero

5. ¿Con qué vienen los pollos enteros?
   a. arroz, frijoles, salsa y tortillas
   b. refrescos y verduras con tortillas
   c. sólo tortillas de maíz

[1] pound   [2] free

▼25 Un producto delicioso | 👥

Escribir • Hablar

La compañía Productos Festivales quiere crear un anuncio de radio para uno de sus productos, las galletas Zum Zum. La compañía también va a ofrecer precios especiales para las galletas Zum Zum por un tiempo limitado.

① Trabaja con otro(a) estudiante y escriban un anuncio para la radio.

   Modelo
   Con galletas Zum Zum, tus niños estarán* más contentos. No compren otras galletas . . .

② Presenten su anuncio a la clase.

*To say "they will be," use *estarán*.

NUEVO PRODUCTO:
¡GALLETAS ZUM ZUM!
- Es un producto divertido y está dirigido a los niños.
- Galleta dulce, tipo sandwich, con crema de distintos sabores.
- Vienen en deliciosos sabores de vainilla, chocolate, fresa y dulce de leche.
- Tienen calcio y vitaminas.
- Vienen también en paquetes individuales que son perfectos para llevar a la escuela.
- A los adultos también les gustan estas galletas porque calman el hambre.

Más práctica (GO)	realidades.com | print	
Instant Check	✔	
Guided WB p. 268	✔	✔
Core WB pp. 147–148	✔	✔
Comm. WB pp. 141, 144	✔	✔
Hispanohablantes WB pp. 278–279, 281		✔

▶ **Read about a forest in Puerto Rico**

▶ **Anticipate information to help you understand what you read**

▶ **Compare and contrast the *coquí* with animals in the United States**

Lectura

El Yunque

> **Estrategia**
>
> **Anticipating meaning**
> What kind of information would you expect to receive at the information center of a major national park? Look through the reading and see if you find the information you listed.

¡Bienvenidos al Bosque Nacional del Caribe, El Yunque!

El Yunque es una de las atracciones más visitadas de Puerto Rico. Es el único bosque tropical[1] en el Sistema de Bosques Nacionales de los Estados Unidos. El bosque es un espectáculo maravilloso que comprende aproximadamente 28,000 acres. Más de 240 especies de árboles coexisten con animales exóticos, como el coquí y la boa de Puerto Rico.

La mejor forma de explorar este parque es caminando por las varias veredas[2] que pasan por el bosque. Hay más de 13 millas de veredas recreativas que sólo se pueden recorrer a pie (no se permiten ni caballos ni motocicletas ni bicicletas de montaña). También hay varias áreas de recreación con comodidades para hacer picnics y parrilladas y está permitido acampar en muchas áreas del bosque. ¡Venga y disfrute del parque!

La cotorra puertorriqueña es un ave en peligro de extinción.

Vereda la Mina

La Vereda la Mina es la más popular del parque. Tiene una longitud de 0.7 millas (1.2 kilómetros) y se tarda entre 30 y 45 minutos en recorrer solamente el camino de ida.[3] Empiece a caminar en el Centro de Información y el área de recreación Palo Colorado. Este camino va al lado del río de la Mina y se termina en la magnífica Cascada la Mina, un salto de agua[4] de 35 pies de altura que forma una bonita piscina, donde puede usted bañarse para refrescarse después de una larga caminata. Tenga los ojos bien abiertos para ver la cotorra[5] puertorriqueña, una de las diez aves[6] en mayor peligro de extinción[7] en el mundo. En El Yunque sólo hay aproximadamente 40 cotorras.

---

[1]rain forest [2]paths [3]one way [4]waterfall [5]parrot [6]birds [7]endangered

Consejos para el caminante

1 Nunca camine solo. Siempre vaya acompañado.
2 Traiga agua y algo para comer.
3 Use repelente para insectos.
4 No abandone las veredas para no perderse[8].
5 No toque[9] las plantas del bosque.
6 No moleste ni alimente[10] a los animales.
7 ¡No tire basura en el parque! Por favor, ¡ayúdenos a mantener limpio este parque!

Cascada la Mina

[8]to get lost   [9]touch   [10]feed

▼ Fondo Cultural

El coquí es una ranita (*little frog*) que es un símbolo importante para los puertorriqueños. Hay muchas variedades de estas ranitas y algunas viven sólo en Puerto Rico. Por la noche, el coquí empieza a cantar, y recibe su nombre por el sonido de su canto: *co-quí, co-quí*. En Puerto Rico, se han escrito muchos poemas, canciones e historias sobre esta rana misteriosa y encantadora.

• ¿Hay algún animal tan importante como el coquí en tu región? ¿Y en los Estados Unidos?

¿Comprendiste?

Escribe *C* si la frase es cierta o *F* si la frase es falsa.

1. Casi nadie visita El Yunque.
2. No hay animales exóticos en el bosque.
3. Las veredas del bosque se pueden recorrer en bicicleta de montaña.
4. Se puede hacer una parrillada en el parque.
5. Se puede alimentar a los animales del parque.
6. Si quieres caminar la Vereda la Mina, para caminar desde el Centro de Información hasta la Cascada y volver tardas (*you take*) una hora y media.

Más práctica	GO

realidades.com | print

Guided WB p. 269	✔	✔
Comm. WB pp. 145, 269	✔	✔
Hispanohablantes **WB**		
pp. 280, 282–283		✔
Cultural Reading Activity	✔	

Perspectivas del mundo hispano

La comida mexicana al aire libre

Has salido a caminar con unas amigas. Después de unas horas Uds. tienen hambre. Están cerca de una calle en la que hay muchos puestos de comida o comedores al aire libre. En algunos de los comedores hay tortillas amarillas y delgadas. Se pone la comida dentro de la tortilla, se enrolla[1] y ya está listo el taco. Unos vendedores venden pollo y chuletas de cerdo a la parrilla.

Haciendo tortillas de maíz

Otros venden tamales, que son pasteles de maíz envueltos[2] en hojas[3] de plátano y hervidos en agua. Para acompañar al plato principal, todos los vendedores ofrecen arroz y frijoles.

Los refrescos son jugos naturales de frutas tropicales: mango, piña, papaya. De postre hay quesos de varias clases, dulces y más frutas. ¡Ummm! Todo está recién hecho.[4] ¿Comemos?

En muchos países hispanohablantes es muy popular pasear y comer con familia y amigos en los comedores al aire libre. La comida que se puede comprar es deliciosa y no cuesta mucho. También se puede descansar y divertirse.

Preparando la comida al aire libre

¡Compruébalo! ¿Donde se vende comida al aire libre en los Estados Unidos? ¿Cuáles son algunos lugares en tu comunidad? (Piensa, por ejemplo, en el béisbol.) ¿Hay algunos en tu barrio? ¿Qué clase de comida venden? ¿Cuál es la comida al aire libre favorita de tus compañeros(as) de clase?

¿Qué te parece? ¿Por qué es popular la comida al aire libre? ¿Qué influencia tiene el clima en la popularidad de los lugares donde se vende la comida al aire libre?

[1] rolled up   [2] wrapped   [3] leaves   [4] freshly made

Comprando helados de frutas frescas

Presentación escrita

Comiendo al aire libre

▶ Create a poster of cookout rules
▶ Use brainstorming to generate ideas

Task

A local school that many Spanish-speaking children attend is planning summer activities. You have been asked to prepare a poster on safety and fun at cookouts.

1 **Prewrite** Think about safety and fun at cookouts. Make two lists telling children what to do and what not to do before and during the cookout, such as:

Antes de la parrillada
- la comida que deben comprar
- cosas que deben traer
- el lugar que van a escoger

Durante la parrillada
- cómo deben preparar el lugar
- qué van a hacer para preparar la comida
- cómo van a limpiar el lugar

2 **Draft** Choose what you will write from the information in the lists you have brainstormed. Present the information in a logical sequence and in an attractive format.

Modelo

Antes de la parrillada
Escojan un lugar seco.

Estrategia

Brainstorming
Brainstorming can help you come up with ideas that you may not have otherwise thought of. When listing items for your poster, write down all the tasks you could possibly suggest. Then, when your list is complete, select the best items.

3 **Revise** Review the spelling, vocabulary, and commands. Share your ideas with a classmate, who will check:
- Is what you have written easy to understand?
- Have you included appropriate commands?
- Should you change or add anything?

4 **Publish** Make changes and add art to represent the commands.

5 **Evaluation** The following rubric will be used to grade your presentation.

Rubric	Score 1	Score 3	Score 5
How easy it is to understand your poster	You have few visuals to support your information.	You have some visuals to support your information.	You have many visuals to support your information.
Attractiveness and clarity of your poster	Your layout is confusing and contains visible error corrections and smudges.	Your layout is somewhat clear and contains visible error corrections and smudges.	Your layout is clear and attractive, and contains no error corrections and smudges.
Your use of vocabulary and grammar	You use very little variation of vocabulary and have frequent grammatical errors.	You use limited vocabulary and have some grammatical errors.	You use an extended variety of vocabulary and have very few grammatical errors.

En busca de la verdad

Episodio 10

Antes de ver el video

"Por fin se ha resuelto el misterio de mi vida".

Nota cultural En América Latina las celebraciones familiares son muy importantes. Cualquier evento agradable es motivo de celebración. Todos los miembros de la familia se reúnen y siempre invitan a los amigos más cercanos para estar juntos. Normalmente se preparan comidas, se toca música, se canta o se baila. ¡En este videomisterio, la noticia sobre el abuelo es un buen motivo para celebrar!

"Aquí traigo las respuestas a todas nuestras preguntas sobre el abuelo".

Resumen del episodio

En este episodio Roberto finalmente descubre la verdad sobre su abuelo Federico. Regresa a Guanajuato y toda la familia se reúne para celebrar la noticia sobre el abuelo.

Palabras para comprender

pertenece belongs to

cuenta de ahorros savings account

póliza de seguro insurance policy

sobreviviente survivor

Has tenido razón. You were right.

"¡Y ahora hay que celebrar!"

Después de ver el video

¿Comprendiste?

A. ¿Qué personaje dice cada una de las siguientes frases?

(Tomás Toledo / Roberto / Nela / Federico / Linda)

1. "Tengo que regresar a Guanajuato con mi familia".

2. "Qué bien que por fin se resolvió este misterio".

3. "Nunca me ha gustado tocar el pasado".

4. "Nunca me imaginé todo esto. Tanto tiempo . . . tanto tiempo".

5. "Por fin se ha resuelto el misterio de mi vida".

6. "Ahora ya sabes la verdad. No me olvides".

7. "Hola. ¿Cómo estás?"

B. Contesta las siguientes preguntas.

1. ¿Cuál ha sido tu personaje favorito de *En busca de la verdad?* ¿Por qué?

2. ¿Cuál ha sido tu escena favorita? ¿Por qué?

3. ¿Qué va a pasar cuando Linda regrese a Guanajuato en la primavera con el programa de intercambio?

Más práctica GO

realidades.com | print

Actividades ✔

Repaso del capítulo

Vocabulario y gramática

to talk about the outdoors

al aire libre	outdoors
el cielo	sky
dar una caminata	to take a walk
dentro de	inside
fuera (de)	outside
la hormiga	ant
la mosca	fly
la nube	cloud
la piedra	rock
el sendero	trail
el suelo	ground, floor

to talk about eating outdoors

la fogata	bonfire
el fósforo	match
hacer una parrillada	to have a barbecue
la leña	firewood
a la parrilla	on the grill
el puesto	(food) stand

to talk about foods

el aguacate	avocado
asado, -a	grilled
asar	to grill, to roast
la carne de res	steak
la cereza	cherry
la cesta	basket
la chuleta de cerdo	pork chop
el durazno	peach
los frijoles	beans
la harina	flour
el maíz	corn
la mayonesa	mayonnaise
el melón, *pl.* los melones	melon
la mostaza	mustard
el olor	smell, odor
el pavo	turkey
la piña	pineapple
el sabor	taste
la salsa de tomate	ketchup
la sandía	watermelon

For *Vocabulario adicional,* see pp. 498–499.

to describe foods and the outdoors

dulce	sweet
grasoso, -a	fatty
mojado, -a	wet
picante	spicy
seco, -a	dry

other useful words

acompañar	to accompany

using *usted* and *ustedes* commands

To form an *Ud.* or *Uds.* command, drop the *-o* of the present-tense *yo* form and add *-e* and *-en* for *-ar* verbs, and *-a* and *-an* for *-er* and *-ir* verbs.

Regular *Ud.* and *Uds.* commands:

preparar:	prepare(n)
comer:	coma(n)
servir:	sirva(n)

Irregular *Ud.* and *Uds.* commands:

dar:	dé, den
estar:	esté, estén
ir:	vaya, vayan
ser:	sea, sean

using *por* in sentences

To indicate length of time or distance
To indicate movement through, along, or around
To indicate an exchange of one thing for another
To indicate reason or motive
To indicate a substitution or action on someone's behalf
To indicate means of communication or transportation

Más repaso (GO) realidades.com | print

Instant Check ✔
Puzzles ✔
Core WB pp. 149–150 ✔
Comm. WB pp. 270, 271–273 ✔ ✔

Preparación para el examen

On the exam you will be asked to . . .	Here are practice tasks similar to those you will find on the exam . . .	For review go to your print or digital textbook . . .

Interpretive

1 Escuchar Listen and understand as people talk about their likes and dislikes about outdoor cooking

A group of teenagers is discussing whether to have a picnic or a dinner at someone's home next Saturday to welcome a group of new students. As you listen to their opinions, decide whether the person is in favor or not in favor of an outdoor picnic.

pp. 374–377 *Vocabulario en contexto*
p. 378 Actividad 5

Interpersonal

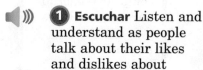

2 Hablar Give instructions to a group about what to do to prepare for a cookout

You have volunteered to help a troop leader organize a group of ten-year-old boy scouts to make their first campfire. What would you instruct them to do? For example, you might begin by saying: *Busquen un lugar seco.*

p. 381 Actividad 12
p. 384 Actividad 16

Interpretive

3 Leer Read and understand typical signs you would see in a park or overnight camping site

As you look for firewood around the campgrounds, you come across several signs that give instructions to park visitors. Read the signs below. Which signs focus on: (a) hiking; (b) cooking; (c) using the cabins?

pp. 376–377 *Videohistoria*
p. 379 Actividad 6
p. 385 Actividad 17
pp. 390–391 *Lectura*

1 Apaguen los incendios completamente con agua.

2 Apaguen las radios después de las once de la noche.

3 No recojan las flores del sendero.

Presentational

4 Escribir Write a list of instructions for an upcoming outdoor party

You are asked to write a "How to" guide for first time campers who are planning to cook outdoors. Write a list of instructions that include: (a) things to take with you; (b) getting the fire started; (c) suggestions for food to eat or grill; (d) rules campers need to follow.

p. 378 Actividad 4
p. 379 Actividad 6
p. 382 Actividad 13
p. 388 Actividad 23
p. 393 *Presentación escrita*

Cultures

5 Pensar Demonstrate an understanding of outdoor food markets in Spanish-speaking countries

Your friend is going to Buenos Aires, Argentina, on vacation and wants to know about the food. What could you tell her about outdoor food markets? How might the places where people buy things to eat be different there?

p. 392 *Perspectivas del mundo hispano*

Vocabulario Repaso

lugares y atracciones

el campo
la ciudad
el estadio
el hotel
el lago
el lugar
el mar
el mercado
las montañas
el museo
la obra de teatro
el país
el parque de diversiones
el parque nacional
el partido
la piscina
la playa
el teatro
el zoológico

actividades

bucear
comprar recuerdos
dar una caminata
descansar
esquiar
ir de cámping
ir de compras
ir de pesca
ir de vacaciones
montar a caballo
montar en bicicleta
pasar tiempo
pasear en bote
regresar
salir
viajar
visitar
tomar el sol

▼1 ¿Qué puedo hacer allí?

Escribir

En una hoja de papel, haz dos columnas. En la columna a la izquierda, escribe una lista de ocho lugares adonde se puede ir de vacaciones. En la columna a la derecha, escribe una actividad que se puede hacer en cada lugar. Trata de variar las actividades en la segunda columna.

Modelo

Lugares	**Actividades**
las montañas	*esquiar*

▼2 Lugares y actividades |

Hablar

Usa las listas de la Actividad 1 y pregúntale a otro(a) estudiante si ha ido a estos lugares de vacaciones y si ha hecho las diferentes actividades.

▶ **Modelo**

A —¿*Has ido de vacaciones a las montañas alguna vez?*

B —*Sí, he ido a las montañas varias veces.*

A —¿*Has esquiado en las montañas?*

B —*No, hemos ido allí en el verano. Hemos dado caminatas en las montañas.*

Gramática Repaso

The infinitive in verbal expressions

Remember that the infinitive is used in many types of expressions with verbs.

To express plans, desires, and wishes:

desear   pensar
encantar   preferir
gustar   querer
ir + a

Este verano mis padres **quieren ir** a las montañas, pero mis hermanos y yo **preferimos pasar** tiempo en la playa.

To express obligation:

deber   tener que
necesitar

Cuando vas a un país latinoamericano, **debes visitar** un mercado al aire libre.

In impersonal expressions:

es divertido   es necesario
es importante   hay que
es interesante

En Chile **es divertido ir** de cámping y **dar** caminatas en los parques nacionales.

▼3 Tus intereses | ___

Escribir • Hablar

Piensa en las vacaciones que te interesan. Escribe cinco frases usando los verbos de *Gramática* para decir cuándo y dónde prefieres ir y qué te gusta hacer. Lee tus frases a otro(a) estudiante para ver si Uds. tienen los mismos intereses.

▶ Modelo

preferir
A —*En el invierno mi familia y yo preferimos ir a Utah para esquiar.*
B —*¿De veras? Nosotros preferimos ir a un lugar donde hace calor, como la Florida.*

Más práctica	GO

realidades.com | print

A ver si recuerdas with Study Plan ✔
Guided WB pp. 271–272   ✔   ✔
Core WB pp. 151–152   ✔   ✔
Hispanohablantes WB p. 290   ✔

▼4 Recomendaciones para | 👥 ___ turistas

Escribir • Hablar

Escoge un lugar turístico y escribe un párrafo con recomendaciones para lo que se debe hacer allí. Usa las expresiones de *Gramática* en tu párrafo. Luego, con otro(a) estudiante, intercambien *(exchange)* papeles y haz comentarios o preguntas sobre el lugar.

▶ Modelo

Cuando vas a Puerto Rico, es muy divertido visitar el Viejo San Juan. Es interesante ver los edificios antiguos. También debes . . .
A —*Me gustaría mucho visitar Puerto Rico. ¿Cuándo debo ir?*
B —*Pues, el clima es fantástico durante todo el año, pero hay muchos turistas en el invierno. Creo que debes ir en el verano.*

8A Un viaje en avión

▼ Chapter Objectives

Communication
By the end of this chapter you will be able to:
- Listen to and read about travel recommendations
- Talk and write about suggestions for safe and enjoyable trips
- Exchange information about planning a trip

Culture
You will also be able to:
- Understand historical record-keeping
- Compare airports and transportation in Spanish-speaking countries with those in the U.S.

You will demonstrate what you know and can do:
- Presentación oral, p. 421
- Preparación para el examen, p. 423

You will use:

Vocabulary
- Travel plans
- Airports

Grammar
- The present subjunctive
- Irregular verbs in the subjunctive

Exploración del mundo hispano

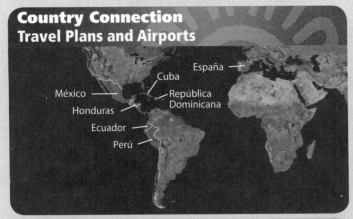

Country Connection
Travel Plans and Airports

España
Cuba
México
República Dominicana
Honduras
Ecuador
Perú

realidades.com (GO)

 Reference Atlas
 Videocultura y actividad

 Mapa global interactivo

En el Aeropuerto Internacional de la Ciudad de México

Arte y cultura | España

Aureliano de Beruete (1845–1912) nació en Madrid. Fue un representante del impresionismo español y le gustaba pintar al aire libre. Pintó este cuadro de Cuenca, un antiguo pueblo de Castilla-La Mancha. Hoy Cuenca es un destino popular para excursiones de un día o de fin de semana desde Madrid. Este pueblo medieval se declaró sitio del Patrimonio Mundial en el año 1996 y se lo conoce por las Casas Colgadas *(hanging)*.

• ¿Por qué piensas que muchos turistas visitan Cuenca? ¿Piensas que es un pueblo tranquilo o con mucha actividad? ¿Te gustaría visitarla?

"Vista de Cuenca", Aureliano de Beruete (1910)

Read, listen to, and understand information about
▶ visiting an airport
▶ planning a trip
▶ traveling safely

Vocabulario en contexto

❝ Mi hermano Antonio y yo vamos a **hacer un viaje** a Nicaragua para visitar a nuestros abuelos. Para **planear** el viaje, fuimos con nuestros padres a una agencia de viajes ❞.

la tarjeta de embarque

hacer la maleta

la agencia de viajes

los turistas

la maleta

el equipaje

el agente de viajes

el pasaporte

—Les he hecho **las reservaciones.** Tienen dos boletos **de ida y vuelta** entre Miami y Managua. Aquí están sus boletos electrónicos. Van a recibir sus tarjetas de embarque en **el aeropuerto.** Ya tienen los asientos 8D y 8F. Antes de llegar a Managua van a **hacer escala** en Tegucigalpa, Honduras, porque no hay **vuelo directo** a Managua.

—Muchas gracias, Sr. Salazar. ¿Y qué más necesitamos?

—Necesitan sus pasaportes. **Las líneas aéreas** sugieren que **lleguen** al aeropuerto dos horas antes de **la salida** del vuelo para **facturar** el equipaje. También insisten en que **pasen** por la **inspección de seguridad.**

Más vocabulario

sugerir (e→ie) to suggest

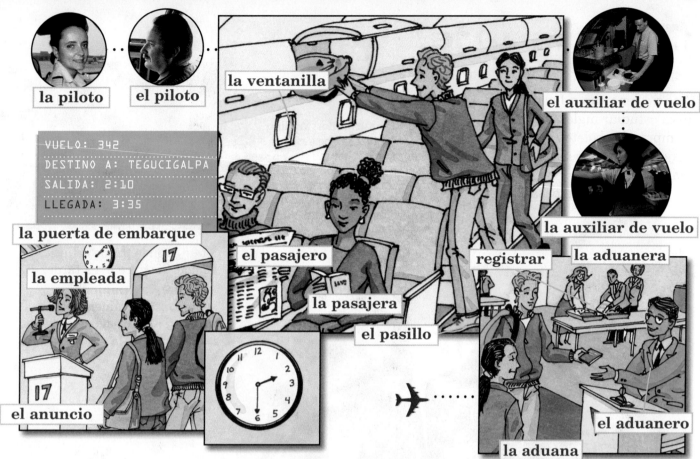

la piloto | el piloto

la ventanilla

el auxiliar de vuelo

la auxiliar de vuelo

VUELO: 342
DESTINO A: TEGUCIGALPA
SALIDA: 2:10
LLEGADA: 3:35

la puerta de embarque

la empleada

el pasajero

la pasajera

el pasillo

registrar

la aduanera

el anuncio

el aduanero

la aduana

"Lo sentimos mucho. Hay un pequeño **retraso** en la salida del vuelo 342 **con destino a** Tegucigalpa, Honduras. Dentro de 20 minutos **tendremos** más información sobre la salida del vuelo 342".

"El vuelo 342 con destino a Tegucigalpa está **listo.** En unos minutos vamos a **abordar.** Favor de pasar a la puerta número 17 de la Terminal A".

—**Bienvenido** a Managua. ¿Qué tiene?

—Una maleta y una mochila.

—Pase a la izquierda. Tendremos que ver qué cosas tiene dentro de su equipaje. Ese señor va a registrar el equipaje. Aquí está su pasaporte.

▼1 En el aeropuerto | 🔊

Escuchar

Estás en un aeropuerto esperando tu vuelo. Oyes muchas conversaciones entre los pasajeros y muchos anuncios. Si escuchas buenas noticias, señala con el pulgar hacia arriba. Si escuchas malas noticias, señala con el pulgar hacia abajo.

▼2 ¿Quién lo dice? | 🔊

Escuchar

Escucha cada frase, y en una hoja de papel escribe quién lo dijo: una pasajera, una agente de viajes, una auxiliar de vuelo o una aduanera.

Más práctica	GO	
realidades.com	print	
Instant Check	✔	
Guided WB pp. 273–278	✔	✔
Core WB pp. 153–154	✔	✔
Comm. WB p. 152	✔	✔
Hispanohablantes WB p. 292		✔

¡Buen viaje!

Ana y Elena van a Londres para estudiar inglés. Compran los boletos para el viaje en una agencia de viajes, pero hay un problema. Lee para saber qué pasa.

Estrategia

Scanning for basic understanding
Reading a new text can be easier if you already know what the story is about. Before reading the *Videohistoria*, scan it for cognates and words you already know. Based on the words you find, predict what the story is about.

Ana: ¿Dónde puede estar Elena? Siempre llega tarde.

Agente: Ten paciencia, señorita. Seguramente llega pronto. Nuestra agencia está **abierta** hasta la una y media.

la agente de viajes

Elena

Ana

Elena: ¿Cuánto **dura** el viaje?

Agente: Un poco más de 14 horas.

Elena: Es muy largo.

Ana: Puedes dormir en el tren.

Agente: Te va a gustar. Es muy divertido.

Elena: Muy bien. Vamos a hacer las reservaciones.

Agente: Aquí tenéis* los boletos. ¡Buen viaje!

Elena: ¡Caramba! Vamos a mirar los boletos.

Ana: A ver. ¿Dónde están? ¿No los tienes tú?

Elena: No. ¿Los dejamos en la agencia de viajes?

---

* Remember that in Spain, the *vosotros(as)* form is used when speaking to a group of people you would address individually with *tú*.

Ana: Elena, ¿por qué no llegas a tiempo?

Elena: Eres tan impaciente. Tenemos mucho tiempo.

Ana: Queremos hacer reservaciones para ir de Madrid a Londres.

Agente: ¿En avión?

Ana: Creo que sí.

Agente: Hay un vuelo directo que cuesta 92 euros.

Ana: ¿Qué más hay?

Agente: Hay un tren.

Elena: ¿Un tren?

Ana: ¿Por qué no? ¿Cuánto cuesta?

Agente: El boleto para estudiantes es muy barato. Muchos estudiantes **extranjeros** toman el tren.

Ana: Está **cerrada.** ¿Qué hacemos?

Elena: Mira. Allí están nuestros boletos.

Ana: ¿A qué hora abren otra vez?

Elena: A las cuatro y media. Ten paciencia, Ana. Tenemos que esperar.

> **Más vocabulario**
> extranjero, -a foreign

▼3 ¿Comprendiste?

Escribir

Usa cada palabra de la lista en una frase completa para indicar lo que pasó en la *Videohistoria.*

Modelo
tarde
Ana está enojada porque Elena llega tarde.

1. impaciente
2. Madrid a Londres
3. 92 euros
4. el tren
5. la agencia de viajes
6. cerrado, -a
7. a las cuatro y media

Más práctica	GO

realidades.com | print

Instant Check	✔	
Guided WB pp. 279–282	✔	✔
Core WB pp. 155–156	✔	✔
Comm. WB pp. 146–148, 149	✔	✔
Hispanohablantes WB p. 293		✔

| ▼ **Objectives**

▷ **Talk about airline regulations**
▷ **Discuss air travel**
▷ **Listen to travel advice**
▷ **Write about modes of transportation**

Vocabulario en uso

▼4 Unos consejos

Leer • Escribir

Cuando viajas por primera vez, vas a tener muchas preguntas. Lee los consejos *(advice)* y escribe la palabra apropiada para completar cada frase.

1. Si vas a un país *(extranjero/pasajero)* insisten en que tengas un pasaporte.

2. Puedes recibir información sobre los vuelos en una *(agente de viajes/agencia de viajes)*. Si está *(cerrada/llegada)*, puedes hacer una búsqueda en la Red.

3. Si no quieres hacer *(reservación/escala)*, sugiero que busques un vuelo directo.

4. Es más cómodo tener un asiento en el *(pasillo/retraso)* o al lado de la *(llegada/ventanilla)*.

5. Debes llegar al *(aeropuerto/pasillo)* dos horas antes de la *(salida/llegada)* de un vuelo internacional.

6. Cuando los empleados de la línea aérea están *(listos/abiertos)* para abordar el vuelo, hacen un *(directo/anuncio)*.

7. Antes de abordar el avión vas a pasar por *(la tarjeta de embarque/la puerta de embarque)*.

8. A veces hay un *(retraso/vuelo)* a causa del mal tiempo o problemas mecánicos. Hay que tener *(paciencia/equipaje)* y no enojarse con los empleados.

▼5 Escucha y escribe | 🔊

Escuchar • Escribir

Hay cosas que vas a necesitar para tu viaje. Escucha estos consejos y escribe la cosa que necesitas.

Modelo

(escuchas) La necesitas hacer con la línea aérea antes de comenzar el viaje.
(escribes) *la reservación*

> **También se dice . . .**
>
> **la maleta** = la valija *(Argentina)*; la petaca *(México)*
>
> **el boleto** = el billete *(España)*; el pasaje *(Bolivia)*

Debes llegar temprano al aeropuerto.

▼6 ¿Quién hace qué? |

Hablar

Una persona que no ha viajado mucho tiene muchas preguntas sobre quiénes hacen diferentes cosas durante el viaje y la preparación para el viaje. Trabaja con otro(a) estudiante para hacer preguntas y contestarlas.

▶ **Modelo**

pasar por el pasillo con bebidas
A —¿*Quién pasa por el pasillo con bebidas?*
B —*La auxiliar de vuelo pasa por el pasillo con bebidas.*

Estudiante A

1. sugerir los vuelos y hacer las reservaciones
2. llevar su pasaporte y tarjeta de embarque
3. facturarles el equipaje a los pasajeros
4. ayudar al pasajero a planear el viaje
5. pasar por la inspección de seguridad
6. registrar las maletas en la aduana
7. decir cuánto dura el vuelo
8. hacer un anuncio sobre la llegada de un vuelo
9. decir "Bienvenidos" a la ciudad adonde llegas

Estudiante B

 Fondo Cultural | El mundo hispano

Los nombres de los aeropuertos tienen un significado histórico. Por ejemplo, el aeropuerto de San Juan, Puerto Rico, se llama Luis Muñoz Marín, el nombre del gobernador de la isla entre 1949 y 1965. El aeropuerto de La Habana, Cuba, se llama José Martí por el poeta y patriota cubano. El aeropuerto de Lima, Perú, se llama Jorge Chávez para conmemorar al gran aviador peruano que murió cuando intentó volar sobre los Alpes en 1910. El aeropuerto de Buenos Aires se llama Ministro Pistarini, por un político que empezó la construcción del aeropuerto. De esta forma, los aeropuertos son parte de la cultura del país porque los nombres reconocen a las personas importantes de su historia.

• ¿Cómo se llama el aeropuerto más cercano a tu ciudad? ¿Por qué tiene ese nombre?

El aeropuerto de La Habana, Cuba

▼7 Los vuelos internacionales | |

Hablar

Para decir más . . .
procedente de arriving from

En el aeropuerto de Buenos Aires, Argentina, los pasajeros tienen muchas preguntas sobre los vuelos internacionales. Trabaja con otro(a) estudiante. Hagan y contesten las preguntas según la información en el letrero electrónico.

▶ **Modelo**

llegar de / Lima

A —*Perdone, señor (señorita), ¿a qué hora llega el vuelo 358 de Lima?*

B —*Un momento, por favor. El avión llega de Lima a la 1:50. Tiene un retraso de 40 minutos.*

Vuelo	Ciudad	Llegada	Salida	Observaciones
927	Asunción		12:45	a tiempo
358	Lima	1:50		retraso de 40 minutos
486	Montevideo		2:05	más información pronto
564	Miami	3:30		vuelo cancelado
872	Río de Janeiro		4:15	a tiempo
199	Santiago		5:35	retraso de 30 minutos
731	La Paz	6:20		a tiempo

Estudiante A

1. salir para / Montevideo
2. salir para / Santiago
3. llegar de / Miami
4. salir para / Asunción
5. llegar de / La Paz
6. salir para / Río de Janeiro

Estudiante B

Un momento, por favor.
Lo siento.
con destino a
procedente de
Sale / Llega a tiempo.

Tiene un retraso de . . .
Tuvieron que cancelar el vuelo.
Tendremos más información muy pronto.
Tenga paciencia, por favor.

▼8 En la revista de la línea aérea | |

Leer • Dibujar • Hablar

Muchas líneas aéreas tienen su propia revista, que generalmente está en tu asiento en el avión. Las revistas tienen una sección que se llama *A bordo*. Esta sección les da a los pasajeros reglas sobre los vuelos.

❶ Lee las reglas. Para cada regla, haz un dibujo que se puede usar para explicar la idea principal de la regla.

❷ Muéstrale *(Show)* el dibujo para una de las reglas a otro(a) estudiante. Tu compañero(a) tiene que decir, en sus propias palabras, la regla que se representa con el dibujo.

•**El abordaje** Las reservaciones se pueden cancelar si usted se presenta en la puerta de embarque menos de diez minutos antes del despegue[1] en vuelos domésticos.

•**Equipaje de mano** Las piezas de equipaje de mano deben ponerse debajo del asiento del pasajero o en un compartimiento arriba. Los perros y animales domésticos a bordo deben quedarse en todo momento en sus receptáculos correspondientes.

•**Dispositivos[2] electrónicos portátiles** Algunos dispositivos electrónicos portátiles pueden interferir con los equipos de navegación de los aviones.

Se permite el uso de estos dispositivos mientras el avión está en tierra[3] con la puerta de abordaje abierta y durante el vuelo cuando los auxiliares de vuelo así lo permitan.

•**Teléfonos celulares** Se permite el uso de los teléfonos celulares sólo cuando el avión está en la puerta de embarque y la puerta del avión está abierta.

•**Tabaco** Se prohíbe fumar[4] y usar tabaco sin humo en todos los vuelos de esta línea aérea. Se le puede poner una multa de hasta US $2,200 por obstruir los detectores de humo de los servicios.[5]

[1]take off [2]devices [3]ground [4]to smoke [5]rest rooms

9 El autobús latinoamericano

Observar • Escribir • Hablar

El autobús es un medio *(means)* de transporte común en América Latina. Observa el autobús que es arte folklórico de Colombia. Luego contesta las preguntas.

1. ¿Qué llevan los pasajeros en el autobús? ¿Qué crees que indican estas cosas sobre sus vidas?

2. ¿Adónde crees que van las personas en el autobús? ¿Piensas que sus viajes duran mucho o poco tiempo? ¿Por qué?

▼ Fondo Cultural | El mundo hispano

El transporte más usado en los países hispanohablantes es el autobús. Hay autobuses de lujo *(luxury)*, de primera clase y de segunda clase. Llevan pasajeros, maletas y hasta animales. En algunos países los autobuses de segunda clase no tienen rutas fijas *(fixed)* y sirven más como taxis. Hay varios nombres para los autobuses. En Colombia y Ecuador, los autobuses se llaman *flotas* y se usan para viajar entre provincias. En España, se llaman *autocares* y en los países del Caribe son *guaguas.* En México y Bolivia los autobuses también se llaman *camiones.*

- ¿Por qué crees que los autobuses son populares en muchos países hispanohablantes?

Una flota de Montecristi, Ecuador

---

10 Dos medios de transporte |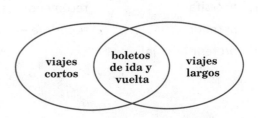

Pensar • Comparar • Hablar • Escribir

El avión y el autobús son dos medios de transporte populares. Trabaja con otro(a) estudiante para comparar estos dos medios.

1 Copien el diagrama de Venn en una hoja de papel y escriban palabras y expresiones para describir los dos medios de transporte.

2 Escriban un resumen de los dos medios de transporte. Pueden incluir impresiones de cómo se viaja en los países hispanohablantes y en los Estados Unidos.

viajes cortos | boletos de ida y vuelta | viajes largos

el autobús   el avión

Modelo

Las personas que hacen viajes cortos frecuentemente van en autobús, especialmente en los países hispanohablantes. Si hacen un viaje largo, por ejemplo a un país extranjero, muchas veces van en avión. Para los dos medios de transporte se puede comprar boletos de ida y vuelta . . .

| ▼ **Objectives**

▶ Listen to and write about travel recommendations
▶ Talk and write about household rules and recommendations for students

Gramática Repaso

The present subjunctive

The subjunctive mood is used to say that one person influences the actions of another.

> Recomendamos **que Uds. hablen** con un agente de viajes.
>
> *We recommend **that you speak** with a travel agent.*
>
> ¿Quiere Ud. **que escribamos** nuestros nombres en las maletas?
>
> *Do you want **us to write** our names on our suitcases?*

Note that the subjunctive sentences have two parts, each with a different subject, connected by the word *que:*

| Ella sugiere | que | yo aprenda francés. |

The first part uses the present indicative verb (recommendation, suggestion, prohibition, and so on) + *que,* and the second part uses the present subjunctive verb (what should happen).

Verbs that are often followed by *que* + subjunctive:

decir	prohibir
insistir en	querer (e → ie)
necesitar	recomendar (e → ie)
permitir	sugerir (e → ie)
preferir (e → ie)	

> **¿Recuerdas?**
>
> Until now you have used verbs in the indicative mood, used to talk about facts or actual events.
>
> • **Aprendo** francés para mi viaje.

The present subjunctive is formed in the same way as negative *tú* commands and all *Ud. / Uds.* commands. You drop the *-o* of the present-tense indicative *yo* form and add present-tense subjunctive endings.

hablar

hable	hablemos
hables	habléis
hable	hablen

aprender / escribir

aprenda escriba	aprendamos escribamos
aprendas escribas	aprendáis escribáis
aprenda escriba	aprendan escriban

The present subjunctive has the same spelling changes and irregular *yo* form changes used with the negative *tú* commands and *Ud. / Uds.* commands.

llegar

llegue	lleguemos
llegues	lleguéis
llegue	lleguen

hacer

haga	hagamos
hagas	hagáis
haga	hagan

Más ayuda | **realidades.com**

 GramActiva Video
Tutorials: Regular forms of the present subjunctive (Spanish version), Regular forms of the present subjunctive (English version), Spelling changes in present subjunctive
Animated Verbs

 Canción de hip hop: *Un viaje de avión*

 GramActiva Activity

▼11 Escucha y escribe | 🔊

Escuchar • Escribir

Escucha a una persona que viaja mucho dar recomendaciones sobre su viaje. Escribe sus seis recomendaciones. Después subraya *(underline)* el verbo en la expresión de recomendación y traza *(draw)* un círculo alrededor del verbo que indica lo que debes hacer.

Modelo

Les <u>recomiendo</u> que ⃝hagan⃝ las reservaciones temprano.

▼12 Juego |

Escribir • GramActiva

❶ En el pizarrón (*chalkboard*), tu profesor(a) va a dibujar dos triángulos. Cada uno tiene cinco secciones y representa una montaña.

❷ La clase se divide en dos equipos. Una persona de cada equipo va al pizarrón. Tu profesor(a) les da un verbo. Los estudiantes deben conjugar el verbo en el presente del subjuntivo, empezando con la forma *yo* en la base de la "montaña". Si cometen un error, su profesor(a) dice *avalancha* y tienen que borrar (*erase*) las palabras y empezar otra vez. El equipo que escribe todas las formas primero gana un punto.

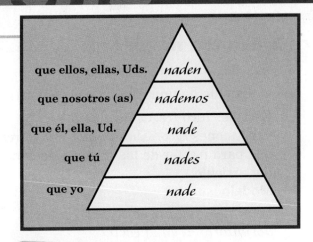

que ellos, ellas, Uds.	*naden*
que nosotros (as)	*nademos*
que él, ella, Ud.	*nade*
que tú	*nades*
que yo	*nade*

▼13 Un programa de intercambio

Leer • Escribir

Lee el anuncio sobre un programa de intercambio en Tegucigalpa, Honduras, y contesta las preguntas.

1. ¿Cuáles son las ventajas (*advantages*) de asistir a un programa como éste?

2. ¿Por cuánto tiempo puedes quedarte allí?

3. ¿Cómo dan la bienvenida a los estudiantes que vienen al programa?

4. ¿Te gustaría participar en un programa como éste? ¿Por qué?

¡Vive con una familia en Tegucigalpa, Honduras!

JÓVENES DE LAS AMÉRICAS

Clases de español diarias • Discursos sobre la cultura e historia hondureña • Excursiones dentro y fuera de la ciudad • Vuelos directos desde los Estados Unidos • Programas que duran de tres semanas a tres meses

Nuestros empleados bilingües te esperan en el aeropuerto y te ayudan a pasar por la aduana. Luego te llevan a la casa de tu familia hondureña.

Llama al 525-8557
www.viveenhonduras.com

▼14 Tres semanas en Honduras |

Hablar

El programa de intercambio en Tegucigalpa les envía una carta con recomendaciones a los estudiantes que van a participar. ¿Cuáles son las recomendaciones? Habla con otro(a) estudiante sobre ellas.

▶ **Modelo**

recomendar
A —¿Qué recomiendan?
B —Recomiendan que llevemos ropa cómoda de algodón.

Estudiante A

1. sugerir	4. querer
2. recomendar	5. insistir en
3. prohibir	6. decirnos

Estudiante B

usar el teléfono de la familia
comprar un regalo para la familia
sacar fotos
traer sólo una maleta y una mochila

llevar ropa cómoda de algodón
tener un diccionario
sólo beber agua en botellas
¡Respuesta personal!

▼15 Estudia mejor | 👥

Leer • Escribir • Hablar

Lee el artículo de una revista para jóvenes.

❶ Escribe cinco frases usando las expresiones *recomiendan que* y *sugieren que* para hablar de las recomendaciones del artículo.

Modelo

Recomiendan que no estudies ni en el dormitorio ni en la cocina.

❷ Escribe tres frases adicionales en que das tus propias recomendaciones sobre cómo puedes prepararte para un examen difícil.

Modelo

Sugiero que escojas un lugar lejos del televisor.

❸ Lee tus frases a otro(a) estudiante. ¿Está de acuerdo con tus recomendaciones? ¿Por qué?

¡Puedes sacarte un diez!

Seguramente te ha pasado que justo cuando tienes el examen más difícil de tu vida no puedes concentrarte para estudiar. El secreto está en encontrar el lugar perfecto para estudiar, y créelo o no, tu dormitorio y la cocina no son buenas opciones. El lugar ideal tiene una ventana porque la luz natural te ayuda a desestresarte*. Pero, ¡cuidado! Se recomienda no mirar directamente la ventana porque siempre hay distracciones en el exterior.

En el lugar ideal, también hay un escritorio con sólo los materiales necesarios para estudiar. Con este sistema de estudio, será posible sacarse un diez y con él puedes impresionar a tus padres y a tus profesores.

*relax, release stress

▼16 Reglas de la casa | 👥 | ♻

Escribir • Hablar

Probablemente hay muchas cosas que tus padres quieren o no quieren que hagas.

❶ Escribe frases sobre cinco cosas que quieren (o no quieren) que hagas. Usa las expresiones *quieren que*, *insisten en que*, *necesitan que*, *me dicen que* y *me prohíben que*.

❷ Trabaja con otros dos estudiantes. Comparen sus listas. Escriban una lista para su grupo de las cosas en que insisten los padres en general. Presenten sus listas a la clase.

Modelo

Mis padres me prohíben que gaste mucho dinero en la ropa.

▼ Fondo Cultural | El mundo hispano

Los programas de intercambio ofrecen la oportunidad de vivir con una familia anfitriona *(host)*. Es la mejor manera de aprender el idioma y conocer la cultura del país. Los estudiantes de intercambio deben respetar las diferencias culturales y las reglas de la familia. Sobre todo, hay que mantener una actitud positiva y abierta.

• ¿Qué consejos te gustaría dar a un(a) estudiante de intercambio que llega a tu comunidad? ¿Qué sería *(would be)* lo más difícil para él (ella)?

Más práctica (GO)

realidades.com | print

Instant Check	✔	
Guided WB pp. 283–287	✔	✔
Core WB p. 157	✔	✔
Comm. WB pp. 150, 153, 274	✔	✔
Hispanohablantes WB pp. 294–297		✔

Gramática

Irregular verbs in the subjunctive

Verbs that have irregular negative *tú* and *Ud. / Uds.* commands also have irregular subjunctive forms.

dar

dé	demos
des	deis
dé	den

estar

esté	estemos
estés	estéis
esté	estén

ir

vaya	vayamos
vayas	vayáis
vaya	vayan

saber

sepa	sepamos
sepas	sepáis
sepa	sepan

ser

sea	seamos
seas	seáis
sea	sean

El agente sugiere que **vayamos** a la puerta de embarque.

*The agent suggests that **we go** to the boarding gate.*

Más ayuda · **realidades.com**

▶ **GramActiva** Video
Tutorial: Irregular present subjunctive

▼17 Un viaje con la profesora

Escribir

Unos estudiantes acaban de llegar al aeropuerto para hacer un viaje al extranjero *(abroad)*. Completa lo que dice su profesora sobre lo que quiere que todos hagan. Usa una forma de los verbos *dar, estar, ir, saber* o *ser* en cada frase.

1. Quiero que Uds. ____ dónde están sus pasaportes.
2. El empleado necesita que nosotros le ____ los pasaportes antes de facturar el equipaje.
3. Les prohíbo que ____ fuera del aeropuerto.
4. Insisto en que todos ____ cerca de la puerta de embarque media hora antes de la salida del vuelo.
5. Necesito que todos Uds. ____ responsables.
6. Insisto en que todos Uds. ____ listos para abordar el avión.
7. Quiero que el viaje ____ una buena experiencia.

Un aeropuerto peruano

▼18 Algunas sugerencias |

Hablar

Unos amigos están planeando un viaje al extranjero. Tú acabas de regresar de un viaje similar y tienes muchas sugerencias para darles. Trabaja con otro(a) estudiante para dar tus recomendaciones.

▶ **Modelo**

A —¿Cuándo debemos estar en el aeropuerto?

B —Les sugiero que lleguen dos horas antes de la salida del vuelo.

Estudiante A

1. qué / saber sobre la inspección de seguridad
2. qué / darles a los empleados de la línea aérea
3. qué forma de identificación / tener
4. qué / decir en la aduana
5. cómo / ir al hotel

Estudiante B

todas las reglas sobre lo que no puedes llevar en el avión
en taxi porque no van a conocer la ciudad todavía
un número de teléfono donde van a estar en el extranjero
que son estudiantes y turistas norteamericanos
un pasaporte y un permiso de manejar

▼19 ¡No viajes sin leer esto!

Leer • Escribir • Hablar

¿Qué recomiendan los expertos que hagas para no tener problemas financieros durante un viaje al extranjero? Lee el artículo y contesta las preguntas según el modelo.

Modelo

¿Qué recomiendan para no tener problemas financieros cuando viajas al extranjero?
Te recomiendan que tomes precauciones.

Para no tener problemas financieros en un viaje al extranjero, toma precauciones.

✦ **Tarjeta de crédito**
Con ella puedes pagar las compras, comidas y otros gastos, y sacar dinero de cajeros automáticos, pero hay que tener cuidado de no perderla. Por eso se debe llevar en un lugar seguro[1] muy cerca de tu cuerpo y saber el teléfono del banco para informar de su pérdida.

✦ **Cheques de viajero**
Se aceptan exactamente como el dinero en efectivo y se reembolsan[2] en menos de 24 horas si los pierdes o te los roban. Se deben firmar y escribir sus números antes de salir del banco, así otra persona no los puede usar. En muchos lugares hay que mostrar[3] una forma de identificación para usarlos.

✦ **"Cash"**
Si traes dinero en efectivo, ponlo en diferentes bolsillos.[4] Cuando llegues a tu destino, pregunta en el hotel por un lugar donde se puede obtener moneda local. En muchos países las casas de cambio[5] son más accesibles para efectuar esta transacción que los bancos.

[1]safe [2]they are refunded [3]show [4]pockets [5]currency exchange offices

---

1. ¿Qué sugieren para no perder la tarjeta de crédito?
2. ¿Qué recomiendan saber si pierdes la tarjeta de crédito?
3. ¿Qué recomiendan hacer con los cheques de viajero?
4. ¿En qué insisten muchos lugares para usar los cheques de viajero?
5. ¿Dónde sugieren poner el dinero en efectivo?
6. ¿Adónde dicen ir para cambiar *(exchange)* el dinero?

▼20 Un viaje sin estrés | 👥

Escribir • Hablar

❶ Dos amigos tuyos planean un viaje al extranjero. Escribe seis frases para ayudarles a hacer las preparaciones, pasar por el aeropuerto y abordar el avión. Usa expresiones como *sugiero que* y *recomiendo que*.

❷ Lean las recomendaciones de otros dos estudiantes, decidan cuáles son las tres mejores y preséntenlas a la clase.

Modelo

Sugiero que vayan a una agencia de viajes para planear su viaje.

Modelo

Recomendamos que siempre lleven los pasaportes durante el viaje.

▼21 La República Dominicana | 🗨️👥 | 🌎

Leer • Hablar

Vas de vacaciones con tu familia. Imagina que otro(a) estudiante es el (la) agente de viajes. Hablen sobre lo que le gustaría a tu familia hacer allí.

▶️ **Modelo**

a mí / sacar fotos

A —*A mí me gusta sacar fotos.*
B —*Recomiendo que vaya a la zona colonial.*

Pasándolo bien en la República Dominicana

Zona Colonial
Es uno de los lugares favoritos de los jóvenes, por sus cafés y sus tiendas al aire libre. Aquí hay muchos edificios históricos, como la catedral.

Las Terrenas
En la costa norte de la isla, se encuentra la playa más larga y bonita de todo el país. Aquí se puede tomar el sol o bucear en las tranquilas aguas.

Los Haitises
Es un parque nacional formado por un grupo de islas cubiertas de selva tropical.* Aquí se pueden apreciar diferentes especies de plantas, pájaros y animales exóticos.

Altos del Chavón
Es un lugar muy bonito situado en una montaña. Aquí se puede estudiar en la escuela de arte, visitar el museo arqueológico, o escuchar conciertos y festivales de jazz en el gran anfiteatro.

*covered with rain forests

1. a nosotros / visitar playas bonitas
2. a mí / tomar lecciones de arte
3. a mis hermanos / observar los pájaros
4. a mi madre / bucear
5. a mi hermana / ir de compras
6. a mis padres / escuchar música

▼22 Viajar y sentirse bien |

Leer • Hablar • Escribir

Estos ejercicios se recomiendan a los pasajeros de vuelos largos para estimular y estirar *(stretch)* los músculos.

1 Lee las instrucciones con otro(a) estudiante. Luego observen los diagramas y decidan qué diagrama corresponde a cada ejercicio.

Conexiones | La salud

1. Círculos de tobillo
Levantar los pies del piso. Hacer un círculo con las puntas de los pies moviéndolas en direcciones contrarias.

2. Flexiones de pie
Tres pasos: Con los talones *(heels)* en el piso, llevar las puntas de los pies hacia arriba. Poner luego los dos pies en el piso. Levantar después los talones y dejar las puntas en el piso.

3. Elevaciones de rodilla
Levantar la pierna con la rodilla doblada. Alternar las piernas. Repetir 20 a 30 veces con cada pierna.

4. Rotación de hombros
Mover los hombros hacia adelante, luego moverlos hacia arriba, hacia atrás y hacia abajo con un movimiento circular.

2 Escojan dos de los ejercicios y escriban las recomendaciones que les pueden hacer a los pasajeros.

Modelo
Les recomendamos que muevan los hombros hacia adelante . . .

3 Lean sus recomendaciones a otro grupo. Ellos van a seguir sus instrucciones.

▼ Pronunciación | 🔊 | (Talk!)

Linking sounds

When people speak a language fluently, they run words together rather than pausing in between them. This is done in English when the five-word question *Do you want to go?* comes out sounding like *Jawanna go?* Here are ways sounds are linked in Spanish.

Two identical sounds are pronounced together as one sound. Listen and repeat:

> tarjeta‿de‿embarque
> línea‿aérea
> va‿a‿hacer la maleta

Two vowels are usually run together. Listen and repeat:

> de‿ida‿y‿vuelta
> la‿empleada
> su‿equipaje‿amarillo

The consonant at the end of a word is linked with the next word. Listen and repeat:

> país‿extranjero
> hablar‿al‿agente
> insisten‿en

¡Compruébalo! Practice reading this riddle as a poem, connecting the sounds. Then figure out its meaning.

> **Sin ser ángel tengo alas,[1]**
> **sin ser auto tengo motor,**
> **y viajo sobre las aguas,**
> **sin ser yate ni vapor.[2]**
> **¿Quién soy yo?**

[1]wings [2]steamship

▼23 Para una visita divertida | | ♻

Hablar • Escribir

Unos amigos de un país hispanohablante vienen a tu ciudad para pasar el verano.

❶ Trabaja con otro(a) estudiante y escriban seis recomendaciones de lo que deben hacer y ver mientras estén allí. Pueden comenzar sus frases con *recomendar que, sugerir que, querer que* y *preferir que*. Pueden incluir estas ideas u otras:

- adónde ir
- dónde y qué comer
- qué partidos, espectáculos y más ver
- dónde dar una caminata o hacer otras actividades al aire libre
- cómo pasar el tiempo libre
- cómo viajar o llegar

❷ Trabajen con otra pareja. Lean sus recomendaciones. ¿Están de acuerdo con sus ideas? Presenten sus ideas a la clase y hagan una lista completa de ideas para visitantes.

▼24 Y tú, ¿qué dices? | (Talk!)

Escribir • Hablar

1. ¿Adónde has viajado? ¿Qué hiciste para planear el viaje? ¿Qué le sugieres a un(a) amigo(a) para planear un viaje?

2. Escoge tres lugares interesantes para visitar en los Estados Unidos. ¿Cómo sugieres que alguien viaje de tu ciudad a estos lugares? ¿Por qué?

3. ¿Qué recomiendas que una persona lleve en su maleta o mochila para no aburrirse en un vuelo largo?

Más práctica	GO	
realidades.com	print	
Instant Check	✔	
Guided WB p. 288	✔	✔
Core WB pp. 158–159	✔	✔
Comm. WB pp. 150–151, 154	✔	✔
Hispanohablantes WB pp. 298–301		✔

El español en la comunidad

Las personas de los países hispanohablantes que visitan los Estados Unidos a veces necesitan ayuda porque han perdido su pasaporte o tienen otro problema. Los países hispanohablantes tienen representantes en los Estados Unidos para ayudar a sus ciudadanos *(citizens)*. Uno de éstos es el cónsul, un diplomático que tiene funciones políticas y económicas en un país extranjero. Ayuda al turista de su país y también ofrece información cultural sobre su propio país y, a veces, hace presentaciones culturales para grupos de estudiantes o adultos.

- Busca información sobre un consulado o embajada *(embassy)* de un país hispanohablante que está cerca de tu comunidad. Pide información sobre cómo se puede visitar el consulado o invitar a un representante a tu escuela.

Lectura

ECUADOR
país de maravillas

El Ecuador está en la costa Pacífica del norte de América del Sur y representa un país típico de la zona andina. Es un país pequeño, pero tiene paisajes para todos los gustos¹. Desde playas tropicales hasta montañas nevadas, desde ciudades coloniales hasta parques naturales, el Ecuador es una joya que deleita² al visitante. Le invitamos a descubrir este país de maravillas.

Estrategia

Previewing
Before you read a magazine article, look at the photos and read the title, subheads, and photo captions. This will help you determine what type of information you will be reading. What do the title and subheads of this article tell you about the information it's likely to contain? What types of places are featured in the photos?

La Iglesia de la Compañía de Jesús, Quito

la altitud, le puede resultar difícil respirar y puede sentirse cansado.

Declarada parte del patrimonio mundial por la UNESCO en 1978, Quito mantiene el centro histórico colonial mejor preservado de América Latina. La Iglesia de la Compañía de Jesús, con un interior muy rico en oro, representa el estilo barroco típico de Quito. Otras iglesias interesantes para el turista son la Iglesia de San Francisco y la Catedral.

Quito
Quito, la capital del Ecuador, es una ciudad cosmopolita situada en un valle rodeado por las cimas³ nevadas de Pichincha y de Cotopaxi. La ciudad está a 9,200 pies de altura. Para el visitante que no está acostumbrado a

Mitad del Mundo
A 30 minutos al norte de Quito está el monumento a la Mitad del Mundo. Se llama así porque la Línea Ecuatorial que divide al planeta en dos hemisferios pasa por este lugar. Los turistas se divierten tomando fotos con un pie en el hemisferio norte y el otro en el hemisferio sur. ¡De un lado, es invierno, y del otro, verano! Durante los equinoccios alrededor del 21 de marzo y del 23 de septiembre, las personas y los objetos no tienen sombra⁴.

La Mitad del Mundo

¹tastes ²delights ³peaks ⁴shadow

Haciendo tejidos en un mercado, Otavalo, Ecuador

Islas Galápagos

Las islas Galápagos representan una de las atracciones turísticas más importantes del Ecuador. Estas islas, así llamadas por las gigantescas tortugas galápagos que viven allí, están en el océano Pacífico a más de 600 millas de la costa del Ecuador. El archipiélago tiene 125 islas e islotes. Para proteger las especies de animales que viven en las islas, como las iguanas, los leones marinos[8] y la gran variedad de pájaros, los turistas no pueden visitar las islas por su cuenta[9]. Tienen que tomar una excursión organizada dirigida por un guía naturalista.

Dentro del monumento hay un museo que celebra las distintas culturas indígenas del Ecuador. De hecho, el 25 por ciento de la población del país es de origen indígena. Entre los grupos más conocidos están los salasacas, los shuars y los otavalos. Cada grupo se viste de una manera diferente, habla su propio idioma y se especializa en algún tipo de artesanía, como los tejidos, los sombreros, las joyas o las canastas[5].

El Ecuador le ofrece al visitante un viaje inolvidable por su gran riqueza cultural y natural. Como dijo el científico Humboldt[6], "Un viaje por el Ecuador se puede comparar con un viaje desde la Línea Ecuatorial casi hasta el Polo Sur"[7].

La mejor manera de llegar a las islas es por avión desde el aeropuerto de Quito o de Guayaquil. Vuelos diarios[10] salen hacia la isla de Baltra. De ahí, se llega a la isla de Santa Cruz, donde está la Estación Científica Charles Darwin. El científico inglés visitó las islas en el siglo XIX y su teoría de la evolución se basa en los estudios que hizo durante su viaje. Desde la isla de Santa Cruz salen barcos para explorar el archipiélago. La mejor época del año para visitar las islas es entre los meses de enero y mayo porque las temperaturas son más cálidas. Los turistas pueden disfrutar de[11] actividades al aire libre, como el buceo y las caminatas que les permite entrar en contacto con la inmaculada naturaleza de estas bellas islas.

Las islas Galápagos

[5]baskets   [6]German scientist who traveled extensively in Latin America   [7]South Pole   [8]sea lions   [9]on their own   [10]daily   [11]enjoy

¿Comprendiste?

1. ¿Por qué crees que el Ecuador es una destinación turística tan popular?

2. ¿Por qué puede ser difícil un viaje al Ecuador?

3. ¿Por qué es tan importante el centro histórico de Quito?

4. ¿Por qué se llama así el monumento a la Mitad del Mundo?

5. ¿Por qué son importantes las culturas indígenas en el Ecuador?

6. ¿Qué hace el gobierno del Ecuador para preservar las islas Galápagos?

Y tú, ¿qué dices?

1. ¿Qué partes del Ecuador te gustaría visitar? ¿Por qué?

2. ¿Crees que el turismo es bueno para las islas Galápagos? ¿Por qué?

Más práctica	GO

realidades.com | print

Guided WB p. 289	✔	✔
Comm. WB pp. 155, 275	✔	✔
Hispanohablantes **WB** pp. 302–303		✔
Cultural Reading Activity	✔	

La cultura en vivo

Los códices

Antiguamente los indígenas americanos viajaban de un sitio a otro para explorar nuevos lugares, comunicarse con otros grupos indígenas y buscar rutas para el transporte de sus productos. A veces, los viajes eran largos, y cuando se alejaban mucho[1] necesitaban anotar el camino para poder regresar a sus casas. Para recordar el camino de regreso, las cosas que veían y los resultados de sus intercambios comerciales, anotaban sus observaciones en unos libros llamados *códices*.

Los antiguos indígenas americanos anotaban sus observaciones en códices.

Objetivo

• Contar un viaje imitando un códice

Materiales

• papel para dibujar (sirven las bolsas de papel)

• marcadores o pinturas acuarelas[2]

• pinceles[3] y lápices

Instrucciones

1 Piensa en un viaje que quieres contar en tu códice. Incluye entre cuatro a seis eventos.

2 Escoge los momentos importantes y represéntalos siguiendo una secuencia lógica. Haz un esquema[4] en una hoja de papel para planear el códice. Piensa en cómo vas a representar con dibujos y símbolos los lugares, medios de transporte, actividades y otros detalles importantes.

3 Dibuja el códice usando una variedad de colores. Lo más importante es que el lector pueda leer la historia de tu viaje por medio del códice. El códice debe ser un dibujo continuo.

4 Cuando termines los dibujos, dobla[5] el códice como lo hacían los aztecas.

Algunos códices famosos: Código Florentino, Códice Borgia, Códice de Tlaxcala, Códice Mendocino, Códice Madrid

Algunos códices muestran el contacto entre los indígenas americanos y los europeos.

[1]traveled far from home   [2]water colors   [3]brushes   [4]outline   [5]fold

Presentación oral

Un viaje al extranjero

Task
You have a job at a travel agency. A client wants to take her family on a summer trip to a Spanish-speaking country. She wants to spend a few days in a nice city, a day or two visiting ruins or historical sites, and a few days at the beach. Recommend a country and provide key travel information.

❶ Prepare Choose a country that meets the client's criteria. Research the following information:

- **Lugar:** ¿Qué país, ciudad, lugares históricos y playas recomiendas que visiten? ¿Qué itinerario sugieres?
- **Documentos:** ¿Necesitan un pasaporte u otro documento?
- **Transporte y equipaje:** ¿Cómo recomiendas que viajen? ¿Cuánto cuesta? ¿Cuánto equipaje pueden llevar? ¿Qué ropa deben llevar?

❷ Practice Go through your presentation. You can use your notes in practice, but not when you present. Try to:

- provide all the information on each point
- speak clearly
- present in a logical sequence

Modelo
Recomiendo que Uds. viajen a . . . Allí pueden ver . . . La ciudad de . . . es muy grande y les ofrece mucho a los turistas . . .

❸ Present Present the trip to your client. You may want to include a map or visuals.

❹ Evaluation The following rubric will be used to grade your presentation.

Estrategia
Brainstorming with a word web
To make sure you have all the information you need for your presentation, start by making a word web. Begin by writing the country you choose in the center of a piece of paper. Around the country name, write the words *lugar, documentos,* and *transporte y equipaje.* For each topic, write as many related ideas as you can. This way, you will have your ideas on paper in an organized format.

Rubric	Score 1	Score 3	Score 5
Your completeness of research	You consulted one source for information and cited the source.	You consulted two sources for information and cited sources.	You consulted three or more sources and cited sources.
Amount of information you communicated	You included one of the following: place, documents needed, travel directions, and luggage.	You included two of the following: place, documents needed, travel directions, and luggage.	You included all of the following: place, documents needed, travel directions, and luggage.
How easily you are understood	You are difficult to understand and make many grammatical errors.	You are fairly easy to understand and make occasional grammatical errors.	You are easy to understand and make very few grammatical errors.

Repaso del capítulo

Vocabulario y gramática

to talk about making travel plans

la agencia de viajes	travel agency
el / la agente de viajes	travel agent
el equipaje	luggage
extranjero, -a	foreign
hacer un viaje	to take a trip
la maleta	suitcase
hacer la maleta	to pack the suitcase
el pasaporte	passport
planear	to plan
la reservación, *pl.* las reservaciones	reservation
la tarjeta de embarque	boarding pass
el / la turista	tourist

to talk about airports

abordar	to board
la aduana	customs
el aduanero, la aduanera	customs officer
el aeropuerto	airport
el anuncio	announcement
el / la auxiliar de vuelo	flight attendant
con destino a	going to
de ida y vuelta	round-trip
directo, -a	direct
durar	to last
el empleado, la empleada	employee
facturar	to check (*luggage*)
hacer escala	to stop over
la inspección, *pl.* las inspecciones de seguridad	security checkpoint
la línea aérea	airline
la llegada	arrival
el pasajero, la pasajera	passenger
el pasillo	aisle
el / la piloto	pilot
la puerta de embarque	departure gate
registrar	to inspect, to search (*luggage*)

el retraso	delay
la salida	departure
la ventanilla	(*airplane*) window
el vuelo	flight

other useful words and expressions

abierto, -a	open
bienvenido, -a	welcome
cerrado, -a	closed
insistir en	to insist
listo, -a	ready
sugerir (*e → ie*)	to suggest
tendremos	we will have
tener paciencia	to be patient

verbs often followed by *que* + subjunctive

decir	prohibir
insistir en	querer (*e → ie*)
necesitar	recomendar (*e → ie*)
permitir	sugerir (*e → ie*)
preferir (*e → ie*)	

present subjunctive

hablar

hable	hablemos
hables	habléis
hable	hablen

aprender / escribir

aprenda escriba	aprendamos escribamos
aprendas escribas	aprendáis escribáis
aprenda escriba	aprendan escriban

irregular verbs in the subjunctive

dar   ir   ser

estar   saber

(*To see these verbs fully conjugated in the present subjunctive, refer to p. 413.*)

For *Vocabulario adicional*, see pp. 498–499.

Más repaso (GO) realidades.com | print

Instant Check	✔
Puzzles	✔
Core WB pp. 160–161	✔
Comm. WB p. 276	✔ ✔

Preparación para el examen

On the exam you will be asked to . . .	Here are practice tasks similar to those you will find on the exam . . .	For review go to your print or digital textbook . . .

Interpretive

 1 Escuchar Listen and understand as someone gives travel recommendations

A student from Spain gives travel tips to students who are thinking of traveling there this summer. Decide if the suggestion includes: (a) planning tips; (b) packing tips; (c) airport arrival tips; or (d) in-flight tips.

pp. 402–405 *Vocabulario en contexto*
p. 406 Actividad 5
p. 410 Actividad 11

Interpersonal

 2 Hablar Make recommendations for planning a stress-free trip

Your teacher asks you to give the class travel tips. You might talk about (a) getting to the airport; (b) checking in at the airline desk; (c) going through security checks; and (d) things to do on the plane. Begin with: *Sugiero que llegues al aeropuerto dos horas antes de la salida de tu vuelo.*

p. 407 Actividad 6
p. 411 Actividad 14
p. 414 Actividades 18–19
p. 415 Actividades 20–21
p. 417 Actividad 24
p. 421 *Presentación oral*

Interpretive

 3 Leer Read and understand a pamphlet about air travel

While at a travel agency, you pick up the pamphlet *Sugerencias para viajar a España*. Look at their suggestions and place them in order, starting with the planning stages and ending with your arrival in Madrid. Label them from A–D.

_1._ Recomendamos que hagas una reservación seis meses antes de tu viaje. _2._ Sugerimos que duermas durante el vuelo. _3._ Recomendamos que bebas mucha agua antes de abordar el vuelo. _4._ Sugerimos que pases por la aduana con todos los documentos necesarios.

pp. 402–403 *Vocabulario en contexto*
p. 406 Actividad 4
p. 408 Actividad 8
p. 414 Actividad 19
p. 416 Actividad 22

Presentational

 4 Escribir Write suggestions for a safe and enjoyable vacation

A travel agency asked your class to design a Web page for its Spanish-speaking clients. You are writing the section *Sugerencias para un buen viaje*. Write four suggestions or more. Include advice about such things as planning your trip through a travel agent vs. on the Internet, packing your suitcase, or asking for a particular seat on the plane.

p. 410 Actividad 11
p. 413 Actividad 17
p. 414 Actividad 19
p. 415 Actividades 20–21
p. 417 Actividad 24

Cultures

 5 Pensar Demonstrate an understanding of historical record-keeping

Explain how accounts of travel and trade were recorded by the indigenous peoples and Spaniards in Latin America. What information was recorded? What purpose did the documents serve? Who used the documents? What modern documents perform a similar function?

p. 420 *La cultura en vivo*

▼ Chapter Objectives

Communication

By the end of this chapter you will be able to:

- Listen to and read about travel recommendations and vacation postcards
- Talk and write about vacations and travel tips
- Exchange information about ways to be a good tourist

Culture

You will also be able to:

- Understand cultural practices related to travel in Spanish-speaking countries
- Compare lodging options in Spanish-speaking countries

You will demonstrate what you know and can do:

- Presentación escrita, p. 445
- Preparación para el examen, p. 447

You will use:

Vocabulary

- Sites of interest in a city
- Staying in a hotel
- Tourist activities and behaviors

Grammar

- Present subjunctive with impersonal expressions
- Present subjunctive of stem-changing verbs

Exploración del mundo hispano

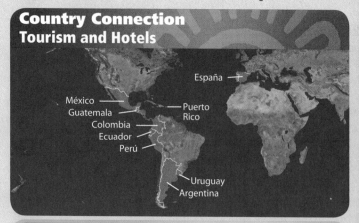

Country Connection
Tourism and Hotels

España
México
Guatemala
Puerto Rico
Colombia
Ecuador
Perú
Uruguay
Argentina

realidades.com GO

📖 **Reference Atlas**

▶ *Videocultura y actividad*

🌐 *Mapa global interactivo*

Las ruinas de Tulum en México

Arte y cultura | México

Artesanía de Oaxaca En Oaxaca, México, el tallado de madera *(wood carving)* es una tradición de los indígenas zapotecas. Los tallados más famosos se llaman alebrijes. Son figuras de animalitos como gatos, caballos, iguanas y vacas, y de animales fantásticos como dragones y monstruos míticos. Hoy en día, en Oaxaca hay alrededor de 200 familias que tallan madera.

• ¿Cuáles son algunos ejemplos de artesanía típica de la región donde vives? ¿En qué sentido *(way)* son similares a los alebrijes de Oaxaca? ¿En qué sentido son diferentes?

Alebrije *(Oaxacan wood carving)* de un armadillo

▼ Objectives

Read, listen to, and understand information about
▶ staying in a hotel
▶ appropriate tourist behavior
▶ traveling in a foreign city

Vocabulario en contexto

❝Aquí tienen nuestro **itinerario**. Vamos a pasar diez días visitando Madrid, la capital de España, la ciudad **histórica** de Toledo y la ciudad de Valencia❞.

El Palacio Real en Madrid

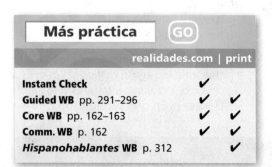

El Escorial

Ciudad de las Artes y las Ciencias, Valencia

ITINERARIO
para el grupo de la Sra. Guzmán

Día 1 — Llegada al Aeropuerto de Barajas en Madrid. Transporte en autobús al hotel en Madrid.

Días 2 a 4 — Primero vamos a **hacer una gira** de la capital y en los días **siguientes** vamos a regresar a los lugares más **famosos** de la ciudad.
- La Plaza Mayor: un lugar histórico con tiendas y cafés al aire libre
- **El Palacio** Real: palacio ceremonial de **los reyes**
- El Parque del Buen Retiro: un parque **bello**, originalmente lugar privado de los reyes
- El Museo del Prado: uno de los museos de arte más grandes y famosos del mundo

Día 5 — Lugares cerca de Madrid. El autobús sale a las 8:00 A.M. **en punto;** no vamos a salir tarde.
- El Escorial: palacio impresionante de Felipe II, **el rey** de España entre los años 1556 y 1598
- El Valle de los Caídos: monumento a los españoles que murieron en la Guerra Civil (1936–1939)

Día 6 — **Excursión** a Toledo. El autobús sale a las 7:30 A.M. y regresa a las 5:00 P.M.
- El Alcázar: originalmente un palacio árabe y después palacio del rey Carlos V en 1545
- La Iglesia de Santo Tomé: para ver el famoso cuadro de El Greco, "El entierro del conde de Orgaz" (1586–88)
- **La Catedral:** un buen ejemplo de la arquitectura gótica y una de las catedrales más **estupendas** del mundo

Más práctica   GO

realidades.com | print

Instant Check	✔	
Guided WB pp. 291–296	✔	✔
Core WB pp. 162–163	✔	✔
Comm. WB p. 162	✔	✔
Hispanohablantes WB p. 312		✔

Madrid • Toledo • Valencia

Días 7 a 8 Viaje en tren a Valencia. Dos días de excursiones en Valencia.
- Ciudad de las Artes y las Ciencias: un lugar con un poco de todo
- Museo Nacional de Cerámica: una colección de cerámica en un edificio histórico

Día 9 Descansar en la playa cerca de Valencia. Con el permiso de sus padres, pueden hacer surf de vela, esquí acuático y moto acuática. También podemos ir con nuestro **guía** a **navegar** en un bote de vela.

el surf de vela

la moto acuática

el esquí acuático

el bote de vela

Día 10 Regresamos a los Estados Unidos en el vuelo 519.

REGLAS PARA EL VIAJE

Para **disfrutar de** este viaje a España, tenemos que ser buenos turistas. Por eso necesitamos prestar atención a las siguientes reglas.

Durante el viaje hay que . . .

POR FAVOR
GRACIAS

- Ser **cortés.** Los buenos modales siempre son importantes.

- Estar en **la habitación** a las 11:00 en punto. No debes **hacer ruido** en las habitaciones.

- Darle **una propina** al hombre que lleva el equipaje. Es una costumbre que debes **observar.**

- Estar muy **atento.** Prestar atención a los (las) guías cuando hacemos excursiones y giras.

- Quedarse en grupos y ser **puntual.** Es necesario llegar a tiempo.

CASA DE CAMBIO

- Usar el tiempo libre para **cambiar** dinero. Se puede ir a **una casa de cambio,** al banco o se puede usar **el cajero automático.**

▼1 ¿Madrid, Toledo o Valencia?

Escuchar

Vas a escuchar varias descripciones de lugares en España. En una hoja de papel, escribe el nombre de la ciudad (Madrid, Toledo o Valencia) donde se encuentra cada lugar.

▼2 ¿Es buena idea o no?

Escuchar

Imagina que eres turista en España con tu clase de español. Escucha lo que dicen tus compañeros y si es buena idea, señala con el pulgar hacia arriba. Si es mala idea, señala con el pulgar hacia abajo.

Un día en Toledo

¡Acompaña a Ignacio y a Javier durante su visita a la ciudad de Toledo!

Estrategia

Using prior experience
Have you ever taken a trip to a historical site or seen a movie about one? Think about experiences such as checking into the hotel, reading a guide book, walking to various destinations, and buying a souvenir. Prior to reading, look at the visuals to see if Javier's experience is similar.

1

Ignacio: Me dijeron que nuestro hotel queda muy cerca de aquí. ¿Dejamos nuestras cosas y vamos a caminar por la ciudad? ¿Quieres conocerla?

Javier: Sí, me gustaría mucho y **tal vez** comprar recuerdos, como **artesanía** de la ciudad.

Javier

Ignacio

5

Javier: Hay mucho que ver aquí en Toledo.

Ignacio: Sí, la catedral, **el castillo,** el museo de El Greco . . .

Javier: Y no te olvides que quiero comprar algo **típico.**

Ignacio: Sí, después de ver los museos buscamos una tienda de artesanía.

6

Ignacio: Aquí está el museo de El Greco. . . . pero está cerrado. Mejor vamos a una tienda.

Javier: Sí, buena idea.

Ignacio: Entonces vamos a buscar una tienda de artesanía.

7

Ignacio: ¡Qué grande es esta espada!

Javier: Sí, debe ser muy cara. ¿Podemos ofrecerle menos dinero?

Ignacio: No, hombre. No se puede **regatear** aquí. No estamos en un mercado. Vas a **ofender** al **vendedor.**

Javier: Entonces creo que sólo voy a comprar **unas tarjetas postales.**

2

3

4

*Están en **la recepción** del hotel.*

Empleado: ¿Queréis* **una habitación doble** o dos **habitaciones individuales?**

Ignacio: Una habitación doble, por favor.

Empleado: Bien, pues aquí está **la llave.**

Ignacio: Vamos a subir la escalera.

Javier: De acuerdo. No me gusta esperar **el ascensor.**

Javier: ¿Adónde vamos primero?

Ignacio: Necesitamos **conseguir** un libro sobre la ciudad.

Ignacio: Este **quiosco** tiene una buena selección. Esta **guía** parece muy buena. Tiene mucha información y mapas de Toledo. Vamos a empezar el tour.*

*Hacer una gira is common usage for planning to take a tour of a city, but *el tour* is also used in many Spanish-speaking countries.

8

Javier: Es mejor. No cuestan tanto. Toledo sí que es una ciudad muy bella.

Ignacio: Tienes razón. Hemos visto muchas cosas interesantes e históricas. Pero ahora debemos descansar un poco. Mañana tenemos un partido de fútbol muy importante.

**Remember that in Spain, the *vosotros(as)* form of verbs is used when speaking to a group of people you would address individually with *tú*.

▼**3** **¿Comprendiste?**

Escribir • Hablar

1. ¿Por qué están Javier e Ignacio en Toledo?
2. ¿Adónde van primero después de llegar a Toledo?
3. ¿Qué les da el empleado del hotel?
4. ¿Qué compra Ignacio después de salir del hotel?
5. ¿Qué visitan los dos jóvenes en Toledo?
6. ¿Por qué no entran en el museo de El Greco?
7. ¿Por qué no compra Javier la espada?
8. ¿Qué decide comprar Javier? ¿Por qué?
9. ¿Qué van a hacer los dos después de salir de la tienda?

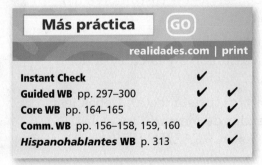

Más práctica (GO)

realidades.com | print

Instant Check	✔	
Guided WB pp. 297–300	✔	✔
Core WB pp. 164–165	✔	✔
Comm. WB pp. 156–158, 159, 160	✔	✔
Hispanohablantes WB p. 313		✔

▶ **Talk about being a tourist in another country**
▶ **Discuss water sports**
▶ **Listen to descriptions of tourist behavior and hotel preferences**
▶ **Write about tourist activities**

Vocabulario en uso

▼**4** ¿Qué clase de turista eres? | 👥 _____

Leer • Escribir • Hablar

Piensa en lo que hace un(a) turista bueno(a) en un país extranjero.

> **Nota**
>
> _La guía_ is both a book you refer to when you travel and a female tour guide. _El guía_ always refers to a male tour guide.

❶ Lee las frases y escribe las palabras correctas para completarlas.

1. Cuando llegas a tu habitación, no _(haces ruido/disfrutas)_ porque no quieres molestar a las otras personas en el hotel.

2. Tratas de _(ofender/observar)_ a las personas en un país extranjero para aprender más de su cultura.

3. Consultas tu _(itinerario/llave)_ para saber las horas de salida de las excursiones y los vuelos para no llegar tarde. Eres una persona muy _(bella/puntual)_.

4. Estás muy _(famoso/atento)_. Prestas atención al guía durante una gira.

5. Le dejas una _(propina/recepción)_ para la persona que te sirvió en un restaurante.

6. Compras la _(artesanía/habitación)_ típica del país que visitas y les preguntas a los _(castillos/vendedores)_ sobre quiénes la han hecho.

7. Haces una gira de los lugares _(siguientes/históricos)_ para saber más de la historia del lugar que visitas.

8. Tienes buenos modales y eres _(típico/cortés)_. Siempre les dices _por favor_ y _gracias_ a los demás.

❷ En otra hoja escribe los números del 1 al 8 y lee las frases de arriba otra vez. Usa los siguientes números para indicar con qué frecuencia haces cada cosa.

⑤ siempre ② a veces
④ casi siempre ① casi nunca
③ a menudo

❸ Suma _(Add up)_ tus puntos. Luego explícale a otro(a) estudiante qué clase de turista eres.

▼ Turistas en un mercado en Ixtapa, México

(40–32) Eres un(a) turista estupendo(a). Sabes lo que debes hacer en el extranjero _(abroad)_.

(31–23) Eres un(a) turista bueno(a). Vas a disfrutar de tus viajes si observas las costumbres del país que visitas.

(22–14) Eres un(a) turista típico(a). Debes estar más atento(a) a las costumbres y la cultura del país que visitas.

(13–0) Eres el (la) típico(a) turista feo(a). Debes leer otra vez y aprender de memoria todos los _Fondos culturales_ en _REALIDADES_ 1 y 2.

▼5 Recomendaciones para los turistas |

Hablar

Habla con otro(a) estudiante y hagan
recomendaciones para los turistas.

dejar

▶ **Modelo**
A —¿Dónde dejo el equipaje?
B —Debes ir a la habitación.

Estudiante A

1. pedir
2. conseguir
3. cambiar
4. regatear con los vendedores sobre
5. ver la residencia de
6. sacar
7. subir a

Estudiante B

usar   buscar
ir a   visitar

▼6 Escucha y escribe |

Escuchar • Escribir

Vas a escuchar lo que puede hacer un(a) turista en un país
extranjero. En una hoja de papel, haz dos columnas. Sobre
una columna, escribe *cortés*. Sobre la otra columna, escribe
descortés (impolite). Escribe cada acción que escuchas en la
columna correcta.

cortés	descortés

▼ Fondo Cultural | El mundo hispano

Regatear es una costumbre de negociar precios,
y es muy común en los mercados de los países
hispanohablantes. En cambio, es una costumbre menos
común en las tiendas. Si quieres comprar algo en un
mercado, le pides el precio al vendedor. El vendedor y el
cliente ofrecen y piden precios hasta acordar *(agree)* un
precio final. Si no sabes si debes regatear o no, puedes
preguntar: "¿Son precios fijos *(fixed)*?".

• Imagina que eres vendedor(a) en un mercado. ¿Te
gustaría regatear con los clientes para vender tus
cosas? ¿Por qué?

En el mercado de Otavalo, en el Ecuador

7 Vacaciones en Punta del Este |

Leer • Escribir • Hablar

Lee el siguiente anuncio para Punta del Este, Uruguay. Luego contesta las preguntas.

Punta del Este:
Destino acuático

EL CLUB NÁUTICO PUNTA DEL ESTE, FAMOSO A NIVEL[1] NACIONAL Y LOCAL, TIENE MUCHAS ACTIVIDADES NÁUTICAS PARA LOS TURISTAS EN, TAL VEZ, EL LUGAR MÁS BELLO DE URUGUAY.

Tanto en el puerto[2] como en la playa se encuentran lugares que alquilan pequeños botes de vela para navegar dentro de la bahía[3] o para llegar hasta la isla Gorriti.

Para los aficionados de la moto acuática, también puede alquilarlas en la playa. Infórmese de los lugares designados para el deporte porque no se permite su práctica en todas partes.

El surf de vela es un deporte muy popular en Punta del Este. Se pueden encontrar escuelas de surf de vela y hay la posibilidad de alquilar tablas[4] en el arroyo[5] Maldonado y en la laguna del Diario. En los días de mucho viento siempre es posible ver la habilidad de los navegantes con sus tablas de salto.

Gracias a la tranquilidad de las aguas del área, Punta del Este es un lugar estupendo para hacer esquí acuático. Hay varias escuelas aquí donde se puede encontrar un gran número de expertos que ofrecen sus servicios de instructor en el arroyo Maldonado y en la laguna del Diario.

¹level ²port ³bay ⁴surfboards ⁵stream

1. ¿Qué deportes puedes practicar en Punta del Este?

2. ¿Qué palabras indican que Punta del Este es un buen lugar para los turistas?

3. Si no sabes hacer ni el surf de vela ni el esquí acuático, ¿puedes disfrutar de unas vacaciones en Punta del Este? ¿Por qué?

4. Imagina que no puedes llevar tu propio equipo para practicar los deportes acuáticos en Punta del Este. ¿Qué puedes hacer?

8 Los deportes acuáticos | |

Hablar

Habla con otro(a) estudiante sobre los deportes acuáticos que se mencionan en el anuncio de Punta del Este. Puedes hacer preguntas como:

- ¿Has hecho . . . alguna vez?
- ¿Dónde lo (la) practicas (practicaste)?
- ¿Te diviertes (divertiste) mucho practicando . . . ?

- ¿Te gustaría practicarlo(la) alguna vez?
- ¿Cuál de los deportes te parece más interesante?

▼9 Los mejores hoteles | ♻ | ◀))

Leer • Escuchar

Imagina que eres agente de viajes y puedes recomendarles a tus clientes uno de los hoteles en estos anuncios. Lee los anuncios. Después escucha las preferencias de las personas y escribe *Hotel Real, Hotel Canarias* o *los dos hoteles* según la información en los anuncios.

El centro turístico de Cancún, el **Hotel Real** está sobre una de las más bellas playas de arena[1] blanca y frente a la Laguna Nichupté. Su arquitectura moderna y servicios de primera clase, hacen el hotel ideal para cualquier[2] vacacionista.

Habitaciones: Tenemos 300 habitaciones que están perfectamente equipadas con aire acondicionado, televisión a color vía satélite, teléfono directo, balcón privado, tina de baño[3] y secadora de pelo.

Servicios adicionales:
• **Restaurantes (3)**
• **Piscina y gran Jacuzzi**
• **Salones de reuniones**

De enero hasta abril:
Habitación individual o doble: $146
De abril hasta diciembre:
Habitación individual o doble: $78

Tel: 289-06-59

Hotel Real

[1]sand [2]any [3]bathtub

El Hotel Canarias, en la República Dominicana, es uno de los más bellos y exclusivos destinos turísticos / vacacionales del Caribe. Este centro turístico se extiende sobre unos 7,000 acres con árboles tropicales y ofrece villas, habitaciones hoteleras, campos de golf (3), canchas de tenis (13), piscinas (19), así como la playa Minitas.

También ofrecemos:
• Restaurantes (9: desde gourmet hasta informal)
• Tiendas de regalo
• Salones de belleza
• Aeropuerto privado
• Oficina de aerolínea
• Gimnasio
• Banco

Tel: 59-28-59

Villas de 2 a 6 habitaciones: $136 hasta $615

▼ Fondo Cultural | El mundo hispano

Cinco estrellas Un sistema internacional de evaluar un hotel es el sistema de estrellas: cinco estrellas es el mejor. ¿Qué necesita tener un hotel de cinco estrellas? En España, el hotel necesita tener aire acondicionado y calefacción *(heating)*, salones sociales, garaje y salón de belleza. En México, tiene que tener un restaurante, cafetería, discoteca y seguridad.

• ¿Prefieres un hotel con muchos servicios?, ¿una habitación de gran lujo? Si vas a un país extranjero, ¿es mejor gastar tu dinero en un hotel de cinco estrellas, en restaurantes caros o en comprar recuerdos?

Gramática

Present subjunctive with impersonal expressions

Sometimes you use an impersonal expression to express how you influence another person's actions.

Here are some impersonal expressions that are often followed by *que* + subjunctive:

es importante   es necesario   es mejor   es bueno

Es necesario que Uds. tengan buenos modales.

Es mejor que consigamos una habitación doble.

It's necessary that you have good manners.

It's better that we get a double room.

> **¿Recuerdas?**
> You know that the subjunctive mood is used to say that one person influences the actions of another.

- Note that in the examples above, a specific person is mentioned in the second half of the sentence. If no person is specified, the infinitive is used without *que*. Compare the following sentences.

Para ser un buen turista, **es importante ser** muy cortés.

Es importante que seas un turista cortés.

*To be a good tourist, **it's important to be** very polite.*

It's important that you be a polite tourist.

Más ayuda   **realidades.com**

 GramActiva Video
Tutorial: Use of subjunctive in noun clauses after impersonal expressions

 Canción de hip hop: *Turistas*

 GramActiva Activity

▼10 Para ser cortés . . .

Leer • Escribir

Para ser cortés en un país extranjero, ¿qué debes hacer? Completa las frases con la forma apropiada del verbo.

Modelo

Es importante que no *(hacer / ser)* mucho ruido en la habitación del hotel.
Es importante que no hagas mucho ruido en la habitación del hotel.

El Viejo San Juan, Puerto Rico

1. Es mejor que no *(llegar / llevar)* pantalones cortos si visitas la catedral.

2. Es importante que le *(dar / ir)* una propina al hombre que te ayuda con el equipaje.

3. Es necesario que *(ser / ver)* puntual para no enojar a los otros miembros de tu grupo.

4. Es bueno que les *(ofender / ofrecer)* a los ancianos tu asiento en el autobús.

5. Es mejor que *(poder / ponerse)* algo sobre tu traje de baño cuando entras en el hotel.

6. Es importante que *(observar / asistir)* las costumbres de las personas que viven allí.

▼11 Debes visitar Cartagena

Leer • Escribir

Lee el correo electrónico de un joven, Isidoro, que visitó Cartagena, Colombia. Completa sus recomendaciones a Daniela con la forma apropiada de uno de los verbos del recuadro.

acompañar	pasar
buscar	usar
decir	ver
ir	

Querida Daniela:

Me preguntaste sobre qué lugares en América del Sur les recomiendo para pasar unas vacaciones estupendas. Pues, en mi opinión, es necesario que Uds. __1.__ a Cartagena, Colombia. Es una combinación de lugares históricos y de playas bellas. Es mejor que un guía local los __2.__ a Uds. Es importante que Uds. __3.__ los servicios de un guía profesional licenciado. Es necesario que Uds. le __4.__ al guía que quieren hacer una gira por el castillo, la catedral y la antigua universidad. También es importante que __5.__ el Museo del Oro—un museo impresionante. Es bueno también que __6.__ por los barrios coloniales para ver las casas históricas. Para más información, es mejor que __7.__ en la Red, porque hay unos sitios Web muy buenos sobre Cartagena.

Tu amigo,
Isidoro

▼12 En la Red

Leer • Escribir

Lee la información que Daniela encuentra en la Red sobre Cartagena, Colombia. Daniela quiere que su familia vaya allí. Completa las frases usando la información del artículo y otras ideas.

Modelo

es bueno / los policías *(estar)* en las playas porque . . .
Es bueno que los policías estén en las playas porque así no hay ningún problema para los turistas.

1. es importante / nosotros *(planear)* ir a las playas porque . . .

2. es bueno / los turistas *(tomar)* el autobús a las playas porque . . .

3. es mejor / nosotros *(ir)* a una de las playas populares porque . . .

4. es mejor / nosotros *(mirar)* la artesanía de los vendedores porque . . .

5. es necesario / Uds. *(hablar)* con un agente de viajes sobre Cartagena porque . . .

Cartagena

Cartagena está rodeada[1] por el Mar Caribe. Sus bellas playas se encuentran a pocos metros del centro histórico. A menos de 35 minutos en autobús desde la Ciudad Vieja, se pueden encontrar las playas llamadas La Boquilla y Manzanillo. Para que los turistas disfruten de estas playas, el gobierno local las limpia todas las noches. Además, las playas son patrulladas[2] por la policía para evitar cualquier problema. Aquí los vendedores se acercan a los turistas para ofrecerles artesanías.

La gente de Cartagena es muy sociable y está acostumbrada a tratar a los turistas. Todas las playas de Cartagena se consideran seguras[3] para bañarse. Estas playas no tienen corrientes fuertes[4]. Las playas más frecuentadas tienen banderas de seguridad que informan a los bañistas sobre el estado del tiempo.

¡Cartagena lo tiene TODO!

[1]surrounded   [2]patrolled   [3]safe   [4]strong currents

▾13 Para disfrutar de las vacaciones |

Hablar

Con otro(a) estudiante, habla de lo que es necesario que hagan tu familia y tú para disfrutar de las vacaciones. Usen las expresiones *es importante, es necesario, es mejor* y *es bueno*.

1. quedarse en un hotel elegante
2. comer comidas típicas del país
3. sacar fotos de todo

▶ **Modelo**

ver edificios históricos

A —*Para mí, es importante que veamos los edificios históricos de una ciudad.*

B —*Para mí, no. No es importante que veamos edificios históricos. Prefiero ir a un cine.*

4. practicar deportes acuáticos
5. hacer una gira de una ciudad principal
6. observar con cuidado el itinerario

▾ Exploración del lenguaje

The suffix -ero(a)

The Spanish suffix *-ero(a)* indicates *someone* or *something* that performs an action:

> Alguien que **viaja** es un(a) **viajero(a)**.

> Algo que muestra (*shows*) **letras** es un **letrero**.

¡Compruébalo! Here are some words that you have learned so far. Complete each sentence with the logical word to tell what the people do or where they work.

1. Alguien que trabaja en la **aduana** es un(a) ___.
2. Algo que te trae **noticias** es un ___.
3. Esa señora es **cocinera**. Ella ___ bien.
4. Mi tía es **florera**. Es artística y trabaja con ___.
5. Cuando fui al ___ hablé con una **banquera** sobre cómo conseguir cheques de viajero.

Refrán

Zapatero, a tus zapatos.

▾ Fondo Cultural | El mundo hispano

Los hostales y albergues son una opción popular para jóvenes turistas. Ellos pueden visitar el campo y las ciudades grandes y sentirse seguros y cómodos sin gastar mucho dinero. En estos lugares los jóvenes también pueden conocer a otros turistas de todo el mundo.

• ¿Por qué crees que los hostales y albergues son tan populares entre los jóvenes?

Un cartel (*sign*) de un hostal en México

Más práctica GO   realidades.com | print

Instant Check	✔	
Guided WB pp. 301–302	✔	✔
Core WB p. 166	✔	✔
Comm. WB pp. 160, 163, 277	✔	✔
Hispanohablantes **WB** pp. 314–317		✔

Gramática

Present subjunctive of stem-changing verbs

Stem-changing verbs ending in -ar and -er have the same stem changes in the subjunctive as in the indicative.

recordar (o → ue)

recuerde	recordemos
recuerdes	recordéis
recuerde	recuerden

perder (e → ie)

pierda	perdamos
pierdas	perdáis
pierda	pierdan

¿Recuerdas?

You know that stem-changing verbs in the present indicative have a stem change in all forms except *nosotros* and *vosotros*.

Es importante que **recordemos** los buenos modales.

Es mejor que no te **pierdas** en el centro. Cómprate una guía.

Stem-changing verbs ending in -ir have changes in all forms of the present subjunctive.

pedir (e → i)

pida	pidamos
pidas	pidáis
pida	pidan

divertirse (e → ie), (e → i)

me divierta	nos divirtamos
te diviertas	os divirtáis
se divierta	se diviertan

dormir (o → ue), (o → u)

duerma	durmamos
duermas	durmáis
duerma	duerman

Es necesario que **pidas** la llave.

Queremos que **se diviertan**.

Es bueno que **duermas** durante el vuelo.

| **Más ayuda** | **realidades.com** |

GramActiva Video
Tutorial: Stem-changes in the present subjunctive
Animated Verbs

GramActiva Activity

▼14 ¿Qué debemos hacer?

Escribir

Si vas a otro país con un grupo de estudiantes, ¿qué deben y no deben hacer Uds.? Escribe frases usando *es importante, es necesario, es mejor* y *(no) es bueno*.

Modelo

conseguir cheques de viajero antes de salir
Es importante que consigamos cheques de viajero antes de salir.

1. sentirse superiores a los demás
2. reírse de las costumbres de otras personas
3. seguir las instrucciones de los líderes
4. mentir en la aduana
5. dormir durante el vuelo muy largo
6. divertirse mucho en el viaje

▼15 Una excursión en Ponce | ♻

Leer • Escribir

En Ponce, Puerto Rico, en medio de la zona histórica turística, está el Museo Castillo Serralles. Completa las reglas del guía de una gira del castillo.

El castillo Serralles originalmente fue la casa de la familia Serralles, una familia que ganó mucho dinero con la producción de azúcar en los años 30.

1. Quiero que Uds. *(entender / perder)* mis explicaciones. ¿Hablo muy rápidamente?

2. Es necesario que me *(seguir / conseguir)* siempre. No pueden ir solos a otras partes del castillo.

3. Si tienen preguntas sobre algún aspecto del castillo, prefiero que me *(poder / pedir)* que se lo explique.

4. Si Uds. quieren que yo *(repetir / reír)* algo, sólo tienen que decírmelo.

5. Es importante *(pensar / recordar)* que muchos de los objetos en el comedor son de los años 30.

6. En la Sala doña Mercedes, no permitimos que *(sentirse / sentarse)* en las sillas ni en los sofás.

7. Por favor, le pido a la última persona que entra en la sala que *(despertar / cerrar)* la puerta.

8. Después de la gira, recomiendo que *(volver / competir)* a los jardines para disfrutar de las vistas impresionantes de la ciudad y del mar.

9. Si quieren hacer otra gira, es necesario que *(conseguir / despedirse)* otro boleto para entrar.

▼16 Una entrenadora frustrada | | ♻

Hablar

Una entrenadora está bastante frustrada con las jugadoras en su equipo. Trabaja con otro(a) estudiante para describir el problema y dar recomendaciones.

▶ Modelo

no tener energía durante las prácticas
A —*Las jugadoras no tienen energía durante las prácticas.*
B —*Es importante que almuercen comida que es buena para la salud.*

Estudiante A

1. estar cansadas durante las prácticas
2. parecer estar aburridas durante los partidos
3. no saber qué hacer durante un partido
4. jugar como personas que no se conocen
5. no llegar a las prácticas a tiempo

Estudiante B

es importante
es necesario
les pido
les recomiendo
insisto en
sugiero

jugar con entusiasmo
empezar a jugar como un equipo unido
acostarse a las 11:00 de la noche en punto
seguir mis instrucciones
vestirse 15 minutos antes de la práctica

▼17 Una carta de Pablo

Leer • Escribir

Pablo aprendió mucho durante su viaje a Panamá. Lee su carta a su madre y, según las experiencias de Pablo, escribe seis recomendaciones para los viajeros al extranjero.

Modelo

Es importante que no pierdas tu pasaporte.

Querida mamá:
He aprendido mucho aquí en Panamá. Por ejemplo, mi maleta era demasiado grande y tuve que facturarla. No sabía que aquí hace tanto calor y tuve que comprar más ropa.

Compré unos recuerdos en el mercado, pero probablemente pagué demasiado porque no regateé con los vendedores. Aprendí que en Panamá ahora se aceptan los dólares estadounidenses.

En el hotel tuve algunos problemas. Olvidé el número de mi habitación y perdí mi llave y tuve que conseguir otra. Pero afortunadamente no he perdido mi pasaporte. Las habitaciones aquí son muy cómodas, pero es difícil dormir porque a veces algunos estudiantes hacen ruido en el hotel.

Un abrazo,
Pablo

▼18 Juego | 👥 | ♻

Escribir • Hablar • GramActiva

❶ Trabajen en grupos de tres. En pequeñas hojas de papel o tarjetas, escriban tres preguntas sobre el tema de viajar. Pongan todas las preguntas en una bolsa para cada equipo.

❷ El (La) profesor(a) divide a la clase en dos equipos, "México" y "España".

❸ Una persona del equipo "México" lee una de las preguntas que está en la bolsa a una persona del equipo "España". Si esta persona puede contestar correctamente usando el subjuntivo y la información apropiada, gana una letra de su país, "España," para su equipo. ¡El primer equipo que gana todas las letras de su país gana el juego!

Modelo

México: *¿Adónde voy para cambiar un cheque de viajero?*
España: *Recomiendo que vayas a una casa de cambio.*

¿Adónde voy para cambiar un cheque de viajero?

¿Qué tengo que conseguir antes de ir a un país extranjero?

¿Dónde se puede regatear por la artesanía?

El español en el mundo del trabajo

Hoy en día el turismo en los países hispanohablantes es más popular que nunca. Los turistas de todo el mundo están descubriendo la riqueza histórica y cultural del mundo hispano. Muchas compañías de turismo ofrecen giras a varios países y necesitan empleados que hablan español, conocen la cultura hispana y tienen interés en ayudar a sus clientes.

• ¿Cómo puedes usar el español trabajando para una compañía de turismo o una agencia de viajes? ¿Qué le recomiendas a alguien que quiere hacer este tipo de trabajo?

▼19 Recomendaciones |

Hablar • Pensar • Escribir

Trabajen en grupos de cuatro estudiantes y hagan recomendaciones sobre las vacaciones. Dos estudiantes van a escribir cinco recomendaciones para las personas que no gastan mucho en las vacaciones y dos van a escribir cinco recomendaciones para las personas que gastan demasiado. Compartan sus recomendaciones con las del otro grupo. Preparen reacciones a las recomendaciones y explíquenselas al otro grupo.

Modelo
Grupo 1: *Para no gastar tanto en las vacaciones, es importante que viajen en coche y no en avión.*
Grupo 2: *Muchas veces no es posible viajar en coche. Queremos ir de vacaciones a Puerto Rico.*

▼20 Y tú, ¿qué dices? | (Talk!)

Escribir • Hablar

1. Para aprender a hablar español muy bien, ¿qué es importante que haga un(a) estudiante?

2. ¿Qué es muy importante que una persona haga para indicar que es cortés?

3. ¿Qué recomiendas que haga un(a) turista cuando acaba de llegar a un país extranjero?

Más práctica	GO	
	realidades.com | print	
Instant Check	✔	
Guided WB pp. 303–304	✔	✔
Core WB pp. 167–168	✔	✔
Comm. WB pp. 161, 164	✔	✔
Hispanohablantes WB pp. 318–319		✔

Fondo Cultural | España

El Parador de Sigüenza es uno de los muchos paradores que hay en España. Estos edificios históricos fueron restaurados y convertidos en alojamientos *(lodgings)* por el gobierno español. Aunque son lujosos *(luxurious)*, quedarse en un parador no es muy caro, y es una manera muy conveniente de conocer España.

- ¿Por qué crees que estos edificios se llaman paradores? ¿Qué palabra que ya sabes forma parte de la palabra parador? ¿Qué prefieres tú, una habitación en un albergue juvenil, en un hotel de cinco estrellas o en un parador? ¿Por qué?

El Parador de Sigüenza, España

▼21 Las vacaciones |

Hablar • Leer • Pensar • Escribir

¿Crees que los estadounidenses y los españoles piensan lo mismo sobre la importancia de gastar dinero en las vacaciones?

Conexiones | Las matemáticas

- Pregúntales a tres adultos si creen que los estadounidenses gastan demasiado en las vacaciones. Escribe el nombre de la persona y su respuesta.

- Compartan y sumen *(add up)* las respuestas a la pregunta con tres estudiantes. Calculen el porcentaje de personas que contestaron afirmativamente y de las que contestaron negativamente.

- Estudia la gráfica que representa cómo contestó un grupo de adultos españoles la misma pregunta. Copia la gráfica y añade la información de tu clase. Luego contesta las siguientes preguntas.

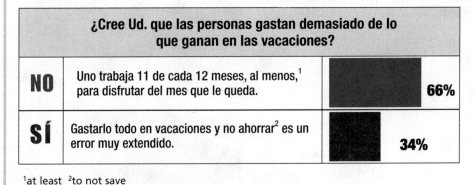

¿Cree Ud. que las personas gastan demasiado de lo que ganan en las vacaciones?		
NO	Uno trabaja 11 de cada 12 meses, al menos,[1] para disfrutar del mes que le queda.	**66%**
SÍ	Gastarlo todo en vacaciones y no ahorrar[2] es un error muy extendido.	**34%**

[1]at least [2]to not save

1. ¿En qué sentido son similares las respuestas de los estadounidenses y de los españoles? ¿En qué sentido son diferentes?

2. Para tu familia y las familias de tus amigos, ¿es importante pasar tiempo de vacaciones? ¿Adónde van y qué hacen durante las vacaciones?

▼22 Mi ciudad |

Escribir • Hablar

❶ Tienes que crear un anuncio para promocionar el turismo en tu comunidad. Escribe sobre cuatro o cinco lugares que recomiendas que visiten los turistas. Usa las expresiones *es mejor que, es importante que, es necesario que, sugiero que* y *recomiendo que*. Incluye consejos *(advice)* sobre lo siguiente:

- la mejor estación para visitar tu ciudad
- lugares para comer, atracciones culturales, los horarios y los precios
- lugares para ir de compras y lo que se puede comprar allí
- consejos sobre las costumbres y los modales
- puntos de interés y actividades divertidas

❷ Compara tus recomendaciones con las de otro(a) estudiante y hablen de ellas.

Lectura

Antigua, una ciudad colonial

Estrategia

Using heads and subheads
Heads and subheads help to organize information. Before you read each section, use its subhead to think about the information you're likely to read.

SITUADA a 45 minutos de la Ciudad de Guatemala, Antigua le fascina al turista por sus calles de piedras, su arquitectura colonial y sus ruinas de iglesias y monasterios. El español Francisco de la Cueva fundó la ciudad el 10 de marzo de 1543. La "Ciudad de las Perpetuas Rosas," nombrada así por sus jardines con flores, tiene un clima muy agradable y preserva un sabor colonial único. Caminar por sus calles es como visitar el pasado y descubrir una ciudad típica española del siglo[1] XVII. ¡Los invitamos a venir y a disfrutar de esta ciudad!

¡Bienvenidos a la hermosa ciudad de Antigua!

HOTELES

Antigua ofrece una gran variedad de hoteles. Los precios pueden variar entre $35.00 y $300.00 la noche. El mejor hotel de Antigua es la Casa de Santo Domingo. Este hotel de cinco estrellas, construido en un antiguo convento, tiene muchas comodidades modernas, como computadoras, piscina, sauna y varios jacuzzis. Las ruinas del convento están todavía en el hotel y así el visitante puede apreciar lo moderno con lo antiguo.

RESTAURANTES

La ciudad de Antigua tiene toda clase de restaurantes; desde restaurantes donde preparan platos guatemaltecos típicos hasta pizzerías. Le recomendamos La Fonda de la Calle Real, establecida en 1975. Este restaurante ofrece comida típica de Guatemala, como la deliciosa carne adobada[2] y muchos postres típicos.

◀ La Iglesia La Merced, Antigua

Una linterna de una casa guatemalteca, Antigua ▶

[1]century   [2]marinated

▲ El Templo I de la Gran Plaza, Tikal

¿Comprendiste?

1. ¿Qué palabra en inglés es similar a la palabra *antigua?* ¿Por qué piensas que Antigua se llama así?

2. ¿Qué puedes ver en Antigua que representa su historia colonial?

3. ¿Qué puedes ver del mundo moderno en esta ciudad?

4. Según este folleto de turismo *(travel brochure)*, ¿cuáles son los lugares más interesantes para visitar?

¿Qué hay que ver en la ciudad de Antigua?

La ciudad de Antigua tiene muchos sitios de interés. Se puede apreciar toda la historia de esta ciudad mirando sus casas y monumentos coloniales. En el centro de la ciudad está la Plaza Mayor. Los edificios principales son el Ayuntamiento[3], la Catedral y el Palacio de los Capitanes.

Vaya al reino de la cultura maya

Si le interesan las ruinas, le recomendamos que haga planes para visitar Tikal, una de las ciudades más importantes de la cultura maya. Desde el aeropuerto de la Ciudad de Guatemala, un avión lo lleva a Flores, la entrada a la zona arqueológica de Tikal. Duerma en uno de los pequeños hoteles de la región. ¡Esperamos[4] que disfrute de esta excursión!

Una experiencia inolvidable

La ciudad de Antigua no es sólo un lugar turístico para visitar parques, volcanes y monumentos históricos. Su gente es tan simpática que usted va a sentirse como en su propia casa. ¡Visite Antigua, lo(a) esperamos con anticipación!

[3]City hall   [4]We hope

 El Ayuntamiento, Antigua ▶

Más práctica   GO

realidades.com | print

Guided WB p. 305	✔	✔
Comm. WB pp. 165, 278	✔	✔
Hispanohablantes **WB** pp. 322–323		✔
Cultural Reading Activity		✔

Perspectivas del mundo hispano

La Red Nacional de Ferrocarriles Españoles

¿Te gustaría viajar por un país hispanohablante en un vehículo moderno, cómodo, rápido, seguro, limpio y económico? Puedes hacerlo en España si viajas en los trenes de la Red Nacional de Ferrocarriles Españoles (RENFE). El ferrocarril, o tren, es un medio de transporte muy popular en España y en toda Europa. El tren es una buena alternativa al automóvil porque transporta a muchos pasajeros y mercancías. Consume menos energía y por eso es más limpio y contamina menos.

La red[1] ferroviaria española tiene más de 15,000 kilómetros y se extiende por todo el país. Hay servicios de metro[2] en Madrid, Barcelona, Valencia y Bilbao y trenes que comunican la ciudad con los suburbios, con otras ciudades de la región y con ciudades lejanas en el país y en otros países. RENFE ofrece billetes[3] más baratos para jóvenes y personas mayores.

RENFE ofrece muchas líneas de trenes de alta velocidad, o AVE, que viajan a velocidades superiores a los 300 kilómetros por hora y recorren largas distancias. Con estos servicios tan rápidos, mucha gente prefiere viajar en tren en vez de en avión.

El AVE, España

¡Compruébalo! ¿Hay metro en tu ciudad? ¿Tiene tu estado un sistema de ferrocarriles? ¿Qué servicios ofrece? ¿Lo has usado alguna vez? ¿Lo usa algún miembro de tu familia?

¿Qué te parece? ¿Qué te parece el transporte por ferrocarril? ¿Cuáles son algunas de sus ventajas[4] y desventajas[5]?

[1]system [2]subway [3]tickets [4]advantages [5]disadvantages

Presentación escrita

Viajemos juntos

Task
You are going on a class trip to a Spanish-speaking country. Prepare a brochure for your group.

La Plaza de Armas en Lima, Perú

❶ Prewrite Think of the preparations you must make before your trip. Answer these questions:

- ¿Qué país van a visitar y cómo van a viajar?
- ¿Qué deben llevar? ¿Una cámara? ¿Unos anteojos de sol?
- ¿Qué lugares van a visitar? ¿Qué excursiones o giras van a hacer? ¿Qué actividades van a hacer?
- ¿Cómo deben vestirse? ¿Hay restricciones de vestimenta?

❷ Draft Use your responses to develop a brochure that will help your group prepare. Include photos or drawings.

❸ Revise Check the spelling, vocabulary, verb usage, and agreement. A classmate will check the following:

- Is the information clear and well organized?
- Have you included all the necessary information?
- Are the visuals useful?
- Is there anything you should add or change?
- Are there any errors?

❹ Publish Make a new version with the changes. Make a final copy for your teacher or your portfolio.

❺ Evaluation The following rubric will be used to grade your brochure.

Estrategia

Using key questions
Key questions are a good way to brainstorm. Jot down answers to a wide range of questions and you will have many ideas to help you with your writing.

Ruinas de una misión, en la Argentina

Rubric	Score 1	Score 3	Score 5
Amount of information provided	You only address some of the questions in your brochure.	You address most of the questions in your brochure.	You address all of the questions in your brochure.
Attractiveness and clarity of your brochure	Your layout is confusing and contains visible error corrections and smudges.	Your layout is somewhat clear but contains visible error corrections and smudges.	Your layout is clear and attractive and contains no error corrections or smudges.
Your use of vocabulary and grammar	You use very little variation of vocabulary and make frequent usage errors.	You use limited vocabulary and have some usage errors.	You use an extended variety of vocabulary and make very few usage errors.

Repaso del capítulo

Vocabulario y gramática

to talk about places to visit in a city

el cajero automático	ATM
la casa de cambio	currency exchange
el castillo	castle
la catedral	cathedral
histórico, -a	historical
el palacio	palace
el quiosco	newsstand

to talk about staying in a hotel

el ascensor	elevator
conseguir *(e → i)*	to obtain
la habitación, *pl.* las habitaciones	room
la habitación doble	double room
la habitación individual	single room
la llave	key
la recepción	reception desk

to talk about appropriate tourist behaviors

atento, -a	attentive
cortés	polite
hacer ruido	to make noise
observar	to observe
ofender	to offend
la propina	tip
puntual	punctual

For *Vocabulario adicional,* see pp. 498–499.

to talk about tourist activities

la artesanía	handicrafts
el bote de vela	sailboat
cambiar	to change, to exchange
disfrutar de	to enjoy
el esquí acuático	waterskiing
la excursión, *pl.* las excursiones	excursion, short trip
el guía, la guía	guide
la guía	guidebook
hacer una gira	to take a tour
el itinerario	itinerary
la moto acuática	personal watercraft
navegar	to sail, to navigate
regatear	to bargain
el surf de vela	windsurfing
la tarjeta postal	postcard
el vendedor, la vendedora	vendor

other useful words and expressions

bello, -a	beautiful
en punto	exactly *(time)*
estupendo, -a	stupendous, wonderful
famoso, -a	famous
el rey, *pl.* los reyes	king, king and queen
siguiente	next, following
tal vez	maybe, perhaps
típico, -a	typical

present subjunctive with impersonal expressions

Es bueno que los estudiantes **hagan** la tarea.

Es importante que comas un buen desayuno.

Es mejor que no **vayamos** al museo hoy.

Es necesario que hagas una gira de la ciudad.

present subjunctive of stem-changing verbs

recordar *(o → ue)*	divertirse *(e → ie),* *(e → i)*
perder *(e → ie)*	
pedir *(e → i)*	dormir *(o → ue),* *(o → u)*

(To see these verbs fully conjugated in the present subjunctive, see p. 437.)

Repaso

Más repaso (GO) realidades.com | print

Instant Check	✔
Puzzles	✔
Core WB pp. 169–170	✔
Comm. WB pp. 279, 280–282	✔ ✔

Preparación para el examen

On the exam you will be asked to . . .	Here are practice tasks similar to those you will find on the exam . . .	For review go to your print or digital textbook . . .

Interpretive

 ① Escuchar Listen and understand as people make recommendations for travel

You need some advice for your trip to Mexico. Listen to these recommendations and determine what is the most important thing to do when you get there. What is the best thing to do there?

pp. 426–429 *Vocabulario en contexto*
p. 431 Actividad 6
p. 433 Actividad 9

Interpersonal

 ② Hablar Talk about ways to have an enjoyable vacation when you travel away from home

Give a group at a Spanish Club meeting some advice about travel in Mexico. How can they be "good" tourists? What is the best way to get to know the city they visit?

p. 430 Actividad 4
p. 431 Actividad 5
p. 432 Actividad 7
p. 436 Actividad 13
p. 440 Actividades 19–20

Interpretive

 ③ Leer Read and understand vacation postcards from friends and family

Read a postcard from a classmate in Mexico. Is the person: (a) having a good or bad trip; (b) using Spanish; and (c) learning about Mexico?

Querido Juan:

Estoy aquí en Cancún. Es muy divertido pasar tiempo en la playa y luego ir al mercado. Me encanta hablar español para regatear. Es importante que no ofendas a los vendedores cuando regateas por el mejor precio.

p. 432 Actividad 7
p. 433 Actividad 9
p. 434 Actividad 10
p. 435 Actividades 11–12
p. 439 Actividad 17
pp. 442–443 *Lectura*

Presentational

 ④ Escribir Write a "tip sheet" for students planning to travel to a foreign country

You are developing a Web site for teen travelers. Complete the following sentences with at least three suggestions per topic: (a) Para ser un(a) turista bueno(a), es importante que . . . ; (b) Para disfrutar mucho de tu viaje, te recomiendo que . . .

p. 430 Actividad 4
p. 434 Actividad 10
p. 435 Actividades 11–12
p. 437 Actividad 14
p. 439 Actividad 17
p. 445 *Presentación escrita*

Cultures

 ⑤ Pensar Demonstrate an understanding of cultural practices related to travel in Spanish-speaking countries

Think about how American tourists would most likely travel within a Spanish-speaking country. To get from one city to another, what kind of transportation would they use? How would this compare with how tourists would travel while visiting the United States?

pp. 442–443 *Lectura*
p. 444 *Perspectivas del mundo hispano*

Vocabulario Repaso

las plantas y los animales

el árbol, *pl.* los árboles
la flor, *pl.* las flores
el mono
el oso
el pájaro
el pez, *pl.* los peces
el tigre

los lugares

al aire libre
el jardín, *pl.* los jardines
el lago
el mar
las montañas
el mundo
el parque nacional
el río
el zoológico

el reciclaje

el centro de reciclaje
reciclar
recoger
separar
tirar
trabajar como voluntario, -a
usar

los materiales

la botella
el cartón
la lata
el papel
el periódico
el plástico
la revista
el vidrio

▼1 ¿Qué es? | 👥

Escribir • Hablar

❶ Lee las siguientes definiciones y escribe la palabra que se define.

1. lugar donde se ven los animales

2. animal que come plátanos

3. publicación que da las noticias

4. material usado para hacer cajas

5. rosa, tulipán, orquídea

❷ Ahora escribe tres definiciones más. Léelas a otro(a) estudiante para ver si puede decir la palabra que se define.

▼2 Lugares interesantes

Escribir • Hablar

Contesta las siguientes preguntas.

1. ¿Cuál es el zoológico más impresionante que has visitado? ¿Por qué te pareció tan fantástico?

2. ¿En tu comunidad hay parques o jardines públicos? Describe uno.

3. ¿Has ido alguna vez a un parque nacional? ¿Cómo era? ¿Qué había? ¿Qué hiciste allí?

4. ¿Has trabajado como voluntario(a) en un centro de reciclaje alguna vez? ¿Qué hacen los voluntarios allí?

Gramática Repaso

Verbs with spelling changes in the present tense

Remember that some verbs have spelling changes in the present tense to preserve the pronunciation of the infinitive in the conjugated forms.

Remember that *g* has a hard or soft sound depending on the vowel that follows it. To maintain the soft consonant sound before the vowel *o*, verbs that end in *-ger*, like *escoger* and *recoger*, change from *g* to *j* in the present-tense *yo* form.

> **Recojo** basura en la calle y la tiro en el basurero. Otras personas no la **recogen**.

In the present-tense *yo* form of verbs like *seguir* and *conseguir*, the silent *u* used in the infinitive and other forms in which the *g* is followed by *e* or *i* is dropped to preserve the sound of *g* as in *get*.

> En el jardín botánico, algunos turistas **siguen** a una guía por los senderos. Yo no la **sigo**; prefiero caminar solo.

Verbs like *enviar* and *esquiar* have an accent mark on the *i* in all present-tense forms except *nosotros* and *vosotros*.

> **Enviamos** cartas a las compañías que destruyen los árboles. Yo también **envío** información por correo electrónico.

▼3 Una semana de vacaciones

Leer • Escribir

Lee lo que dice una muchacha sobre sus vacaciones. Completa su historia con las formas apropiadas de los verbos *escoger, esquiar* y *seguir*.

Cada año mi familia y yo vamos a las montañas para esquiar. Yo __1.__ muy bien porque hace cinco años que tomo lecciones de esquí. Mis padres me dicen, "Amalia, __2.__ : o esquías con nosotros o tomas una lección". Yo siempre __3.__ un día de lecciones porque los instructores __4.__ estupendamente. Escucho con atención y __5.__ sus instrucciones. Algunos chicos en las lecciones son demasiado atrevidos y no __6.__ instrucciones.

Más práctica · (GO)

realidades.com | print

A ver si recuerdas with Study Plan ✔
Guided WB pp. 307–308 ✔ ✔
Core WB pp. 171–172 ✔ ✔
Hispanohablantes WB p. 330 ✔

▼4 Un proyecto en la comunidad

Escribir

Un grupo de personas de una escuela decide ayudar a limpiar su comunidad. Escribe frases para decir qué hacen.

Modelo
mi profesor de ciencias / conseguir permiso para . . .
Mi profesor de ciencias consigue permiso para hacer el proyecto.

1. yo
2. mis amigos
3. mi mejor amigo(a)
4. nosotros
5. nuestros profesores

enviar cartas a la comunidad para . . .
recoger basura en . . .
seguir las instrucciones de . . .
escoger el lugar donde . . .
conseguir bolsas de plástico para . . .

▼ Chapter Objectives

Communication

By the end of this chapter you will be able to:

- Listen to and read about students' future plans
- Talk and write about high school activities and career plans
- Exchange information about what high school will be like for new students

Culture

You will also be able to:

- Understand folk art from Spanish-speaking countries
- Compare education in the Spanish-speaking world with that in the U.S.

You will demonstrate what you know and can do:

- Presentación oral, p. 471
- Preparación para el examen, p. 473

You will use:

Vocabulary

- Professions
- The future

Grammar

- The future tense
- The future tense: irregular verbs

Exploración del mundo hispano

Country Connection
Future Plans and Professions

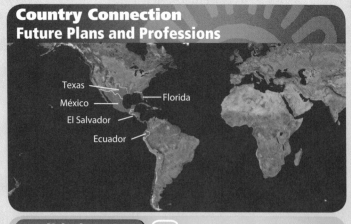

- Texas
- México
- El Salvador
- Ecuador
- Florida

realidades.com (GO)

 Reference Atlas

 Videocultura y actividad

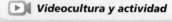 **Mapa global interactivo**

El pintor David Alfaro
Siqueiros trabajando
en su taller, 1966

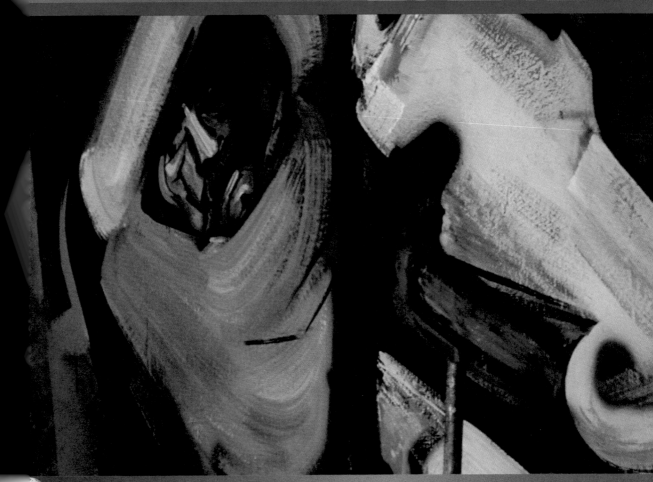

Arte y cultura | México

David Alfaro Siqueiros (1896–1974) En una de las paredes principales de la Universidad Nacional Autónoma de México está este gran mural del famoso artista mexicano David Alfaro Siqueiros. La Universidad le pidió a Siqueiros una obra pública, monumental, relacionada con la educación. Los estudiantes representados en el mural comparten sus conocimientos con el pueblo mexicano. Siqueiros terminó el mural en 1956.

- ¿Hay algún mural o alguna obra de arte monumental en tu escuela o tu comunidad? ¿Cómo es?

"El Pueblo a la Universidad y la Universidad al Pueblo" (1950–1954), David Alfaro Siqueiros ▶

(Detail) © 2010 Artists Rights Society (ARS), New York/SOMAAP, Mexico City/photo: Paul Almasy/Corbis

Vocabulario en contexto

▼ Objectives

Read, listen to, and understand information about
▶ professions
▶ making plans for the future
▶ earning a living

Exposición de carreras

❝Bienvenidos a la Exposición de **carreras.** Hoy les vamos a hablar sobre las posibilidades que hay para Uds. después de **graduarse** del **colegio.** Después de **la graduación** de la escuela secundaria, algunos de Uds. asistirán a **la universidad** y estudiarán para **una profesión.** Otros irán a **una escuela técnica,** y otros conseguirán un trabajo inmediatamente. Tenemos información para todos❞.

el hombre de negocios

la mujer de negocios

la oficina — el (la) secretario(a)

el (la) contador(a)

En el mundo de los negocios es importante tener a personas **bilingües.** En el futuro hablar dos **idiomas,** como el inglés y el español, será más importante.

el (la) arquitecto(a)

el (la) diseñador(a)

el (la) técnico(a)

Habrá carreras importantes en la tecnología: arquitectos para la construcción de casas y edificios y diseñadores para sitios Web y juegos de computadoras.

el juez, la jueza

Algunos de Uds. seguirán la carrera de **derecho** y tendrán un programa de estudios muy interesante.

el (la) abogado(a)

Para ser abogado o juez hay que ir a la universidad y estudiar **leyes** seis u ocho años.

el (la) agricultor(a)

el (la) cartero(a)

Hay muchas otras oportunidades de trabajo: carreras de agricultor, mecánico, bombero o cartero, por ejemplo. Tal vez algunos seguirán una carrera militar.

el (la) mecánico(a)

66 Me gusta estudiar ciencias sociales. Creo que seguiré una carrera en **la política**99.

el (la) político(a)

el (la) ingeniero(a)

66 Las matemáticas siempre han sido fáciles para mí. Me gustaría ser ingeniero99.

el (la) científico(a)

el (la) gerente

66 Hace dos años que trabajo como dependiente en una tienda de ropa. Quisiera ser gerente de la tienda99.

el (la) veterinario(a)

66 Me interesa el estudio de la medicina, pero también me gustan los animales. Estudiaré para ser veterinaria99.

66 A mí me encantan las ciencias. Seré científica y trabajaré en un laboratorio99.

▼1 Las profesiones | 🔊

Escuchar

Escucha las descripciones de diferentes profesiones. Mira los dibujos y las fotos y señala la profesión que se describe en cada frase.

▼2 ¿Lógico o no? | 🔊

Escuchar

¿Qué sabes sobre las profesiones y las carreras? Levanta una mano si lo que escuchas es lógico y levanta las dos manos si no es lógico.

Más práctica GO	realidades.com | print	
Instant Check	✔	
Guided WB pp. 309–316	✔	✔
Core WB pp. 173–174	✔	✔
Comm. WB p. 172	✔	✔
Hispanohablantes **WB** p. 332		✔

Y tú, ¿qué vas a ser?

¿Qué van a ser Angélica, Esteban y Pedro? ¿Qué le pasa a Pedro? Lee la historia.

Estrategia

Activating background knowledge
As you read the *Videohistoria*, think about what you already know about the professions being discussed.

• What do the characters need to do in order to work in their chosen professions?

1

Angélica: Hola, Pedro, ¿qué tal?

Pedro: Hola. Muy bien, ¿y tú? ¿Está Esteban?

Angélica: ¿Adónde van?

Esteban: A la escuela. Hay un concurso de arte, de dibujos. Y Pedro va a participar.

Angélica   Lisa   Pedro   Esteban

5

Pedro: No sé. Es difícil ganarse la vida como **artista**. Quizás podré ser **escritor**. Sabes que también me gusta mucho escribir. Y tú, ¿qué piensas hacer?

6

Esteban: Pues a mí me gustan las profesiones técnicas. Quiero estudiar para ingeniero o arquitecto . . .

7

Directora: Todos los trabajos son excelentes, pero uno de ellos es el mejor . . . ¡Pedro Ríos! ¡Felicidades!

Pedro: Y bien, ¿qué te parece?

Esteban: ¡Genial!

Angélica: A mí no me gusta.

Esteban: Porque tú no comprendes el mundo de las artes.

Angélica: Sí, lo comprendo, pero . . .

Angélica: Algún día prefiero **ganarme la vida** como mujer de negocios. Tendré **un salario** decente y **beneficios.**

Esteban: Sí, y querrás ser **dueña** de tu negocio . . .

Pedro: Mejor vamos o llegaremos tarde al concurso.

Esteban: Oye, creo que eres muy talentoso. Algún día podrás ser **pintor . . .**

Lisa: ¡Felicidades, Pedro!

Pedro: Gracias, Lisa. Es un momento muy importante para mí.

Esteban: ¿Un autógrafo, por favor?

Pedro: ¿Cómo? Ah, sí, por supuesto. Voy a ser un pintor muy famoso.

▼3 ¿Comprendiste?

Escribir • Hablar

1. ¿Adónde van Pedro y Esteban? ¿Por qué?

2. ¿Qué más piensa hacer Angélica en el futuro? ¿Por qué?

3. ¿Qué más le gusta hacer a Pedro? ¿Qué profesión piensa seguir?

4. ¿Qué profesión le gustaría seguir a Esteban?

5. ¿Quién ganó el concurso? ¿Qué le pide Esteban a Pedro?

Más práctica	GO	
realidades.com | print		
Instant Check	✔	
Guided WB pp. 317–320	✔	✔
Core WB pp. 175–176	✔	✔
Comm. WB pp. 166–168, 169, 170	✔	✔
Hispanohablantes WB p. 333		✔

| ▼ **Objectives**

▸ **Talk about professions**
▸ **Discuss career plans**
▸ **Listen to people describe their careers**
▸ **Write about future plans and employment ads**

Vocabulario en uso

▼4 ¡A trabajar en el periódico!

Escribir

Un joven trabaja en un periódico y tiene que organizar los anuncios clasificados. Escribe la profesión que no corresponde a cada una de estas categorías.

Modelo
la tecnología: arquitecta, contador, diseñador, técnica
contador

1. los negocios: contadora, secretario, gerente, mecánica
2. las artes: pintora, artista, escritor, cartero
3. la política y el derecho: agricultor, jueza, político, abogada
4. la tecnología: diseñadora, arquitecta, juez, ingeniero
5. las ciencias: veterinario, científico, médica, mujer de negocios
6. el servicio público: policía, cartera, política, cantante

▼5 Así es mi trabajo |

Escuchar • Escribir

Copia la tabla en una hoja de papel. Vas a escuchar a seis personas hablar de su trabajo. Escribe lo que escuchas sobre los estudios de cada persona, lo que hace en su trabajo y cuál es su profesión.

los estudios	lo que hace	su profesión

▼6 Una carrera en negocios internacionales

Leer • Escribir

Lee la historia de un hombre que ahora tiene una carrera en los negocios internacionales. Escoge y escribe las palabras apropiadas para completar la descripción de su preparación profesional y de su trabajo ahora.

colegio	programa de estudios
idioma	universidad
me gradué	

Hace nueve años __1.__ del colegio. Decidí asistir a la __2.__ para seguir un __3.__ en los negocios. Durante mis años en el __4.__ , estudié español y quería seguir estudiando este __5.__ en la universidad también. Por eso tomé clases avanzadas de español.

beneficio	me gano la vida
bilingüe	oficinas
hombre de negocios	salario

Soy __6.__ ahora y por eso conseguí un trabajo como __7.__ con una compañía internacional después de graduarme de la universidad. Uno de los buenos aspectos de mi carrera en los negocios internacionales es que __8.__ viajando a varios países de América del Sur durante el año. Otro __9.__ es que recibo un __10.__ muy bueno porque puedo comunicarme con los empleados que trabajan en nuestras __11.__ en estos países.

▼7 Los planes para el futuro | (Talk!)

Hablar

Con otro(a) estudiante, hablen de sus planes para el futuro.

▶ **Modelo**

A —*¿Piensas seguir una carrera en el mundo de las artes después de graduarte del colegio?*

B —*Posiblemente. Algún día me gustaría ser pintor(a).*

o: —*No, no quiero ser pintor(a). Quisiera ganarme la vida como ingeniero(a) en el futuro.*

1.

2.

3.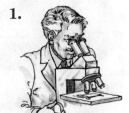

4.

5.

▼8 Las profesiones de mis amigos |

Escribir • Hablar

Piensa en las personas a quienes conoces. ¿Qué profesión tendrán ellos en el futuro?

❶ Para cada dibujo, escribe la profesión de la persona. Luego escribe el nombre de una persona a quien conoces que puede tener esta profesión en el futuro.

❷ Trabaja con otro(a) estudiante. Usen lo que escribieron y hablen sobre quiénes tendrán estas profesiones en el futuro.

▶ Modelo

A —¿Quién será *ingeniero* algún día?
B —*Mi primo Alejandro* será *ingeniero*. Le gusta mucho estudiar *matemáticas*.

1.

2.

3.

4.

5.

6.

▼9 Juego | 👥 | ♻

Escribir • Hablar

❶ Tu profesor(a) va a dividir a la clase en grupos de cuatro o cinco estudiantes. Va a decir una categoría de trabajo y cada grupo va a escribir diferentes carreras y profesiones para esta categoría.

❷ Cuando tu profesor(a) indica que no hay más tiempo, un grupo lee su lista en voz alta. El grupo recibe un punto por cada carrera o profesión que tiene y que otro grupo no tiene. Luego otro grupo lee las carreras o profesiones que no leyó el primer grupo. Van a seguir hasta no tener más carreras o profesiones diferentes.

❸ Luego el (la) profesor(a) les da otra categoría. El grupo con más puntos al final gana. Van a usar las listas de carreras y profesiones en la Actividad 10.

LOS VIAJES:
agente de
viajes
auxiliar de
vuelo
piloto
empleado de una
línea aérea
guía

▼Fondo Cultural | El mundo hispano

La educación básica en los países hispanohablantes incluye *(includes)* la educación preescolar, la primaria y la secundaria. Todos los jóvenes tienen que completarla; es decir, es obligatoria. La educación secundaria dura tres años (de los 13 a los 15 años). Luego sigue el bachillerato y los estudios medios profesionales. En la secundaria, muchos jóvenes aprenden un oficio *(trade)* relacionado con los servicios o la educación tecnológica.

• ¿Te parece similar o diferente la educación básica en los países hispanohablantes a cómo es en los Estados Unidos?

▼10 Se busca . . . | 👥 | ♻

Hablar • Escribir • Escuchar

Usa las listas de carreras y profesiones de la Actividad 9 para crear anuncios clasificados de un periódico en línea.

❶ Trabaja con otro(a) estudiante y escriban tres anuncios. Cada anuncio debe indicar el trabajo, describir lo que necesita hacer o saber la persona e indicar un beneficio del trabajo.

❷ Lean los anuncios clasificados a otro grupo, sin decir el trabajo que se busca. El otro grupo tiene que escuchar y decirles a Uds. la persona que se busca, según la descripción.

Modelo

Se busca secretario bilingüe. Debe tener experiencia trabajando en una oficina. Es necesario que hable inglés y español y que sepa usar la computadora. No hay que trabajar los fines de semana.

▼11 Y tú, ¿qué dices? | (Talk!)

Escribir • Hablar

1. Describe a un adulto a quien conoces bien. ¿Qué profesión tiene? ¿Se preparó para su carrera en la universidad? ¿En una escuela técnica? ¿Qué programa de estudios siguió?

2. ¿Qué vas a hacer después de graduarte del colegio? ¿Piensas asistir a la universidad o a una escuela técnica, o comenzar a trabajar?

3. ¿Te gustaría seguir una carrera militar? ¿Crees que hay beneficios de una carrera militar? ¿Cuáles son?

4. ¿Te interesa ser dueño(a) de tu propio negocio algún día? ¿Por qué?

▼ Pronunciación | 🔊 | (Talk!)

Diéresis

As you have seen, when *gu* is used before *e* and *i*, the *u* is silent. To indicate that the *u* is pronounced, it is written with a *diéresis* (ü). Listen to and say the following sentences:

Ramón **Gue**vara es bilin**güe**. Quiere se**guir** una carrera como **guí**a para los turistas extranjeros.

¡Compruébalo! Listen to the sentences as they are read. Complete the spelling of the words by adding *güe* or *güi*. ¡Ojo! In one case, you will also have to add a written accent mark to the *e* or *i*.

1. Un ave *(bird)* graciosa de la Antártida es el pin___no.
2. Si hablas sólo un idioma, eres monolin___.
3. El estudio de lenguaje *(language)* se llama la lin___stica.

¡Trabalenguas!

Gárgaras
Gla-gle-gli-glo-glu-güe-güi,
¡qué difícil es así!
Güi, güe, glu, glo, gli, gle, gla,
¡qué trabajo igual me da!

Gramática

The future tense

Another way to talk about future events is to use the future tense. The future tense expresses what will happen. To form the future tense of regular -*ar,* -*er,* and -*ir* verbs, use the same set of endings for all verbs and add them to the infinitive.

-é	-emos
-ás	-éis
-á	-án

(yo)	trabajaré seré viviré	(nosotros) (nosotras)	trabajaremos seremos viviremos
(tú)	trabajarás serás vivirás	(vosotros) (vosotras)	trabajaréis seréis viviréis
Ud. (él) (ella)	trabajará será vivirá	Uds. (ellos) (ellas)	trabajarán serán vivirán

¿Recuerdas?

You already know two ways to talk about future events.

Using the present tense:

• Mañana **comenzamos** el trabajo.
Tomorrow we begin work.

Using *ir* + *a* + infinitive:

• El futuro **va a ser** mejor.
The future is going to be better.

Note that all forms have a written accent mark except *nosotros(as).*

Mañana **comenzaremos** el trabajo.
Tomorrow we will begin work.

El futuro **será** mejor.
The future will be better.

| **Más ayuda** | **realidades.com** |

 GramActiva **Video**
Tutorials: Formation of regular future tense (Spanish), Formation of regular future tense (English)
Animated Verbs

 GramActiva **Activity**

▼12 Escucha y escribe | 🔊 _____

Escuchar • Escribir

Un estudiante va a escribir un artículo para el periódico de su escuela sobre los planes de los estudiantes que se graduarán del colegio este año. Escucha los planes de sus compañeros y escríbelos según el modelo.

Modelo

Escuchas: Voy a ir de vacaciones a Costa Rica.
Escribes: *Iré de vacaciones a Costa Rica.*

Estrategia

Using memory cues
To learn the endings for the future tense, remember the present-tense forms of *haber (he, has, ha, hemos, habéis, han).* The sound of these is identical for all forms except *vosotros(as).*

Haciendo deportes en las playas de Florida

▼13 ¿Y ustedes? | Talk!

Escribir • Hablar

En la Actividad 12, Uds. escucharon los planes de unos estudiantes después de terminar el año escolar. Ahora van a hablar sobre los planes de otras personas para el verano.

❶ Escribe frases sobre qué van a hacer estas personas.

Modelo

mi profesor(a) de . . .
Mi profesora de matemáticas tomará cursos en la universidad.

1. yo
2. mis amigos(as) y yo
3. muchos estudiantes
4. mi mejor amigo(a)

❷ Trabaja con otro(a) estudiante. Comparen sus ideas para el verano.

▶ **Modelo**

A —*Mi profesora de matemáticas tomará cursos en la universidad.*

B —*¿De veras? Mi profesor de español viajará por América Central.*

▼14 Las profesiones del futuro

Leer • Escribir

Lee el artículo del periódico y escribe qué van a hacer las personas en las profesiones del futuro.

Modelo

trabajar
Los técnicos médicos trabajarán en consultorios y hospitales.

• **Ciencias ambientales**[1]
Las compañías del futuro __1.__ *(entender)* que la planificación[2] y la conservación de nuestro planeta __2.__ *(ser)* esenciales.

• **Experto en turismo** La gran demanda de turismo pronto __3.__ *(resultar)* que no exista ninguna parte del planeta sin ser visitada. Los expertos en turismo __4.__ *(ayudar)* a los clientes a escoger las vacaciones apropiadas.

• **Ingeniero de robots**
Los robots __5.__ *(estar)* en nuestras casas y lugares de trabajo con más frecuencia. Por eso (nosotros) __6.__ *(necesitar)* miles de diseñadores y técnicos para crear y reparar las máquinas.[3]

• **Médico** Los ancianos __7.__ *(visitar)* a sus médicos con más frecuencia. Y los científicos __8.__ *(tratar)* de encontrar nuevas curas para las enfermedades que existen hoy en día.

[1]environmental   [2]planning   [3]machines

▼15 Y tú, ¿qué dices? |  Talk!

Escribir • Hablar

1. En tu opinión, de los cuatro grupos de profesiones mencionados en el artículo, ¿cuál será más importante? ¿Por qué?

2. Escoge uno de los cuatro grupos y escribe tres frases diciendo lo que las personas van a hacer en el futuro en estas carreras.

3. ¿Qué serás tú algún día? ¿Crees que tu profesión será tan importante en el futuro como es ahora? ¿Por qué?

Más práctica	GO	
realidades.com	print	
Instant Check	✔	
Guided WB pp. 321–322	✔	✔
Core WB p. 177	✔	✔
Comm. WB pp. 170, 173	✔	✔
Hispanohablantes WB pp. 334–337, 340		✔

Gramática

▼ Objectives

- Talk and write about future plans
- Make predictions

The future tense: irregular verbs

Irregular verbs in the future use the same endings as regular verbs, but the stems are irregular. Here are some irregular future stems:

hacer	har-	¿Qué clase de trabajo **hará** ella?
poder	podr-	En el futuro **podremos** usar el Internet para seguir más carreras.
saber	sabr-	¿**Sabrás** hablar más de dos idiomas en el futuro?
tener	tendr-	Algún día **tendré** un trabajo con un salario muy bueno.
haber	habr-	**Habrá** muchas oportunidades para usar el español en mi carrera.

¿Recuerdas?

Future-tense endings

-é	-emos
-ás	-éis
-á	-án

Más ayuda realidades.com

- ***GramActiva* Video**
- ***Canción de hip hop:*** *¿Qué profesión tendrás?*
- ***GramActiva* Activity**

▼16 Una carta de una amiga

Leer • Escribir

Dos chicas son muy buenas amigas, pero ya no viven en la misma ciudad. Las dos se graduaron y están haciendo sus planes para ir a la universidad. Lee la carta y escribe la forma apropiada de los verbos en el futuro.

Querida Manola:

¿Cómo estás? No puedo creer que por fin me gradué y que en agosto yo __1.__ (empezar) a estudiar en la universidad. Estoy muy emocionada. Todavía no sé qué clases tomaré, así que __2.__ (tener) que hablar primero con un representante de la universidad. Él __3.__ (saber) qué cursos debo tomar. Y tú, ¿has decidido a qué universidad __4.__ (asistir)? Claro que __5.__ (sentirse) triste si no puedes ir conmigo a la Universidad del Norte, pero si no, tú y yo __6.__ (poder) tomar las vacaciones juntas, ¿no? Bueno, nosotras __7.__ (tener) tiempo para hablar de eso en julio. ¡Estoy muy emocionada que vengas a visitarme! Tengo mucho que contarte, y ¡por supuesto __8.__ (haber) mucho que hacer! Estoy segura que nosotras __9.__ (hacer) muchas cosas con nuestras familias y por supuesto, ¡con los amigos también! Bueno, eso es todo por ahora. Escríbeme pronto.

Con cariño,

Mónica

▼17 La vida profesional

Escribir

Los consejeros *(counselors)* del colegio saben que los intereses que tienen los estudiantes mientras están en el colegio afectarán mucho a su vida profesional en el futuro. Lee la primera parte de lo que dicen y escribe el resultado usando un verbo del recuadro.

asistir	ganar	poder	tener
estudiar	ganarse la vida	ser	trabajar
enseñar	haber	seguir	usar

1. Si eres buen(a) estudiante de matemáticas, . . .
2. Si a los jóvenes les interesan mucho las ciencias sociales, . . .
3. Si a una persona le gusta dar discursos y sabe mucho de leyes, . . .
4. Si una persona trabaja ahora en una tienda, . . .
5. Si te gusta mucho trabajar al aire libre, . . .
6. Si un(a) estudiante tiene talento en música o drama, . . .

Nota

The future tense is often used with *si* + a present-tense verb.

- Si tenemos suficiente dinero, **podré** asistir a la universidad.

*If we have enough money, **I will be able** to attend the university.*

Modelo

Si te interesan mucho los animales, . . .
Si te interesan mucho los animales, podrás ser veterinaria algún día.

▼18 La vida en el campo | 👥

Hablar • Escribir

¿Cómo es la vida diaria en los pueblos pequeños? En esta pintura, Fausto Pérez muestra la vida diaria en un pueblo rural de su país.

1 Trabaja con otro(a) estudiante para escribir tres frases sobre el futuro de las personas que viven en este pueblo.

2 Lean sus frases a la clase y decidan qué grupo tiene las ideas más originales.

Modelo

Los agricultores trabajarán todos los días . . .

"El Granjero" by Fausto Pérez, 2009, mixed media

▼ Fondo Cultural | El Salvador

Fausto Pérez, un artista de El Salvador, vivió en una granja *(farm)* cuando era joven y pasó mucho tiempo al aire libre disfrutando de la naturaleza *(nature)* con sus abuelos. Ahora la vida sencilla del campo y las memorias de su niñez *(childhood)* son la inspiración para sus pinturas.

- ¿Expresa el pintor una actitud positiva o negativa hacia el pueblo rural en el cuadro? ¿Por qué piensas esto?

▼19 ¿Cómo será esta escuela?

Escribir • Hablar

Tienes que escoger los cursos para el año que viene. Tus amigos y tú tienen muchas preguntas para los profesores.

1 Escribe cinco preguntas que puedes hacerles a los profesores. Puedes usar verbos como *tener (que), poder, dar, permitir, haber, hacer, empezar, terminar, escribir* y *leer.*

2 Trabaja con otro(a) estudiante. Hagan los papeles de un(a) estudiante y un(a) profesor(a).

Modelo

¿Tendremos mucha tarea? ¿Podremos llevar gorras en la clase?

▶ **Modelo**

A —*¿Tendremos mucha tarea?*
B —*Sí, por supuesto que tendrán mucha tarea en la clase.*
o: —*No, pero tendrán que escuchar y trabajar en la clase.*

▼20 Un programa de televisión

Hablar • Escribir

A veces los programas de televisión parecen ser verdaderos y pensamos en lo que les pasará a nuestros personajes favoritos.

1 Piensa en dos o tres programas de televisión. Es mejor que escojas programas que cuentan alguna historia, como una telenovela o un programa de detectives. Busca a otro(a) estudiante en tu clase que conozca uno de los programas que has escogido.

2 Con tu compañero(a), escribe cinco predicciones sobre lo que pasará en este programa. Luego léeles las predicciones a otros grupos para ver si están de acuerdo con Uds.

Modelo

En la telenovela Días trágicos, *Raquel se casará con el hermano de su médico.*

▼21 Juego

Escribir • Hablar • GramActiva

1 Vas a recibir tres tiras *(strips)* de papel. En cada papel, escribe una frase sobre tu propio futuro.

Modelo

En diez años viviré en España.
Tendré una esposa y tres hijos.

2 Trabaja con un grupo de cuatro estudiantes. Todos van a poner sus papeles en una cesta. Saca una tira de papel y léela. Si es tu propio papel, devuélvelo a la cesta y saca otro. Pregúntale a otro(a) estudiante si él (ella) hará esto en el futuro.

Si contesta *sí* la primera vez, recibes cinco puntos. Si contesta *no*, pregunta a otro(a) estudiante y si contesta *sí*, recibes tres puntos y la persona que escribió la frase recibe cinco puntos. La persona con más puntos al final gana.

Modelo

Roberto, ¿vivirás en España en diez años?

▼22 Los niños que trabajan | 🧑‍🤝‍🧑 | ♻

Leer • Hablar

Lee la información sobre el Programa del Muchacho Trabajador en Ecuador.
Después trabaja con otro(a) estudiante y contesten las preguntas.

¿Sabías que en algunos países pobres muchos niños comienzan a trabajar a los ocho o diez años de edad?

El Programa del Muchacho Trabajador (PMT) en Ecuador fue fundado en 1983 para proteger y hacer efectivas las leyes sobre los derechos de los niños[1]. El PMT también ayuda a los niños y jóvenes que viven en condiciones de pobreza[2].

Los Espacios Alternativos que están en 29 barrios de ocho ciudades del país ofrecen un lugar seguro para los niños. Voluntarios del mundo entero vienen a ayudarlos. Alejandro Morales, por ejemplo, viene de México.

Él dice: "En este mundo hay muchas personas y hay que tratar de ayudar a que todas las personas lleguen al triunfo". Laura Soulié, una voluntaria de Argentina, afirma: "Odio la mentira, la violencia y la injusticia".

Las instituciones como el Programa del Muchacho Trabajador son muy importantes porque permiten establecer un mundo en el cual los niños pueden tener una vida mejor.

Muchos niños tienen que trabajar en las plantaciones de banano.

[1]children's rights
[2]poverty

1. ¿A qué edad comienzan a trabajar los niños en algunos países?

2. ¿Cómo ayuda a los niños el Programa del Muchacho Trabajador?

3. ¿Conoces otras instituciones como el PMT en los Estados Unidos o en otro país?

4. ¿Te gustaría trabajar como voluntario(a) en una de estas organizaciones? ¿Por qué?

▼23 Algunas soluciones | 🧑‍🤝‍🧑 | ♻

Escribir • Hablar

Imagina que eres el (la) presidente de una organización internacional. Tienes que sugerir soluciones para la situación de los niños trabajadores. Trabaja con otro(a) estudiante para escribir tres cosas que podremos hacer nosotros o que podrán hacer en Ecuador. Compartan sus ideas con la clase.

Modelo

1. *Construiremos más Espacios Alternativos para ayudar a los niños.*
2. *No compraremos productos hechos por compañías en las cuales trabajan niños.*

▼**24** **¿Qué harás en el futuro?** | 👥

Hablar • Pensar • Escribir

¿Qué profesión tendrás en el futuro? Haz una encuesta en la clase y suma los resultados para determinar cuáles son las profesiones más populares.

Conexiones | Las matemáticas

① Trabaja con un grupo de cuatro o cinco personas. Hagan una tabla con las profesiones indicadas. Indiquen el número de estudiantes del grupo que trabajará en cada profesión.

② Escriban una o dos frases sobre la tabla y compartan la información con la clase.

Modelo
Dos personas de nuestro grupo trabajarán en el mundo de la tecnología . . . y una persona es indecisa (undecided).

③ Reúnan las tablas de la clase y sumen entre todos el número de estudiantes que trabajará en cada profesión.

④ Hagan entre todos una gráfica circular *(pie chart)* para indicar el porcentaje *(percentage)* de estudiantes que trabajará en cada profesión. Expliquen la gráfica circular.

Modelo
El 33 por ciento de los estudiantes en la clase seguirán una carrera en la tecnología. Asistirán a la universidad o a una escuela técnica para ser ingenieros o diseñadores.

Profesiones	Número de estudiantes
Tecnología	✓✓
Técnica / Mecánica	
Artes	✓
Ciencias	
Negocios	✓
Derecho	
Música / Drama	
Servicio público	
Política	
Indecisos / Otros	✓

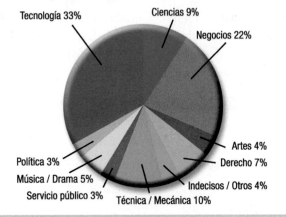

Tecnología 33% Ciencias 9% Negocios 22% Artes 4% Derecho 7% Indecisos / Otros 4% Técnica / Mecánica 10% Servicio público 3% Música / Drama 5% Política 3%

▼ Fondo Cultural | El mundo hispano

Los centros de educación superior en América Latina y España están muy diversificados. Después de graduarse del colegio, los estudiantes pueden continuar sus estudios en la universidad para graduarse como abogados, arquitectos, ingenieros o médicos. Los estudiantes que desean ser maestros pueden continuar sus estudios en las Escuelas Normales o de Magisterio y los que quieren ser técnicos en computación o enfermería asisten a las Escuelas Politécnicas. Los que quieren ser artistas pueden estudiar en los conservatorios y las escuelas de drama.

• Si quieres continuar los estudios después de graduarte del colegio, ¿qué opciones hay en la región donde vives?

▼25 En la exposición de carreras |

Escribir • Hablar

Imaginen que Uds. asisten a la exposición de carreras.

1 Con otro(a) estudiante, escriban preguntas que los jóvenes pueden hacerles a los adultos sobre la universidad o las escuelas técnicas, las carreras, el salario y otra información.

Modelo

¿Tendremos que asistir a la universidad si queremos seguir una carrera en la música?

2 Formen un grupo de cuatro estudiantes. Una pareja de los jóvenes hace las preguntas y los adultos tienen que contestarlas. Después cambien papeles.

Una exposición de carreras en una escuela secundaria

▼26 Y tú, ¿qué dices? |

Escribir • Hablar

1. ¿Qué clases tienes ahora? ¿Crees que estudiarás estas materias en la universidad? ¿Por qué?

2. ¿Has pensado en qué profesión tendrás en el futuro? ¿Cómo será? ¿Podrás ganar un buen salario? ¿Qué otros beneficios habrá?

3. ¿Qué cosas hay hoy en día que no habrá en el futuro? ¿Qué cosas habrá que no existen ahora?

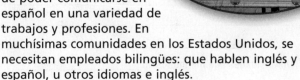

El español en la comunidad

Ya sabes la importancia de poder comunicarse en español en una variedad de trabajos y profesiones. En muchísimas comunidades en los Estados Unidos, se necesitan empleados bilingües: que hablen inglés y español, u otros idiomas e inglés.

• ¿En qué trabajos o profesiones en tu comunidad es necesario ser bilingüe? ¿Qué idiomas se hablan en tu comunidad?

Más práctica GO

realidades.com | print

Instant Check	✔	
Guided WB pp. 323–324	✔	✔
Core WB pp. 178–179	✔	✔
Comm. WB pp. 171, 174, 283	✔	✔
***Hispanohablantes* WB**		
pp. 338–339, 341		✔

Lectura

¿Qué vas a hacer después de graduarte?
Visita un centro de carreras para decidir.

Estrategia

Using heads and subheads
You can quickly learn what an article or brochure is about by reading the heads and subheads. Quickly read the heads in the following brochure to find out what information is provided.

¡Descubre tu futuro!

El Centro de Carreras les ofrece servicios e información a todos los estudiantes de nuestra comunidad que desean ir a la universidad. Nosotros pensamos que todos los jóvenes que tienen este sueño[1] deben tener la oportunidad de hacerlo.

Los estudiantes que vienen al centro pueden . . .

* crear y mantener un portafolio personal de las notas y actividades escolares
* buscar información sobre cientos de universidades del país
* investigar diferentes carreras y explorar las opciones
* asistir a presentaciones sobre cómo financiar los estudios
* buscar y solicitar becas,[2] ayuda financiera y préstamos[3]
* recibir información sobre distintos planes de ahorro[4]
* conversar con consejeros[5] que hablan español

El portafolio personal es una carpeta con toda tu información académica del colegio. Después de terminar las clases y recibir las notas, escribe la información en tu portafolio. El portafolio te ayudará cuando completes las solicitudes[6] universitarias porque tendrás toda la información necesaria en un sólo lugar.

Nombre: _____

Dirección: _____

Clases y Notas

Grado:

9 _____

10 _____

11 _____

12 _____

Intereses extracurriculares: _____

_____

_____

_____

Universidades que me interesan: _____

_____

_____

[1]dream [2]scholarships [3]loans [4]savings [5]counselors [6]fill out applications

Una prueba de aptitud puede ayudarte a encontrar la mejor profesión para ti. Lo primero que debes hacer es determinar tu personalidad. Lee las siguientes descripciones. ¿Cuál te describe?

✳ Personalidad

a. realista
b. investigadora
c. artística
d. sociable
e. emprendedora[7]
f. analítica

✳ Te gusta . . .

a. trabajar con animales, máquinas[8] y herramientas.[9]
b. estudiar y resolver problemas de ciencias o de matemáticas.
c. participar en actividades creativas como el arte, el teatro y la música.
d. hacer cosas con otras personas.
e. ser el líder.
f. trabajar con números y máquinas de manera ordenada.

✳ Prefieres . . .

a. cosas prácticas que se pueden tocar y ver.
b. las ciencias.
c. actividades creativas.
d. enseñar o ayudar a otras personas.
e. la política y los negocios.
f. el éxito en los negocios.

✳ Evitas[10] . . .

a. situaciones sociales.
b. ser el líder.
c. actividades repetitivas.
d. las máquinas, los animales y las herramientas.
e. actividades científicas.
f. actividades desordenadas.

Profesiones

Para saber la carrera más relacionada a tus gustos e intereses, revisa tus respuestas. Haz la suma para ver qué letra marcaste más y compara este resultado con la siguiente información. Si marcaste dos letras diferentes o más, puede ser que tengas aptitud para varias carreras.

✳ Si marcaste más la letra *a*, debes ser ingeniero(a) o arquitecto(a).

✳ Si marcaste más la letra *b*, debes ser científico(a) o médico(a).

✳ Si marcaste más la letra *c*, debes ser actor o actriz o diseñador(a) de ropa.

✳ Si marcaste más la letra *d*, debes ser profesor(a) o enfermero(a).

✳ Si marcaste más la letra *e*, debes ser vendedor(a) o abogado(a).

✳ Si marcaste más la letra *f*, debes ser contador(a) o cajero(a).

---

[7]enterprising   [8]machines   [9]tools   [10]You avoid

¿Comprendiste?

1. ¿Qué es un centro de carreras? ¿Qué servicios ofrece?

2. ¿Qué información debes incluir en tu portafolio personal?

3. ¿Para qué sirve una prueba de aptitud?

Más práctica GO	realidades.com | print
Guided WB p. 325	✔ ✔
Comm. WB pp. 175, 284	✔ ✔
Hispanohablantes **WB** pp. 342–343	✔
Cultural Reading Activity	✔

Y tú, ¿qué dices?

1. ¿Crees que una visita a un centro de carreras sería útil *(would be useful)* para ti? ¿Por qué?

2. ¿Cuál es tu profesión ideal según la prueba? ¿Crees que tiene razón la prueba? Si no, ¿qué te gustaría cambiar para mejorarla?

La cultura en vivo

Los artistas *naif*

Hay un grupo de artistas en los países hispanohablantes que producen arte de origen campesino[1]. Este estilo se conoce como arte *naif*, arte ingenuo o arte campesino. Generalmente los artistas *naif* no tienen una educación artística académica. Sus obras están relacionadas con escenas de la vida rural y los trabajos del campo. Las imágenes son sencillas, espontáneas y llenas de fantasía. Algunas veces los artistas y artesanos añaden los materiales que usan en su trabajo o también productos de la naturaleza, como flores secas, piedras, conchas[2] y pedazos de madera[3].

"Targelia, Christmas Eve" (1990), Julio Toaquiza
Photo courtesy of the Art Archive / Picture Desk, Kobal Collection.

Objetivo

Hacer una pintura[4] imitando el estilo de los artistas *naif*.

Materiales

Busca materiales sencillos, objetos de la naturaleza o cosas que usas en tus actividades diarias. Quizás necesites pintura y pincel[5].

Instrucciones

1 Estudia los cuadros de las artesanías en esta página. Piensa en sus características.

2 Escoge una escena que quieres pintar.

3 ¡Recuerda! Los artistas *naif* usan ideas sencillas.

4 Antes de empezar el trabajo, haz un dibujo del proyecto.

Opciones

Puedes mostrar el trabajo en clase y explicar qué características del arte *naif* has usado, qué representa tu trabajo y por qué escogiste ese tema.

"Paisaje" (1984), Patricia Tobaldo

[1]peasant [2]shells [3]wood [4]painting [5]paintbrush

Presentación oral

Mi vida hoy y en el futuro

Task
Prepare a presentation about the jobs you expect to have in the future, based on your current interests.

1 Prepare Think about your life today: favorite subjects in school, what you do for fun, jobs that appeal to you. Then think about how these interests might influence your future job choices. Make a chart to organize your thoughts.

	Ahora	En el futuro
cursos favoritos	las matemáticas y el arte	diseñadora en una escuela técnica
diversiones	trabajo en la computadora	crearé diseños nuevos

Estrategia

Using charts
Create a chart to help you think through the key information you want to talk about. This will help you speak more effectively.

2 Practice Rehearse your presentation. You can use your notes in practice, but not when you present. Try to:

- provide as much information as you can
- use complete sentences
- speak clearly

Modelo
Ahora mis cursos favoritos son . . .
Estudiaré para ser . . .

3 Present Tell the audience about your interests today and how they will impact your job choices in the future.

4 Evaluation The following rubric will be used to grade your presentation.

Rubric	Score 1	Score 3	Score 5
How complete your preparation is	You provide the information but not the chart.	You provide the information, but the chart is only partially completed.	You provide the information and a completed chart.
Amount of information communicated	You include one of the following: classes, leisure activities, potential jobs.	You include two of the following: classes, leisure activities, potential jobs.	You include all of the following: classes, leisure activities, potential jobs.
How easily you are understood	You are difficult to understand and make many grammatical errors.	You are fairly easy to understand and make occasional grammatical errors.	You are easy to understand and make very few grammatical errors.

Repaso del capítulo

Vocabulario y gramática

to talk about professions in science and technology

el agricultor, la agricultora	farmer
el arquitecto, la arquitecta	architect
el científico, la científica	scientist
el diseñador, la diseñadora	designer
el ingeniero, la ingeniera	engineer
el mecánico, la mecánica	mechanic
el técnico, la técnica	technician
el veterinario, la veterinaria	veterinarian

to talk about professions in business

el cartero, la cartera	mail carrier
el contador, la contadora	accountant
el dueño, la dueña	owner
el / la gerente	manager
el hombre de negocios	businessman
la mujer de negocios	businesswoman
los negocios	business
el secretario, la secretaria	secretary

to talk about professions in the arts

las artes	the arts
el / la artista	artist
el escritor, la escritora	writer
el pintor, la pintora	painter

For *Vocabulario adicional,* see pp. 498–499.

to talk about professions in law and politics

el abogado, la abogada	lawyer
el derecho	*(study of)* law
el juez, la jueza, *pl.* los jueces	judge
la ley	law
la política	politics
el político, la política	politician

to talk about the future

algún día	someday
los beneficios	benefits
bilingüe	bilingual
la carrera	career
el colegio	high school
la escuela técnica	technical school
el futuro	future
ganarse la vida	to make a living
la graduación	graduation
graduarse *(u → ú)*	to graduate
habrá	there will be
el idioma	language
militar	military
la oficina	office
la profesión, *pl.* las profesiones	profession
el programa de estudios	course of studies
el salario	salary
seguir *(e → i)* (una carrera)	to pursue (a career)
la universidad	university

the future tense: irregular verbs

haber	habr-
hacer	har-
poder	podr-
saber	sabr-
tener	tendr-

future-tense endings

-é	-emos
-ás	-éis
-á	-án

Más repaso GO realidades.com | print

Instant Check	✔
Puzzles	✔
Core WB pp. 180–181	✔
Comm. WB p. 285	✔ ✔

Preparación para el examen

On the exam you will be asked to . . .	Here are practice tasks similar to those you will find on the exam . . .	For review go to your print or digital textbook . . .

Interpretive

 ① Escuchar Listen and understand as people talk about their future plans

At the Senior Send-off Assembly, some graduating seniors are asked what they will do after they graduate. Listen and identify: (a) what they will do next year; (b) what professions they will pursue; and (c) what they think their salary will be.

pp. 452–455 *Vocabulario en contexto*
p. 456 Actividad 5
p. 459 Actividad 10
p. 460 Actividad 12

Interpersonal

 ② Hablar Talk to incoming students about what high school will be like in your school

You volunteer to help incoming Spanish-speaking students enroll for classes. How would you describe what high school will be like for them? You could talk about: (a) classes; (b) extracurricular activities; and (c) advice on how to meet new people. Give as many details as you can.

p. 458 Actividad 8
p. 459 Actividad 11
p. 464 Actividades 19–21
p. 466 Actividad 24
p. 467 Actividad 25
p. 471 *Presentación oral*

Interpretive

 ③ Leer Read and understand notes sent to graduating seniors about their future

On the inside of Miguel's graduation card is a note from his mother. As you read it, determine what she predicts college will be like for him.

p. 461 Actividad 14
p. 462 Actividad 16
pp. 468–469 *Lectura*

Querido hijo:

El año que viene irás a la universidad. Tú y tus amigos comenzarán una vida nueva en la universidad y tendrán oportunidades de conocer a gente interesante. Tu padre y yo sabemos que sacarás buenas notas.

Con mucho amor,

Mamá

Presentational

 ④ Escribir Write about your future plans

As part of an application for a summer job, you are asked to write a short paragraph about your future career plans. For example, you might include: *Estudiaré en la universidad por seis años para prepararme para ser veterinario(a).*

p. 458 Actividad 8
p. 460 Actividad 12
p. 461 Actividades 13–14
p. 462 Actividad 16
p. 463 Actividades 17–18
p. 467 Actividades 25–26

Cultures

 ⑤ Pensar Demonstrate an understanding of folk art from Spanish-speaking countries

A classmate is going on a trip to South America. Your teacher asks the student to bring back typical handicrafts from the countries she visits. Based on what you have learned in this chapter, what would you expect the student to bring back?

p. 470 *La cultura en vivo*

▼ Chapter Objectives

Communication

By the end of this chapter you will be able to:

- Listen and read about the environment and predictions about the future
- Talk and write about your impact on the environment and recommendations to protect it
- Exchange information about what you will do to improve the environment

Culture

You will also be able to:

- Understand efforts to protect natural resources in the Spanish-speaking world
- Compare ways the environment is protected and harmed in Spanish-speaking countries and in the U.S.

You will demonstrate what you know and can do:

- Presentación escrita, p. 495
- Preparación para el examen, p. 497

You will use:

Vocabulary

- The planet Earth
- Energy
- The environment

Grammar

- The future tense: other irregular verbs
- The present subjunctive with expressions of doubt

Exploración del mundo hispano

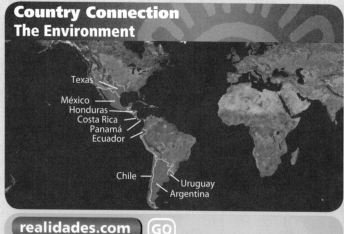

Country Connection
The Environment

Texas
México
Honduras
Costa Rica
Panamá
Ecuador
Chile
Uruguay
Argentina

 realidades.com GO

 Reference Atlas

▶ *Videocultura y actividad*

Mapa global interactivo

Un ocelote en un árbol, Costa Rica

Arte y cultura

| Estados Unidos | México

Alfredo Arreguín nació en Michoacán, México, en 1935. Desde 1958 ha vivido en Seattle, donde estudió arte en la Universidad de Washington. Muchos de sus cuadros tienen elementos de la cultura de su país nativo y de la naturaleza de la región donde vive actualmente *(currently)*. Las garzas *(herons)* viven cerca del agua. Habitan en los Estados Unidos y también en México.

• Cuando miras este cuadro, ¿qué te hace sentir el artista?

"Las garzas" (2002), Alfredo Arreguín ▼
Oil on canvas, 42 x 60 in. Courtesy of Alfredo Arreguín.

Read, listen to, and understand information about
▶ what the world may be like in the future
▶ problems facing the environment
▶ solutions for problems in our environment

Vocabulario en contexto

❝La destrucción de nuestro **medio ambiente** afecta a cada persona. Tenemos que **luchar contra** este problema **grave.**

Para la salud de la gente de nuestro pueblo, hay que **eliminar** la contaminación del aire y del agua.

la contaminación

el aire **contaminado**

el pueblo

el agua **contaminada**

la calefacción solar

Tenemos que **reducir*** el uso de **la electricidad** y usar otras **fuentes** de **energía.**

Debemos **proteger*** a los animales que están **en peligro de extinción.**

la paz

Para **mejorar** la situación del mundo es necesario **resolver*** los problemas entre los países. Es importante que **haya** paz y que no haya **guerra❞.**

*Reducir has a *c → zc* spelling change in the *yo* form of the present tense.

*Proteger is a regular *-er* verb with a spelling change in the *yo* form of the present tense: *protejo.*

*Resolver has an *o → ue* stem change in the present tense.

¡**HAY** MUCHAS **MANERAS** EN QUE UDS. PUEDEN AYUDAR A PROTEGER LA BELLEZA DE NUESTRA **NATURALEZA** . . .

• • • EN **EL ESPACIO!**

EN **LAS SELVAS TROPICALES!**

EN **LOS BOSQUES!**

EN **LOS DESIERTOS!**

la Luna

la planta

la colina

la Tierra

el valle

66**Júntense** con amigos y participen en uno de los grupos **ecológicos** de nuestra comunidad hoy99.

1 En las noticias | 🔊))

Escuchar

Escucha lo que dice el señor del grupo ecológico en la página 476. Señala con el dedo qué parte de la escena se describe.

2 ¿Cierta o falsa? | 🔊))

Escuchar

En una hoja de papel, escribe los números del 1 al 7. Si la frase que escuchas es cierta, escribe *C*. Si es falsa, escribe *F*.

Más práctica (GO)

realidades.com | print

Instant Check	✔	
Guided WB pp. 327–332	✔	✔
Core WB pp. 182–183	✔	✔
Comm. WB p. 181	✔	✔
Hispanohablantes WB p. 352		✔

¡Caramba, qué calor!

Hoy hace mucho calor en San Antonio. Lee la historia para saber qué hacen Esteban y Pedro.

Estrategia

Recognizing cognates
Before you read the *Videohistoria,* focus on the boldfaced words.

• Which of these words are cognates? Can you find other cognates that have not been boldfaced?

1

Esteban: ¿Qué pasa?

Pedro: No sé, pero creo que no tenemos **aire acondicionado.**

Esteban: ¿Cómo? ¿Con este calor? Imposible. Mamá, ¿qué pasa con el aire acondicionado?

Esteban   Angélica   Pedro

5

6

7

Pedro: Esteban, ¿no te gustaría tener el aire acondicionado solar?

Esteban: ¿Por qué?

Pedro: Pues, **conserva** energía y reduce el uso de la electricidad. Debemos usar mejor lo que ya tenemos. ¿Ves? El autobús es muy **eficiente.**

Esteban: Sí, **es cierto.** También es **económico.**

Pedro: El aire contaminado es un problema grave. Para tener aire más **puro** debemos montar en bicicleta.

Esteban: Sí, pero con tanto calor el coche es más cómodo y más rápido.

Pedro: ¡Ay, Esteban, pero así podemos **ahorrar** energía y dinero al mismo tiempo!

Esteban: ¿No **funciona** el aire acondicionado?

Cajera: No, y dudo que funcione mañana tampoco.

Angélica: ¿Qué necesitas, Esteban? Mamá no está.

Esteban: Pues, parece que el aire acondicionado está mal. No lo oigo. ¿Puedes ver lo que pasa?

Angélica: ¡Por supuesto que no! Hazlo tú. **Además,** ¡no hace tanto calor!

Pedro: ¡Silencio! Yo mismo voy a ver lo que pasa.

Pedro: Me parece que el aire acondicionado se rompió. **Dudo que sea** la electricidad.

Esteban: No podemos quedarnos aquí. ¿Por qué no vamos al cine? Angélica, ¿nos puedes llevar en el coche?

Angélica: Bueno, pero tendrán que esperar media hora. Tengo que terminar algo.

Pedro: ¿Por qué no caminamos? El cine no está muy lejos.

Esteban: Sí, Angélica. Aquí, Esteban. Oye, ¿nos puedes venir a recoger en tu coche?

Angélica: ¡Esteban!

▼3 ¿Comprendiste?

Escribir • Hablar

1. ¿Dónde están los jóvenes? ¿Cuál es el problema?

2. ¿Quién piensa que hace mucho calor, Angélica o Esteban?

3. ¿Adónde deciden ir Pedro y Esteban? ¿Cómo van a ir?

4. Según Pedro, ¿por qué es bueno usar el aire acondicionado solar?

5. Según Pedro, ¿qué pueden hacer para no crear más contaminación del aire?

6. ¿Qué pasa cuando Pedro y Esteban llegan al cine? ¿Qué solución tiene Esteban?

Más práctica GO

realidades.com | print

Instant Check	✔	
Guided WB pp. 333–336	✔	✔
Core WB pp. 184–185	✔	✔
Comm. WB pp. 176–178, 179	✔	✔
Hispanohablantes **WB** p. 353		✔

▼ Objectives

▶ Talk about nature
▶ Discuss ways to protect the environment
▶ Listen to descriptions of nature
▶ Write about nature and the environment

Vocabulario en uso

▼4 Descripciones del medio ambiente |

Escuchar • Escribir

Escucha las descripciones del medio ambiente. En una hoja de papel, escribe los números del 1 al 8. Escribe el nombre de lo que está describiendo.

Modelo

Escuchas: Es un lugar donde llueve mucho y donde hay muchos árboles y plantas.
Escribes: *la selva tropical*

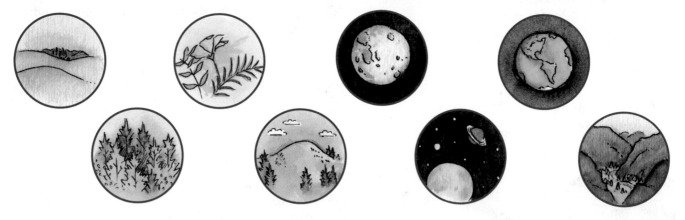

▼5 ¿Dónde se encuentra . . . ? |

Hablar

Para cada dibujo de la Actividad 4, piensa en dónde se encuentra este aspecto del medio ambiente. Puede estar cerca de tu comunidad, en un país hispanohablante que has estudiado o en el espacio. Habla con otro(a) estudiante sobre los lugares.

▶ **Modelo**

A —¿*Dónde se encuentran* <u>*desiertos*</u>?
B —*Hay* <u>*desiertos*</u> *en* <u>*Chile*</u>.

El desierto de Atacama, en Chile

▼6 Las analogías | ♻

Leer • Pensar • Escribir

Completa cada analogía según el modelo.
Usa las palabras del recuadro.

Modelo
flor : jardín :: árbol : *bosque*

ahorrar	económico	guerra
calefacción	energía	luchar
dudar	espacio	

1. resolver : problema :: conservar : _____
2. volver : regresar :: pelear : _____
3. llegar : salir :: gastar : _____
4. verano : aire acondicionado :: invierno : _____
5. puro : contaminado :: paz : _____
6. añadir : eliminar :: creer : _____
7. océano : la Tierra :: la Luna : _____
8. quizás : tal vez :: barato : _____

▼7 Una reunión del club de ecología | ♻

Leer • Escribir

Un estudiante asistió a una reunión del club de ecología.
Tomó apuntes *(notes)* para después escribir un artículo para
el periódico. Escribe los verbos que completan las frases.

Modelo
*Para resolver los problemas
ecológicos, hay que tener leyes
estrictas.*

1. Tendremos que hacer leyes más estrictas para _____ (luchar / mejorar) el medio ambiente.

2. Si reciclamos las latas, los periódicos y el cartón, podemos _____ (reducir / conservar) la basura que está en el mundo.

3. Si queremos vivir en un mundo limpio, debemos _____ (eliminar / mejorar) la destrucción del medio ambiente.

4. Es importante _____ (luchar / mejorar) contra la destrucción de las selvas tropicales.

5. Las leyes que protegen la naturaleza no pueden _____ (reducir / funcionar) si no las obedecemos.

6. Todos deben _____ (juntarse / dudar) con otras personas para participar en una organización que trabaja por la protección del medio ambiente.

Fondo Cultural | Argentina | Chile

Los pingüinos *(penguins)* de la Patagonia, una región al
sur de Argentina y Chile, comen peces. Están amenazados
(threatened) por la pesca excesiva y la contaminación de la
industria petrolera. Antes los buques petroleros *(oil tankers)*
descargaban *(unloaded)* en el mar el agua de lastre *(ballast)*
sucia, y la contaminación petrolera causó la muerte de más de
40,000 pingüinos al año. Ahora, para proteger a los pingüinos,
los buques petroleros pasan por rutas más alejadas de la costa.

• ¿Qué impacto tienen las industrias de tu comunidad en el
medio ambiente?

Pingüinos magallánicos, Argentina

▼8 Un artículo para el periódico

Leer • Escribir

cierto	eficiente
contaminado	grave
ecológico	puro
económico	solar

El estudiante de la Actividad 7 ha comenzado a escribir su artículo. Completa el párrafo con las formas apropiadas de los adjetivos en el recuadro.

Tenemos una situación __1.__ en nuestro pueblo. Los ríos y lagos están __2.__ y cada día mueren más peces. Si no reducimos la contaminación, no habrá ni agua __3.__ para beber ni aire para respirar. ¿Cómo podemos resolver estos problemas? Primero, los científicos deben buscar otras fuentes de energía __4.__, como la calefacción __5.__. Segundo, debemos usar nuestros coches menos y usar el transporte público más. Es mejor para el medio ambiente y más __6.__. Tercero, podemos trabajar en alguna organización __7.__ que trata de conservar el medio ambiente. Es __8.__ que nuestra comunidad tiene un problema, pero si luchamos juntos, podemos resolverlo.

▼9 ¿Cómo se puede . . . ? |

Hablar

Habla con otro(a) estudiante sobre lo que se puede hacer para conservar el medio ambiente.

▶ Modelo

A —¿*Cómo se puede reducir la basura?*
B —*Se puede reciclar las botellas de vidrio y de plástico.*

Estudiante A

1. proteger — la electricidad
2. resolver — el medio ambiente
3. conservar — a los animales en peligro de extinción
4. mejorar — energía
5. ahorrar — el problema de la contaminación del agua
6. salvar — la condición de la Tierra

Estudiante B

luchar contra la destrucción de . . .
reciclar . . .
no usar el coche y . . .
apagar . . .

no tirar basura en . . .
buscar . . .
juntarse con . . .
eliminar . . .

▼ Exploración del lenguaje

Antonyms

You have learned many ways to increase your vocabulary. One of these is learning words as antonym, or opposite, pairs. Write the antonyms for the following words:

puro ≠ __?__   aire acondicionado ≠ __?__

falso ≠ __?__   construcción ≠ __?__

¡Compruébalo! Here is a series of popular *refranes* using *Más vale* ("It's better, worth more"). Complete each *refrán* with the antonym of the word in bold type.

Más vale uno en **paz** que ciento en _____.

Más vale **antes** que _____.

Más vale **algo** que _____.

Más vale perro **vivo** que león _____.

▼10 Animales en peligro de extinción

Leer • Escribir • Hablar

Según los científicos en México, más del 20 por ciento de los animales del país están en peligro de extinción. A causa de la contaminación, la destrucción de su hábitat y la caza *(hunting)*, animales como el oso negro, la ballena *(whale)* gris, la tortuga marina y muchos más podrán desaparecer si no se encuentran soluciones a este grave problema ecológico.[1] En 2002, el Banco de México anunció un programa que podrá ayudar a los animales. Lee el anuncio y contesta las preguntas.

1. Según los científicos, ¿por qué están en peligro de extinción algunos animales en México?

2. ¿Qué programa ofrece el Banco de México? ¿Qué piensas del programa?

3. ¿Te gustaría comprar una moneda? ¿Por qué?

[1]Fuente: *El Universal*, 25 de agosto de 2002

¡Ayuda a proteger el medio ambiente!

Monedas y especies

El Banco de México presenta su colección exclusiva de doce monedas de plata con imágenes de animales en peligro de extinción en México. Con cada moneda que Ud. compra, el Banco de México dona[2] dinero a proyectos de conservación del medio ambiente.

De venta en:
Banamex
Bital
Bancomer
BanRegio

[2]donates

▼Fondo Cultural | Panamá

El Parque Nacional Darién, en el Panamá, es el parque nacional más grande de América Central. Fue creado en 1980 para proteger la gran selva tropical del Darién, que se encuentra en la frontera entre el Panamá y Colombia. Hay siete especies de mamíferos y cinco especies de pájaros que sólo viven en esta selva. Además, tres grupos indígenas precolombinos todavía viven en el Darién: los kunas, los emberá y los wounaan.

• ¿Hay un parque cerca de tu comunidad creado para proteger y conservar la naturaleza? Descríbelo.

Un águila arpía, ave nacional del Panamá

▼11 Y tú, ¿qué dices? | (Talk!) _____

Escribir • Hablar

1. Describe la naturaleza que existe cerca de tu comunidad. ¿Te gusta estar afuera?

2. ¿Dónde prefieres pasar tiempo: en un bosque, en una selva tropical o en un desierto? Explica por qué.

3. ¿Cuáles son los peores problemas ecológicos de tu región? ¿Cómo se puede mejorar la situación?

4. Además de la electricidad, ¿qué otras fuentes de energía se usan en tu región? ¿Son eficientes y económicas? ¿El uso de estas fuentes de energía conserva o destruye el medio ambiente?

Gramática

The future tense: other irregular verbs

Other verbs that have irregular stems in the future tense are:

decir	dir-
poner	pondr-
querer	querr-
salir	saldr-
venir	vendr-

En el futuro **dirán** que la destrucción de las selvas tropicales causó muchos problemas ecológicos.
*In the future **they will say** that the destruction of the rain forests caused many ecological problems.*

Pondremos más plantas en nuestra casa.
***We will put** more plants in our house.*

Querremos luchar contra la guerra y por la paz.
***We will want** to fight against war and for peace.*

Saldré muy temprano por la mañana. ¿**Vendrás** conmigo?
***I will leave** very early in the morning. **Will you come** with me?*

¿Recuerdas?

You know how to form irregular verbs in the future using the same endings that you use for regular verbs *(-é, -ás, -á, -emos, -éis, -án)*. You already know these irregular verbs:

haber	**habr-**
hacer	**har-**
poder	**podr-**
saber	**sabr-**
tener	**tendr-**

Más ayuda **realidades.com**

GramActiva Video
Tutorial: Verbs with irregular stems in future tense

GramActiva Activity

▼12 Escucha y escribe | ♲ | ◀))

Escuchar • Escribir

Unos jóvenes hablan de sus experiencias como voluntarios en un centro de reciclaje. Hablan de lo que ocurre siempre y de lo que ocurrirá en el futuro. Escucha las seis frases y escríbelas. Después escribe *presente* si ocurre ahora o *futuro* si ocurrirá en el futuro.

Contenedores de reciclaje

▼13 Vamos al centro de reciclaje

Leer • Escribir

Lee la conversación entre dos jóvenes que van a trabajar en el centro de reciclaje. Escribe la forma correcta de los verbos en el futuro.

Angélica: Oye, Pedro. El sábado voy al centro de reciclaje. ¿ __1.__ (Venir) tú conmigo?

Pedro: Está bien. __2.__ (Ir) contigo pero sólo tengo dos horas. ¿Qué __3.__ (hacer) nosotros?

Angélica: Primero nosotros __4.__ (tener) que llevar estas cajas al centro. Luego __5.__ (poner) los periódicos, el cartón y el vidrio en sus cajas.

Pedro: Y si no podemos quedarnos por más de dos horas, ¿qué les __6.__ (decir)?

Angélica: La verdad. Yo les __7.__ (decir) que tengo que estudiar. Y tú __8.__ (poder) salir al mismo tiempo. No __9.__ (haber) ningún problema.

Fondo Cultural | Ecuador

El ecoturismo en el Ecuador Hay varias compañías de ecoturismo que ofrecen excursiones que benefician al medio ambiente y a las comunidades que los turistas visitan. Por ejemplo, en el Ecuador los turistas visitan la región del Amazonas y se quedan en casas típicas de la región. Esto no causa problemas para el medio ambiente. Además, los guías son indígenas de la región y con las excursiones ganan dinero para sus comunidades.

• ¿Cómo pueden causar problemas los turistas y el turismo en una región de mucha belleza ecológica? Compara las excursiones ecológicas que puedes hacer en Ecuador con las que puedes hacer en los Estados Unidos.

Selva tropical en la región amazónica del Ecuador

▼14 El turismo | | ♻

Hablar

Unos amigos tratan de decidir adónde irán de vacaciones, pero es difícil decidir porque no están de acuerdo. Con otro(a) estudiante, pregunta y contesta según el modelo.

▶ Modelo

A —*Saldremos en julio. Iremos a la ciudad. ¿De acuerdo?*

B —*Pero nos dirán que no hay habitaciones libres.*

julio

Estudiante A

1. junio   2. octubre

3. agosto   4. julio

Estudiante B

a. Miles de turistas *(estar)* allí. Todos *(ponerse)* los trajes de baño y *(venir)* a la playa.

b. Las plantas y los árboles *(ser)* muy bonitos pero *(haber)* muchos mosquitos y moscas y *(llover)* todos los días.

c. *(Hacer)* demasiado calor. Además el aire *(ser)* muy seco. *(Querer)* encontrar un lugar con aire acondicionado.

d. No *(saber)* si *(hacer)* frío o calor. *(Querer)* dar caminatas pero no *(poder)* si hay mucha nieve en los valles.

▼15 En el presente y en el futuro | 👥

Hablar • Escribir

¿Crees que tu vida en el futuro será muy diferente de tu vida ahora?

yo (ahora)	yo (futuro)	mi compañero(a) (ahora)	mi compañero(a) (futuro)
en una tienda de descuentos	en una oficina de abogados		

❶ Trabaja con otro(a) estudiante. Copia la tabla en una hoja de papel. Para cada verbo del recuadro, escribe la información que describe tu vida ahora y cómo crees que será en el futuro. Después escribe las respuestas de tu compañero(a).

> ▶ **Modelo**
>
> **A** —*Ahora trabajo en una tienda de descuentos. En el futuro, trabajaré en una oficina de abogados. ¿Y tú?*
> **B** —*Ahora trabajo . . .*

querer

saber (+ *infinitive*)

salir con

tener que

vivir

¡Respuesta personal!

❷ Escribe cinco frases para describir las semejanzas (*similarities*) o diferencias entre la vida de tu compañero(a) ahora y su vida en el futuro.

▼16 ¿Qué resultará? | 👥

Escribir • Hablar

¿Qué resultará de las situaciones que existen ahora? Usa los verbos del recuadro para escribir un posible resultado para cada situación. Luego, con otro(a) estudiante, compara los resultados que han escrito. ¿Son muy similares o muy diferentes sus ideas sobre el futuro?

decir	poder	salir
haber	poner	ser
hacer	querer	tener
ir	saber	venir

Modelo

Cada día se destruyen las selvas tropicales.
Habrá más animales en peligro de extinción.

1. Mis padres quieren usar la energía de una manera más eficiente en la casa.
2. Vamos a recoger la basura en el parque.
3. Tratamos de ahorrar la electricidad en la escuela.
4. Los científicos quieren explorar el espacio.
5. La contaminación del aire en la ciudad es muy grave.
6. Hay muchos grupos ecológicos que tratan de conservar el medio ambiente.

Más práctica (GO)

realidades.com | print

Instant Check	✔	
Guided WB pp. 337–338	✔	✔
Core WB p. 186	✔	✔
Comm. WB pp. 180, 182	✔	✔
Hispanohablantes WB pp. 354–357, 360		✔

Gramática

The present subjunctive with expressions of doubt

You have used the subjunctive to say that one person tries to persuade another to do something. It is also used after verbs and expressions that indicate doubt or uncertainty.

Dudamos que puedan resolver todos los problemas.

We doubt that they can solve all the problems.

No es cierto que protejan las selvas tropicales.

It is not certain that they will protect the rain forests.

Other expressions that indicate doubt or uncertainty are:

no creer que	to not believe
no estar seguro, -a de que	to be unsure
es imposible que	it is impossible
es posible que	it is possible

When the verb or expression indicates certainty, use the indicative, *not* the subjunctive.

Estoy seguro de que destruyen los bosques.

I'm sure that they are destroying the forests.

Creemos que es importante proteger la naturaleza.

We believe that it is important to protect nature.

• The subjunctive form of *hay* is *haya*, from *haber*.

Es posible que haya suficiente electricidad.

It is possible that there is enough electricity.

Más ayuda · **realidades.com**

▶ **GramActiva** Video

🔊 **Canción de hip hop:** ¿Qué haremos para mejorar el mundo?

✎ **GramActiva** Activity

▼17 ¿Cierto o no?

Leer • Escribir

Lee lo que dicen estas personas sobre el futuro y decide si es necesario usar el subjuntivo o el indicativo. Luego escribe la forma apropiada del verbo.

1. No creo que _____ (haber) soluciones fáciles para los problemas ecológicos en la Tierra.

2. Dudamos que la contaminación del medio ambiente se _____ (mejorar) pronto.

3. Es posible que las leyes estrictas _____ (poder) ayudar a reducir la contaminación.

4. Es cierto que muchos animales _____ (estar) en peligro de extinción.

5. Estoy seguro de que el reciclaje _____ (eliminar) la destrucción de las selvas tropicales.

Modelo

Es imposible que sólo las leyes protejan los bosques de la contaminación.

6. El profesor no cree que las guerras _____ (ir) a terminar nunca.

7. No estoy seguro de que las leyes para proteger el medio ambiente _____ (funcionar) muy bien.

8. Es verdad que la calefacción solar _____ (ser) mejor para el medio ambiente que la electricidad.

18 En 15 años |

Hablar

Imagina que otro(a) estudiante y tú van a filmar una película sobre qué pasará en el mundo en 15 años. Hablen de si están seguros de que las cosas ocurrirán.

▶ **Modelo**

A —¿Crees que haya paz en la Tierra en 15 años?

B —No, no creo que haya paz.

o: —Sí, estoy seguro(a) de que habrá paz.

> **Nota**
>
> In a question, *creer que* is followed by the subjunctive if the speaker has doubts about, or suggests the possibility of, the action.

Estudiante A

1. haber guerras
2. funcionar los coches con energía solar
3. viajar a otros planetas
4. encontrar nuevas fuentes de energía
5. tener una mujer como Presidenta
6. todos ser bilingües

Estudiante B

(no) dudar que
es (im)posible que
(no) creer que
(no) estar seguro, -a de que
(no) es cierto que

19 Y ahora, tu opinión |

Escribir • Hablar

¿Será posible resolver los problemas ecológicos de hoy? Escribe tus opiniones sobre lo que van a hacer las personas de la lista en el futuro. Luego trabaja con otro(a) estudiante y di si Uds. están de acuerdo o no en sus opiniones.

Modelo

Creo que viviremos en la Luna algún día.

o: *Es imposible que vivamos algún día en la Luna.*

los científicos	los problemas ecológicos
nosotros	el aire acondicionado solar
yo	por la paz y contra la guerra
el Presidente	a los animales en peligro de extinción
toda la gente	la destrucción de las selvas tropicales
¡Respuesta personal!	**¡Respuesta personal!**

▼20 La contaminación acústica

Leer • Escribir • Hablar

Cuando pensamos en la contaminación, casi siempre nos referimos al aire y al agua. Pero la contaminación acústica (*noise*) es también un gran problema, especialmente en las grandes ciudades. Lee este artículo sobre la contaminación acústica en Buenos Aires y contesta las preguntas.

¡Baja el volumen!

¿Sabías que Buenos Aires es la ciudad más ruidosa de América Latina? Según los especialistas, a este problema se lo llama la contaminación acústica. Este tipo de contaminación se produce cuando el nivel[1] del sonido[2] es muy alto y se cambian las condiciones normales del ambiente.

En algunas zonas de Buenos Aires, los niveles de ruido son tan altos que algunas personas tienen problemas hasta para trabajar. Roberto, un vendedor, dice: "A veces hay tanto ruido que no se puede conversar con los clientes. ¡Es terrible!"

Pero, ¿cómo afecta el ruido a la salud? Es verdad que mientras el ruido de una motocicleta puede ser insoportable[3] para algunos, a otros ese ruido no les molesta. El hecho es que la contaminación acústica tiene muchos efectos negativos para la salud: estrés y problemas para escuchar y dormir son algunos ejemplos.

¿QUÉ SE PUEDE HACER?

Aunque muchas personas dudan que se pueda eliminar la contaminación acústica, es posible reducirla siguiendo estos consejos[4]:

- hablar en un tono de voz normal
- controlar el volumen del televisor y de la radio
- hablar en público por el celular en voz baja
- evitar los gritos innecesarios
- no usar los aparatos eléctricos ruidosos en la noche

[1] level [2] sound [3] unbearable [4] pieces of advice

1. ¿Estás de acuerdo de que un sonido puede ser agradable para una persona y no para otra? Da otro ejemplo de esto.

2. ¿Crees que la contaminación acústica es un gran problema donde vives? ¿Por qué? ¿Qué recomendaciones resolverían (*would solve*) problemas acústicos en tu comunidad?

3. ¿Qué leyes o reglas hay en tu escuela o comunidad para reducir la contaminación acústica? ¿Crees que funcionan?

4. Escribe otras dos sugerencias que puedan ayudar a reducir la contaminación acústica.

▼21 ¿La campaña puede tener éxito? |

Hablar

¿Crees que sea posible reducir la contaminación acústica? Usa ideas de la página Web de "¡Baja el volumen!" y tus propias ideas de la Actividad 20 para decirle a otro(a) estudiante si crees que la campaña pueda tener éxito. Usa también las expresiones de la Actividad 18 de la página 488.

Modelo

Dudo que muchas personas reduzcan el volumen de su televisor o radio.

22 Dos lugares muy distintos

Pensar • Escribir

Joaquín Torres-García nació en Uruguay, un país urbano y moderno. José Antonio Velásquez nació en Honduras, un país más rural y menos moderno que Uruguay. En los cuadros de estos dos artistas, vemos dos mundos diferentes.

"Paisaje hondureño de San Antonio de Oriente" (1972), José Antonio Velásquez

Oil on canvas, 47 1/4" x 60 1/2". Museum of Modern Art of Latin America, Washington D.C.

1. Describe el primer cuadro. ¿Qué cosas puedes identificar? ¿Ves algún elemento de la naturaleza? ¿Cómo te hace sentir?

2. Describe el segundo cuadro. ¿Qué elementos de la naturaleza ves? ¿Qué cosas hechas por personas hay? ¿Cómo te hace sentir?

3. Compara los cuadros. ¿Qué crees que los artistas están tratando de decirnos sobre la gente y su relación con la naturaleza? ¿Con cuál estás de acuerdo? ¿Por qué?

"Nueva York a vista de pájaro" (1920), Joaquín Torres-García

Gouache and watercolor on cardboard, 33.8 x 48.5. Yale University Art Gallery, Gift of Collection Societé Anonymé.

23 El uso y abuso del agua

Leer • Pensar • Escribir • Hablar

Trabajen en grupos de cuatro y observen los dibujos. Túrnense para leer las sugerencias para ahorrar el agua. Luego contesta las preguntas.

Conexiones | La ecología

1. Tomar duchas más cortas. Si se usa la bañera,[1] llenarla sólo hasta la mitad.[2]

2. Lavar las verduras en un recipiente y no bajo el grifo.[3]

3. Cerrar el grifo cuando se cepilla los dientes.

4. Regar[4] el jardín por la mañana o al anochecer[5] para que el sol no evapore el agua.

5. Usar la lavadora sólo cuando esté llena de ropa.

[1]bathtub [2]halfway [3]faucet [4]Water [5]dusk

1. ¿En tu comunidad hay restricciones sobre el uso del agua? ¿Cuáles son?

2. Trabaja con otro(a) estudiante. Escriban cuatro frases para decir qué sugerencias darán más resultado en sus casas y qué sugerencias dudan que tengan resultado.

▼24 El Día de la Tierra

Leer • Escribir • Hablar

Lee el lema *(slogan)* que usó Costa Rica para su Día de la Tierra y contesta las preguntas.

1. ¿Qué aspectos del medio ambiente y qué problemas ecológicos se incluyen en el lema?

2. Usa lo que has aprendido sobre Costa Rica y explica por qué se preocupan *(worry)* los costarricenses.

3. Explica lo que entiendes de "entenderemos que no se puede comer el dinero".

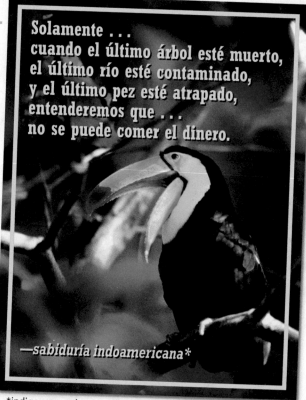

Solamente . . .
cuando el último árbol esté muerto,
el último río esté contaminado,
y el último pez esté atrapado,
entenderemos que . . .
no se puede comer el dinero.

—*sabiduría indoamericana**

*indigenous saying

▼25 La conservación

Escribir • Dibujar • Hablar

Trabaja con otro(a) estudiante. Creen su propio lema para animar *(encourage)* a otras personas a pensar en la conservación.

❶ Hagan una lista de los problemas ecológicos que quieren mencionar y escriban un lema basado en la lista.

❷ Pongan su lema en un cartel o una camiseta. Añadan dibujos o fotos. Preséntenlo a la clase.

El español en el mundo del trabajo

Conservation International (CI) es una de varias organizaciones sin fines de lucro *(nonprofit)* cuya misión es proteger el medio ambiente. Tiene sus oficinas principales en Washington, D.C., pero muchos de sus empleados hablan español o portugués. Gran parte de sus esfuerzos *(efforts)* ecológicos se centran en los países de América Central y América del Sur. Por eso, también tiene empleados en México, Costa Rica, Panamá, Ecuador, Bolivia y Perú.

• Además de hablar español, ¿cómo debe ser la persona que trabajará para *Conservation International*? ¿Qué le interesará a esta persona?

Más práctica (GO)

realidades.com | print

Instant Check	✔	
Guided WB pp. 339–341	✔	✔
Core WB pp. 187–188	✔	✔
Comm. WB pp. 180, 183, 286	✔	✔
Hispanohablantes **WB** pp. 358–359, 361		✔

Lectura

▼ Objectives

▶ Read about the Antarctic and Tierra del Fuego

▶ Use key passages to identify the author's point of view

Protejamos la Antártida

Estrategia

Detecting point of view
When reading an article, you need to be aware that the author might have strong opinions about certain issues. While you read this article, try to identify those passages and sentences that support the point of view of the author. Do you agree or disagree?

Pingüinos juanitos

Con un área de 16.5 millones de kilómetros cuadrados, la Antártida es un continente de hielo, y es el quinto en tamaño de la Tierra. El 90 por ciento del hielo de la Tierra se encuentra en la Antártida. Es un desierto frígido donde casi nunca llueve. El continente está rodeado por islas que tienen un clima menos frío y por esto hay una variedad de plantas. Estas plantas mantienen un gran número de pájaros y animales. La existencia de especies está limitada por el clima y el hielo, pero existe una abundancia de vida en el agua: plancton, coral, esponjas, peces, focas,[1] ballenas y pingüinos.

¡Estamos en peligro!

Las regiones polares son muy importantes para la supervivencia[2] de la Tierra entera. Los casquetes de hielo[3] en las zonas polares reflejan luz solar y así regularizan la temperatura de la Tierra. Cuando se destruyen estos casquetes, hay menos luz solar que se refleja y la Tierra se convierte en un receptor termal. Esto se llama el efecto de invernadero.[4] Es en la Antártida que en 1985 se reportaron por primera vez los hoyos[5] en la capa[6] del ozono y aquí es donde hoy día se trata de encontrar una solución.

El Tratado Antártico

A través de los años, muchos países han declarado soberanía de derechos[7] sobre la Antártida y esto ha producido problemas, especialmente en la Argentina y Chile. Pero el 1ro de diciembre de 1959, los problemas se acabaron con el Tratado[8] Antártico.

[1]seals [2]survival [3]ice caps [4]greenhouse effect [5]holes [6]layer [7]sovereign land rights [8]Treaty

Ushuaia, Argentina

medidas[9] para proteger el medio ambiente de la Antártida. La región de Tierra del Fuego dividida entre Chile y la Argentina es hoy un centro de investigación científica polar. La ciudad de Ushuaia se ha convertido en el punto de partida[10] para los que visitan la Antártida.

Ushuaia

Es la ciudad más al sur del mundo. Desde aquí salen equipos científicos a la Antártida para estudiar el clima, la naturaleza, el hielo y la roca. También salen excursiones turísticas dirigidas por

científicos especializados en el medio ambiente de la región. Los barcos tardan dos días en llegar a la Antártida y los visitantes pueden quedarse en las bases de actividad científica que se encuentran en el continente.

Un crucero, la Antártida

El tratado estableció reglas para el uso de la región. Las dos más importantes son el uso pacífico del continente para objetivos científicos y la prohibición de la explotación minera. La Argentina y Chile, entre otros, han tomado

Base científica de la Argentina, Antártida

[9]have taken steps [10]departure

¿Comprendiste?

1. Según el artículo, ¿cómo afectan las regiones polares al medio ambiente?

2. ¿Por qué se considera la Antártida un desierto?

3. ¿Por qué fue importante el Tratado Antártico?

Y tú, ¿qué dices? | (Talk!)

¿Te gustaría visitar la Antártida? ¿Por qué?

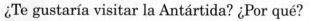

Más práctica	GO
realidades.com	print	

Guided WB p. 342	✔	✔
Comm. WB pp. 184, 287	✔	✔
Hispanohablantes **WB** pp. 362–363		✔
Cultural Reading Activity	✔	

Perspectivas del mundo hispano

La deforestación de los bosques tropicales

La selva amazónica

La selva o el bosque tropical son bosques con una vegetación rica y abundante, situados alrededor de la zona de la línea ecuatorial. En América Latina y el Caribe, los bosques cubren[1] el 47 por ciento del área total, y la región del río Amazonas tiene el 33 por ciento de todos los bosques tropicales del mundo.

Hace tres o cuatro mil años, los bosques tropicales cubrían el 14 por ciento de la Tierra. Hoy en día los bosques tropicales sólo cubren el dos por ciento de la Tierra. La mayoría de la deforestación ha ocurrido en los últimos 250 años, producida por el aumento[2] de la producción industrial y de la población. El 84 por ciento de la deforestación en América Latina es causada por la expansión de áreas para la agricultura, el 12.5 por ciento se debe a la tala[3] de árboles y el 3.5 por ciento a la construcción de carreteras, puentes y otras obras públicas.

Es importante proteger los bosques porque en ellos viven personas y animales que están perdiendo sus hogares.[4] Además, los bosques tropicales son una fuente muy importante de recursos naturales y medicinas.

La deforestación en la zona amazónica, Brasil

¡Compruébalo! Busca información en Internet sobre el porcentaje[5] de bosques en tu estado.[6] ¿Ha aumentado[7] o bajado en los últimos 50 años? ¿Hay programas para proteger los bosques? Descríbelos.

¿Qué te parece? Compara el problema de la deforestación de los bosques tropicales con la situación que existe en tu estado. ¿En qué sentido es similar? ¿En qué sentido es diferente?

[1]cover   [2]increase   [3]logging   [4]homes
[5]percentage   [6]state   [7]increased

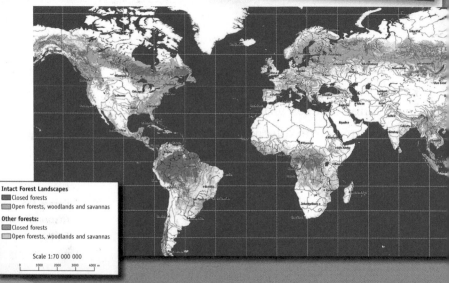

Intact Forest Landscapes
■ Closed forests
■ Open forests, woodlands and savannas

Other forests:
■ Closed forests
■ Open forests, woodlands and savannas

Scale 1:70 000 000

0   1000   2000   3000   4000 km

▼ Objectives | **Aplicación**
▸ Write a newspaper article about a community improvement project
▸ Use key questions to organize your article

Presentación escrita

Prestemos servicio

Task
You have been asked to write an article for the daily paper explaining a summer volunteer project you have organized.

1 Prewrite To write your article, answer the following:
- ¿Qué . . . ?
- ¿Quién(es) . . . ?
- ¿Por qué . . . ?
- ¿Dónde . . . ?
- ¿Cuándo . . . ?
- Para más información . . .

2 Draft Using the answers, write the first draft of your article. Use a title that captures the interest of your readers. Present your ideas in a logical, concise, and interesting format.

3 Revise Check the spelling, agreement, verb forms, and use of vocabulary. Have a classmate check:
- Did you present your plan in a logical, concise format?
- Did you include all the necessary information?
- Should you add or change anything?
- Are there errors in spelling, verb forms, or agreement?

4 Publish Rewrite the article, making the necessary corrections and changes. Make a copy for your teacher and include another in your portfolio.

5 Evaluation The following rubric will be used to grade your article.

Estrategia

Key questions
Before writing an article, it's always a good idea to organize the information you will need. Questions such as Who?, What?, When?, Where?, and Why? are useful in planning your article.

Proyecto	
¿Qué?	
¿Quién?	
¿Por qué?	
¿Dónde?	
¿Cuándo?	

Rubric	Score 1	Score 3	Score 5
Logical presentation of your ideas	Your ideas do not have a logical sequence and your writing is not concise.	Your ideas have a somewhat logical sequence and your writing is somewhat concise.	Your ideas have a logical sequence and your writing is concise.
Completeness of your information	You answer two key questions in the article.	You answer four key questions in the article.	You answer all key questions in the article.
Your accuracy in using the future and present subjunctive	You use one verb in each tense with grammatical errors.	You use two verbs in each tense with some grammatical errors.	You use three or more verbs in each tense with very few grammatical errors.

Repaso del capítulo
Vocabulario y gramática

to talk about Earth

el bosque	forest
la colina	hill
el desierto	desert
el espacio	(outer) space
la Luna	the moon
la naturaleza	nature
la planta	plant
el pueblo	town
la selva tropical	rain forest
la Tierra	Earth
el valle	valley

to talk about energy

ahorrar	to save
el aire acondicionado	air conditioning
la calefacción	heat
económico, -a	economical
eficiente	efficient
la electricidad	electricity
la energía	energy
solar	solar

to talk about the environment

conservar	to conserve
la contaminación	pollution
contaminado, -a	polluted
contra	against
la destrucción	destruction
ecológico, -a	ecological
eliminar	to eliminate
en peligro de extinción	endangered, in danger of extinction
la fuente	source
funcionar	to function, to work
grave	serious
la guerra	war
juntarse	to join
luchar	to fight
la manera	way, manner
el medio ambiente	environment
mejorar	to improve

la paz	peace
proteger (g→j)	to protect
puro, -a	pure
reducir (c→zc)	to reduce
resolver (o→ue)	to solve

other useful words and expressions

además (de)	in addition (to), besides
dudar	to doubt
es cierto	it is certain
haya	there is, there are (subjunctive)

other verbs that have irregular stems in the future tense

decir	dir-
poner	pondr-
querer	querr-
salir	saldr-
venir	vendr-

the present subjunctive with expressions of doubt

No creo que los estudiantes **lleguen** a tiempo.

Dudamos que el aire acondicionado **funcione.**

Ramón **no está seguro de que** el concierto **empiece** a las siete.

Es posible que veamos al Presidente.

Es imposible que la gente **viva** en el espacio.

No es cierto que el agua del río **sea** pura.

For *Vocabulario adicional,* see pp. 498–499.

Más repaso (GO) realidades.com | print

Instant Check	✔	
Puzzles	✔	
Core WB pp. 189–190		✔
Comm. WB pp. 288, 289–291	✔	✔

Preparación para el examen

On the exam you will be asked to . . .	Here are practice tasks similar to those you will find on the exam . . .	For review go to your print or digital textbook . . .

Interpretive

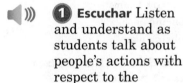 **1 Escuchar** Listen and understand as students talk about people's actions with respect to the environment

In honor of "*Día de la Tierra*", a class is discussing what people currently do or will do to improve the environment. Listen to their comments, and write *presente* if their statements deal with the present or *futuro* if they deal with the future.

pp. 476–479 *Vocabulario en contexto*
p. 480 Actividad 4
p. 484 Actividad 12

Interpersonal

 2 Hablar Tell what you will do personally to save the environment

The director from the Hispanic Youth Center asks you to talk to a group about five things that *you* will do this year to make a positive impact on the environment. For example, you might say: *Trabajaré en un centro de reciclaje.*

p. 482 Actividad 9
p. 483 Actividad 10
p. 486 Actividad 16
p. 488 Actividad 19
p. 489 Actividades 20–21
p. 490 Actividad 23
p. 491 Actividad 25

Interpretive

 3 Leer Read and understand a description of the future

Read a description of a film director's portrayal of how the world will be in 30 years. Where will people live? What will we use for energy? Does he include anything you consider impossible?

En el futuro, habrá apartamentos debajo del océano o en las estaciones del espacio. Dudo que usemos la gasolina para los coches. Será necesario usar la energía solar. Para conservar la energía, no tendremos más que una computadora y un televisor en cada apartamento.

p. 481 Actividad 7
p. 482 Actividad 8
p. 485 Actividad 13
p. 487 Actividad 17
p. 490 Actividad 23
p. 491 Actividad 24

Presentational

 4 Escribir Write information to include on a "*Proteger nuestro medio ambiente*" poster

Your science teacher asks you to write a Spanish version of an environmental poster. What recommendations would you include on the poster? For example, you might write: *Sugerimos que reciclen los periódicos.*

p. 481 Actividad 7
p. 482 Actividad 8
p. 487 Actividad 17
p. 488 Actividad 19
p. 491 Actividades 24–25
p. 495 *Presentación escrita*

Cultures

 5 Pensar Demonstrate an understanding of efforts to protect natural resources in the Spanish-speaking world

Think about what you have learned in this chapter about how the people and governments in Spanish-speaking countries address environmental problems. Compare these efforts to those in the United States. Does this seem to be a regional or a worldwide problem?

p. 481 *Fondo cultural*
p. 483 Actividad 10, *Fondo cultural*
p. 485 *Fondo cultural*
p. 494 *Perspectivas del mundo hispano*

Vocabulario adicional

realidades.com **GO**

 Bilingual Visual Dictionary

Tema 1

Las actividades en la clase

anotar to take notes

el ensayo essay

reflexionar to reflect on, to think about

responder (a) to respond

el resumen, *pl.* **los resúmenes** summary

Las cosas de la escuela

el borrador, *pl.* **los borradores** eraser

el marcador, *pl.* **los marcadores** marker

el pisapapeles, *pl.* **los pisapapeles** paperweight

el pizarrón *pl.* **los pizarrones** blackboard

el sujetapapeles, *pl.* **los sujetapapeles,** paper clip

la tiza chalk

Tema 2

Las cosas para arreglarse

el esmalte de uñas nail polish

la espuma de afeitar shaving foam

el fijador hair spray

el lápiz de labios, *pl.* **los lápices de labios** lipstick

la loción, *pl.* **las lociones** lotion

la loción astringente astringent

la loción humectante moisturizing lotion

la loción para después de afeitarse aftershave lotion

la maquinilla de afeitar razor

la sombra de ojos eye shadow

Las compras de ropa

estar pasado, -a de moda to be out of style

Los precios

accesible affordable

Tema 3

Los lugares en la comunidad

el asilo para ancianos senior citizen home

el ayuntamiento city hall

el centro cultural cultural center

el centro de salud health center

En la tienda deportiva

los anteojos de esquí / de natación goggles

el balón, *pl.* **los balones** ball (football, soccer, and so on)

el bate de béisbol baseball bat

el casco helmet

el guante de béisbol baseball glove

el uniforme del equipo team uniform

En el banco

el billete bill

el cambio change

la cuenta corriente checking account

depositar un cheque to deposit a check

En el correo

el correo aéreo air mail

el correo urgente express mail

el sobre envelope

Para manejar

la acera sidewalk

el bache pothole

Para el metro

bajar de to get off

hacia toward

la parada (del autobús, del metro, . . .) (bus, metro, . . .) stop

subir a to get on

Tema 4

Los eventos especiales

agradecer *(c → zc)* to be grateful for, to be appreciative of

el bautizo baptism

brindar to propose a toast

el Día de Acción de Gracias Thanksgiving

el Día de San Valentín Saint Valentine's Day

la Nochebuena Christmas Eve

la Víspera del Año Nuevo New Year's Eve

Los miembros de la familia

el bisabuelo great-grandfather

la bisabuela great-grandmother

el cuñado brother-in-law

la cuñada sister-in-law

el nieto grandson

la nieta granddaughter

el padrino godfather

la madrina godmother

el sobrino nephew

la sobrina niece

Para describir cómo era de niño(a)

creativo, -a creative

inquieto, -a restless

juguetón, juguetona playful

mentiroso, -a fibber

prudente prudent, sensible

El equipo para niños

el cajón de arena sandbox

el carrusel merry-go-round

el columpio swing

el patio de recreo playground

la subibaja seesaw

el tobogán, *pl.* **los toboganes** slide

Los animales en las fábulas

el águila, *pl.* **las águilas** *f.* eagle

el conejo rabbit

el cuervo raven

la gallina hen

el gallo rooster

la oveja sheep

la rana frog

el toro bull

la vaca cow

el zorro, la zorra fox

Tema 5

Las emergencias

la alergia allergy

el análisis, *pl.* **los análisis** medical test

el antibiótico antibiotic

la aspirina aspirin

la camilla stretcher

el cirujano, la cirujana surgeon

estar resfriado to have a cold

estornudar to sneeze

la fiebre fever

la fractura fracture

la **gripe** flu

la **hinchazón** swelling

el **jarabe** cough syrup

la **lesión**, *pl.* **las lesiones** injury

el **oído** ear (inner)

la **operación**, *pl.* **las operaciones** operation

el **pecho** chest

la **picadura** sting

sufrir to suffer

la **tos** cough

Los desastres naturales

el **ciclón**, *pl.* **los ciclones** cyclone

el **daño** damage

el **derrumbe** landslide

la **erupción volcánica** volcanic eruption

huir *(i → y)* to flee

el **maremoto** tidal wave

seguro, -a safe

sobrevivir to survive

la **tempestad** storm

el **tifón**, *pl.* **los tifones** typhoon

el **tornado** tornado, twister

Las noticias

los **detalles** details

en vivo live

el / la **periodista** journalist, reporter

el **titular** headline

Tema 6

Los eventos deportivos

el **atletismo** track and field

la **carrera** race

la **corona** crown

empatar to tie

la **meta** finish line (in a race)

el **resultado** score

el **torneo** tournament

el **trofeo** trophy

vencer *(c → z)* to defeat, to conquer

Los sentimientos

alegrarse to be happy

estar conmovido, -a to be moved

El cine

el **bandido**, la **bandida** bandit

el / la **culpable** guilty person

el / la **delincuente** delinquent

el **documental** documentary

el **festival de cine** film festival

filmar to shoot, film

el **monstruo** monster

Tema 7

Las cosas de la cocina

la **cafetera** coffee maker

el **cucharón**, *pl.* **los cucharones** ladle

la **licuadora** blender

el **molde** baking pan

las **tazas para medir** measuring cups

Las comidas al aire libre

el **aceite de oliva** olive oil

el **ají** pepper; hot sauce made with this pepper

el **apio** celery

los **calamares** squid

el **chorizo** sausage

la **ciruela** plum

el **cordero** lamb

los **espárragos** asparagus

las **espinacas** spinach

la **fruta de estación** seasonal fruit

el **hígado** liver

la **langosta** lobster

el **pepino** cucumber

la **ternera** veal

la **toronja** grapefruit

Para describir comidas

agrio, -a bitter

cocido, -a cooked

crudo, -a raw

jugoso, -a juicy

salado, -a salty

Tema 8

Los viajes

acampar to camp

el / la **excursionista** excursionist

la **expedición**, *pl.* **las expediciones** expedition

el **explorador**, la **exploradora** explorer

ir al extranjero to go abroad

el **paisaje** landscape

el **paseo** trip

el **recorrido** route

la **tienda de acampar** tent

el / la **trotamundos** globe-trotter, world traveler

En el avión

abrocharse el cinturón to fasten one's seat belt

la **almohada** pillow

aterrizar *(z → c)* to land

el **compartimiento sobre la cabeza** overhead compartment

despegar to take off

procedente de arriving from

la **tripulación** crew

la **turbulencia** turbulence

la **salida de emergencia** emergency exit

la **señal de no fumar** no smoking sign

Expresiones y palabras

asombroso, -a amazing

extraordinario, -a extraordinary

glorioso, -a glorious

maravilloso, -a wonderful

tradicional traditional

único, -a unique, special

Tema 9

Los trabajos

el / la **electricista** electrician

el **horario fijo** regular schedule

el / la **intérprete** interpreter

el **plomero**, la **plomera** plumber

el **programador**, la **programadora** computer programmer

el **puesto** job position

el **tiempo completo** full time

el **tiempo parcial** part time

el **título universitario** college degree

el **trabajador social**, la **trabajadora social** social worker

el **traductor**, la **traductora** translator

El medio ambiente

el **aluminio** aluminum

prevenir to prevent

la **reserva natural** nature reserve

Resumen de gramática
Grammar Terms

Adjectives describe nouns: *a **red** car.*

Adverbs usually describe verbs; they tell when, where, or how an action happens: *He read it **quickly**.* Adverbs can also describe adjectives or other adverbs: ***very** tall, **quite** well.*

Articles are words in Spanish that can tell you whether a noun is masculine, feminine, singular, or plural. In English, the articles are ***the, a,*** and ***an.***

Commands are verb forms that tell people to do something: ***Study!, Work!***

Comparatives compare people or things.

Conjugations are verb forms that add endings to the stem in order to tell who the subject is and what tense is being used: *escribo, escrib**iste**.*

Conjunctions join words or groups of words. The most common ones are ***and, but,*** and ***or.***

Direct objects are nouns or pronouns that receive the action of a verb: *I read the **book**. I read **it**.*

Future tense is used to talk about actions in the future and to express what will happen: *Tomorrow **we will begin** working.*

Gender in Spanish tells you whether a noun, pronoun, or article is masculine or feminine.

Imperfect tense is used to talk about actions that happened repeatedly in the past; to describe people, places, and situations in the past; to talk about a past action or situation where no beginning or end is specified; and to describe an ongoing action in the past. The imperfect tense may also be used to tell what time it was or to describe weather in the past and to describe the past physical, mental, and emotional states of a person or thing.

Imperfect progressive tense is used to describe something that was taking place over a period of time in the past: *He **was skiing** when he broke his leg.*

Indirect objects are nouns or pronouns that tell you to whom / what or for whom / what something is done: *I gave **him** the book.*

Infinitives are the basic forms of verbs. In English, infinitives have the word "to" in front of them: ***to walk.***

Interrogatives are words that ask questions: ***What** is that? **Who** are you?*

Nouns name people, places, or things: ***students, Mexico City, books.***

Number tells you if a noun, pronoun, article, or verb is singular or plural.

Prepositions show relationship between their objects and another word in the sentence: *He is **in** the classroom.*

Present tense is used to talk about actions that always take place, or that are happening now: *I always **take** the bus; I **study** Spanish.*

Present perfect tense is used to say what a person *has done: We **have seen** the new movie.*

Present progressive tense is used to emphasize that an action is happening *right now: I **am doing** my homework; he **is finishing** dinner.*

Preterite tense is used to talk about actions that were completed in the past: *I **took** the train yesterday; I **studied** for the test.*

Pronouns are words that take the place of nouns: ***She** is my friend.*

Reflexive verbs are used to say that people do something to or for themselves: *I **wash my** hair.* Other reflexive verbs often describe a change in mental, emotional, or physical state, and can express the idea that someone "gets" or "becomes": *They **became** angry.*

Subjects are the nouns or pronouns that perform the action in a sentence: ***John** sings.*

Subjunctive mood is used to say that one person influences the actions of another: ***I recommend that you speak** with your doctor; **it is important that she have** good manners.* It is also used after verbs and expressions that indicate doubt or uncertainty: ***It's possible that there's** enough food.*

Superlatives describe which things have the most or least of a given quality: *She is the **best** student.*

Verbs show action or link the subject with a word or words in the predicate (what the subject does or is): *Ana **writes**; Ana **is** my sister.*

Nouns, Number, and Gender

Nouns refer to people, animals, places, things, and ideas. Nouns are singular or plural. In Spanish, nouns have gender, which means that they are either masculine or feminine.

Singular Nouns	
Masculine	Feminine
libro	carpeta
pupitre	casa
profesor	noche
lápiz	ciudad

Plural Nouns	
Masculine	Feminine
libros	carpetas
pupitres	casas
profesores	noches
lápices	ciudades

Definite Articles

El, la, los, and *las* are definite articles and are the equivalent of "the" in English. *El* is used with masculine singular nouns; *los* with masculine plural nouns. *La* is used with feminine singular nouns; *las* with feminine plural nouns. When you use the words *a* or *de* before *el,* you form the contractions *al* and *del: Voy **al** centro; Es el libro **del** profesor.*

Masculine	
Singular	**Plural**
el libro	los libros
el pupitre	los pupitres
el profesor	los profesores
el lápiz	los lápices

Feminine	
Singular	**Plural**
la carpeta	las carpetas
la casa	las casas
la noche	las noches
la ciudad	las ciudades

Indefinite Articles

Un and *una* are indefinite articles and are the equivalent of "a" and "an" in English. *Un* is used with singular masculine nouns; *una* is used with singular feminine nouns. The plural indefinite articles are *unos* and *unas.*

Masculine	
Singular	**Plural**
un libro	unos libros
un baile	unos bailes

Feminine	
Singular	**Plural**
una revista	unas revistas
una mochila	unas mochilas

Pronouns

Subject pronouns tell who is doing the action. They replace nouns or names in a sentence. Subject pronouns are often used for emphasis or clarification: *Gregorio escucha música. **Él** escucha música.*

A *direct object* tells who or what receives the action of the verb. To avoid repeating a direct object noun, you can replace it with a *direct object pronoun.* Direct object pronouns have the same gender and number as the nouns they replace: *¿Cuándo compraste **el libro? Lo** compré ayer.*

An *indirect object* tells to whom or for whom an action is performed. *Indirect object pronouns* are used to replace an indirect object noun: ***Les** doy dinero. (I give money to them.)* Because *le* and *les* have more than one meaning, you can make the meaning clear, or show emphasis, by adding *a* + the corresponding name, noun, or pronoun: ***Les** doy el dinero a **ellos.***

A *reflexive pronoun* is used to show that someone does an action to or for herself or himself. Each reflexive pronoun corresponds to a different subject and always agrees with the subject pronoun: *Todos los días **me ducho** y **me arreglo** el pelo.* You know that a verb is reflexive if its infinitive form ends with the letters *se: ducharse, arreglarse.*

After most prepositions, you use *mí* and *ti* for "me" and "you." The forms change with the preposition *con: conmigo, contigo.* For all other persons, you use subject pronouns after prepositions.

The personal a

When the direct object is a person, a group of people, or a pet, use the word *a* before the object. This is called the "personal *a*": *Visité **a** mi abuela. Busco **a** mi perro, Capitán.*

Subject Pronouns		Direct Object Pronouns		Indirect Object Pronouns		Reflexive Pronouns		Objects of Prepositions	
Singular	**Plural**	**Singular**	**Plural**	**Singular**	**Plural**	**Singular**	**Plural**	**Singular**	**Plural**
yo	nosotros, nosotras	me	nos	me	nos	me	nos	(para) mí, conmigo	nosotros, nosotras
tú	vosotros, vosotras	te	os	te	os	te	os	(para) ti, contigo	vosotros, vosotras
usted (Ud.), él, ella	ustedes (Uds.), ellos, ellas	lo, la	los, las	le	les	se	se	Ud., él, ella	Uds., ellos, ellas

Adjectives

Words that describe people and things are called adjectives. In Spanish, most adjectives have both masculine and feminine forms, as well as singular and plural forms. Adjectives must agree with the nouns they describe in both gender and number. When an adjective describes a group including both masculine and feminine nouns, use the masculine plural form.

Masculine	
Singular	**Plural**
alto	altos
inteligente	inteligentes
trabajador	trabajadores
fácil	fáciles

Feminine	
Singular	**Plural**
alta	altas
inteligente	inteligentes
trabajadora	trabajadoras
fácil	fáciles

Shortened Forms of Adjectives

When placed before masculine singular nouns, some adjectives change into a shortened form.

bueno	→	buen chico
malo	→	mal día
primero	→	primer trabajo
tercero	→	tercer plato
grande	→	gran señor

One adjective, **grande,** changes to a shortened form before any singular noun: *una **gran** señora, un **gran** libro.*

Possessive Adjectives

Possessive adjectives are used to tell what belongs to someone or to show relationships. Like other adjectives, possessive adjectives agree in number with the nouns that follow them.

Only *nuestro* and *vuestro* have different masculine and feminine endings. *Su* and *sus* can have many different meanings: *his, her, its, your,* or *their.*

The long forms of possessive adjectives are used for emphasis and come *after* the noun. They may also be used without a noun: *Esta chaqueta es **tuya?** Sí, es **mía.***

Singular	Plural
mi	mis
tu	tus
su	sus
nuestro, -a	nuestros, -as
vuestro, -a	vuestros, -as
su	sus

Singular	Plural
mío/mía	míos/mías
tuyo/tuya	tuyos/tuyas
suyo/suya	suyos/suyas
nuestro/nuestra	nuestros/nuestras
vuestro/vuestra	vuestros/vuestras
suyo/suya	suyos/suyas

Demonstrative Adjectives

Like other adjectives, demonstrative adjectives agree in gender and number with the nouns that follow them. Use *este, esta, estos, estas* ("this" / "these") before nouns that name people or things that are close to you. Use *ese, esa, esos, esas* ("that" / "those") before nouns that name people or things that are at some distance from you.

Use *aquel, aquella, aquellos,* or *aquellas* ("that [those] over there") before nouns that name people or things that are far from both you and the person to whom you are speaking.

Singular	Plural
este libro	estos libros
esta casa	estas casas
ese niño	esos niños
esa manzana	esas manzanas
aquel bolso	aquellos bolsos
aquella blusa	aquellas blusas

Interrogative Words

You use interrogative words to ask questions. When you ask a question with an interrogative word, you put the verb before the subject. All interrogative words have a written accent mark.

¿Adónde?	¿Cuándo?	¿Dónde?
¿Cómo?	¿Cuánto, -a?	¿Por qué?
¿Con quién?	¿Cuántos, -as?	¿Qué?
¿Cuál?	¿De dónde?	¿Quién?

Comparatives and Superlatives

Comparatives Use *más . . . que* or *menos . . . que* to compare people or things: *más interesante que . . . , menos alta que . . .*

When talking about number, use *de* instead of *que: Tengo más de cien monedas en mi colección.*

To compare people or things that are equal, use *tan . . . como: tan* popular **como** . . . *Tanto / tanta . . . como* is used to say *"as much as"* and *tantos / tantas . . . como* is used to say "as many as": **tanto** dinero **como . . . tantas** amigas

como . . . Tanto and *tanta* match the number and gender of the noun to which they refer.

Superlatives Use this pattern to express the idea of "most" or "least."

el
la   + *noun* + más / menos + *adjective*
los
las

*Es **el programa de televisión más interesante.***
*Son **los perritos más pequeños.***

Several adjectives are irregular when used with comparisons and superlatives.

older	mayor
younger	menor
better	mejor
worse	peor

To say that something is "the most," "the least," "the best," or "the worst" in a group or category, use *de.*

*Es **la chica más seria de** la clase.*
*Es **la mejor película del** festival de cine.*

Affirmative and Negative Words

To make a sentence negative in Spanish, *no* usually goes in front of the verb or expression. To show that you do not like either of two choices, use *ni . . . ni.*

Alguno, alguna, algunos, algunas and *ninguno, ninguna* match the number and gender of the noun to which they refer. When *alguno* and *ninguno* come before a masculine singular noun, they change to *algún* and *ningún.*

Affirmative	Negative
algo	nada
alguien	nadie
algún	ningún
alguno, -a, -os, -as	ninguno, -a
siempre	nunca
también	tampoco

Adverbs

To form an adverb in Spanish, *-mente* is added to the feminine singular form of an adjective. This *-mente* ending is equivalent to the "-ly" ending in English. If the adjective has a written accent, such as *rápida, fácil,* and *práctica,* the accent appears in the same place in the adverb form.

general	→ generalmente
especial	→ especialmente
fácil	→ fácilmente
feliz	→ felizmente
rápida	→ rápidamente
práctica	→ prácticamente

Verbos

Regular Present, Preterite, Imperfect, Future, and Subjunctive

Here are the conjugations for regular -ar, -er, and -ir verbs in the present, preterite, imperfect, future, and subjunctive tenses.

Infinitive	Present		Preterite		Imperfect		Future		Subjunctive	
estudiar	estudio	estudiamos	estudié	estudiamos	estudiaba	estudiábamos	estudiaré	estudiaremos	estudie	estudiemos
	estudias	estudiáis	estudiaste	estudiasteis	estudiabas	estudiabais	estudiarás	estudiaréis	estudies	estudiéis
	estudia	estudian	estudió	estudiaron	estudiaba	estudiaban	estudiará	estudiarán	estudie	estudien
correr	corro	corremos	corrí	corrimos	corría	corríamos	correré	correremos	corra	corramos
	corres	corréis	corriste	corristeis	corrías	corríais	correrás	correréis	corras	corráis
	corre	corren	corrió	corrieron	corría	corrían	correrá	correrán	corra	corran
vivir	vivo	vivimos	viví	vivimos	vivía	vivíamos	viviré	viviremos	viva	vivamos
	vives	vivís	viviste	vivisteis	vivías	vivíais	vivirás	viviréis	vivas	viváis
	vive	viven	vivió	vivieron	vivía	vivían	vivirá	vivirán	viva	vivan

Present Progressive and Imperfect Progressive

When you want to emphasize that an action is happening *right now*, you use the present progressive tense.

To describe something that was taking place over a period of time *in the past*, use the imperfect progressive.

Infinitive	Present Progressive				Imperfect Progressive	
estudiar	estoy	estudiando	estamos	estudiando	estaba estudiando	estabámos estudiando
	estás	estudiando	estáis	estudiando	estabas estudiando	estabais estudiando
	está	estudiando	están	estudiando	estaba estudiando	estaban estudiando
correr	estoy	corriendo	estamos	corriendo	estaba corriendo	estábamos corriendo
	estás	corriendo	estáis	corriendo	estabas corriendo	estabais corriendo
	está	corriendo	están	corriendo	estaba corriendo	estaban corriendo
vivir	estoy viviendo		estamos viviendo		estaba viviendo	estábamos viviendo
	estás viviendo		estáis viviendo		estabas viviendo	estabais viviendo
	está viviendo		están viviendo		estaba viviendo	estaban viviendo

Present Perfect Tense

When you want to say what a person *has done*, use the present perfect tense.

Infinitive	Present Perfect	
estudiar	he estudiado	hemos estudiado
	has estudiado	habéis estudiado
	ha estudiado	han estudiado
correr	he corrido	hemos corrido
	has corrido	habéis corrido
	ha corrido	han corrido
vivir	he vivido	hemos vivido
	has vivido	habéis vivido
	ha vivido	han vivido

Commands

When telling a friend, a family member, or a young person to do something, use an affirmative *tú* command. To give these commands for most verbs, use the same present-tense forms that are used for *Ud., él, ella*. Some verbs have an irregular affirmative *tú* command.

When telling a friend, a family member, or a young person *not* to do something, use a negative *tú* command. To give these commands for most verbs, drop the *-o* of the present-tense *yo* form and add *-es* for *-ar* verbs and *-as* for *-er* and *-ir* verbs. Some verbs have an irregular negative *tú* command.

To give affirmative or negative commands in the *Ud.* or *Uds.* form, drop the *-o* of the present-tense *yo* form and add *-e* or *-en* for *-ar* verbs and *-a* or *-an* for *-er* and *-ir* verbs. Some verbs have an irregular *Ud.* or *Uds.* command.

For stem-changing and spelling-changing verbs see the tables on pages 506–509.

Infinitive	Tú	Negative *tú*	Usted	Ustedes
estudiar	estudia	no estudies	(no) estudie	(no) estudien
correr	corre	no corras	(no) corra	(no) corran
vivir	vive	no vivas	(no) viva	(no) vivan

Infinitive	Tú	Negative *tú*	Usted	Ustedes
dar	da	no des	(no) dé	(no) den
decir	di	no digas	(no) diga	(no) digan
estar	está	no estés	(no) esté	(no) estén
hacer	haz	no hagas	(no) haga	(no) hagan
ir	ve	no vayas	(no) vaya	(no) vayan
poner	pon	no pongas	(no) ponga	(no) pongan
salir	sal	no salgas	(no) salga	(no) salgan
ser	sé	no seas	(no) sea	(no) sean
tener	ten	no tengas	(no) tenga	(no) tengan
venir	ven	no vengas	(no) venga	(no) vengan

Stem-changing Verbs

Here is a list of stem-changing verbs. Only conjugations with changes are highlighted.

Infinitive in -ar

Infinitive	Present Indicative		Present Subjunctive	
pensar (e→ie)	pienso	pensamos	piense	pensemos
	piensas	pensáis	pienses	penséis
	piensa	piensan	piense	piensen

Verbs like **pensar**: calentar, comenzar,[1] despertar(se), empezar, recomendar, tropezar

contar (o→ue)	cuento	contamos	cuente	contemos
	cuentas	contáis	cuentes	contéis
	cuenta	cuentan	cuente	cuenten

Verbs like **contar**: acostar(se), almorzar, costar, encontrar(se), probar(se), recordar

jugar (u→ue)	juego	jugamos	juegue	juguemos
	juegas	jugáis	juegues	juguéis
	juega	juegan	juegue	jueguen

Infinitive in -er

	Present Indicative		Present Subjunctive	
entender (e→ie)	entiendo	entendemos	entienda	entendamos
	entiendes	entendéis	entiendas	entendáis
	entiende	entienden	entienda	entiendan

Verbs like **entender**: encender, perder

devolver (o→ue)	devuelvo	devolvemos	devuelva	devolvamos
past participle:	devuelves	devolvéis	devuelvas	devolváis
devuelto	devuelve	devuelven	devuelva	devuelvan

Verbs like **devolver**: mover(se), resolver, torcer(se),[2] volver (past participle: **vuelto**)

[1]Remember that verbs like *comenzar* and *tropezar* also have a spelling change *(z → c)* in all forms of the present subjunctive. See p. 508 for a complete conjugation of *empezar*.

[2]Verbs like *torcer(se)* also have a spelling change *(c → z)* in all forms of the present subjunctive. See p. 509 for a complete conjugation of *torcer(se)*.

Stem-changing Verbs (continued)

Infinitive in -*ir*

	Indicative				Subjunctive	
	Present		**Preterite**		**Present**	
pedir (e→i) (e→i)	pido	pedimos	pedí	pedimos	pida	pidamos
present participle: pidiendo	pides	pedís	pediste	pedisteis	pidas	pidáis
	pide	piden	pidió	pidieron	pida	pidan
Verbs like **pedir**: conseguir,* despedir(se), repetir, seguir, servir, vestir(se)						
preferir (e→ie) (e→i)	prefiero	preferimos	preferí	preferimos	prefiera	prefiramos
present participle:	prefieres	preferís	preferiste	preferisteis	prefieras	prefiráis
prefiriendo	prefiere	prefieren	prefirió	prefirieron	prefiera	prefieran
Verbs like **preferir**: divertir(se), hervir, mentir, sugerir						
dormir (o→ue) (o→u)	duermo	dormimos	dormí	dormimos	duerma	durmamos
present participle:	duermes	dormís	dormiste	dormisteis	duermas	durmáis
durmiendo	duerme	duermen	durmió	durmieron	duerma	duerman
Verbs like **dormir**: morir(se) (past participle: muerto)						

*Verbs like *conseguir* and *seguir* also have a spelling change *(gu → g)* in all forms of the present subjunctive. See p. 509 for a complete conjugation of *seguir*.

Spelling-changing Verbs

These verbs have spelling changes in the present, preterite, and/or subjunctive. The spelling changes are indicated in boldface blue type.

Infinitive, Present Participle, Past Participle	Present		Preterite		Subjunctive	
almorzar (z → c) almorzando almorzado	See stem-changing verbs		**almorcé** almorzaste almorzó	almorzamos almorzasteis almorzaron	**almuerce** **almuerces** **almuerce**	**almorcemos** **almorcéis** **almuercen**
buscar (c → qu) buscando buscado	See regular -ar verbs		**busqué** buscaste buscó	buscamos buscasteis buscaron	**busque** **busques** **busque**	**busquemos** **busquéis** **busquen**
comunicarse (c → qu) comunicándose comunicado	See reflexive verbs		See reflexive verbs and **buscar**		See reflexive verbs and **buscar**	
conocer (c → zc) conociendo conocido	**conozco** conoces conoce	conocemos conocéis conocen	See regular -er verbs		**conozca** **conozcas** **conozca**	**conozcamos** **conozcáis** **conozcan**
creer (i → y) creyendo creído	See regular -er verbs		creí creíste **creyó**	creímos creísteis **creyeron**	See regular -er verbs	
destruir (i → y) destruyendo destruido	**destruyo** **destruyes** **destruye**	destruimos destruís **destruyen**	destruí destruiste **destruyó**	destruimos destruisteis **destruyeron**	**destruya** **destruyas** **destruya**	**destruyamos** **destruyáis** **destruyan**
empezar (z → c) empezando empezado	See stem-changing verbs		**empecé** empezaste empezó	empezamos empezasteis empezaron	**empiece** **empieces** **empiece**	**empecemos** **empecéis** **empiecen**
enviar (i → í) enviando enviado	**envío** **envías** **envía**	enviamos enviáis **envían**	See regular -ar verbs		**envíe** **envíes** **envíe**	enviemos enviéis **envíen**
escoger (g → j) escogiendo escogido	**escojo** escoges escoge	escogemos escogéis escogen	See regular -er verbs		**escoja** **escojas** **escoja**	**escojamos** **escojáis** **escojan**
esquiar (i → í) esquiando esquiado	See **enviar**		See regular -ar verbs		See **enviar**	
jugar (g → gu) jugando jugado	See stem-changing verbs		**jugué** jugaste jugó	jugamos jugasteis jugaron	See stem-changing verbs	
leer (i → y) leyendo leído	See regular -er verbs		See **creer**		See regular -er verbs	
obedecer (c → zc) obedeciendo obedecido	See **conocer**		See regular -er verbs		See **conocer**	

Spelling-changing Verbs (continued)

Infinitive, Present Participle Past Participle	Present		Preterite		Subjunctive	
ofrecer (c → zc) ofreciendo ofrecido	See **conocer**		See regular *-er* verbs		See **conocer**	
pagar (g → gu) pagando pagado	See regular *-ar* verbs		See **jugar**		pague pagues pague	paguemos paguéis paguen
parecer (c → zc) pareciendo parecido	See **conocer**		See regular *-er* verbs		See **conocer**	
practicar (c → qu) practicando practicado	See regular *-ar* verbs		See **buscar**		See **buscar**	
recoger (g → j) recogiendo recogido	See **escoger**		See regular *-er* verbs		See **escoger**	
reír(se) (e → i)* riendo (riéndose) reído	me río te ríes se ríe	nos reímos os reís se ríen	me reí te reíste se rió	nos reímos os reísteis se rieron	me ría te rías se ría	nos riamos os riáis se rían
reunirse (u → ú)* reuniéndose reunido	me reúno te reúnes se reúne	nos reunimos os reunís se reúnen	See regular *-ir* verbs		me reúna te reúnas se reúna	nos reunamos os reunáis se reúnan
sacar (c → qu) sacando sacado	See regular *-ar* verbs		See **buscar**		See **buscar**	
seguir (e → i) (gu → g)* siguiendo seguido	sigo sigues sigue	seguimos seguís siguen	See stem-changing verbs: **pedir**		siga sigas siga	sigamos sigáis sigan
tocar (c → qu) tocando tocado	See regular *-ar* verbs		See **buscar**		See **buscar**	
torcer(se) (o → ue) (c → z) torciendo torcido	me tuerzo te tuerces se tuerce	nos torcemos os torcéis se tuercen	See regular *-er* verbs		me tuerza te tuerzas se tuerza	nos torzamos os torzáis se tuerzan

*Verbs like **reír(se)**: sonreír, freír (past participle: fr**ito**)

*Verbs like **reunirse**: graduarse (present: *me gradúo, te gradúas, se gradúa, nos graduamos, os graduáis, se gradúan;* preterite: see preterite of regular *-ar* verbs; subjunctive: *me gradúe, te gradúes, se gradúe, nos graduemos, os graduéis, se gradúen*)

*Verbs like **seguir**: conseguir

Irregular Verbs

These verbs have irregular patterns.

Infinitive Present Participle Past Participle	Present		Preterite	
dar dando dado	doy das da	damos dais dan	di diste dio	dimos disteis dieron
decir diciendo dicho	digo dices dice	decimos decís dicen	dije dijiste dijo	dijimos dijisteis dijeron
estar estando estado	estoy estás está	estamos estáis están	estuve estuviste estuvo	estuvimos estuvisteis estuvieron
haber habiendo habido	he has ha	hemos habéis han	hube hubiste hubo	hubimos hubisteis hubieron
hacer haciendo hecho	hago haces hace	hacemos hacéis hacen	hice hiciste hizo	hicimos hicisteis hicieron
ir yendo ido	voy vas va	vamos vais van	fui fuiste fue	fuimos fuisteis fueron
oír* oyendo oído	oigo oyes oye	oímos oís oyen	oí oíste oyó	oímos oísteis oyeron
poder pudiendo podido	puedo puedes puede	podemos podéis pueden	pude pudiste pudo	pudimos pudisteis pudieron
poner poniendo puesto	pongo pones pone	ponemos ponéis ponen	puse pusiste puso	pusimos pusisteis pusieron

*Verbs like **oír**: caerse

Irregular Verbs (continued)

4		5		6	
Imperfect		**Future**		**Subjunctive**	
daba	dábamos	daré	daremos	dé	demos
dabas	dabais	darás	dareis	des	deis
daba	daban	dará	darán	dé	den
decía	decíamos	diré	diremos	diga	digamos
decías	decíais	dirás	diréis	digas	digáis
decía	decían	dirá	dirán	diga	digan
estaba	estábamos	estaré	estaremos	esté	estemos
estabas	estabais	estarás	estaréis	estés	estéis
estaba	estaban	estará	estarán	esté	estén
había	habíamos	habré	habremos	haya	hayamos
habías	habíais	habrás	habréis	hayas	hayáis
había	habían	habrá	habrán	haya	hayan
hacía	hacíamos	haré	haremos	haga	hagamos
hacías	hacíais	harás	haréis	hagas	hagáis
hacía	hacían	hará	harán	haga	hagan
iba	íbamos	iré	iremos	vaya	vayamos
ibas	ibais	irás	iréis	vayas	vayáis
iba	iban	irá	irán	vaya	vayan
oía	oíamos	oiré	oiremos	oiga	oigamos
oías	oíais	oirás	oiréis	oigas	oigáis
oía	oían	oirá	oirán	oiga	oigan
podía	podíamos	podré	podremos	pueda	podamos
podías	podíais	podrás	podréis	puedas	podáis
podía	podían	podrá	podrán	pueda	puedan
ponía	poníamos	pondré	pondremos	ponga	pongamos
ponías	poníais	pondrás	pondréis	pongas	pongáis
ponía	ponían	pondrá	pondrán	ponga	pongan

Irregular Verbs (continued)

Infinitive Present Participle Past Participle	Present		Preterite	
querer queriendo querido	quiero quieres quiere	queremos queréis quieren	quise quisiste quiso	quisimos quisisteis quisieron
saber sabiendo sabido	sé sabes sabe	sabemos sabéis saben	supe supiste supo	supimos supisteis supieron
salir saliendo salido	salgo sales sale	salimos salís salen	salí saliste salió	salimos salisteis salieron
ser siendo sido	soy eres es	somos sois son	fui fuiste fue	fuimos fuisteis fueron
tener teniendo tenido	tengo tienes tiene	tenemos tenéis tienen	tuve tuviste tuvo	tuvimos tuvisteis tuvieron
traer trayendo traído	traigo traes trae	traemos traéis traen	traje trajiste trajo	trajimos trajisteis trajeron
venir viniendo venido	vengo vienes viene	venimos venís vienen	vine viniste vino	vinimos vinisteis vinieron
ver viendo visto	veo ves ve	vemos veis ven	vi viste vio	vimos visteis vieron

Irregular Verbs (continued)

	4 Imperfect		5 Future		6 Subjunctive	
	quería	queríamos	querré	querremos	quiera	queramos
	querías	queríais	querrás	querréis	quieras	queráis
	quería	querían	querrá	querrán	quiera	quieran
	sabía	sabíamos	sabré	sabremos	sepa	sepamos
	sabías	sabíais	sabrás	sabréis	sepas	sepáis
	sabía	sabían	sabrá	sabrán	sepa	sepan
	salía	salíamos	saldré	saldremos	salga	salgamos
	salías	salíais	saldrás	saldréis	salgas	salgáis
	salía	salían	saldrá	saldrán	salga	salgan
	era	éramos	seré	seremos	sea	seamos
	eras	erais	serás	seréis	seas	seáis
	era	eran	será	serán	sea	sean
	tenía	teníamos	tendré	tendremos	tenga	tengamos
	tenías	teníais	tendrás	tendréis	tengas	tengáis
	tenía	tenían	tendrá	tendrán	tenga	tengan
	traía	traíamos	traeré	traeremos	traiga	traigamos
	traías	traíais	traerás	traeréis	traigas	traigáis
	traía	traían	traerá	traerán	traiga	traigan
	venía	veníamos	vendré	vendremos	venga	vengamos
	venías	veníais	vendrás	vendréis	vengas	vengáis
	venía	venían	vendrá	vendrán	venga	vengan
	veía	veíamos	veré	veremos	vea	veamos
	veías	veíais	verás	veréis	veas	veáis
	veía	veían	verá	verán	vea	vean

Reflexive Verbs

Infinitive and Present Participle	Present	
lavarse lavándose	me lavo	nos lavamos
	te lavas	os laváis
	se lava	se lavan
	Preterite	
	me lavé	nos lavamos
	te lavaste	os lavasteis
	se lavó	se lavaron
	Subjunctive	
	me lave	nos lavemos
	te laves	os lavéis
	se lave	se laven

Familiar *(tú)* Commands
lávate
no te laves

Formal *(Ud. and Uds.)* Commands
lávese
no se lave

Sometimes the reflexive pronouns *se* and *nos* are used to express the idea "(to) each other." These are called reciprocal actions: **Nos** *dábamos la mano.*

Vocabulario español–inglés

The *Vocabulario español-inglés* contains all active vocabulary from the text, including vocabulary presented in the grammar sections.

A dash (—) represents the main entry word. For example, **pasar la —** after **la aspiradora** means **pasar la aspiradora.**

The number following each entry indicates the chapter in which the word or expression is presented. A Roman numeral (I) indicates that the word was presented in REALIDADES 1.

The following abbreviations are used in this list: *adj.* (adjective), *dir. obj.* (direct object), *f.* (feminine), *fam.* (familiar), *ind. obj.* (indirect object), *inf.* (infinitive), *m.* (masculine), *pl.* (plural), *prep.* (preposition), *pron.* (pronoun), *sing.* (singular).

A

a to *(prep.)* (I)

— **...le gusta(n)** he/she likes (I)

— **...le encanta(n)** he/she loves (I)

— **casa** (to) home (I)

— **causa de** because of (5A)

— **la derecha (de)** to the right (of) (5A)

— **la izquierda (de)** to the left (of) (I)

— **la una de la tarde** at one (o'clock) in the afternoon (I)

— **las ocho de la mañana** at eight (o'clock) in the morning (I)

— **las ocho de la noche** at eight (o'clock) in the evening / at night (I)

— **menudo** often (I)

— **mí también** I do (like to) too (I)

— **mí tampoco** I don't (like to) either (I)

¿— **qué hora?** (At) what time? (I)

— **tiempo** on time (1A)

— **veces** sometimes (I)

— **ver.** Let's see. (I)

al (a + el), a la to the (I)

abierto, -a open (8A)

el **abogado, la abogada** lawyer (9A)

abordar to board (8A)

abrazar(se) to hug (4B)

el **abrigo** coat (I)

abril April (I)

abrir to open (I)

el **abuelo, la abuela** grandfather, grandmother (I)

los **abuelos** grandparents (I)

aburrido, -a boring (I)

aburrir to bore (I)

aburrirse to get bored (6A)

me aburre(n) it bores me (they bore me) (I)

acabar de + *inf.* to have just ... (I)

el **accidente** accident (5B)

acción: película de — action film (6B)

el **aceite** cooking oil (7A)

acompañar to accompany (7B)

acostarse (o →ue) to go to bed (2A)

las **actividades extracurriculares** extracurricular activities (1B)

el **actor** actor (I)

la **actriz,** *pl.* **las actrices** actress (I)

la **actuación** acting (6B)

acuerdo:

Estoy de —. I agree. (I)

No estoy de —. I don't agree. (I)

además (de) in addition (to), besides (9B)

adhesiva: la cinta — transparent tape (1A)

¡Adiós! Good-bye! (I)

¿Adónde? (To) where? (I)

la **aduana** customs (8A)

el **aduanero, la aduanera** customs officer (8A)

el **aeropuerto** airport (8A)

afeitarse to shave (2A)

el **aficionado, la aficionada** fan (6A)

afortunadamente fortunately (5A)

la **agencia de viajes** travel agency (8A)

el / la **agente de viajes** travel agent (8A)

agitado, -a agitated (6A)

agosto August (I)

el **agricultor, la agricultora** farmer (9A)

el **agua** *f.* water (I)

el **— de colonia** cologne (2A)

el **aguacate** avocado (7B)

ahora now (I)

ahorrar to save (9B)

aire: al — libre outdoors (7B)

el **aire acondicionado** air conditioning (9B)

el **ajedrez** chess (1B)

el **ajo** garlic (7A)

al *(a + el),* **a la** to the (I)

— **aire libre** outdoors (7B)

— **final** at the end (6A)

— **horno** baked (7A)

— **lado de** next to (I)

alegre happy (6A)

la **alfombra** rug (I)

algo something (I)

¿— **más?** Anything else? (I)

el **algodón** cotton (2B)

alguien someone, anyone (1A)

algún, alguno, -a some (1A)

— **día** some day (9A)

algunos, as some, any (1A)

allí there (I)

el **almacén,** *pl.* **los almacenes** department store (I)

almorzar (o→ue) (z→c) to have lunch (1A)

el **almuerzo** lunch (I)

en el — for lunch (I)

alquilar to rent (6B)

alrededor de around (4B)

alto, -a tall (I); high (2B)

amarillo, -a yellow (I)

la ambulancia ambulance (5B)

el amor love (6B)

anaranjado, -a orange (I)

ancho, -a wide (3B)

el anciano, la anciana older man, older woman (I)

los ancianos older people (I)

el anillo ring (I)

el animador, la animadora cheerleader (1B)

el animal animal (I)

el aniversario anniversary (4B)

anoche last night (I)

los anteojos de sol sunglasses (I)

antes de before (I, 2A)

antiguo, -a old, antique (4B)

anunciar to announce (2B)

el anuncio announcement (8A)

añadir to add (7A)

no añadas don't add (7A)

el año year (I)

el — pasado last year (I)

¿Cuántos —s tiene(n)...? How old is / are ...? (I)

Tiene(n)...—s. He / She is / They are ...(years old). (I)

apagar (g → gu) to put out (fire) (5A); to turn off (7A)

el apartamento apartment (I)

aplaudir to applaud (6A)

aprender (a) to learn (I)

— de memoria to memorize (1A)

apretado, -a tight (2B)

aproximadamente approximately (3B)

aquel, aquella that (over there) (2B)

aquellos, aquellas those (over there) (2B)

aquí here (I)

el árbol tree (I)

los aretes earrings (I)

el argumento plot (6B)

el armario closet, locker (I, 1A)

el arquitecto, la arquitecta architect (9A)

arreglar (el cuarto) to straighten up (the room) (I)

arreglarse (el pelo) to fix (one's hair) (2A)

arrestar to arrest (6B)

el arroz rice (I)

el arte: la clase de — art class (I)

las artes the arts (9A)

las — marciales martial arts (1B)

la artesanía handicrafts (8B)

el artículo article (5A)

el artista, la artista artist (9A)

artístico, -a artistic (I)

asado, -a grilled (7B)

asar to grill, to roast (7B)

el ascensor elevator (8B)

asco: ¡Qué —! How awful! (I)

el asiento seat (1A)

asistir a to attend (1B)

asustado, -a frightened (5A)

atención: prestar to pay attention (1A)

atento, -a attentive (8B)

el / la atleta athlete (6A)

la atracción, pl. las atracciones attraction (I)

atrevido, -a daring (I)

la audición, pl. las audiciones audition (2A)

el auditorio auditorium (6A)

el autobús, pl. los autobuses bus (I)

el / la auxiliar de vuelo flight attendant (8A)

la avenida avenue (3B)

el avión airplane (I)

¡Ay! ¡Qué pena! Oh! What a shame / pity! (I)

ayer yesterday (I)

la ayuda help (1A)

ayudar to help (I)

el azúcar sugar (I)

azul blue (I)

B

bailar to dance (I)

el bailarín, la bailarina, pl. los bailarines dancer (1B)

el baile dance (I)

bajar to go down (5A)

bajar (información) to download (I)

bajo, -a short (stature) (I); low (2B)

el banco bank (3A)

la banda (musical) band (1B)

la bandera flag (I)

bañarse to take a bath (2A)

el baño bathroom (I)

el traje de — swimsuit (I)

barato, -a inexpensive, cheap (I)

el barco boat, ship (I)

el barrio neighborhood (I)

basado, -a: estar — en to be based on (6B)

el básquetbol: jugar al — to play basketball (I)

Basta! Enough! (3B)

bastante enough, rather (I)

batir to beat (7A)

el bebé, la bebé baby (4B)

beber to drink (I)

las bebidas drinks (I)

béisbol: jugar al — to play baseball (I)

bello, -a beautiful (8B)

los beneficios benefits (9A)

besar(se) to kiss (4B)

la biblioteca library (I)

bien well (I)

— educado, -a well-behaved (4A)

bienvenido, -a welcome (8A)

bilingüe bilingual (9A)

el bistec beefsteak (I)

blanco, -a white (I)

los bloques blocks (4A)

la blusa blouse (I)

la boca mouth (I)

la boda wedding (2A)

el **boleto** ticket (I)

el **bolígrafo** pen (I)

los **bolos: jugar a los —** to bowl (1B)

la **bolsa** bag, sack (I)

el **bolso** purse (I)

el **bombero, la bombera** firefighter (5A)

bonito, -a pretty (I)

el **bosque** forest (9B)

las **botas** boots (I)

el **bote:**

    pasear en — to go boating (I)

    el **— de vela** sailboat (8B)

la **botella** bottle (I)

el **brazo** arm (I)

bucear to scuba dive, to snorkel (I)

bueno (buen), -a good (I)

    Buenas noches. Good evening. (I)

    Buenas tardes. Good afternoon. (I)

    Buenos días. Good morning. (I)

buscar (c→qu) to look for, to search (for) (I)

la **búsqueda** search (1B)

    hacer una — to do a search (1B)

el **buzón,** *pl.* **los buzones** mailbox (3A)

C

el **caballo: montar a —** to ride horseback (I)

la **cabeza** head (I)

cada día every day (I)

la **cadena** chain (I)

caerse to fall (5B)

    (yo) me caigo I fall (5B)
    (tú) te caes you fall (5B)

    se cayó he/she fell (5B)

    se cayeron they/you fell (5B)

el **café** coffee, café (I)

la **caja** box (I); cash register (2B)

el **cajero, la cajera** cashier (2B)

el **— automático** ATM (8B)

los **calcetines** socks (I)

la **calculadora** calculator (I)

el **caldo** broth (7A)

la **calefacción** heat (9B)

calentar (e→ie) to heat (7A)

caliente hot (7A)

la **calle** street, road (I)

calor:

    Hace —. It's hot. (I)

    tener — to be warm (I)

la **cama** bed (I)

    hacer la — to make the bed (I)

la **cámara** camera (I)

    la **— digital** digital camera (I)

el **camarero, la camarera** waiter, waitress (I)

el **camarón,** *pl.* **los camarones** shrimp (7A)

cambiar to change, to exchange (8B)

caminar to walk (I)

la **caminata** walk (7B)

    dar una — take a walk (7B)

el **camión,** *pl.* **los camiones** truck (3B)

la **camisa** shirt (I)

la **camiseta** T-shirt (I)

el **campamento** camp (I)

el **campeón, la campeona,** *pl.* **los campeones** champion (6A)

el **campeonato** championship (6A)

el **campo** countryside (I)

el **canal** (TV) channel (I)

la **canción,** *pl.* **las canciones** song (I, 1B)

canoso: pelo — gray hair (I)

cansado, -a tired (I)

el / la **cantante** singer (1B)

cantar to sing (I)

capturar to capture (6B)

la **cara** face (2A)

cara a cara face-to-face (I)

caramba good gracious (3A)

la **carne** meat (I)

    la **— de res** steak (7B)

el **carnet de identidad** ID card (1A)

caro, -a expensive (I)

la **carpeta** folder (I)

    la **— de argollas** three-ring binder (I)

la **carrera** career (9A)

la **carretera** highway (3B)

la **carta** letter (I, 3A)

    echar una — to mail a letter (3A)

el **cartel** poster (I)

la **cartera** wallet (I)

el **cartero, la cartera** mail carrier (9A)

el **cartón** cardboard (I)

la **casa** home, house (I)

    a — (to) home (I)

    en — at home (I)

    — de cambio currency exchange (8B)

casarse (con) to get married (to) (4B)

casi almost (I, 3A)

castaño: pelo — brown (chestnut) hair (I)

el **castillo** castle (8B)

la **catedral** cathedral (8B)

catorce fourteen (I)

la **causa** cause (5A)

a — de because of (5A)

la **cebolla** onion (I)

celebrar to celebrate (I)

la **cena** dinner (I)

el **centro** center, downtown (I, 3A)

    el **— comercial** mall (I)

    el **— de reciclaje** recycling center (I)

cepillarse (los dientes) to brush (one's teeth) (2A)

el **cepillo** brush (2A)

    el **— de dientes** toothbrush (3A)

cerca (de) close (to), near (I)

el **cerdo** pork (7B)

    la **chuleta de —** pork chop (7B)

el **cereal** cereal (I)

la **cereza** cherry (7B)

cero zero (I)

cerrado, -a closed (8A)

cerrar to close (3A)

la **cesta** basket (7B)

el **champú** shampoo (3A)

la **chaqueta** jacket (I)

charlar to chat (4B)

el **cheque:**

    cobrar un — to cash a check (3A)

    el — de viajero traveler's check (2B)

    el — (personal) (personal) check (2B)

la **chica** girl (I)

el **chico** boy (I)

    chocar (c→qu) con to crash into, to collide with (5B)

la **chuleta de cerdo** pork chop (7B)

el **cielo** sky (7B)

cien one hundred (I)

las **ciencias:**

    la clase de — naturales science class (I)

    la clase de — sociales social studies class (I)

el **científico, la científica** scientist (9A)

(es) cierto (it is) certain (9B)

cinco five (I)

cincuenta fifty (I)

el **cine** movie theater (I)

la **cinta adhesiva** transparent tape (1A)

el **cinturón, pl. los cinturones** belt (2A)

la **cita** date (2A)

la **ciudad** city (I)

claro, -a light (color) (2B)

la **clase** class (I)

    la sala de clases classroom (I)

¿Qué — de ...? What kind of ...? (I)

el **club, pl. los clubes** club (1B)

    el — atlético athletic club (1B)

cobrar un cheque to cash a check (3A)

el **coche** car (I)

la **cocina** kitchen (I)

cocinar to cook (I)

el **codo** elbow (5B)

la **colección, pl. las colecciones** collection (4A)

coleccionar to collect (4A)

el **colegio** secondary school, high school (9A)

la **colina** hill (9B)

el **collar** necklace (I)

el **color, pl. los colores** color (I)

    ¿De qué — ...? What color ...? (I)

    de sólo un — solid-colored (2B)

la **comedia** comedy (I)

el **comedor** dining room (I)

el **comentario** commentary (6A)

comenzar (e →ie) (z →c) to start (5A)

comer to eat (I)

cómico, -a funny, comical (I)

la **comida** food, meal (I)

como like, as (I)

¿Cómo?:

    ¿— eres? What are you like? (I)

    ¿— es? What is he / she like? (I)

    ¿— está Ud.? How are you? *formal* (I)

    ¿— estás? How are you? *fam.* (I)

    ¿— lo pasaste? How was it (for you)? (I)

    ¿— se dice...? How do you say ...? (I)

    ¿— se escribe...? How is...spelled? (I)

    ¿— se hace...? How do you make...? (7A)

    ¿— se llama? What's his / her name? (I)

    ¿— se va...? How do you go to...? (3B)

    ¿— te llamas? What is your name? (I)

    ¿— te queda(n)? How does it (do they) fit (you)? (I)

¡Cómo no! Of course! (3A)

la **cómoda** dresser (I)

cómodo, -a comfortable (2A)

compartir to share (I)

la **competencia** competition (6A)

competir (e→i) to compete (6A)

complicado, -a complicated (I, 3B)

la **composición, pl. las composiciones** composition (I)

comprar to buy (I)

comprar recuerdos to buy souvenirs (I)

comprender to understand (I)

la **computadora** computer (I)

    la — portátil laptop computer (I)

    usar la — to use the computer (I)

comunicarse (c→qu) to communicate (I)

    (tú) te comunicas you communicate (I)

    (yo) me comunico I communicate (I)

la **comunidad** community (I)

con with (I)

    — destino a going to (8A)

    — mis / tus amigos with my / your friends (I)

    ¿— qué se sirve? What do you serve it with? (7A)

    ¿— quién? With whom? (I)

el **concierto** concert (I)

el **concurso** contest (2A)

    el — de belleza beauty contest (6A)

    el programa de —s game show (I)

el **conductor, la conductora** driver (3B)

congelado, -a frozen (7A)

conmigo with me (I)

conocer (c→zc) to know, to be acquainted with (I, 1A)

conseguir (e → i) to obtain (8B)

consentido, -a spoiled (4A)

conservar to conserve (9B)

el **consultorio** doctor's /dentist's office (3A)

el **contador, la contadora** accountant (9A)

la **contaminación** pollution (9B)

contaminado, -a polluted (9B)

contar (o→ue) (chistes) to tell (jokes) (4B)

contento, -a happy (I)

contestar to answer (1A)

contigo with you (I)

contra against (9B)

la **corbata** tie (I)

el **coro** chorus, choir (1B)

el **correo** post office (3A)

el **correo electrónico** e-mail (I)

escribir por — to write e-mail (I)

correr to run (I)

cortar to cut (I, 7A)

— el césped to mow the lawn (I)

—se to cut oneself (5B)

—se el pelo to cut one's hair (2A)

cortés, *pl.* **corteses** polite (8B)

las **cortinas** curtains (I)

corto, -a short *(length)* (I)

los **pantalones —s** shorts (I)

la **cosa** thing (I)

costar (o→ue) to cost (I)

¿Cuánto cuesta(n)...? How much does (do) … cost? (I)

la **costumbre** custom (4B)

crear to create (I)

— una página Web to create a Web page (1B)

creer (i→y):

Creo que... I think... (I)

Creo que no. I don't think so. (I)

Creo que sí. I think so. (I)

el **crimen** crime (6B)

el / la **criminal** criminal (6B)

el **crítico, la crítica** critic (6B)

el **cruce de calles** intersection (3B)

cruzar to cross (3B)

el **cuaderno** notebook (I)

la **cuadra** block (3B)

el **cuadro** painting (I)

¿Cuál? Which? What? (I)

¿— es la fecha? What is the date? (I)

¿Cuándo? When? (I)

¿Cuánto?:

¿— cuesta(n)...? How much does (do)...cost? (I)

¿— tiempo hace que...? How long...? (1B)

¿Cuántos, -as? How many? (I)

¿—s años tiene(n)...? How old is / are...? (I)

cuarenta forty (I)

cuarto, -a fourth (I)

y — quarter past *(in telling time)* (I)

el **cuarto** room (I)

cuatro four (I)

cuatrocientos, -as four hundred (I)

la **cuchara** spoon (I)

la **cucharada** tablespoon(ful) (7A)

el **cuchillo** knife (I)

el **cuello** neck (5B)

la **cuenta** bill (I)

la **cuerda** rope (4A)

el **cuero** leather (2B)

cuidar a to take care of (3A)

el **cumpleaños** birthday (I)

¡Feliz —! Happy birthday! (I)

cumplir años to have a birthday (4B)

el **cupón de regalo,** *pl.* **los cupones de regalo** gift certificate (2B)

el **curso: tomar un curso** to take a course (I)

D _____

dar to give (I)

— + *movie or TV program* to show (I)

— de comer al perro to feed the dog (I)

— puntadas to stitch *(surgically)* (5B)

— un discurso to give a speech (1A)

— una caminata to take a walk (7B)

dar(se) la mano to shake hands (4B)

de of, from (I)

— acuerdo. OK. Agreed. (3B)

— algodón cotton (2B)

— cuero leather (2B)

¿— dónde eres? Where are you from? (I)

— ida y vuelta round trip (8A)

— la mañana / la tarde / la noche in the morning / afternoon / evening (I)

— lana wool (2B)

— moda in fashion (2B)

— negocios business (9A)

— niño as a child (4A)

— oro gold (2A)

— pequeño as a child (4A)

— plata silver (2A)

— plato principal as a main dish (I)

— postre for dessert (I)

— prisa in a hurry (5A)

¿— qué color ...? What color ...? (I)

¿— qué está hecho, -a? What is it made of? (2B)

— repente suddenly (5A)

— seda silk (2B)

— **sólo un color** solid-colored (2B)

— **tela sintética** synthetic fabric (2B)

¿— veras? Really? (I)

— **vez en cuando** once in a while (4A)

debajo de underneath (I)

deber should, must (I)

decidir to decide (I)

décimo, -a tenth (I)

decir to say, to tell (I)

¿Cómo se dice ...? How do you say ...? (I)

dime tell me (I)

¡No me digas! You don't say! (I)

¿Qué quiere — ...? What does...mean? (I)

Quiere — ... It means ... (I)

Se dice... You say... (I)

las **decoraciones** decorations (I)

decorar to decorate (I)

el **dedo** finger (I)

Déjame en paz. Leave me alone. (3B)

dejar to leave (*something*), to let (3B)

no dejes don't leave, don't let (7A)

delante de in front of (I)

delicioso, -a delicious (I)

los **demás, las demás** others (I)

demasiado too (I)

el / la **dentista** dentist (3A)

dentro de inside (7B)

depende it depends (2A)

el **dependiente, la dependienta** salesperson (I)

deportista athletic, sports-minded (I)

derecha: a la — (de) to the right (of) (I)

derecho straight (3B)

el **derecho** (*study of*) law (9A)

el **desayuno** breakfast (I)

en el — for breakfast (I)

descansar to rest, to relax (I)

los **descuentos: la tienda de —** discount store (I)

desde from, since (3B)

desear to wish (I)

¿Qué desean (Uds.)? What would you like? *formal* (I)

el **desfile** parade (4B)

el **desierto** desert (9B)

desobediente disobedient (4A)

el **desodorante** deodorant (2A)

desordenado, -a messy (I)

despacio slowly (3B)

el **despacho** office (home) (I)

despedirse (e→i) (de) to say good-bye (*to*) (4B)

el **despertador** alarm clock (I)

despertarse (e→ie) to wake up (2A)

después (de) afterwards, after (I)

destino: con — a going to (8A)

la **destrucción** destruction (9B)

destruir (i→y) to destroy (5A)

el / la **detective** detective (6B)

detrás de behind (I)

devolver (o→ue) (un libro) to return (a book) (3A)

el **día** day (I)

Buenos —s. Good morning. (I)

cada — every day (I)

el — festivo holiday (4B)

¿Qué — es hoy? What day is today? (I)

todos los —s every day (I)

la **diapositiva** slide (I)

dibujar to draw (I)

el **diccionario** dictionary (I)

diciembre December (I)

diecinueve nineteen (I)

dieciocho eighteen (I)

dieciséis sixteen (I)

diecisiete seventeen (I)

los **dientes** teeth (2A)

cepillarse — to brush one's teeth (2A)

el cepillo de — toothbrush (2A)

diez ten (I)

difícil difficult (I)

digital: la cámara — digital camera (I)

dime tell me (I)

el **dinero** money (I)

el **dinosaurio** dinosaur (4A)

la **dirección,** *pl.* **las direcciones** direction (6B)

la — electrónica e-mail address (I)

directo, -a direct (8A)

el **director, la directora** (*school*) principal (6B)

el **disco compacto** compact disc (I)

grabar un — to burn a CD (I)

el **discurso** speech (1A)

discutir to discuss (1A)

el **diseñador, la diseñadora** designer (9A)

disfrutar de to enjoy (8B)

divertido, -a amusing, fun (I)

divertirse (e→ie) (e→i) to have fun (4B)

doblar to turn (3B)

doce twelve (I)

el **documento** document (I)

doler (o→ue) to hurt (I, 5B)

el **dolor** pain (5B)

domingo Sunday (I)

dónde:

¿—? Where? (I)

¿De — eres? Where are you from? (I)

dormido, -a asleep (5A)

dormir (o→ue) (o→u) to sleep (I)

—se to fall asleep (6A)

el **dormitorio** bedroom (I)

dos two (I)

los / las dos both (I)

doscientos, -as two hundred (I)

el **drama** drama (I)

la **ducha** shower (2A)

ducharse to take a shower (2A)

dudar to doubt (9B)

el **dueño, la dueña** owner (9A)

dulce sweet (7B)

los **dulces** candy (I)

durante during (I)

durar to last (I, 8A)

el **durazno** peach (7B)

E

echar una carta to mail a letter (3A)

ecológico, -a ecological (9B)

económico, -a economical (9B)

el **edificio de apartamentos** apartment building (5A)

la **educación física: la clase de —** physical education class (I)

efectivo: en — cash (2B)

los **efectos especiales** special effects (6B)

eficiente efficient (9B)

ejemplo: por — for example (2A)

el **ejercicio: hacer —** to exercise (I)

el *m. sing.* the (I)

él he (I)

la **electricidad** electricity (9B)

los **electrodomésticos: la tienda de —** household-appliance store (I)

electrónico, -a: la dirección — e-mail address (I)

elegante elegant (2A)

eliminar to eliminate (9B)

ella she (I)

ellas *f.* they (I)

ellos *m.* they (I)

emocionado, -a excited, emotional (6A)

emocionante touching (I)

el **empate** tie (6A)

empezar (e→ie) (z→c) to begin, to start (I, 1A)

el **empleado, la empleada** employee (8A)

en in, on (I)

— **+** *vehicle* by, in, on (I)

— **casa** at home (I)

— **efectivo** cash (2B)

— **la ... hora** in the ... hour (class period) (I)

— **la Red** online (I)

— **línea** online (1B)

— **medio de** in the middle of (3B)

— **peligro de extinción** endangered, in danger of extinction (9B)

— **punto** exactly *(time)* (8B)

¿— **qué puedo servirle?** How can I help you? (I)

— **realidad** really (2B)

— **seguida** right away (3A)

enamorado, -a de in love with (6B)

enamorarse (de) to fall in love (with) (6B)

encantado, -a delighted (I)

encantar to please very much, to love (I)

a él / ella le encanta(n) he / she loves (I)

me / te encanta(n)... I / you love ... (I)

encender (e→ie) to turn on, to light (7A)

encima de on top of (I)

encontrar (o→ue) to find (2B)

la **energía** energy (9B)

enero January (I)

el **enfermero, la enfermera** nurse (5B)

enfermo, -a sick (I)

enlatado, -a canned (7A)

enojado, -a angry (6A)

enojarse to get angry (6A)

enorme enormous (4B)

la **ensalada** salad (I)

la — de frutas fruit salad (I)

ensayar to rehearse (1B)

el **ensayo** rehearsal (1B)

enseñar to teach (I)

entender (e→ie) to understand (1A)

entonces then (I)

la **entrada** entrance (2B)

entrar to enter (I)

entre among, between (1B)

entregar to turn in (1A)

el **entrenador, la entrenadora** coach, trainer (6A)

la **entrevista** interview (6A)

entrevistar to interview (6A)

entusiasmado, -a excited (2A)

enviar (i→í) to send (I, 3A)

el **equipaje** luggage (8A)

facturar el — to check luggage (8A)

el **equipo** team (1B)

el — de sonido sound (stereo) system (I)

el — deportivo sports equipment (3A)

¿**Eres...?** Are you ...? (I)

es is; (he / she / it) is (I)

— **cierto** it's true (9B)

— **el** *(number)* **de** *(month)* **it is the... of...** *(in telling the date)* (I)

— **el primero de** *(month)*. It is the first of ... (I)

— **la una.** It is one o'clock. (I)

— **necesario.** It's necessary. (I)

— **un(a) ...** It's a ... (I)

la **escala** stopover (8A)

la **escalera** stairs, stairway (I), ladder (5A)

escaparse to escape (5A)

la **escena** scene (6B)

escoger (g→j) to choose (2B)

esconder(se) to hide (oneself) (5A)

escribir:

¿**Cómo se escribe ...?** How

is ... spelled? (I)

    — **cuentos** to write stories (I)

    — **por correo electrónico** to write e-mail (I)

    — **un informe sobre...** to write a report about...

    Se escribe ... It's spelled ... (I)

el **escritor, la escritora** writer (9A)

el **escritorio** desk (I)

escuchar música to listen to music (I)

la **escuela primaria** primary school (I)

la **escuela técnica** technical school (9A)

ese, esa that (I, 2B)

eso: por — that's why, therefore (I)

esos, esas those (I, 2B)

el **espacio** (outer) space (9B)

los **espaguetis** spaghetti (I)

la **espalda** back (5B)

el **español: la clase de —** Spanish class (I)

especial special (2A)

especialmente especially (I)

el **espejo** mirror (I)

esperar to wait (3B)

la **esposa** wife (I)

el **esposo** husband (I)

el **esquí acuático** waterskiing (8B)

esquiar to ski (I)

la **esquina** corner (3B)

Está hecho, -a de ... It is made of ... (2B)

esta noche this evening (I)

esta tarde this afternoon (I)

la **estación,** *pl.* **las estaciones** season (I)

    la — de servicio service station (3A)

el **estadio** stadium (I)

el **estante** shelf, bookshelf (I)

estar to be (I)

    ¿Cómo está Ud.? How are

you? *formal* (I)

¿Cómo estás? How are you? fam. (I)

— + *present participle* to be + *present participle* (I)

    — **basado, -a en** to be based on (6B)

    — **de moda** to be in fashion (2B)

    — **en línea** to be online (I, 1B)

    — **enamorado, -a de** to be in love with (6B)

    — **seguro, -a** to be sure (3B)

    No estoy de acuerdo. I don't agree. (I)

la **estatua** statue (3B)

este, esta this (I, 2B)

este fin de semana this weekend (I)

el **estilo** style (2B)

el **estómago** stomach (I)

estos, estas these (I, 2B)

    ¿Qué es esto? What is this? (I)

estrecho, -a narrow (3B)

la **estrella (del cine)** (movie) star (6B)

el / la **estudiante** student (I)

estudiar to study (I)

estudioso, -a studious (I)

la **estufa** stove (7A)

estupendo, -a stupendous, wonderful (8B)

el **evento especial** special event (2A)

exagerado, -a outrageous (2B)

el **éxito** success (6B)

    tener — to be successful (6B)

examinar to examine, to check (5B)

la **excursión,** *pl.* **las excursiones** excursion, short trip (8B)

la **experiencia** experience (I)

explicar to explain (1A)

la **explosión,** *pl.* **las explosiones** explosion (5A)

extracurricular extracurricular

(1B)

extranjero, -a foreign (8A)

el / la **extraterrestre** alien (6B)

F

fácil easy (I)

facturar to check (luggage) (8A)

la **falda** skirt (I)

faltar to be missing (I)

famoso, -a famous (8B)

fantástico, -a fantastic (I)

la **farmacia** pharmacy (3A)

fascinante fascinating (I)

fascinar to fascinate (6B)

favorito, -a favorite (I)

febrero February (I)

la **fecha: ¿Cuál es la —?** What is the date? (I)

¡Felicidades! Congratulations! (4B)

felicitar to congratulate (4B)

¡Feliz cumpleaños! Happy birthday! (I)

fenomenal phenomenal (6A)

feo, -a ugly (I)

la **fiesta** party (I)

    la — de sorpresa surprise party (4B)

el **fin de semana:**

    este — this weekend (I)

    los fines de semana on weekends (I)

final: al final at the end (6A)

flojo, -a loose (2B)

la **flor,** *pl.* **las flores** flower (I)

la **fogata** bonfire (7B)

el **fósforo** match (7B)

la **foto** photo (I)

la **fotografía** photography (1B)

el **fotógrafo, la fotógrafa** photographer (1B)

el **fracaso** failure (6B)

frecuentemente frequently (4B)

el **fregadero** sink (7A)

freír (e→í) to fry (7A)

las **fresas** strawberries (I)

fresco, -a fresh (7A)

los **frijoles** beans (7B)

el **frío:**

Hace —. It's cold. (I)

tener — to be cold (I)

frito, -a fried (7A)

fue it was (I)

— un desastre. It was a disaster. (I)

el **fuego** fire (7A)

los **fuegos artificiales** fireworks (4B)

la **fuente** fountain (3B); source (9B)

fuera (de) outside (7B)

funcionar to function, to work (9B)

furioso, -a furious (6A)

el **fútbol: jugar al —** to play soccer (I)

el **fútbol americano: jugar al —** to play football (I)

el **futuro** future (9A)

G —————

el **galán,** *pl.* **los galanes** leading man (6B)

la **galleta** cookie (I)

ganar to win (I); to earn *(money)* (1B)

—se la vida to make a living (9A)

la **ganga** bargain (2B)

el **garaje** garage (I)

la **gasolina** gasoline (3A)

gastar to spend (2B)

el **gato** cat (I)

el **gel** gel (2A)

generalmente generally (I)

generoso, -a generous (4A)

¡Genial! Great! (I)

la **gente** people (I)

el / la **gerente** manager (9A)

la **gimnasia** gymnastics (1B)

hacer — to do gymnastics (1B)

el **gimnasio** gym (I)

gira: — hacer una — to take a tour (8B)

el **globo** balloon (I)

el **gol** goal (in sports) (6A)

meter un — to score a goal (6A)

el **golf: jugar al —** to play golf (I)

la **gorra** cap (I)

grabar to record (1B)

— un disco compacto to burn a CD (I)

gracias thank you (I)

gracioso, -a funny (I)

la **graduación,** *pl.* **las graduaciones** graduation (9A)

graduarse (u→ú) to graduate (9A)

los **gráficos** computer graphics (I)

grande large (I)

la **grapadora** stapler (1A)

grasoso, -a fatty (7B)

grave serious (9B)

gris gray (I)

gritar to scream (5A)

los **guantes** gloves (I)

guapo, -a good-looking (I)

la **guardería infantil** day-care center (4A)

la **guerra** war (9B)

el / la **guía** guide (8B)

la **guía** guidebook (8B)

los **guisantes** peas (I)

gustar:

a él / ella le gusta(n) he / she likes (I)

(A mí) me gusta ... I like to ... (I)

(A mí) me gusta más... I like to ... better (I prefer to ...) (I)

(A mí) me gusta mucho ... I like to ... a lot (I)

(A mí) no me gusta ... I don't like to ... (I)

(A mí) no me gusta nada ... I don't like to...at all. (I)

Le gusta ... He / She likes... (I)

Me gusta ... I like... (I)

Me gustaría... I would like ... (I)

Me gustó. I liked it. (I)

No le gusta ... He / She doesn't like ... (I)

¿Qué te gusta hacer? What do you like to do? (I)

¿Qué te gusta hacer más? What do you like better (prefer) to do? (I)

Te gusta ... You like ... (I)

¿Te gusta ...? Do you like to ...? (I)

¿Te gustaría? Would you like? (I)

¿Te gustó? Did you like it? (I)

H —————

haber to have *(as an auxiliary verb)* (6B)

había there was / there were (4B)

la **habitación,** *pl.* **las habitaciones** room (8B)

la — doble double room (8B)

la — individual single room (8B)

hablar to talk (I)

— por teléfono to talk on the phone (I)

habrá there will be (9A)

hacer to do (I)

¿Cómo se hace...? How do you make...? (7A)

¿Cuánto tiempo hace que...? How long...? (1B)

hace + *time expression* ago (I)

Hace + *time* **+ que ...** It has been ... (1B)

Hace calor. It's hot. (I)

Hace frío. It's cold. (I)

Hace sol. It's sunny. (I)

— ejercicio to exercise (I)

— el papel de to play the role of (6B)

— escala to stop over (8A)

— gimnasia to do gymnastics

(1B)

— la cama to make the bed (I)

— la maleta to pack the suitcase (8A)

— ruido to make noise (8B)

— un picnic to have a picnic (4B)

— un viaje to take a trip (8A)

— un video to videotape (I)

— una búsqueda to do a search (1B)

— una gira to take a tour (8B)

— una parrillada to have a barbecue (7B)

— una pregunta to ask a question (1A)

¿Qué hiciste? What did you do? (I)

¿Qué tiempo hace? What is the weather like? (I)

(tú) haces you do (I)

(yo) hago I do (I)

hambre: Tengo —. I'm hungry. (I)

la **hamburguesa** hamburger (I)

la **harina** flour (7B)

has visto you have seen (6B)

hasta until (3A); as far as, up to (3B)

— luego. See you later. (I)

— mañana. See you tomorrow. (I)

— pronto. See you soon. (3A)

hay there is, there are (I)

— que one must (I)

haya *(subjunctive)* there is, there are (9B)

haz *(command)* do, make (I)

he visto I have seen (6B)

hecho: ¿De qué está — ? What is it made of? (2B)

el **helado** ice cream (I)

herido, -a injured (5A)

el **herido, la herida** injured person (5A)

el **hermano, la hermana** brother, sister (I)

el **hermanastro, la hermanastra** stepbrother, stepsister (I)

los **hermanos** brothers, brother(s) and sister(s) (I)

el **héroe** hero (5A)

la **heroína** heroine (5A)

hervir (e→ie) (e→i) to boil (7A)

el **hijo, la hija** son, daughter (I)

los **hijos** children, sons (I)

histórico, -a historical (8B)

el **hockey** hockey (1B)

la **hoja de papel** sheet of paper (I)

¡Hola! Hello! (I)

el **hombre** man (I)

el **— de negocios** businessman (9A)

el **hombro** shoulder (5B)

la **hora: en la... —** in the...hour (class period) (I)

¿A qué —? (At) what time? (I)

el **horario** schedule (I)

la **hormiga** ant (7B)

el **horno** oven (7A)

al — baked (7A)

horrible horrible (I)

el **horror: la película de —** horror movie (I)

el **hospital** hospital (I)

el **hotel** hotel (I)

hoy today (I)

hubo there was, there were (5A)

el **hueso** bone (5B)

los **huevos** eggs (I)

el **humo** smoke (5A)

el **huracán,** *pl.* **los huracanes** hurricane (5A)

I _____

ida y vuelta round-trip (8A)

identidad: carnet de — ID card

el **idioma** language (9A)

la **iglesia** church (I)

igualmente likewise (I)

impaciente impatient (I)

importante important (I)

importa(n): me/te — it matters (it's important)/they matter to me/to you (2B)

impresionante impressive (I)

el **incendio** fire (5A)

increíble incredible (I)

infantil childish (I)

la **información** information (I)

el **informe** report (I, 1A)

el **ingeniero, la ingeniera** engineer (9A)

el **inglés: la clase de —** English class (I)

el **ingrediente** ingredient (7A)

inmediatamente immediately (2B)

inolvidable unforgettable (I)

insistir en to insist (8A)

la **inspección,** *pl.* **las inspecciones de seguridad** security checkpoint (8A)

inteligente intelligent (I)

el **interés** interest (1B)

interesante interesting (I)

interesar to interest (I)

me interesa(n) it interests me (they interest me) (I)

la **inundación,** *pl.* **las inundaciones** flood (5A)

investigar (g → gu) to investigate (5A)

el **invierno** winter (I)

la **inyección,** *pl.* **las inyecciones** injection, shot (5B)

poner una — to give an injection (5B)

ir to go (I)

— a + *inf.* to be going to + *verb* (I)

— a la escuela to go to school (I)

— a pie to go on foot (3A)

— de cámping to go camping (I)

— de compras to go shopping (I)

— de pesca to go fishing (I)

— **de vacaciones** to go on vacation (I)

¡Vamos! Let's go! (I)

el **itinerario** itinerary (8B)

la **izquierda: a la — (de)** to the left (of) (I)

J

el **jabón** soap (3A)

el **jardín,** *pl.* **los jardines** garden, yard (I)

los **jeans** jeans (I)

joven *adj.* young (I)

el / la **joven** young man, young woman (I)

los **jóvenes** young people (1B)

las **joyas (de oro, de plata)** (gold, silver) jewelry (2A)

la **joyería** jewelry store (I)

las **judías verdes** green beans (I)

jueves Thursday (I)

el **juez, la jueza,** *pl.* **los jueces** judge (9A)

el **jugador, la jugadora** player (6A)

jugar (a) (u→ue) (g→gu) to play *(games, sports)* (I)

— **a los bolos** to bowl (1B)

— **al básquetbol** to play basketball (I)

— **al béisbol** to play baseball (I)

— **al fútbol** to play soccer (I)

— **al fútbol americano** to play football (I)

— **al golf** to play golf (I)

— **al tenis** to play tennis (I)

— **al vóleibol** to play volleyball (I)

— **videojuegos** to play video games (I)

el **jugo:**

el — **de manzana** apple juice (I)

el — **de naranja** orange juice (I)

el **juguete** toy (I)

julio July (I)

junio June (I)

juntarse to join (9B)

L

la **the** *f. sing.* (I); it, her *f. dir. obj. pron.* (I)

los **labios** lips (2A)

el **laboratorio** laboratory (I, 1A)

el **lado: al — de** next to (I)

el **ladrón, la ladrona,** *pl.* **los ladrones** thief (6B)

el **lago** lake (I)

la **lámpara** lamp (I)

la **lana** wool (2B)

el **lápiz,** *pl.* **los lápices** pencil (I)

largo, -a long (I)

las **the** *f. pl.;* them, you *formal pl. f. dir. obj. pron.* (I)

— **dos, los dos** both (I)

lástima: ¡Qué —! What a shame! (5B)

lastimarse to hurt oneself (5B)

la **lata** can (I)

lavar to wash (I)

— **el coche** to wash the car (I)

— **la ropa** to wash the clothes (I)

— **los platos** to wash the dishes (I)

—**se la cara** to wash one's face (2A)

le (to / for) him, her, you *formal sing. ind. obj. pron.* (I)

— **gusta ...** He / She likes... (I)

— **traigo ...** I will bring you ... (I)

No — gusta ... He / She doesn't like ... (I)

la **lección,** *pl.* **las lecciones de piano** piano lesson (class) (I)

tomar lecciones to take lessons (1B)

la **leche** milk (I)

la **lechuga** lettuce (I)

el **lector DVD** DVD player (I)

leer (i→y) revistas to read magazines (I)

lejos (de) far (from) (I)

lentamente slowly (2A)

la **leña** firewood (7B)

les (to / for) them; you *(formal) pl. ind. obj. pron.* (I)

el **letrero** sign (2B)

levantar pesas to lift weights (I)

levantarse to get up (2A)

la **ley** law (9A)

la **librería** bookstore (I)

el **libro** book (I)

la **liga** league (6A)

la **limonada** lemonade (I)

limpiar el baño to clean the bathroom (I)

limpio, -a clean (I)

la **línea:**

estar en — to be online (I, 1B)

la — aérea airline (8A)

la **liquidación,** *pl.* **las liquidaciones** sale (2B)

listo, -a ready (8A)

llamar:

— **por teléfono** to call on the phone (5A)

¿Cómo se llama? What's his / her name? (I)

¿Cómo te llamas? What is your name? (I)

Me llamo ... My name is ... (I)

la **llave** key (8B)

el **llavero** key chain (I)

la **llegada** arrival (8A)

llegar: llegar tarde to arrive late (1A)

llenar (el tanque) to fill (the tank) (3A)

llevar to wear (I); to take, to carry, to bring (I)

llevarse bien / mal to get along well / badly (4B)

llorar to cry (4B)

llover (o→ue) to rain (5A)

Llueve. It's raining. (I)

la lluvia rain (5A)

lo it, him, you *formal m. dir. obj. pron.* (I)

— siento. I'm sorry. (I)

lo que what (1A)

loco, -a: volverse (o→ue) — to go crazy (6A)

el locutor, la locutora announcer (5A)

los the *m. pl.* (I); them, you *formal pl. m. dir. obj. pron.* (I)

— dos, las dos both (I)

— fines de semana on weekends (I)

— lunes, los martes... on Mondays, on Tuesdays... (I)

luchar to fight (9B)

luego then (2A)

el lugar place (I)

la Luna the moon (9B)

lunes Monday (I)

los lunes on Mondays (I)

la luz, *pl.* **las luces** light (I)

M

la madrastra stepmother (I)

la madre (mamá) mother (I)

el maíz corn (7B)

mal bad, badly (I)

la maleta suitcase (8A)

hacer la — to pack the suitcase (8A)

malo, -a bad (I)

manejar to drive (3B)

la manera way, manner (9B)

la mano hand (I)

darse la — to shake hands (4B)

mantener: para — la salud to maintain one's health (I)

la mantequilla butter (I)

la manzana apple (I)

el jugo de — apple juice (I)

mañana tomorrow (I)

la mañana:

a las ocho de la — at eight

(o'clock) in the morning (I)

de la — in the morning (I)

el maquillaje make-up (2A)

el mar sea (I)

la marca brand (2B)

los mariscos shellfish (7A)

marrón *pl.* **marrones** brown (I)

martes Tuesday (I)

los martes on Tuesdays (I)

marzo March (I)

más:

¿Qué —? What else? (I)

— ...que more...than (I)

— de more than (I)

— o menos more or less (I)

matar to kill (6B)

las matemáticas: la clase de — mathematics class (I)

los materiales supplies, materials (1A)

mayo May (I)

la mayonesa mayonnaise (7B)

mayor, *pl.* **mayores** *adj.* older (I)

los mayores grown-ups (4B)

me (to / for) me *dir., ind. obj. pron.* (I)

— aburre(n) it / they bore(s) me (I)

— estás poniendo nervioso, -a. You are making me nervous. (3B)

— falta(n) ... I need ... (I)

— gustaría I would like (I)

— gustó. I liked it. (I)

— importa(n) it matters (it's important) they matter to me (2B)

— interesa(n) it / they interest(s) me (I)

— llamo ... My name is ... (I)

— parece it seems to me (2B)

— queda(n) bien / mal. It / They fit(s) me well / poorly. (I)

— quedo en casa. I stay at home. (I)

¿— trae...? Will you bring me ...? *formal* (I)

el mecánico, la mecánica mechanic (9A)

media, -o half (I)

y — thirty, half past (I)

mediano, -a medium (2B)

la medicina medicine (5B)

el médico, la médica doctor (3A)

medio ambiente environment (9B)

mejor:

el/ la —, los / las —es the best (I)

—(es) que better than (I)

mejorar to improve (9B)

el melón, *pl.* **los melones** melon (7B)

memoria: aprender de — to memorize (1A)

menor younger (I)

menos:

más o — more or less (I)

— ... que less / fewer ... than (I)

— de less / fewer than (I)

mentir (e→ie) (e→i) to lie (4A)

el menú menu (I)

menudo: a — often (I)

el mercado market (2B)

el mes month (I)

la mesa table (I)

poner la — to set the table (I)

la mesita night table (I)

meter: — un gol to score a goal (6A)

el metro subway (3B)

mezclar to mix (7A)

la mezquita mosque (I)

mi, mis my (I)

mí:

a — también I do (like to) too (I)

a — tampoco I don't (like to) either (I)

para — in my opinion, for me (I)

el microondas microwave (7A)

el miedo: tener — (de) to be

scared (of), to be afraid (of) (I)

el miembro member (1B)

ser — to be a member (1B)

mientras (que) while (4B)

miércoles Wednesday (I)

mil thousand (I)

militar *(adj.)* military (9A)

un millón de / millones de a million / millions of (6A)

mío, -a, -os, -as mine (2A)

mirar to look (at) (I)

mismo, -a same (I)

la mochila bookbag, backpack (I)

moda: de — in fashion (2B)

los modales manners (4B)

mojado, -a wet (7B)

molestar to bother (4A)

el momento: un — a moment (I)

la moneda coin (4A)

el mono monkey (I)

las montañas mountains (I)

montar:

— a caballo to ride horse back (I)

— en bicicleta to ride a bicycle (I)

— en monopatín to skateboard (I)

el monumento monument (I)

morado, -a purple (I)

morirse (o →ue)(o →u) to die (6A)

se murieron they died (5A)

la mosca fly (7B)

la mostaza mustard (7B)

la moto acuática jet skiing (8B)

moverse (o→ue) to move (5B)

mucho, -a a lot (I)

— gusto pleased to meet you (I)

muchos, -as many (I)

los muebles furniture (5A)

muerto, -a dead (5A)

la mujer woman (I)

la — de negocios

businesswoman (9A)

las muletas crutches (5B)

la multa ticket (3B)

el mundo world (4A)

la muñeca doll (4A); wrist (5B)

el muñeco action figure (4A)

el músculo muscle (5B)

el museo museum (I)

el músico, la música musician (1B)

muy very (I)

— bien very well (I)

N _____

nacer to be born (4B)

nada nothing (I)

(A mí) no me gusta — ... I don't like to...at all. (I)

nadar to swim (I)

nadie no one, nobody (1A)

la naranja: el jugo de — orange juice (I)

la nariz, *pl.* **las narices** nose (I)

la natación swimming (1B)

la naturaleza nature (9B)

navegar to sail, to navigate (8B)
— en la Red to surf the Web (I, 1B)

necesario: Es —. It's necessary. (I)

necesitar:

necesitas you need (I)

necesito I need (I)

los negocios business (9A)

el hombre de — business man (9A)

la mujer de — business woman (9A)

negro: el pelo negro black hair (I)

nervioso, -a nervous (2A)

nevar (e→ie) to snow (5A)

Nieva. It's snowing. (I)

ni ... ni neither ... nor, not ... or (I)

ningún, ninguno, -a no, none, not any (1A)

el niño, la niña young boy, young girl (I)

los niños children (I)

No comas. Don't eat. (7A)

No dejes Don't leave, don't let (7A)

No escribas. Don't write. (7A)

No estoy de acuerdo. I don't agree. (I)

No hables. Don't speak. (7A)

¡No me digas! You don't say! (I)

no ... todavía not yet (6B)

la noche:

a las ocho de la — at eight (o'clock) in the evening, at night (I)

Buenas —s. Good evening. (I)

de la — in the evening, at night (I)

esta — this evening, tonight (I)

nos (to / for) us *dir., ind. obj. pron.* (I)

¡— vemos! See you later! (I)

nosotros, -as we (I)

la nota grade, mark (in school) (1A)

sacar una buena — to get a good grade (1A)

el noticiero newscast (5A)

novecientos, -as nine hundred (I)

noveno, -a ninth (I)

noventa ninety (I)

noviembre November (I)

el novio, la novia boyfriend, girlfriend (I)

la nube cloud (7B)

nuestro, -a, -os, -as our, ours (I)

nueve nine (I)

nuevo, -a new (I)

el número shoe size (2B)

nunca never (I)

O _____

o or (I)

obedecer (c→zc) to obey (4A)

obediente obedient (4A)

la **obra de teatro** play (I)

observar to observe (8B)

ochenta eighty (I)

ocho eight (I)

ochocientos, -as eight hundred (I)

octavo, -a eighth (I)

octubre October (I)

ocupado, -a busy (I)

ocurrir to occur (5A)

ofender to offend (8B)

la **oficina** office (9A)

ofrecer (c→zc) to offer (4A)

oír to hear (5A)

el **ojo** eye (I)

la **olla** pot (7A)

el **olor** smell, odor (7B)

olvidarse de to forget about (7A)

   no te olvides de don't forget about / to (7A)

   se me olvidó I forgot (3A)

once eleven (I)

la **oportunidad** opportunity (1B)

ordenado, -a neat (I)

el **oro** gold (2A)

la **orquesta** orchestra (1B)

os (to / for) you *pl. fam. dir., ind. obj. pron.* (I)

oscuro, -a dark (2B)

el **oso** bear (I)

   el — de peluche teddy bear (4A)

el **otoño** fall, autumn (I)

otro, -a other, another (I)

otra vez again (I)

¡Oye! Hey! (I)

P _____

la **paciencia** pacience (8A)

   tener — to be patient (8A)

paciente *adj.* patient (I)

el **padrastro** stepfather (I)

el **padre (papá)** father (I)

los **padres** parents (I)

pagar (por) to pay (for) (I)

la **página Web** Web page (I)

el **país** country (I)

el **pájaro** bird (I)

la **palabra** word (1A)

el **palacio** palace (8B)

el **palo de golf** golf club (3A)

el **pan** bread (I)

   el — tostado toast (I)

la **pantalla** (computer) screen (I)

los **pantalones** pants (I)

   los — cortos shorts (I)

las **papas** potatoes (I)

   las — fritas French fries (I)

el **papel** role (6B)

   el — picado cut-paper decorations (I)

   hacer el — de to play the role of (6B)

la **papelera** wastepaper basket (I)

para for (I)

   — + *inf.* in order to (I)

   — la salud for one's health (I)

   — mantener la salud to maintain one's health (I)

   — mí in my opinion, for me (I)

   ¿ — qué sirve? What's it (used) for? (I)

   — ti in your opinion, for you (I)

el **paramédico, la paramédica** paramedic (5A)

parar to stop (3B)

parecer:

   me parece que it seems to me (2B)

   ¿Qué te parece? What do you think? / How does it seem to you? (2B)

la **pared** wall (I)

los **parientes** relatives (4B)

el **parque** park (I)

   el — de diversiones amusement park (I)

   el — nacional national park (I)

parrilla: a la — on the grill (7B)

participar (en) to participate (in) (1B)

el **partido** game, match (I)

el **pasajero, la pasajera** passenger (8A)

el **pasaporte** passport (8A)

pasar to pass, to go (3B)

   ¿Cómo lo pasaste? How was it (for you)? (I)

   — la aspiradora to vacuum (I)

   — tiempo con amigos to spend time with friends (I)

   ¿Qué pasa? What's happening? (I)

   ¿Qué te pasó? What happened to you? (I, 5B)

el **pasatiempo** pastime (1B)

pasear en bote to go boating (I)

el **pasillo** aisle (8A)

la **pasta dental** toothpaste (3A)

pastel *adj.* pastel *(color)* (2B)

el **pastel** cake (I)

los **pasteles** pastries (I)

las **pastillas** pills (5B)

patinar to skate (I)

los **patines** skates (3A)

el **patio de recreo** playground (4A)

el **pavo** turkey (7B)

la **paz** peace (9B)

el **peatón,** *pl.* **los peatones** pedestrian (3B)

el **pedazo** piece, slice (7A)

pedir (e→i) to order, to ask for (I)

   — ayuda to ask for help (1A)

   — prestado, -a (a) to borrow (from) (2A)

el **peine** comb (2A)

pelar to peel (7A)

pelearse to fight (4A)

la **película** film, movie (I)

   la — de acción action film (6B)

   la — de ciencia ficción science fiction movie (I)

   la — de horror horror movie

(I)

la — policíaca crime movie, mystery (I)

la — romántica romantic movie (I)

ver una — to see a movie (I)

(en) peligro de extinción in danger of extinction, endangered (9B)

peligroso, -a dangerous (3B)

pelirrojo, -a red-haired (I)

el **pelo** hair (I, 2A)

el **— canoso** gray hair (I)

el **— castaño** brown (chestnut) hair (I)

el **— negro** black hair (I)

el **— rubio** blond hair (I)

la **pelota** ball (3A)

peluche: el oso de — teddy bear (4A)

pensar (e→ie) to plan, to think (I)

peor:

el / la **—, los / las —es** the worst (I)

—(es) que worse than (I)

pequeño, -a small (I)

perder (e→ie) to lose (6A)

Perdón. Excuse me. (I)

perezoso, -a lazy (I)

el **perfume** perfume (I)

el **periódico** newspaper (I)

el **permiso de manejar** driver's license (3B)

permitir to permit, to allow (4A)

pero but (I)

el **perrito caliente** hot dog (I)

el **perro** dog (I)

la **persona** person (I)

el **personaje principal** main character (6B)

pesas: levantar — to lift weights (I)

el **pescado** fish (as a food) (I)

el **pez,** pl. **los peces** fish (4A)

picante spicy (7B)

picar to chop (7A)

el **picnic** picnic (4B)

el **pie** foot (I)

la **piedra** rock (7B)

la **pierna** leg (I)

el / la **piloto** pilot (8A)

la **pimienta** pepper (I)

pintarse (las uñas) to paint, to polish (one's nails) (2A)

el **pintor, la pintora** painter (9A)

la **piña** pineapple (7B)

la **piñata** piñata (I)

la **piscina** swimming pool (I)

el **piso** story, floor (I)

primer — second floor (I)

segundo — third floor (I)

la **pizza** pizza (I)

planear to plan (8A)

la **planta** plant (9B)

la **planta baja** ground floor (I)

el **plástico** plastic (I)

la **plata** silver (2A)

el **plátano** banana (I)

el **plato** plate, dish (I)

de — principal as a main dish (I)

el **— principal** main dish (I)

la **playa** beach (I)

la **plaza** plaza (3B)

pobre poor (I)

pobrecito, -a poor thing (5B)

poco: un — (de) a little (I)

poder (o→ue) to be able to (I)

(tú) puedes you can (I)

(yo) puedo I can (I)

se puede you can (7A)

el / la **policía** police officer (3B)

policíaca: la película — crime movie, mystery (I)

la **política** politics (9A)

el **político, la política** politician (9A)

el **pollo** chicken (I)

poner to put, to place (I)

pon (command) put, place (I)

— la mesa to set the table (I)

— una inyección to give an injection (5B)

— una multa to give a ticket (3B)

—se to apply, to put on (clothing, make up, etc.) (2A); + adj. to become (6A)

(tú) pones you put (I)

(yo) pongo I put (I)

por for (how long) (3A); by, around, along, through (3B)

— ejemplo for example (2A)

— eso that's why, therefore (I)

— favor please (I)

— lo general in general (4A)

¿— qué? Why? (I)

— supuesto of course (I)

— ... vez for the ... time (6A)

porque because (I)

portarse bien / mal to behave well / badly (4A)

la **posesión,** pl. **las posesiones** possession (I)

el **postre** dessert (I)

de — for dessert (I)

la **práctica** practice (1B)

practicar (c→qu) deportes to play sports (I)

práctico, -a practical (I)

el **precio** price (I, 2B)

preferir (e→ie) (e→i) to prefer (I)

(tú) prefieres you prefer (I)

(yo) prefiero I prefer (I)

la **pregunta** question (1A)

hacer una — to ask a question (1A)

el **premio** prize (6A)

preparar to prepare (I)

—se to get ready (2A)

la **presentación,** pl. **las presentaciones** presentation (I)

el **presentador, la presentadora** presenter (6A)

prestar atención to pay attention (1A)

la **primavera** spring (I)

primer (primero), -a first (I)

   — piso second floor (I)

el **primo, la prima** cousin (I)

los **primos** cousins (I)

   prisa hurry (3B)

     de — in a hurry (5A)

     tener — to be in a hurry (3B)

   probar (o→ue) to taste, to try (7A)

   probarse (o→ue) to try on (2B)

el **problema** problem (I)

la **profesión,** *pl.* **las profesiones** profession (9A)

el **profesor, la profesora** teacher (I)

el **programa** program, show (I)

   el — de concursos game show (I)

   el — de dibujos animados cartoon (I)

   el — de entrevistas interview program (I)

   el — de estudios course of studies (9A)

   el — de la vida real reality program (I)

   el — de noticias news program (I)

   el — deportivo sports program (I)

   el — educativo educational program (I)

   el — musical musical program (I)

   prohibir: se prohíbe it is forbidden (1A)

   pronto soon (3A)

     Hasta —. See you soon. (3A)

la **propina** tip (8B)

   propio, -a own (I)

   proteger (g→j) to protect (9B)

el **proyecto** project (1A)

   el — de construcción construction project (I)

el **público** audience (6A)

el **pueblo** town (9B)

   puede: se — you can (7A)

puedes: (tú) — you can (I)

puedo: (yo) — I can (I)

el **puente** bridge (3B)

la **puerta** door (I)

   la — de embarque departure gate (8A)

pues well *(to indicate pause)* (I)

el **puesto** (food) stand (7B)

la **pulsera** bracelet (I)

   el reloj — watch (I)

las **puntadas** stitches (5B)

   dar — to stitch *(surgically)* (5B)

puntual punctual (8B)

el **pupitre** desk (I)

puro, -a pure (9B)

Q

que who, that (I)

qué:

   ¿Para — sirve? What's it (used) for? (I)

   ¡— + *adj.!* How ...! (I)

   ¡— asco! How awful! (I)

   ¡— buena idea! What a good / nice idea! (I)

   ¿— clase de...? What kind of ... ? (I)

   ¿— desean (Uds.)? What would you like? *formal* (I)

   ¿— día es hoy? What day is today? (I)

   ¿— es esto? What is this? (I)

   ¿— hiciste? What did you do? (I)

   ¿— hora es? What time is it? (I)

   ¡— lástima! What a shame! (5B)

   ¿— más? What else? (I)

   ¿— pasa? What's happening? (I)

   ¡— pena! What a shame / pity! (I)

   ¿— quiere decir... ? What does ... mean? (I)

   ¿— tal? How are you? (I)

   ¿— tal es ...? How is (it)...? (6B)

¿— te gusta hacer? What do you like to do? (I)

¿— te gusta hacer más? What do you like better (prefer) to do? (I)

¿— te parece? What do you think? / How does it seem to you? (I, 2B)

¿— te pasó? What happened to you? (I, 5B)

¿— tiempo hace? What's the weather like? (I)

quedar to fit, to be located (I, 3B)

quedarse to stay (3A)

el **quehacer (de la casa)** (household) chore (I)

quemar(se) to burn (oneself), to burn up (5A)

querer (e→ie) to want (I)

   ¿Qué quiere decir...? What does...mean? (I)

   Quiere decir... It means... (I)

   quisiera I would like (I)

   (tú) quieres you want (I)

   (yo) quiero I want (I)

¿Quién? Who? (I)

quince fifteen (I)

quinientos, -as five hundred (I)

quinto, -a fifth (I)

el **quiosco** newsstand (8B)

quisiera I would like (I)

quitar to take away, to remove (3B)

   — el polvo to dust (I)

quizás maybe (I)

R

la **radiografía** X-ray (5B)

   sacar una — to take an X-ray (5B)

rápidamente quickly (I, 2A)

la **raqueta de tenis** tennis racket (3A)

el **ratón,** *pl.* **los ratones** (computer) mouse (I)

   razón: tener — to be correct (I)

   realista realistic (I)

la **recepción** reception desk (8B)

la **receta** prescription (5B); recipe (7A)

recetar to prescribe (5B)

recibir to receive (I)

reciclar to recycle (I)

recientemente recently (2B)

recoger (g→j) to collect, to gather (I)

recomendar (e→ie) to recommend (6B)

recordar (o→ue) to remember (4B)

los **recuerdos** souvenirs (I)

comprar — to buy souvenirs (I)

la **Red:**

en la — online (I)

navegar (g→gu) en la — to surf the Web (I, 1B)

reducir to reduce (9B)

el **refresco** soft drink (I)

el **refrigerador** refrigerator (7A)

regalar to give (a gift) (4B)

el **regalo** gift, present (I)

regatear to bargain (8B)

registrar to inspect, to search *(luggage)* (8A)

la **regla** rule (1A)

regresar to return (I)

regular okay, so-so (I)

la **reina** queen (6A)

reírse (e→í) to laugh (4B)

el **reloj** clock (I)

el **— pulsera** watch (I)

repente: de — suddenly (5A)

repetir (e → i) to repeat (1A)

el **reportero, la reportera** reporter (5A)

rescatar to rescue (5A)

la **reservación,** *pl.* **las reservaciones** reservation (8A)

reservado, -a reserved, shy (I)

resolver (o→ue) to solve (9B)

respetar to respect (1A)

el **restaurante** restaurant (I)

resultar to result, to turn out (6A)

el **retraso** delay (8A)

la **reunión,** *pl.* **las reuniones** meeting (1B); gathering (4B)

reunirse (u→ú) to meet (4B)

el **rey,** king *pl.* **los reyes** king and queen (8B)

rico, -a rich, tasty (I)

el **río** river (I)

robar to rob, to steal (6B)

la **rodilla** knee (5B)

rojo, -a red (I)

romántico, -a: la película — romantic movie (I)

romper to break (I)

—se to break, to tear (5B)

la **ropa: la tienda de —** clothing store (I)

rosado, -a pink (I)

roto, -a broken (5B)

rubio, -a blond (I)

ruedas: silla de — wheelchair (5B)

el **ruido** noise (8B)

s

sábado Saturday (I)

saber to know (how) (I, 1B)

(tú) sabes you know (how to) (I)

(yo) sé I know (how to) (I)

el **sabor** taste (7B)

sabroso, -a tasty, flavorful (I)

el **sacapuntas,** *pl.* **los sacapuntas** pencil sharpener (I)

sacar (c→qu):

— fotos to take photos (I)

— la basura to take out the trash (I)

— un libro to take out, to check out a book (3A)

— una buena nota to get a good grade (1A)

— una radiografía to take an X-ray (5B)

la **sal** salt (I)

la **sala** living room (I)

la **— de clases** classroom (I)

la **— de emergencia** emergency room (5B)

el **salario** salary (9A)

la **salchicha** sausage (I)

la **salida** exit (2B); departure (8A)

salir to leave, to go out (I)

el **salón de belleza,** *pl.* **los salones de belleza** beauty salon (2A)

los **salones de chat** chat rooms (1B)

la **salsa** salsa, sauce (7A)

la **— de tomate** ketchup (7B)

saltar (a la cuerda) to jump (rope) (4A)

la **salud:**

para la — for one's health (I)

para mantener la — to maintain one's health (I)

saludar(se) to greet (4B)

salvar to save (5A)

la **sandía** watermelon (7B)

el **sándwich de jamón y queso** ham and cheese sandwich (I)

la **sangre** blood (5B)

la **sartén** frying pan (7A)

se abre opens (3A)

se cierra closes (3A)

se me olvidó I forgot (3A)

se murieron they died (5A)

se prohíbe ... it's forbidden ... (1A)

se puede you can (7A)

sé: (yo) — I know (how to) (I)

el **secador** blow dryer (2A)

secarse to dry (2A)

seco, -a dry (7B)

el **secretario, la secretaria** secretary (9A)

sed:
Tengo —. I'm thirsty. (I)

la **seda** silk (2B)

seguida: en — right away (3A)

seguir (e→i) to follow, to continue (3B)

— **una carrera** to pursue a career (9A)

según according to (I)

— **mi familia** according to my family (I)

segundo, -a second (I)

— **piso** third floor (I)

seguro, -a sure (3B)

seis six (I)

seiscientos, -as six hundred (I)

el **sello** stamp (3A)

la **selva tropical** rain forest (9B)

el **semáforo** stoplight (3B)

la **semana** week (I)

este fin de — this weekend (I)

la — pasada last week (I)

los fines de — on weekends (I)

el **sendero** trail (7B)

sentirse (e→ie) (e→i) to feel (5B)

la **señal** sign (3A)

la — de parada stop sign (3B)

señor (Sr.) sir, Mr. (I)

señora (Sra.) madam, Mrs. (I)

señorita (Srta.) miss, Miss (I)

separar to separate (I)

septiembre September (I)

séptimo, -a seventh (I)

ser to be (I)

¿Eres...? Are you...? (I)

es he / she is (I)

fue it was (I)

no soy I am not (I)

soy I am (I)

ser: será it, he, she will be (6B)

serio, -a serious (I)

la **servilleta** napkin (I)

servir (e→i) to serve, to be useful (I)

¿En qué puedo —le? How can I help you? (I)

¿Para qué sirve? What's it (used) for? (I)

sirve para it is used for (I)

sesenta sixty (I)

setecientos, -as seven hundred (I)

setenta seventy (I)

sexto, -a sixth (I)

si if, whether (I)

sí yes (I)

siempre always (I)

siento: Lo —. I'm sorry. (I)

siete seven (I)

siguiente next, following (8B)

la **silla** chair (I)

la — de ruedas wheelchair (5B)

simpático, -a nice, friendly (I)

sin without (I)

— **duda** without a doubt (5A)

la **sinagoga** synagogue (I)

el **sitio Web** Web site (I)

sobre on, about (I, 1A)

sociable sociable (I, 1A)

el **software** software (I)

el **sol:**

Hace —. It's sunny. (I)

los anteojos de — sunglasses (I)

tomar el — to sunbathe (I)

solar solar (9B)

sólo only (I)

de — un color solid-colored (2B)

solo, -a alone (I)

Son las... It is ... *(in telling time)* (I)

sonreír (e→í) to smile (4B)

la **sopa de verduras** vegetable soup (I)

la **sorpresa** surprise (4B)

el **sótano** basement (I)

soy I am (I)

su, sus his, her, your *formal,* their (I)

subir to go up (5A)

sucio, -a dirty (I)

la **sudadera** sweatshirt (I)

el **suelo** ground, floor (7B)

sueño: tener — to be sleepy (I)

el **suéter** sweater (I)

sugerir (e→ie) (e→i) to suggest (8A)

el **supermercado** supermarket (3A)

supuesto: por — of course (I)

el **surf de vela** windsurfing (8B)

suyo,-a,-os,-as his, hers, yours, theirs (2A)

T

tal: ¿Qué — ? How are you? (I)

¿Qué — es? How is it? (6B)

tal vez maybe, perhaps (8B)

talentoso, -a talented (I)

la **talla** size (2B)

también also, too (I)

a mí — I do (like to) too (I)

tampoco: a mí — I don't (like to) either (I)

tan so (2B)

— + *adj.* so + adj. (2B)

— + *adj.* + como as + *adj.* + as (1B)

el **tanque** tank (3A)

el **tanteo** score (6A)

tanto so much (I)

tantos, -as + *noun* + como as much / many + *noun* + as (1B)

tarde late (I)

la — afternoon (I)

a la una de la — at one (o'clock) in the afternoon (I)

Buenas —s. Good afternoon.(I)

de la — in the afternoon (I)

esta — this afternoon (I)

llegar (g→gu) — to arrive late (1A)

la **tarea** homework (I)

la **tarjeta** card (I, 3A)

la — de crédito credit card (2B)

la — de embarque boarding pass (8A)

la — postal postcard (8B)

la **taza** cup (I)

te (to / for) you *sing. dir., ind. obj. pron.* (I)

¿**— gusta ... ?** Do you like to...? (I)

¿**— gustaría?** Would you like? (I)

¿**— gustó?** Did you like it? (I)

— importa(n) it matters (it's important), they matter to you (2B)

— ves (bien) you look (good) (2A)

el **té** tea (I)

el **— helado** iced tea (I)

el **teatro** theater (I)

el **teclado** (computer) keyboard (I)

el **técnico, la técnica** technician (9A)

la **tecnología** technology / computers (I)

la clase de — technology / computer class (I)

la **tela sintética** synthetic fabric (2B)

la **telenovela** soap opera (I)

el **televisor** television set (I)

el **templo** temple, Protestant church (I)

temprano early (I)

tendremos we will have

el **tenedor** fork (I)

tener to have (I)

¿**Cuántos años tiene(n) ...?** How old is / are...? (I)

— calor to be warm (I)

— cuidado to be careful (3B)

— éxito to succeed, to be successful (6B)

— frío to be cold (I)

— miedo (de) to be scared (of), to be afraid (of) (I)

— paciencia to be patient (8A)

— prisa to be in a hurry (3B)

— razón to be correct (I)

— sueño to be sleepy (I)

Tengo hambre. I'm hungry. (I)

Tengo que ... I have to... (I)

Tengo sed. I'm thirsty. (I)

Tiene(n)...años. He / She is / They are ... (years old). (I)

el **tenis: jugar al —** to play tennis (I)

tercer (tercero), -a third (I)

terminar to finish, to end (I)

el **terremoto** earthquake (5A)

ti you *fam. after prep.*

¿**Y a —?** And you? (I)

para — in your opinion, for you (I)

el **tiempo:**

a — on time (1A)

¿**Cuánto — hace que...?** How long have you been...? (1B)

el — libre free time (I)

pasar — con amigos to spend time with friends (I)

¿**Qué — hace?** What's the weather like? (I)

la **tienda** store (I)

la — de descuentos discount store (I)

la — de electrodomésticos household-appliance store (I)

la — de ropa clothing store (I)

Tiene(n)...años. He / She is / They are ... (years old). (I)

la **Tierra** Earth (9B)

las **tijeras** scissors (1A)

tímido, -a timid (4A)

típico, -a typical (8B)

el **tío, la tía** uncle, aunt (I)

los **tíos** uncles, aunt(s) and uncle(s) (I)

tirar to spill, to throw away (7A)

no tires don't spill, don't throw away (7A)

la **toalla** towel (2A)

el **tobillo** ankle (5B)

tocar (c→qu) la guitarra to play the guitar (I)

el **tocino** bacon (I)

todavía still (3A)

no... — not yet (6B)

todo el mundo everyone (4A)

todos, -as all (I)

— los días every day (I)

tomar:

— el sol to sunbathe (I)

— lecciones to take lessons (1B)

— un curso to take a course (I)

los **tomates** tomatoes (I)

tonto, -a silly, stupid (I)

torcerse (o→ue) (c→z) to twist, to sprain (5B)

la **tormenta** storm (5A)

la **tortuga** turtle (4A)

trabajador, -ora hardworking (I)

trabajar to work (I)

el **trabajo** work, job (I)

el — voluntario volunteer work (I)

traer:

Le traigo... I will bring you... (I)

¿**Me trae ...?** Will you bring me ...? *formal* (I)

el **tráfico** traffic (3B)

el **traje** suit (I)

el — de baño swimsuit (I)

tranquilo, -a calm (2A)

tratar de to try to (5A)

tratarse de to be about (6B)

travieso, -a naughty, mischievous (4A)

trece thirteen (I)

treinta thirty (I)

treinta y uno thirty-one (I)

tremendo, -a tremendous (I)

el **tren** train (I)

el — eléctrico electric train (4A)

tres three (I)

trescientos, -as three hundred (I)

el **triciclo** tricycle (4A)

triste sad (I)

tropezar (e→ie) (z→c) (con) to trip (over) (5B)

tu, tus your (I)

tú you *fam.* (I)

el / la **turista** tourist (8A)

tuyo, -a, -os, -as yours (2A)

U

Ud. (usted) you *formal sing.* (I)

Uds. (ustedes) you *formal pl.* (I)

¡Uf! ugh!, yuck! (I)

último, -a the last / final (6A)

un, una a, an (I)

— **poco (de)** a little (I)

la **una: a la —** at one o'clock (I)

la **universidad** university (9A)

uno one (I)

unos, -as some (I)

las **uñas** nails (2A)

usado, -a used (I)

usar la computadora to use the computer (I)

usted (Ud.) you *formal sing.* (I)

ustedes (Uds.) you *formal pl.* (I)

las **uvas** grapes (I)

V

las **vacaciones: ir de —** to go on vacation (I)

valiente brave (5A)

el **valle** valley (9B)

¡Vamos! Let's go! (I)

varios, -as various, several (3A)

el **vaso** glass (I)

el **vecino, la vecina** neighbor (4A)

veinte twenty (I)

veintiuno, -a (veintiún) twenty-one (I)

la **vela** sail (8B)

la **venda** bandage (5B)

el **vendedor, la vendedora** vendor (8B)

vender to sell (I)

venir to come (I)

la **ventana** window (I)

la **ventanilla** (airplane) window (8A)

ver to see (I)

a — ... Let's see... (I)

¡Nos vemos! See you later! (I)

te ves (bien) you look good (2A)

— **la tele** to watch television (I)

— **una película** to see a movie (I)

el **verano** summer (I)

veras: ¿De —? Really? (I)

la **verdad** truth (4A)

¿Verdad? Really? (I)

verde green (I)

el **vestido** dress (I)

vestirse (e→i) to get dressed (2A)

el **veterinario, la veterinaria** veterinarian (9A)

la **vez,** *pl.* **las veces:**

a veces sometimes (I)

de — en cuando once in a while (4A)

otra — again (I)

por ... — for the ... time (6A)

viajar to travel (I)

el **viaje** trip (I)

la **víctima** victim (6B)

la **vida** life (5A)

el **video** video (I)

los **videojuegos: jugar —** to play video games (I)

el **vidrio** glass (I)

viejo, -a old (I)

viernes Friday (I)

el **vinagre** vinegar (7A)

la **violencia** violence (6B)

violento, -a violent (I)

visitar to visit (I)

— **salones de chat** to visit chat rooms (I, 1B)

vivir to live (I)

vivo, -a bright (color) (2B); living, alive (5A)

el **vóleibol: jugar al —** to play volleyball (I)

volver (o→ue) to return (1B)

—**se loco, -a** to go crazy (6A)

la **voz,** *pl.* **las voces** voice (1B)

el **voluntario, la voluntaria** volunteer (I)

vosotros, -as you *fam. pl.* (I)

el **vuelo** flight (8A)

vuestro, -a, -os, -as your, yours (I)

W

Web: crear una página Web to create a Web page (1B)

Y

y and (I)

¿— a ti? And you? (I)

— **cuarto** quarter past (I)

— **media** thirty *(in telling time)* (I)

¿— tú? And you? *fam.* (I)

¿— usted (Ud.)? And you? *formal* (I)

ya already (I, 3B)

el **yeso** cast (5B)

yo I (I)

el **yogur** yogurt (I)

Z

las **zanahorias** carrots (I)

la **zapatería** shoe store (I)

los **zapatos** shoes (I)

el **zoológico** zoo (I)

English-Spanish Vocabulary

The *English-Spanish Vocabulary* contains all active vocabulary from the text, including vocabulary presented in the grammar sections.

A dash (—) represents the main entry word. For example, **to play** — after **baseball** means **to play baseball**

The number following each entry indicates the chapter in which the word or expression is presented. A Roman numeral (I) indicates that the word was presented in REALIDADES 1.

The following abbreviations are used in this list: *adj.* (adjective), *dir. obj.* (direct object), *f.* (feminine), *fam.* (familiar), *ind. obj.* (indirect object), *inf.* (infinitive), *m.* (masculine), *pl.* (plural), *prep.* (preposition), *pron.* (pronoun), *sing.* (singular).

A

a, an un, una (I)

a little un poco (de) (I)

a lot mucho, -a (I)

able: to be — **to** poder (o → ue) (I)

about sobre (I, 1A)

    to be — tratarse de (6B)

accident el accidente (5B)

to **accompany** acompañar (7B)

according to según (I)

    — my family según mi familia (I)

accountant el contador, la contadora (9A)

acquainted: to be — with conocer (c → zc) (I, 1B)

acting la actuación (6B)

action figure el muñeco (4A)

action film la película de acción (6B)

actor el actor (I)

actress la actriz, *pl.* las actrices (I)

to **add** añadir (7A)

    addition: in — (to) además (de) (9B)

    address: e-mail — la dirección electrónica (I)

afraid: to be — (of) tener miedo (de) (I)

after después de (I)

afternoon:

    at one (o'clock) in the afternoon a la una de la tarde (I)

    Good —. Buenas tardes. (I)

    in the — de la tarde (I)

    this — esta tarde (I)

afterwards después (I)

again otra vez (I)

against contra (9B)

agitated agitado, -a (6A)

ago hace + *time expression* (I)

agree:

    I —. Estoy de acuerdo. (I)

    I don't —. No estoy de acuerdo. (I)

Agreed. De acuerdo. (3B)

air conditioning el aire acondicionado (9B)

airline la línea aérea (8A)

airplane el avión (I)

airport el aeropuerto (8A)

aisle el pasillo (8A)

alarm clock el despertador (I)

alien el / la extraterrestre (6B)

alive vivo, -a (5A)

all todos, -as (I)

almost casi (I, 3A)

alone solo, -a (I)

along por (3B)

already ya (I, 3B)

also también (I)

always siempre (I)

am:

    I — (yo) soy (I)

    I — not (yo) no soy (I)

ambulance la ambulancia (5B)

among entre (1B)

amusement park el parque de diversiones (I)

amusing divertido, -a (I)

and y (I)

    — you? ¿Y a ti? *fam.* (I); ¿Y tu? *fam.* (I); ¿Y usted (Ud.)? *formal* (I)

angry enojado, -a (6A)

    to get — enojarse (6A)

animal el animal (I)

ankle el tobillo (5B)

anniversary el aniversario (4B)

to **announce** anunciar (2B)

announcement el anuncio (8A)

announcer el locutor, la locutora (5A)

another otro, -a (I)

to **answer** contestar (1A)

ant la hormiga (7B)

antique antiguo, -a (4B)

any algunos, -as (1A)

anyone alguien (1A)

Anything else? ¿Algo más? (I)

apartment el apartamento (I)

    — building el edificio de apartamentos (5A)

to **applaud** aplaudir (6A)

apple la manzana (I)

    — juice el jugo de manzana (I)

approximately aproximadamente (3B)

April abril (I)

architect el arquitecto, la arquitecta (9A)

Are you ... ? ¿Eres ... ? (I)

arm el brazo (I)

around por (3A, 3B); alrededor de (4B)

to **arrest** arrestar (6B)

arrival la llegada (8A)

to **arrive late** llegar (g → gu) tarde (1A)

art class la clase de arte (I)

article el artículo (5A)

artist el artista, la artista (9A)

artistic artístico, -a (I)

arts las artes (9A)

    martial — las artes marciales (1B)

as como (I)

    — a child de niño (4A); de pequeño (4A)

    — a main dish de plato principal (I)

    — far as hasta (3B)

as much / many + *noun* + as tantos, -as + *noun* + como

as + *adj.* + as tan + *adj.* + como (1B)

to **ask for** pedir (e → i) (I)

    — help pedir ayuda (1A)

to **ask a question** hacer una pregunta (1A)

asleep dormido, -a (5A)

    to fall—dormirse (6A)

at:

    — eight (o'clock) a las ocho (I)

    — eight (o'clock) at night a las ocho de la noche (I)

    — eight (o'clock) in the evening a las ocho de la noche (I)

    — eight (o'clock) in the morning a las ocho de la mañana (I)

    — home en casa (I)

    — one (o'clock) a la una (I)

    — one (o'clock) in the afternoon a la una de la tarde (I)

    — the end al final (6A)

    — what time? ¿A qué hora? (I)

athlete el / la atleta (6A)

ATM el cajero automático (8B)

to **attend** asistir a (1B)

attentive atento, -a (8B)

attention: to pay — prestar atención (1A)

attraction(s) la atracción, *pl.* las atracciones (I)

audience el público (6A)

audition la audición, *pl.* las audiciones (2A)

auditorium el auditorio (6A)

August agosto (I)

aunt la tía (I)

aunt(s) and uncle(s) los tíos (I)

autumn el otoño (I)

avenue la avenida (3B)

avocado el aguacate (7B)

B

baby el / la bebé (4B)

back la espalda (5B)

backpack la mochila (I)

bacon el tocino (I)

bad malo, -a (I); mal (I)

badly mal (I)

bag la bolsa (I)

baked al horno (7A)

ball la pelota (3A)

balloon el globo (I)

banana el plátano (I)

band *(musical)* la banda (1B)

bandage la venda (5B)

bank el banco (3A)

barbecue: to have a — hacer una parrillada (7B)

bargain la ganga (2B)

to **bargain** regatear (8B)

baseball: to play — jugar al béisbol (I)

based: to be — on estar basado, -a en (6B)

basement el sótano (I)

basket la cesta (7B)

basketball: to play — jugar al básquetbol (I)

bathroom el baño (I)

to **be** ser (I); estar (I)

    He / She is / They are ... (years old). Tiene(n) ... años. (I)

    How old is / are ... ? ¿Cuántos años tiene(n)...? (I)

    to — + *present participle* estar + *present participle* (I)

    to — a member ser miembro (1B)

    to — able to poder (o → ue) (I)

    to — about tratarse de (6B)

    to — acquainted with conocer (c → zc) (I)

    to — afraid (of) tener miedo (de) (I)

    to — based on estar basado, -a en (6B)

    to — born nacer (4B)

    to — careful tener cuidado (3B)

    to — cold tener frío (I)

    to — correct tener razón (I)

    to — going to + *verb* ir a + *inf.* (I)

    to — in a hurry tener prisa (3B)

    to — in fashion estar de moda (2B)

    to — in love with estar enamorado, -a de (6B)

    to — located quedar (I, 3B)

    to — online estar en línea (I, 1B)

    to — scared (of) tener miedo (de) (I)

    to — sleepy tener sueño (I)

    to — sure estar seguro, -a (3B)

    to — useful servir (I)

    to — warm tener calor (I)

beach la playa (I)

beans los frijoles (7B)

bear el oso (I)

to **beat** batir (7A)

beautiful bello, -a (8B)

beauty contest el concurso de belleza (6A)

beauty salon el salón de belleza, *pl.* los salones de belleza (2A)

because porque (I)

    — of a causa de (5A)

to **become** ponerse (6A)

bed la cama (I)

    to go to — acostarse (o → ue) (2A)

    to make the — hacer la cama (I)

bedroom el dormitorio (I)

beefsteak el bistec (I)

before antes de (I, 2A)

to **begin** empezar (e → ie) (I)

to **behave well / badly** portarse bien / mal (4A)

behind detrás de (I)

belt el cinturón, *pl.* los cinturones (2A)

benefits los beneficios (9A)

besides además (de) (9B)

best: the — el / la mejor, los / las mejores (I)

better than mejor(es) que (I)

between entre (1B)

bicycle: to ride a — montar en bicicleta (I)

bilingual bilingüe (9A)

bill la cuenta (I)

binder: three-ring — la carpeta de argollas (I)

bird el pájaro (I)

birthday el cumpleaños (I)

    Happy —! ¡Feliz cumpleaños! (I)

    to have a — cumplir años (4B)

black hair el pelo negro (I)

block la cuadra (3B)

blocks los bloques (4A)

blond hair el pelo rubio (I)

blood la sangre (5B)

blouse la blusa (I)

blow dryer el secador (2A)

blue azul (I)

to **board** abordar (8A)

boarding pass la tarjeta de embarque (8A)

boat el barco (I)

    sail — el bote de vela (8B)

boating: to go — pasear en bote (I)

to **boil** hervir (e → ie) (e → i) (7A)

bone el hueso (5B)

bonfire la fogata (7B)

book el libro (I)

bookbag la mochila (I)

bookshelf el estante (I)

bookstore la librería (I)

boots las botas (I)

to **bore** aburrir (I)

    it / they bore(s) me aburre(n) (I)

    to get bored aburrirse (6A)

boring aburrido, -a (I)

born: to be — nacer (4B)

to **borrow (from)** pedir (e → i) prestado, -a (a) (2A)

both los dos, las dos (I)

to **bother** molestar (4A)

bottle la botella (I)

to **bowl** jugar a los bolos (1B)

box la caja (I)

boy el chico (I)

    young — el niño (I)

boyfriend el novio (I)

bracelet la pulsera (I)

brand la marca (2B)

brave valiente (5A)

bread el pan (I)

to **break** romper (I); romperse (5B)

breakfast el desayuno (I)

    for — en el desayuno (I)

bridge el puente (3B)

bright *(color)* vivo, -a (2B)

to **bring** traer (I); llevar (I)

    I will — you ... Le traigo ... (I)

    Will you — me ... ? ¿Me trae ... ? (I)

broken roto, -a (5B)

broth el caldo (7A)

brother el hermano (I)

brothers; brother(s) and sister(s) los hermanos (I)

brown marrón (I)

    — (chestnut) hair el pelo castaño (I)

brush el cepillo (2A)

    tooth — el cepillo de dientes (3A)

to **brush (one's teeth)** cepillarse (los dientes) (2A)

to **burn a CD** grabar un disco compacto (I)

to **burn (oneself), to burn up** quemar(se) (5A)

bus el autobús, *pl.* los autobuses (I)

business los negocios (9A)

    — man el hombre de negocios (9A)

    — woman la mujer de negocios (9A)

busy ocupado, -a (I)

but pero (I)

butter la mantequilla (I)

to **buy** comprar (I)

    — souvenirs comprar recuerdos (I)

by por (3B)

    — + *vehicle* **en +** *vehicle* (I)

C

café el café (I)

cake el pastel (I)

to **call: to — on the phone** llamar por teléfono (5A)

calculator la calculadora (I)

calm tranquilo, -a (2A)

camera la cámara (I)

    digital — la cámara digital (I)

camp el campamento (I)

can la lata (I)

can:

    I — (yo) puedo (I)

    you — (tú) puedes (I); se puede (7A)

candy los dulces (I)

canned enlatado, -a (7A)

cap la gorra (I)

to **capture** capturar (6B)

car el coche (I)

card la tarjeta (I, 3A)

    credit — la tarjeta de crédito (2B)

    ID — el carnet de identidad (I)

    post — la tarjeta postal (8B)

cardboard el cartón (I)

care: to take — of cuidar a (3A)

career la carrera (9A)

careful: to be — tener cuidado (3B)

carrots las zanahorias (I)

to **carry** llevar (I)

cartoon el programa de dibujos animados (I)

cash en efectivo (2B)

to **cash a check** cobrar un cheque (3A)

cash register la caja (2B)

cashier el cajero, la cajera (2B)

cast el yeso (5B)

castle el castillo (8B)

cat el gato (I)

cathedral la catedral (8B)

cause la causa (5A)

CD: to burn a — grabar un disco compacto (I)

to **celebrate** celebrar (I)

center el centro (I, 3A)

cereal el cereal (I)

certain: it is — es cierto (9B)

chain la cadena (I)

chair la silla (I)

> **wheel —** la silla de ruedas (5B)

champion el campeón, la campeona, *pl.* los campeones (6A)

championship el campeonato (6A)

to **change** cambiar (8B)

channel *(TV)* el canal (I)

character: main — el personaje principal (6B)

to **chat** charlar (4B)

chat rooms los salones de chat (1B)

cheap barato, -a (I)

check:

> **to cash a —** cobrar un cheque (3A)

> **traveler's —** el cheque de viajero (2B)

personal — el cheque personal (2B)

to **check** *(luggage)* facturar (el equipaje) (8A); examinar (5B)

to **check out** sacar (c → qu) (3A)

cheerleader el animador, la animadora (1B)

cherry la cereza (7B)

chess el ajedrez (1B)

chicken el pollo (I)

child: as a — de niño (4A); de pequeño (4A)

childish infantil (I)

children los hijos (I); los niños (I)

choir el coro (1B)

to **chop** picar (c → qu) (7A)

chore: household — el quehacer (de la casa) (I)

chorus el coro (1B)

to **choose** escoger (g → j) (2B)

church la iglesia (I)

> **Protestant —** el templo (I)

city la ciudad (I)

class la clase (I)

classroom la sala de clases (I)

clean limpio, -a (I)

to **clean the bathroom** limpiar el baño (I)

clock el reloj (I)

to **close** cerrar (3A)

close (to) cerca (de) (I)

closed cerrado, -a (8A)

closes se cierra (3A)

closet el armario (I)

clothing store la tienda de ropa (I)

cloud la nube (7B)

club el club, *pl.* los clubes (1B)

> **athletic —** el club atlético (1B)

coach el entrenador, la entrenadora (6A)

coat el abrigo (I)

coffee el café (I)

coin la moneda (4A)

cold:

> **It's —.** Hace frío. (I)

> **to be —** tener frío (I)

to **collect** recoger (g → j) (I)

to **collect** coleccionar (4A)

collection la colección, *pl.* las colecciones (4A)

to **collide with** chocar (c → qu) con (5B)

cologne el agua de colonia (2A)

color:

> **What — ... ?** ¿De qué color ... ? (I)

> **—s** los colores (I)

comb el peine (2A)

to **come** venir (I)

comedy la comedia (I)

comfortable cómodo, -a (2A)

comical cómico, -a (I)

commentary el comentario (6A)

to **communicate** comunicarse (c → qu) (I)

> **I —** (yo) me comunico (I)

> **you —** (tú) te comunicas (I)

community la comunidad (I)

compact disc el disco compacto (I)

> **to burn a —** grabar un disco compacto (I)

to **compete** competir (e → i) (6A)

competition la competencia (6A)

complicated complicado, -a (I, 3B)

composition la composición, *pl.* las composiciones (I)

computer la computadora (I)

> **— graphics** los gráficos (I)

> **— keyboard** el teclado (I)

> **— mouse** el ratón (I)

> **— screen** la pantalla (I)

> **—s / technology** la tecnología (I)

> **laptop —** la computadora portátil (I)

> **to use the —** usar la computadora (I)

concert el concierto (I)

to **congratulate** felicitar (4B)

Congratulations! ¡Felicidades! (4B)

to **conserve** conservar (9B)

construction project el proyecto de construcción (I)

contest el concurso (2A)

    beauty — el concurso de belleza (6A)

to **continue** seguir (e → i) (3B)

to **cook** cocinar (I)

cookie la galleta (I)

cooking oil el aceite (7A)

corn el maíz (7B)

corner la esquina (3B)

correct: to be — tener razón (I)

to **cost** costar (o → ue) (I)

    How much does (do) ... —? ¿Cuánto cuesta(n)? (I)

cotton el algodón (2B)

country el país, *pl.* los países (I)

countryside el campo (I)

course:

    to take a — tomar un curso (I)

    — of studies el programa de estudios (9A)

cousin la prima, el primo (I)

    —s los primos (I)

to **crash into** chocar (c → qu) con (5B)

crazy: to go – volverse loco, -a (6A)

to **create** crear (I)

    to — a Web page crear una página Web (1B)

credit card la tarjeta de crédito (2B)

crime el crimen (6B)

    — movie la película policíaca (I)

criminal el / la criminal (6B)

critic el crítico, la crítica (6B)

to **cross** cruzar (3B)

crutches las muletas (5B)

to **cry** llorar (4B)

cup la taza (I)

currency exchange la casa de cambio (8B)

curtains las cortinas (I)

custom la costumbre (4B)

customs la aduana (8A)

customs officer el aduanero, la aduanera (8A)

to **cut** cortar (I, 7A)

    to — oneself cortarse (5B)

    to — one's hair cortarse el pelo (2A)

    to — the lawn cortar el césped (I)

cut-paper decorations el papel picado (I)

D

dance el baile (I)

to **dance** bailar (I)

dancer el bailarín, la bailarina *pl.* los bailarines (1B)

dangerous peligroso, -a (3B)

daring atrevido, -a (I)

dark oscuro, -a (2B)

date: What is the —? ¿Cuál es la fecha? (I)

date la cita (2A)

daughter la hija (I)

day el día (I)

    every — todos los días (I); cada día (I)

    What — is today? ¿Qué día es hoy? (I)

day care center la guardería infantil (4A)

dead muerto, -a (5A)

December diciembre (I)

to **decide** decidir (I)

to **decorate** decorar (I)

decorations las decoraciones (I)

delay el retraso (8A)

delicious delicioso, -a (I)

delighted encantado, -a (I)

dentist el / la dentista (3A)

deodorant el desodorante (2A)

department store el almacén,

pl. los almacenes (I)

departure la salida (8A)

departure gate la puerta de embarque (8A)

depend: it depends depende (2A)

desert el desierto (9B)

designer el diseñador, la diseñadora (9A)

desk el pupitre (I); el escritorio (I)

dessert el postre (I)

    for — de postre (I)

to **destroy** destruir (i → y) (5A)

destruction la destrucción (9B)

detective el / la detective (6B)

dictionary el diccionario (I)

Did you like it? ¿Te gustó? (I)

to **die** morirse (o→ue) (o→u) (6A)

difficult difícil (I)

digital camera la cámara digital (I)

dining room el comedor (I)

dinner la cena (I)

dinosaur el dinosaurio (4A)

direct directo, -a (8A)

direction la dirección, *pl.* las direcciones (6B)

director el director, la directora (6B)

dirty sucio, -a (I)

disaster: It was a —. Fue un desastre. (I)

discount store la tienda de descuentos (I)

to **discuss** discutir (1A)

dish el plato (I)

    as a main — de plato principal (I)

    main — el plato principal (I)

disobedient desobediente (4A)

to **do** hacer (I)

    — (command) haz (I)

    — you like to ... ? ¿Te gusta ... ? (I)

I — (yo) hago (I)

to — a project hacer un proyecto (1A)

to — a search hacer una búsqueda (1B)

to — gymnastics hacer gimnasia (1B)

you — (tú) haces (I)

What did you —? ¿Qué hiciste? (I)

doctor el médico, la médica (3A)

doctor's / dentist's office el consultorio (3A)

document el documento (I)

dog el perro (I)

to feed the — dar de comer al perro (I)

doll la muñeca (4A)

Don't eat. No comas. (7A)

Don't leave, Don't let No dejes (7A)

Don't speak. No hables. (7A)

Don't write. No escribas. (7A)

door la puerta (I)

double room la habitación doble (8B)

doubt: without a — sin duda (5A)

to doubt dudar (9B)

to download bajar (información) (I)

downtown el centro (3A)

drama el drama (I)

to draw dibujar (I)

dress el vestido (I)

dressed: to get — vestirse (2A)

dresser la cómoda (I)

to drink beber (I)

drinks las bebidas (I)

to drive manejar (3B)

driver el conductor, la conductora (3B)

driver's license el permiso de manejar (3B)

dry seco, -a (7B)

to dry secarse (c → qu) (2A)

dryer: blow — secador (2A)

during durante (I)

to dust quitar el polvo (I)

DVD player el lector DVD (I)

E

e-mail:

— address la dirección electrónica (I)

to write — escribir por correo electrónico (I)

to earn ganar (1B)

to enjoy disfrutar de (8B)

early temprano (I)

to earn (money) ganar (1B)

earrings los aretes (I)

Earth la Tierra (9B)

earthquake el terremoto (5A)

easy fácil (I)

to eat comer (I)

ecological ecológico, -a (9B)

economical económico, -a (9B)

educational program el programa educativo (I)

efficient eficiente (9B)

eggs los huevos (I)

eight ocho (I)

eight hundred ochocientos, -as (I)

eighteen dieciocho (I)

eighth octavo, -a (I)

eighty ochenta (I)

either tampoco (I)

I don't (like to) — a mí tampoco (I)

elbow el codo (5B)

electric train el tren eléctrico (4A)

electricity la electricidad (9B)

elegant elegante (2A)

to eliminate eliminar (9B)

elevator el ascensor (8B)

eleven once (I)

else:

Anything —? ¿Algo más? (I)

What —? ¿Qué más? (I)

emergency room la sala de

emergencia (5B)

emotional emocionado, -a (6A)

employee el empleado, la empleada (8A)

end: at the — al final (6A)

to end terminar (I)

endangered en peligro de extinción (9B)

energy la energía (9B)

engineer el ingeniero, la ingeniera (9A)

English class la clase de inglés (I)

to enjoy disfrutar de (8B)

enormous enorme (4B)

enough bastante (I)

Enough! ¡Basta! (3B)

to enter entrar (I)

entrance la entrada (2B)

environment medio ambiente (9B)

to escape escaparse (5A)

especially especialmente (I)

evening:

Good —. Buenas noches. (I)

in the — de la noche (I)

this — esta noche (I)

every day cada día (I), todos los días (I)

everyone todo el mundo (4A)

exactly en punto (8B)

to examine examinar (5B)

example: for — por ejemplo (2A)

excited entusiasmado, -a (2A); emocionado, -a (6A)

exchange: currency — la casa de cambio (8B)

to exchange cambiar (8B)

excursion la excursión, pl. las excursiones (8B)

Excuse me. Perdón. (I)

to exercise hacer ejercicio (I)

exit la salida (2B)

expensive caro, -a (I)

experience la experiencia (I)

to **explain** explicar (c → qu) (1A)

explosion la explosión, *pl.* las explosiones (5A)

extinction: in danger of — en peligro de extinción (9B)

extracurricular extracurricular (1B)

— **activities** las actividades extracurriculares (1B)

eye el ojo (I)

F

fabric: synthetic — la tela sintética (2B)

face la cara (2A)

face-to-face cara a cara (I)

failure el fracaso (6B)

to **fall** caerse (5B)

I — (yo) me caigo (5B)

to — asleep dormirse (o→ue) (o→u) (6A)

to — in love (with) enamorarse (de) (6B)

you — (tú) te caes (5B)

fall el otoño (I)

famous famoso, -a (8B)

fan el aficionado, la aficionada (6A)

fantastic fantástico, -a (I)

far (from) lejos (de) (I)

farmer el agricultor, la agricultora (9A)

to **fascinate** fascinar (6B)

fascinating fascinante (I)

fashion: to be in — estar de moda (2B)

fast rápidamente (I)

father el padre (papá) (I)

fatty grasoso, -a (7B)

favorite favorito, -a (I)

February febrero (I)

to **feed the dog** dar de comer al perro (I)

to **feel** sentirse (e → ie) (e → i) (5B)

fewer:

— **... than** menos ... que (I)

— **than ...** menos de ... (I)

fifteen quince (I)

fifth quinto, -a (I)

fifty cincuenta (I)

to **fight** luchar (9B)

to **fight** pelearse (4A)

to **fill (the tank)** llenar (el tanque) (3A)

film la película (I)

final último, -a (6A)

to **find** encontrar (o → ue) (2B)

finger el dedo (I)

to **finish** terminar (I)

fire el incendio (5A); el fuego (7A)

firefighter el bombero, la bombera (5A)

firewood la leña (7B)

fireworks los fuegos artificiales (4B)

first primer (primero), -a (I)

fish el pescado (I); el pez, *pl.* los peces (4A)

to go —ing ir de pesca (I)

to **fit: It / They —(s) me well / poorly.** Me queda(n) bien / mal. (I)

five cinco (I)

five hundred quinientos, -as (I)

to **fix (one's hair)** arreglarse (el pelo) (2A)

flag la bandera (I)

flavorful sabroso, -a (I)

flight el vuelo (8A)

flight attendant el / la auxiliar de vuelo (8A)

flood la inundación, *pl.* las inundaciones (5A)

floor el piso (I); el suelo (7B)

ground — la planta baja (I)

second — el primer piso (I)

third — el segundo piso (I)

flour la harina (7B)

flower la flor, *pl.* las flores (I)

fly la mosca (7B)

folder la carpeta (I)

to **follow** seguir (e → i) (3B)

following siguiente (8B)

food la comida (I)

food stand el puesto (7B)

foot el pie (I)

football: to play — jugar (u → ue) (g → gu) al fútbol americano (I)

for para (I); por (3A)

— **breakfast** en el desayuno (I)

— **example** por ejemplo (2A)

— **lunch** en el almuerzo (I)

— **me** para mí (I)

— **the ... time** por ... vez (6A)

— **you** para ti (I)

for (how long) por (3A)

forbidden: It is —. Se prohíbe. (1A)

foreign extranjero, -a (8A)

forest el bosque (9B)

rain — la selva tropical (9B)

to **forget about/to** olvidarse de (7A)

don't — no te olvides de (7A)

forgot: I — se me olvidó (3A)

fork el tenedor (I)

fortunately afortunadamente (5A)

forty cuarenta (I)

fountain la fuente (3B)

four cuatro (I)

four hundred cuatrocientos, -as (I)

fourteen catorce (I)

fourth cuarto, -a (I)

free time el tiempo libre (I)

French fries las papas fritas (I)

frequently frecuentemente (4B)

fresh fresco, -a (7A)

Friday viernes (I)

fried frito, -a (7A)

friendly simpático, -a (I)

frightened asustado, -a (5A)

from de (I); desde (3B)

Where are you —? ¿De dónde eres? (I)

frozen congelado, -a (7A)

fruit salad la ensalada de frutas (I)

to **fry** freír (e → í) (7A)

frying pan la sartén, *pl.* las sartenes (7A)

fun divertido, -a (I)

    to have — divertirse (e → ie) (e → i) (4B)

to **function** funcionar (9B)

funny gracioso, -a (I); cómico, -a (I)

furious furioso, -a (6A)

furniture los muebles (5A)

future el futuro (9A)

G

game el partido (I)

game show el programa de concursos (I)

garage el garaje (I)

garden el jardín, *pl.* los jardines (I)

garlic el ajo (7A)

gasoline la gasolina (3A)

to **gather** recoger (g → j) (I)

gathering la reunión, *pl.* las reuniones (4B)

gel el gel (2A)

general: in — por lo general (4A)

generally generalmente (I)

generous generoso, -a (4A)

get:

    to — a good grade sacar (c → qu) una buena nota (1A)

    to — along well / badly llevarse bien / mal (4B)

    to — angry enojarse (6A)

    to — bored aburrirse (6A)

    to — dressed vestirse (e → i) (2A)

    to — married casarse (con) (4B)

    to — ready prepararse (2A)

    to — up levantarse (2A)

gift el regalo (I)

gift certificate el cupón de

regalo, *pl.* los cupones de regalo (2B)

girl la chica (I)

    young — la niña (I)

girlfriend la novia (I)

to **give** dar (I); regalar (4B)

    to — a speech dar un discurso (1A)

    to — a ticket poner una multa (3B)

    to — an injection poner una inyección (5B)

glass el vaso (I); el vidrio (I)

gloves los guantes (I)

to **go** ir (I); pasar (3B)

    Let's —! ¡Vamos! (I)

    to be —ing to + *verb* ir a + *inf.* (I)

    to — to bed acostarse (o → ue) (2A)

    to — boating pasear en bote (I)

    to — camping ir de cámping (I)

    to — crazy volverse (o → ue) loco, -a (6A)

    to — down bajar (5A)

    to — fishing ir de pesca (I)

    to — on foot ir a pie (3A)

    to — on vacation ir de vacaciones (I)

    to — out salir (I)

    to — shopping ir de compras (I)

    to — to bed acostarse (o → ue) (2A)

    to — to school ir a la escuela (I)

    to — up subir (5A)

goal *(in sports)* el gol (6A)

    to score a — meter un gol (6A)

going to con destino a (8A)

gold el oro (2A)

golf:

    — club el palo de golf (3A)

    to play — jugar (u → ue) (g → gu) al golf (I)

good bueno (buen), -a (I)

    — afternoon. Buenas tardes. (I)

    — evening. Buenas noches. (I)

    — gracious caramba (3A)

    — morning. Buenos días. (I)

Good-bye! ¡Adiós! (I)

good-looking guapo, -a (I)

grade *(in school)* la nota (1A)

    to get a good — sacar una buena nota (1A)

to **graduate** graduarse (u → ú) (9A)

graduation la graduación, *pl.* las graduaciones (9A)

grandfather el abuelo (I)

grandmother la abuela (I)

grandparents los abuelos (I)

grapes las uvas (I)

gray gris (I)

    — hair el pelo canoso (I)

greasy grasoso, -a (7B)

Great! ¡Genial! (I)

green verde (I)

    — beans las judías verdes (I)

to **greet** saludar(se) (4B)

to **grill** asar (7B)

grill: on the — a la parrilla (7B)

grilled asado, -a (7B)

ground el suelo (7B)

ground floor la planta baja (I)

grown-ups los mayores (4B)

guide el / la guía (8B)

guidebook la guía (8B)

guitar: to play the — tocar la guitarra (I)

gym el gimnasio (I)

gymnastics la gimnasia (1B)

H

hair el pelo (I, 2A)

    black — el pelo negro (I)

    blond — el pelo rubio (I)

    brown (chestnut) — el pelo castaño (I)

gray — el pelo canoso (I)

to cut one's — cortarse el pelo (2A)

to fix one's — arreglarse el pelo (2A)

half media, -o (I)

— **past** y media (*in telling time*) (I)

ham and cheese sandwich el sándwich de jamón y queso (I)

hamburger la hamburguesa (I)

hand la mano (I)

to shake —s darse la mano (4B)

handicrafts la artesanía (8B)

happy contento, -a (I); alegre (6A)

— **birthday!** ¡Feliz cumpleaños! (I)

hardworking trabajador, -ora (I)

to **have** tener (I)

I — **to ...** tengo que + *inf.* (I)

to — **a barbecue** hacer una parrillada (7B)

to — **a birthday** cumplir años (4B)

to — **a picnic** hacer un picnic (4B)

to — **fun** divertirse (e → ie) (e → i) (4B)

to — **just...** acabar de + *inf.* (I)

to — **lunch** almorzar (o → ue) (z → c) (1A)

to **have** haber (*as an auxiliary verb*) (6B)

he él (I)

he / she is es (I)

He / She is / They are ... (years old). Tiene(n) ... años. (I)

head la cabeza (I)

health:

for one's — para la salud (I)

to maintain one's — para mantener la salud (I)

to **hear** oír (5A)

heat el fuego (7A); la calefacción (9B)

to **heat** calentar (e → ie) (7A)

Hello! ¡Hola! (I)

to **help** ayudar (I)

How can I — **you?** ¿En qué puedo servirle? (I)

help la ayuda (1A)

Help! ¡Socorro! (5A)

her su, sus *possessive adj.* (I); la *dir. obj. pron.* (I); le *ind. obj. pron.* (I)

hers suyo, -a (2A)

here aquí (I)

hero el héroe (5A)

heroine la heroína (5A)

Hey! ¡Oye! (I)

to **hide (oneself)** esconder(se) (5A)

high alto, -a (2B)

high school el colegio (9A)

highway la carretera (3B)

hill la colina (9B)

him lo *dir. obj. pron.* (I); le *ind. obj. pron.* (I)

his su, sus (I); suyo, -a (2A)

historical histórico, -a (8B)

hockey el hockey (1B)

holiday el día festivo (4B)

home la casa (I)

at — en casa (I)

— **office** el despacho (I)

(to) — a casa (I)

homework la tarea (I)

horrible horrible (I)

horror movie la película de horror (I)

horseback: to ride — montar a caballo (I)

hospital el hospital (I)

hot caliente (7A)

— **dog** el perrito caliente (I)

It's —. Hace calor. (I)

hotel el hotel (I)

hour: in the ... — en la ... hora (*class period*) (I)

house la casa (I)

household:

—**appliance store** la tienda de electrodomésticos (I)

— **chore** el quehacer (de la casa) (I)

how!

— + *adj.!* ¡Qué + *adj.!* (I)

— **awful!** ¡Qué asco! (I)

How? ¿Cómo? (I)

— **are you?** ¿Cómo está Ud.? *formal* (I); ¿Cómo estás? *fam.* (I); ¿Qué tal? *fam.* (I)

— **can I help you?** ¿En qué puedo servirle? (I)

— **do you go to ... ?** ¿Cómo se va...? (3B)

— **do you make ... ?** ¿Cómo se hace ...? (7A)

— **do you say ... ?** ¿Cómo se dice... ? (I)

— **does it (do they) fit (you)?** ¿Cómo te queda(n)? (I)

— **does it seem to you?** ¿Qué te parece? (2B)

— **is ... spelled?** ¿Cómo se escribe ... ? (I)

— **is (it) ... ?** ¿Qué tal es...? (6B)

— **long ... ?** ¿Cuánto tiempo hace que...? (1B)

— **many?** ¿Cuántos, -as? (I)

— **much?** ¿Cuánto?

— **much does (do) ... cost?** ¿Cuánto cuesta(n) ... ? (I)

— **old is / are ... ?** ¿Cuántos años tiene(n) ... ? (I)

— **was it (for you)?** ¿Cómo lo pasaste? (I)

to **hug** abrazar(se) (z → c) (4B)

hundred: one — cien(to) (I)

hungry: I'm —. Tengo hambre. (I)

hurricane el huracán, *pl.* los huracanes (5A)

hurt doler (o → ue) (I, 5B)

to **hurt oneself** lastimarse (5B)

hurry prisa (3B)

in a — de prisa (5A)

to be in a — tener prisa (3B)

husband el esposo (I)

I

I yo (I)

— **am** soy (I)

— **am not** no soy (I)

— **don't think so.** Creo que no. (I)

— **have seen** he visto (6B)

— **stay at home.** Me quedo en casa. (I)

— **think ...** Creo que ... (I)

— **think so.** Creo que sí. (I)

— **will bring you ...** Le traigo ... (I)

—**'m hungry.** Tengo hambre. (I)

—**'m sorry.** Lo siento. (I)

—**'m thirsty.** Tengo sed. (I)

I do too a mí también (I)

I don't either a mí tampoco (I)

I forgot se me olvidó (3A)

I would like Me gustaría (I); (yo) quisiera (I)

ice cream el helado (I)

iced tea el té helado (I)

ID card el carnet de identidad (1A)

if si (I)

immediately inmediatamente (2B)

impatient impaciente (I)

important importante (I)

impressive impresionante (I)

to **improve** mejorar (9B)

in en (I)

— **danger of extinction** en peligro de extinción (9B)

— **front of** delante de (I)

— **general** por lo general (4A)

— **love with** enamorado, -a de (6B)

— **my opinion** para mí (I)

— **order** to para + *inf.* (I)

— **the ... hour** en la ... hora *(class period)* (I)

— **the middle of** en medio de (3B)

— **your opinion** para ti (I)

incredible increíble (I)

inexpensive barato, -a (I)

information la información (I)

ingredient el ingrediente (7A)

injection la inyección, *pl.* las inyecciones (5B)

to give an — poner una inyección (5B)

injured herido, -a (5A)

injured person el herido, la herida (5A)

inside dentro de (7B)

to **insist** insistir en (8A)

to **inspect** registrar (8A)

intelligent inteligente (I)

interest el interés (1B)

to **interest** interesar (I)

it / they interest(s) me me interesa(n) (I)

interesting interesante (I)

intersection el cruce de calles (3B)

interview la entrevista (6A)

— **program** el programa de entrevistas (I)

to **interview** entrevistar (6A)

to **investigate** investigar (g → gu) (5A)

is es (I)

he / she — es (I)

it — **true** es cierto (9B)

it la, lo *dir. obj. pron.* (I)

— **depends** depende (2A)

— **fits (they fit) me well / poorly.** Me queda(n) bien / mal. (I)

— **has been ...** Hace + *time* + que ... (1B)

— **is ...** Son las *(in telling time)* (I)

— **is forbidden ...** Se prohíbe ... (1A)

— **is made of ...** Está hecho, -a de ... (2B)

— **is one o'clock.** Es la una. (I)

— **is the ... of ...** Es el *(number)* de *(month) (in telling the date)* (I)

— **is the first of ...** Es el primero de *(month).* (I)

— **seems to me** me parece que (2B)

— **was** fue (I)

— **was a disaster.** Fue un desastre. (I)

—**'s a ...** es un / una ... (I)

—**'s cold.** Hace frío. (I)

—**'s hot.** Hace calor. (I)

—**'s necessary.** Es necesario. (I)

—**'s raining.** Llueve. (I)

—**'s snowing.** Nieva. (I)

—**'s sunny.** Hace sol. (I)

it / he / she will be será (6B)

itinerary el itinerario (8B)

J

jacket la chaqueta (I)

January enero (I)

jeans los jeans (I)

jet skiing la moto acuática (8B)

jewelry (gold, silver) las joyas (de oro, de plata) (2A)

jewelry store la joyería (I)

job el trabajo (I)

to **join** juntarse (9B)

judge el juez, la jueza, *pl.* los jueces (9A)

juice:

apple — el jugo de manzana (I)

orange — el jugo de naranja (I)

July julio (I)

to **jump (rope)** saltar (a la cuerda) (4A)

June junio (I)

just: to have — ... acabar de + *inf.* (I)

K

ketchup la salsa de tomate (7B)

key la llave (8B)

key chain el llavero (I)

keyboard (computer) el teclado (I)

to kill matar (6B)

kind: What — of ... ? ¿Qué clase de ... ? (I)

king el rey (8B)

to kiss besar(se) (4B)

kitchen la cocina (I)

knee la rodilla (5B)

knife el cuchillo (I)

to know saber (I); conocer (c → zc) (I, 1A)

    I — (yo) conozco (I)

    I — (how to) (yo) sé (I)

    you — (tú) conoces (I)

    you — (how to) (tú) sabes (I)

L

laboratory el laboratorio (I, 1A)

ladder la escalera (5A)

lake el lago (I)

lamp la lámpara (I)

language el idioma (9A)

laptop computer la computadora portátil (I)

large grande (I)

last último, -a (6A)

last:

    — night anoche (I)

    — week la semana pasada (I)

    — year el año pasado (I)

to last durar (I, 8A)

late tarde (I)

to arrive — llegar tarde (1A)

later: See you — ¡Hasta luego!; ¡Nos vemos! (I)

to laugh reírse (e → í) (4B)

law la ley (9A); *(study of)* el derecho (9A)

lawyer el abogado, la abogada (9A)

lazy perezoso, -a (I)

leading man el galán, *pl.* los galanes (6B)

league la liga (6A)

to learn aprender (a) (I)

leather el cuero (2B)

to leave salir (I); *(something)* dejar (3B)

    don't — no dejes (7A)

Leave me alone. Déjame en paz. (3B)

left: to the — (of) a la izquierda (de) (I)

leg la pierna (I)

lemonade la limonada (I)

less:

    — ... than menos ... que (I)

    — than menos de (I)

lessons: to take — tomar lecciones (1B)

to let dejar (3B)

    don't — no dejes (7A)

Let's go! ¡Vamos! (I)

Let's see ... A ver ... (I)

letter la carta (I, 3A)

    to mail a — echar una carta (3A)

lettuce la lechuga (I)

library la biblioteca (I)

to lie mentir (e → ie) (e → i) (4A)

life la vida (5A)

to lift weights levantar pesas (I)

to light encender (e → ie) (7A)

light *(color)* claro, -a (2B); la luz, *pl.* las luces (I)

like como (I)

to like:

    Did you — it? ¿Te gustó? (I)

    Do you — to ... ? ¿Te gusta ... ? (I)

    He / She doesn't — ... No le gusta ... (I)

    He / She —s ... Le gusta ... (I); A él / ella le gusta(n) ... (I)

    I don't — to ... (A mí) no me gusta ... (I)

    I don't — to ... at all. (A mí) no me gusta nada ... (I)

    I — ... Me gusta ... (I)

    I — to ... (A mí) me gusta ... (I)

    I — to ... a lot (A mí) me gusta mucho ... (I)

    I — to ... better (A mí) me gusta más ... (I)

    I —d it. Me gustó. (I)

    I would — Me gustaría (I); quisiera (I)

    What do you — better (prefer) to do? ¿Qué te gusta hacer más? (I)

    What do you — to do? ¿Qué te gusta hacer? (I)

    What would you — ? Qué desean (Uds.)? (I)

    Would you —? ¿Te gustaría? (I)

    You — ... Te gusta ... (I)

likewise igualmente (I)

lips los labios (2A)

to listen to music escuchar música (I)

little: a — un poco (de) (I)

to live vivir (I)

living vivo, -a (5A)

    to make a — ganarse la vida (9A)

living room la sala (I)

located: to be — quedar (3B)

locker el armario (1A)

long largo, -a (I)

    How — ? ¿Cuánto tiempo hace que ...? (1B)

to look:

    to — (at) mirar (I)

    to — for buscar (c → qu) (I)

    you — (good) te ves (bien) (2A)

loose flojo, -a (2B)

to lose perder (e → ie) (6A)

    lot: a — mucho, -a (I)

to love encantar (I)

    He / She —s ... A él / ella le encanta(n) ... (I)

I / You — ... Me / Te encanta(n) ... (I)

love el amor (6B)

    to be in — with estar enamorado, -a de (6B)

    to fall in — with enamorarse de (6B)

low bajo, -a (2B)

luggage el equipaje (8A)

    to check — facturar el equipaje (8A)

lunch el almuerzo (I)

    for — en el almuerzo (I)

    to have — almorzar (o → ue) (z → c) (1A)

M

madam (la) señora (Sra.) (I)

made:

    It's — of ... Está hecho, -a de (2B)

    What's it — of? ¿De qué está hecho, -a?

magazines: to read — leer revistas (I)

mail:

    — carrier el cartero, la cartera (9A)

    —box el buzón, *pl.* los buzones (3A)

    to — a letter echar una carta (3A)

main:

    — character el personaje principal (6B)

    — dish el plato principal (I)

        as a — de plato principal (I)

to maintain one's health para mantener la salud (I)

to make:

    — *(command)* haz (I)

    to — a living ganarse la vida (9A)

    to — noise hacer ruido (8B)

    to — the bed hacer la cama (I)

You are making me nervous. Me estás poniendo nervioso, -a. (3B)

make-up el maquillaje (2A)

mall el centro comercial (I)

man el hombre (I)

    leading — el galán *pl.* los galanes (6B)

    older — el anciano (I)

    business— el hombre de negocios (9A)

manager el / la gerente (9A)

manner la manera (9B)

manners los modales (4B)

many muchos, -as (I)

    as — as tantos, -as + *noun* + como (1B)

    How —? ¿Cuántos, -as? (I)

March marzo (I)

mark (in school) la nota (1A)

    to get a good — sacar (c → qu) una buena nota (1A)

market el mercado (2B)

married: to get — (to) casarse (con) (4B)

martial arts las artes marciales (1B)

match el fósforo (7B); el partido (I)

materials los materiales (1A)

mathematics class la clase de matemáticas (I)

matter: It (They) matter(s) to me / to you me / te importa(n) (2B)

May mayo (I)

maybe quizás (I); tal vez (8B)

mayonnaise la mayonesa (7B)

me me *ind., dir. obj. pron* (I)

    for — para mí (I), me (I)

    it matters / they matter to — me importa(n) (2B)

    it seems to — me parece que (2B)

    — too a mí también (I)

    to — me (I)

    with — conmigo (I)

meal la comida (I)

to mean:

    It —s ... Quiere decir ... (I)

    What does ... —? ¿Qué quiere decir ... ? (I)

meat la carne (I)

mechanic el mecánico, la mecánica (9A)

medicine la medicina (5B)

medium mediano, -a (2B)

to meet reunirse (u → ú) (4B)

meeting la reunión, *pl.* las reuniones (1B)

melon el melón, *pl.* los melones (7B)

member el miembro (1B)

    to be a — ser miembro (1B)

to memorize aprender de memoria (1A)

menu el menú (I)

messy desordenado, -a (I)

microwave el microondas (7A)

middle: in the — of en medio de (3B)

military *(adj.)* militar (9A)

milk la leche (I)

million un millón (6A)

    —s of millones de (6A)

mine mío, -a, -os, -as (2A)

mirror el espejo (I)

mischievous travieso, -a (4A)

Miss (la) señorita (Srta.) (I)

missing: to be — faltar (I)

to mix mezclar (7A)

moment: a — un momento (I)

Monday lunes (I)

    on —s los lunes (I)

money el dinero (I)

money exchange la casa de cambio (8B)

monkey el mono (I)

month el mes (I)

monument el monumento (I)

moon la Luna (9B)

more:

    — ... than más ... que (I)

    — or less más o menos (I)

    — than más de (I)

morning:

    Good — Buenos días. (I)

    in the — de la mañana (I)

mosque la mezquita (I)

mother la madre (mamá) (I)

mountains las montañas (I)

mouse (computer) el ratón, *pl.* los ratones (I)

mouth la boca (I)

to **move** moverse (o → ue) (5B)

movie la película (I)

    action — la película de acción (6B)

    — theater el cine (I)

    to see a — ver una película (I)

to **mow the lawn** cortar el césped (I)

Mr. (el) señor (Sr.) (I)

Mrs. (la) señora (Sra.) (I)

much:

    as — tanto, -a (1B)

    how —? ¿Cuánto? (I)

    so — tanto (I)

muscle el músculo (5B)

museum el museo (I)

music:

    to listen to — escuchar música (I)

musical program el programa musical (I)

musician el músico, la música (1B)

must deber (I)

    one — hay que (I)

mustard la mostaza (7B)

my mi (I); mis (I)

    — name is ... Me llamo ... (I)

mystery la película policíaca (I)

N

nails las uñas (2A)

name:

    My — is ... Me llamo ... (I)

    What is your —? ¿Cómo te llamas? (I)

    What's his / her —? ¿Cómo se llama? (I)

napkin la servilleta (I)

narrow estrecho, -a (3B)

national park el parque nacional (I)

nature la naturaleza (9B)

naughty travieso, -a (4A)

to **navigate:** navegar (g → gu) (8B)

near cerca (de) (I)

neat ordenado, -a (I)

necessary: It's —. Es necesario. (I)

neck el cuello (5B)

necklace el collar (I)

to **need:**

    I — necesito (I)

    I — ... Me falta(n) ... (I)

    you — necesitas (I)

neighbor el vecino, la vecina (4A)

neighborhood el barrio (I)

neither ... nor ni ... ni (I)

nervous nervioso, -a (2A)

never nunca (I)

new nuevo, -a (I)

news program el programa de noticias (I)

newscast el noticiero (5A)

newspaper el periódico (I)

newsstand el quiosco (8B)

next siguiente (8B)

    — to al lado de (I)

nice simpático, -a (I)

night:

    at — de la noche (I)

    last — anoche (I)

    — table la mesita (I)

nine nueve (I)

nine hundred novecientos, -as (I)

nineteen diecinueve (I)

ninety noventa (I)

ninth noveno, -a (I)

no no (I); ningún, ninguno (1A)

no one nadie (1A)

nobody nadie (1A)

noise el ruido (8B)

none ningún, ninguno, -a (1A)

nose la nariz, *pl.* las narices (I)

not:

    — yet no ... todavía (6B)

    — ... or ni ... ni (I)

notebook el cuaderno (I)

nothing nada (I)

November noviembre (I)

now ahora (I)

nurse el enfermero, la enfermera (5B)

O

obedient obediente (4A)

to **obey** obedecer (c → zc) (4A)

to **observe** observar (8B)

to **obtain** conseguir (e → i) (8B)

to **occur** ocurrir (5A)

o'clock:

    at eight — a las ocho (I)

    at one — a la una (I)

October octubre (I)

odor el olor (7B)

of de (I)

    — course por supuesto (I), ¡Cómo no! (3A)

    What is it made —? ¿De qué está hecho, -a? (2B)

to **offend** ofender (8B)

to **offer** ofrecer (c → zc) (4A)

office (home) el despacho (I)

office la oficina (9A)

often a menudo (I)

Oh! What a shame / pity! ¡Ay! ¡Qué pena! (I)

okay regular (I); De acuerdo. (3B)

old viejo, -a (I); antiguo, -a (4B)

    He / She is / They are ... years —. Tiene(n) ... años. (I)

How — is / are ... ? ¿Cuántos años tiene(n) ... ? (I)

   —er mayor, *pl.* mayores (I)

   —er man el anciano (I)

   —er people los ancianos (I)

   —er woman la anciana (I)

on en (I), sobre (1A)

   — Mondays, on Tuesdays ... los lunes, los martes ... (I)

   — the grill a la parrilla (7B)

   — time a tiempo (1A)

   — top of encima de (I)

   — weekends los fines de semana (I)

once in a while de vez en cuando (4A)

one uno (un), -a (I)

   at — (o'clock) a la una (I)

   — hundred cien (I)

   — must hay que (I)

   — thousand mil (I)

onion la cebolla (I)

online en la Red (I)

   to be — estar en línea (I, 1B)

only sólo (I)

to **open** abrir (I)

open abierto, -a (8A)

opens se abre (3A)

opinion: in my — para mí (I)

opportunity la oportunidad (1B)

or o (I)

orange anaranjado, -a (I)

   — juice el jugo de naranja (I)

orchestra la orquesta (1B)

to **order** pedir (e→ i) (I)

other otro, -a (I)

others los / las demás (I)

our nuestro(s), -a(s) (I)

ours nuestro(s), nuestra(s) (2A)

outdoors al aire libre (7B)

outer space el espacio (9B)

outrageous exagerado, -a (2B)

outside fuera (de) (7B)

oven el horno (7A)

own propio, -a (I)

owner el dueño, la dueña (9A)

P

to **pack the suitcase** hacer la maleta (8A)

page: Web — la página Web (1B)

pain el dolor (5B)

to **paint (one's nails)** pintarse (las uñas) (2A)

painter el pintor, la pintora (9A)

painting el cuadro (I)

palace el palacio (8B)

pants los pantalones (I)

paper: sheet of — la hoja de papel (I)

parade el desfile (4B)

paramedic el paramédico, la paramédica (5A)

parents los padres (I)

park el parque (I)

   amusement — el parque de diversiones (I)

   national — el parque nacional (I)

to **participate** (in) participar (en) (1B)

party la fiesta (I)

   surprise — la fiesta de sorpresa (4B)

to **pass** pasar (3B)

passenger el pasajero, la pasajera (8A)

passport el pasaporte (8A)

pastel *(colors)* pastel *adj.* (2B)

pastime el pasatiempo (1B)

pastries los pasteles (I)

patience la paciencia (8A)

patient paciente (I)

   to be — tener paciencia (8A)

to **pay (for)** pagar (g → gu) (por) (I)

to **pay attention** prestar atención (1A)

peace la paz (9B)

peach el durazno (7B)

peas los guisantes (I)

pedestrian el peatón, *pl.* los peatones (3B)

to **peel** pelar (7A)

pen el bolígrafo (I)

pencil el lápiz, *pl.* los lápices (I)

   — sharpener el sacapuntas, *pl.* los sacapuntas (I)

people la gente (I)

   older — los ancianos (I)

   young — los jóvenes (1B)

pepper la pimienta (I)

perfume el perfume (I)

perhaps tal vez (8B)

to **permit, to allow** permitir (4A)

person la persona (I)

pharmacy la farmacia (3A)

phenomenal fenomenal (6A)

phone: to talk on the — hablar por teléfono (I)

photo la foto (I)

   to take —s sacar (c → qu) fotos (I)

photographer el fotógrafo, la fotógrafa (1B)

photography la fotografía (1B)

physical education class la clase de educación física (I)

piano lesson (class) la lección de piano (I)

picnic el picnic (4B)

piece el pedazo (7A)

pills las pastillas (5B)

pilot el / la piloto (8A)

piñata la piñata (I)

pineapple la piña (7B)

pink rosado, -a (I)

pizza la pizza (I)

place el lugar (I)

to **place** poner (I)

to **plan** pensar (e → ie) + *inf.* (I); planear (8A)

plant la planta (9B)

plastic el plástico (I)

plate el plato (I)

play la obra de teatro (I)

to **play** jugar (u → ue) (g → gu) (a) *(games, sports)* (I); tocar *(an instrument)* (I)

to — baseball jugar al béisbol (I)

to — basketball jugar al básquetbol (I)

to — football jugar al fútbol americano (I)

to — golf jugar al golf (I)

to — soccer jugar al fútbol (I)

to — sports practicar deportes (I)

to — tennis jugar al tenis (I)

to — the guitar tocar la guitarra (I)

to — the role of hacer el papel de (6B)

to — video games jugar videojuegos (I)

to — volleyball jugar al vóleibol (I)

player el jugador, la jugadora (6A)

playground el patio de recreo (4A)

plaza la plaza (3B)

please por favor (I)

to — very much encantar (I)

pleased to meet you mucho gusto (I)

plot el argumento (6B)

police officer el / la policía (3B)

to **polish (one's nails)** pintarse (las uñas) (2A)

polite cortés, *pl.* corteses (8B)

politician el político, la política (9A)

politics la política (9A)

polluted contaminado, -a (9B)

pollution la contaminación (9B)

pool la piscina (I)

poor pobre (I)

— thing pobrecito, -a (5B)

pork el cerdo (7B)

— chop la chuleta de cerdo (7B)

possession la posesión, *pl.* las posesiones (I)

postcard la tarjeta postal (8B)

post office el correo (3A)

poster el cartel (I)

pot la olla (7A)

potatoes las papas (I)

practical práctico, -a (I)

practice la práctica (1B)

to **prefer** preferir (e → ie) (e → i) (I)

I — (yo) prefiero (I)

I — to ... (a mí) me gusta más ... (I)

you — (tú) prefieres (I)

to **prepare** preparar (I)

to **prescribe** recetar (5B)

prescription la receta (5B)

present el regalo (I)

presentation la presentación, *pl.* las presentaciones (I)

presenter el presentador, la presentadora (6A)

pretty bonito, -a (I)

price el precio (I, 2B)

principal *(of a school)* el director, la directora (6B)

primary school la escuela primaria (I)

prize el premio (6A)

problem el problema (I)

profession la profesión, *pl.* las profesiones (9A)

program el programa (I)

project el proyecto (1A)

Protestant church el templo (I)

to **protect** proteger (g → j) (9B)

punctual puntual (8B)

pure puro, -a (9B)

purple morado, -a (I)

purse el bolso (I)

to **pursue a career** seguir (e → i) una carrera (9A)

to **put** poner (I)

— *(command)* pon (I)

I — (yo) pongo (I)

to — on *(clothing, make-up, etc.)* ponerse (2A)

to — out *(fire)* apagar (g → gu) (5A)

you — (tú) pones (I)

Q

quarter past y cuarto (I)

queen la reina (6A)

question la pregunta (1A)

to ask a — hacer una pregunta (1A)

quickly rápidamente (I, 2A)

R

rain la lluvia (5A)

rain forest la selva tropical (9B)

to **rain** llover (o → ue) (5A)

It's —ing. Llueve. (I)

rather bastante (I)

to **read magazines** leer revistas (I)

ready listo, -a (8A)

to get — prepararse (2A)

realistic realista (I)

reality program el programa de la vida real (I)

really en realidad (2B)

Really? ¿Verdad? (I); ¿De veras? (I)

to **receive** recibir (I)

recently recientemente (2B)

reception desk la recepción (8B)

recipe la receta (7A)

to **recommend** recomendar (e → ie) (6B)

to **record** grabar (1B)

to **recycle** reciclar (I)

recycling center el centro de reciclaje (I)

red rojo, -a (I)

—-haired pelirrojo, -a (I)

to **reduce** reducir (9B)

refrigerator el refrigerador (7A)

rehearsal el ensayo (1B)

to **rehearse** ensayar (1B)

relatives los parientes (4B)

to **relax** descansar (I)

to **remember** recordar (o → ue) (4B)

to **remove** quitar (3B)

to rent alquilar (6B)

to repeat repetir (e → i) (1A)

report el informe (I, 1A)

reporter el reportero, la reportera (5A)

to rescue rescatar (5A)

reservation la reservación, *pl.* las reservaciones (8A)

reserved reservado, -a (I)

to respect respetar (1A)

to rest descansar (I)

restaurant el restaurante (I)

to result resultar (6A)

to return regresar (I); volver (o→ue) (1B)

    to — a book devolver (o → ue) (un libro) (3A)

rice el arroz (I)

rich rico, -a (I)

to ride:

    to — a bicycle montar en bicicleta (I)

    to — horseback montar a caballo (I)

right:

    to the — (of) a la derecha (de) (I)

    — away en seguida (3A)

ring el anillo (I)

river el río (I)

road la calle (I)

to roast asar (7B)

to rob robar (6B)

rock la piedra (7B)

role el papel (6B)

    to play the — of hacer el papel de (6B)

romantic movie la película romántica (I)

room el cuarto (I); la habitación, *pl.* las habitaciones (8B)

    chat — el salón de chat, *pl.* los salones de chat (1B)

    double — la habitación doble (8B)

    single — la habitación individual (8B)

to straighten up the — arreglar el cuarto (I)

rope la cuerda (4A)

round-trip ida y vuelta (8A)

ruins las ruinas (8B)

rug la alfombra (I)

rule la regla (1A)

to run correr (I)

S _____

sack la bolsa (I)

sad triste (I)

to sail navegar (g → gu) (8B)

sailboat el bote de vela (8B)

salad la ensalada (I)

    fruit — la ensalada de frutas (I)

salary el salario (9A)

sale la liquidación, *pl.* las liquidaciones (2B)

salesperson el dependiente, la dependienta (I)

salon: beauty — el salón de belleza, *pl.* los salones de belleza

salsa la salsa (7A)

salt la sal (I)

same mismo, -a (I)

sandwich: ham and cheese — el sándwich de jamón y queso (I)

Saturday sábado (I)

sausage la salchicha (I)

to save ahorrar (9B); salvar (5A)

to say decir (I)

    How do you —? ¿Cómo se dice? (I)

    to — good-bye despedirse (e → i) de (4B)

    You — ... Se dice ... (I)

    You don't —! ¡No me digas! (I)

scared: to be — (of) tener miedo (de) (I)

scene la escena (6B)

schedule el horario (I)

school la escuela (I)

    high — el colegio (9A)

    primary — la escuela primaria (I)

    technical — la escuela técnica (9A)

science:

    — class la clase de ciencias naturales (I)

    — fiction movie la película de ciencia ficción (I)

scientist el científico, la científica (9A)

scissors las tijeras (1A)

score el tanteo (6A)

to score (a goal) meter un gol (6A)

to scream gritar (5A)

screen: computer — la pantalla (I)

to scuba dive bucear (I)

sea el mar (I)

search la búsqueda (1B)

    to do a — hacer una búsqueda (1B)

to search (for) buscar (I)

season la estación, *pl.* las estaciones (I)

seat el asiento (1A)

second segundo, -a (I)

    — floor el primer piso (I)

secretary el secretario, la secretaria (9A)

security checkpoint la inspección, *pl.* las inspecciones de seguridad (8A)

to see ver (I)

    Let's — A ver ... (I)

    — you later! ¡Nos vemos!; Hasta luego. (I)

    — you soon. Hasta pronto. (3A)

    — you tomorrow. Hasta mañana. (I)

    to — a movie ver una película (I)

seem:

    How does it — to you? ¿Qué te parece? (2B)

    it —s to me me parece (2B)

seen:

    I have — he visto (6B)

    you have — has visto (6B)

to **sell** vender (I)

to **send** enviar (i → í) (I, 3A)

to **separate** separar (I)

September septiembre (I)

serious serio, -a (I); grave (9B)

to **serve** servir (e → i) (I)

    What do you — it with?
    ¿Con qué se sirve? (7A)

service station la estación de servicio (3A)

to **set the table** poner la mesa (I)

seven siete (I)

seven hundred setecientos, -as (I)

seventeen diecisiete (I)

seventh séptimo, -a (I)

seventy setenta (I)

several varios, -as (3A)

shake hands dar(se) la mano (4B)

shame: What a —! ¡Qué lástima! (5B)

shampoo el champú (3A)

to **share** compartir (I)

to **shave** afeitarse (2A)

she ella (I)

sheet of paper la hoja de papel (I)

shelf el estante (I)

shellfish los mariscos (7A)

ship el barco (I)

shirt la camisa (I)

    T— la camiseta (I)

shoe store la zapatería (I)

shoes los zapatos (I)

shoe size el número (2B)

short bajo, -a *(stature)*; corto, -a *(length)* (I)

shorts los pantalones cortos (I)

shot la inyección, *pl.* las inyecciones (5B)

should deber (I)

shoulder el hombro (5B)

show el programa (I)

to **show** + *movie or TV program* dar (I)

shower la ducha (2A)

    to take a — ducharse (2A)

shrimp el camarón, *pl.* los camarones (7A)

shy reservado, -a (I)

sick enfermo, -a (I)

sign el letrero (2B); la señal (3A)

    stop — la señal de parada (3B)

silk seda (2B)

silly tonto, -a (I)

silver la plata (2A)

since desde (3B)

to **sing** cantar (I)

singer el / la cantante (1B)

sink el fregadero (7A)

sir (el) señor (Sr.) (I)

sister la hermana (I)

site: Web — el sitio Web (I)

six seis (I)

six hundred seiscientos, -as (I)

sixteen dieciséis (I)

sixth sexto, -a (I)

sixty sesenta (I)

size *(shoe)* el número, la talla (2B)

to **skate** patinar (I)

to **skateboard** montar en monopatín (I)

skates los patines (3A)

to **ski** esquiar (i → í) (I)

skirt la falda (I)

sky el cielo (7B)

to **sleep** dormir (o→ue) (o → u) (I)

to **fall asleep** dormirse (o → ue) (o → u) (6A)

sleepy: to be — tener sueño (I)

slice el pedazo (7A)

slide la diapositiva (I)

slowly lentamente (2A); despacio (3B)

small pequeño, -a (I)

smell el olor (7B)

to **smile** sonreír (e → í) (4B)

smoke el humo (5A)

to **snorkel** bucear (I)

to **snow:** nevar (e → ie) (5A)

    It's —ing. Nieva. (I)

so tan (2B)

so + *adj.* tan + *adj.* (1B)

so much tanto (I)

so-so regular (I)

soap el jabón (3A)

soap opera la telenovela (I)

soccer: to play — jugar (u → ue) (g → gu) al fútbol (I)

sociable sociable (I)

social studies class la clase de ciencias sociales (I)

socks los calcetines (I)

soft drink el refresco (I)

software el software (I)

solar solar (9B)

solid-colored de sólo un color (2B)

to **solve** resolver (o → ue) (9B)

some unos, -as (I); algún, alguno, -a (1A)

    — day algún día (9A)

someone alguien (1A)

something algo (I)

sometimes a veces (I)

son el hijo (I)

    —s; —(s) and daughter(s) los hijos (I)

song la canción, *pl.* las canciones (I, 1B)

soon pronto (3A)

    See you —. Hasta pronto. (3A)

sorry: I'm —. Lo siento. (I)

sound (stereo) system el equipo de sonido (I)

soup: vegetable — la sopa de verduras (I)

source la fuente (9B)

souvenirs los recuerdos (I)

    to buy — comprar recuerdos (I)

space el espacio (9B)

spaghetti los espaguetis (I)

Spanish class la clase de español (I)

special especial (2A)

special effects los efectos especiales (6B)

special event el evento especial (2A)

speech el discurso (1A)

to spell:

How is ... spelled? ¿Cómo se escribe ... ? (I)

It's spelled ... Se escribe ... (I)

to spend gastar (2B)

to — time with friends pasar tiempo con amigos (I)

spicy picante (7B)

to spill tirar (7A)

don't — no tires (7A)

spoiled consentido, -a (4A)

spoon la cuchara (I)

sports:

— equipment el equipo deportivo (3A)

—-minded deportista (I)

— program el programa deportivo (I)

to play — practicar (c → qu) deportes (I)

spring la primavera (I)

stadium el estadio (I)

stairs, stairway la escalera (I)

stamp el sello (3A)

stand (food) el puesto (7B)

stapler la grapadora (1A)

star: movie — la estrella (del cine) (6B)

to start empezar (e → ie) (I); comenzar (e → ie) (z → c) (5A)

statue la estatua (3B)

to stay: quedarse (3A)

I — at home. Me quedo en casa. (I)

steak la carne de res (7B)

to steal robar (6B)

stepbrother el hermanastro (I)

stepfather el padrastro (I)

stepmother la madrastra (I)

stepsister la hermanastra (I)

stereo system el equipo de sonido (I)

still todavía (3A)

to stitch (surgically) dar puntadas (5B)

stitches las puntadas (5B)

stomach el estómago (I)

to stop parar (3B)

to stop over hacer escala (8A)

stop sign la señal de parada (3B)

stoplight el semáforo (3B)

stopover la escala (8A)

store la tienda (I)

book— la librería (I)

clothing — la tienda de ropa (I)

department — el almacén, pl. los almacenes (I)

discount — la tienda de descuentos (I)

household-appliance — la tienda de electrodomésticos (I)

jewelry — la joyería (I)

shoe — la zapatería (I)

stories: to write — escribir cuentos (I)

storm la tormenta (5A)

story el piso (I)

stove la estufa (7A)

to straighten up the room arreglar el cuarto (I)

straight derecho (3B)

strawberries las fresas (I)

street la calle (I)

student el / la estudiante (I)

studies: course of — el programa de estudios (9A)

studious estudioso, -a (I)

to study estudiar (I)

stupendous estupendo, -a (8B)

stupid tonto, -a (I)

style el estilo (2B)

subway el metro (3B)

to succeed tener éxito (6B)

success el éxito (6B)

to be —ful tener éxito (6B)

suddenly de repente (5A)

sugar el azúcar (I)

to suggest sugerir (e → ie) (e → i) (8A)

suit el traje (I)

suitcase la maleta (8A)

summer el verano (I)

to sunbathe tomar el sol (I)

Sunday domingo (I)

sunglasses los anteojos de sol (I)

sunny: It's —. Hace sol. (I)

supermarket el supermercado (3A)

supplies los materiales (1A)

sure seguro, -a (3B)

to surf the Web navegar (g → gu) en la Red (I, 1B)

surprise la sorpresa (4B)

sweater el suéter (I)

sweatshirt la sudadera (I)

sweet dulce (7B)

to swim nadar (I)

swimming la natación (1B)

swimsuit el traje de baño (I)

synagogue la sinagoga (I)

synthetic fabric la tela sintética (2B)

T

T-shirt la camiseta (I)

table la mesa (I)

to set the — poner la mesa (I)

tablespoon(ful) la cucharada (7A)

to take llevar (I)

to — a bath bañarse (2A)

to — a course tomar un curso (I)

to — a shower ducharse (2A)

to — a tour hacer una gira (8B)

to — a trip hacer un viaje (8A)

to — a walk dar una caminata (7B)

to — away quitar (3B)

to — care of cuidar a (3A)

to — lessons tomar lecciones (1B)

to — out sacar (c → qu) (3A)

to — out the trash sacar la basura (I)

to — photos sacar fotos (I)

to — an X-ray sacar una radiografía (5B)

talented talentoso, -a (I)

to **talk** hablar (I)

to — on the phone hablar por teléfono (I)

tall alto, -a (I)

tank el tanque (3A)

tape: transparent — la cinta adhesiva (1A)

taste el sabor (7B)

to **taste** probar (o → ue) (7A)

tasty sabroso, -a (I); rico, -a (I)

tea el té (I)

iced — el té helado (I)

to **teach** enseñar (I)

teacher el profesor, la profesora (I)

team el equipo (1B)

to **tear** romperse (5B)

technical school la escuela técnica (9A)

technician el técnico, la técnica (9A)

technology / computers la tecnología (I)

technology / computer class la clase de tecnología (I)

teddy bear el oso de peluche (4A)

teeth los dientes (2A)

to brush one's — cepillarse los dientes (2A)

television: to watch — ver la tele (I)

television set el televisor (I)

to **tell** decir (I)

— me dime (I)

to — jokes contar (o → ue) (chistes) (4B)

temple el templo (I)

ten diez (I)

tennis: to play — jugar (u → ue) (g → gu) al tenis (I)

tennis racket la raqueta de tenis (3A)

tenth décimo, -a (I)

thank you gracias (I)

that que (I); ese, esa (I); *(over there)* aquel, aquella (2B)

—'s why por eso (I)

the el, la (I) los, las (I)

— best el / la mejor, los / las mejores (I)

— worst el / la peor, los / las peores (I)

theater el teatro (I)

movie — el cine (I)

their su, sus (I)

theirs suyo, -a, suyos, -as (2A)

them las, los *dir. obj. pron.* (I), les *ind. obj. pron.* (I)

then entonces (I); luego (2A)

there allí (I)

— is / are hay (I); haya *(subjunctive)* (9B)

— was hubo (5A)

— was / — were había (4B)

— will be habrá (9A)

therefore por eso (I)

these estos, estas (I)

they ellos, ellas (I)

they died se murieron (5A)

thief el ladrón, la ladrona, *pl.* los ladrones (6B)

thing la cosa (I)

to **think** pensar (e → ie) (I)

I don't — so. Creo que no. (I)

I — ... Creo que ... (I)

I — so. Creo que sí. (I)

What do you — (about it)? ¿Qué te parece? (I)

third tercer (tercero), -a (I)

third floor el segundo piso (I)

thirsty: I'm —. Tengo sed. (I)

thirteen trece (I)

thirty treinta (I); y media *(in telling time)* (I)

thirty-one treinta y uno (I)

this este, esta (I)

— afternoon esta tarde (I)

— evening esta noche (I)

— weekend este fin de semana (I)

What is — ? ¿Qué es esto? (I)

those esos, esas (I); (over there) aquellos, aquellas (2B)

thousand: a — mil (I)

three tres (I)

three hundred trescientos, -as (I)

three-ring binder la carpeta de argollas (I)

through por (3B)

to **throw away** tirar (7A)

Thursday jueves (I)

ticket el boleto (I); la multa (3B)

to give a — poner una multa (3B)

tie la corbata (I); el empate (6A)

tight apretado, -a (2B)

time:

At what —? ¿A qué hora? (I)

for the ... — por ... vez (6A)

free — el tiempo libre (I)

on — a tiempo (1A)

to spend — with friends pasar tiempo con amigos (I)

What — is it? ¿Qué hora es? (I)

timid tímido, -a (4A)

tip la propina (8B)

tired cansado, -a (I)

to a *prep.* (I)

in order — para + *inf.* (I)

— the a la, al (I)

— the left (of) a la izquierda (de) (I)

— the right (of) a la derecha (de) (I)

toast el pan tostado (I)

today hoy (I)

tomatoes los tomates (I)

tomorrow mañana (I)

See you —. Hasta mañana. (I)

tonight esta noche (I)

too también (I); demasiado (I)

I do (like to) — a mí también (I)

me — a mí también (I)

toothbrush el cepillo de dientes (3A)

toothpaste la pasta dental (3A)

top: on — of encima de (I)

touching emocionante (I)

tour: to take a — hacer una gira (8B)

tourist el / la turista (8A)

towel la toalla (2A)

town el pueblo (9B)

toy el juguete (I)

traffic el tráfico (3B)

trail el sendero (7B)

train el tren (I)

electric — el tren eléctrico (4A)

trainer el entrenador, la entrenadora (6A)

transparent tape la cinta adhesiva (1A)

to **travel** viajar (I)

travel agency la agencia de viajes (8A)

travel agent el / la agente de viajes (8A)

tree el árbol (I)

tremendous tremendo, -a (I)

tricycle el triciclo (4A)

trip el viaje (I)

to take a — hacer un viaje (8A)

to **trip** (over) tropezar (e → ie) (z → c) (con) (5B)

tropical rain forest la selva tropical (9B)

truck el camión, *pl.* los camiones (3B)

truth la verdad (4A)

to **try** probar (o → ue) (7A)

to **try on** probarse (o → ue) (2B)

to **try to** tratar de (5A)

Tuesday martes (I)

on —s los martes (I)

turkey el pavo (7B)

to **turn** doblar (3B)

to — in entregar (g → gu) (1A)

to — off apagar (g → gu) (7A)

to — on encender (e → ie) (7A)

to — out resultar (6A)

turtle la tortuga (4A)

TV channel el canal (I)

twelve doce (I)

twenty veinte (I)

twenty-one veintiuno (veintiún) (I)

to **twist** torcerse (o → ue) (c → z) (5B)

two dos (I)

two hundred doscientos, -as (I)

typical típico, -a (8B)

U _____

Ugh! ¡Uf! (I)

ugly feo, -a (I)

uncle el tío (I)

uncles; uncle(s) and aunt(s) los tíos (I)

underneath debajo de (I)

to **understand** comprender (I); entender (e → ie) (1A)

university la universidad (9A)

unforgettable inolvidable (I)

until hasta (3A)

up to hasta (3B)

us: (to / for) — nos *dir., ind. obj. pron.* (I)

to **use:**

to — the computer usar la computadora (I)

What's it —d for? ¿Para qué sirve? (I)

used usado, -a (I)

useful:

to be — servir (e → i) (I)

is — for sirve para (I)

V _____

vacation: to go on — ir de vacaciones (I)

to **vacuum** pasar la aspiradora (I)

valley el valle (9B)

various varios, -as (3A)

vegetable soup la sopa de verduras (I)

vendor el vendedor, la vendedora (8B)

very muy (I)

— well muy bien (I)

veterinarian el veterinario, la veterinaria (9A)

victim la víctima (6B)

video el video (I)

video games: to play — jugar videojuegos (I)

to **videotape** hacer un video (I)

vinegar el vinagre (7A)

violence la violencia (6B)

violent violento, -a (I)

to **visit** visitar (I)

to — chat rooms visitar salones de chat (I, 1B)

voice la voz, *pl.* las voces (1B)

volleyball: to play — jugar (u → ue) (g → gu) al vóleibol (I)

volunteer el voluntario, la voluntaria (I)

— work el trabajo voluntario (I)

to **wait** esperar (3B)

waiter, waitress el camarero, la camarera (I)

to **wake up** despertarse (e → ie) (2A)

to **walk** caminar (I)

  to take a — dar una caminata (7B)

wall la pared (I)

wallet la cartera (I)

to **want** querer (e → ie) (I)

  I — (yo) quiero (I)

  you — (tú) quieres (I)

war la guerra (9B)

warm: to be — tener calor (I)

was fue (I)

to **wash** lavar (I)

  to — the car lavar el coche (I)

  to — the clothes lavar la ropa (I)

  to — the dishes lavar los platos (I)

  to — one's face lavarse la cara (2A)

wastepaper basket la papelera (I)

watch el reloj pulsera (I)

to **watch television** ver la tele (I)

water el agua (I)

watermelon la sandía (7B)

waterskiing el esquí acuático (8B)

way la manera (9B)

we nosotros, -as (I)

to **wear** llevar (I)

weather: What's the — like? ¿Qué tiempo hace? (I)

Web:

  to create a — page crear una página Web (1B)

  to surf the — navegar (g → gu) en la Red (I, 1B)

  — page la página Web (I, 1B)

  — site el sitio Web (I)

Wednesday miércoles (I)

wedding la boda (2A)

week la semana (I)

  last — la semana pasada (I)

weekend:

  on —s los fines de semana (I)

  this — este fin de semana (I)

welcome bienvenido, -a (8A)

well bien (I); pues ... *(to indicate pause)* (I)

  very — muy bien (I)

  — -behaved bien educado, -a (4A)

wet mojado, -a (7B)

What? ¿Cuál? ¿Qué? (I)

  — are you like? ¿Cómo eres? (I)

  (At) — time? ¿A qué hora? (I)

  — color ... ? ¿De qué color ... ? (I)

  — day is today? ¿Qué día es hoy? (I)

  — did you do? ¿Qué hiciste? (I)

  — do you like better (prefer) to do? ¿Qué te gusta hacer más? (I)

  — do you like to do? ¿Qué te gusta hacer? (I)

  — do you serve it with? ¿Con qué se sirve? (7A)

  — do you think (about it)? ¿Qué te parece? (I, 2B)

  — does ... mean? ¿Qué quiere decir ... ? (I)

  — else? ¿Qué más? (I)

  — happened to you? ¿Qué te pasó? (I, 5B)

  — is it made of? ¿De qué está hecho, -a? (2B)

  — is she / he like? ¿Cómo es? (I)

  — is the date? ¿Cuál es la fecha? (I)

  — is this? ¿Qué es esto? (I)

  — is your name? ¿Cómo te llamas? (I)

  — kind of . . . ? ¿Qué clase de . . . ? (I)

  — time is it? ¿Qué hora es? (I)

  — would you like? ¿Qué desean (Uds.)? (I)

  —'s happening? ¿Qué pasa? (I)

  —'s his / her name? ¿Cómo se llama? (I)

  —'s it (used) for? ¿Para qué sirve? (I)

  —'s the weather like? ¿Qué tiempo hace? (I)

what!:

  — a good / nice idea! ¡Qué buena idea! (I)

  — a shame / pity! ¡Qué pena! (I); ¡Qué lástima! (5B)

what lo que (1A)

wheelchair la silla de ruedas (5B)

When? ¿Cuándo? (I)

Where? ¿Dónde? (I)

  — are you from? ¿De dónde eres? (I)

  (To) —? ¿Adónde? (I)

whether si (I)

Which? ¿Cuál? ¿Cuáles? (I)

while mientras (que) (4B)

  once in a — de vez en cuando (4A)

white blanco, -a (I)

who que (I)

Who? ¿Quién? (I)

Why? ¿Por qué? (I)

wide ancho, -a (3B)

wife la esposa (I)

will be será (6B)

Will you bring me ... ? ¿Me trae ... ? (I)

to **win** ganar (1B)

window la ventana (I)

window *(airplane)* la ventanilla (8A)

windsurfing el surf de vela (8B)

winter el invierno (I)

with con (I)

— me conmigo (I)

— my / your friends con mis / tus amigos (I)

— whom? ¿Con quién? (I)

— you *familiar* contigo (I)

What do you serve it —? ¿Con qué se sirve? (7A)

without sin (I)

— a doubt sin duda (5A)

woman la mujer (I)

older woman la anciana (I)

business— la mujer de negocios (9A)

wonderful estupendo, -a (8B)

wool la lana (2B)

word la palabra (1A)

work el trabajo (I)

volunteer — el trabajo voluntario (I)

to   **work** trabajar (I); funcionar (9B)

world el mundo (4A)

worse than peor(es) que (I)

worst: the — el / la peor, los / las peores (I)

Would you like? ¿Te gustaría? (I)

wrist la muñeca (5B)

to   **write:**

to — e-mail escribir por correo electrónico (I)

to — stories escribir cuentos (I)

writer el escritor, la escritora (9A)

X
─────────────────────

X-ray la radiografía (5B)

Y
─────────────────────

yard el jardín, *pl.* los jardines (I)

year el año (I)

last — el año pasado (I)

yellow amarillo, -a (I)

yes sí (I)

yesterday ayer (I)

yet: not — no ... todavía (6B)

yogurt el yogur (I)

you *fam. sing.* tú (I); *formal sing.* usted (Ud.) (I); *fam. pl.* vosotros, -as (I); *formal pl.* ustedes (Uds.) (I); *fam. after prep.* ti (I); *sing. ind., dir. obj. pron* te (I), *pl. fam. ind. obj. pron.* os (I), *formal ind. obj. pron.* le, les (I), *formal dir. obj. pron.* lo, la, los, las

And —? ¿Y a ti? (I)

for — para ti (I)

it matters (it's important), they matter to — te importa(n) (2B)

to / for — *fam. pl.* os (I)

to / for — *fam. sing.* te (I)

with — contigo (I)

— can se puede (7A)

— don't say! ¡No me digas! (I)

— have seen has visto (6B)

— look (good) te ves (bien) (2A)

— say ... Se dice ... (I)

young joven (I)

— boy / girl el niño, la niña (I)

— man el joven (I)

— people los jóvenes (1B)

— woman la joven (I)

—er menor, *pl.* menores (I)

—est el / la menor, los / las menores (I)

your *fam.* tu (I); *fam.* tus, vuestro(s), -a(s) (I); *formal* su, sus (I)

yours *fam.* tuyo, -a, -os, -as, *formal* suyo, -a, -os, -as (2A)

yuck! ¡Uf! (I)

Z
─────────────────────

zero cero (I)

zoo el zoológico (I)

Grammar Index

Structures are most often presented first in *A primera vista,* where they are practiced lexically in conversational contexts. They are then explained in a *Gramática* section or are placed as reminders in a *¿Recuerdas?* or *Nota.* Lightface numbers refer to the pages where these structures are initially presented lexically or, after explanation, where student reminders occur. Lightface numbers also refer to pages that review structures first presented in Level 1. **Boldface numbers** refer to pages where new structures are explained.

a personal with **conocer** 56

absolute superlatives 183

accents:
    to separate diphthongs 254
    written 144

adjectives:
    agreement of 3
    demonstrative 102, 104, **114,** 124
    making comparisons with 47, **53**
    possessive 76, **88,** 96
    used as nouns **116**

adverbs, formation of 79

affirmative and negative words 19, 20, **31**

cardinal numbers 99

commands:
    affirmative *tú* 158–159, **168,** 353
    irregular affirmative *tú* 159, **168,** 180
    irregular negative *tú* **356,** 370
    negative *tú* 350, **356,** 370, 382
    usted, ustedes 375, **382,** 396

como: *see* comparisons

comparisons 46, 47, **53**

conocer:
    with **alguien, nadie** 32
    with personal **a** 32, 56
    vs. **saber** 56, 68

contractions 43

creer que + subjunctive 488

dar, preterite of 142

decir:
    affirmative *tú* command 168
    present 155

diéresis 459

diminutives **(-ito, -ita)** 183

direct object pronouns; *see* pronouns

estar vs. **ser** 86, 96

exclamations with **¡Qué!** 237

Exploración del lenguaje:
    antonyms 482
    compound words 383
    false cognates 272
    gestos 170
    origins of words from Arabic 113
    prefixes: **des-, im-, in-, ir-** 221
    suffix **-ero(a)** 436
    suffixes: **-oso(a), -dor(a)** 327
    verbs and corresponding **-ción** nouns 60

future tense:
    of regular verbs 452, **460,** 462, 463, 472
    of irregular verbs **decir, poner, querer, salir, venir** 463, **484,** 496
    of irregular verbs **haber, hacer, poder, saber, tener** 452, **462,** 463, 472, 484

haber:
    imperfect 222, **248**
    preterite 240, **248**

hacer:
    affirmative *tú* command 168
    irregular *yo* form of present tense 15, 155
    with time expressions 46, **58**

hay que 19

imperfect and preterite 248, 272, 307

imperfect progressive 288
    and preterite 266, **277**

imperfect tense:
    of **haber** 222, **248**

    of irregular verbs **ir, ser, ver** 186, 189, **196,** 208
    of **jugar, ser, tener** 208
    of regular verbs 186, 188–189, **194**
    other uses of **248**
    to describe a situation 213, **219,** 234, 307
    to describe weather; physical, mental, emotional states; states of being 241, **248**

impersonal **se** 350–351, **360**

indicative mood 410
    of stem-changing verbs 437

indirect object pronouns; *see* pronouns

infinitive:
    in verbal expressions 399
    used after prepositions 81
    with certain verbs and expressions 71

ir:
    affirmative *tú* command 168
    imperfect **196,** 208
    ir + a + infinitive 43, 460
    present 43
    to indicate future 460

nationalities 6

nouns, making comparisons with 46, **53**

numbers:
    cardinal numbers 99
    in telling time 127

oír:
    ¡Oye! 250
    present **250,** 262
    preterite **250,** 262

para 24

parecer 116

past participles **331,** 342

personal **a,** with **conocer** 56

poner:
    affirmative *tú* command 168
    irregular *yo* form of present 15, 155

Acknowledgments

Maps All maps created by XNR Productions.

Photographs Every effort has been made to secure permission and provide appropriate credit for photographic material. The publisher deeply regrets any omission and pledges to correct errors called to its attention in subsequent editions.

Unless otherwise acknowledged, all photographs are the property of Pearson Education, Inc.

Photo locators denoted as follows: Top (T), Center (C), Bottom (B), Left (L), Right (R), Background (Bkgd)

Cover (L) Floresco Productions/OJO Images/Getty Images; **(CL)** SuperStock/Alamy Images; **(CR)** Alamy Images; **(R)** Michelle Chaplow/Alamy Images

Front Matter vii (C) Alamy, (BC, BR) NASA, (BL) StockTrek/SuperStock; viii (BR) ©David Woods/Corbis; xviii (L) ©Reuters NewMedia/Corbis, (Bkgd) ©Danny Lehman/Corbis; xix (BR) ©Gary Yim/Shutterstock; xx (Bkgd) ©Kevin Schafer/Corbis; xxii (Bkgd) ©Don Hebert/Getty Images, (L) NewsCom; xxiv (Bkgd) ©Chris Huxley/eStock Photo; xxvi (Bkgd) ©Bob Krist/Corbis; xxviii (BL) Getty Images, (Bkgd) ©Michael Busselle/Corbis; xxix (BR) ©Sean Sprague/The Image Works, Inc.; xxx (Bkgd) NewsCom, (BC) ©Bob Daemmrich/The Image Works, Inc.; xxxi (BR) ©Bill Ross/Corbis; xxxii (B) ©Bob Daemmrich/Alamy Images.

1 (BR) John Phelan/DDB Stock Photography; 3 ©Reuters/Corbis; 4 ©Richard T. Nowitz/Corbis; 7 (BL) ©Stan Fellerman/Corbis, (TC) Alamy, (CL, CC) Corbis, (TL, CR, BC) Getty Images, (T, C) Jupiter Images, (CR) Valueline/Punchstock; 11 (CR) NewsCom; 14 ©Bob Daemmrich/Daemmrich Photography; 16 ©dbimages/Alamy Images; 17 Danita Delimont/Alamy Images; 24 (BL) ©Russell Gordon/Danita Delimont Photography/NewsCom; 25 (BR) ©Rudi von Briel/PhotoEdit; 26 Hero Images Inc./Alamy; 28 (BR) ©Latin Stock Collection/Corbis; 29 (TR) Ralf-Finn Hestoft/PhotoLibrary Group, Ltd.; 32 (BR) ©Keith Dannemiller/Alamy Images; 33 Courtesy of Craig Reubelt; 35 ©Bayard Presse, (CR) ©David R. Frazier Photolibrary, Inc./Alamy Images; 38 (B) ©Buddy Mays/Corbis, (C) ©Danny Lehman/Corbis, (T) ©Jack Kurtz/The Image Works; 39 (TR) ©Danny Lehman/Corbis, (C) ©geogphotos/Alamy Images; 42 ©Bob Daemmrich/Daemmrich Photography; 44 NewsCom; 45 Antonio Berni (1905–1981), "Club Atlético Nueva Chicago" (New Chicago Athletic Club), 1937, oil on canvas, 6' 3/4" × 9' 10 1/4". Inter-American Fund (645.1942). The Museum of Modern Art/Licensed by Scala-Art Resource, NY. Digital Image ©2004 Museum of Modern Art, New York/Art Resource, NY; 50 Loona/ABACAPRESS/NewsCom; 51 ©Todd Powell; 54 John R. Amelia/Fotolia; 55 (BR) ©Jeremy Horner/Corbis, (TC) Fernando Botero, "The Musicians", 1979, oil on canvas, 74 (1).75 × 85.5 in. ©Fernando Botero/Courtesy Marlborough Gallery, NY, (TR) Fernando Botero, "Three Musicians", 1983, oil on canvas, 64.5 × 48.5 in. ©Fernando Botero/Courtesy Marlborough Gallery, NY; 57 Keith Dannemiller/Alamy Images; 59 (CL) ©AFP/Getty Images, (BC) ©Michael Ochs Archives/Getty Images; 61 (BR) ©Ghislain & Marie David de Lossy/Getty Images, (TL) ©William R. Sallaz/Getty Images, (C) Tom Rosenthal/SuperStock; 62 (BR) ©Jimmy Dorantes/Latin Focus, (BC) Ilene Perlman/Alamy Images; 63 (T)

©Bonnie Kamin/PhotoEdit, NewsCom; 66 (BR) ©Andre Jenny/Alamy Images, (CR) ©Danny Lehman/Corbis, (TR) ©Michael S. Yamashita/Corbis; 67 (TR) ©Macduff Everton/Corbis, (C) ©Stephen Simpson/Getty Images; 72 ©Keith Dannemiller/Alamy Images; 73 Diego Rivera, "Dance in Tehuantepec", 1935. Charcoal and watercolor. 18 15/16 × 23 7/8 in. Los Angeles County Museum of Art. Gift of Mr. and Mrs. Milton W. Lipper, from the Milton W. Lipper Estate. Photograph ©2003 Museum Associates/LACMA. ©Banco de México Diego Rivera & Frida Kahlo Museums Trust. Av. Cinco de Mayo No. 2, Col. Centro, Del Cuauhtemoc 06059, México, D.F. Reproduction authorized by the Instituto Nacional de Bellas Artes y Literatura/Los Angeles County Museum of Art; 79 (BR) Alamy Images; 82 (BR) ©Bob Daemmrich/Daemmrich Photography, (TR) ©Rob Van Petten/Getty Images; 83 (CR) ©Image Source; 84 Daemmrich Photography; 85 (CL) ©Marisol Diaz/Latin Focus, (CR) ©Nik Wheeler/Corbis; 86 ©Bob Daemmrich/Daemmrich Photography; 88 (BR) ©Ronald de Hommel; 90 (BL, B) ©Carlos Goldin/DDB Stock Photography; 91 (TR) ©Charles Westerman/ImageState, (CR) ©Exactostock/SuperStock; 92 (TR) ©Jeremy Horner/Corbis, (CR) ©Tiziana and Gianni Baldizzone/Corbis; 93 ImagesBazaar / Alamy (CR) ©Francesco Venturi/Corbis; 94 (BL) Danny Lehman Photography; 95 (TR, C) ©Danny Lehman/Corbis, (TC) Danny Lehman Photography; 98 Alamy Images; 100 ©Alex Segre/Alamy Images; 101 Infanta Margarita (1651–73) in Blue, 1659 (oil on canvas). Diego Rodríguez de Silva y Velázquez (1599–1660)/Kunsthistorisches Museum, Vienna, Austria/Bridgeman Art Library; 108 (TR, BR) Alamy; 109 Isaac Hernández/Mercury Press; 112 (BL) ©Bob Daemmrich/Daemmrich Photography, (BR) ©The Granger Collection, NY; 113 (BL) ©Bettmann/Corbis, (BR) EUREKA SLIDE; (T) ©Free Agents Limited/Corbis; 115 (CR) ©Daniel Ciccone, (TR) ©First Light/Alamy Images; 117 (BR) Alamy Images, (T) Flashpoint/WENN/NewsCom; 118 ©Bettmann/Corbis; 119 (CL) ©Bettmann/Corbis, (CR) ©Paul A. Souders/Corbis, (CL) Rick Piper Photography/Alamy Images; 120 (B) Alamy Images, (CR) Somos Images/AGE Fotostock; 121 (TR) Blend Images/Alamy; 122 (TR) ©David Pollack/Corbis, (BR) Corbis; 123 (C) ©Jimmy Dorantes/Latin Focus, (TR) Courtesy of the U.S. Latino & Latina WWII Oral History Project, Nettie Lee Benson Latin American Collection, University of Texas at Austin; 126 (TR) ©Ray Juno/Corbis, (TL) Alamy Images; 128 ©Gregory Wrona/Alamy Images; 129 Julio Alpuy, "Buenos Aires", 1957/Courtesy of Cecilia de Torres Ltd., New York City; 135 (BR) ©Dave G. Houser/Corbis; 137 (TR) ©Bjorn Svensson/Alamy Images, (CR) ©graficart/Alamy; 139 ©Bob Thomas/Getty Images; 140 Alin Dragulin/AGE Fotostock; 141 ©RDA/Hulton Archive/Getty Images; 142 (BR) Radius Images/Alamy; 143 (CR, CC) Getty Images; 144 (BR) Alamy Images; 145 ©Jimmy Dorantes/Latin Focus; 147 ©Gavin Hellier/Getty Images, ©L. Clarke/Corbis; 148 (BR) ©Jeremy Horner/Corbis, (TR) ©Paul Almasy/Corbis; 149 (TR) ©Gisela Damm/eStock Photo; 156 ©Jon Hicks/Corbis; 157 Diego Rivera, The Making of a Fresco Showing the Building of a City, 1931, fresco, 271 by 357 inches, gift of William Gerstle. Photo by David Wakely/San Francisco Art Institute; 162 Alamy Images; 164 (CR) ©DK Images, (TC) ©Steve Vidler/eStock Photo; 165 (BR) ©Sime s.a.s./eStock Photo, (CR) Paul Franklin/©DK Images; **167** ©D. Hurst/Alamy, (TC) ©John Tomaselli/Alamy; **169** (BR) ©Bettmann/Corbis; **171** ©SuperStock Inc./SuperStock; **172** ©Daniel Ciccone; **173** (C) Frida Kahlo, "El camión", 1929. Oil on canvas. 26 × 55 cm. ©Banco de México Diego Rivera & Frida Kahlo Museums Trust. Av. Cinco de Mayo No. 2, Col. Centro, Del. Cuauhtemoc 06059, México, D. F. Reproduction authorized by the Instituto Nacional de Bellas Artes y Literatura/Schalkwijk/Art Resource, NY; **173** (BR) ©Washington, DC Convention and Tourism Corporation; **174** (L) Alamy Images, Shutterstock; **175** Paul Kennedy/Alamy Images, Shutterstock; **176** (TR) ©Richard Glover/Corbis, (CR) ©Rudi von Briel/PhotoEdit, (BR) Alamy Images; **177** (TR) Nobilior/Fotolia; **182** eStock Photo; **183** Getty Images; **184** ©Danita Delimont/Alamy Images; **185** Pablo Picasso (1881–1973), "First Steps", 1943, oil on canvas, 130.2 × 97.1 cm (51 1/4 × 38 1/4 in.). Yale University Art Gallery, Gift of Stephen Carlton Clark, B. A. 1903. ©2004 Estate of Pablo Picasso/Artists Rights Society ARS, New York/Art Resource, NY; **186** (TC) ©DK Images, (CR) ©Elmer Frederick/Corbis, (TR) Getty Images, Jupiter Images, (TL) Paul Barton/Corbis, (CL) Photodisc/Getty Images; **190** Getty Images; **191** ©Robert Van Der Hilst/Getty Images; **192** ©Bob Daemmrich/Alamy Images; **193** (TL) Getty Images; **194** (BR) Alamy Images; **196** (BR) NewsCom; **197** ©The Granger Collection, NY; **198** George Eastman House/Nickolas Muray/Courtesy George Eastman House; **200** (BR) Alejandro Reyna, "Los niños del futuro" ©Lorenzo Armendariz/Latin Focus, (B) Bridgeman Art Library; **201** (CR) Francisco José de Goya y Lucientes (1746–1828), "Don Manuel Osorio Manrique de Zúñiga", c. 1790s, oil on canvas, 127 × 101.6 cm. Metropolitan Museum of Art, New York, USA/Bridgeman Art Library; **210** ©Peter Adams Photography Ltd/Alamy Images; **211** "Desfile cívico escolar" (Schoolchildren on Parade), 1936, Antonio Ruiz. Oil on canvas, 24.5 × 33.5 cm./©Secretaría de Hacienda y Crédito Público; **216** (B) ©Javier Larrea/AGE Fotostock; **218** (BR) NewsCom; **220** (CR) ©Stewart Aitchison/DDB Stock Photography, (BC) Peggy Boyles; **221** ©Tony Freeman/PhotoEdit; **222** Carmen Lomas Garza (b. 1948), "Tamalada" (Making Tamales), 1988, oil on linen mounted on wood, 24" × 32". ©1988 Carmen Lomas Garza. Photo credit: M. Lee Featherree. Collection of Paula Maciel-Benecke and Norbert Benecke, Aptos, California/Carmen L. Garza; **223** (TR, BR) ©Bettmann/Corbis; **224** Alamy Images; **225** ©Steve Dunwell/PhotoLibrary Group, Ltd.; **226** ©Jacques Jangoux/Getty Images; **227** (BR) ©Andy Caulfield, (BR) Alamy, (TL) Alamy Images; **229** (BL) ©Suzanne Murphy-Larronde/DDB Stock Photography, (CR) Peggy Boyles; **230** (BR) ©J. P. Courau/DDB Stock Photography, (BC) Getty Images, (TR) Jimmy Dorantes/Latin Focus; **231** NewsCom; **236** (TL) ©David Papazian/Corbis, (TR, TC) ©Massimo Listri/Corbis; **238** JUAN MABROMATA/AFP/Getty Images/NewsCom; **239** The Storm by Zulia Gotay de Anderson, 2002/©Zulia Gotay de Anderson; **240** (BC) ©Bill Gentile/Corbis, (BL, BC) ©Reuters/Corbis, (C) ©Robert Brenner/PhotoEdit, (BR) ©Tomás del Amo/PhotoLibrary Group, Ltd., (CR) Getty Images, (Bkgd) Horizon International Images Limited/Alamy Images; **245** ©Pablo Corral Vega/Corbis; **246** ©AFP Photo/EPA/EFE/Robin Townsend/NewsCom; **247** NewsCom; **251** Rodrigo Abd/©Associated Press; **252** (TR)

©Bettmann/Corbis, (BR) Fernando Botero (b. 1933), "Terremoto en Popayán" (Earthquake in Popayán), 1999, oil on canvas, 173 × 112 cm. Museo Botero, Banco de la República de Colombia. ©Fernando Botero./Courtesy Marlborough Gallery, NY; **255** ©Hector Mata/AFP/Getty Images; **256** ©Bettmann/Corbis; **257** ©Bettmann/Corbis; **258** (TR) ©Dave G. Houser/Corbis; **259** (T) Bettmann/Corbis; **264** RIANE KADOCH SWISA KRT/NewsCom; **265** Diego Rivera (1866–1957). "The History of Medicine in Mexico, The People Demanding Health", 1953. Fresco, approx. 7.4 × 10.8 m. Hospital de la Raza, Mexico City, D. F., Mexico. Photo: ©2003 Banco de México Diego Rivera & Frida Kahlo Museums Trust. Av. Cinco de Mayo No. 2, Col. Centro, Del. Cuauhtemoc 06059, México, D. F. Reproduction authorized by the Instituto Nacional de Bellas Artes y Literatura/Art Resource, NY; **271** (BR) pf/Alamy; **273** (BR) ©Ted Spiegel/Corbis; **274** (BR) DDB Stock Photography; **276** ©Ronnie Kaufman/Corbis; **278** (BR) ©Alex Cook/©PAC-Antioquia; **279** (BR) ©Franck Seguin/TempSport/Corbis, (TR) ©Jim Cummins/Corbis; **280** (CR) ©Albert Gea/Reuters Media, (BR) ©Pablo San Juan/Corbis; **282** (BL) NewsCom, (CR) Pan American Health Organization; **283** (TR, TL) NewsCom, Peace Corps; **284** (TR) ©Spencer Grant/PhotoEdit, (CR) Getty Images; **285** (TR) David Burch/Glow Images (BR) ©Tom Stewart/Corbis; **290** NewsCom; **292** ©Jonathan Larsen/Diadem Images/Alamy Images; **293** "El futbolista" (The Football Player), 1973, lithograph on zinc, 19 × 24 by Salvador Dalí (1904–1989)/©The Salvador Dalí Foundation/Artists Rights Society (ARS), NY; **294** (TL) ©AFP Photo/Jorge Uzon/NewsCom, (TC) ©Reuters/Corbis; **298** ©Patricio Crooker/fotosbolivia/The Image Works; **299** ©Francisco J. Rangel; **300** (BR) ©Albert Gea/Reuters/Corbis, (CR) ©Duomo/Corbis; **301** (TL, BR) NewsCom; **303** (CR) ©Clive Rose/Getty Images, (TR) ©Stu Forster/Getty Images; **304** (C) ©Jan Butchofsky-Houser/Corbis, (CL) Corbis, (C) JSC/NASA, (TR) NewsCom; **305** (BR) ©Luis Diez Solano/COVER/The Image Works; **307** (CR) "Las pantallas" by Mariano Sapia/Mariano Sapia, (BL) NewsCom; **308** (BR) NewsCom; **310** (L) ©John Gibson/AFP/Getty Images; **311** (CL, CC) ©Comité Olímpico Argentino/Amateur Athletic Foundation, (TR) ©Martin Bernetti/Getty Images, (CR) ©mtrommer/Fotolia, (C) COMITE ORGANIZADOR JOGOS PAN AMERICANOS RIO 2007/©AP Photo; **312** NewsCom; **313** (TR) ©Spencer Rowell/Getty Images; **318** Russell Gordon/DanitaDelimont "Danita Delimont Photography"/NewsCom; **319** TORNASOL FILMS/NewsCom; **325** (BR) Billie L. Porter/Photofest, (CR) NewsCom; **326** KCSPresse/Splash News/NewsCom; **328** (BR) ©Warner Brothers/Photofest; **330** Alamy; **332** NewsCom; **333** ©Telepix/Alamy Images; **334** Alamy; **335** NewsCom; **336** (CL, BR) NewsCom; **337** NewsCom; **338** (CR) Alamy Images, (TR) NewsCom; **344** ©Pat LaCroix/Getty Images; **346** ©Ingolf Pompe 52/Alamy Images; **347** Christie's Images Ltd./SuperStock; **352** ©Takehiko Sunada/HAGA/The Image Works; **353** (BR) Santiago Cornejo/Fotolia (CR) ©Becky Luigart-Stayner/Corbis, (BL) ©Michelle Garrett/Corbis, (CL) ©Paul_Brighton/Shutterstock; **355** (BR) ©holbox/Shutterstock, (TR) ©Norman Owen Tomalin/Photoshot; **357** ©foodcolors/Fotolia; **358** (TR) ©Morton Beebe/Corbis, (BR) ©Pablo Corral V/Corbis; **359** ©Chris Everard/Getty Images; **360** (BL) ©Japack Company/AGE Fotostock, (TR) ©Lynda Richardson/Corbis, (BR) helenedevun/Fotolia (CR) ©Michelle Garrett/Corbis, (TC) ©Nik Wheeler/Corbis, (CL) ©Norman Owen Tomalin/Photoshot, (CR) ©Paul Webster/Getty Images, (TL) ©JJAVA/Fotolia, Shutterstock; **361** ©Jennifer Blau/PhotoLibrary Group, Ltd.; **362** ©Danny Lehman/Corbis; **363** (CR) ©Danny Lehman/Corbis, (BR) ©Jimmy Dorantes/Latin Focus, (BL) ©Michael Newman/PhotoEdit; **365** (TL) ©RDA/Hulton Archive/Getty Images; **366** (TR) JJAVA/Fotolia; **372** ©imagebroker/Alamy; **373** Carmen Lomas Garza (b. 1948), "Sandía" (Watermelon), 1986, gouache painting on paper, 20 × 28 in. Photo Credit: Wolfgang Dietze. Collection of Dudley D. Brooks and Tomás Ybarra-Frausto, New York, NY/Carmen L. Garza; **378** SuperStock; **380** (CL) ©Index Stock Imagery/PhotoLibrary Group, Ltd., (BL) Getty Images, (BR) SuperStock; **381** ©Lois Ellen Frank/Corbis; **383** Elena Climent (b. 1955), "Tienda de legumbres" (Vegetable Store), 1992, oil on canvas, 36 × 44 1/8 in. /©Elena Climent; **384** ©Thomas Hoeffgen/ Getty Images; **385** SuperStock; **386** ©Alison Wright/Corbis; **387** (BR) ©Antonio Perez/Latin Focus; **388** National Geographic Image Collection; **389** (TR) ©WoodyStock/Alamy Images; **390** (BL) ©Angelina Lax/Photo Researchers, Inc., (CR) ©Kevin Schafer/Corbis, (Bkgd) SuperStock; **391** (BL) ©Bob Krist/Corbis, (C) ©John Mitchell/Photo Researchers, Inc., (CR) ©Kevin Schafer/Corbis, (TC) Chip Peterson and Rosa María de la Cueva Peterson; **392** (TR, CR, BR) ©Jimmy Dorantes/Latin Focus; **393** (BR) ©Lawrence Sawyer/Index Stock Imagery/PhotoLibrary Group, Ltd., (TR) ©Paul Barton/Corbis; **398** (CR) ©Buddy Mays/Corbis, (TL) ©Doug Stamm/Seapics, (TR) ©Michael S. Yamashita/ Corbis, (CL) ©Paul Steel/Steel Photography Pty.Ltd; **400** Bloomberg/Getty Images; **401** Photri Images/SuperStock; **403** (TR) ©James Marshall/Corbis, (TC) ©Mark Peterson/Corbis, (CR) ©Najlah Feanny/Saba/Corbis, (TL) ©WINS; **406** ©Larry Luxner/Luxner News, Inc.; **407** (BR) ©AG/Latin Focus; **409** (CR) ©Pablo Corral V/Corbis; **411** (CR) ©Alain Le Garsmeur/Corbis; **412** ©Jupiterimages/Comstock/Thinkstock; **413** (BR) Alamy Images; **415** (CL) ©Abbie Enock; Travel Ink/Corbis, (BC) ©Franz-Marc Frei/Corbis, (TC) ©Giraud Philippe/Sygma/Corbis, (BR) ©Suzanne Murphy-Larronde; **417** (BR) ©Larry Luxner/Luxner News, Inc.; **418** (BC) ©Pablo Corral/Corbis, (CL) ©Paul Rodriguez/Latin Focus, (BR) ©Tim Whitby/Alamy Images; **419** (TL) ©Albrecht G. Schaefer/Corbis, (C) ©Dr. Morley Read/Shutterstock, (TR) ©Owen Franken/Corbis; **420** (TR, CR) ©Nettie Lee Benson Latin American Collection/University of Texas Libraries/University of Texas-Austin; **421** Alamy Images; **424** ©All Canada Photos/SuperStock; **425** ©Jimmy Dorantes/Latin Focus; **426** (CL) jorgedasi/Shutterstock (BR) ©José Fuste Raga/Corbis, (C) ©Nik Wheeler/Corbis; **430** ©Jan Butchofsky-Houser/Corbis; **431** ©David J. Simchock; **432** (CR) ©D. Stonek/Latin Focus, (C) ©Jimmy Dorantes/Latin Focus; **433** (CL) ©David Stoecklein/Corbis, (CR) ©Tony Arruza/Corbis; **434** ©Suzanne Murphy-Larronde; **435** ©Jeremy Horner/Corbis; **436** ©Mike Hipple/Alamy Images; **438** ©Sven Martson/The Image Works; **439** (BR) ©Jason Lindsey/Alamy Images; **440** (BR) Photolibrary Group, Inc.; **442** (R) ©Massimo Listri/Corbis, (BL) ©Peter M. Wilson/Corbis; **443** (BL) ©Larry Luxner/Luxner News, Inc., (T) ©ML Sinibaldi/Corbis; **444** (TR) ©Sappa/Photo Researchers, Inc.; **445** (TR) ©Bettmann/Corbis, (BR) ©Hubert Stadler/Corbis; **448** ©Paul A. Souders/Corbis; **450** ©Farrell Grehan/Corbis; **451** ©2010 Artists Rights Society (ARS), New York/SOMAAP, Mexico City/photo: Paul Almasy/Corbis; **458** ©Daniel Ciccone; **460** ©Bob Daemmrich/Daemmrich Photography; **461** (T) ©iStockphoto; **463** Fausto Pérez/FaustoPérez/Galería Hidalgo; **465** (CR) ©Owen Franken/Corbis, (TR) ©Pablo Corral V/Corbis; **467** (TR, BC) ©Bob Daemmrich/Daemmrich Photography; **468** (CR) Michael Newman/PhotoEdit (BL) ©Monika Graff/The Image Works, Inc.; **469** (CR) ©Bill Bachmann/Alamy Images, (CR) Alamy; **470** (B) Album/Oronoz/NewsCom, (TR) Toaquiza, Julio, "Targelia, Christmas Eve", ca. 1990s. Photo ©Pablo Corral V/Corbis; **471** Bob Daemmrich/Alamy Images; **474** LOOK Die Bildagentur der Fotografen GmbH/Alamy Images; **475** Alfredo Arreguín; **477** (C) ©Andre Nantel/Shutterstock, (Inset) ©BsChan/Shutterstock, (TR) ©Didier Dorval/Masterfile Corporation, (CC) ©Donald Barger/Shutterstock, (CL) ©Mark Garlick/Photo Researchers, Inc., (TC) ©szefei/Shutterstock; **480** ©Albert Mendelewski/Shutterstock; **481** ©Charles Philip/Painet Stock Photos; **483** ©W. Perry Conway/Corbis, (T) Coins courtesy of Don Bailey Numismatic Service; **484** (R) AGE Fotostock; **485** (TR) ©Dr. Morely Read/Shutterstock; **490** (CR) ©2009 VEGAP, Madrid/Artists Rights Society (ARS), NY, (TR) "Paisaje hondureño de San Antonio de Oriente" (1972), José Antonio Velásquez/Art Museum of the Americas; **491** (TR) ©David Stoecklein/Corbis; **493** (C) ©George D. Lepp/Corbis, (CR) ©iStockphoto, (TL) ©SF Photo/Shutterstock; **494** (BR) ©Greenpeace, (CR) ©Mark Edwards/PhotoLibrary Group, Inc., Dr. Morley Read/Shutterstock; **495** ©/Jupiter Images.

Text

Grateful acknowledgment is made to the following for copyrighted material:

Agencia Literaria Carmen Balcells

"Oda a la cebolla" and "Oda al tomate" from the work Odas elementales, by Pablo Neruda. Copyright © Fundación Pablo Neruda, 2011. "Oda a las papas fritas" from the work Navegaciones y regresos, by Pablo Neruda. Copyright © Fundación Pablo Neruda, 2011. Used by permission of Agencia Literaria Carmen Balcells S.A.

Bayard Revistas, S.A.

"Reglas de oro para estudiar mejor" from Okapi, May 2002 © Okapi Bayard Presse. Reprinted by permission.

El Universal

"En Riesgo de extinción 20% de los animales en México" by Julián Sánchez from EL UNIVERSAL domingo, el 25 de agosto de 2002.

Organización Panamericana de la Salud — PAHO

"Campeones de la Salud" from ORGANIZACIÓN PANAMERICANA DE LA SALUD. Reprinted by permission of the Pan American Health Organization.

Note: Every effort has been made to locate the copyright owner of material reproduced in this component. Omissions brought to our attention will be corrected in subsequent editions.